MISTEL

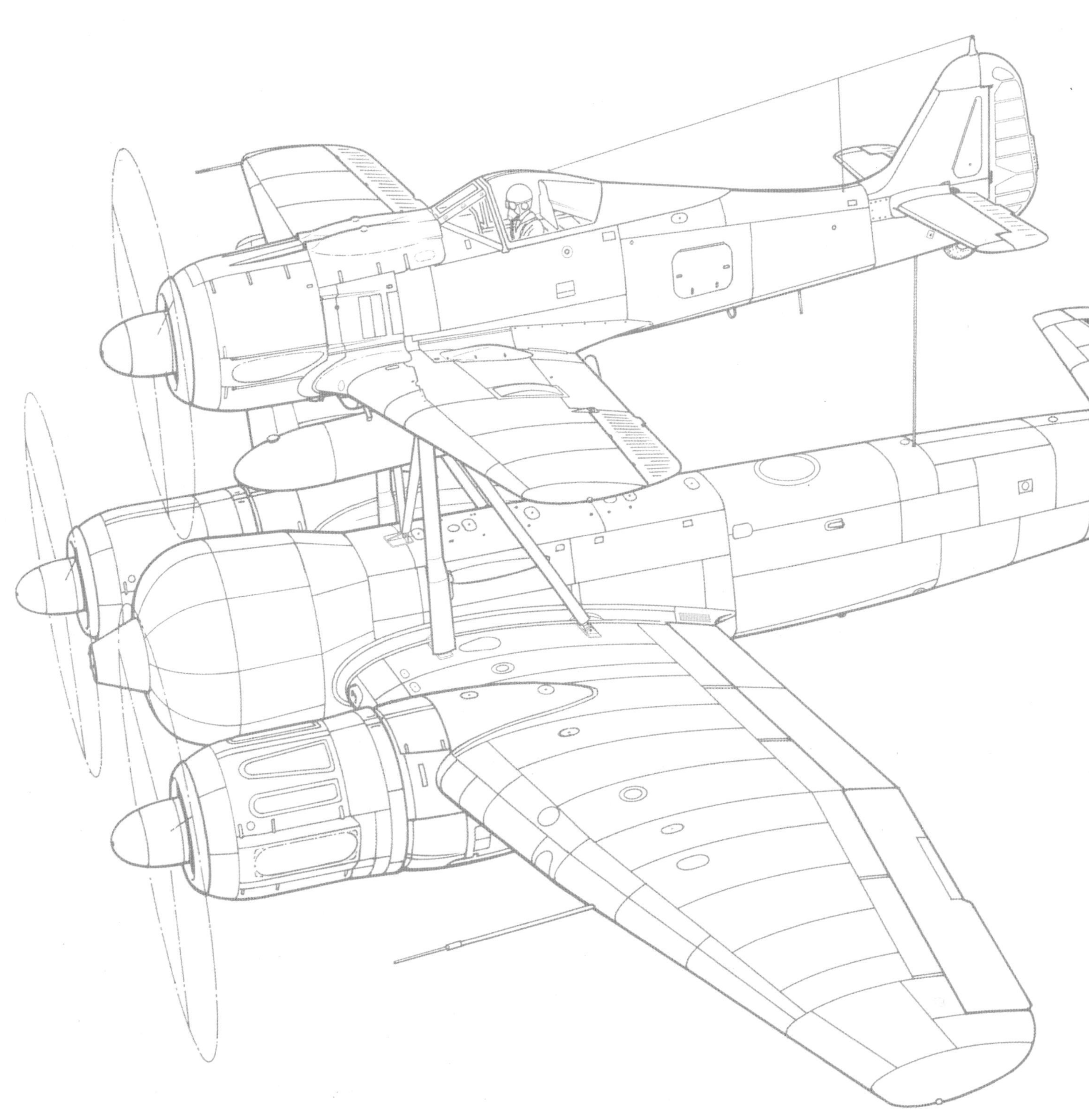

An Imprint of
Crécy Publishing

MISTEL 1942-1945

GERMAN COMPOSITE AIRCRAFT AND OPERATIONS

ROBERT FORSYTH

with

Eddie J. Creek
Stephen Ransom
Werner Stocker

Technical Drawings:
Arthur L. Bentley &
Eddie J. Creek

Colour Artwork:
Tom Tullis &
Dennis Davison

THE AUTHOR

Robert Forsyth is an author, editor and publisher, specialising in military aviation and military history. After working in the shipping industry, he co-founded a publishing and book production business in 1995 with Eddie J. Creek which has produced some 250 illustrated reference books on military aviation, armoured warfare, vintage motor sport, history, biography and wildlife.

He is the author of thirty books on the aircraft, units and operations of the Luftwaffe, an interest he has held since boyhood, and he has been consulted for television on the same subject. He has written articles for *The Aviation Historian, Aerojournal, Aeroplane Monthly, Aviation News, Combat Aircraft,* and *FlyPast* and he is a member of the Editorial Board of *The Aviation Historian*.

The first edition of *Mistel – German Composite Aircraft and Operations 1942-1945* was his third book and was published originally in 2001.

The author with Rudi Riedl, former Mistel pilot of 6./KG 200, in Bremen during research for this book in February 1999.

Mistel © 2020
Robert Forsyth

First published 2001
This revised edition 2020

ISBN 978 1 91080 981 5

Produced by Chevron Publishing Limited
Project Editor: Robert Forsyth
Book design: Mark Nelson

Published by Crécy Publishing Ltd.

An imprint of Crécy Publishing Ltd.
1a Ringway Trading Estate,
Shadowmoss Road, Manchester, M22 5LH

Visit the Crécy Publishing website at:
www.crecy.co.uk

Printed in Bulgaria by Multiprint

An Imprint of
Crécy Publishing

CONTENTS

INTRODUCTION TO REVISED EDITION

LOOKING back over the twenty years since the original publication of this book, what strikes me is how the *Mistel* remains, in equal measures, a strangely impressive, remarkably efficient, resourceful and yet, many would think, a reckless concept. Certainly, the pilots who flew the combination in action were proficient and brave – but they spoke well of it. Perhaps the blend of all these attributes is what continues to give the composite an enduring fascination for aviation enthusiasts.

Certainly, the inspiring early designs of Alberto Santos-Dumont, John Porte, Robert Hobart Mayo, Hugo Junkers, Claude Dornier and Fritz Stamer did not necessarily foresee a military or offensive role for the composite, but they all shared the inherent fundamental quality of invention borne of necessity. Perhaps it was inevitable then that from 1939, as Europe became ensnared in war, skilled, experienced and inventive aviators and engineers like Siegfried Holzbaur, Horst-Dieter Lux and Dietrich Peltz, would adapt what had been intended as a mail and commercial transport concept for war.

It was not easy to discover fresh material on *Mistel* operations back in the mid-1990s, but I was fortunate to be able to meet then with several *Mistel* pilots and to obtain their recollections at first-hand. A little over twenty years later, that opportunity has now passed, but what new and additional material has come my way, I have included in this book.

I must thank Jeremy Pratt of Crécy Publishing for offering me the opportunity to re-visit the *Mistel* and to revise and expand the original edition. My thanks too to Mark Nelson for giving the book a visual reboot. The following individuals have also kindly assisted with this revised edition and I am most grateful to them: Martin Frauenheim, Neil Page, Nick Stroud, Phil Jarrett, Ralph Pegram, William A. Medcalf and Ryan Noppen

Robert Forsyth
2020

PREFACE AND ACKNOWLEDGEMENTS TO FIRST EDITION (2001)

ACCORDING to the Oxford Dictionary a 'Preface' should explain a book's 'scope, intention and method.'

At conception, it was my intention that this book should tell the story of the development and use of the composite aircraft before and during the Second World War – not just by Germany, but also by Great Britain, a country which pioneered some of the first civil and military types and which, as the reader will discover, provided inspiration to the German designers and aviators who subsequently adapted the composite for use in war.

The Second World War saw unparalleled military inventiveness and technical innovation on the part of all main belligerents, from the German *Enigma* cypher machine to *Ultra*, the system which defeated it; from General Percy Hobart's armoured 'funnies' to Dr Barnes Wallis's 'bouncing bomb'; from the German *Goliath* mini demolition vehicle to the V-2 rocket. Such inventions and innovations have, thankfully, been well-documented by writers and historians since 1945 and their record has been secured in history. Sadly, many other worthy and perhaps not so worthy, but no less fascinating, inventions have lacked such attention. One example is the *Mistel* – a concept born of inventiveness and circumstance.

In the first part of this book, I have attempted to provide the reader with an insight into how the *Mistel* came to be and to place it in its historical context. In the second part, I have endeavoured to collate as much information as possible relative to the weapon's sporadic deployment and its dramatic yet questionable effectiveness.

I have been fortunate to have been able to draw upon a multitude of sources to do this: books, contemporary documents and reports, and the memories of those who designed and flew this daunting contraption. This would not have been conceivable without the generosity, advice, knowledge, patience and support of many aviation researchers, writers and historians and my only hope is that what is contained in the pages that follow reflects their kind and invaluable assistance.

There are five specific individuals, without whom this book would have been impossible to write and I would like to record my grateful thanks to each of them.

Firstly, my good friend, Stephen Ransom, for so willingly giving up his time and extending this project his assistance in the form of his considerable technical and historic knowledge and linguistic skills on my behalf. His contribution, suggestions, patience and support were, at times, way beyond what I could possibly hope for. Many thanks also for kindly accompanying me during my research trips to Germany.

Secondly to *Dipl.-Ing.* Christian Teuber who, like Stephen, provided tremendous support in the writing of this book. Christian, too, translated countless documents and letters and made his apartment available for interviews on more than one occasion. I wish him the very best of luck with his own autogyro design and building projects.

Also my thanks to Rudi Riedl, a former *Mistel* pilot with 6./KG 200, whose belief in this project from its early days helped to 'open doors' that may otherwise have understandably stayed closed. I am honoured and grateful that his wartime recollections are contained within these pages.

I would also like to express my thanks to Werner Stocker in the USA who kindly translated endless documents and diaries and who offered his valued opinions and suggestions during the writing of this book.

Eddie Creek gave me his time and support and accompanied me during my visit to a KG(J) 30 *Treffen* in Germany. His knowledge, linguistic and photographic skills, humour and patience were invaluable.

In Germany, I would like to thank Arno Rose for allowing me access to the papers which formed his own research material for his book on the *Mistel*. I would also like to thank Alfred W. Krüger for his advice, hospitality, translation skills and support, and *Dipl.-Ing.* Karl Kössler for his assistance with photographs and information. Jürgen Rosenstock also helped with translation during the early stages of research. I benefited from receiving the assistance of Marton Szigeti, Helmut Rosenboom, Hans-Justus Meier, Peter Achs, P.W. Stahl, Peter Petrick, Sven Carlsen, Burkhard Otto, *Dr.* Brigitte Weyl of Südverlag GmbH and *Dr.* Kristina Zerges and Christian Hohlfeld of the *Pressestelle* at the Techische Universität in Berlin.

I was fortunate enough to have received help and recollections from several former *Mistel* pilots. In particular, I would like to offer my thanks to the former Junkers acceptance pilot, Heinz Schreiber, (who probably flew more *Mistel* on more occasions than any other man), for extending me his hospitality and recollections and to Karl Russmeyer, formerly of 3./KG(J) 30, for allowing me his time and access to key records, and for providing me with some stories from the past. My thanks must also go to Heinz Frommhold who kindly arranged for Eddie Creek and myself to attend the KG(J) 30 *Treffen* at Bernried in September 2000 and who has offered invaluable help in checking the manuscript for accuracy in respect to *Mistel* operations during Operation *Eisenhammer* and over the Oder bridges. I am also grateful to Heinz Frommhold and Rudolf Kainz for allowing me to draw upon the excellent *Staffelchronik* of 3./KG(J) 30. Hans Altrogge, Walter Fledlink, Fred Gottgetreu (Canada), Toni Grögel, Alfred Hansen, Herbert Kuntz, Alfred Lew, Fritz Lorbach, Carl-Ernst Mengel, Balduin Pauli and Karlheinz Wiesner also contributed photographs and recollections and I am grateful to them all.

In England I owe a special thank you to J. Richard Smith for allowing me to incorporate his own research into this study and in this regard acknowledgement also goes to Chris Mendosa and Mike Norton. Nick Beale once again helped me with many contributions of information and suggestions on how to locate further material. I am, as always, indebted to the other former members of the *'Staffel'* who provided information and suggestions: Steve Coates, Martin Pegg and Jerry Scutts. The 'final result' has been unquestionably enhanced by the inclusion of Arthur Bentley's unequalled technical illustrations. Wally Carter advised me on hollow-charge warheads and David Irving, Geoff Thomas, Phil Jarrett, Mark Healy and Roger Freeman contributed advice, information, documents and photographs. I am extremely grateful to Barry Blunt and Bob Dickens of the The Mosquito Aircrew Association who put me in contact with John Waters and Noel Le Long, without whose assistance and contributions the details of the Tirstrup raid would not have been forthcoming. I must also mention Wally Lake, the National Secretary of the Royal New Zealand Air Force Association. I wish to thank Les Gentry for his enthusiastic help in providing information on HMS *Nith* as well as vividly recalling his own experiences of how it felt to be on the receiving end of a *Mistel* attack. Thanks also to Peter Meryon, Roy Adam and John Collins.

In the USA, Jerry Crandall, John M. Gray, Robert Foose, Lillian Howes, James H. Kitchens, James V. Crow, Richard Lutz, Robert M. Littlefield, Steve Blake and Tom Tullis all provided information, photographs and expertise. I am also grateful to Stephen Fochuk and Jack Dunn in Canada for providing me with key information on the RCAF's encounters with the *Mistel*. John Bradley and Dave Wadman also contributed valuable information. From The Netherlands, Marcel van Heijkop assisted me with information on the activities of I./KG 66 and I wish Marcel the best of luck in his own research into that unit's operations. My thanks also to Jörn Junker, Eric Mombeek and Kees Mol.

RF
2001

Author's Note

During the course of my research, it became apparent that neither the RLM nor the Luftwaffe applied firm or common designations to the different *Mistel* variants. Often I came across misleading and conflicting reports. In the post-war years, most writers have tended to settle on the basis that the '*Mistel* 1' was a Bf 109-fitted *Mistel*, while the '*Mistel* 2' comprised an Fw 190 upper component. Unfortunately, I have come across too many instances which conflict with this assumption or simply offer a contrary view to accept any firm nomenclature.

For example, the '*Mistel* 2' *Bedienungsvorschrift* to be found in the Appendix to this book, is dated as early as May 1944 and covers the Bf 109/Ju 88 combination. Former *Mistel* pilots whom I have interviewed and with whom I have corresponded seem to recall no hard and fast variant assignations. The only consistent designation is the prefix 'S' (i.e., '*Mistel* S1') which denotes a *Schule* or training aircraft.

My text is based on what is contained in the documents I have found. Where first-hand accounts are used, variants are quoted verbatim. Otherwise, I am afraid I too have sought refuge in the seemingly unsubstantiated post-war designations.

FOREWORD

HEINZ FROMMHOLD

Formerly Pilot in 3. *Staffel, Kampfgeschwader*(J) 30

WHEN Robert Forsyth asked me to write an introduction to this book I had some reservations because, in view of the following remarks, I feel sure that some of my fellow countrymen may wish to brand me as militaristic, ultra-nationalist or right wing. However, that is unavoidable if I am to express my beliefs, for I consider it quite natural that participants in particular circumstances should be asked to describe them, even if they occurred more than fifty years ago and may, today, be considered controversial. After all, who better to relate those occurrences than those who experienced them?

A modern historian recently remarked that to rely on the descriptions of an historic event from a single participant can only impair the total, objective view. If one acknowledges the fact that every person experiences an occurrence as an individual and that a number of witnesses to a single event may each describe it completely differently, then one would have to agree with this view. One would have to accept also that the reader of eyewitness accounts may himself have yet another interpretation. However, historical studies are lacking if the eyewitness's accounts are not taken into consideration, for then history may become merely a record by a detached observer, perhaps from a different generation, cultural background, or idealistic predisposition, who may weigh historical events against his own values. The consequence is that truth becomes distorted and suffers as a result.

It is almost impossible to recall, effectively, a period of more than fifty years ago without referring to documents, photographs and verbal recollections. In this respect I am fortunate to have surviving comrades of KG 30 with whom I can talk about shared experiences. During 1998 I had to compile an account of events between September 1944 and May 1945 as part of a history, or *Chronik*, of KG 30. For a better understanding of that history, I included information on the technical and tactical development of the *Mistel* concept and was therefore already well acquainted with the subject when Robert Forsyth asked me to support him in his quest for information from former members of KG 30.

The results of his labours are now complete and I am proud to have played a part – indeed, only a small part – in the completion of this project, and to be able to comment here about his work. I wish to commend the author firstly for his obsession to discover *everything* about his subject; secondly, for his ability to record in words and photographs (even though he was unable to obtain as many photographs as he wished) the history of a weapon which preceded what we today take for granted in a modern weapons system; and thirdly, for his desire and ability to view things as we ourselves saw them when we were young men, rather than conform to what seems to be the prevalent *Zeitgeist* (spirit of the times) required by the majority of today's publishers.

Over the past fifty years, public interest in military aviation has largely been concerned with those individuals who, during the war years, stood in the limelight as fighter pilots. I most certainly do not begrudge my fighter pilot comrades this fame, but little is ever written about reconnaissance, ground-attack or transport pilots and their crews and, with only a few exceptions, what has been written on the subject of bomber aircraft and the fellows who crewed them has been negative.

Now Robert Forsyth has written this book about the men who served in a bomber group, or *Kampfgeschwader*, and in particular of a very special mission they were assigned in March 1945. The weapon to be used was, in terms of the personnel and material expenditure involved, as well as its technical finesse, unique. The period during the last war which the author describes was one in which I was involved intensively and I know of no other publication about the *'Beethoven-Gerät'*, especially one which tells the story of the people and events in the way which we ourselves experienced them. All the people, all the machines, all the successes – and the failures – are recorded here.

Robert Forsyth has carried out the most intensive consultation possible of sources; he has searched for and located many of the participants and has interviewed them critically. He has made a great effort to put together as many illustrations and photographs as are available into this book and his efforts, from my viewpoint, are a complete success.

If I was allowed to acquire only one book, it would be this one. For that I thank Robert Forsyth and his collaborators and am pleased to have contributed this Foreword.

Heinz Frommhold

INTRODUCTION

RUDI RIEDL

Formerly Pilot in 6. *Staffel, Kampfgeschwader* 200

From the Birch Tree to the *Mistel*

I AM often asked how I first became interested in flying. The answer to the fulfilment of my childhood dream was simple; my uncle was a pilot during the First World War and he told me many vivid, wonderful stories, spiced with humour, about flying, which left me with the feeling that I had somehow been his co-pilot. Not far from where my grandmother lived stood two slender birch trees, almost twelve metres high. When the wind blew and they swayed to and fro, I often sat high among their branches living my dream as a pilot.

I was born in Grünberg, in the Sudetenland, now part of the Czech Republic. Then came Hitler, our 'liberator'. We were not his friends. My stepfather was sent to the concentration camp at Dachau and I had to report twice weekly to the Gestapo. I was then given some good advice and volunteered for flying duties in the Luftwaffe. I saw this as one way of escaping the interest of the Gestapo. My training as a pilot began in the summer of 1940. Afterwards, I became a blind-flying instructor at the *Blindflugschule* B9 at Pretsch-an-der-Elbe. The school was disbanded in the summer of 1944 and some of us were transferred to Burg, near Magdeburg. There we joined

KG 200 under the command of its *Kommodore, Oberst* Werner Baumbach. From then on we belonged to the 6. *Staffel*, II. *Gruppe*. Our *Staffelkapitän* in the *Mistel* squadron – or as we called them, 'Father and Son' – was *Oberleutnant* Pauli. We received training on the Bf 109 and Fw 190 in order to master the art of flying the *Mistel* and we experienced little difficulty converting to these types; after all, we had been told we were an élite group of pilots. Flying exercises, tactical studies and learning about our targets brought us closer to the start of operations. In the meantime the *Mistel* had reached maturity. It was an extremely dangerous weapon and was predestined and in a position to successfully undertake the most difficult operations ever mounted by the *Luftwaffe*. Suddenly, the *Mistel* became so important that even Göring wanted to use it.

The British Royal Navy was to feel its might; an attack was planned on Scapa Flow, named Operation *Drachenhöhle*. On 14 February 1945, as we were about to climb aboard our aircraft for our ride to hell, we heard the sounds of engines and machine guns firing. Incredulity followed shock. Was it a coincidence? Had someone revealed our plans? The fact was that two RAF Mosquitos crewed by Flight Lieutenant Craft and Flying Officer Waters and Flying Officer LeLong and Flying Officer McLaren had rendered two of our *Mistel* useless. With that, the prestige attack was called off.

Be that as it may, these daring fellows had prevented an inferno taking place at Scapa Flow affecting both sides. For this act they deserve recognition.

The author, Robert Forsyth, understands his craft well. Through painstaking research he has been able to relate the history of the *Mistel* – the 'Father and Son' – with a clarity and truth that is seldom found. As a pilot and member of one of the *Mistel* units, I greatly value this work and hope that it will find its own special place amongst the many studies of Second World War aviation.

When I look back, despite pleasant and unpleasant events, I am still the boyhood pilot, flying high in the birch trees...

Rudi Riedl

PART ONE | INVENTION

An introduction to early British composite experiments

'LIKE A DOVE FROM A ROOF'

Completed at Friedrichshafen and commissioned in July 1915, the L13 was commanded by Kapitänleutnant Heinrich Mathy the following September when it bombed central London. Mathy flew 14 airship bombing missions over England, more than any other German naval airman.

EARLY COMPOSITE AIRCRAFT EXPERIMENTS

IN 1905, nine years before the outbreak of the First World War, Alberto Santos-Dumont, the wealthy, dapper, French-domiciled son of a Brazilian coffee planter, and a pioneering balloonist and airship pilot, experimented with what was probably the first ever 'composite' aircraft arrangement when he successfully used one of his dirigible envelopes to lift an aeroplane into the air for testing. The same year, John J. Montgomery, Professor of Physics at Santa Clara College in California, launched a man-carrying glider in another experiment which probably owed much to Gustav Koch, an Austrian who, in 1891, had published a paper in which he proposed testing a prone-piloted hang-glider by attaching it to a balloon, towing it to a high altitude and then releasing it so that it could glide to earth.

Although these early experiments seemed only to provoke an attitude of bemused indifference from the international media and the aeronautical fraternity, in June 1912 Fred T. Jane wrote to the British *Flight* magazine asking: 'How long before dirigibles will grow bigger and carry aeroplanes to use against aeroplanes which attack them?'

War broke out and by the spring of 1916, the German Zeppelin bombing campaign against the British Isles had reached its peak. The *Oberste Heeresleitung* (German Supreme Headquarters) had recognised the significant offensive contribution which the airship was making to the overall conduct of the war. Throughout the previous year both army and navy airships had mounted several successful attacks against London and other targets, such as Folkestone in the south of England and Hull and Tyneside in the north of the country.

From late April and throughout May 1915, the first 32,000 m3 ship, LZ38, operated over Harwich, Southend, Ramsgate and then on the night of 31 May, over central London, dropping 1,400 kg of grenades and incendiary bombs into the docks during this first *London-Angriff*. On this occasion, the vivid blasts of the explosions below were clearly visible to the crew of LZ38. But for the frustrated British anti-aircraft gunners below, the enemy airship remained invisible because of the high altitude at which it flew and the murky prevailing weather conditions. Nine aircraft took off to intercept but failed to locate the Zeppelin due to the weather. Nevertheless, LZ38's commander, *Hptm.* Erich Linnarz, realised that the British would quickly and vigorously enhance their defences.

The short summer nights brought a lull in operations, but raids resumed that September. On the night of 7-8 September, *Hptm.* George's LZ74, loaded with 2,000 kg of general purpose and incendiary bombs attacked London accompanied by a wooden-framed Schütte-Lanz type airship, SL2, under the command of *Hptm.* Richard von Wobesser. Again, the target was the Surrey Commercial

A scene of destruction somewhere in East London in 1915 following a German bombing raid.

Docks and the West India Docks located to the east of the city as well as the railway stations at Bow and Bethnal Green in the East End. *Hptm.* George wrote that large fires had been observed during the attack and though his craft had been fired upon by British batteries, LZ74 escaped undamaged. Eighteen Londoners were killed and another 38 injured.

Less than 24 hours later, four Navy Zeppelins took part in the fourth *Geschwader-Angriff* over England. On this occasion more than 4,800 kg of bombs rained down on London, Middlesbrough and Norwich, resulting in the heaviest raid directed against Britain for the entire war. The commander of Airship L13 was *Kapitänleutnant* Heinrich Mathy who would take part in more airship raids than any other Navy Zeppelin flier, flying fourteen operational missions and dropping 34,000 kg of bombs; he wrote of the 8 September raid:

> 'Navigation from Kings Lynn to London was straightforward because the landscape was completely dark and most of the cities were still lit up. London was still very brightly illuminated and was recognisable from Cambridge. Orientation over the entire capital was very easy because Regent's Park was located precisely and the city centre was lit up as if in peacetime. After passing Regent's Park the crew began dropping bombs near High Holborn at an altitude of 2,500 m.'

Immediately twenty searchlights picked out the airship and the English anti-aircraft batteries started to find L13 with quick-firing rounds. L13 climbed to 3,400 m and reached a small cloud in order to hide. After all the bombs had been released, the airship retired to Cambridge and from there to the coast.

The raid left 22 dead, 87 injured and there was serious damage to property and business premises. In total, the German Navy mounted thirty Zeppelin raids against England during 1915 and dropped 37,000 kg of bombs. Over the course of the next eighteen raids, 111 airships dropped 166,000 kg on targets in London and the Midlands. The appearance of these monstrous machines in the skies over England and the increasing number of shattered buildings caused panic and even riots amongst a civilian population which had always assumed that wars were fought on foreign soil.

Standard British tactics to combat the Zeppelins usually centred around tenacious attacks by individual fighters – often B.E.2c two-seat biplanes – armed with bombs or aerial darts which were dropped manually onto the enemy airship. A chain of observers was established across the north-east of London and in the event that a Zeppelin was spotted, a coloured rocket was fired with the colour indicating from which direction the airship was approaching. At this signal the Home Defence Squadrons were alerted, hopefully soon enough to allow just one aircraft to be sent up to an altitude of 8,000 ft. Once at this height, the pilot was to patrol over his own field for up to 90 minutes and to take offensive action if the airship was spotted. If not, he was to return to his airfield, firing a green signal flare to indicate his approach in the darkness at which point the ground crew would respond with a similar light to confirm that the landing area was clear and then light a string of 5 gallon kerosene/gasoline filled fuel cans to outline the runway. These fighters were usually modified as single-seat night-interceptors, with the space for the observer converted to accommodate more fuel. However, despite a theoretical top speed of 93 mph, it took the B.E.2c nearly an hour to reach the Zeppelin's comfortable ceiling of 3,658 m, a height which then had to be exceeded in order to position the aircraft above the airship so as to be able to bomb it.

At least one pilot carried specially made petrol bombs which were pushed by hand through a tube in the cockpit floor of his BE 2c fighter. When pushed through the tube, an electrical contact lighted the fuse, whereupon the bomb burst into flames, discharging a bunch of large fish-hooks. It was hoped that the hooks would catch inside the Zeppelin's envelope and the flames would destroy the enemy craft. However, little – if any – success was achieved with these weapons.

On other occasions, the pilots of the Home Defence Squadrons simply tried to empty a drum or two of Lewis gun bullets into a Zeppelin, but this had little more effect than diverting the attention of German crew members who were compelled to conduct emergency repairs. Certainly, it was rare that sufficient damage was inflicted to bring a Zeppelin down.

The first destruction of a Zeppelin by another aircraft occurred on 7 June 1915 when Flight Sub-Lieutenant R.A.J. Warneford of the Royal Naval Air Service (RNAS) dropped six 25-lb bombs on LZ37 over Belgium, a feat for which Warneford was awarded the Victoria Cross. In other instances, land-based anti-aircraft fire either contributed to, or accounted for, the destruction of a Zeppelin.

In a measure designed to intercept the Zeppelins before they reached the English coast, a small seaplane carrier, the *Vindex*, was fitted with a flying deck from which it was intended to operate a pair of Bristol Scout fighters. The Royal Naval Air Service (RNAS) already deployed Bristol Scouts as anti-Zeppelin fighters from aerodromes in eastern and southern England, but success had so far proved elusive. The ship-borne Scouts were dismantled once on board and stowed in a purpose-built 'hangar'. Offensive armament for RNAS anti-Zeppelin operations usually comprised two containers of explosive Ranken darts carried directly under the pilot's seat, each container holding 24 darts. On 3 November 1915, on a dead calm sea, with *Vindex* steaming at 25 knots, Flight Lieutenant H.F. Towler made the first successful deck take-off accomplishing it in under 30 ft, but subsequent operations mounted from the carrier resulted in failure. Aircraft were forced to ditch into the North Sea and other disadvantages included the lengthy reassembly of dismantled aircraft on board ship which meant interception sorties could not be flown at short notice.

In 1915, Commander N.F. Usborne, a well-known British pioneer aviator and commander of Kingsnorth airship station in Kent, embarked upon another radical anti-Zeppelin experiment. The intention was to design and develop an anti-Zeppelin aircraft capable of long endurance. A composite aircraft, known as the AP.1, or 'Airship Plane 1', was assembled comprising a B.E.2c fighter (S/N 989) attached to an SS ('Sea Scout') Type airship envelope. It was intended that the airship would carry the fighter to the altitude at which Zeppelins operated and then remain 'on station' using minimum fuel. If a Zeppelin was sighted, the envelope would be released and the B.E.2c would close in to attack.

Although the concept appeared to be sound, difficulties were experienced when the release gear became entangled during a trial flight on 21 February 1916, causing premature release at 4,000 ft. The B.E.2c inverted and crashed into the goods yard of Strood railway station, throwing out and killing both Commander Usborne and his fellow officer, Lt. Commander de Courcy W.P. Ireland.

On a calm sea on 3 November 1915, F/Lt. H.F. Towler, RN, flying Bristol Scout C, No. 1255, made the first take-off from a carrier ship in wartime when he successfully left the deck of HMS *Vindex*, a small seaplane carrier used for operations against German Zeppelin airships.

Described as the 'the first aeroplane ship', the Airship Plane 1 combination of a Sea Scout airship acting as a carrier for a B.E.2c fighter, was flown by Commander N.F. Usborne over north Kent, England, in 1916. Usborne's intention was that the airship would carry the fighter to its zone of operation and in the eventuality of contact with a Zeppelin, the B.E.2c fighter would be released for attack. This was one of the earliest known airworthy composites. Usborne and another airman were killed in the machine in February 1916.

The Admiralty promptly banned any further experiments with AP.1 and a later version, the AP.2, though completed, never flew.

On 16 May 1916, an intriguing contraption comprising a flying boat carrier aircraft with a Bristol Scout C fighter mounted on its upper wing – effectively the first known aeroplane composite arrangement – slid down the slipway at the RNAS Station at Felixstowe on the east coast of England to mark the beginning of an innovative experiment to improve further on the strike response time of carrier-borne intercepts.

The mastermind behind this experiment was 33-year-old Irish-born Squadron Commander John Porte, the commander of the Felixstowe Station.

Commander John Porte (left) glances at the camera from the hull of the *America* flying boat in late 1914/early 1915. As commander of the RNAS Felixstowe he would develop and build the first known composite to incorporate two powered aircraft.

JOHN PORTE

JOHN PORTE joined the Royal Navy in 1898 as an officer cadet and following his initial training, volunteered for the submarine service. In January 1908, he was appointed to command his first submarine and a successful naval career seemed assured just over two years later when he was offered command of one of the Navy's most modern and sophisticated submarines, the C38.

Porte's ambitions, however, were dealt an unexpected blow when, in early 1911, he was invalided out of the Navy with pulmonary tuberculosis.

Fortunately, his illness did little to daunt his enthusiasm for his great interest in aeronautical experimentation. While a serving naval officer, he had as early as 1909 experimented with a glider which was tested on a wooden track on Portsdown Hill near Portsmouth. In 1910 he built his own version of the Santos-Dumont *Demoiselle* and also a biplane made with a tubular steel frame powered by a 40-hp engine. The same year he learned to fly on a Deperdussin monoplane at Rheims in France where facilities for flying instruction were considered better than in England.

By 1912 he had been appointed technical director and designer at the British Deperdussin Company with whom he built a reputation as an excellent pilot at the company's flying school at Hendon.

Following the closure of the Hendon school in August 1913, Porte became test pilot for White and Thompson Co. Ltd, the company which had acquired the British rights for the products of the Curtiss Aeroplane Company of Hammondsport, New York. In October 1913, Glenn Curtiss personally delivered one of his latest types of flying boat to White and Thompson's representative in Brighton, England. Porte was so impressed by what he saw there that he resigned his position with White and Thompson and moved to Hammondsport to work for Curtiss.

In America Porte became involved in the building of a flying boat capable of crossing the Atlantic. The boat was called *America* and had been commissioned in response to a prize of £10,000 offered by a leading British newspaper, the *Daily Mail*, in 1913 for the first successful completion of a trans-Atlantic flight. *America's* design incorporated a wingspan of 72 ft, two 90 hp Curtiss engines and a crew of two, one of whom was to be John Porte. Porte was backed in this venture by Rodman Wanamaker, scion of John Wanamaker, the department store tycoon, and a number of successful flights were made over Lake Keuka in July 1914. Sadly, however, just as *America* neared completion, war broke out in Europe and Porte immediately returned to England, contacted the Admiralty offering his services and was subsequently appointed to command the RNAS Training School at Hendon.

His first move was to persuade the Admiralty to purchase two *America* class flying boats which arrived at Felixstowe in November 1914 where they engaged in trials. The results of the trials proved promising and an order for a further fifty boats fitted with more powerful engines was made in March 1915 with delivery of the machines following during the second half of the year under the designation Curtiss H.4.

By the autumn of 1915, Porte was working to find ways in which to improve and modify the Curtiss H.4 into a fully seaworthy and operationally capable flying boat. Again, his sense of experimentation prevailed and modifications involving hull extension fins and tail extensions were made to five Curtiss hulls.

In late 1915, Porte commenced work on the prototype of a large three-engined flying boat of his own design known as the Porte 'Baby'. In many ways, this bore a remarkable similarity to the Curtiss H.4 in areas such as the wing configuration. In its prototype version, the machine was powered by three 250-hp water-cooled V-12 Rolls-Royce Eagle engines, two positioned outboard and driving tractor airscrews, the third located centrally and operating as a pusher. Although underpowered for its size, the Baby could nevertheless achieve a very acceptable maximum speed of 78 mph. The 57-ft plywood-covered hull incorporated an enclosed cockpit for the pilot, with further accommodation for four more crew.

Initial trials conducted in a following sea pointed to a loss of stability and the Baby wallowed badly, but this deficiency was overcome by introducing a 3-ft extension to the bows which subsequently improved water performance. On the morning of 11 May 1916, in what were described as 'fine but overcast conditions' at Felixstowe and over a moderate sea, Lt. Helbert took the Baby – more officially known as 'The Porte Flying Boat' – for a test. Things went well and Porte later recorded: '*Porte Flying Boat was tested and gave much satisfaction. Speed has increased to 68 knots and she rises more easily from the water.*'

Over the next few days, further tests were conducted – apparently successfully – with Commander Hope Vere at the controls accompanied by passengers – as many as six on one such flight.

An order for twenty production Babies was placed with May, Harden and May of Southampton Water, a subsidiary of the Aircraft Manufacturing Company. The production models differed little from the prototype.

Thought to have been the largest aeroplane built in England at the time, the Porte Baby seaplane lies on the slipway at Felixstowe in 1916. With a span of 124 ft and a loaded weight of 16,500 lbs, the Baby had a maximum speed of 78 mph and could climb to 9,000 ft in nine minutes. The aircraft was chosen by John Porte for the lower component of his composite experiment.

For example, the prototype, RNAS Serial No.9800, incorporated a diamond-shaped structure of four struts at the rear of the outboard engines but this was later modified to include an improved engine installation and revised strut design comprising a standard straight interplane strut fitted between the rear spars of the upper and lower mainplanes in line with the engines and all subsequent production aircraft carried this modification. Most production machines were powered by Rolls-Royce Eagle engines, with the later examples receiving improved performance from Eagle VIIIs. Ultimately however, only ten Porte Babies were completed.

Between 1917-1918, the Porte Baby saw operational service with the RNAS stations at Felixstowe and Killingholme but they proved to be vulnerable due to their low speed and lack of manoeuvrability. During the afternoon of 1 October 1917, a Baby suffered a 20-minute attack by three enemy aircraft near the North Hinder Light Vessel. Despite damage to two of its engines, the crew managed to conduct repairs at sea and taxi the machine back to the English coast, north of Orfordness. The Babies were known to carry machine guns for defensive armament, probably on mountings in the hatchway immediately behind the cockpit and also behind the wings. The prototype, which was equipped experimentally with a six-pounder non-recoil gun mounted on the bows thought to have been intended for anti-submarine operations, was also most likely used as the carrier for Porte's composite experiment of May 1916 which used a Bristol Scout C biplane as the upper component.

The Bristol Scout was a tried and tested single-seat biplane, used by both the Royal Flying Corps (RFC) and the RNAS, and had first entered service in August 1914. Designed by Frank Barnwell at the Bristol works of the British and Colonial Aeroplane Co., it developed a reputation for excellent handling qualities combined with superior structural strength. In July 1915 Captain Lanoe G. Hawker of No.6 Squadron won the first Victoria Cross to be awarded for air-to-air combat whilst flying a Scout armed only with a single-shot cavalry carbine. Hawker was able to drive one enemy aircraft down, damage another and shoot down a third.

In total, 80 Scouts went to France although RFC use there was generally limited to the protection of reconnaissance machines, with one or two Scouts serving with each squadron. The aircraft never fully equipped one complete unit and by the opening of the Somme offensive in July 1916, only two Squadrons had the type on strength. In RNAS employment, the Scout C was used both operationally and for training. Unlike many of the RFC aircraft which were fitted with an 80-hp Le Rhône engine, the RNAS machines, which were envisaged as operating more frequently over the sea, were given the 80-hp Gnôme engine which was considered a more reliable power unit. However, some Scout Cs were fitted with the 80-hp Clerget rotary engine.

Scout C Serial No.3028 – one of the machines previously employed on the *Vindex* – was selected to serve as the upper component in Commander Porte's anti-Zeppelin composite experiment at Felixstowe. Porte's method was to mount the Scout in a central position on a

Bristol Scout D, No.5574 with non-standard cowling. A Scout was to serve as the upper component in Commander John Porte's composite experiment of 1916.

Commander John Porte's composite, featuring the Porte Baby seaplane as the lower component and a Bristol Scout C as the upper component, waits on the slipway at the RNAS Felixstowe in May 1916.

Porte Baby's upper wing. The Scout's undercarriage was positioned immediately in front of the leading edge of the flying boat's wing, the wheels resting in special crutches carried on struts from the engine bearers of the Baby's central engine. The Scout's tail skid was secured by a quick-release toggle controlled by the fighter's pilot.

At 1050 hrs on 17 May 1916, in fine weather and over a moderate sea, the Baby took to the air in what was to be the first and only successful flight and airborne separation of the Scout-Baby composite. The Scout played no active part in the take-off and its engine remained switched off throughout.

Described by Porte for official reasons as simply '*an extended flight*', an element of mystery surrounds the composite's debut. With Porte at the controls of the Baby, the Composite climbed over Shotley and Felixstowe. Once the combination had reached a height of 1,000 ft over Harwich, the pilot of the Scout, Flight Lieutenant M.J. Day, switched on his engine, ran it up to full power and, according to one commentator, lifted away from the flying-boat 'like a dove from a roof.' Despite deteriorating visibility, this whole episode could clearly be seen from both the air station at Felixstowe as well as from other points along the coast and by vessels at sea, yet strangely, Porte made no reference to this sensational aeronautical achievement in his 'Daily Report' for the RNAS, his entry stating merely that the '*...Porte Flying Boat carried out non-stop flight of 4 hours 50 minutes. Fog prevented further flying. Engines ran perfectly.*'

There is a further oddity; Porte also stated that it had not been him flying the Baby, but Commander Hope Vere. One can only speculate that for reasons of embarrassment or official disapproval, Porte intended to cover up the flight of the Composite.

Shortly afterwards, F/Lt Day landed the Scout safely at nearby Martlesham. The experiment was never repeated.

Two days later, Vere is recorded as flying the Baby on another 'extended flight' and towards the end of the month, the flying boat transferred to the RNAS Establishment on the Isle of Grain for armament and altitude tests. On a flight on 28 May 1916, Vere reached 5,600 ft. The last recorded mention of the Porte Baby is on 30 May 1916 when it was listed as undergoing overhaul.

John Porte went on to work with more experimental flying-boat designs, including the Felixstowe F.1, F.2, F.3 and F.5. Perhaps his most ambitious project was the Felixstowe Fury, known unofficially as the 'Porte Super Baby', which was a massive triplane flying boat with a wing span of 123 ft, fuel capacity of 1,500 gallons and powered by five Rolls-Royce Eagle VII engines. At one stage, it was proposed to fly the Fury across the Atlantic but financial limitations prevented this.

After the war, in August 1919, John Porte joined the Gosport Aviation Company Ltd and designed a series of passenger, mail and freight-carrying boats. Unfortunately, in October of that year, he finally succumbed to the tuberculosis which had plagued him for several years. Despite it being unknown to him, the successful outcome of the brief experiment performed at Felixstowe three years earlier would remain one of his most extraordinary and lasting legacies, the principles of which would surface again firstly at Felixstowe and then as used by the German Luftwaffe on a greater scale and in a much more offensive form during the course of the next world conflict.

'I AM NOT CONVINCED THAT IT HAS ANY REAL USEFULNESS'

BRITISH PRE-WAR COMPOSITE AIRCRAFT

Inspired by Norman Macmillan's 1928 patent for 'aircraft coupled in pairs or trains', a Fairey III F is seen here at the Royal Navy base at Gosport on the south coast of England in 1933. The aircraft has been fitted with support struts on its upper wing to carry and air-launch a gunnery target glider which was partially gyro-stabilized.

TO what extent, if any at all, John Porte's composite experiment in 1916 influenced the minds of post-war British aircraft designers is not known. In 1928 however, Norman Macmillan, test pilot at the Fairey aircraft company, obtained a patent for 'aircraft coupled in pairs or trains'. Macmillan envisaged a method whereby an aircraft carried above itself a 'gliding bomb' loaded with either ammunition, stores or mail and which, if necessary, could also 'be used for attack'. Ultimately though, Macmillan's idea was adopted only as a means to launch target gliders for anti-aircraft gunnery practice by the Royal Navy. At least one such composite arrangement was assembled and used at Gosport in 1933 when a partially gyro-stabilised target glider was fitted to a Fairey IIIF, although the naval gunners disapproved of the target since it proceeded in a series of stalls and dives.

There, it seems, the notion rested until April 1932 when another patent was granted to Major Robert Hobart Mayo, the General Manager (Technical) for Britain's Imperial Airways for 'aircraft carrying other aircraft.' Born in 1890, Mayo possessed an acute mind. A Cambridge graduate in mathematics, he joined the Royal Aircraft Factory at Farnborough and just before the First World War was appointed head of the experimental department. On the outbreak of war, he resigned and joined the RFC with which he served on the Western Front, but was recalled to Britain to work as a test pilot at the Aeroplane Experimental Establishment at Martlesham Heath in Suffolk. Subsequently he joined the Air Ministry heading the Design (Aeroplane) Section, Technical Department and after working for a period as a consultant joined Imperial Airways at the beginning of the 1930s. Mayo's job at the airline was to draw up specifications of new aircraft and to work closely with aircraft manufacturers. The origins of his application for a composite lay in response to the problem of the carriage of airmail between Britain and North America.

Mail had first been carried by air in 1919 when the British Post Office granted the first contracts of carriage under which mail was sent by air (though only at a substantial surcharge), thus ending the ocean-going 'monopoly' previously enjoyed by the big shipping lines. As traffic increased, so the surcharges applied came down and in 1927 Imperial Airways took over the Cairo-Baghdad desert airmail route which had been established by the RAF six years earlier, incorporating it into the route to India as a lucrative additional and alternative source of revenue to the carriage of passengers. By 1930 airmail charges had become standardised for all European destinations and in December 1934 Parliament approved a flat rate at which all first-class mail would be carried before June 1937 by air throughout the British Empire, except to Canada and the West Indies. However, Imperial Airways and Qantas who, in 1931 had jointly experimented in running pioneering air mail services to Australia, had already concluded that, in the interests of cost and reliability, a new standard type of flying boat was needed for the long-haul routes. Unlike such overland services operated in America, the cost of running purely airmail services over long-distance sea and jungle crossings, especially during monsoons, was not economically viable. However, the Dutch carrier, KLM, together with the Netherlands Post Office, had proved it could be done by operating a successful mail/passenger route between Amsterdam and Batavia (now Jakarta). Thus, acting on Robert Mayo's advice, Imperial Airways issued a specification for a large, four-engined flying boat for employment on the arterial African, Indian and Australian routes.

One of the companies which tendered for the flying boat contract was the Rochester-based firm of Short Brothers, established by three enterprising brothers in 1908 – Horace, Eustace and Oswald Short.

Horace, the elder brother, had spent several years travelling and working abroad and when he returned to England in 1895, he moved to London with his widowed mother and two brothers, where he patented a steam or compressed air-powered sound-amplifying device which he had invented.

Eustace and Oswald meanwhile had developed a fascination for ballooning and in 1904 collaborated with Horace on the design of a high-altitude hydrogen-filled balloon. The following year, the brothers won a contract to supply three reconnaissance balloons for the Indian Army and in April 1907, following the completion of other balloons, won a gold medal for excellence of manufacture from the Aero Club of the United Kingdom.

The break into aircraft manufacture came in 1908 when Wilbur Wright, who, with his brother Orville had startled the world with the invention of their aeroplane, offered the licence to build British versions of their Flyer to the newly registered partnership of Short Brothers.

With a factory established at Leysdown on the Isle of Sheppey, production of the Short-Wright Flyers commenced. Whilst Horace concentrated on the development and production of aeroplanes, Eustace and Oswald continued their involvement with balloons and built several examples including the 79,000 ft^3 Planet which competed in the 1909 Gordon Bennett race from Zurich to Poland.

In 1913, a new factory was built at Rochester on the River Medway in Kent. The First World War saw Short Brothers designing and producing many single-engined twin-float seaplanes. Expansion followed with a further factory being built at Cardington near Bedford for the construction of rigid airships for the Admiralty.

Upon Horace Short's death in April 1917, the firm diversified and Oswald dabbled in using duralumin in the construction of wing ribs and seaplane floats. In July 1920, using this material, he attracted American attention with his Silver Streak seaplane. The company also kept busy by building motorboats, barges and ships' lifeboats, though a financial disaster during the 1923-24 depression was only averted by a timely contract to supply vehicle bodies for a London bus company. Throughout the interwar years, the company used its experience in seaplane production to build a variety of successful flying boats such as the Singapore and Calcutta/Rangoon types which saw service with the RAF and Imperial Airways overseas and the Valetta which was used for a 12,300-mile survey and route-proving flight along the Nile to Central Africa in 1931. The previous year, an enlarged version of the Singapore had been built for the Japanese Navy.

Imperial Airways became a good customer of the company throughout the 1930s, ordering a number of four-engined Kents (the replacement for the Calcutta). The airline was pleased with the aircraft since, despite five years' exposure to the elements and climatic changes, they showed no signs of corrosion. Two landplane variants were also ordered by the carrier, each capable of taking 39 passengers.

Biplane flying boat production ended in June 1932, the year of Eustace Short's death, with the launch of the six-engined, 5,000 hp Sarafand and a year later, the company sold 22 of its smaller six-seat Scion monoplanes, powered by two 90-hp Pobjoy engines.

A successful bid for the four-engined flying boat tender from Imperial Airways resulted in the series production of the famous Empire flying boat. No fewer than 28 of these aircraft were ordered straight off the drawing board and they became a recognisable and enduring symbol of the British Empire throughout Africa, India and Australia, carrying both passengers and mail.

Meanwhile, whilst the challenge of establishing regular and reliable air mail routes to the east had been met, the problem of extending such airmail services to North America still remained. The truth was that the Empire flying boat would only just be able to cross the Atlantic if all its disposable load was turned over to fuel. Another method was needed.

Geographically, the most direct route to North America was the Great Circle route via Ireland to Newfoundland but again for an aircraft, the prevailing westerly winds demanded very large and impractical reserves of fuel. A sub-Arctic route with staging via Iceland and Greenland was possible but only under extremely favourable summer conditions. The other, more practical option was to stage via the Azores and Bermuda, but even this was not feasible. Bermuda possessed an adequate seaplane base but the only harbour in the Azores at Horta on the island of Faial, was considered too small and busy for large, heavily-laden flying boats and the open sea was too dangerous.

Three potential solutions emerged. The first originated with a method adopted by Deutsche Lufthansa (DLH) for its early airmail service to New York. On 22 July 1929, a Heinkel He 12 seaplane, registered D-1717, was launched by a compressed air-powered K.2 catapult from the upper sun deck of the Norddeutsche Lloyd's ocean-going liner Bremen. Designed by Heinkel, the catapult's compressed air tube ran through one of the vessel's enormous smokestacks, down to the engine room, where it was connected with the ship's compressed air installation. The Bremen was on her maiden voyage westbound across the North Atlantic and the Heinkel – carrying 11,000 letters – was launched at a point some 45 minutes flying time from New York. Ernst Heinkel, the aircraft designer, was on board and witnessed the launch; he wrote:

> '... the ship's post office was crowded with people, particularly women, who wanted to send a letter by this new method. It would bear a catapult-mail postmark. Shortly before the start, 60,000 Marks' worth of post was loaded on the He 12, but that hardly worried me. At the official starting time, everyone was out on the sun deck. To the last second, I was afraid something untoward would happen... The ship was travelling at a good 28 knots, as my catapult calmly and without a sound, turned into the wind. The Hornet engine[1] was throttled back, Studnitz and Kirchhoff[2] climbed into their seats. I wonder how many of the spectators realised that they were witnessing

[1] The He 12 was powered by a 500 hp American Pratt and Whitney Hornet engine.

[2] Captain von Studnitz – DLH pilot and Kirchhof, his radio operator.

Watched by curious passengers, Heinkel He 12, D-1717, takes off from Norddeutsche Lloyd's ocean-going liner *Bremen* on the first catapult-launched airmail flight to New York on 22 July 1929. The compressed air catapult installed on the upper sun deck of the *Bremen*, measured 27 metres in length. Aircraft designer, Ernst Heinkel who was on board at the time wrote: 'Long before the spectators could grasp what had happened, the plane was over the Atlantic swell.'

The Heinkel He 12, D-1717, lies on the water in New York harbour on 22 July 1929 as mail is unloaded and thrown down to a waiting launch.

a historical moment in the history of flying. Schwärzler, at the control panel, tightened the starting cable and two red lights went on in the cockpit. This told Studnitz that the catapult was ready to start. He flashed back the "OK" signal and Schwärzler[3] pushed the lever to start.

'Even the giant ship herself swayed a little beneath us as the compressed air hissed out and the plane was launched, at great speed, along the runway. Long before the spectators could grasp what had happened, the plane was over the Atlantic swell. Like a tiny line in the sky the wings grew smaller and smaller and soon disappeared as the bows of the *Bremen* threw up higher waves, proving that the ship was at full speed once more.'

The flight was a success and the Heinkel arrived in New York harbour five hours ahead of its mother ship which had also just won the Blue Riband from Cunard Line's *Mauretania* for the fastest Atlantic crossing. The system continued until 1935.

In June 1932, DLH tested its revolutionary new long-distance mail service from Berlin to Buenos Aries via Barcelona, Seville and Las Palmas, and Bathurst in the Gambia. From Bathurst, a Dornier 15 Wal flying boat would fly across the Atlantic to a dedicated support ship. Landing near the vessel, the Wal would then be hauled by a massive crane up a 'dragsail', a semi-rigid blanket which reached into the water from over the stern and which acted as a slipway. The flying boat was then moved to the bow from where it was launched into the air, to embark upon the Natal-bound leg of its journey, off a 103-ft ramp at 94 mph using a compressed air catapult.

Regular scheduled services were expanded in 1937 with the introduction of the elegant Blohm und Voss Ha 139 A which suited DLH's requirements for a long-range floatplane. Two such aircraft were used: the Ha 139 V1, registered D-AJEY and named Nordwind, and the Ha 139 V2, registered D-AMIE and named Nordmeer. Supported by the depot/catapult ships Schwabenland and Friesenland, the Ha 139s took between 14-19 hours to complete the east-west transatlantic journey from the Azores to Newfoundland. However, various instability faults with the aircraft were discovered and trials were stopped at the end of November 1937.

[3] Schwärzler – an Austrian engineer who worked for Heinkel.

This method was barely acceptable, because despite the fact that the aircraft did not carry passengers, the DLH crews found the launch accelerations – up to 4.5 g – difficult to tolerate. Nevertheless, Major Rupert Penny at the British Air Ministry proposed utilising specially converted barges for catapult launching, complete with refuelling and repair facilities, though this proposal was rejected on the grounds that the climb for a heavily-laden mailplane from a sea-level launch to its operating altitude would incur too great a cost in terms of both fuel and time.

A second prospective solution to the problem of crossing the Atlantic non-stop stemmed from a proposal by Sir Alan Cobham, the renowned aviator and barnstormer, whereby an Empire flying boat would take off at normal weight with a moderate fuel load and rendezvous for air-to-air refuelling from a tanker aircraft out of Horta. It was known that a flying boat starting from Lisbon could be refuelled over the Azores, provided that a firm rendezvous could be guaranteed. This method was actually adopted later on the Ireland-Newfoundland route once the techniques of coupling hoses and transferring fuel had been improved.

The third and perhaps most radical solution lay in Major Mayo's 1932 proposal for a composite aircraft. Mayo's plan called for a heavily laden mailplane to be fitted on top of a larger more lightly loaded carrier aircraft which would then transport the mailplane to its operational

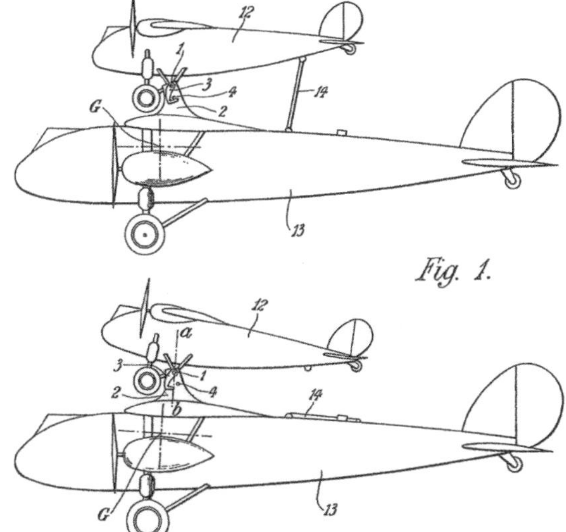

Drawings from Robert Mayo's patent for a composite aircraft dated 27 April 1933. In the US patent from July 1935 the concept was described as a means of launching aircraft in the air at such speed and altitude as to ensure safe continuation of flight without having to attain minimum flying speed while taxying over land or water.

altitude, at which point the components would separate. The mailplane would then continue to its destination burning enough fuel en route to be below its maximum permitted weight for landing. The lower aircraft or 'component' would then return to its base either to perform another launch or to operate in its own right as a short-haul transport until required again for an aerial launch.

In his memoirs, the Australian-born former RAF pilot, Captain Donald C.T. Bennett, who later flew the upper component mailplane wrote:

> 'Bob Mayo was the typical scientist, tall and thin, slightly drooping – he had the most meek voice and mild manner of any relatively senior official I have ever known. In fact, his position in Imperial Airways was only one stage from the top, yet his manner was that of a shy schoolboy. Behind his quiet exterior, however, he packed a very fine intellect, and indeed quite a strong character which he only showed when really necessary. His work technically was of a high order, and his contribution to Imperial Airway's success was undoubtedly great. His only weakness was that often he would not stand up, particularly against the commercial interests of the company, in a manner which we pilots would have liked to have seen. He was certainly one of the kindest people for whom I have ever worked.'

Both the Air Ministry and Imperial Airways viewed Mayo's proposal favourably for, at an estimated total cost of £60,000 and on the basis that both components were to be seaplanes, the project would be much cheaper and more workable than installing catapults on barges and would be ready years before efficient in-flight refuelling. In 1935, a contract for the construction of a single 'Mayo Composite' was awarded to Short Brothers, the cost being shared between the British Treasury and Imperial Airways.

When completed, the lower component was designated the S.21, registered G-ADHK and named *Maia*. In many respects, *Maia* resembled an Empire flying boat but with one or two noticeable differences. Firstly, the machine had a slightly wider beam than the Empire boat as well as flared chines and a tumblehome cross section bringing the wing-roots closer together. In order to give adequate clearance for the floats of the upper component, *Maia's* engine nacelles were mounted farther along the wing which had the same overall span as the Empire, but was greater in area by 250 sq ft. There were also increases in the chord and area of the tail surfaces and changes to the hull in the stern which raised the tailplane in relation to the wing. Accommodation was provided for 18 passengers. Power came from four 920-hp Pegasus Xc 9-cylinder air-cooled radial engines.

The upper component was designated S.20, registered G-ADHJ and named *Mercury*. It was a four-engined, twin-float, mid-wing seaplane with an oval section-fuselage which was of standard Short Brothers monocoque construction. It had the benefit of a strong longitudinal box-beam which could accommodate a load of over 5,000 lb when carried by a single attachment hook under the centre of gravity. Powered by four Napier-Halford Rapier engines, this neatly designed machine had a total fuel capacity of 1,200 gallons allowing a cruising range of 3,000 miles. The fuel could be jettisoned early into a flight in the case of an emergency.

The whole machine was skinned with Alclad sheet except for the control services which were fabric-covered; the rudders and elevators had inset trim tabs. The enclosed cockpit in which pilot and navigator sat in tandem was positioned well forward of the wing. The hold, located under and aft of the wing, could accommodate 1,000 lb of mail, the port-side loading door also serving as crew entry.

When coupled, the two components of the Mayo Composite effectively functioned as one aircraft, the controls of the upper machine being locked and its pilot only contributing to thrust and lift. The Composite's higher centre of gravity required more positive lateral stability on the water and this was achieved by increasing the beam of the planing bottom and the displacement of the wing floats, which were also lowered so that with full load, both were awash simultaneously.

Mayo's original intention had been to allow separation of the two components by means of the upper component's elevator control, but this was discarded as too risky and later design centred around using the differential lift-coefficients of aerofoils for the two components arranged in such a way that, as speed increased, the upper component took a greater share of the total lift than the lower, thus creating a positive separating force strong enough to overcome spring detents intended to hold the components together.

In the case of *Maia* and *Mercury*, the controls of the upper component, except the trim tabs, were all locked in the neutral position to prevent relative yawing forces being applied before separation from the lower component. To ensure that the S.20 was correctly trimmed fore and aft upon release from the S.21 and also to provide the pilot with some initial control, the S.20 pilot was allowed a small degree of movement in pitch. Nose- or tail-heaviness was indicated to the lower pilot by lights. The lower pilot waited until four lights on his instrument panel flicked on simultaneously – forward trim, aft trim, 3,000 lb tension, 5,000 lb tension – and then pulled his release lever.

The Short S.21, G-ADHK, *Maia*, sits on the slipway with its four 920-hp Bristol Pegasus Xc radial engines idle.

The elegant Short S.20, G-ADHJ, *Mercury*, seen on a rain-dampened slipway.

He then spoke by telephone to the S.20's pilot, whose own lights would be showing 3,000 lb and 5,000 lb tension, to advise that the hook was free. At that point, the S.21 pilot would pull his release lever and a third securing hook would be released automatically as soon as the tension exceeded 5,000 lb by a pre-set spring-controlled load.

On release, the S.20 would rise in level attitude and accelerate, whilst the S.21 would fall away eliminating any risk of collision following separation, though for a few moments, neither pilot was able to see the other aircraft.

Maia first flew for 20 minutes on 27 July 1937 with Shorts chief test pilot, John Lankester Parker, at the controls. Following this flight, the support structure for the S.20 *Mercury* upper component was fitted and the aircraft was installed with temporary four-bladed wooden airscrews. Two more trial flights were performed, without incident, before three-blade variable-pitch airscrews were fitted ready for a level test at 6,000 ft, which took place on 9 August. Three days later, the aviation press had a chance to see *Maia* fly during a demonstration flight.

Mercury embarked upon its maiden flight on 5 September when Parker flew it for 15 minutes, followed by a 40-minute handling flight the next day. On 8 September, *Mercury*, too, was shown to an intrigued group of press reporters.

For the remainder of 1937, both components continued to be flown separately whilst stability and positioning tests were made. On 1 January 1938, Parker began taxying trials with the complete Composite assembly. During one such flight, the Composite accidentally became airborne for a short time whilst the Shorts designer and project manager, Bill Hambrook, was observing the release gear while still standing on top of the lower component. He was left to grasp firmly onto the support pylon!

Parker made the first 20-minute combined flight on 20 January with Harold Piper at the controls of *Mercury*. Though the Composite handled well on this occasion, no separation was attempted due to incorrectly set load indicators. Adjustments were made to rectify this problem and on 5 February the Composite flew for a second time, but rough weather foiled a further attempt at separation. Then, on the following day, in excellent prevailing weather conditions but without any prior planning, the first separation took place during the course of a 30-minute flight over the River Medway. The event passed without any problems and went virtually unnoticed, being witnessed by only a few residents in the nearby riverside towns of Rochester and Strood. However, the British Movietone News ciné cameras were ready when, on 23 February, Parker, accompanied by Captain A.S. Wilcockson of Imperial Airways as co-pilot, achieved perfect separation at 700 ft over the Medway during a public demonstration flight. Wilcockson told curious journalists after the flight: 'I think the chief thing we discovered was that it wasn't a fluke the first time.'

Others were more sceptical; writing on the Mayo Composite in The Aeroplane that month, C.G. Grey scoffed:

> 'I am not convinced that it has any real usefulness... Personally if I had to cross the Atlantic in a hurry by air I would rather do it in a helium-filled Zeppelin with heavy-oil Diesel motors than in any other way. But if I had plenty of time I would rather go by a small one-class boat which would take eight or nine days to do the job and would not receive endless messages or issue a daily news bulletin.'

Major Robert H Mayo (right), General Manager (Technical) of Imperial Airways and inventor of the Short-Mayo Composite, with Short Bros test pilot John Lankester Parker photographed on 6 February 1938. Short's S.21, G-ADHK, *Maia* is on the water behind.

The Short-Mayo Composite moored on the River Medway.

Captain A.S.Wilcockson (centre) of Imperial Airways, flew the *Maia* lower component of the Short-Mayo composite during fuel consumption tests and in-flight separation trials. Wilcockson is seen here on the occasion of the commencement of the England-India air route in March 1929.

Captain Donald C.T. Bennett of Imperial Airways who flew the S.20 *Mercury* upper component. He found the delays to the completion of the Composite 'insufferable.' Bennett is seen here later in his career as an Air Vice Marshal in the RAF.

In a caustic article, Grey scorned the 'heretical doctrine' which lay behind the concept of the Composite and he questioned the aspects of passenger safety and cost: 'Whoever may be financing the Mayo Composite scheme has got to spend a few more hundreds of thousands before the scheme can be put to any practical use…'

The following month, the Composite was delivered in separate components to the Marine Aircraft Experimental Establishment (MAEE) at Felixstowe where full-load tests and, eventually, full-load separations were performed by both the Shorts team of Parker and Piper (in *Mercury*) and Squadron Leaders Martin and Pickles of the MAEE. However, according to Donald Bennett of Imperial Airways, things did not always go smoothly at Felixstowe:

> 'The laborious processes were unbelievable, and I really think that if I had not been present during the whole of the tests the Felixstowe staff would have taken at least two years to complete them. Fortunately, their governmental inefficiency was somewhat offset by the fact that a very good friend of mine, tall and cheerful Percy Pickles, was the pilot allotted to the aircraft… Finally, with summer well advanced, we managed to wrest *Mercury* and *Maia* away from Felixstowe…'

Following the successful conclusion of these tests, the Composite components were then returned separately to Shorts. In June, *Mercury's* Rapier V engines were upgraded to supercharged Rapier VIs, at which point the whole Composite was handed over to Captains Wilcockson (*Maia*) and Bennett (*Mercury*) for fuel consumption tests at Hythe in Southampton Water on the south coast of England. These tests proved eventful for Bennett; just before the first such flight he avoided serious injury when he slipped on a mixture of water and hydraulic fluid which coated *Maia's* smooth upper surface. In the darkness of the early morning, clutching some valuable technical equipment, he fell off the aircraft into the chill water below. Fortunately for Bennett, he avoided colliding with the motor-launch which had ferried him to the Composite and which had until only moments earlier, been tethered to *Maia*! He recalled:

> 'On the second of these test flights the intercommunication between the lower half and the upper half failed, and I regret to say, so did our intended drill, covering such an eventuality. It speaks volumes for the care which Major Mayo had put into the design that in spite of this we separated without trouble. The sensation of separating in a composite aircraft is exactly the same as that of dropping a heavy bomb.'

After a string of delays, which Bennett found 'insufferable', he bullied the Air Ministry sufficiently enough so that on 14 July 1938 a further separation was performed over Southampton, following which Bennett, accompanied by his radio operator, A.J. Coster and an Air Ministry observer, flew 2,040 miles to Foynes on the Shannon in Ireland and out over the Atlantic to a sufficient distance from where shortwave radio contact was made with both Foynes and Botwood in Newfoundland, Canada. Encouraged by these gratifying accomplishments, Mayo and Bennett next wanted to attempt to fly *Mercury* all the way to Newfoundland, land, reload and return to the UK without *Maia*.

The Air Ministry, however, remained unimpressed and sceptical. At a meeting attended by Mayo, Bennett and Wilcockson and representatives from the Ministry, the case for further development of the Composite was presented. Bennett recalled:

> 'To me it was a new experience, the pattern of which repeated itself in my life many times in the years that followed. Lashings of civil servants, some said to be scientific and some admittedly not, sat around and solemnly and formally told us that *Mercury* with a full load of petrol could barely do the trip from Foynes to Botwood, and that its return flight without *Maia* to help it off the ground was quite impossible. They based their opinion on the Felixstowe test figures, and it seemed to be that dear old Bob Mayo, a somewhat sensitive man, was going to shrivel up and disappear. Fortunately, Percy Pickles provided me with the knowledge that Felixstowe, somewhat ignorant of the peculiarities of Exactor hydraulic controls, had carried out all the fuel consumption tests on rich mixture. Fortunately, Imperial Airways were themselves responsible, and although the Air Ministry still had most serious doubts about what I said, they gracefully stood aside and let us continue with the projected flights.'

Mercury was launched again over Foynes shortly before 2000 hrs on 21 July. This time she carried 600 lb of newspapers, press photographs and newsreels.

> 'Headwinds were forecast,' wrote Bennett, 'and therefore immediately after the separation, I dropped down from 2,000 ft to cross the last little piece of Ireland. Thereafter, whilst daylight lasted, I cruised at about 50 ft above the surface, avoiding as far as possible the effect of the headwinds. There was an automatic pilot on *Mercury*, and fortunately it was a good one. With a compass excellently sited and very accurately swung, I found *Mercury* a wonderful aircraft to navigate… Never before nor since have I experienced such an excellent navigational arrangement, nor have I achieved more accurate results...'

Twenty-four hours and 20 minutes later, Bennett and Coster touched down in a blaze of publicity at Boucherville, Montreal in Canada with 80 gallons of fuel still in the tanks. This meant that consumption was less than 54 gallons per hour, substantially better than specified and much better than the Air Ministry's pessimistic calculations. Without delay, *Mercury* was refuelled. She took off for Port Washington, Long Island, from where, after a short stop, she flew on to Botwood via Boucherville on 25 July. The next day she headed to Horta and then, via Lisbon, to Hythe on the south coast of England on the 27th. The average speed for the entire round trip was calculated to have been over 160 mph.

In August 1938, the first prototype of the new German four-engined Focke-Wulf Fw 200 *Condor* airliner, the Fw 200 V1 was redesignated Fw 200 S-1 (the 'S' suffix denoting *Sonder* or 'special'), and renamed *Brandenburg* with the registration D-ACON. On the 10th of that month, the aircraft took off on a non-stop long-distance publicity flight from Berlin to New York. Despite strong headwinds, the Fw 200's pilots, Alfred Henke and Rudolf von Moreau, covered the 6,558 km to Bennett aerodrome, New York in 24 hours and 55 minutes at an average speed of 264 km/h. The return journey was accomplished in only 19 hours and 47 minutes at an average speed of 330 km/h.

It was this feat which prompted Bennett to suggest to the British Secretary of State for Air, Sir Howard Kingsley Wood, that the S.20 *Mercury* should be used for an attempt on the world seaplane distance record. Not wishing to be

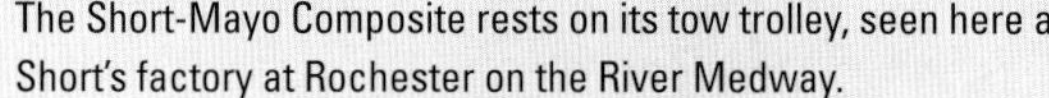

With *Mercury* safely attached to *Maia*, the Composite is prepared for its short tow towards the water.

The Short-Mayo Composite receives final checks on the slipway.

The Short-Mayo Composite on the River Medway with engines running and gathering speed.

The Short-Mayo Composite rests on its tow trolley, seen here at Short's factory at Rochester on the River Medway.

The Short-Mayo Composite in flight over the Kent countryside, early 1938.

Moment of separation: the S.20 *Mercury* lifts away from the S.21 *Maia*.

The Short S.20 banks low over the water's edge on its return flight following separation from S.21.

In early 1939 following an increase in airmail traffic, Imperial Airways considered a plan to use two adapted Armstrong Whitworth AW 27 Ensigns as lower components in an enhanced version of the Short-Mayo Composite. The Ensigns would carry a landplane variant of the S.20. The scheme was ultimately abandoned.

surpassed by the German achievement, the Air Ministry agreed to Bennett's proposal and on 6 October, the Composite took off from Dundee in Scotland and *Mercury* was launched with her course set for Cape Town, South Africa, which it was hoped would be reached non-stop. To facilitate this, *Mercury's* floats had been sealed in Rochester for use as transfer tanks which increased the machine's fuel capacity to 2,130 gallons.

The trip was tough; firstly, icing over southern England forced Bennett and his co-pilot, Ian Harvey, to take *Mercury* down from the intended cruising altitude of 10,000 ft to 3,000 ft and high wind tore off an engine cowling which subsequently increased drag. After ten hours flying time, *Mercury* crossed the Algerian coast. However, severe winds over the Sahara and tropical thunderstorms over Equatorial Africa meant that the chances of reaching the Cape on the available fuel were slim. Furthermore, the electric pumps designed to draw fuel from the float reserves failed and Bennett and Harvey were forced to use the manual hand-pump, an exhausting task at 12,000 ft without oxygen.

Eventually, *Mercury* landed on the Orange River, close to the Alexander Bay diamond mine settlement, having flown 6,045 miles in just over 42 hours. After refuelling from five 40-gallon drums floated out to the seaplane, *Mercury* reached Cape Town and, later, Durban, where she was inspected and the flight duly recorded as an international seaplane record for distance in a straight line at 5,997.5 miles.

The South African trip almost heralded the end of Composite operations. In a bitter reflection, Bennett wrote: 'After this flight, which was one of the major world air records, I received no official reception, no trace of recognition of any sort from the Government and no celebrations from Imperial Airways, from Short Bros or from Napiers, the makers of the engines. I wonder if such a flight could have occurred in any other country without at least some form of celebration on the return?'

Upon return to Southampton, *Mercury* underwent various trials with de-icing boots along the wing, fin and tailplane leading edges as well as tests involving modified engine intakes. However, these were brought to an abrupt stop in November 1938, when an unprecedented accumulation of Christmas airmail stretched Imperial Airway's resources to their limit. On 29 November, *Mercury* was again pressed into service and launched from *Maia* over Southampton. This time, in the first of two such flights, she was loaded to capacity – a one-ton payload with mail bags even packed into her floats. Bennett and Coster flew 2,200 miles non-stop to Alexandria, Egypt at 152 mph. The second flight took place on 12 December.

The Alexandria trips were to be the last Composite flights which *Mercury* would perform. Ice at Botwood prevented any more flights to Newfoundland and the resumption of summer services the following year was frustrated by the threat of war in Europe and the diversion of effort towards in-flight refuelling trials. *Mercury* remained inactive for over a year, whilst *Maia* was fitted out to accommodate ten passengers for flights between Southampton and Foynes before being used for navigational training. On 11 May 1941, whilst under BOAC jurisdiction and with the support pylons for *Mercury* removed, *Maia* was destroyed during a German night raid on Poole harbour.

In June 1940, *Mercury* wax delivered by Bennett to the RAF's 320 (Netherlands) Squadron, whose personnel had managed to escape their homeland ahead of the German invasion. The unit subsequently undertook coastal reconnaissance duties using *Mercury* for training purposes. During 1941, 320 Squadron was re-equipped with Hudsons and *Mercury* was returned to Felixstowe for scrapping. The RAF flew the aircraft back to Rochester on 9 August 1941 where it was broken up soon afterwards.

In a damning indictment of the apparent disregard shown by both the British government and BOAC to Mayo's work on the Composite concept, Air Vice-Marshal D.C.T. Bennett wrote in his post-war memoirs:

> '... the pioneers of the Empire air routes were given no recognition whatever... Major Bob Mayo, the General Manager Technical [never] received any honours for the grand pioneering work [he] had done... It is deplorable as it is typical that the country of [his] birth gave him no honour.'

There had been a glimmer of a chance for further development of Robert Mayo's concept in late 1938/early 1939 when the favourable airmail volumes carried by the Composite induced Imperial Airways to consider placing an order for a small fleet of landplane composite variants based on four S.20 upper components and two adapted Armstrong Whitworth Ensigns serving as the lower components.

Designed and built as a large four-engined 'Empire route airliner', Imperial Airways initially intended to deploy the Ensign on the European and Eastern passenger routes. Unfortunately, the limited numbers of aircraft built by Christmas 1938 were proving underpowered and prone to malfunctions and mechanical problems. Imperial Airways hesitated and in January 1939, Armstrong Whitworth informed the airline that, lacking a positive decision, it was too late to convert the eleventh and twelfth aircraft and that work on the thirteenth and fourteenth was virtually at a standstill pending instructions one way or another. The new composite scheme was eventually abandoned.

Despite its relatively low cost, the Air Ministry also rejected the proposal on the grounds that the segregation of mail and passengers did not form part of long-term policy. In an attempt to soothe Imperial Airways' disappointment, the Mayo Composite was offered to them at no cost, an offer which the airline gladly took up.

'FOR HEAVEN'S SAKE, DON'T LET THIS COME UP AGAIN'

BRITISH WARTIME DEVELOPMENT, DILEMMAS AND DISAGREEMENT

The Fw 200 Condor – the aircraft which Churchill described as 'formidable' and which forced the British to consider the possibility of using composite aircraft to protect convoys in the Mediterranean. The Fw 200 C-2 of 1./KG 40 seen here on patrol over the Bay of Biscay was shot down during a night mission off the east coast of England in July 1940.

ALTHOUGH the Shorts-Mayo Composite was the only arrangement of its type known to have flown in England, at least one other radical British designer had been sufficiently attracted by the composite concept to commence initial construction of his own design.

The designer in question was Noel Pemberton Billing. Pemberton Billing was viewed by many as a paradox; on one hand, a devoted advocate of the development and expansion of aviation, blessed with a quick, fertile and imaginative mind, whilst on the other, an unpredictable extremist and entrepreneur with a tendency towards the impractical. Born in London in January 1881, Pemberton Billing ran away from home at the age of 13 and found his way to Delagoa Bay, Mozambique aboard a sailing tramp. From Durban where he found employment as a bricklayer and tram conductor, he travelled to Natal and joined the Natal Mounted Police, becoming their champion boxer at the age of 16. Twice wounded during the Boer War, he returned to England and opened a garage.

He attempted his first aeronautical flight in 1904 in a home-made glider by flying from the roof of his house in East Grinstead, Sussex – a feat which nearly cost him his life. Undeterred, he established an airfield at Fambridge, Essex in 1909, affording it the somewhat grandiose title, 'The Colony of British Aerocraft'.

On 17 September 1913, he was awarded his RAeC Aviator's Certificate as a result of a wager of £500 with Frederick Handley Page that he would learn to fly and qualify for his Certificate before breakfast!

It was during the same month that the title 'Supermarine' was adopted as the name of a small aircraft factory founded by Pemberton Billing at Woolston near Southampton. Nothing particularly remarkable came out of Supermarine at this time, the company concentrating its efforts on a somewhat unremarkable range of seaplane designs, some of which were distinguished by removable wings, without which the hull was intended to function as a cabin cruiser.

With the outbreak of the First World War, Pemberton Billing enlisted for service in the RNAS as a Flight Lieutenant and his short war service career is perhaps best noted for his masterminding an audacious 'cloak-and-dagger' style air raid on the German Zeppelin factory at Friedrichshafen. The operation was fraught with difficulties and unexpected hitches, but it left one new Zeppelin completely destroyed and the factory severely damaged, forcing the Germans to conduct a hurried reorganisation of the Zeppelin works, involving the diversion of valuable military resources away from the front to guard an installation previously thought safe from attack.

At the beginning of 1916, Pemberton Billing left the RNAS with the rank of Temporary Squadron Commander. He also sold the Supermarine Aviation Works to embark on a career in politics and write his first book, *Air War, How To Wage It*. Having been involved at first hand in the war against the Zeppelins and with public fears mounting as a result of the airship raids on England's cities, he supported the various xenophobic media campaigns running in England for some kind of concerted retaliation

Noel Pemberton Billing, an unpredictable yet inventive man who devised the concept of the 'slip-wing' as an alternative to the composite.

against Germany. Pemberton Billing stood for candidacy in two by-elections. The second of these elections saw him successfully elected MP for East Hertfordshire and he promoted himself as the 'First Air Member of Parliament'. He immediately began to promote one of his key campaign themes – a ruthless policy of direct retaliation against German civilians. This, he argued, could only be achieved through the creation of an independent air force established specifically to bomb Germany. He was supported by other 'air-minded' MPs such as Winston Churchill, though on one occasion, he was expelled from the chamber of the House of Commons when his 'expostulations' against the unprepared state of British air defences grew too extreme.

Nevertheless, Pemberton Billing's demands forced the creation of a new all-party Parliamentary Air Committee which was intended to promote the idea of raids against Germany. For a time, it seemed that he had become too preoccupied with politics to afford time to designing aeroplanes, but during the mid-1930s, this changed.

The P.B.37 is thought to have originated in 1936 – the height of Pemberton Billing's design renaissance, though further development did not really occur until later. Though he was aware of Robert Mayo's Composite design, Pemberton Billing considered the idea to be economically flawed because the lower component of Mayo's creation had to be larger and heavier than the aircraft it was to carry into the air. Pemberton Billing subsequently set about designing his alternative to the Composite based around a so-called 'slip-wing' which took the form of a powered and piloted glider with twice the wing area of the lower aircraft upon which it was mounted. This reduced the wing loading of the complete composite to a figure sufficiently low to allow a normal take-off run.

Once airborne at a safe height, the lower component – either a heavy transport aircraft or a bomber – separated from the slip-wing and performed its assigned mission. This meant that the lower component could have wings of less area than it would need for a conventional take-off and yet still be able to operate from limited airfields, a distinct advantage in military terms. Furthermore, its cruising speed would be enhanced by the reduction in wing area following the release of the slip-wing which would then return to its base ready for re-use.

In the spring of 1940, with RAF bombers flying their first missions against German shipping in the North Sea and conducting leaflet-dropping sorties over Germany and occupied Europe, Noel Pemberton Billing joined the Manchester-based firm of F Hills and Son. This company, located in the former Ford factory at Trafford Park, gave the designer complete freedom to work on his Air Ministry-approved composite project and allocated staff to him under the project manager, A.E. Clarke. Quite how Pemberton Billing was able to acquire clearance for the use of the materials he needed at a time when the war in the air was just beginning to intensify, remains a mystery, but work began in earnest in a sectioned-off area of the factory known as the 'Experimental Unit'. After just five weeks, the wooden, single-seat, mid-wing monoplane upper component with its tricycle undercarriage, cruciform tail and 135 ft² wing area was virtually completed. This was powered by a 40 hp two-cylinder air-cooled engine driving a two-bladed wooden propeller.

Despite being of a more complex construction, work progressed with equal speed on the lower component. It took eleven weeks to complete the uncovered airframe and install the 290-hp in-line engine mid-fuselage where it would drive a pair of low-speed pusher propellers behind the wing trailing edges via a high-speed shaft from the engine to a gearbox with two speeds and reverse. The fuselage took the form of a welded-steel-tube box girder, faired to oval cross section and fabric covered. The 67 ft² wing area and tailplane were wooden and fabric covered. The engine was completely enclosed offering what Pemberton Billing considered to be 'exceptional visibility for the pilot with the highest possible aerodynamic efficiency.'

The two components were coupled by a simple four-point attachment connected to a single release button which was controlled by the pilot of the lower component.

It was estimated that the P.B.37 could carry a 1,000-lb payload for 1,000 miles at 240 mph with a top speed of 260 mph at 10,000 ft.

In the early summer of 1940, work on the P.B.37 was halted. In a bitter article to *Flight* magazine in November 1941, Pemberton Billing complained of lack of official assistance or financial cooperation from the Air Ministry with his composite project and, as with his earlier projects, the venture never saw completion.

Still Pemberton Billing would not rest. As the Battle of Britain was fought and London experienced the *Blitz*, so the designer studied tactical and strategic necessities more closely and this was reflected in at least three of his later slip-wing projects, the P.B.41, P.B.47 and P.B.49.

The first-mentioned of these was intended as a means with which to increase the endurance of a standard fighter – flying as the lower component of a slip-wing composite – to enable longer standing patrols over large cities with the specific hope of intercepting German bombers at night. Pemberton Billing opined that a Hawker Hurricane would be the most suitable option and that it could be attached to a twin-boom pusher biplane or strut-braced high-wing monoplane as the upper component. Powered by a de Havilland Gypsy engine with a crew of two, the upper component would also be equipped with a skid undercarriage, radio equipment, flares and a nose-mounted searchlight. It would also feature large fuel tanks from which the fighter would draw fuel.

Tactically, it was intended that the upper-component crew would to all intents and purposes fly the patrol, thus allowing the fighter pilot to rest until an enemy aircraft was spotted. At this point, the fighter's engine would be opened up and the slip-wing's engine started. The fighter would then release the slip-wing by breaking the connection with the four holding points located on its upper fuselage. Once in action, it was rather naively thought that the fighter could be assisted by the low-powered slip-wing as it dropped parachute flares and/or applied its searchlight upon the enemy aircraft.

The P.B.47 and P.B.49 projects both dated from 1940 and were based on high-speed bombers. In the P.B.47, Pemberton Billing hoped to create a small but fast single-seat bomber able to carry 2,000 lb of ordnance for 2,000 miles – far enough to reach several German cities – its take-off assisted by a high-wing strut-braced powered slip-wing, thus reducing the wing area of the bomber to around 160 ft² which was 100 ft² less than that of a Hurricane fighter. The maximum speed was set at 530 mph but as Pemberton Billing wrote:

> '...there are features which do not appeal to the Air Force authorities. The fact that it is a single-seater prevents the use of a bomb-aimer so dear to our hypocritical hearts, and the discarding of military equipment is demanding greater sacrifice on the part of the pilot, but surely these

minor sacrifices are worth putting up with for the sake of a weapon against which there can be no effective defence?'

The P.B.49 was effectively a larger variation of the P.B.47 and utilised a compact and well-designed twin-engined long-range bomber about half the size of a Vickers Wellington and powered by two 2,000 hp liquid-cooled engines underslung on the wings and mounted as pushers driving contra-rotating propellers. The take-off run was approximately 900 ft and the initial rate of climb was calculated at 1,070 ft per minute. Again, as with the P.B.47, wing-loading was drastically reduced by using a high-wing strut-braced slip-wing with a 210 hp engine to help the bomber into the air. Once release had been achieved, the bomber, with a wing area of 420 ft^2 and a span of only 61 ft, could easily carry a 10,000 lb bomb load at a cruising speed of 400 mph. Range was 5,000 miles with an endurance of 12.5 hours, though Pemberton Billing boasted that with careful handling, range could be extended to 8,000 miles. The crew of three – pilot, co-pilot/bomb-aimer and navigator/wireless operator – effectively sat surrounded by fuel tanks capable of holding 1,400 gallons of fuel. Alternatively, the bomb load could be increased allowing up to 20,000 lb of explosive to be carried to Berlin.

However, despite Pemberton Billing's eccentric genius and creativity, his well-meant if seemingly unfeasible composite projects were met with little more than bemused derision by the Air Ministry.

By 1941, with Shorts' *Maia* destroyed by enemy action and *Mercury* broken up, Noel Pemberton Billing's P.B.37 languishing in a forgotten corner of a Manchester factory and aeronautical experts continually working on longer-range aircraft with improved performance, there seemed little likelihood that the Composite concept would ever resurface. However, this was not the case for that same year the devastating effect on Allied convoys of the Luftwaffe's long-range anti-shipping operations and the demands for safe escort of Allied shipping in the Mediterranean forced senior commanders, for a while at least, to consider otherwise.

In his post-war memoirs, Winston Churchill summarised British fears about the danger posed to merchant shipping from German air attack:

> '*To the U-boat scourge was now added air attack far out on the ocean by long-range aircraft. Of these the Focke-Wulf 200, known as the Condor, was the most formidable... They could start from Brest or Bordeaux, fly right round the British island, refuel in Norway, and then make a return journey the next day. On their way they would see far below them the very large convoys of forty or fifty ships to which scarcity of escort had forced us to resort... They could attack these convoys, or individual ships, with destructive bombs, or they could signal the positions to which the waiting U-boats should be directed in order to make interceptions...* '

Few individual German aircraft types achieve specific mention in Churchill's memoirs but the fact that the Fw 200 does, is testimony to just how much the long-range Luftwaffe reconnaissance-bomber increasingly became a painful thorn in the side of British maritime interests during early 1941. Throughout the last half of 1940 and into early 1941, the Fw 200s of I./KG 40, under the command of *Major* Edgar Petersen, had been exacting a debilitating campaign against British merchant shipping around the British Isles. Petersen had been ordered by the Chief of the Luftwaffe General Staff, *General der Flieger* Hans Jeschonnek, to select an aircraft capable of undertaking long-range maritime patrol and strike operations until the new Heinkel He 177 became available in 1942. He opted for the Fw 200 primarily because, unlike one alternative, the Ju 90, there were twelve such aircraft readily available.

Operating out of Bordeaux-Merignac on the French Atlantic coast, the *Gruppe* was predominantly equipped with the Fw 200 C-1. With a crew of five and powered by four 830 hp BMW 132 radial engines, the aircraft was capable of carrying mixed offensive loads of 250-kg and 500-kg bombs. Cooperating closely with the German Navy's *Marine Gruppe West* at Lorient, these aircraft were able to search/patrol across the Bay of Biscay and range in a wide arc over the Atlantic to the west coast of Ireland and then north towards their landing bases in Norway.

During August and September 1940, I./KG 40 sank more than 90,000 tons of Allied shipping. On 26 October, the unit enjoyed a spectacular success when *Oblt.* Bernhard Jope bombed and crippled the 42,500-ton Canadian Pacific liner *Empress of Britain* off the north-west coast of Ireland. The vessel was en route to Liverpool from Cape Town carrying more than 600 service personnel and passengers, most of them on their way home from the Middle East. The liner was torpedoed and sunk by a U-boat two days later.

Throughout November and December there were regular low-level bombing and strafing attacks on unarmed merchant vessels and convoys off the west coast of Ireland. On 30 December, Admiral Karl Dönitz, the *Befelhshaber der U-boote*, demanded at a staff meeting: 'Just let me have a minimum of 20 Fw 200s solely for reconnaissance purposes and U-boat successes will go sky high!' In January 1941, Hitler placed I./KG 40 under the direct control of the German Navy.

During the period 1 August 1940 to 9 February 1941, 85 ships totalling 363,000 tons were sunk by the *Gruppe*. This was despite the fact that actual serviceability was usually only six to eight aircraft, operating one or two sorties a day over the Biscay area but often extending their patrols to the north-west coast of Ireland. By the end of February, the *Condors* had accounted for 22 ships sunk that month, totalling 84,515 tons. Tactically, despite lack of a reliable bombsight, the *Condors* made their attacks low enough to ensure that at least one bomb out of a stick of five would hit. As Petersen recalled: 'You could hardly miss... provided you kept low enough.'

In the spring of that year, Colonel Stewart Menzies, the head of Britain's Secret Intelligence Service, aroused Churchill's interest in the possibility of deploying a 'small fighter plane pick-a-back on a large one to attack the Focke-Wulf in the North Western Approaches.'

Quite why Menzies was involving himself in issues so far divorced from the world of intelligence is not clear, though the spymaster was known to have many influential friends in London's corridors of power and it is possible that he was acting on behalf of other interested parties. Certainly by this time, a scheme to place a Hawker Hurricane fighter on top of an Armstrong Whitworth Whitley twin-engine bomber had been proposed by at least one section of the Air Staff, following recommendations by RAF Coastal Command.

On 2 March 1941, Churchill, in his capacity as Minister of Defence, wrote to his Chief of Staff, Major-General Sir Hastings Ismay, asking for further details in respect to the technical and military practicalities of Menzies' suggestion. Ismay was a man used to acting as the

During the spring of 1941, RAF Coastal Command put forward a proposal to mount a Hawker Hurricane fighter on top of an Armstrong Whitworth Whitley bomber in an attempt to combat the Fw 200. In the photograph to above left, are Hurricane IICs of No. 87 Sqn, RAF seen in August 1942 when the unit's aircraft were deployed on night-intruder missions.Above right, Whitleys of No. 102 Sqn, RAF. During the early war period, these aircraft were employed on leaflet-dropping missions over Germany and 'security patrols' over the Frisian Islands.

link between Churchill and the Chiefs of Staff – a task that demanded extraordinary ability, tact and strength of character. One close aide to Churchill considered that "... nobody did more to oil the wheels on the bumpy road between the service chiefs and the politicians."

Ismay passed the matter to Air Chief Marshal Sir Charles Portal, the somewhat obstinate Chief of Air Staff. Portal, who would skirmish with Churchill months later over his firm reluctance to consider the introduction of a long-range fighter aircraft to protect British bombers on daylight raids over Germany, showed equal reluctance over the feasibility of a 'pick-a-back' fighter for deployment against the *Condor*. He replied to Ismay:

> 'Some time ago I considered the idea of using a fighter mounted pick-a-back on a large aircraft but I have no hope that it will help us defeat the Focke-Wulf. All attempts to deal with commerce raiding aircraft by means of shore-based fighters or reconnaissance aircraft are open to fundamental objection that the number of machines required to maintain patrols at long range would be out of all proportion to the number of interceptions which we could hope to effect. At moderate range, the Beaufighter would be more efficient than the Whitley-Hurricane combination. This particular scheme has the additional drawback that the only large aircraft available are large bombers and it would be wasteful in the highest degree to divert still more of our scanty bomber force from the task of attacking targets which they know they can.'

Portal's sentiments won the support of Sir Henry Tizard, a former RFC pilot and Chairman of the Aeronautical Research Committee, a body of airmen, government scientists, administrators and university scientific staff established to explore and analyse the question of air defence. In fairness, Tizard took the view that no proposal, however improbable, should be discounted if there was the remotest chance of it being used successfully to repel an enemy air attack. However, on the question of a composite aircraft he was forthright in his opposition. Already, a proposal made by Short Brothers in the light of that company's experiences with the Short-Mayo Composite, had landed on his desk. As an alternative method of extending the range of a Hurricane fighter so as to provide escort for long-range Atlantic patrols, Short Brothers proposed mounting a Hurricane II on top of a Liberator. On 24 March 1941, Tizard wrote to Portal:

> 'I hear that you are giving your personal attention to the problem of the Mayo Composite machine owing to the Prime Minister's interest... I have never thought that there was a clear case for the operational use of a Mayo Composite. Some little time ago, however, Coastal Command got very keen on it and was supported by one section of the Air Staff, but not by another. I was pressed to have experiments made. I said what I usually do in such circumstances, i.e. if we are going to do an experiment, let us do it properly. I therefore rejected some suggestions that were put forward and selected a Liberator-Hurricane combination for the experiment... We made, with considerable trouble, all arrangements to see the experiment through.

Winston Churchill poses for a photograph with his Chiefs of Staff in the garden at 10 Downing Street, London in May 1945. In March 1941, Churchill wrote to Major-General Sir Hastings Ismay (standing at right) inquiring as to the technical and military practicalities of a British composite design which would be suitable for protecting convoys in the Western Approaches. Ismay passed the matter to Air Chief Marshal Sir Charles Portal (far left, front row), the Chief of Air Staff, who firmly disagreed with such proposals. It was Portal's opinion that: 'at short ranges the Beaufighter would be at least as efficient as the Composite. The range of the Composite may prove to be too little, if any, more than the Beaufighter.' Churchill eventually agreed.

'At the end of last week the Minister[1] told me that after consultation with you, he had decided that the whole experiment should drop. Before giving instructions, I went to the Air Ministry and saw Freeman and Harris[2], discussed the problem on broader lines with them, agreed with their conclusion that it was hardly worth the effort and left the room saying: "Now for Heaven's sake don't let this come up again because I am afraid that if you don't do the experiment properly someone will always be bringing it up again on the highest level and we shall be back where we started."

'It is this kind of thing that is really detrimental to progress. I don't think even you can have any idea of the time and efforts that are wasted over reconsidering old ideas brought forward by someone new which have something to be said for them but are not of sufficient importance to warrant the time spent. Do not let us half do things. If this is going to be dropped now I hope we shan't hear of it again during the war...'

Two days later, Portal assured Tizard: 'You can rely on me to see that the question is not raised again during the present war.'

Portal then drafted his response to Churchill. In a brusque memo to the Prime Minister dated 26 March he listed the impracticalities and shortcomings of deploying Composite aircraft against the Fw 200:

'At short ranges the Beaufighter would be at least as efficient as the Composite. The range of the Composite may prove to be too little, if any, more than the Beaufighter... At long ranges, the use of shore-based aircraft is an extremely uneconomical means of providing constant protection to a convoy. Up to two squadrons may be necessary for each aircraft maintained over a convoy... The Composite idea is most unlikely to be efficient. The idea arose out of the need to assist an overloaded aircraft into the air and was never intended for use on long flights. The crew of the lower component would have a difficult aircraft to handle and the pilot of the upper component would have to spend long hours in the Hurricane cockpit with a good chance of being drowned if he sighted a Focke-Wulf anywhere except near the convoy... I am more convinced that employing a number of heavy bombers over the Focke-Wulf factory and airfield would do far more towards meeting the menace than they could achieve by carrying fighters over the Atlantic.'

'These reasons are conclusive against the plan,' Churchill replied. 'Proceed as you propose.'

However, despite Portal's attempts to end the Composite debate for good, the idea still found favour with other elements of the armed forces. Hearing of Portal's machinations, in late April 1941 the First Sea Lord, the Rt. Hon. Albert Victor Alexander, urged the Air Ministry not to abandon the further development and trials of composite aircraft. Not surprisingly, the Navy welcomed any measures which would offer much-needed protection of both its own vessels and the vital merchant tonnage which plied waters well within range of I./KG 40's Fw 200s or other Luftwaffe aircraft. Allied merchant shipping lost as a result of enemy air action for the last quarter of 1940 reached 90,080 tons (32 ships), but for the first quarter of 1941 this escalated to 281,216 tons (88 ships). As far as Alexander was concerned the facts spoke for themselves.

The firm of Short Bros., builders of the Short-Mayo Composite, proposed mounting a Hawker Hurricane fighter on top of a B-24 Liberator bomber so as to provide escort for long-range Atlantic air patrols. The idea was rejected by Sir Henry Tizard, Chairman of the Aeronautical Research Committee. Here Liberator IIIs of RAF Coastal Command's No. 120 Sqn are lined up at Aldergrove in April 1943.

Alexander believed, perhaps misguidedly, that the Composite, if adopted, could offer benefits in addition to convoy protection; he suggested that, by their nature, composites could offer long-range fighter cover for landings on enemy-held coasts, provide fighter protection for long-range bombers and assist in the reinforcement of overseas airfields with fighter aircraft. All of these proposals were quickly demolished by Sir Archibald Sinclair, the Secretary of State for Air; contrary to Alexander's suggestions it was felt that composite operations over a landing area would require a 'prohibitive' number of machines, they would be vulnerable to fighter attack and the parent aircraft could better be deployed as bombers in the tactical support role for the landing forces. Furthermore, the idea of long-range fighter escort for bombers was dismissed; 'The loss of fighters would be prohibitive,' Sinclair warned, 'Their range is short and they would be unable to return to their base after being launched.'

In Sinclair's view, the replenishment of overseas airfields with fighters was also 'open to objection.'

'The parent aircraft were never intended for long ranges – merely for launching overloaded aircraft,' Sinclair wrote on 1 May. 'And an enormous diversion of effort would be necessary in proportion to the number of fighters delivered.'

However, with the benefit of hindsight, it is possible to see some justification in Alexander's ideas. The very urgent need for the airborne protection of merchant convoys against German air attack had led to the introduction of still untested Fighter Catapult Ships, former cargo ships refitted to carry a

The Rt. Hon. Albert Victor Alexander, the British First Sea Lord, seen here, left, arriving on deck following an inspection of a Royal Navy submarine at Holy Loch, Scotland in June 1942. Alexander urged the Air Ministry not to abandon development and trials of composite aircraft. He believed that composites could offer convoy protection, long-range fighter cover for landings on enemy-held coasts, provide fighter protection for long-range bombers and assist in the reinforcement of overseas airfields with fighter aircraft.

1 Sir Archibald Sinclair, Secretary of State for Air.
2 Air Chief Marshal Sir Wilfrid Freeman and Marshal of the Royal Air Force Sir Arthur Harris.

Sir Archibald Sinclair, the Secretary of State for Air, disagreed with the principle of the Composite. Among several reasons, Sinclair stated that composite operations over a landing area would require a 'prohibitive' number of machines, be vulnerable to fighter attack with parent aircraft better deployed as bombers in the tactical support role for landing forces. Sinclair is seen here (in civilian suit) talking with USAAF officers during a visit to an RAF base in 1942.

catapult from which it was intended to launch either Fairey Fulmar or Sea Hurricane fighters in defence of a convoy when threatened from the air.

The performance of the Fulmar Mk II matched that of the Sea Hurricane Mk IA at 5,000 ft and it was faster in a dive. Its realistic range of 830 miles doubled that of the Hurricane, which gave its crew a greater chance of reaching land after launching. However, the fact was that there were more Hurricane Mk Is available for conversion to Sea Hurricane Mk IAs than there were Fulmars, which in any case were needed by the Fleet. But although the Sea Hurricane may have been available in more plentiful numbers, the real crux came in its performance comparison with the Fw 200. Most likely disadvantaged by hard service during the Battle of Britain, the average Sea Hurricane – unlike a standard Hurricane Mk I – carried additional weight in the shape of catapult spools, a heavy fuel load and strengthening panels. This reduced speed and the truth was that, at 254 km/h, a Fw 200 minus its bomb load, flying at full throttle in evasive action still stood a chance of outpacing a Hurricane. There was also the not entirely irrelevant drawback that, in all probability, once launched from its catapult the aircraft would have to be ditched in the sea and the pilot picked up by escort vessels.

Although sea trials had commenced in March 1941, the Admiralty recognised that there would be problems in the quick development and conversion of catapult-equipped vessels. Siting the catapult above holds would be unsafe, and an athwartships operation would require a vessel to turn its beam to the wind, an impractical option for a laden merchant ship. There was also the fact that when in ballast or only lightly loaded in a rolling sea, conditions on a merchant vessel would be too difficult to launch an aircraft, not to mention the fact that the actual installation of a catapult would mean that a valuable cargo vessel would be out of use for three months – an unacceptable period of time. Maintenance and repairs at sea would also involve complications, and the need for a large number of pilots and maintenance crews to be on board ship for long periods would result in a waste of resources and a lack of training.

The *Springbank*, one of the first such vessels to be converted, underwent considerable modification in preparation for her role as a catapult ship. Searchlights had to be repositioned, a deckhouse was removed and cabins and cranes had to be rearranged to make room for the catapult. Even the arc of fire of her forward guns became limited as a result of the installation of the crane which lifted the fighter onto the catapult.

The situation was not helped by the fact that on 27 April the *Patia*, one of the original four Fighter Catapult Ships to be converted, was attacked and sunk by an enemy aircraft, thought to have been an He 111, off Newcastle-upon-Tyne.

When, on 20 June 1941, Alexander penned a reply to Sinclair, tonnage sunk by enemy aircraft for the quarter beginning April had amounted to 531,170 tons (222 ships) and the remaining Fighter Catapult Ships had been with their respective convoys for some six weeks, though had yet to claim their first victory over a Fw 200.

> 'As we see it,' Alexander wrote, 'the right aircraft to deal with the ocean raiding aircraft is the "cruiser" or "battlecruiser aircraft", provided the superiority of speed and armament is there in order to catch and kill the raider. You say this is the case at present as regards Liberator vis-à-vis Focke-Wulf, but will this be the case in say six months' time? We must expect an improved performance from the enemy at any time.
>
> 'Would it not then be as well to be able to produce the high-class fighter on the spot at the right moment to make full use of the principle of surprise and ensure the kill? For that reason, I should like each long-range aircraft to be fitted to carry a fighter when working over the sea or when on convoy protection provided her performance is not appreciably affected. No doubt the Mosquito may prove a better answer, but I have doubts about its ability to navigate to find a convoy in order to give the protection; and will not the fatigue of the pilot preclude its use at the distances at which the big aircraft can be used?'

Just one month earlier on 21 May, the aircraft carrier *Furious* had steamed through the Mediterranean to Malta, carrying the Hurricanes of 213 and 229 Squadrons intended as reinforcements for the hard-pressed British and Commonwealth fighter contingent in Egypt. Aware of the risks, Alexander issued a warning:

> 'The Composite would also be invaluable for the reinforcement of Egypt, about which I am gravely concerned. The *Furious* will take Hurricanes out via Malta, but if she gets hit whilst in the Mediterranean her whole cargo will be a write-off. She is very vulnerable and there is nothing to take her place.
>
> 'If you can deal with these and similar problems without using the Composite, I will press you no more, but I do ask you to give it your further earnest consideration, and, if you see fit, propose to the Prime Minister that his decision be reconsidered and the experiment completed so that should the operational need arise we may not be caught unprepared. Speed is essential.'

There is little evidence to suggest that Churchill, Sinclair or any other members of the War Cabinet paid

On 23 July 1941 the British destroyer, HMS *Fearless* (seen here on fire to the left) was attacked and sunk by German aircraft south of Sardinia whilst escorting convoy GM.1 comprising six merchant ships bound for Malta. A cruiser and merchant vessel were also damaged during the Luftwaffe attacks. A month earlier, the British First Sea Lord had written to the Secretary of State for Air: 'I should like each long-range aircraft to be fitted to carry a fighter when working over the sea or when on convoy protection provided her performance is not appreciably affected.'

heed to Alexander. Not until nearly a year later, in April 1942, did Churchill again raise the question of the employment of composite aircraft. This time however, his enquiry was for bombers to carry fighters for escort purposes. By now, the Wellingtons, Stirlings and Whitleys of RAF Bomber Command were making regular night raids on German cities and a new aircraft, the Lancaster, had also recently made its operational debut over Germany. The American Eighth Air Force, with its policy of precision daylight bombing, had yet to arrive in England and Bomber Command was the only part of Britain's armed forces which could strike at Germany's western territories and thus offer some support to the Russians who were fighting so bitterly in the east. Simultaneously however, the Luftwaffe had established an efficient nightfighter control network based on the use of long- and short-range radar. These radars would assist in guiding the increasingly proficient German nightfighter crews towards their targets. Portal had selected 43 key German industrial targets – representing a combined population of fifteen million people – which would be subjected to continual air bombardment. To do this he secured Churchill's agreement to provide and maintain a force of 4,000 bombers. But Churchill was concerned at the enormous risks being placed upon the shoulders of his bomber crews. Did the Composite offer a practical, if not unconventional, solution?

In late April Churchill asked his Scientific Adviser, Lord Cherwell (previously Professor Sir Frederick Lindemann) whether he believed that the Composite as a 'fighter-carrier' would prove to be an economical proposition in the war over Europe. Historians have viewed Cherwell as something of a *bête noire*; indeed, one writer has commented that Cherwell's 'fatal weakness was that he rarely found it possible to believe in an idea unless he had been at least a midwife at its delivery.'

This aspect of his character may explain the tone of his reply to the Prime Minister:

> 'The combination would be absurdly vulnerable; if the fighter left his bomber he would seldom be able to reach a friendly base. In any event, it seems doubtful whether either of the machines could carry arms or ammunition if they were to reach their maximum range.
>
> 'Save in the case of the Liberator, no very great ranges seem likely to be feasible. A Whitley-Hurricane combination would probably not get much more than 1,200 miles; a Liberator-Spitfire combination, even over-loading the undercarriage and refuelling the Spitfire in the air, would probably have a maximum range of 2,400 miles.
>
> 'With extra fuel tanks it is possible to give our fighters a range of 1,500 miles, so that they could get to the Middle East in three hops. If still greater ranges were necessary it might be easier to strengthen their undercarriages so that even greater petrol loads could be imposed on them than to face the enormous complications of the composite aircraft and the expense which would be involved in making and manning the mother aircraft.'

In discussion with Portal a few days later, Churchill discussed Cherwell's memo and asked the Chief of Air Staff whether, from a different viewpoint, he considered that composites could be used to replenish aircraft carriers with fighters at sea. Portal replied that he wanted to investigate the matter with his 'technical advisers' and would revert. On 6 May 1942, Portal wrote to Churchill:

A Hawker Sea Hurricane IA is loaded on board a British merchant ship at a Scottish port prior to catapult launch trials.

> 'There is no doubt that composite aircraft could, in theory, be used in the way you suggest. The question is whether we should be wise to divert from constructing and improving aircraft of tried operational types which are urgently needed in every theatre of war the enormous effort required to build these elaborate and vulnerable composite aircraft whose utility is so doubtful. My technical advisers are unanimous and emphatic in supporting Lord Cherwell's opinion that we should not, and I am confident that they are right.'

In a short two word reply from 10 Downing Street two days later, Churchill simply stated: 'I agree.'

From this point, it seems that further mention of the Composite ceased and the idea was quietly shelved. In Germany however, things were remarkably different.

SECRET

5

COPY Offices of the War Cabinet,
Great George Street,
S.W.1.

28th April, 1942.

PRIME MINISTER.

Composite Aircraft.

I do not believe that using bombers to carry fighters is an economical proposition.

Save in the case of the Liberator, no very great ranges seem likely to be feasible. A Whitley - Hurricane combination would probably not get much more than 1,200 miles; a Liberator - Spitfire combination, even over-loading the undercarriage and refuelling the Spitfire in the air, would probably have a maximum range of 2,400 miles.

The combination would be absurdly vulnerable; if the fighter left his bomber he would seldom be able to reach a friendly base. In any event it seems doubtful whether either of the machines could carry arms or ammunition if they were to reach their maximum range.

With extra fuel tanks, it is possible to give our fighters a range of 1,500 miles, so that they could get to the Middle East in three hops. If still greater ranges were necessary it might be easier to strengthen their undercarriages, so that even greater petrol loads could be imposed on them than to face the enormous complications of the composite aircraft and the expense which would be involved in making and manning the mother aircraft.

(Signed) CHERWELL.

C.A.S.

What do you say ?

(Init) W.S.C. 2/5/42.

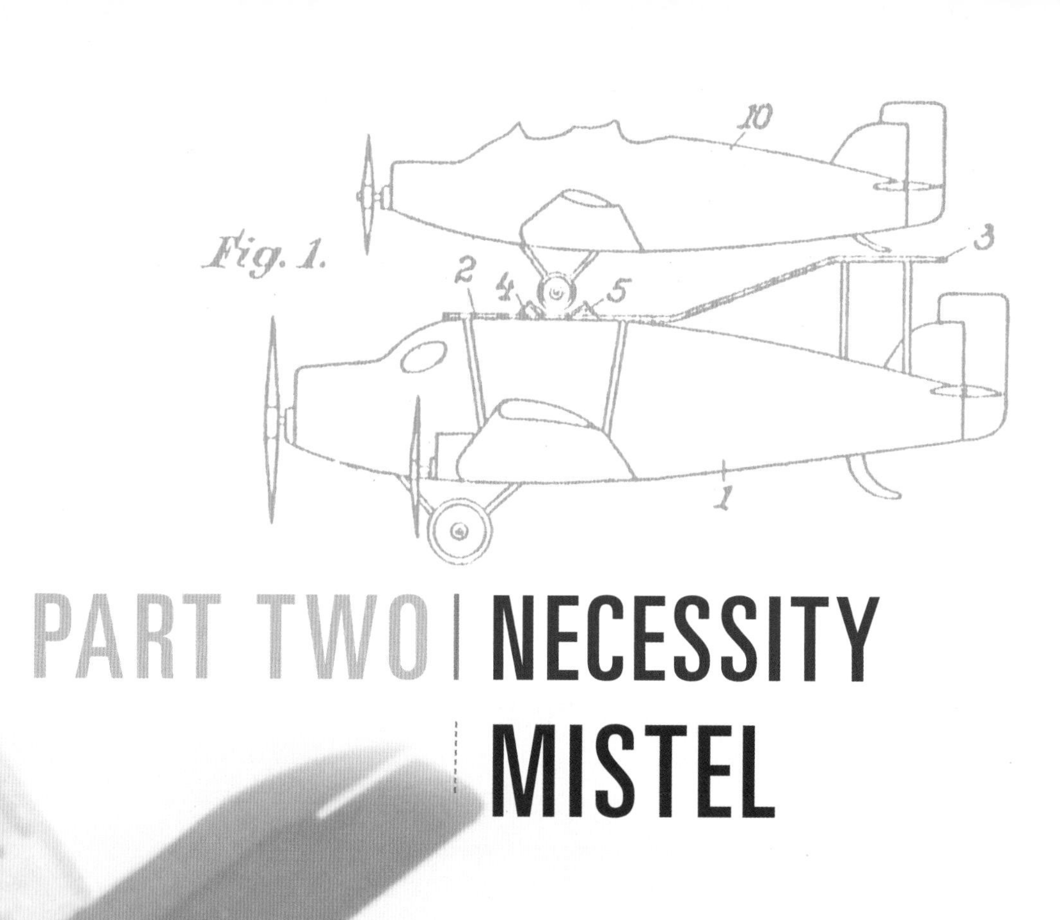

PART TWO | NECESSITY MISTEL

'THIS ADVENTUROUS CREATION'

BIRTH OF THE *MISTEL* CONCEPT

In 1927, Professor Hugo Junkers (centre), the eminent German aircraft designer, filed a patent for a composite aircraft design in which 'a flying machine is placed on or connected with another flying machine of some suitable type, which serves for imparting to the machine to be started an additional acceleration and, if desired, to support it in the air until a predetermined altitude has been attained.' Junkers is seen here flanked by the record-breaking test pilots Johann Risticz, a Hungarian, who broke the endurance record when he remained airborne for more than 52 hours, and Wilhelm Zimmermann, who achieved a new speed, distance and duration record with a Junkers G38 on 10 April 1930.

EIGHT years before his death in February 1935 and eleven years prior to the inaugural flight of the Short-Mayo Composite in England, the eminent German aircraft designer, Professor Hugo Junkers, filed German and US patents for the 'Start of Flying Machines'.

By 1927, the embittered 67-year-old Professor had expended a part of his considerable energies fighting a protracted legal battle against the German government in an attempt to retain majority ownership of the business he had founded and built. An ill-fated venture with the Russian government during the early 1920s had almost resulted in financial disaster for his Dessau-based company, the Junkers Flugzeugwerke. Suffering from the restrictions enforced by the Treaty ofVersailles and fearful of the severe economic consequences of war reparation payments sought by Britain and France, Germany was eager to cooperate in any bilateral ventures with Russia so as to allow continued if not covert development of its aircraft industry. By signing the Treaty of Rapello, Russia had declared herself willing to place airfields, aircraft manufacturing facilities and labour at Germany's disposal in return for German technical knowledge and training.

Following the First World War, and aided, in part, by the moderate nature of the Treaty of Versailles on the manufacture of civil aircraft, Junkers had built the revolutionary F-13 all-metal, six-seat monoplane transport which had first flown on 25 June 1919 – three days before the signing of the Treaty. Such was the success and reliability of this aircraft that by the late 1920s, F-13s were in service in Germany and nine other nations. In 1921, Junkers had established his own airline, Junkers-Luftverkehrs AG, which operated no fewer than 60 F-13s and which, amongst other accomplishments, performed pioneering exploratory flights to China.

The potential for large-scale manufacturing of aircraft in Russia free of Allied intervention, however, was irresistible. In November 1922, encouraged and supported by the German government to the tune of 100 million Marks, Junkers signed a contract with the Russian government to build airframes and engines for use by the Soviet Air Force at the former Russo-Baltic factory at Fili, near Moscow. Professor Junkers was well aware that a lucrative market existed for military as well as civil aircraft and that, wherever possible, every commercial type should be built with potential military conversion in mind.

In 1924, additional subsidies were offered to the Junkers Flugzeugwerke AG to expand production at Fili, but by the following year expectations had not materialised; apparently Junkers chose to use the money merely to cover domestic wage costs. Furthermore, there were complaints from the Russians, and German desire to continue cooperation with Russia was waning. A request to Junkers was made to repay all outstanding credits. Simultaneously, all existing credit arrangements with Junkers were stopped and the company was asked for repayment. For a while the company struggled on, weighed by the burden of heavy debt repayment, but finally, on 3 October 1925, Junkers Flugzeugwerke AG ran out of money. The Government threw out a rescue line in the

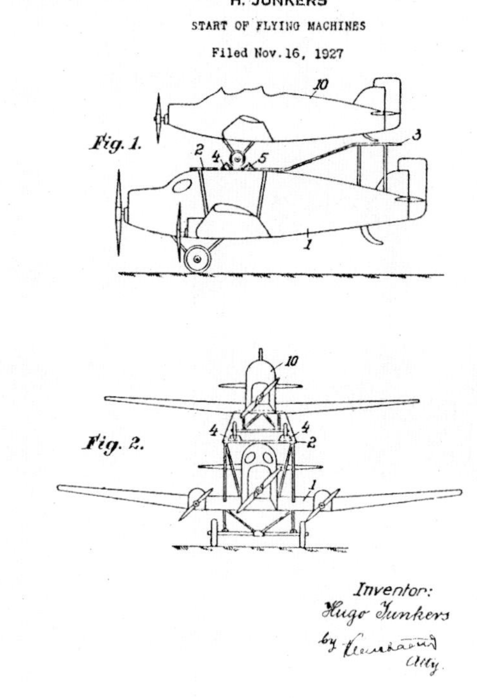

Professor Hugo Junkers' patent application for the 'Start of Flying Machines' as filed with the United States Patent Office on 26 February 1929. The drawing is based on a Junkers G 24/Junkers A 20 combination.

Patented Feb. 26, 1929. 1,703,488

UNITED STATES PATENT OFFICE.

HUGO JUNKERS, OF DESSAU, GERMANY.

START OF FLYING MACHINES.

Application filed November 16, 1927, Serial No. 233,708, and in Germany July 13, 1927.

My invention refers to flying machines and more especially to a method and the means for starting them, it being a particular object of the invention to provide starting means which are more efficient than those hitherto used.

According to the present invention a flying machine is placed on or connected with another flying machine of some suitable type, which serves for imparting to the machine to be started an additional acceleration and, if desired, to support it in the air until a predetermined altitude has been attained.

I am aware that it has already been suggested in order to facilitate the starting of a flying machine to place it on a truck or slide arranged to be propelled by some suitable source of energy, such as an engine, drop weight, gas pressure, or the like. As these starting means add an additional accelerating power to the accelerating power created by the power plant of the machine to be started, the craft can be imparted the velocity necessary for the floating in air already after a comparatively short distance. However these starting means involve a drawback, inasmuch as they do not allow acting on the craft after it has once started floating in the air, as is desirable in all cases where the craft is required to rise directly after the start, for instance in order to fly over obstacles placed near the starting point. A quick rising of the craft is connected with particular difficulties in the case of flying machines which are heavily loaded per unit of carrying surface and have little spare energy left for propulsion.

If according to the present invention the craft to be started is supported by another flying machine, preferably the craft to be started is placed from above onto an auxiliary flying machine provided with means for supporting the craft, and in such a case simple means must only be provided for preventing any undesirable relative displacement of the crafts. The machine to be started can separate itself from the auxiliary craft as soon as the supporting surfaces (wings) of the craft to be started have attained the lift required for free flight. It is however also possible to suspend the craft to be started from the auxiliary flying machine, where the landing or floating gear of the auxiliary craft is arranged in such manner is not to hinder the detaching of the craft to be started from the auxiliary machine.

In the drawings accompanying this specification and forming part thereof two modifications of flying machines embodying my invention are illustrated diagrammatically by way of example.

In the drawings

Fig. 1 is a side elevation, and

Fig. 2 is a front elevation of a flying machine to be started, the machine being placed on top of an auxiliary machine.

Referring first to Figs. 1 and 2, 1 is the auxiliary flying machine, 2 is a platform erected on the wings and extending above the fuselage of the auxiliary machine, 3 being a stage connected with the platform and serving as a support for the spike of the machine to be started. Blocks 4 and 5 placed in front and behind the starting wheels of the machine 10 which shall be started, prevent relative displacement of the two crafts.

The machine 10 which shall be started is placed on top of the auxiliary machine 1, the engines of both machines are started, and the auxiliary flying machine 1 now starts rolling until it comes free from the ground, whereupon both crafts together can rise to a predetermined altitude, when the separation of the craft 10 to be started from the auxiliary supporting craft 1 can be effected by suitably adjusting the rudders or ailerons of the crafts, if desired in connection with a slacking down of the engine of the supporting craft.

This new starting method can be used for starting on land and on the water surface. The machine to be started and the auxiliary or supporting craft can be of any desired type and a flying machine having an ordinary landing carriage can be started from the surface of the water, while the machine 10 shown in Fig. 1 might as well be replaced by a hydroplane placed on top of the auxiliary machine 1.

I wish it to be understood that I do not desire to be limited to the exact details of construction shown and described for obvious modifications will occur to a person skilled in the art.

I claim:—

The method of starting a flying machine having the usual landing gear but which is incapable of rising by its own power from

shape of a final one-off subsidy, but the price was 66 per cent of Junkers Flugzeugwerke AG shares and 80 per cent of the stock in the airline, Junkers-Luftverkehrs AG.

According to one official history of the Luftwaffe, by 1926 'Germany was already the most air-minded nation in Europe.' Significant developments were taking place within the commercial air transport sector and, in January of that year, the three surviving commercial airlines, Deutscher Aero Lloyd, Junkers Luftverkehrs AG and the Deutsch-Russische Luftverkehrsgesellschaft, merged to form a new national airline, Deutsche Lufthansa AG (DLH).

Throughout 1926, indignant to what he perceived as bully-boy nationalisation, Junkers fought to re-establish control over his fallen business empire and by December he had reached a compromise with the government whereby he was able to reacquire the shareholding in Junkers Flugzeugwerke AG and the Jumo Motorenwerke AG he had lost the previous year. In return, he agreed to sell to the government the remaining 20 per cent shareholding in the Junkers airline and to repay 1 million Marks. He was also committed to supplying aircraft worth 2.7 million Marks.

Thus, once more back in control of aircraft design and manufacturing, Professor Junkers set about concentrating on a series of new and typically radical designs in a sector in which his company excelled, namely transport aircraft. Throughout the early and mid-1920s Junkers manufactured various configurations of transport including the open-cockpit K16, the small, two-seat A20, the A35, and the three-engined G23 and G24 – all of them featuring all-metal construction, a trademark design.

However, as aerial trade routes opened up and extended and demand for longer ranges with greater load capacities grew, a problem which began to emerge was the difficult question of take-off assistance for heavily loaded aircraft. Although once airborne, many contemporary aircraft were perfectly flightworthy, take-off was often not possible without some form of assistance.

Solutions did exist; as has been detailed in Chapter Two, the catapult was used successfully by Lufthansa for seaborne operations and it had also been tried on land along with towed starts, but all of these options had their drawbacks. In September 1925, Junkers Flugzeugwerke was approached by the rocket propulsion pioneer, Max Valier, who proposed converting either a G23 or G24 three-engine machine with mixed power by replacing the two outboard engines with rocket units.

Valier's proposal was eventually turned down, but it did prompt the engineers at Dessau to continue to investigate the take-off assistance problem, leading them to experiment with both jettisonable rockets, as attached to a Junkers W33 on at least one flight in July 1929, and a far more innovative concept – the *Huckepack* or 'pick-a-back' method.

On 18 July 1927, Hugo Junkers lodged an application in Germany for an 'invention' in which,

> 'A flying machine is placed on or connected with another flying machine of some suitable type, which serves for imparting to the machine to be started an additional acceleration and, if desired, to support it in the air until a predetermined altitude has been attained.'

According to Junkers:

> '… the aircraft to be started is supported by another flying machine. Preferably the craft to be started is placed from above onto an auxiliary flying machine provided with means for supporting the craft, and in such a case simple means must only be provided for preventing any undesirable relative displacement of the craft. The machine to be started can separate itself from the auxiliary craft as soon as the supporting surfaces [wings] of the craft to be started have attained the lift required for free flight.'

Junkers intended that 'any desired type' of aircraft could be used for both components of the *Huckepack* composite arrangement. However study of the drawings which accompanied Junkers' patent reveals that the Professor was probably intending to convert his theory into practical experiment by utilising a Junkers G24 passenger aircraft as

The Junkers G24 was powered by three 310-hp Junkers L5 engines and was the aircraft included as the lower component in Professor Junkers' composite proposal of 1927. The G24 is seen here in a novel arrangement with a small sportsplane positioned on its port wing.

the 'auxiliary flying machine' or lower component. The G24 was essentially an enlarged development of the Junkers G23, the forerunner of many successive Junkers multi-engined, all-metal, cantilever transport aircraft. First flown in mid-1925, the G24 was designed as a commercial landplane with accommodation for three crew and nine passengers, the former occupying semi-enclosed cockpits on some machines whilst enjoying fully enclosed flight decks on others. The prototype was powered by three 230 hp Junkers L2a engines while most of the later aircraft had three 310 hp Junkers L5s or a combination of two L2as and one L5.

It is possible that Professor Junkers' choice for the lower component of his proposed composite arrangement was influenced by the impressive endurance and distance records achieved by the G24. On 24 July 1926, almost a year to the day before Junkers filed his patent, two G24s took off from Berlin to commence a marathon 20,000-km route-proving flight across Siberia to the Far East. Landing at Peking on 30 August, the two aircraft began the return journey nine days later, arriving back in Berlin on 26 October. Each aircraft had flown 140 hours. Five months later a G24 established eleven world endurance and distance records carrying 500, 1,000 and 2,000-kg payloads.

The proposed upper component of the Junkers composite – or to use the Professor's own words, 'the craft' – is identifiable in the patent drawing, as a two-seater open-cockpit A20. This seems logical in light of the type of commercial role, at least outwardly, the composite was intended to fulfil. The A20, which first flew in 1923, was a low-wing monoplane built for the carriage of freight and mail and so would have been the judicious choice on the part of Junkers. Power was provided either by a 160 hp Mercedes D IIIa in the case of those aircraft manufactured by Junkers, or by a 220 hp Junkers L2 in the case of aircraft built by the Swedish-based Junkers subsidiary, AB Flygindustri. However, some aircraft were fitted with BMW IIIa and IV engines.

The A20 was operated by Junkers Luftverkehr on its overnight mail service between Warnemünde and Karlshamm in Sweden, while Lufthansa used at least ten aircraft for the carriage of night mail, newspapers and general freight. Other users included a Swiss carrier and Turkey's Inspectorate of Air Forces. A small quantity was also built at Fili for the Soviet Air Force.

Had such a composite combination ever been constructed in accordance with Junkers' proposals, the combined empty weight of the G24 (4,800 kg) and the A20 (940 kg) would have been 5,740 kg.

The Junkers A20, a low wing monoplane built for the carriage of freight and mail, was Professor Junkers' choice as the upper component in his 1927 composite proposal.

Professor Junkers intended that a support platform was to have been added to the wings of the lower aircraft, extending above and over this machine's fuselage with a further platform or 'stage' reaching back towards and over the vertical stabiliser and acting as a support for the upper machine's tail skid. Wheel chocks attached to the platform were intended to prevent any displacement occurring during take-off or flight. According to Junkers,

> 'The [upper] machine is placed on top of the auxiliary machine, the engines of both machines are started, and the auxiliary machine now starts rolling until it comes free from the ground, whereupon both craft together can rise to a predetermined altitude, when the separation of the [upper] craft can be effected by suitably adjusting the rudders or ailerons of the craft, if desired in connection with a slackening down of the engine of the supporting craft.'

Junkers foresaw that such a principle could be adapted for both land and water take-offs and landings.

Several historians have attributed Junkers' death eight years later to the increasing pressures placed upon him by the ambitious and combative *Staatsekretär* (State Secretary) of the *Reichsluftfahrtministerium* (RLM, Reich Air Ministry), *Generalmajor* Erhard Milch. A former employee of the Junkers airline, Milch had victimised the Professor following the old man's resistance to his demanding aircraft production programmes which included placing all of Junkers' patents and factories at the disposal of the Reich. In a deliberate campaign of persecution, Milch ensured that every detail of the financial mismanagement which had taken place at Fili was made public.

Placed under house arrest, Junkers' reputation as a pacifist and democrat was tarnished still further by a public

The patent application lodged by Dr.-Ing. Claude Dornier in October 1927, as it appeared in the German aviation journal *Flugsport* of May 1932 and covering a method of increasing the load capability of large, multi-engined aircraft.

c 27 Pat. **541520** v. 6. 10. 27. veröff. 13. 1. 32. **Dornier-Metallbauten G. m. b. H. u. Dr.-Ing. e. h. Claude Dornier. Friedrichshafen a. B.** *Mehrmotoriges Großflugzeug von hoher Flächenbelastung mit Mitteln zur Mehrbelastung.*

Patentanspruch:

Mehrmotoriges Großflugzeug von hoher Flächenbelastung mit Mitteln zur Leistungssteigerung, dadurch

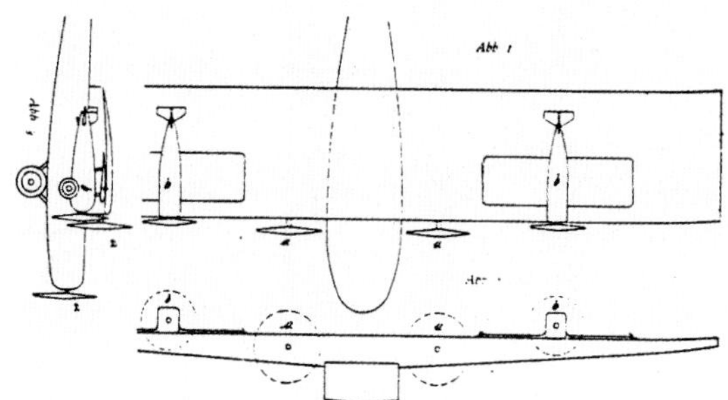

gekennzeichnet, daß außer normalen Motoren vorzugsweise auf oder unter den Tragflügeln noch ablösbare, nur die Leistungsbelastung des Flugzeuges vorübergehend erhöhende Aggregate angeordnet sind, die aus einem Motor mit einer verkümmerten, jedoch eine Notlandung noch sicherstellenden Schwebe-, Steuer- und Landevorrichtung bestehen.

Below: A page from the journal *Flugsport* dated May 1938 featuring details of the Short-Mayo Composite. Mayo attempted to raise official interest in his Composite concept in Germany in the mid/late 1930s but his efforts were in vain despite the fact that it intrigued many in the aeronautical fraternity there.

Steiggeschw. am Boden 7,1 m/sec, Gipfelhöhe praktisch 6100 m, Reichweite 1350 km.

Das Tochterflugzeug „Mercury" ist ein Ganzmetallhochdecker mit vier Napier-Rapier-Motoren von je 340 PS Höchstleistung.

Die Flügelbauweise ähnelt derjenigen des Empire-Bootes. Kastenholme aus T-Profilen, Rohrdiagonalen. Das Mittelstück wird von einem der V-Form angepaßten Brennstofftank mit 5400 l Inhalt ausgefüllt. Der Behälter nimmt einen Teil der Verdrehkräfte des Flügels auf. Einige Zwischenwände mit nach innen gerichteten Rückschlagventilen verhindern ein Ablaufen des Brennstoffes nach einer Seite. Da mit der höchstmöglichsten Brennstofflast eine Wasserung schwie-

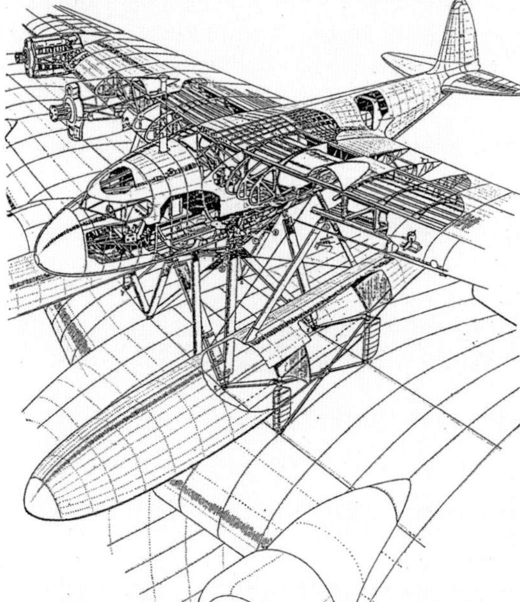

Befestigung des Tochterflugzeuges „Mercury" auf dem Flugboot „Maia". A. Verbindungslasche, B. elektrischer Kontakt, C. Arretiereinrichtung für die Steuerung des „Mercury", solange die Maschinen miteinander verbunden sind, D. Hebel für die Lösung der Sicherung für die Verbindung (unterer Pilot), E. Fußpunkt der Pyramide, auf der die Hauptlast des oberen Flugzeuges ruht, F. Befestigungspunkt der Stützstreben für die Schwimmer (letztere sind durch zwei Spante X und Y besonders für die Aufnahme dieser Kräfte geeignet), G. H. I. Träger, an denen die Schwimmerstreben und die Auslösevorrichtung angeschlossen sind, K. Strebenknoten des „Mercury". Zeichnung: The Aeroplane

investigation led by *Oberst* Albert Kesselring, head of the Administrative Office within the RLM. This brought forward charges of association with various leftist and Jewish causes. The pressure proved too much and the Professor finally yielded, selling the controlling interests in his company in October 1934 and resigning his directorships the following month.

Hugo Junkers died at his home in Bavaria on 3 February 1935, his 76th birthday. Milch sent a wreath.

On 6 October 1927, three months after Junkers had lodged his patent application for a composite aircraft, fellow German aircraft designer, *Dr.-Ing. e.h.* Claude Dornier of the Dornier-Metallbauten GmbH, lodged a patent application for 'Methods of increasing the load capability of large, heavily-loaded, multi-engined aircraft.'

In his application, Dornier proposed that:

'A large, heavily-loaded aircraft be fitted with additional separable/jettisonable aircraft, the latter's engines providing additional power to improve the take-off and climb-out performance of the large aircraft. The jettisonable aircraft may be attached to the upper or lower surface of the large aircraft's wing and they are fitted with control surfaces which will allow them to fly back to the ground once they have been jettisoned.'

To date no further information on the Dornier proposal has come to light and with it, it seems, initial German research into composite aircraft ended. No further development, experimentation or testing in this direction is known to have taken place either within Junkers or Dornier or any other German aircraft manufacturer for several years.

At least one source suggests that the origins of what would become the Luftwaffe's future composite concept – the *Mistel* – may have lain in pre-war discussions between Major Robert Mayo, the British designer of the Short-Mayo Composite and Milch. Certainly, Milch visited England in October 1937 as head of a high-ranking Luftwaffe delegation which toured airfields and aircraft factories in the Midlands on a 'goodwill' mission. *Generalleutnant* Milch's busy itinerary included meetings and dinners with various British politicians and dignitaries including Winston Churchill, Lord Swinton, the Air Minister, and a number of senior air commanders who would direct the RAF in its future war against the Luftwaffe. It is believed that Milch also met Major Mayo at this time who was keen to promote his design, if not a little frustrated at apparent British inertia over it.

By the time of Milch's visit, both the Short S.21 *Maia*, the lower component of the Short-Mayo Composite, and its upper component, the S.20 *Mercury*, had flown separately on test flights. According to one writer however, Milch 'showed interest' in the composite, but 'did not initiate any development.'

A more likely answer is that Mayo's patents for both his seaplane and projected landplane composites were published in editions of the German *Flugsport* magazine in 1935 and 1936 respectively. Certainly, *Flugsport's* editor, Oskar Ursinus, avidly ensured that any interesting international aeronautical developments were reported through the pages of his journal. In any event, the declaration of war in 1939 brought an end to all these purely peaceful projects and experiments, both British and German.

* * *

By October 1942, Adolf Hitler was faced with dangerous and draining military predicaments both on the Eastern Front and in Africa. There was virtual deadlock at Stalingrad where Sixth Army was fighting against the Russians amidst the rain-drenched ruins of the city, clawing its way forward street by street, factory by factory. There was still no success to report.

In Egypt the British, under Montgomery, had launched a major attack involving 150,000 men supported by 1,000 tanks and 800 aircraft against German forces. With fuel and ammunition virtually expended, there was little that Rommel could do but retreat. Word was also reaching the *Führer* of an Allied invasion fleet heading for North Africa, and in the night skies over the Reich RAF bombers were inflicting heavy damage on Germany's industrial cities.

Far away from the battlefront however, in the relative peace and safety of the south German town of Ainring nestling in the foothills of the Alps, creative minds were at work. The *Deutsche Forschungsanstalt für Segelflug* (DFS, German Research Institute for Gliders) had been formed in 1925 from the Rhön-Rossitten-Gesellschaft. Intended specifically for research into glider flight, this company was founded at the Wasserkuppe under the leadership of *Dr.* Walter Georgii, an internationally renowned meteorologist, but it was later transferred to Darmstadt-Griesheim in 1933. As the organisation's work increased,

A pre-war view of Ainring airfield. Located close to the Alps, it was the location for many of the DFS Mistel experiments.

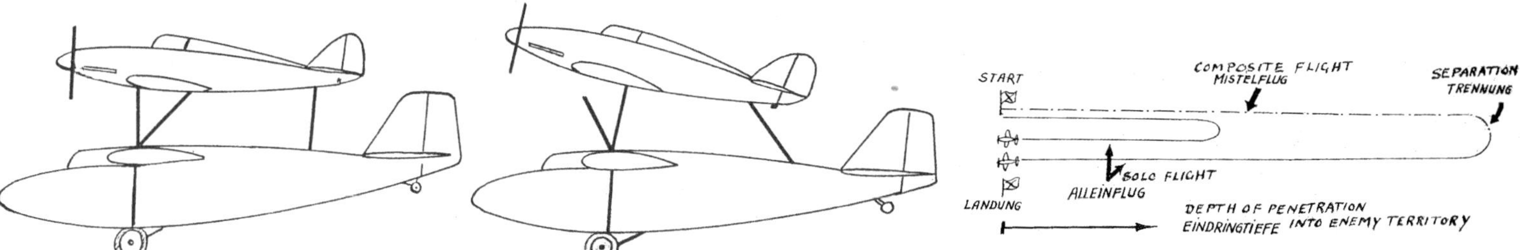

Two sketches drawn by Fritz Stamer from a post-war report prepared for the Allies in which the former Managing Director of the DFS outlined the thinking behind his *Mistelschlepp* concept.

Above: A sketch drawn by Fritz Stamer to illustrate the range benefits of deploying the *Mistelschlepp* method for delivering assault troops or for increasing the range of a fighter aircraft over and above that of a solo aircraft.

another move was made to Ainring airfield, located 7 km west of Salzburg. A civilian airfield before the war, Ainring's claim to fame was that it was used on occasions before and during the war by Hitler when visiting his residence at Berchtesgaden, 20 km to the south-east. It also played a role in the development of the Fieseler Fi 103 flying bomb when, during the spring of 1941, a DFS 230 A-1 transport glider fitted with an Argus pulse jet under each wing took off from the field, making the first stratospheric glider flight by reaching an altitude of 11,640 m. As the war progressed, the number of Ainring's hangars was increased and *Flak* positions were installed. Accommodation was plentiful in the shape of the pre-war gliding school barracks.

It was here, as the position at Stalingrad worsened and the military situation in North Africa deteriorated, that Fritz Stamer proposed a radical scheme for delivering troop-carrying gliders. Instead of a glider being towed behind a powered aircraft, Stamer's idea was to mount it rigidly beneath one and then to jettison it over the target area. He would later describe the concept as 'this adventurous creation.'[1]

As we have seen, since Hugo Junkers' earlier proposals there had been no further practical work carried out in Germany on the possible utilisation of composite aircraft and by 1942 the seemingly insurmountable difficulty of performing a safe in-flight separation still frustrated attempts at further experiments.

British pre-war progress in this area, however, was well known to the Germans; *Flight* magazine published articles

[1] Stamer writing in *Der Flieger*, date unknown.

FRITZ STAMER

FRITZ STAMER was born in Hannover in November 1897 and joined the German Youth Movement in 1913. His studies for a career as an architect were interrupted by the outbreak of the First World War. Joining the *Luftstreitkräfte*, he was shot down during a reconnaissance flight over the Western Front in September 1918. Following two years of captivity in France, he returned to Germany but abandoned his pre-war aspirations to practise architecture. Instead, by 1921, he had become active in the gliding community on the Wasserkuppe. His first assignment was with Weltensegler GmbH, but during the winter of 1923-24 he transferred to Arthur Martens' flying school. The following year he joined the Rhön-Rossitten-Gesellschaft and, in 1928, made the first 35 second flight in the *Ente* ('Duck') a rocket-powered aircraft fitted with a 'radically new engine' launched by a rubber shock cord and designed by Alexander Lippisch, the then head of the technical department for aerodynamic research. By 1933 Stamer was working as head of the *Institut für Flugversuche* (Institute for Aeronautical Experiment) at the DFS Darmstadt, but following Walter Georgii's appointment to the RLM's *Forschungsabteilung* (Research Department), Stamer became Managing Director of the DFS.

Fritz Stamer sits in an early tailless glider in 1923. This radical craft never flew, having been damaged during transport.

Fritz Stamer (second from left), the mastermind behind *Mistelschlepp*, or the Mistel method of towing, in discussion with aeronautical luminaries including Graf Isenburg (third from left), Gerd von Hoeppner (second from right) and Oskar Ursinus (far right) during the 1920s. Ursinus published details of Robert Mayo's patents and the Short-Mayo Composite in his magazine, *Flugsport*.

on the British Short-Mayo composite in early 1938 and the information gleaned from these articles appeared in detail in *Flugsport* later that year. However, to give Stamer due credit, although details of Mayo's ideas were freely available as a result of considerable coverage in the aeronautical press, his subsequent experiments showed a marked difference and therefore innovation from Mayo in his designs for coupling and separation.

Stamer assembled a group of technicians, aerodynamicists and pilots from the Flight Trials Department at Ainring in order to meet the challenge of developing a composite aircraft or the so-called '*Mistel* Method of Towing', intended for 'transport and operational applications'. Precisely who originated the word '*Mistel*' (Mistletoe) is not clear, but former members of II./KG 200, a Luftwaffe unit which flew the composite operationally later in the war, recount at least one credible analogy; Mistletoe grows on the sides of trees, particularly oaks, and it takes nourishment from the parent tree, in the same way the upper component of the composite would take its fuel from the lower component.

Stamer's team included Paul Kiefel, Erich Klöckner, Karl von Jan, Kurt Oppitz, Karl Schieferstein, Paul Stämmler and Hermann Zitter. It was a very experienced assembly of men.

Karl Schieferstein, a former glider pilot, test pilot and instructor, who would fly the upper components of the planned composite, had joined the DFS in September 1936. Walter Georgii considered that Schieferstein,

> '...distinguished himself through his calmness, level-headedness, innate teaching ability and comradeliness, as well as by his thorough flying and technical knowledge and capabilities. These qualities made him one of the most liked and successful of instructors. It is to the credit of Schieferstein that flight operations, often accompanied by unusual requirements, could continue to be conducted at the DFS without serious accident right up to the last moment.'

Karl Schieferstein, the DFS test pilot who flew the upper components of the early Mistel combinations. Walter Georgii considered that Schieferstein 'distinguished himself through his calmness, level-headedness, innate teaching ability and comradeliness, as well as by his thorough flying and technical knowledge and capabilities'.

Hermann Zitter, a Wasserkuppe veteran from 1928, had trained for blind-flying with Deutsche Lufthansa in Berlin in 1937 and the same year also trained at the *Erprobungsstelle* Rechlin on powered aircraft. The previous year he had worked as a glider instructor specialising in towing. He joined the DFS at Ainring in 1940 where he used his towing skills to assist Fritz Stamer in his various experiments.

In 1939, Erich Klöckner became the first glider pilot to reach 9,280 metres over the Central Alps, thus establishing a new altitude record, and a year later he reached the edge of the stratosphere in a glider. He would later fly the Bachem *Natter* in early trials.

The first *Mistel* experiments took place in October 1942 and were made with a Klemm Kl 35 lightplane mounted above a DFS 230 B-2 glider.

The Klemm Kl 35 was perhaps the best known and most widely used of all the designs to emerge from the firm of Klemm Leichtflugzeugbau GmbH of Böblingen near Stuttgart. Throughout the 1930s the company suffered a frosty relationship with the Nazi Party and the RLM, largely as a result of *Dr.-Ing.* Hanns Klemm's unashamed Protestant religious convictions which, ultimately, deprived his company of orders. Nevertheless, such problems did not prevent the Kl 35 from becoming one of the standard elementary training aircraft of the Luftwaffe. Originally designed for private ownership as a sportsplane, the Kl 35 first flew in 1935 and was powered by an 80 hp Hirth HM 60R four-cylinder inverted air-cooled engine. It took the form of an elegant, low-wing, two-seat monoplane of wooden construction. Its gull wing had a wood and fabric covering and it had a fixed undercarriage. The main production version, the Kl 35D, was fitted with a 105 hp Hirth HM 504A-2 engine and saw lengthy service throughout the Second World War with both the Luftwaffe's training schools as well as with the air forces of Sweden, Czechoslovakia, Hungary and Rumania. However, production of the Kl 35 had been in steady decline since the outbreak of the war and by the time of the Ainring composite experiments, was down to five per month.

The DFS 230 originated from a requirement by the Rhön-Rossitten-Gesellschaft for a glider with high-aspect ratio wings with which to conduct meteorological research. Designed by Hans Jacobs, the German aviatrix Hanna Reitsch first test-flew it when towed behind a Ju 52 transport. To some, the glider's square, fabric-covered fuselage, shoulder wing and jettisonable skid may have appeared cumbersome and ungainly, but its one-ton empty weight/one-ton load-carrying performance was, in military terms, impressive. In 1937, Reitsch helped to prove this point when she separated from a Ju 52, put the DFS 230 into a dive and made a perfect landing directly in front of a group of Luftwaffe dignitaries including Milch, Kesselring, Udet and von Greim who watched eight fully armed troops charge out of the glider and adopt assault positions.

Following further military evaluation, it was realised that deployment of glider-borne assault troops offered inherent advantages: as with parachute drops, approach was silent with the assault troops sitting straddling a wooden bench which ran down the centre of the craft. On touch-down the Perspex cockpit cover was ejected allowing the pilot and co-pilot to join the assault. The troops exited the aircraft through a pair of doors located to port and starboard and were not scattered in the landing operation. Furthermore, time – dangerous time – was not wasted whilst paratroops untangled themselves from their chutes.

Two subsequent high-profile glider operations involving the DFS 230 supported this view. The first of these was the successful capture of the Belgian fort of Eben-Emael which dominated the Albert Canal defences during the German advance into Belgium in May 1940. Hitler literally hugged himself with joy at the news of the fort's capture and decorated his victorious assault troops personally. The second major occasion in which the DFS glider saw action was during the successful but hard-won German airborne assault on Crete a year later. This time, 53 gliders formed the spearhead of the attack but it was to be a tough and costly operation. Several DFS 230s were scattered owing to the rocky terrain and others crashed and tow cables snapped.

Despite these mishaps, however, Fritz Stamer was convinced that the proposed '*Mistel* method of towing' was a way of eliminating tow-cable problems such as those which occurred on Crete.

Consequently, at Ainring, a DFS 230 B-2 (CB+ZB) was modified in such a way that the first third of the upper surface of each wing close to the wing roots was fitted with a trough-shaped support corresponding to the profile of the wheels of a Kl 35 (D-EXCM), so that the weight of the Kl 35 could be spread evenly over the wing's surface via a reinforcing plate bonded to it with glue. In front of the fin of the DFS 230, a tubular steel trestle was attached to the upper rear fuselage which supported the tail skid of the Kl 35 in a sheet steel shoe.

The two aircraft were fastened to one another by means of a pyramid system of wires attached to four points on the upper fuselage of the DFS 230 and coupled together at a single point under the fuselage of the Kl 35. The four wires comprising the pyramid were tightened to create a combined tension of 1,000 kg. In this condition the sprung undercarriage of the Kl 35 was fully compressed. On release, the undercarriage extended and rotated the upper aircraft by approximately +3° from its normal angle of incidence of +1.5°, thereby assisting aircraft separation.

The DFS 230 retained its normal jettisonable undercarriage but without brakes, although it was not intended to jettison the undercarriage for the purpose of the trials. The trials were viewed only as 'preliminary' since Stamer and his team realised that the performance of the Kl 35 was insufficient to 'lift' a DFS 230 using the *Mistel* method. The low flight speed of such a *Mistel* combination resulted in a reduction of the propeller's efficiency with an ensuing speed reduction of some 60 km/h between a Kl 35 and Kl 35/DFS 230 composite. It was therefore

Below: The instrument panel in a DFS 230.

Left: The DFS 230 B-2, CB+ZB/Kl 35, D-EXCM, Mistel combination in front of the airfield buildings at Ainring in the autumn of 1942. The two aircraft were fastened to one another by means of a pyramid system of wires attached to four points on the upper fuselage of the DFS 230 and coupled together at a single point under the fuselage of the Kl 35.

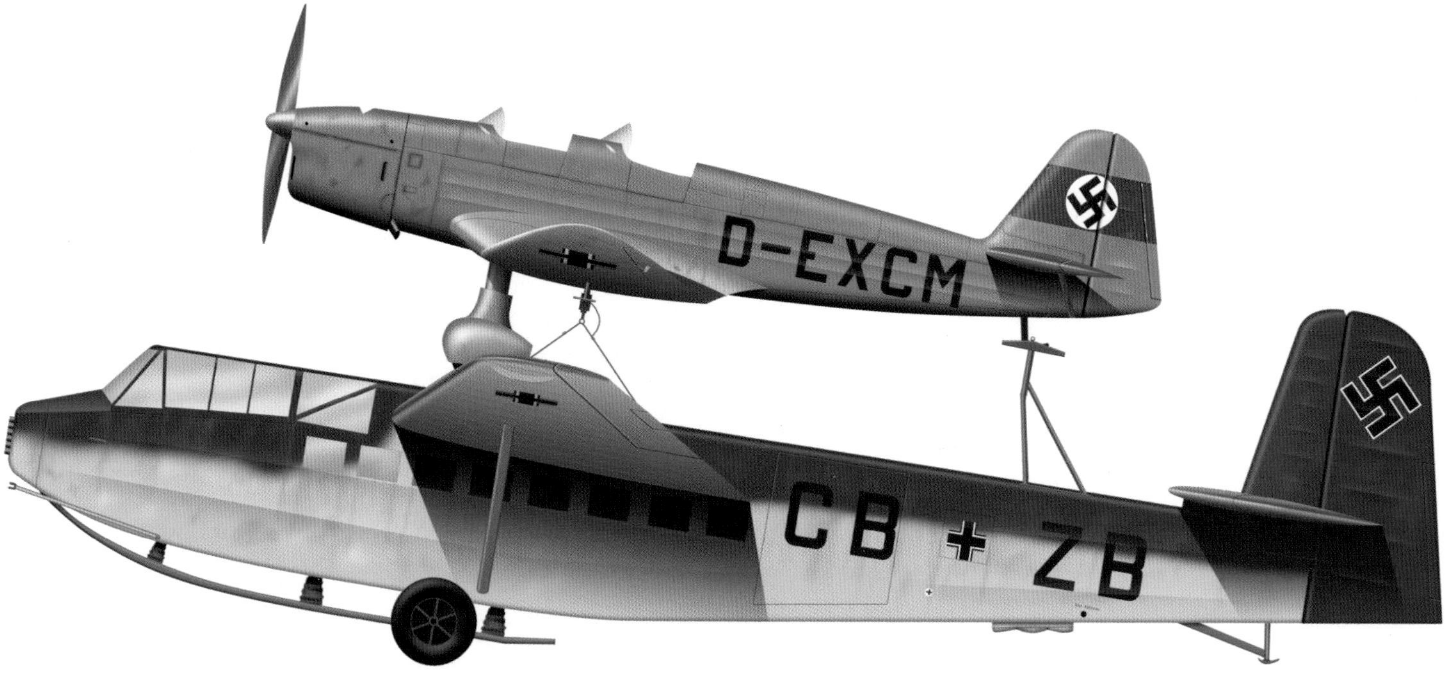

Klemm Kl 35, D-EXCM/DFS 230, CB+ZB, Deutsche Forschungsanstalt für Segelflug 'Ernst Udet', Ainring October 1942

proposed that trials should be conducted using a Ju 52 as a towplane.

An intercom cable to allow the pilots of the upper and lower components to communicate with each other was fastened along one of the pyramid's wires. A simple, pull-out connector was located behind the coupling at the apex of the pyramid.

Separation was planned to take place in horizontal flight at 120 km/h. As a safeguard against problems arising during separation, the DFS 230 was fitted with a brake parachute, the deployment of which was expected to decelerate the glider sufficiently to allow the Kl 35 to fly free.

Stamer brushed aside fears concerning the strength of the DFS 230 should the Kl 35 upper component fail to support its own weight during flight; the weight of the Kl 35, when carrying only one pilot was 600 kg, a weight quite easily carried by the DFS 230 B-2 which had a maximum payload of 1,200 kg. The take-off weight for the Kl 35/DFS 230 combination totalled 1,675 kg; 1,075 kg for the DFS 230 B-2 and 600 kg for the Kl 35.

Flight-testing began on 1 September 1942 when Karl Schieferstein took the controls of the Kl 35 and Kurt Oppitz piloted the DFS 230. On some test flights Paul Stämmler accompanied Oppitz as co-pilot. The combination was linked by means of an 80-metre-long tow line to a Ju 52 (D-AOQA) piloted by Hermann Zitter. With the engine of the Klemm set at full throttle, all take-offs proved trouble-free, the take-off distances being shorter than when the unladen DFS 230 took off alone under towed start.

Controls of both components handled reasonably well in towed flight at 130-150 km/h, though aileron response was considered 'sluggish' when controlled by the DFS 230 and 'poor' when by the Kl 35. The only other noticeable effect was a small nose-down pitching moment which was generated when the Kl 35's throttle was opened to full power. This, however, could be trimmed with the elevator trim tab. The reason for this characteristic is believed to have been due to the propeller slipstream increasing the download on the tailplane of the DFS 230 and thereby effectively raising the thrust axis above the centre-of-gravity.

Prior to the flight tests taking place, Stamer's team had calculated that the optimum speed for separation should be 120 km/h and subsequent flights proved these calculations correct. When separation was ready to be effected, Schieferstein, as pilot of the upper component, was to give the alert, *'Achtung!'* ('Ready!') via his intercom to signal that he was applying full throttle, at which point Oppitz acknowledged with *'Los!'* ('Go!') as he disengaged the lower component.

The compressed undercarriage extended itself on release and, after deployment of a spoiler, the Kl 35 climbed forwards and up and away from the DFS 230 at approximately 30-45 degrees. Trouble-free separation of the aircraft during the various tests took place successively at 1,500 m, 1,000 m, 10 m and 0.5 m above ground level. The brake parachute was not used.

Karl Schieferstein remembers the flight tests:

> 'I was put "on top", possibly because I was a little smaller, and that is exactly where I remained for the rest of the trials. The Kl 35, with its open cockpit, was a breezy but exciting place of work for me! At the very beginning of this trial each pilot made his own control inputs without making his intentions known to the other aircraft. The burden of steering the couple lay with the pilot of the aircraft below, with my assistance from above when I could predict his intentions. The 105 hp powerplant was insufficient to maintain horizontal flight and was most definitely not powerful enough for take-off and climb. The airborne handling and performance of this launch pad was eagerly awaited by all and, when the time came to separate, it actually worked fairly well. The Kl 35 I was flying literally leapt up as the spring-loaded attachment struts launched me upward and away from the glider; I pushed the throttle forward and easily climbed away.'

Landings with the coupled combination were also made without any difficulties. Oppitz instructed Schieferstein via the intercom to close or open the throttle and to pull on the elevators during the last stage of the landing.

A jubilant Stamer later wrote, 'The flight tests revealed trouble-free performance characteristics and the possibility of controlling the combination by either pilot.'

Flight-testing of the DFS 230 B-2, CB+ZB/ Kl 35, D-EXCM, began on 1 September 1942 when the DFS test pilot, Karl Schieferstein, took the controls of the Kl 35 upper component and Kurt Oppitz piloted the DFS 230. With the Alps providing a dramatic backdrop, the wire supports can be seen clearly between the fuselages of the two aircraft.

DFS test pilot, Paul Stämmler, at the controls of a DFS 230. Stämmler flew this type on numerous occasions as a lower component of the Mistel Composite during trials at Ainring in 1942.

The DFS 230 B-2, CB+ZB/Kl 35, D-EXCM, Mistel seen moments after its release from the Junkers 52 towplane piloted by Hermann Zitter during a test flight from Ainring in late 1942.

Above and left: The DFS 230 B-2, CB+ZB/Kl 35, D-EXCM, combination makes its gradual descent into Ainring at the end of a test flight in the autumn of 1942. Generally, landings with the coupled combination were made without difficulty; Kurt Oppitz in the DFS 230 instructed Karl Schieferstein in the Kl 35 upper component via intercom to close or open the throttle and to pull on the elevators during the last stage of approach.

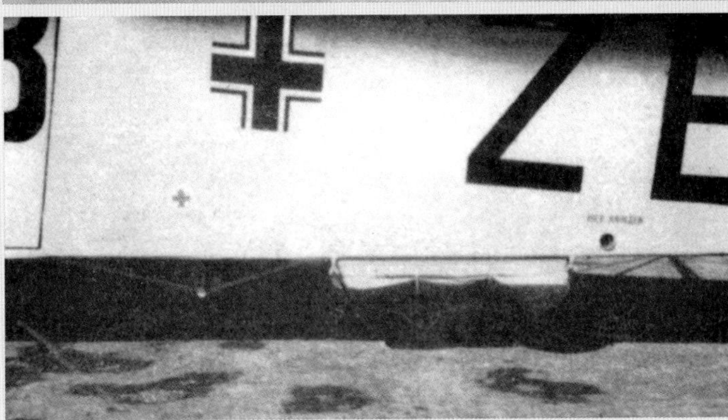

As a safeguard against problems arising during separation of the Mistel, the DFS 230 was fitted with a brake parachute, the deployment of which was expected to decelerate the glider sufficiently to allow the Kl 35 upper component to fly free. This picture shows the brake parachute and its attachment under the tail of the DFS 230.

A dramatic photograph showing DFS 230 B-2, CB+ZB, landing at Ainring with brake parachute deployed during tests with nose-mounted brake rockets.

With the successful conclusion of the Kl 35/DFS 230 combination tests, Stamer embarked on a further series of tests in which the DFS 230 was coupled to a Focke-Wulf Fw 56 *Stösser* trainer. This aerodynamically superior aircraft had evolved as a result of specifications placed by the RLM during the 1930s for a lightweight fighter and advanced trainer.

The Fw 56 was installed with a 240 hp Argus AS 10C in-line engine and had a parasol wing built of spruce and plywood and a fuselage constructed of welded steel tube with an alloy and fabric covering. In 1935, the Fw 56V6 – also the pre-production A-03 (D-IXYO) – was held to be the best aircraft by the RLM due to its strength and handling, qualities which were considered to be on a par with the new Messerschmitt Bf 109 monoplane fighter. No fewer than 1,000 examples were built before construction ceased in 1940, many of these seeing service with the Luftwaffe's fighter schools and the NSFK (*Nationalsozialistischen Fliegerkorps* – National Socialist Flying Corps).

Fritz Stamer's decision to proceed with the *Mistel* experiments using an Fw 56 upper component was primarily based around the greater power of the *Stösser* as compared to the Klemm, particularly at full throttle when climbing. Furthermore, the combination offered a much more favourable overall aerodynamic configuration arising from the high-wing layout of the Focke-Wulf machine.

The Fw 56 was mounted on top of the DFS 230 at the same angle of incidence as the Kl 35 with minor adjustments being made to take into account the difference in overall dimensions. The Fw 56 weighed 985 kg, still within the 1,200 kg payload capability of the DFS glider.

Because it was expected that the location of the upper aircraft's thrust axis would generate a nose-down pitching moment, the attachment of the Fw 56 was arranged so that its centre-of-gravity was 40 mm behind that of the DFS 230.

Flight-testing went ahead with Schieferstein piloting the Fw 56 (CA+GN) and Oppitz flying the DFS 230 (CB+ZB). As with the earlier trials, Hermann Zitter towed the combination into the air using a Ju 52; this was necessary because of the short runway at Ainring which was approximately 800 metres.

Communication between Schieferstein and Oppitz was so arranged that either the pilot of the DFS 230 could fly the combined aircraft, whereby the flight control surfaces of the upper aircraft were held in their neutral position, or both pilots could together fly the combination in the event that control performance proved inadequate, particularly in roll. Tests were also planned to fly the combination solely from the upper aircraft while the control surfaces of the DFS 230 were held in their neutral position. The take-off weight for the Fw 56/DFS 230 combination totalled 2,060 kg: 1,075 kg for the DFS 230B-2 and 985 kg for the Fw 56.

Tests proceeded without any problems in relation to towing, separation or coupled landing. Control performance was comparable with that of the Klemm combination, but to a greater extent more effective and less noticeable nose-down pitching moments were experienced when closing or opening the throttles.

The proposed separation speed of 130 km/h proved acceptable, although it was recognised that separation could be made at lower speeds if necessary without difficulty.

In his report dated 22 October 1942, Stamer wrote:

> 'The flying and control characteristics of the DFS 230/Kl 35 and DFS 230/Fw 56 *Mistel* combinations in tow, free flight, separation and coupled landing have proven so normal, that they can be considered operationally ready.'

There was, however, one problem which Stamer and his team could not overcome: vertical oscillation during take-off. The *Mistel* combination had been designed in such a way as to be equipped for blind-flying. In this respect, and following the successful conclusion of the initial flight tests, the DFS investigated the possibility of rigidly towing the DFS 230/Fw 56 combination with a Heinkel He 111 (RN+EE) as tow-plane. A series of such

Below and below right: Two views of the Fw 56 (CA+GN)/DFS 230 (CB+ZB) Mistel at Ainring in 1942.

Karl Schieferstein gazes at the camera from the cockpit of the DFS Ainring's Fw 56, CA+GN, as a member of the ground crew attends to the upper wing. Note the apex of the pyramid wire support and hook beneath the fuselage.

The Fw 56/DFS 230 Mistel combination receives attention from technicians. Note how the propeller of the Fw 56 clears the open cockpit of the DFS 230.

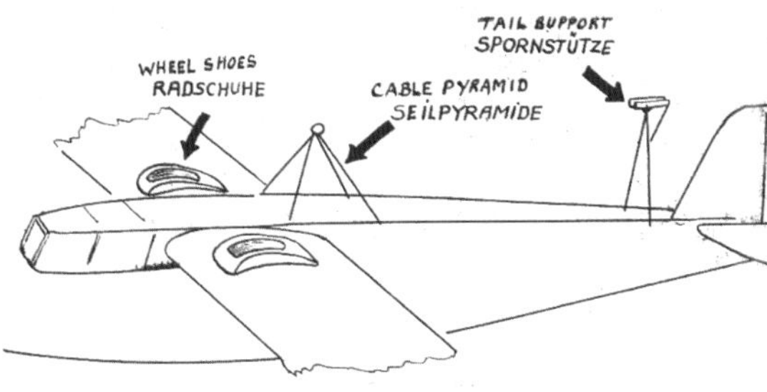

A sketch prepared by Fritz Stamer illustrating the wheel shoes fitted to the wings of the DFS 230 intended to support the wheels of the Fw 56 upper component. Also seen further along the glider's fuselage are the cable pyramid and tail support.

The undercarriage of the Fw 56 sits in the upper wing wheel troughs of the DFS 230. A wire pyramid support was fitted to the upper fuselage of the DFS 230 and incorporated the intercom cable and pull-out connector, and attachment hook to the Fw 56. Here Karl Schieferstein watches the camera from the cockpit of CA+GN.

A view of the left wheel 'shoe' support and reinforcement on the upper surface of the wing of DFS 230 B-2 (CB+ZB). In the background can be seen the wire suppport 'pyramid' structure and intercom cable.

The support for the tail skid of the Fw 56 fitted to the rear fuselage of the DFS 230.

tests were made with the He 111 piloted by Erich Klöckner, with Kurt Oppitz at the controls of the Fw 56 and Paul Stämmler in the DFS 230. These tests revealed considerable difficulties, which seemed to be due to the relationship of the towing attachment point to the high centre-of-gravity, as well as the significantly higher inertia and poor aileron effectiveness of the *Mistel* combination.

On 19 October 1942, near disaster ensued: the He 111 took off to the west along Ainring's runway into a light prevailing wind with the *Mistel* trailing behind it. As the Heinkel gathered speed, so the *Mistel* combination began to bump along the ground – harder and harder; it began to vibrate and then suddenly the towline broke and the combination bounced on the ground, skidded off the runway and came to rest in a field with a damaged starboard wing. Erich Klöckner recalled:

> 'All involved knew this kind of launch was inherently very risky, the instability of this configuration being well known from previous trials, and the centre-of-gravity of the *Mistel* combination did not make it any easier.

Focke-Wulf Fw 56/DFS 230, Deutsche Forschungsanstalt für Segelflug 'Ernst Udet', Ainring October 1942

Though of poor quality, this is the only known photograph showing the Fw 56/DFS 230 in flight.

After lifting off, very light vertical oscillations began, as experienced during solo tow; however, these oscillations increased rapidly to an intensity not previously experienced by the *Mistel* pilots, or by me in the He 111. They quickly became so violent, even during the take-off, that the DFS 230 hit the ground hard on several occasions. Quick thinking as ever, Stämmler, thank God, would release the tow.'

Meanwhile, the Fw 56 had been shaken off its support struts and damaged its tail. Klöckner continued:

'The next impact was so strong that the Fw 56, mounted on top of the cargo glider, was torn from its mounting, damaging the empennage. Half the elevator was broken off, but Kurt Oppitz managed to land the *Stösser* without too much difficulty. The cargo glider, as a result of the hard impact, bounced uncontrolled into the air, hitting the ground in a field outside the airfield boundary, right wing first.'

The He 111 reached the end of the runway, at which point Klöckner pulled up but not before the aircraft's tail had sliced through a hedge.

'There was no take-off abort for me; I had to continue my flight, otherwise I would have landed on the hut containing the non-directional beacon which stood on the extended runway centreline. At the very last moment, I managed to lift off, the wheels and elevator of the He 111 passing through the boundary hedge, but I was airborne.

'Apart from the less than happy result detailed above, the launch nearly ended in catastrophe for another reason. In the right seat next to me sat '*Schorsch*' Keller, the flight mechanic. During the take-off, he suffered some kind of panic attack and jumping from his seat, tore open the top cabin window and began shouting, apparently in fear of his imminent death: "*It's not going to work! It's not going to work!*" He then tried to squeeze himself through the window. There was nothing else for me to do, but to grab him roughly by the seat of his pants and pull him back down into his seat, where he sat motionless until we landed. I felt sorry for him, as '*Schorsch*' was one of our oldest and most respected flight mechanics, but he just did not have the nerve any longer for this type of dangerous situation.'

Luckily, there was no damage and the aircraft was able to land.

Notwithstanding these dramas, the flight team concluded that an 800-metre runway was not long enough and further experiments in rigid-towing were abandoned.

The 1942 experiments at Ainring, however, represented the first stage in developing a *Mistel*

The Bf 109 E/DFS 230 Mistel combination in its initial form in flight over southern Germany in June 1943.

combination which would allow a transport glider to carry a full payload, and for the combination to at least maintain the altitude to which it had been towed and to be able to climb after being towed into the air or, ultimately, to take off under its own power. It was also intended that the operational range of the combination should be increased so that the glider could carry, as a minimum, sufficient fuel for the *Mistel* combination to fly its mission and then, following separation, for the upper component to be able to return with full tanks.

At the conclusion of the trials, Stamer summarised the inherent benefits of the *Mistel* as follows:

1. No modifications were needed to the tail of the powered upper component.
2. Use of a technically simple method of refuelling the upper aircraft from the lower during towing, leading to an increase in the radius of action.
3. The simplest method of carrying an unmanned aircraft through the use of remote control.
4. The possibility of coupled landings.
5. The possibility of using an aircraft with a high wing loading for carrying slower aircraft which cannot be towed by any other method.
6. The application of aircraft as a 'carrier' component which, following separation, could remain fully operational and be able to provide protection for the lower component when landing.
7. The simplest method of providing an operational towing group [*Schleppverband*] with additional means of assisting take-off when using towing aircraft.

In line with point 6, Stamer proposed that the initial operational *Mistel* combination should comprise a DFS 230 glider as the lower component with an early Messerschmitt Bf 109 B fighter as the upper component.

It was also Stamer's intention to continue further experiments with a combination which offered greater range and a higher payload. To this end, he proposed combining the larger capacity DFS 331 glider with a Messerschmitt Bf 110 twin-engine fighter. However, despite the fact that design work on the DFS 331 had been undertaken in 1940, by 1941 only one prototype had been completed by the Gothaer Waggonfabrik. By 1942, the RLM had effectively discounted the type in favour of alternatives which offered higher payload options such as the Go 242. This machine could accommodate 21 fully-equipped troops in its fuselage or, alternatively, a cargo such as a *Kübelwagen* utility vehicle.

Over the next two years such developments appear to have become academic, for as Germany's armies became locked into more and more defensive battles, so it became an unavoidable requirement for the *Mistel* concept – if it was to survive in any practical way – to incorporate faster, more modern types of aircraft.

On 21 June 1943, a new combination comprising a DFS 230 carrying a Messerschmitt Bf 109 E fighter was ready for flight-testing. By this stage of the war, the E variant of the Bf 109 had largely been phased out from the front-line fighter units and had been relegated to the fighter training schools in favour of the up-rated Bf 109 F and G series. Nevertheless, for Stamer's requirements, the Bf 109 E was adequate. He wanted to develop a combination which firstly allowed the pilot in either aircraft to control take-off and also to make a coupled landing and to allow in-flight separation, as well as landings, flight and separation with an unmanned DFS 230.

Following the completion of testing of the individual components and due to the short runway at Ainring, as well as the increased take-off requirements of the DFS 230/ Bf 109 E combination, the two components of the new composite were flown to Hörsching, south of Linz, for flight-testing. Hörsching boasted a 1,700-metre-long concrete runway – ample for Stamer's purposes. As with the previous trials, the test team comprised Zitter, Oppitz and Schieferstein.

Modifications had centred around the increased weight involved in carrying the heavier Bf 109 E since the fuselage structure as well as the undercarriage of the production variant of the DFS 230 was too weak to support the fighter, particularly during a landing.

A solution was devised whereby the weight of the Bf 109 E was transferred directly to a suitably revised undercarriage fitted to the DFS 230. As Stamer wrote:

'The extended undercarriage of the Bf 109 as well as the wheel well on the underside of the wing appeared so aerodynamically unfavourable that it was decided not to use the method of mounting the *Mistel* combinations with the Kl 35 and Fw 56. Instead, the Bf 109 was supported on a swivelling framework mounted on the DFS 230 and not on its own undercarriage.'

A swivelling, tailwheel support structure was also fitted onto the DFS 230's upper fuselage in front of the tailplane. Loads were then transferred via the reinforced rear fuselage structure to the glider's tailwheel. The bearings on this framework could be freed by means of a clutch, and the last stage in releasing the upper aircraft was achieved through the forward rotation of the framework. The attachments on the lower end of the framework, close to the wing roots of the DFS 230, also served to transfer the weight of the Bf 109 directly to the glider's undercarriage.

The revised landing gear design for the DFS 230 incorporated undercarriage legs and wheels from a Junkers W 34 and the sprung tailwheel from an Hs 126.

The Bf 109 E was fitted with a mounting fixture on the underside of the wing close to the wing root and front spar. A similar fitting was added underneath the fuselage in front of the retractable tailwheel. The swivelling framework as well as the tail support were fitted with open, claw-type fittings, in which the opening was arranged upwards at approximately 45 degrees to the vertical. The framework was braced so that it leaned forwards and could be folded down towards the nose of the DFS 230.

The Bf 109 was braced by a wire stretched from a coupling on the underside of its fuselage close to its centre-of-gravity to a point approximately halfway along the fuselage of the DFS 230. At the point of separation, use of the previously mentioned clutch allowed the framework to rotate forwards and free the Bf 109.

It was in this initial form that the *Mistel* combination began its tests with a series of taxying runs conducted at increasingly high speeds to check such factors as directional control and undercarriage brake effectiveness, etc. However, after taxying about 500 metres the combination lifted off the runway, even before full throttle had been applied. The Bf 109 was throttled back, and over the intercom the two pilots discussed the situation. Feeling comfortable with things, they decided to continue with the flight. The ensuing flight lasted 40 minutes, during which a maximum rate of climb of 3.5 metres per second was reached, with an altitude of 2,000 metres. Banking manoeuvres were flown to port and starboard. Speed was held below a maximum of 240 km/h in order not to exceed the maximum allowable towing speed of the DFS 230.

The changes in pitching moment generated when the engine of the Bf 109 was throttled back or opened up were so small that they could be easily controlled or trimmed and a coupled landing was made.

A second take-off was performed immediately following the landing of the first flight. The take-off run on this occasion was estimated to be about 400 m. With the Bf 109 flying at full throttle, separation was performed at an altitude of 2,000 m and at a speed of 180 km/h. The spoilers on the DFS 230 were deployed during the release operation and the Bf 109 flew free according to plan, and during separation maintained its altitude and flight attitude. The DFS 230, however, reared up sharply during the separation procedure and collided with the coupling under the Bf 109, whereby the forward arch of the glider's canopy was slightly damaged.

Karl Schieferstein recalled:

'The difference in wing loading of the two aircraft did seem rather high and therefore the whole concept was judged somewhat risky. For that reason, Zitter opted to fly the DFS 230 from the second pilot's seat, leaving the forward seat, and something of a crumple zone, empty.

'This combination was able to take off without assistance, climb, separate in the air or land still attached. Putting Zitter in the rear seat as a precaution soon paid off because upon release, the tailwheel of the Me 109 went straight through the hood of the cabin, right in front of his nose. He did not like this at all, and neither did I; a more serious collision was only avoided by the quick deployment of the spoilers on the DFS 230, which caused rapid deceleration.' However, each aircraft landed without difficulty.

A further flight was made soon afterwards which was followed by a coupled landing. This flight, like the first, was, according to Stamer, 'completely faultless'.

The composite's encouraging take-off and landing performance, as well as its apparently flawless flight characteristics, allowed testing to be transferred back to Ainring. Subsequently, the combination was flown some 110 km overland from Hörsching. An engine mechanic accompanied the pilot of the DFS 230 on this trouble-free flight and a coupled landing was made at Ainring.

However, due to the earlier collision over Hörsching, it was found necessary to modify the tail mounting framework in such a way that the inclination of one aircraft relative to the other could be increased. Two extra mountings were added close to the rear spar fittings of the Bf 109 and in line with the forward fixtures. The single plane framework mounted to the DFS 230 was rebuilt as an open truss, additional struts being added to the main supports to create a V-shaped structure. The open claw fittings were remounted on the rear struts; flat pads were added at their previous positions to transfer the loads from the fittings near the front spar of the Bf 109.

A latching device was added to the tailwheel support, which was released only after the support had rotated forwards through a predefined angle. The wire anchoring the Bf 109 to the DFS 230 was no longer needed and it was replaced by a coupling located on the centre-line of the Bf 109, in the same plane as the forward struts of the truss structure.

Once the modifications had been satisfactorily completed, flight testing recommenced on 16 July 1943. The first test now showed that the length of the runway at Ainring was more than adequate and, upon completion, a coupled landing was made. There followed another flight in which separation was carried out at an altitude of 1,500 metres. Again, the DFS 230 reared up, and again the truss framework swung forward, but this time the rear struts restraining the Bf 109 lifted, thereby increasing the relative angle between the two aircraft and simplifying their separation. Separation occurred satisfactorily, though on this occasion one of the lateral struts of the truss framework was deformed when it hit the guard on the tailwheel of the Bf 109. Nevertheless, each aircraft landed without difficulty.

These tests revealed the need to fit a dive brake to the truss framework. A further series of solo flight tests was then conducted with the DFS 230 to investigate the effects of extending the dive brake and to check that it produced the desired pitching moment.

The sink speed was found to increase substantially and a nose-down pitching moment was produced. A lattice-type

A sequence of photographs showing the Bf 109 E/DFS 230 Mistel combination in its initial form in flight over southern Germany in June 1943 with Karl Schieferstein piloting the Bf 109 and Hermann Zitter sitting in the rear seat of the DFS 230. A swivelling, tailwheel support structure was fitted onto the upper fuselage in front of the DFS 230's tailplane. The Bf 109 E was fitted with a mounting fixture on the underside of the wing close to the wing root and front spar. A similar fitting was added underneath the fuselage in front of the retractable tailwheel. The swivelling framework as well as the tail support were fitted with open, claw-type fittings, facing upwards at approximately 45° to the vertical. The framework was braced so that it leaned forwards and could be folded down towards the nose of the DFS 230. The Bf 109 was braced by a wire stretched from a coupling on the underside of its fuselage close to its centre-of-gravity to a point approximately halfway along the fuselage of the DFS 230. At the point of separation, use of the clutch allowed the framework to rotate forwards and free the Bf 109. However, a mid-air collision between the two components over Hörsching forced a revision of the support design.

Messerschmitt Bf 109 E/DFS 230, Deutsche Forschungsanstalt für Segelflug 'Ernst Udet', Ainring, January 1944

Evidence from the photographs of this combination indicates that the starboard side of the Bf 109E carried the code letter 'K' whilst the port side carried the code letter 'A' (see photograph page 39, centre)

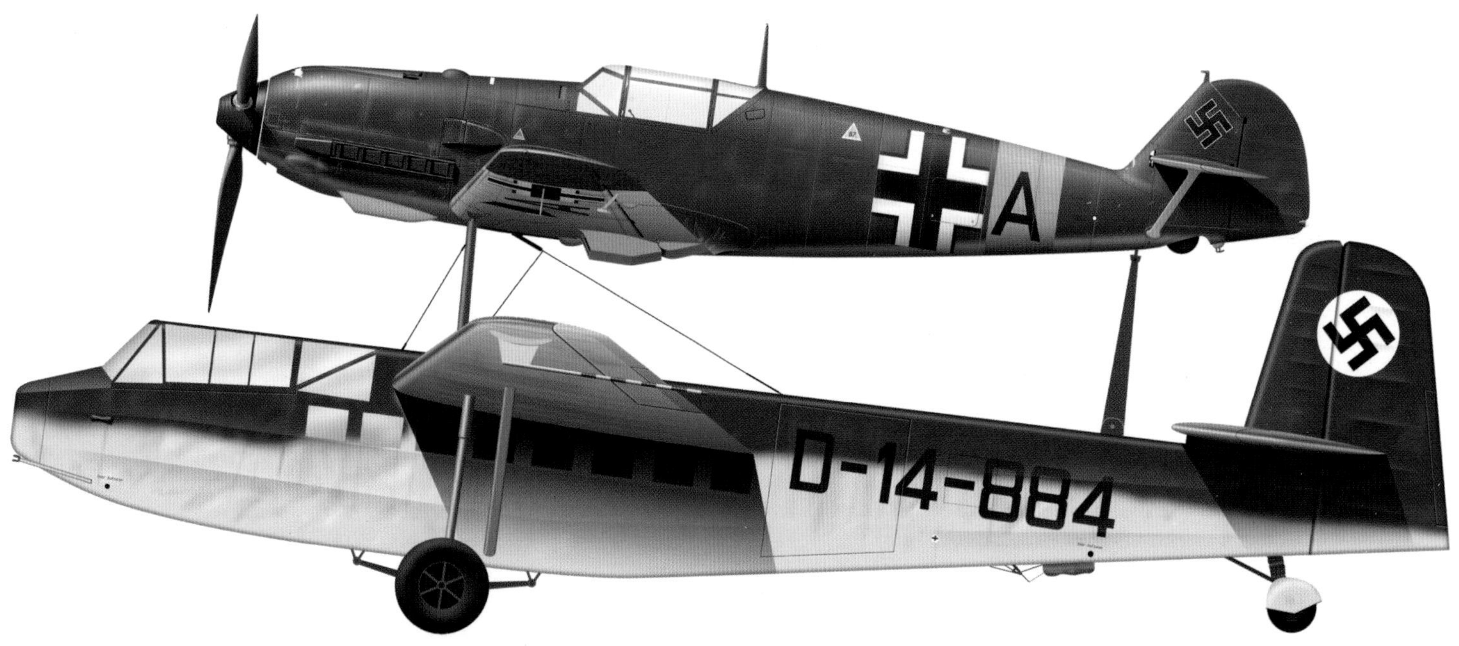

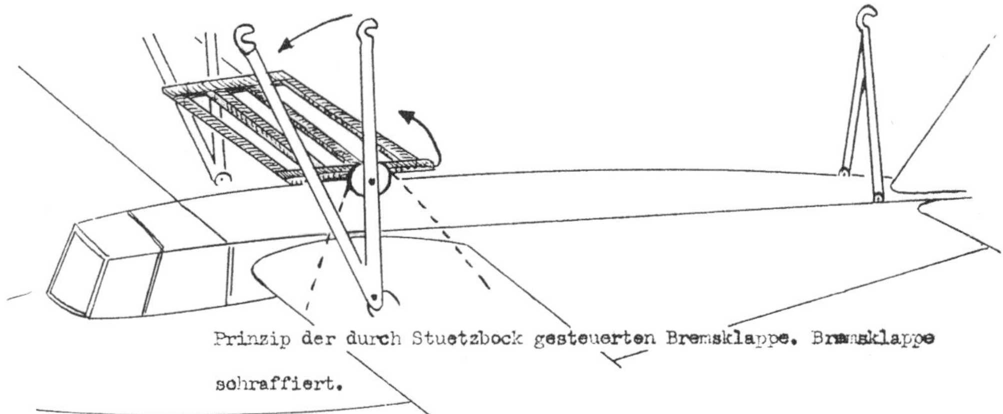

A drawing produced by Fritz Stamer to show the design, location and construction of the modified support structure for the Bf 109 E/DFS 230 Mistel.

The Bf 109E mounted on its modified supports with the dive brake in the deployed position.

The modified support structure for the Bf 109 E/DFS 230 Mistel. Two further mountings were added close to the rear spar fittings of the Bf 109 and in line with the forward fixtures. The single plane framework mounted to the DFS 230 was rebuilt as an open truss, additional struts being added to the main supports to create a V-shaped structure. The open claw fittings were remounted on the rear struts; flat pads were added at their previous positions to transfer the loads from the fittings near the front spar of the Bf 109. A latching device was added to the tailwheel support and was released only after the support had rotated forwards through a pre-defined angle. The wire anchoring the Bf 109 to the DFS 230 was no longer needed and it was replaced by a coupling located on the centre-line of the Bf 109, in the same plane as the forward struts of the truss structure. Note also the intercom connector and the stowed position of the dive brake.

dive brake was mounted and hinged at right angles to the direction of flight and with a large gap between its lower edge and the upper surface of the wing of the DFS 230.

For safety reasons the pilot of the DFS 230 was reseated further back in the cockpit in a position approximately level with the co-pilot's seat. In addition, a side exit door was incorporated to allow the pilot to bail out without having to open the cockpit canopy. The DFS 230 was also equipped with a brake parachute which could be used in an emergency, in the event that the aircraft did not separate properly, despite release of the latches holding the Bf 109 and the extension of the dive brake.

The Bf 109 pilot's view of the DFS 230's wing tips was enhanced by painting them a 'light colour' and single red and white stripes were added to the undersides of each, probably applied in a spanwise or diagonal pattern, though precisely why is not clear.

A series of separations was subsequently conducted during which the dive brake was extended. These separations were accomplished without any difficulties. Remarkably, the pilot of the DFS 230, probably either Kurt Oppitz or Paul Stämmler, became so familiar with the separation procedure during the course of these tests that he was able to separate cleanly without having to extend the dive brake by pitching the aircraft nose down at the right moment.

All flight tests were conducted with the DFS 230 carrying 500–600 kg in excess of its normal all-up weight. This weight resulted from the addition of ballast installed in the nose of the DFS 230 to counterbalance the weights of the rearward location of the pilot's seat, the truss framework, undercarriage, reinforcements to the tail and accommodation of a second crewman. A 100-kg electric battery, intended for tests not associated with the *Mistel* experiments, was also installed and used as ballast.

The second version of the Bf 109 E/ DFS 230 Mistel, photographed at Ainring in the winter of 1943, incorporated modifications to the tail mounting framework designed to increase the inclination between one aircraft and the other.

Additionally, radio equipment, a transformer, a power amplifier and a loudspeaker were installed in the DFS 230. The glider was also equipped with control surface servo-actuators and a bank of pressurised air bottles for trials in which it was to be controlled solely by the pilot of the Bf 109. The total additional weight of this equipment relative to the aircraft's normal all-up weight was 750 kg though it had no effect whatsoever on flight characteristics and an unnoticeable effect on performance.

During the Ainring experiments, the DFS 230 was not flown at its maximum payload of 1,000-1,200 kg. Rather, it was intended to measure the forces on the truss framework at various speeds and with the Bf 109 mounted at different angles of incidence and with various flap settings, in order to determine which of the many possible flight configurations would result in a part of the weight of the Bf 109 being carried by the DFS 230.

The aircraft were controlled throughout these tests by both pilots, though trials did include turning manoeuvres and also flights over long distances of around 60 km solely under the control of the Bf 109. Not unexpectedly, these tests reconfirmed the ineffectiveness of the ailerons. All other control functions were rated highly. Control capabilities, however, were considered 'adequate' for normal weather conditions and wide turns.

Flight tests were also made in which the *Mistel* combination was controlled only from the DFS 230 and the controls of the Bf 109 were unconstrained. In this case, overall control was noticeably better. The sluggishness of the ailerons, however, was pronounced and was due to the considerably larger weight of the combination and high location of the centre-of-gravity of the combined aircraft. The handling of the *Mistel* when flown with combined control functions, apart from a certain degree of aileron sluggishness, was excellent. No problems were encountered, except for the now familiar rearing up of the DFS 230 during separation. This violent manoeuvre of the DFS 230 was traced to effects arising from the downwash behind the Bf 109 on the tailplane and rear fuselage of the glider.

The sink rate of the solo DFS 230 flying at 120 km/h with all additional equipment (truss framework, main undercarriage, tailwheel) was recorded at 3 m/sec according to the static pressure gauge, whereas the unmodified DFS 230 at the same speed was 1.2 m/sec. In cruising flight, the level speed of the *Mistel* combination was 200 km/h, at which speed the Bf 109's normal cooling system was inadequate in warm weather.

There were other dangers, as Karl Schieferstein remembers:

> 'After completing the observations and finishing different tests on the airfield at Hörsching, we wanted to go back to Ainring. It was Christmas Eve and, as a one-off, Zitter had taken our *Segelflug-Startmeister* (Glider Controller) along as a passenger in his DFS 230. While flying cross-country, the left-hand pylon, which held my Me 109 in place, either opened or broke off. We were flying near Salzburg at the time and took the obvious option to separate; however, the right-hand coupling jammed, probably because the Me 109 was then flying tilted to the right by about 15 degrees. In the absence of any other ideas, we continued our flight, although we had no idea if we would be able to land in this unusual and unstable configuration without crashing. I asked Zitter what his passenger thought of the situation and he replied: "Well, I haven't told him anything and he can't see above and behind." We performed a very smooth landing which taxed our flying skills to the limit, and again my Messerschmitt remained on top, still tilted at a jaunty angle. Again, someone must have been watching over us, and we wondered if it had anything to do with it being Christmas.'

By early January 1944, however, Fritz Stamer was able to report:

> 'Flight tests with a *Mistel* combination comprising a DFS 230 below and a Bf 109 E above demonstrated faultless in-flight, take-off and landing characteristics… Control capability was available with only one of the aircraft; with the combined controls of both aircraft, the controllability was good…'

Unfortunately for Stamer, things did not always go according to plan and at one critical stage in its development, the *Mistel* almost faced disaster during a demonstration set up by Stamer for officials from the RLM. As Karl Schieferstein recalled:

> 'Paul Stämmler sat in the DFS 230 and I was in the Me 109. We had planned to make a clean approach. I separated but the mechanism did not work properly. Just as we reached an altitude of only five metres, Stämmler said: "Karl, separate now!" I replied: "I have separated!" Stämmler: "*Oh, my God!*" The ground came closer. We attempted a soft landing. Just as we landed the mechanism freed itself. I felt the movement, gave full throttle, made an elegant turn and landed almost alongside Stämmler, who had just rolled to a stop. The *Mistel* test had been rescued. Everyone had been impressed. Only Fritz Stamer had noticed anything wrong. With his long-legged, stork-like stride he came over to us and asked: "Karl, did you say something?" I countered with: "Is anything wrong, *Herr* Stamer? What's wrong?" He could have strangled me. Unintentionally, it had been a successful demonstration.'

As a result of the Ainring experiments, Germany now had the theoretical and practical proof that the principle of composite aircraft was not to be ignored or dismissed. Indeed, there were those who had already recognised the significant military potential of the *Mistel* as an offensive weapon. The question was how best and how quickly the weapon could be developed and exploited.

'THE WORK FORCE WOULD BE BETTER EMPLOYED ON OTHER TASKS'

Siegfried Holzbaur (left), the Junkers chief test pilot who was regarded as the 'Father of the Mistel'. He is seen here with Luftwaffe personnel during a visit to 2./KG 101's base at St. Dizier, France in June 1944. The unit was the first to use the Mistel operationally.

PROJECT *BEETHOVEN*

THE man perhaps most recognised as being the originator and driving force behind the eventual operational employment of the *Mistel* concept by the Luftwaffe during the Second World War was *Flugkapitän* Siegfried Holzbaur.

In 1939, as war broke out across Europe, Holzbaur formulated the idea for developing a so-called *Grossbombe* or 'Large Bomb' principle whereby an enormous bomb would be delivered to a target such as a ship by a smaller aircraft mounted on top of the bomb's upper surface or even partially embedded into it. It was intended that the bomb would be of the simplest practical design, thus incurring the least cost. This combination was to have taken off by means of a ground-based take-off trolley and was to have been powered in flight by two jet engines. Following its target approach run and separation from the bomb, the control aircraft would return to base.

The inertia shown on the part of the German authorities for such a proposal can, to some extent, be explained by the satisfactory performance of the Luftwaffe against maritime targets in the North Sea, around the British Isles and in the English Channel during 1940. Seven merchantmen were sunk during March for example and on the 16th, aircraft from KG 30 hit and damaged the heavy cruiser HMS *Norfolk* and the gunnery training ship HMS *Iron Duke* at their anchorage in Scapa Flow.

In early April 1940 during operations off the coast of Norway, He 111s of KG 26 and Ju 88s of KG 30 damaged the British battleship HMS *Rodney* and the cruisers *Devonshire*, *Southampton* and *Glasgow*, whilst the destroyer

SIEGFRIED HOLZBAUR

BORN in Stuttgart on 19 December 1915, Siegfried Holzbaur was, like many others of his generation, an avid builder of model aircraft in his youth. Later, he studied mechanical engineering and aircraft construction at the *Staatliche Ingenieurschule* in Esslingen. From an early age he took up both glider and powered sports flying, participating in several major aeronautical sporting competitions and rallies, including the *Rhönflugwettbewerbe* from 1934 to 1938 and the *Olympia-Sternflug* in 1936, during which he took joint second place with Dr.-Ing. Rall. In 1934 he became the 37th recipient of the *Internationale Segelflugleistungsabzeichen 'Silber C'* (International Gliding Badge in Silver) and in 1938 he flew as a member of Adolf Fach's Klemm-equipped DVL team which won second place in the *Deutschlandflug* of that year. In 1935, Holzbaur joined the Stuttgart-based firm of Robert Bosch as a research technician in the development of high pressure fuel injection systems for aero engines as well as a test pilot, in which capacity he flew the Albatross L 84 (W.Nr. 278 D-INYK), with the new BMW VI U engine at the *Erprobungsstelle* Travemünde. From 1938 until the end of the war he was employed by Junkers at their Dessau works as a research engineer and test pilot, initially as a 'project pilot', together with Rupprecht Wendel, for the development of the Ju 88.

As a *Flugkapitän* at Junkers, Holzbaur was accorded the responsibilities of chief test pilot and subsequently performed the maiden flights of various new Junkers aircraft, such as the Ju 87 B dive-bomber, the Ju 288 medium bomber and the Ju 287 V1 jet bomber prototype which he first flew on 8 August 1944. During a flight in the Ju 86 P high-altitude reconnaissance type, fitted with a pressure cabin and Jumo 207A supercharged diesels, Holzbaur reached an altitude of 14,500 metres. Between 1933-1945, he flew more than seventy different types of aircraft, including the Messerschmitt Me 262 jet fighter and the Arado Ar 234 jet bomber. In late 1943, Holzbaur was awarded the *Kriegsverdienstkreuz* (War Service Cross) First Class in recognition for his dedication and pioneering work in flight-testing.

HMS *Gurkha* was sunk west of Stavanger. Throughout the whole Norwegian campaign, Royal Navy warships and transport were subjected to continuous attacks by the Luftwaffe. Later, during the campaign against England, Ju 87s from VIII. *Fliegerkorps* dive-bombed convoys off the south coast of England. Between 1 July and 9 August German aircraft launched some 1,300 anti-shipping sorties around the British Isles. Overseas convoys were forced to abandon passage through the Channel, but coastal traffic still ran the gauntlet and suffered.

Hauptmann Dietrich Peltz, an accomplished Stuka and bomber pilot, visited Siegfried Holzbaur at Dessau in December 1941 and was impressed by the Mistel concept. Together with Werner Baumbach, he brought the idea to the attention of Hermann Göring. Peltz is seen here as an Oberleutnant in October 1940 having been awarded the Ritterkreuz.

The following year however, with defeat over England and heavy air commitments in the east as a result of Operation *Barbarossa*, fortunes changed. Bomber units were transferred to Russia and although Fw 200 *Condors* of KG 40 were operating out of France and Scandinavia, their relatively low speed meant that they could only operate with confidence against unarmed merchant ships. British shipborne defensive measures (such as the introduction of catapult-launched fighters) and armament improved, convoy escort increased and the *Condors* were gradually forced to return to a purely reconnaissance role with attacks only being made when cloud cover was adequate.

On a clear, windless day towards the end of 1941 Siegfried Holzbaur was airborne out of the Junkers works at Dessau, flight-testing a Ju 88 fitted with a reflector bombsight which was intended to be used in conjunction with an automatic pilot. At one point, during what was essentially a routine flight on automatic pilot, he visually aligned the Ju 88 with a factory chimney which rose up from the ground ahead and below him as a dark upright line. At a range of 10-15 km, Holzbaur went into a slight descent towards his 'target'. At a distance of about 3-4 km, he relaxed and allowed the trimmed aircraft to fly itself along the path set by the autopilot. As the aircraft flew on, he became surprised at how accurately the aircraft passed over the top of the chimney. It was at that moment that Holzbaur realised he had inadvertently stumbled across an exciting possibility. With typical enterprise and endeavour, he repeated the 'experiment' several times and became convinced that he had found a method of remotely, yet accurately, steering an aircraft over long distances towards a target. Furthermore, if the aircraft could carry an extremely large explosive charge, there existed the means to deliver significant offensive loads against pre-selected targets. The next day, in order to convince himself of the idea, he undertook further tests. The results, especially in terms of accuracy, were exactly the same as the day before.

On the strength of his unofficial experiments, at the end of December 1941, Holzbaur prepared a report for the Junkers project office in which he proposed mounting a small aircraft above a larger, explosive-filled aircraft which would be used to control, aim and release the latter at a target. The weapon could be used to strike at a heavily-armoured target such as a battleship or gun emplacement. For the upper component, Holzbaur suggested that a fighter aircraft, such as the Messerschmitt Bf 109, be used which would be able to make good its escape at high speed upon separation, and also be well able to defend itself if attacked by hostile fighters. For the lower component, Holzbaur proposed using 'weary' Ju 88 bombers whose airframes and engines had reached their maximum permissible service hours and were thus considered expendable. In addition, he proposed replacing the autopilot with a three-axis control system and a gyro-stabilised sight.

Unfortunately for Holzbaur, the project office received his report with some degree of scepticism and his proposal was judged to be 'a waste of time'. News from the battlefronts painted a rosy, yet misleading picture; Luftwaffe bomber crews were chalking up staggering successes against enemy armies and navies in both Russia and the Mediterranean. The truth however, was that the price of apparently easily won victories was high.

In January 1941, in an attempt to bolster the Axis strength in the Mediterranean following the Italian reverses in Libya, Hitler despatched a small Luftwaffe air contingent, X.*Fliegerkorps*, to Sicily. Also in the Mediterranean at this time was the aircraft carrier HMS *Illustrious*, operating as part of the British Mediterranean Fleet. On 10 January, the recently arrived Ju 87s of I./St.G 1 and II./St.G 2 attacked and badly damaged the aircraft carrier 161 km west of Malta. On the 13th, after reconnaissance aircraft had identified *Illustrious* in Valletta Harbour, the Stukas of *Hptm.* Werner Hozzel's I./St.G 1 laboured into the air, each aircraft carrying specially-fitted 1,000 kg bombs intended for the British carrier. The German dive-bombers launched the first in a series of well executed and determined attacks, but as Hozzel recalled:

> 'This aircraft carrier had become a matter of prestige for the OKL. It had to be sunk under all circumstances. If the Supreme Command of the *Wehrmacht* could report the sinking of an aircraft carrier by German Stukas, both friend and foe would have sat up and taken notice. So we commenced our attacks over Valletta with heavy losses. More than 90 AA batteries spat their fire at us… At the same time, a strong force of Hurricanes interfered with us on the approach and on our departure. In practically every sortie, I lost three or four of my old, battle-tested crews; an irreplaceable loss. It was just impossible to replace those thoroughly trained and experienced pilots and their "back-seaters". During those actions, the carrier was hit by four 1,000 kg bombs, the heaviest a Ju 87 could carry. Still, we did not succeed in sinking it, though she must have suffered terrible internal damage.'

Although the dive-bombers had caused considerable damage to the harbour installations at Valletta, *Illustrious* was sufficiently repaired and she eventually limped to Alexandria from where she departed to America for extensive repairs.

In the Crimea, it was just as tough; during the first months of *Barbarossa*, elements of the Soviet Black Sea Fleet had pounded Constanza, the naval port serving as base to a small Rumanian fleet and an even smaller German fleet. Hitler knew that the capture of the Russian naval base at Sevastopol was crucial in removing the threat posed by the Soviet navy to Axis shipping, especially the supply convoys he planned to use to support the *Wehrmacht's* advance into the Caucasus. However, to his considerable disappointment, attempts by bombers of *Luftflotte* 4 to destroy Russian tonnage resulted in only negligible damage. Later, in September 1941, IV.*Fliegerkorps* launched a series of intensive attacks against Soviet merchant and naval fleets defending Odessa and though several ships were sunk and many others damaged by Luftwaffe dive-bombers, some 350,000 troops and civilians and 200,000 tons of materiel were evacuated from the port to Sevastopol.

The truth began to emerge and with it the sobering fact that success, in terms of enemy tonnage sunk by aircraft, was negated by the unacceptably highly losses in aircraft sustained as a result of anti-shipping operations. For example, by the end of 1941, it was becoming increasingly clear that the Luftwaffe was losing its battle to blockade Britain's maritime lifelines. At the beginning of operations conducted by the *Fliegerführer Atlantik* it had been estimated that one aircraft would be lost for every 30,000 tons of enemy shipping sunk; at the end of 1941, this figure had declined to 10,000 tons for every aircraft loss. It was even worse in the Mediterranean theatre.

Such facts helped to rekindle interest in Holzbaur's proposal. There seemed to be some justification for deliberately sacrificing one or two war-weary, unmanned aircraft in order to achieve a level of success which was, at that time, costing the Luftwaffe considerable numbers of aircraft and crews. Slowly, but surely, any scepticism that there had been over the Holzbaur proposal dissipated, particularly so when the test pilot demonstrated the accuracy of his idea to an engineer from the Junkers project office and an autopilot specialist, both of whom flew with him for the demonstration. Having witnessed the potential of Holzbaur's method for themselves, they needed little convincing to encourage others within the company to view it in the same way.

On 19 December 1941, Siegfried Holzbaur's twenty-seventh birthday, *Hptm.* Dietrich Peltz, one of the Luftwaffe's most experienced and successful bomber pilots, visited the Junkers works at Dessau as a guest of *Flugkapitän* Karl-Heinz Kindermann, the former Junkers chief pilot and then head of the company's *Technischer Aussendienst* (Technical Service Liaison Office). Peltz had formerly served as *Gruppenkommandeur* of II./KG 77 and had been awarded the *Ritterkreuz* in recognition of his bombing missions over England the previous year. Later, on the northern sector of the Eastern Front, he had achieved great success in mounting pinpoint attacks against Soviet trains and railway stations. At the time of his visit to Dessau, Peltz had just been appointed commander of the *Verbandsführerschule für Kampfflieger* at Foggia in Italy. At the youthful age of 27, he was directly responsible for the training of the Luftwaffe's future bomber commanders.

Roughly the same age, Peltz and Holzbaur had, coincidentally, both worked at Daimler-Benz in Stuttgart in their youth. The two men therefore enjoyed much in common and were able to understand each other's objectives. Holzbaur seized the opportunity to explain to Peltz his ideas and ambitions for converting old Ju 88s into unmanned, guided bombs. Peltz, an officer known to embrace radical ideas, immediately became interested and wanted to see Holzbaur's project for himself. The next day, both men were airborne in a Ju 88, with Holzbaur at the controls.

Peltz quickly grasped the military significance of Holzbaur's proposal. In the *Grossbombe* was a method of delivering a large explosive charge to a pinpoint target with a high level of accuracy. It could ideally be used as an anti-shipping weapon and, in Peltz's opinion, further development and subsequent production needed to commence immediately. In an effort to generate more support, Peltz referred the matter to another renowned anti-shipping ace, *Hptm.* Werner Baumbach, *Kommandeur* of I./KG 30. Baumbach had won fame flying Ju 88s over the British Isles and Norway. In June 1941 he became only the second bomber pilot in the Luftwaffe to be awarded the Oakleaves to the *Ritterkreuz*. Baumbach, too, visited Holzbaur at Dessau and he, like Peltz, recognised in the *Grossbombe* the weapon which the Luftwaffe badly needed in its anti-shipping arsenal.

Inspired by the work at Junkers, Peltz consulted another friend whom he had met while at Foggia, *Haupting. Dipl.-Ing.* Horst-Dieter Lux. Lux had been born in Jena on 5 April 1917 and worked as a civilian aeronautical engineer and text pilot assigned on behalf of the RLM to test-fly new types and assess them for acceptance. He recalled:

> 'My flying career started when I was an unborn baby when my very enterprising mother, who was four months' pregnant, climbed into a rickety biplane piloted by her brother and I logged my first hour. Flying was in the family. At the age of about fourteen I joined a private group with the aim of building and flying a glider.'

This enthusiasm for flying was fuelled further when Adolf Hitler rose to power in January 1933. Hitler recognized the tremendous propaganda and potential military value in sports flying and formed the *Nationalsozialistiches Fliegerkorps* (NSFK), a branch of the Nazi Party, to encourage boys from the age of 12 to take up flying. In line with this new 'air-minded' Nazi stance, youth from all over the Reich flocked to embark on courses in fieldcraft, workshop duties, physical fitness and, ultimately, glider-flying. Lux was, by his own admission 'obsessed' by flight and its science:

> 'As much as I was convinced that being a pilot was the life for me, early on the hands-on work on aeroplanes instilled in me a curiosity to know more about what lay behind such terminology as aerodynamics, stress analysis, lift coefficients, stability and much more. I wanted to be a pilot with solid aeronautical engineering knowledge.'

Lux went on to study aeronautical engineering at the Technical University in Berlin and learned to be a test pilot at the DVL. He also spent some time at the Luftwaffe *Erprobungsstelle* at Rechlin and later, after war broke out, made studies and practical tests into dive-bombing. Because of the inclement weather in northern Germany, the test and research team to which Lux was attached was relocated to Foggia in Italy where he met Peltz and the two became friends. By the end of the war he was familiar with Junkers' aircraft having flown the Ju 52, Ju 86, Ju 87, Ju 88 and Ju 188, but he also had hours on several Heinkel, Messerschmitt, Focke-Wulf, Dornier and Siebel types. In September 1944 he also took a brief introductory course on the new Me 262 and Ar 234 jet aircraft with the forward-thinking, if not brave, aim of considering such aircraft as candidates for future composite configuration.

It was at Foggia however that he and Peltz spent considerable time discussing how high losses sustained during attacks on convoys could be reduced. Echoing the vision of Holzbaur, Lux recalled:

> 'In 1941 and 1942, the Luftwaffe lost approximately twenty-five aircraft and crews for one ship sunk in the Mediterranean. The ratio threatened to grow worse and only a new tactic for attacks on ships from the air based on an innovative weapon could improve the situation. The answer came from a look at the Japanese Kamikaze operations. One aircraft – one weapon could sink a ship. But it also demanded the sacrifice of a human pilot. While the loss of one aircraft for the chance to destroy one ship was completely acceptable, the price of a human was not. Japanese mentality may have allowed that, but German mentality could not. The pilot had to be saved.
>
> 'After several ideas, such as ejection from the aircraft with rescue by a submarine, the final concept emerged. The pilot had to fly home. His aircraft would be a fighter mounted on top of a larger bomber which would be

Dipl.-Ing. Horst-Dieter Lux photographed in the 1960s. As a test pilot with the DVL and assigned to the RLM in 1942, he championed the Mistel concept and became a central figure in its development for military use. After the war, in 1953, Lux moved to the USA and joined Lockheed as a research specialist after serving as a development engineer and test pilot with various European aircraft manufacturers. In 1961 he worked on the marketing of F-104 development projects such as the zero-length launch (ZELL) small airfield tactical support (SATS) and side-looking radar (SLR) for the West German Ministry of Defence. In January 1970 he was appointed manager of a $7.5 million USAF foreign military sales programme under which the Lockheed-California Company (CALAC) carried out testing and engineering of a reconnaissance system for the German Navy's F-104Gs.

Flugkapitän Siegfried Holzbaur (eighth from left in darker flying overalls) links arms with two eminent Luftwaffe bomber commanders for a group photograph at Dessau in late 1941/early 1942. This was probably the occasion on which Holzbaur welcomed Hauptmann Werner Baumbach (fifth from right), Kommandeur of I./KG 30, to the Junkers works to inspect the Bf 109F/Ju 88A-4 *Beethoven* prototype. Also in this picture is Flugkapitän Karl-Heinz Kindermann (third from left), the former Junkers chief pilot and then head of the company's Technischer Aussendienst, who authorised the assignment of a small group of aircraft fitters to produce the experimental Mistel in a way which would not interfere with Junkers' normal workload but which would allow the company to cooperate with the DFS. Also identifiable are: far right, Professor Heinrich Hertel, deputy Chairman of Junkers; Joachim Matthies (fourth from right); test pilot Major Erich Bloedorn (seventh from left) Kommodore of KG 30; Hans-Joachim Pancherz (sixth from left) test pilot, and Ernst Zindel (second from left), designer.

unmanned and carried the warhead. The combination of the two aircraft had to be controlled and piloted from the fighter cockpit. For the actuation of landing gear, flaps, throttles and especially the elevator, ailerons and rudder, a "fly-by-wire" system had to be developed. It was not without risk.'

Excited and heartened by what they had seen at Dessau and with support from Lux, Peltz and Baumbach brought Holzbaur's proposal to the attention of *Reichsmarschall* Göring and the *Reichsluftfahrtministerium* (RLM). Much to the bomber pilots' disappointment however, the RLM failed to understand the opportunities presented to them and Göring showed only limited interest in the project; as Baumbach has recorded in his memoirs:

> 'As far back as 17 January 1942, Peltz and I had drawn Göring's attention to the idea of these aircraft... Unfortunately, without result. The accuracy of this weapon which, though new, was assembled from existing aircraft, was about eighty per cent against fixed targets. Its effect was shattering.'

Nevertheless, Göring did go as far as to authorise further tests to be conducted at Dessau, and in early 1942 the Ju 88V21 was fitted with a modified Patin PDS (*Patin-Dreiruderstenerung*) three-axis control system and a gyro-stabilised sight with which target acquisition flights were made, the flight paths being measured with a theodolite fitted with a ciné camera. The aircraft was tracked up to a point close to the target and the subsequent flight path was extrapolated from the measurements. Repeated experiments conducted by Junkers using this system showed that a target measuring 15 metres x 15 metres could be hit with certainty.

Undaunted by earlier indifference, in the spring of 1942 Junkers forwarded the results of these successful tests to Göring and the RLM, but no response was forthcoming. Furthermore, commitments to other contracts then being fulfilled by Junkers did not allow the company enough time to pursue the matter further and the project was shelved. On 17 July, Peltz discussed the matter of '*Flugkapitän* Holzbaur's proposal for pinpoint target tactics using the Ju 88/Me 109' with representatives of the Aircraft Development Department at the office of the *Generalluftzeugmeister*, but here, too, it seems that Peltz could not dispel the mood of apathy and inertia shown earlier.

However, as has been recorded in the previous chapter, during the second half of 1942 and into 1943, the DFS at Ainring had been experimenting with Fritz Stamer's '*Mistel*' method of towing aircraft. On 17 June 1943 the Institute drafted a report for the RLM in which it outlined its understanding of how a Ju 88 A-4/Bf 109 F *Mistel* combination could be used in an offensive military capacity:

> 'The Ju 88 A-4/Bf 109 F *Mistel* combination offers the possibility of using the Ju 88 A-4 as an unmanned *Grossbombe*, remotely controlled by the Bf 109 F to a target on a pre-determined glide path. With a range of 1,500 km, the *Mistel* can still deliver a 3.5-ton payload of high explosive. Such target aircraft can be stripped of all unnecessary equipment and can therefore carry substantial amounts of explosives.
>
> 'This method has the advantage that the fighter can remain outside the range of the anti-aircraft guns of a sea target since it can disengage its payload from out of range of said anti-aircraft fire and escape due to its superior speed from any pursuing fighter cover. Another advantage is that such a mission requires only one pilot.'

The 'unnecessary equipment' was classified as the dive brake hydraulics, automatic dive mechanism, defensive armament, radio and bomb-aiming equipment; it would all be removed. The estimated weight of the composite was envisaged as:

Bf 109 F	
Empty Weight	2,010 kg
Additional Equipment	246 kg
Fully Armed Weight	2,256 kg
Fuel 700 litres	525 kg
Lubrication 30 litres	30 kg
Pilot and Personal Equipment	100 kg
2 MG 17 Belts for 500 Rounds	5 kg
2 x 500 Rounds MG 17 Ammunition	25 kg
MG-FF Drum for 60 Rounds	8 kg
60 Rounds MG-FF Ammunition	12 kg
Weight of Disposable Fuel Tank	18 kg
Additional Total Weight	723 kg
Ju 88 A-4	
Fully Armed Weight	8,715 kg
Fuel	2,450 kg
Lubrication	200 kg
	11,365 kg
Removed Weight	1,500 kg
	9,865 kg
Bf 109 and Ju 88 A	
Total Weight	12,844 kg
Explosives	3,156 kg
Maximum Take-Off Weight	**16,000 kg**

During July and August 1943, Karl-Heinz Kindermann authorised the assignment of a small group of aircraft fitters to produce an experimental composite aircraft comprising a Bf 109 F fighter upper component (CI+MX) coupled to a Ju 88 A-4 lower component in a way which would not interfere with the Junkers workload but which would allow the company to cooperate with the DFS whose design, manufacturing and flight-test departments took on the responsibility of providing and testing a type of towing frame or *Schleppgestell* for the new composite which had been assigned the code name *'Beethoven'*.

Simultaneously, Junkers and Patin installed the PDS flight control system and the DUZ company worked on the transfer of the throttle controls from the Ju 88 to the Bf 109. The composite was constructed in such a way that the Bf 109 rested on two three-legged support structures and was fastened with spherically-aligned bolts. The structures were attached to points on the front and rear spar joints as well as to frame 9 of the Ju 88's fuselage. The third attachment was made in front of the tailwheel well of the Bf 109 via a collapsible strut which enabled the Bf 109's incidence to be increased during separation. The collapsible strut was attached to frame 20 of the Ju 88's fuselage. The Bf 109 was fastened to the support structures by means of explosive bolts. On separation, only the bolt keeping the collapsible strut straight was detonated by the pilot. The subsequent increase in the angle of incidence of the Bf 109 operated a switch to command the detonation of all three bolts holding the aircraft.

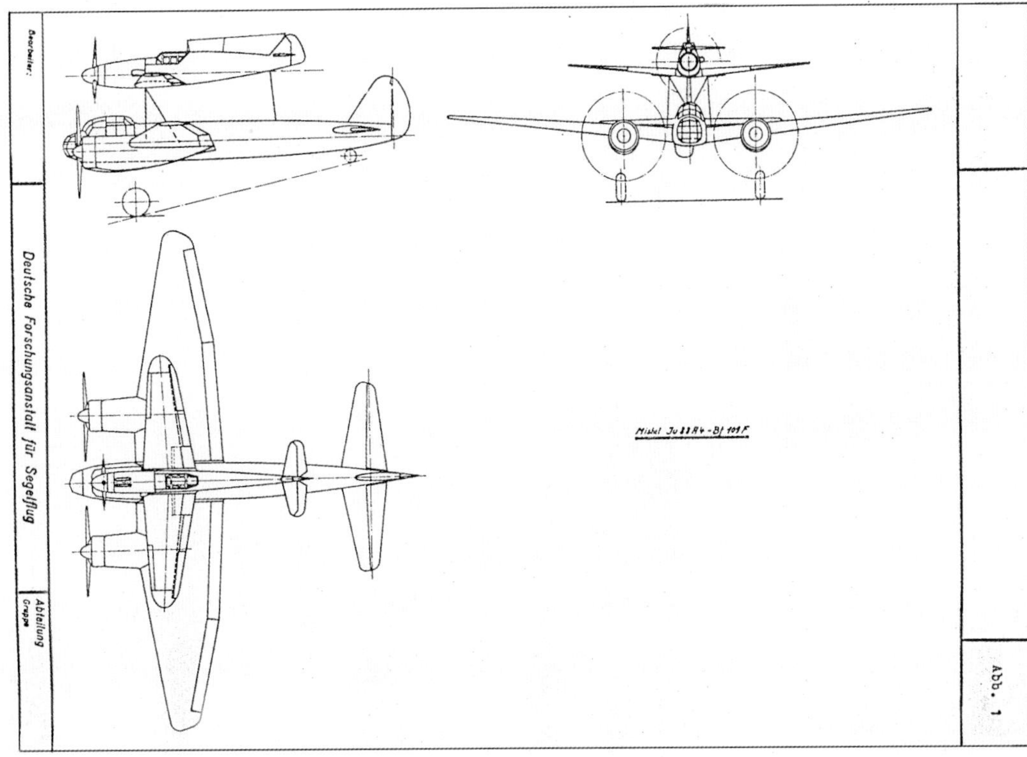

An early drawing of the Ju 88 A-4/Bf 109 F Mistel produced by the DFS.

The Ju 88's engines were throttled mechanically from the Bf 109 via the linkage supplied by DUZ, which during the release sequence was also explosively separated. The throttle levers fitted to the Bf 109 were much longer than those normally found in the Ju 88 in order to overcome the higher friction forces associated with the modified throttle system. Two dual-function instruments indicating engine manifold pressure and engine speed (rpm) were fitted to the Bf 109 to monitor the performance of the Ju 88's engines. The electrical connections between the two aircraft were made with two multi-pin shear connectors. Their halves were secured by locking wire to prevent inadvertent separation.

The PDS control system enabled the *Mistel* combination to fly solely under control from the Bf 109. The system could be operated in two conditions – 'automatic' and 'cruise'. In cruising flight, control movements were measured by potentiometer and transmitted electrically to the servos coupled to the flying control surfaces of the Ju 88. In the 'automatic' flight condition, the Ju 88 could be controlled by switches fitted to the Bf 109's control column and instrument panel. The switches were arranged to send directional and lateral control commands to the Ju 88 in the same way as if the pilot was physically controlling the aircraft.

In 1943, *Dr.-Ing.* Fritz Haber was appointed head of development, construction and flight trials for the *Mistel* project at Junkers. Born in Mannheim on 3 April 1912, Fritz 'Fips' Haber had studied aircraft construction at the *Technische Hochschule* at Darmstadt between 1931 and 1936. In 1939 he was assigned to work as an assistant to *Professor* N. Scheubel at the *Aerodynamisches Institut* and for his doctorate specialised in the workings of parachutes and wind tunnels. Later that year he joined Junkers at the company's Dessau plant where he worked in the Development Office under *Professor* Heinrich Hertel, becoming involved with the development of the Ju 88, Ju 288 and various control surfaces and wind tunnel experiments.

In an unpublished study on the technical aspects of the *Mistel*, Haber wrote:

> 'Of the many problems encountered in the development of the *Mistel*, the most difficult concerned the creation of a flight control system which allowed the composite to be flown from the upper aircraft and ensured that the carrier aircraft, after separation, continued to fly exactly along the path it flew as part of the composite.
>
> 'Because mechanical connections between the control surfaces of the upper and lower aircraft would have resulted in unacceptably high control forces, electrically-powered servo-actuators were developed to ease the pilot's workload. These actuators, at least in Germany, were the only ones to be put into large-scale production and used extensively.
>
> 'Control of the composite during cruising flight used open-loop control principles governed by the *Mistel's* speed. The control rods of the upper aircraft were linked to potentiometers, the movement of which regulated, after attenuation and amplification, the power supply to the electrically-driven servo-actuators fitted to the carrier aircraft's flaps, ailerons, elevators and rudder. The speed at which the system operated was dependent on the differences between the control surface deflections of the upper and lower aircraft. This form of control worked extremely well and, in particular, fulfilled all aircraft handling and performance requirements. Pilots were unanimous in their opinion: flying the composite did not present any problems. Later, it transpired that there was hardly any need for conversion training. Tests successfully demonstrated that the servo-system gave the pilot the impression that his control column and rudder pedals were mechanically linked to the control surfaces of the aircraft beneath him, though this was not the case. These tests also showed the way how future, large and very fast

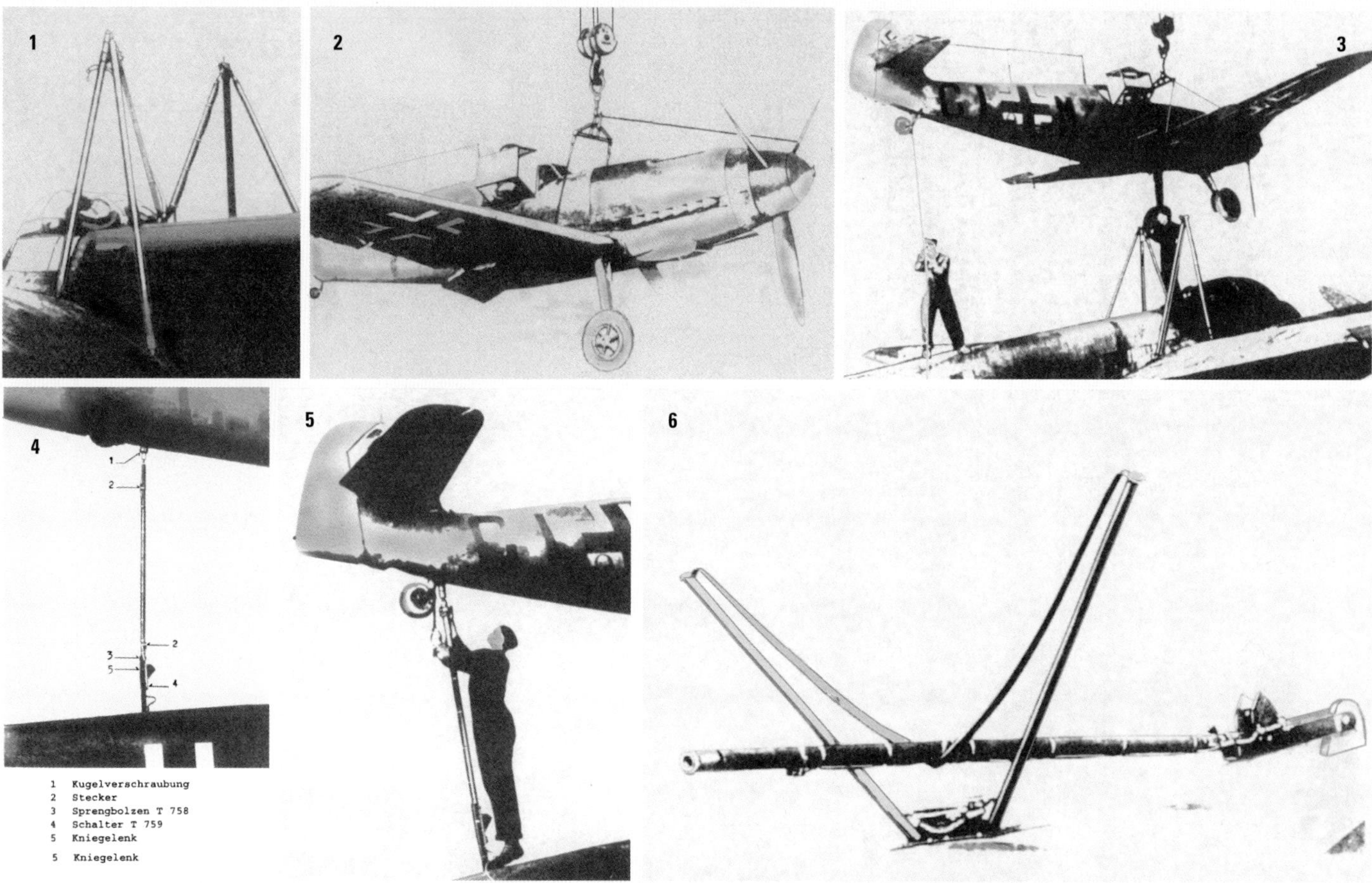

A series of illustrations taken from the 'Mistel 2' instruction manual prepared by Junkers in May 1944 (issued August 1944)
1. The installation of the front support struts on a Ju 88 A-4. **2.** The hoisting arrangement for the Bf 109 upper component as shown in an illustration from the 'Mistel 2' instruction manual prepared by Junkers in May 1944. Junkers supplied one set of hoisting equipment for every five Bf 109s allocated to Mistel conversion. **3.** The first Bf 109 F-4, CI+MX/Ju 88 A-4 Mistel combination is used for a picture in the 'Mistel 2' instruction manual showing the Bf 109 being lowered onto the Ju 88 A-4. The mechanic seen to the left is controlling the positional movement of the Bf 109 with a rope. **4.** The assembly of the collapsible rear strut between the Bf 109 and Ju 88. (1) Ball and socket connection; (2) Electrical connection; (3) Explosive bolts; (4) Switch; (5) Swivel. **5.** A mechanic connects the collapsible rear strut. **6.** The collapsible rear strut and catching stay as fitted to the rear top fuselage of a Ju 88 A-4.

aircraft could be flown under conditions where control forces were likely to exceed the strength of the pilot.

'The above mentioned system could be used during take-off and normal cruising flight. It also automatically steered the carrier aircraft towards its target after separation, control in this case being provided by a three-axis gyro-stabilised platform, which maintained the carrier aircraft's heading and its flight path relative to the horizon while keeping its lateral axis level. The longitudinal inclination of the composite was controlled and determined by the pilot in the upper aircraft. Theoretically, this method of control was not correct, since the inclination of the carrier aircraft's flight path and not its longitudinal inclination should have been held constant during its flight towards the target. This point was of particular importance if the flight path of the carrier aircraft was disturbed by the act of separation; any sudden change to the flight path caused it to miss its target. Theoretical analyses, however, revealed that the control of the lower component's longitudinal inclination after separation did not, in practice, lead to loss of accuracy. In addition, the control system proved capable of correcting flight path disturbances. Three primary sources of disturbance during separation had been identified during the theoretical analyses. The first was caused by pitching moments which attempted to alter the aircraft's inclination. These, however, could easily be brought under control by use of the elevators. The second and third forms of disturbance were produced by forces exerted perpendicular to and along the flight path respectively. In both of these cases, the disturbances could be minimised by adjusting the relative inclination of the joined aircraft to one another and the throttle settings of each aircraft. In addition, the third source was found to be a function of the carrier aircraft's aerodynamic drag which, although normally small, became noticeable at about 10 km from the point of separation.'

When flying as part of the *Mistel* combination the Bf 109 took its fuel from the outer starboard wing tank of the Ju 88. The emergency fuel line leading to this tank was connected to the drop tank fuel line of the Bf 109, a normal drop tank connector being used. The Ju 88's fuel pumps were more than capable of meeting fuel flow demands. It was intended to fit a limit switch to the Bf 109's tanks to ensure that its tanks were completely full before separation took place, but by the time preliminary flight trials had been completed in February 1944, this had yet to be installed. Other modifications still requiring completion at this time were the connection of the engine speed selector lever via a dog-latch to the Ju 88's throttle, so that under certain conditions engine manifold pressure and engine speed

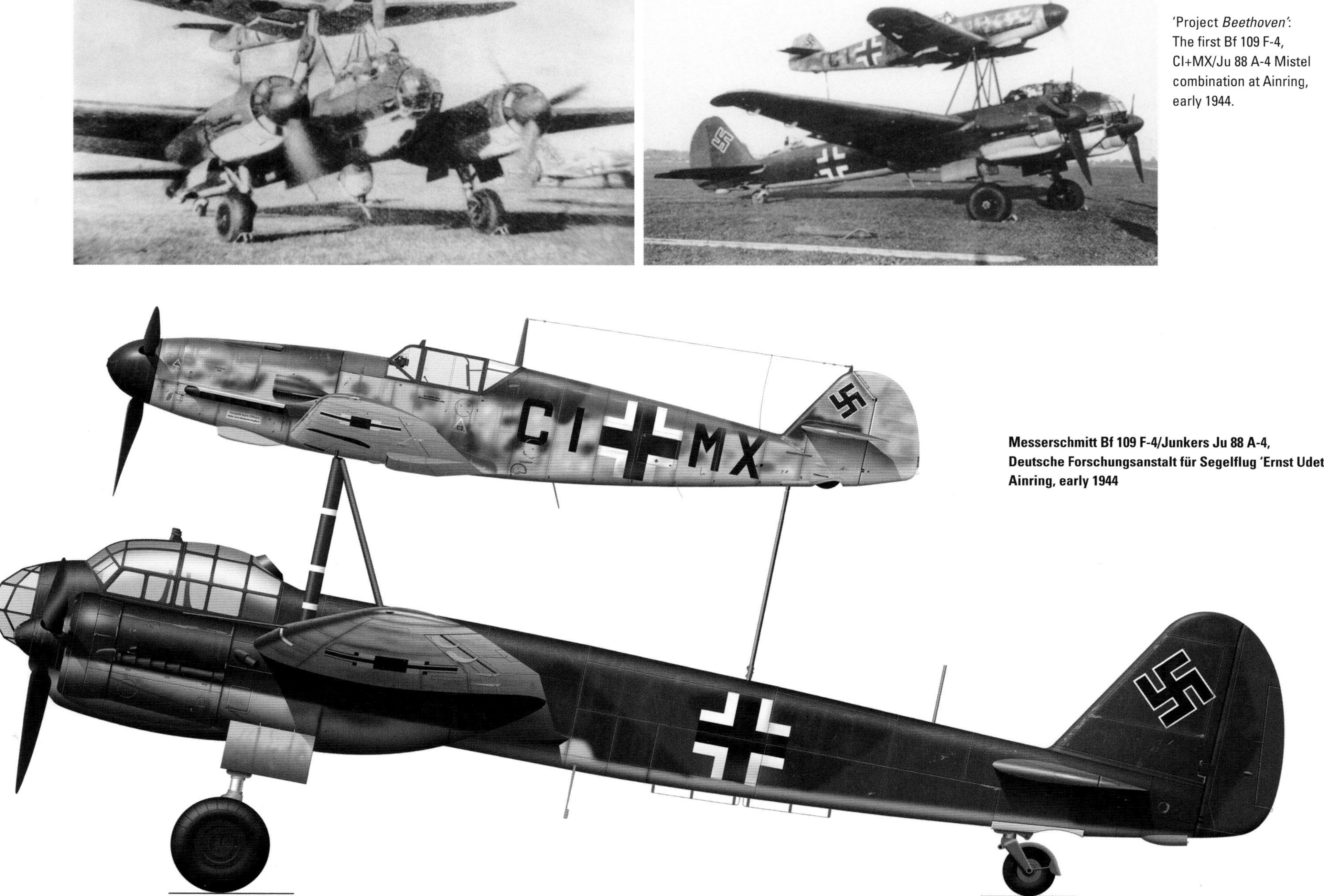

'Project *Beethoven*': The first Bf 109 F-4, CI+MX/Ju 88 A-4 Mistel combination at Ainring, early 1944.

Messerschmitt Bf 109 F-4/Junkers Ju 88 A-4, Deutsche Forschungsanstalt für Segelflug 'Ernst Udet', Ainring, early 1944

The Bf 109 F-4, CI+MX/ Ju 88 A-4 Mistel in flight.

Bf 109 F-4, CI+MX lifts away from its Ju 88 A-4 carrier during flight trials by the DFS at Ainring in early 1944.

settings were not coupled together; the transfer of the propeller feathering switch from the Ju 88 to the Bf 109; the installation of the mechanism for jettisoning the strengthened undercarriage of the Ju 88 by the Bf 109 during operational conditions and the installation of the Bf 109-operated, electro-hydraulic landing flap actuators in the Ju 88.

In his report for the DFS on the Bf 109/Ju 88 *Mistel* dated 9 February 1944, *Dipl.-Ing.* Rudolf Ziegler of the *Abteilung Mustererprobung* (Type Trials Department) described the flight-testing as follows:

'The handling characteristics of the *Mistel* combination are similar to the Ju 88 in cruising flight, on take-off and landing, and during instrument flying, apart from sluggishness caused by the extra weight. The performance of the combination, particularly during take-off, is better than that of the Ju 88 by itself. The *Mistel* combination in cruising flight is 50 km/h faster than the Ju 88 alone. The central position of the Bf 109's engine allows the combination to be flown without difficulty even when one of the Ju 88's engines fails.

'Ten separations were made at speeds of between 300 and 550 km/h during the course of the trials. The rapidity with which the separation can be accomplished is strongly dependent on the incidence setting of the Bf 109's tailplane and this can, at high speeds and in situations where the aircraft is trimmed tail down, lead to structural damage to the Bf 109 during separation. The aircraft was, therefore, trimmed according to the speed at which it was flown. It is recommended that the Bf 109 should always be trimmed nose down with a tailplane setting of 1.5 to 1.7 degrees. At high speeds the Bf 109 will then lift off when the explosive bolts are detonated, without hesitation and without additional control movements. At lower speeds, however, the Bf 109 will only lift off after detonation of the bolt holding the collapsible strut straight, when the aircraft is rotated by elevator movement to a high angle of incidence. The Bf 109's acceleration at separation on these occasions lies between +3 and +4g and -2g. A short, sharp shock is also noticeable in the Ju 88 during separation. The acceleration experienced by the Ju 88 at a speed of 550 km/h is between -1.2g and +2.5g, i.e. the Ju 88 also diverges from and lifts parallel to its flight path as if it had been struck by a gust of wind.

'Twenty-five test flights were conducted with the autopilot. During the last flight the system was, apart from some minor problems, still operating sufficiently well to be able to accept the results of this test. The *Mistel* combination could be flown without difficulty by the Bf 109 with the autopilot set to "cruise". The evaluation and selection criteria for the pilot of the Ju 88, however, must be established beforehand, because the characteristics of the Ju 88 are predominant. A series of take-offs and landings with the autopilot switched on were made solely under the control of the Bf 109. The take-off of the combination, because of its higher inertia, is more pleasant than that of the Bf 109. There is also no tendency for the combination to break away from its flight path when the Bf 109's engine is opened up to full power. Even the landing of the combination with the autopilot switched on is not particularly difficult.

'Homing flights (*Zielanflüge*) made with the autopilot set to "cruise" or "automatic" are possible. Changing the setting from one condition to the other using the switch on the Bf 109's instrument panel did not induce a change in the aircraft's attitude. After separation the Ju 88 continues to fly under the control of the autopilot according to its predefined speed and heading. Without the autopilot the Ju 88 must be trimmed nose down when flown as part of the *Mistel* combination. If the autopilot is switched off after separation, the Ju 88 automatically flies trimmed nose down.'

The flight tests at Ainring did not proceed without some problems. For example, during the climb-out after take-off on the first flight, the port engine of the Ju 88 failed and had to be switched off, though landing with the remaining engines was accomplished without difficulty.

Erich Klöckner recalls events during another test in which he flew the Bf 109:

'As we had hoped, the take-off was normal, and I quickly became accustomed to my position, relatively high above the ground. We climbed to 3,000 metres and began checking the flight characteristics during turns, and in the landing configuration, as well as throttling the lower engines back. These tests also included shallow dives with a brief application of full power. After completion of the programme, the plan was to separate the team. We went into a very shallow dive and I pressed the firing button for the pins; the Me 109 reared up to the left, turning hard right by 10-15 degrees. Then there was a terrible metallic rending and the aircraft jerked free. The violence of the Me 109's initial turn was so abrupt that my head was thrown against the left side of the canopy. A large lump appeared on my left temple, forcing me to go to the medical centre after landing, and get an ice bag for my head. In the meantime, a heated discussion developed over the fact that only the left pin had fired. Fortunately, the one on the right had simply broken off at its predetermined breaking point. It took quite some time for me to recover from the shock, but Oppitz, flying the Ju 88, had noticed nothing untoward!'

Furthermore, the fuses protecting the electrical circuit used for the detonation of the three primary explosive bolts tripped during the first attempt at separation. This was caused by a short-circuit in the Ju 88's electrical system, the end of an electrical cable remaining unattached because it could not be connected to one of the control surface servo-actuators, a part of which had been removed. Although the current in the detonating circuit was still sufficient to trigger the explosive bolt holding the collapsible tail strut straight, it was not enough to detonate the three primary explosive bolts in sequence. Consequently, the explosive in the bolts was heated so slowly that only the front, left-hand bolt detonated and the remaining two bolts, which were not strong enough to withstand the subsequent shock-loads, were torn apart. On separation, the Bf 109 was subjected momentarily to large accelerations (+6.5g and -3g). This resulted in separating the detonating and control circuits and transferring the former to the Bf 109. Thereafter, the separation system functioned faultlessly.

Another problem occurred during the initial flights which involved separation when the automatic circuit-breakers (*Selbstschalter*) in the detonating circuit cut out several times. This was caused by vibration of their covers.

Additionally, the explosive bolt attaching the right-hand DUZ throttle control linkage did not detonate during homing flights and was pulled apart on separation. Consequently, the Ju 88's starboard engine was throttled back to idle. However, it was recognised that the engines had to remain at full power should the explosive bolt in the throttle linkage fail to detonate.

The automatic circuit-breakers for the control system were relocated because the Bf 109's pilot occasionally knocked them unintentionally with his elbow during take-off, causing them to cut out.

Fritz Haber, in his detailed study, recalled another particular aspect of the *Mistel*:

'Another important item of the *Mistel's* equipment was the gyro-stabilised sight. This, once aligned with the target, was capable of remaining "locked on" to the target. The principle of its operation is explained by the following example: assume two points, each travelling at constant speed along two different, straight, convergent paths, meet at the same time where the paths intersect. When the two points are joined by a line at any particular instant in time, it will be noticed that these lines are parallel to one another. If point 1, in the diagram (at right), represents the moving target and point 2 the approaching aircraft, then these lines can be considered to represent the view through the gyro-stabilised sight. As the aircraft flies towards its target, these 'lines-of-sight' move forward parallel to each other. It is, therefore, apparent that the line-of-sight does not coincide with the aircraft's flight direction or its longitudinal axis, i.e. the aircraft is not flown along the line-of-sight. This situation leads to the requirement that the line-of-sight must not be fixed relative to the aircraft's axes and is fulfilled by the use of a gyro-stabilised sight, whereby the line-of-sight is always aligned with the gyro's axis. It is well known that the axis of a gimbally-mounted gyro rotating at very high speed does not move from its initial orientation. Therefore, the aircraft can be rotated around any of its axes and the alignment of the gyro's axis, and hence the line-of-sight, will not change. Thus the requirement allowing movement of the line-of-sight relative to the aircraft's axes is fulfilled. Target acquisition is achieved by initially locking the gyro's axis, and thus the line-of-sight, and aiming the aircraft at the target. The pilot then frees the gyro and afterwards has nothing more to do than align and maintain the target in the sight's reticule. He has then achieved the situation with the correct lead angle depicted in the sketch. It is clear that in this situation, where the target is continually being tracked, the upper aircraft can be separated at any time, because the overall situation will not alter. This is the basic difference between this method of target acquisition and other methods, in which separation must be carried out at a specific time in order to avoid (aiming) errors. Refinements were made to the system to reduce the time needed for target acquisition and to reduce its sensitivity but these did not alter the method described here. The whole method proved extraordinarily simple and required little training in its use, as demonstrated by a number of pilots who, after making only three or four target acquisition training flights during their first flight with the *Mistel*, went on to complete successful operations. It should be noted that the gyro-stabilised sight could not be used for aerial combat or during bombing operations, because the speed of a shell or bomb is not the same as that of the aircraft firing a cannon or dropping bombs. The simplicity and certainty of hitting a target using the Mistel method was based on the premise that the carrier aircraft continued to fly in a straight line and did not have to rely on the calculation of lead angles needed for ballistic flight.'

By November 1943, despite proven cooperation between Junkers and the DFS, development work on the *Mistel* was causing some tensions in the corridors of power at the RLM in Berlin, particularly since it appeared that much of the work was being undertaken unilaterally and

Method of target acquisition using gyro-stabilised sight

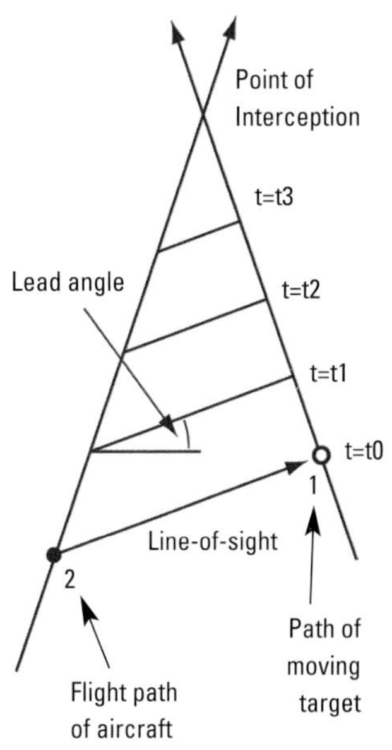

(Speeds of aircraft and target constant)

without the official sanction from certain Ministry departments. In a memo dated 4 November concerning 'Project *Beethoven*', a member of GL/C-E 9/IV B, the department at the *Technisches Amt* (Technical Office) in charge of the development of guided missiles, complained that 'the chance of success was questionable and, based on past experience, the workforce would be better employed on other tasks.'

This attitude was probably brought about by the fact that having received an approach from Peltz and Baumbach, Göring,

'... awarded a contract (to Junkers) without involving the C Departments and unbeknown to C-E 2. Just after C-E 2/II had awarded a similar contract to the DFS, Junkers intervened and claimed prior rights. Today Junkers and the DFS are working together on this task under the supervision of C-E 2/II. It was thereby agreed that GL/C-E 9 would not be involved in the development of this project. The department became aware of this project only after they had been asked about it.'

Nevertheless, this is one of the first signs that the RLM was beginning, albeit begrudgingly in some quarters, to accept the *Mistel* concept as a feasible military possibility. Benefits included minimal personnel requirements (one pilot), the meaningful use of a war-weary airframe and a concept which allowed launch a long way from the target thus affording protection to the control aircraft which, of course, was a fully capable fighter.

In the late autumn of 1943 the RLM authorised the construction of an initial batch of 15 *Mistel* to be built under the control of the Junkers *Technischer Aussendienst* at the company's works at Nordhausen in the Harz mountains where acceptance flight-testing and the installation of the control system were also to be undertaken. For the lower components, 15 restored Ju 88 A-4 airframes were delivered to Nordhausen from the Junkers works at Leipzig. The building programme was to be placed under the day-to-day control of a specially formed 45-man team known as the *Baustelle Schwab/Nordhausen* which was named after its manager, Herbert Schwab, and which mostly comprised civilian staff and technicians. *Dr.-Ing.* Fritz Haber was brought in as head of development and, on the orders of *Hptm.* Dietrich Peltz, *Haupting.* Horst-Dieter Lux was assigned to the project to coordinate Luftwaffe requirements and to develop a pilot-training programme.

Lux recalled his early experiences working on the *Mistel* for Junkers:

'I set up the industry operation along the lines of the "Skunk Works": small, secluded, with extremely tight security and very limited access. The original contract was for ten aeroplanes, half of them for development and experimental flight tests and half as pre-production models. It was a challenging programme. Two aeroplanes, a fighter and a bomber, had to be mounted together, a fly-by-wire system had to be developed so the combined aircraft could be flown from the fighter cockpit and a large warhead had to be mated to the nose of the bomber, replacing the cockpit.

'I made the first flight about two months after the start of the programme. The development of the fly-by-wire system accounted for the bulk of the flight-test programme. Stability and control came a close second, followed by tests to establish safe separation of the two aeroplanes over a wide speed regime, from stall to maximum speed. A single-channel, fly-by-wire system is a hazard in itself, but in 1943-44 it was pure luck if there were no upsets. But there were, ranging from sudden hard-overs, also instability, to explosive bolts which did not explode. Eventually the bugs were worked out...'

In 1888, Charles Edward Munroe, an explosives expert at the Naval Torpedo Station and the Naval War College at Newport, Rhode Island, is believed to have devised the concept of a hollow charge in an experiment conducted against an iron and steel safe.

Based upon data compiled by the DFS, it was estimated that the optimum operational altitude for a *Mistel* was 3,000-5,000 metres. Range would obviously be dependent upon the weight of the warhead carried, the capacity of auxiliary fuel tanks and the removal of all unnecessary spare parts, but 1,500 km was thought possible with a 3.5-ton warhead.

For the warhead of the composite, the German designers turned to the hollow-charge principle. This was by no means a new or unique form of armament since hollow-charge weapons were used throughout the war against tanks. What was unique about the fitting of a hollow-charge warhead to the *Mistel* however, was the sheer size of charge involved – far larger than any previously built. Fritz Haber recorded:

'Once aiming accuracy through the use of the control system and the gyro-stabilised sight could be guaranteed, attention was given to the design of the desired explosive charge. At first, plans were made to fill the wing or fuselage of the carrier aircraft with explosives. Specialists, however, voiced the opinion that this method would not be effective because it would be difficult to detonate all of the explosive at the same time, the part initially detonated blowing apart the remainder. They also considered that the proposed method of packing the explosive would be ineffective against armoured vehicles. The specialists at the RLM, therefore, were presented with the unique chance of creating an explosive charge without having to take into account its ballistic shape and size, characteristics normally needed in designing a free-fall bomb. This warhead was, in effect, an oversized *Panzerfaust*, which was capable of penetrating armour plating 120 cm thick. If built as a normal bomb it would have had a length of 6-7 metres.'

The hollow charge idea is popularly thought to have originated in the USA with the explosives expert Charles Edward Munroe while he was working at the Naval Torpedo Station and the Naval War College at Newport, Rhode Island in 1888. In an article published in 1900 while Professor of Chemistry at the United States Naval Academy at Annapolis in Maryland, Munroe described the effects of a charge he had set up against the wall of a safe that was,

'...twenty-nine inch cube with walls four inches and three quarters thick, made up of plates of iron and steel ...when a hollow charge of dynamite nine pounds and a half in weight and untamped was detonated on it, a hole three inches in diameter was blown clear through the wall, though a solid charge of the same weight and of the same material produced no material effect. The hollow cartridge was made by tying the sticks of dynamite around a tin can, the open mouth of the latter being placed downward...'

The hollow charge, also known in the USA as a 'shaped charge', exploited this discovery. The earliest development of a hollow-charge cartridge, or '*Hohlladung*', in Germany can be traced back to 1883, when Max von Förster, director of the Schießwollefabrik Wolff and Co. at Walsrode, published the results of trials conducted with many different types of hollow-charge cartridges made under a range of different conditions. However, Förster's findings attracted little interest.

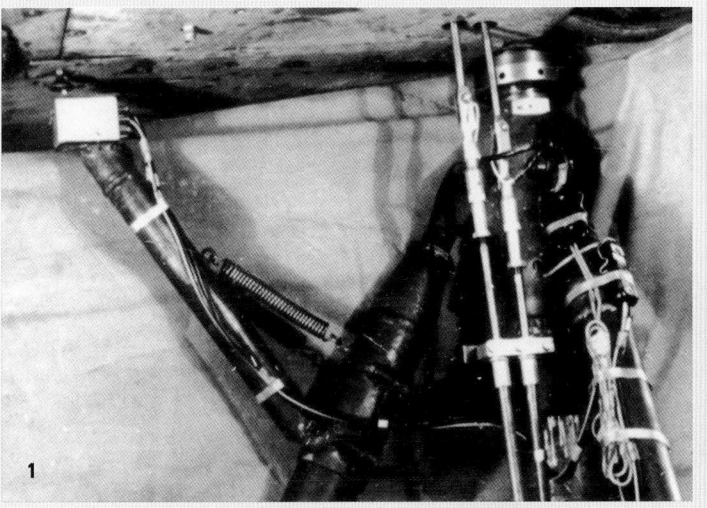

A selection of views showing the connection point details between Bf 109 F-4, CI+MX, and its Ju 88 A-4 lower component as seen on page 48.

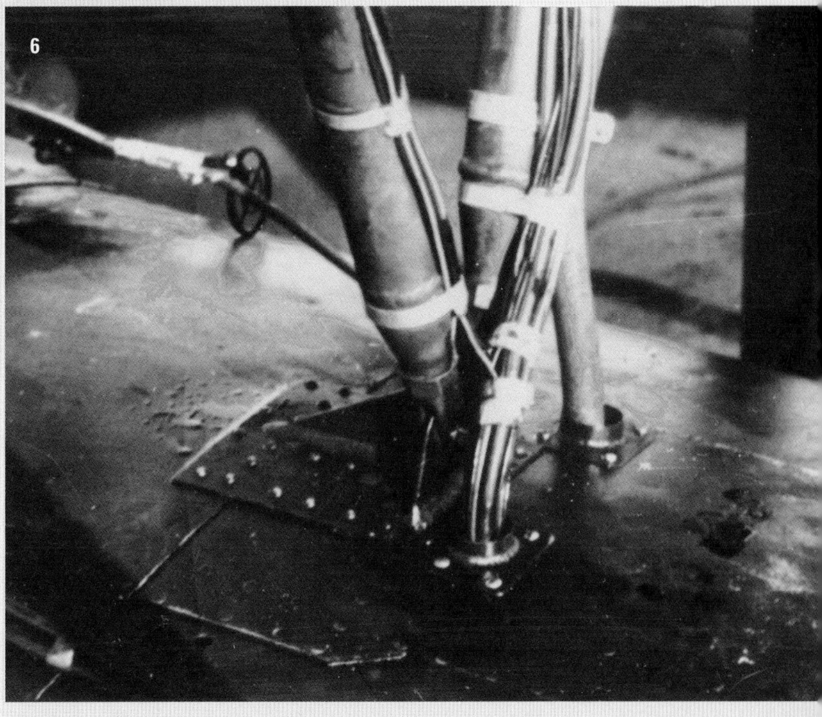

1. The left-hand mounting point on the front spar of the Bf 109 F-4 located in front of the DUZ-modified throttle linkage. The ring clamps were released upon separation of the two components. The switch triggering the explosive retention bolts can be seen on the left.
2. The right-hand mounting point on the front spar of the Bf 109 F-4 upper component. Behind it are the spherical-jointed fuel connection and two electrical multi-pin shear connectors.
3. A view of the front left main attachment point, spherical-jointed fuel connection and throttle linkage, as seen after separation of the two components.
4. The attachment of the collapsible strut to fuselage frame 20 on the Ju 88 A-4 lower component.
5. The attachment of the three-legged support structure to fuselage frame 9 of the Ju 88 A-4 lower component.
6. The attachment of the three-legged support structure on the front spar of the Ju 88 A-4.

It was not until 1937 that *Professor Dr.* Hubert Schardin, Director of the *Luftwaffen-Institut für Ballistik und Kurzzeitphysik* at Berlin-Gatow, conducted further trials on the hollow charge principle which were based on the early work of *Professor* Carl Cranz, the German physicist and ballistics expert, and other research dating back to 1929. One of Schardin's associates feared that a hollow charge delivered from the air would lose its penetrative force and so a way had to be found in which an explosive mass could be compressed and contained against a glass wall. Upon impact with a target, the glass wall would shatter and the explosive would be drawn into an air-free chamber or vacuum. Experiments were conducted and this theory was found to work without any difficulties. Indeed, experiments conducted without the vacuum also worked and it was found that the effect in penetrative force doubled.

Schardin and his team subsequently conducted many tests using metals. It was discovered that when exploded, a powerful detonation wave occurred against the surface of the hollow area. Because the detonation closed the cavity, it produced in it a convergent shock wave. Extremely high pressures and temperatures resulted. If, in addition, the cavity was lined with a metal sheet, the liner was driven inwards and extruded as a very thin, lethal high-velocity liquid jet able to melt and penetrate very thick high-grade steel. Temperatures reached 3,000-4,000 degrees Centigrade, with the speed of penetration measured at 11,000 metres per second.

The British had already conducted experiments with hollow-charge bombs intended for use against capital ships. Initial trials conducted between January and March 1942 against models constructed of ships' plating and representing the *Tirpitz* and HMS *King George V* had shown that complete penetration from deck to bottom could be obtained against the most heavily armoured capital ship if hit at an angle of attack of 30 degrees by a 38-inch-diameter, 5,000-lb soft-nosed bomb weighing approximately one ton and containing 75 per cent explosive. In a report written by a senior technician to Lord Cherwell, Scientific Adviser to the War Cabinet, following full-scale trials carried out in April, it was stated: 'If such a bomb is operationally practicable, it is in my opinion, the most effective anti-ship weapon yet seen.'

The problem now facing the British weapons specialists was finding an aircraft able to carry such a bomb over long distances and to aim accurately from anywhere between 1,500 to 10,000 ft. The solution lay in the Avro Lancaster. In late April and early May 1942, the Boscombe Down-based Aeroplane and Armament Experimental Establishment conducted trials over deep sea at Lyme Bay and then over a hard target area on the downs near Porton using Lancaster I R5609. The aircraft featured specially modified and enlarged bomb doors which were operated by an elastic cord rather than hydraulically. The results of the trials suggested that one direct hit from a 'Capital Ship' bomb was enough to sink a large armoured warship.

Once the concept of a 'CS' bomb had been proved and accepted in principle, it was not long before it was used operationally. On the night of 27/28 August 1942, a force of nine Lancasters of 106 Squadron led by Wing Commander Guy Gibson headed for the port of Gdynia in Poland, some 950 miles from their base, to bomb the new German aircraft carrier, *Graf Zeppelin*, which was thought to be almost ready for sailing. Each aircraft carried a 13-ft-long CS bomb. Only seven Lancasters reached the port, but they were unable to locate the target because of 9/10 cloud at 8,000 ft and the bombs fell in the general harbour area. Although *Graf Zeppelin* was the prize, alongside were the cruisers *Lützow* and *Hipper* and a large troop ship. According to one team of historians[1], had the *Graf Zeppelin* been sunk 'this raid would have ranked as one of the bombing war's epics.'

In Germany the main proponent of using a very heavy hollow-charge warhead on the *Mistel* was *Generalingenieur der Luftwaffe, Dipl.-Ing.* Ernst Marquardt, head of the RLM *Technisches Amt* GL/C-E7, the department responsible for the development of bombs, mines and torpedoes.

Under Marquardt's direction, the *Mistel* warhead, known as the *Schwere Hohlladung* (SHL) 3500, was

[1] Martin Middlebrook and Chris Everitt in *The Bomber Command War Diaries – An Operational Reference Book: 1939-1945* (Penguin Books, 1990).

In mid-1942 the British conducted experiments with hollow-charge bombs intended for use against capital ships and the Aeroplane and Armament Experimental Establishment at Boscombe Down conducted trials with a specially modified Lancaster bomber (R 5609). The aircraft featured enlarged bomb doors which were operated by an elastic cord rather than hydraulically. The results of the trials suggested that one direct hit from a 'Capital Ship' bomb of the type seen here was enough to cause the sinking of a large armoured warship.

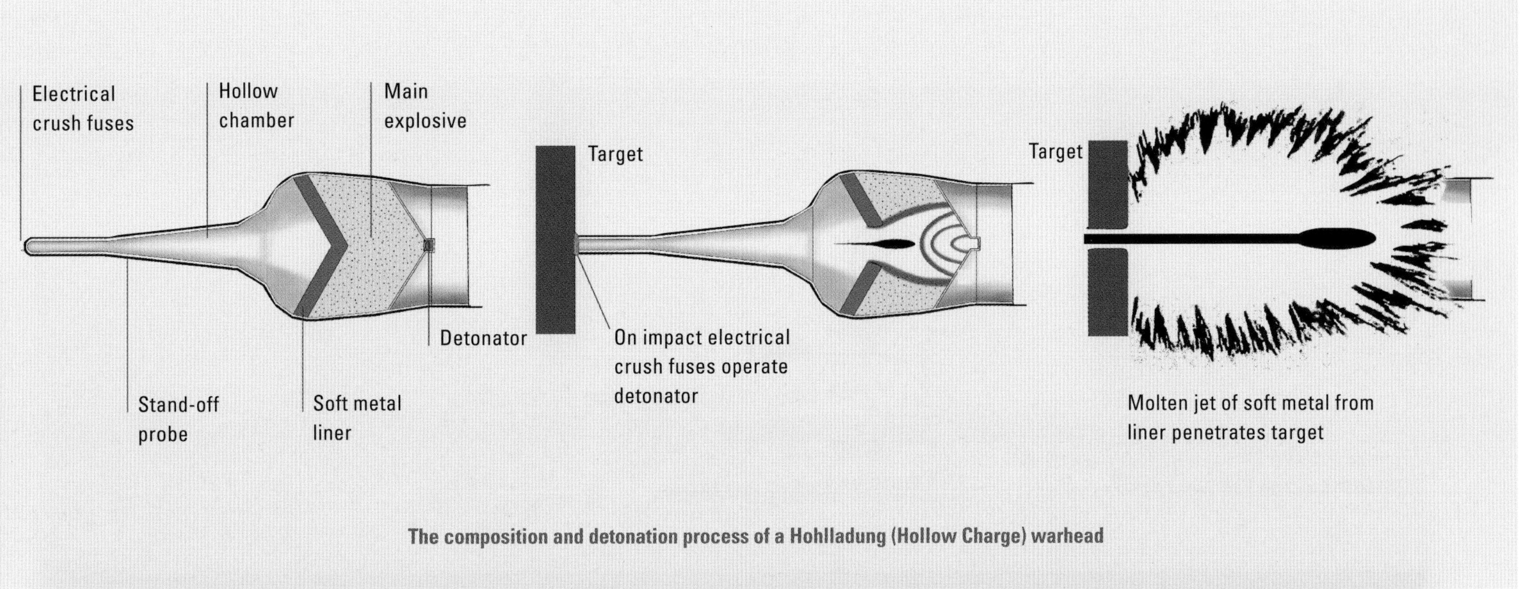

The composition and detonation process of a Hohlladung (Hollow Charge) warhead

developed under great secrecy by the Lauchammer firm at Riesa on the Elbe River, 90 km east of Leipzig. It was designed to pierce the armoured steel of a battleship or blow open a wall of reinforced concrete such as that found on heavy gun emplacements, command bunkers and industrial targets such as factories and power stations. The 1,700 kg of explosive and detonator for the main charge was placed at the rear of the warhead with a conical cavity to the front of it, 1.8 metres in diameter. The cone was lined with a layer of soft metal, either aluminium or copper, with four electrical crush fuses positioned at the tip of a 2.75-metre probe, protruding from the front of the warhead and known as the *Elefantenrüssel* ('Elephant's Trunk'). Soft metal was important, since a harder metal would prevent the hollow charge action from functioning properly. The use of copper is noteworthy since copper was always in short supply in Germany during the war with most stocks being allocated to make brass for the Navy.

When this probe struck the target, the fuses would trigger the detonator behind the explosive charge. The detonator circuit was not closed until the upper aircraft had separated and after some 2-3 seconds had elapsed. In addition, the warhead could not be armed until

A hollow-charge warhead, known as the *'Elefantenrüssel'* (Elephant's Trunk) is fitted to the fuselage bulkhead of a Ju 88 Mistel lower component at an unknown location in late 1944.

One of the French warships captured by the Germans at the naval port of Toulon in southern France was the 25,000-ton French Courbet class dreadnought, *Océan* (formerly *Jean Bart*). She is seen here in 1937. In 1943, she was used as a 'target' for experiments with the SHL 3500 hollow-charge warhead.

Smoke spirals into the sky after a trial detonation of an SHL 3500 hollow-charge warhead on the hulk of an old French navy warship, possibly the battleship *Océan*, at Toulon in late 1943.

The *Océan* photographed after the SHL 3500 tests.

the carrier aircraft's landing flaps had been retracted. This safeguard prevented the warhead from exploding in the event that the upper aircraft was deliberately or unintentionally separated during an aborted take-off. After firing, the charge – a mixture of 70 per cent Hexogen high-explosive and 30 per cent Trinitrotoluol – would focus all its force on the soft metal liner which would then liquefy and project forward in a fine jet. Travelling at over twenty times the speed of sound, the jet could drill a hole through more than 8 metres of armoured steel or 20 metres of reinforced concrete. Once through the outer layer of a target and subsequently confined within it, the jet of metal would vaporise anything in its path.

The length of the probe could be varied to trigger the charge at the optimum distance from the target. When used against armoured steel it could be as long as 2.75 metres, but for less well protected targets, the length was considerably shortened and at least three variants of probes of varying length are known to have been developed. A stand-off probe was necessary in order to allow time for the soft metal liner to form itself into a thin jet before impact. Broadly speaking, the greater the distance between the charge and the target at detonation, the thinner and deeper the hole drilled; the closer to the target, the wider and shallower the penetration. The entire detonation procedure took place within one 10,000th of a second.

Towards the end of 1943, *Gen.-Ing.* Marquardt, in conjunction with specialists from the *Erprobungsstelle* Rechlin, arranged for static tests of a hollow charge similar to the one intended for use on the *Mistel* to be conducted against the old 25,000-ton French Courbet class dreadnought, *Océan* (formerly *Jean Bart*), anchored in the approaches to the naval port of Toulon in southern France. She had been disarmed and converted into an accommodation ship in the port in August 1935 and continued as such after being renamed *Océan*. She had remained at Toulon during the Vichy regime, still used as an accommodation hulk. When the Germans captured the port in November 1942, *Océan* was not among the French vessels scuttled and was captured intact. Subsequently, the *Kriegsmarine* designated the vessel for target use.

The 4-ton charge was directed at the vessel's two main gun turrets. Additional 10-cm steel armour plate had been fitted to the 'target' to make it more representative of modern warships. When the charge was detonated, it shot through the additional 10-cm armour, through the 30-cm armour of one gun turret, passing through the turret and out the opposite side, which was of similar thickness, and through the armour plating of a second turret. The result was an effective total penetration of 28 metres into the ship.

In East Prussia, Siegfried Holzbaur also conducted static trials with the hollow charge against structures made of reinforced concrete. Employing a similar charge to that used by Marquardt, Holzbaur was able to blast his way through some 18 metres of concrete.

It was intended that a warhead with similar capability could be fitted to a purpose-converted Ju 88 with relative ease by trained specialist Luftwaffe armourers in the field. To facilitate this, a Ju 88 would have its crew compartment removed at the aft bulkhead, this process being carried out at a Junkers *Mistel* conversion facility. Four spherically-aligned quick-release bolts would be fitted and the crew compartment re-installed for training purposes or ferrying to an operational airfield.

Then, once delivered to an operational unit and at the time a mission was ordered, the crew compartment would once again be removed and the warhead fitted, again using

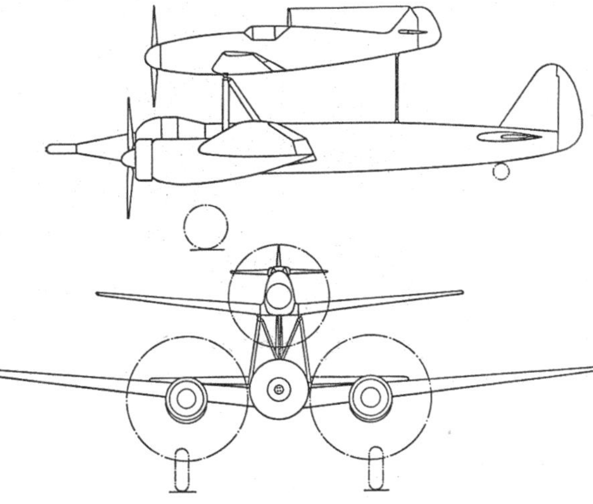

Above and right: An undated Junkers specification guide and drawing for the *'Beethoven-Gerät'* ('Beethoven device) controlled, unmanned aircraft for *Totaleinsatz*. This denoted an aircraft that was to be knowingly sacrificed during operations.

Beethoven - Gerät

Ausgesteuertes, unbemanntes Flugzeug für Totaleinsatz

Hersteller:	Junkers - Flugzeug - u. Motorenwerke A.G., Dessau.	
Einsatzzweck:	Bekämpfung hochwertiger schwer u. schwerstgepanzerter Seeziele.	
Das Gespann besteht aus:	Ju 88 A - 4 (Weiterentwicklung in Ju 88 G - 1) Bf 109 F (-"- -"- in Fw 190 A - 7 / A - 8)	
Leistungsangaben:	Reiseleistung: Kampfleistung: Technische Flugstrecke: Flugdauer: Auftreffgeschwindigkeit: Rückflugstrecke Bf 109:	455 km/h in 5 km Höhe 485 km/h in 5 km Höhe 675 - 710 km bei 455 km/h in 5 km Höhe 1,6 Stunden cirka 600 km/h rund 800 km
Ablösen des Jägers:	1000 - 3000 m vor Ziel.	
Kraftstoff:	Bf 109 400 Ltr. normal, 300 Ltr. Abwurfbehälter } für Rückflug Ju 88 A-4 Tragflügel - Entnahmebehälter 2 × 415 Ltr. - 830 Ltr. Tragflügelbebehälter 2 × 425 Ltr. - 850 Ltr. vorderer Rumpfbehälter 1220 Ltr., hinterer -"- 680 Ltr. } vorwiegend zur Speisung der Bf 109 im Anflug.	
Gewichte:	Ju 88 A - 4 = 14,0 to Bf 109 F = 2,8 to	
Abfluggewicht:	= 16,8 to	
Besatzung:	1 Mann	
Zusätzliche Bauteile:	1.) Patin - Dreiachsensteuerung mit Lagenaufschaltung für den gegebenen Zweck von Junkers abgeändert. 2.) TSA 1 - Visier (Zeiß - Jena) 3.) Hohlladung: SHL 3500 (davon 1700 kg Sprengstoff bestehend aus 70% Hexogen und 30% Trinitrotoluol.) 4.) Verbindungsgerüst für die beiden Flugzeuge.	
Zünder:	Abgeänderter Z 66; empfindlicher, magnetelektrischer Aufschlagzünder (allseitsaufschlagempfindlich). Schärfung erfolgt etwa 3 Sekunden nach Trennung der Flugzeuge automatisch.	
Bemerkungen:	siehe besondere Anlage.	

A rare photograph of an early Beethoven combination in flight somewhere over Germany.

A rare photograph of what is purported to be an experimental third oleo leg, possibly a mock-up or a ground-only working, installed on the fuselage centre-line beneath a Ju 88, directly between the two usual oleos. This was intended to offer additional support for an operational Mistel combination, the weight of which was around 20,000 kg with a warhead.

the quick-release bolts. This process, lasting approximately one day, required a team of six mechanics, two armourers and a crane capable of lifting four tons. After the warhead was attached the composite had to be towed to the take-off position because the pilot of the fighter could not operate the brakes of the Ju 88.

The all-up weight of the operational *Mistel* (i.e. one fitted with a warhead) was about 20,000 kg, some 7,000 kg heavier than a normally loaded Ju 88 and thus approaching the load limits. This placed heavy demands on the undercarriage which really needed to be completely redesigned, but no such modifications were carried out and the undercarriage was extremely prone to collapse on take-off. A safe take-off could only be attempted from a concrete runway which was considered to be in perfect working order. Even the smallest hole or imperfection on a runway's surface could have had dire consequences for the composite and its pilot. The normal tyre for a Ju 88 was the 1,140 x 410 mm type which was rated at a maximum overloaded weight of 20.6 tons on take-off.

As an intended interim solution to this problem it is believed trials were carried out with an experimental third oleo leg installed on the fuselage centre-line beneath the aircraft and directly between the two usual oleos, retracting rearwards into a compartment in the fuselage. Nothing seems to have come of such trials, however, if they took place.

Later in the war, operational variants of the *Mistel* were fitted with large 1,220 x 445 mm tyres which were rated as high as 23.4 tons for take-off; the maximum permissible load at landing was lower so as to avoid tyre 'blow-outs' when touching down, though once in the air a combination fitted with a warhead was impossible to land, so the only choice left to the pilot in an emergency was to jettison the complete lower component.

Apart from a weak undercarriage, another problem was the time lag between the fighter's pilot operating a control and the auto-pilot relaying this to the bomber. The Ju 88 always had a tendency to swing on take-off, and this tendency was magnified by the delay in the time needed to correct. It was not unknown for the combination to swerve off the runway on take-off and it was impossible to fly the *Mistel* in tight formation due to the same problem. Consequently, in the post-war years the machine developed a reputation for not having been easy to fly. However, as we shall see in the chapters that follow, this was not necessarily the view of test pilots or of the pilots who flew the *Mistel* operationally. Indeed, as Fritz Haber recorded:

> 'The relative size of the aircraft chosen to form the *Mistel* proved favourable. It was obvious that during the separation of a very small aircraft from a much larger one there would be negligible disturbance, whereas on separation of aircraft of equal size the disturbance would

be very noticeably large. The relationship of 1:3 in size of the Me 109 relative to that of the Ju 88 was regarded as small.

'Consideration of all of these points led to the conclusion that the control of the carrier aircraft's longitudinal inclination was the only acceptable alternative, mainly because a system capable of controlling the flight path inclination was not available, would have been very difficult to develop and would have incurred much time and testing. Subsequently, the 56 tests made to measure the flight path fully confirmed the calculations and thoughts concerning the method of control. The tests also showed that the aircraft would hit the target with an average dispersion of +/- 6 metres from a distance of 1,000 metres and +/- 12 metres from 2,000 metres.'

The Ju 88 A-4/Bf 109 F-4 combination was designated the *Mistel* 1. Prior to the fitting of the warhead, the prefix 'S' for '*Schule*' was added to the above designation, the *Mistel* S1 being the training version of the *Mistel* 1. The *Mistel* trainer was generally considered a much easier aircraft to handle than the operational variant. It was much lighter because it carried no warhead, and the Ju 88's pilot could also assist should the pilot of the fighter make a mistake. He was also able to land the combination.

Towards the end of 1943, one of the first *Mistel* to be assembled at Nordhausen was transferred to the *Erprobungsstelle der Luftwaffe* at Peenemünde-West on the Baltic coast. It was here, amidst great secrecy, that the Luftwaffe was performing launch trials with the Fi 103 flying bomb, the weapon that was to become infamous as the 'V1' and which would be used to bomb London indiscriminately months later.

At Peenemünde-West, the composite was initially moved well away from the airfield and screened from prying eyes by means of a high wooden fence. Eventually, the machine was transferred to Hangar W1, known also as the *Reins-Halle* after the aircraft engineer, *Dipl.-Ing.* Gerd Reins, who had been killed flying the He 112 in June 1940. It was to the *Reins-Halle* that a warhead was later delivered and fitted.

On a cold, damp day in February 1944, Siegfried Holzbaur arrived at Peenemünde-West for the first time accompanied by *Generalmajor* Dietrich Peltz and *Major* Werner Baumbach, both of whom had come to observe what was to be the first airborne trial of a *Mistel* with a 'live' warhead. Peltz had done well since he had first promoted Holzbaur's idea to Göring more than two years before; he now held the position of *General der Kampfflieger*, was in direct command of the IX. *Fliegerkorps* and had been appointed to the position of *Angriffsführer England* by Göring with responsibility for Operation *Steinbock*, the bombing campaign against the British Isles.

Under the watchful gaze of the assembled officers, *Haupting*. Lux and key members of the *Baustelle Schwab/Nordhausen*, a heavy tow tractor pulled the *Mistel* from the hangar and out to the runway. Holzbaur climbed up the ladder and settled himself into the Bf 109's cockpit. Within a short time, the aircraft was airborne following a faultless take-off, after which it climbed to rendezvous over the sea with its Ju 88 escort.

The target was to be the Møns-Klint, a 110 metre-high chalk cliff on the Danish island of Møn, 120 km to the north-west of Peenemünde. With all three engines running smoothly, instruments functioning normally, dead on course, Holzbaur put the *Mistel* into a steady climb as it approached the southern-most point of the island of Rügen. A light wind from the north-east blew hazy clouds across the Baltic. All appeared to be going well.

Suddenly, the composite lurched in the air and the Ju 88 felt as if it was pulling towards the earth. Holzbaur wrestled with the controls and tried to throttle back the engines in an attempt to correct his course, but the machine refused to respond. Locked together, the two aircraft began to dive unalterably towards Rügen. Holzbaur remained as calm as possible and could only attribute the situation to a break in the electrical feed in the Bf 109's autopilot.

Below, the little coastal village of Thiessow slid into view. The Junkers test pilot decided to enforce an emergency separation. Fritz Haber remembered the incident:

> 'The aircraft suddenly began to dive out of control, for reasons which, even today, have still not been determined. Holzbaur could not bring the composite back under control and he was faced with no other alternative but to separate his aircraft, which he did quickly, leaving the consequences of his action to fate.'

The Bf 109 bucked in the air and climbed away as the explosive-laden Ju 88 plummeted towards Rügen and smashed into the ground just three kilometres from the village. There was a tremendous explosion, a momentary burst of flame and a moment later, a mushroom-shaped cloud of smoke rose 900 metres into the air.

Luftwaffe and civilian experts quickly flew and sailed into Thiessow from Peenemünde to investigate the causes of the accident. Fortunately, no one had been hurt, but nothing whatsoever remained of the Ju 88 and a search around the enormous crater proved fruitless. For reasons of security, and perhaps due to a measure of embarrassment, a cover story was concocted by the military. Horst-Dieter Lux described the aftermath:

> 'The village is in uproar. Windows are broken and houses have lost their roofs, but the devastation is only of secondary importance. The 800 inhabitants are hurrying to the scene of the accident and the secret is in danger of being revealed. The situation is rescued. A lorry bringing first aid personnel and coffins rushes to the scene of the crash, where there is nothing to see but an enormous crater. People attempt to recover what is believed to be the four-man crew of the bomb-laden aircraft, or so it seems. Secrecy is preserved and nobody realises that an unmanned aircraft with a very large bomb has crashed and a crucial test has failed. The previously divided opinion on the *Mistel* among the High Command is now decidedly negative. The engineers at the airfield in central Germany, besides having to overcome technical difficulties, now have to try to retain the interest of the High Command in the *Mistel*.'

Three days later, the 'dead aircrew' were afforded a mock funeral at a cemetery near Karlshagen. They were 'buried' with full military honours.

Later, Holzbaur, who was a well-built man, believed the only possible explanation for the *Mistel's* failure was that in the narrow confines of the Bf 109's cockpit he had inadvertently cut out the main guiding mechanism causing the Ju 88 to fall out of control.

Undaunted by the Rügen accident however, and determined to save the project in the eyes of an increasingly sceptical RLM, Holzbaur arranged another

Two Mistel photographed by Allied reconnaissance aircraft outside the hangars at Peenemünde on 26 April 1944. They have been ringed in crayon by British identification specialists who reported: 'Among the aircraft seen at Peenemünde airfield on 26.4.44 were two Ju 88s, each with a small aircraft mounted on top of its fuselage. The small aircraft, which have the appearance and dimensions of Me 109s, are mounted centrally above the larger aircraft, and shadow indicates that the tails of the small aircraft are raised well above the fuselages of the Ju 88s.'

'live' trial in May 1944. This time, on the 24th, the Møns-Klint area was cleared of its inhabitants by German troops and local dwellings were suitably prepared for the effect of what were warned to be 'violent explosions'.

According to a report received by British Intelligence in June 1944, a number of senior German officers arrived on Møn and sealed off the hinterland immediately behind the cliffs. Observers noted that a large piece of canvas, the size of a sail, was suspended from the cliff face and a catapult ship equipped with a crane had arrived off the coast, together with a tanker.

Bad weather delayed the test for 24 hours, but next day, 25 May, at around 0830 hrs, Holzbaur was in the air approaching the cliffs in a *Mistel* 1. He was escorted by three He 111s and a Fieseler *Storch* observation aircraft accompanied the formation at a higher altitude. As the *Mistel* passed the catapult ship it was seen to separate and the lower component was directed at high speed towards its target. However, as the Ju 88 neared the cliff it 'made a vertical descent, but missed the target by a wide margin.'

According to a report submitted by the OKL *Führungsstab*, the bomber actually overshot by 40 metres whilst the lateral deviation amounted to 100 metres. The aircraft was reported to have crashed into the cliffs some 75 metres away from the target and exploded causing 'a high column of fire and smoke'.

Despite a lack of accuracy, Holzbaur knew he had at least convinced the RLM that the weapon was capable of being successfully delivered. His task now was to improve the guidance system and methods to ensure accuracy. It would not be until August 1944 that he would attempt another test.

In the meantime, activity at Peenemünde had not gone unnoticed. On 26 April 1944, even before Holzbaur had proved the capability of the *Mistel*, an RAF photo-reconnaissance Mosquito had photographed the German test centre and had provided the Allies with the first indication that the Germans were experimenting with a composite aircraft for military purposes. Two composites were captured on film in front of the airfield's main hangars.

The Allied conclusions were unwittingly accurate. On 6 May 1944, Wing Commander G.E.F. Proctor of A.I.2(g), reported that:

> '*A recent photograph of Peenemünde showed two composite aircraft, each consisting of a Ju 88 with a small aircraft mounted on top of its fuselage. The small aircraft cannot be definitely identified but they have the same dimensions and general appearance as the Me 109. It can be definitely stated that the Germans are experimenting with composite aircraft, but with what purpose in view is not yet known.*'

Unknown to Proctor, the new German weapon would be unleashed against the Allies within a matter of weeks.

'MAKE PREPARATIONS FOR AN ATTACK ON SCAPA FLOW'

The British naval base at Gibraltar offered the Luftwaffenführungsstab an attractive target for the Mistel since a successful attack there would shock the British and damage significant enemy naval assets in the Mediterranean. However, any operation mounted from airfields in southern France would face strong aerial defences, such as these Seafires seen on the deck of HMS *Formidable* anchored off Gibraltar in mid-1943.

EARLY OPERATIONAL PLANS

AROUND the same time that the RAF discovered the *Mistel's* existence at Peenemünde in April 1944, and with an apparently marked shift in its earlier attitude, the *Luftwaffenführungsstab* was considering how best to deploy its new weapon in a way that would ensure maximum effect.

Junkers now officially referred to the *Mistel* as '*Beethoven-Gerät: Ausgesteuertes, unbemanntes Flugzeug für Totaleinsatz* (lit. '*Beethoven*-equipment': Automatically controlled, unmanned aircraft for *Totaleinsatz*). The word '*Totaleinsatz*' signified the intention to use this weapon in the full knowledge that it would be expendable. It was envisaged that the *Mistel* would be deployed in operations against heavily armoured maritime targets and would require minimal pilot training.

The officers of the *Luftwaffenführungsstab* no doubt felt some obligation to avenge the sinking of the *Kriegsmarine's* battlecruiser *Scharnhorst* by British warships in Arctic waters off northern Norway in December 1943. The loss of *Scharnhorst* was a catastrophe; nearly 2,000 of her officers and men were drowned.

Out in the Atlantic, U-boat losses were steadily climbing: October 1943 had seen the loss of 23 boats and the wolf-packs were now forced to stay submerged for longer periods, relying more and more on assistance from the dwindling number of Fw 200s provided by the Luftwaffe to find their targets. As 1943 drew to a close, *Großadmiral* Karl Dönitz recommended his commanders to fire blind at greater depth, which wasted torpedoes and led to poor morale among crews. By early 1944, the Allies possessed sufficient numbers of aircraft carriers and shore-based aircraft to provide full cover for every convoy. U-boat losses continued to rise: 9 in January, 12 in February, 12 in March and 11 in April.

The prevailing military situation facing Hitler and his commanders on the battlefronts in April 1944 was precarious. Three months earlier in the East, Leningrad had been liberated by the Russians. In the Ukraine, following the Russian winter offensive and despite a *Führer* Order to the contrary, General Hube's 1. *Panzerarmee* had finally managed to fight its way out of entrapment by Soviet forces at Tarnopol, but along the north coast of the Black Sea von Kleist's Army Group A was under attack and Odessa was given up on 10 April, leaving Rumania open to the Red Army's advance.

In Italy, Allied and German forces were locked in a bitter struggle around Monte Cassino which dominated the route to Rome. Closer to home, Berlin, in addition to all the other German cities under attack, had been bombed several times at night by the RAF since January, and in March the USAAF had launched its first daylight raids accompanied by fighter escort all the way to the capital. The psychological strain placed on the Reich's long-suffering civilian population was beginning to tell. Hitler, usually uninterested in the issue of air defence, had begun to question the effectiveness of the Luftwaffe. Throughout February, the Allies had bombed aircraft production centres, yet the German fighter force seemed unable to perform its vital role of air defence.

On 3 April, British carrier-borne aircraft attacked the battleship *Tirpitz* at its anchorage at Kaafjord in Norway where the vessel was still recovering from the damage inflicted by British midget submarines six months earlier. One hundred and twenty-eight German sailors were killed as a result of the raid, and though the *Tirpitz* remained afloat, she was too badly damaged to put to sea again under her own steam.

For the planners on the *Luftwaffenführungsstab*, the time had come when the Luftwaffe urgently needed to execute a spectacular, high-profile, morale-boosting mission against the enemy; something that would prove to the *Führer* and the German people that their air force was still capable of hurting its enemies where they least expected it and that it could at least match the kind of raids that had been made against significant German naval targets. As one option, they turned to the still untried *Mistel*.

This new type of aircraft offered the possibility to attack specific targets in locations normally well beyond the capability of other bomber aircraft, both in terms of range and safety. According to a report prepared by the *Führungsstab* on 16 April 1944, three targets were considered which offered 'the most promising chances of success': the British naval base at Gibraltar, the British Home Fleet anchorage at Scapa Flow in the Orkney Islands to the north of Scotland, and the Russian fleet at Leningrad.

First page from a study prepared by the Operations Department of the Luftwaffenführungsstab on 16 April 1944 in which the 'operational possibilities' for the Mistel were considered. Paragraph 3 lists the three 'most promising' targets for the composite aircraft as the British naval bases at Gibraltar and Scapa Flow, and the Soviet fleet at Leningrad.

3.99

Den 16.April 1944

Luftwaffenführungsstab
Ia op

S t u d i e

über die Einsatzmöglichkeiten der "Mistel".

1.) Einsatz der "Mistel" ist vorgesehen gegen die schweren Einheiten der feindl. Seestreitkräfte. Bisherige Erprobung lässt erwarten, dass Schlachtschiffe und Flugzeugträger bei Volltreffern zum Sinken gebracht werden.

Über die techn. Unterlagen für den Einsatz der "Mistel" ist eine Vortragsnotiz von Ia/T als Anlage 1 beigefügt.

2.) Nach Abschluss aller Vorbereitungen und der Umschulung der Flugzeugführer wird sofortiger Einsatz vorgeschlagen. Im Falle einer feindl. Grosslandung bieten sich für die "Mistel" keine günstigeren Einsatzbedingungen, da die feindl. schweren Seestreitkräfte ausserhalb der Reichweite eigener FX- und PK-Flugzeuge bleiben werden und mit unmittelbarem Eingreifen zur Unterstützung der Landung nicht zu rechnen ist. Ein Zurückstellen des Einsatzes als "Überraschungswaffe" für diesen Fall wird deshalb nicht für zweckmässig erachtet. Je länger mit dem Einsatz gezögert wird, desto mehr Zeit bleibt dem Feind Abwehrmassnahmen zu treffen, insbesondere da eine unbedingte Geheimhaltung nicht gewährleistet ist.

3.) Von den sich bietenden Einsatzmöglichkeiten – siehe Anlage 2 und 3 – sind als am erfolgversprechendsten herauszuheben:

Gibraltar und
Scapa Flow, ausserdem
Leningrad (russ.Flotte).

292

Vorteil ist, dass beide Ziele von Plätzen vom Festland aus erreichbar sind und damit eine Verlegung der Waffe im Schiffstransport entfällt.

– 2 –

Gibraltar was an attractive target and a successful attack there would shock the British, undermine morale and, hopefully, significantly weaken major enemy naval assets in the Mediterranean. Such a mission could be flown from the French airfields of Rennes, Toulouse and Istres which were between 1,025 and 1,350 km from the target, provided appropriate provisions were made for all *Mistel* deployed to have a combat radius of 1,400 km.

This was an important factor, as the *Führungsstab* recorded in its report:

> 'The target is dependent on the combat radius. Combat radius of 400-500 km is of little interest. Combat radius of 750-800 km is called for by the *Führungsstab* and can be achieved without technical difficulty when using 300-litre auxiliary tanks. Combat radius does not mean here half of the range. There will be only sufficient fuel available for the return flight of the 109 once the aircraft has flown to the limit of the above mentioned combat range. If the requirement for the return flight of the 109 is waived (landing in neutral territory) in favour of achieving a greater combat radius by distributing the fuel to the three engines of the *Mistel*, then only a negligible increase in the combat range of 150 km will be gained. This is of no practical importance, since even very distant enemy bases cannot be reached.'

Of course, there were other major difficulties in attempting to reach Gibraltar; not least of these was Hitler's reluctance to allow the Luftwaffe to fly operational missions over Spanish territory, a mark of his historic wariness of the steadfast and occasionally obstinate dictator, Franco. Furthermore, there was the question of local defences. As the report of 16 April stated:

> 'It is to be expected that the target will be well protected by anti-aircraft defences and by fighters from the local airfield. Because of the importance of this target, it is also to be expected that there will be complete radar coverage.'

The Gibraltar option was abandoned. That left Scapa Flow and Leningrad.

By April 1944, production of the initial batch of 15 *Mistel* was under way. The OKL now faced the dilemma of whether to deploy all of these machines against Scapa, whether to deploy only some of them against this target and the remainder against Leningrad or another target, or whether to make two attacks against the Royal Navy anchorage.

> 'In both cases,' the report continued, 'it is a question of whether a surprise attack can be mounted. A surprise attack is best flown late during a moonlit night to arrive over the target at dawn or during the day at low level and to pull up shortly before the target, but this will naturally allow the enemy the chance to defend himself. It is expected that Leningrad will also be strongly defended and, therefore, there will be little chance of mounting a surprise attack. The largest material losses and psychological effects will be achieved by an attack on Scapa Flow. The destruction of the Russian fleet, should it put to sea, could then still be the responsibility of the German Baltic Fleet. An attack against one target will ease preparations and allow effort to be focused to this end. No more than two battleships and one or two aircraft carriers are expected to be found at Scapa, which is proposed as the primary target.'

To the east lay Leningrad, home to the Soviet fleet. Luftwaffe planners believed that a Mistel attack launched against the Russian anchorage would yield spectacular results.

Certain considerations influenced the *Führungsstab* in their eventual decision. Firstly, Scapa Flow lay some 700 km west of the Luftwaffe airfield at Grove in Denmark. From here, a *Mistel* could reach the target provided that the Bf 109 was fitted with a 300-litre auxiliary fuel tank. Secondly, it was known that a number of the Royal Navy's largest warships, including aircraft carriers and battleships, regularly passed through Scapa Flow whilst assigned to the Home Fleet.

> 'It is expected that a battleship can be destroyed with one direct hit.' wrote *General der Flieger* Karl Koller, the Chief of the *Luftwaffenführungsstab*, 'and, therefore, it should be sufficient to despatch two *Mistel* against each large ship at Scapa, i.e. a total of eight *Mistel* should be sufficient.'

Such targets, if hit, would make headline news. The idea was tempting. Leningrad was thus removed from the list of potential targets. Only Scapa Flow remained.

Scapa Flow is in the Orkney Islands and its origins can be traced back to the Vikings who gave the place its name and who used it as a raiding base as early as the 7th century, even before they colonised the Orkneys. An expanse of relatively peaceful water, sheltered by the cold, windswept and desolate mounds of Holm, Burray, South Ronaldsay, Flotta and Fara, it had played a vital role in British maritime history for over 200 years, serving as the Royal Navy's main home strategic base throughout the First World War and into the Second.

Between 1914-1918, the British Grand Fleet was anchored in Scapa ready to deny the North Sea and the Atlantic to the German High Seas Fleet and merchant ships. Following the Armistice on 11 November 1918, the German Fleet surrendered off the Firth of Forth and was ordered north to Scapa Flow for internment where it was eventually scuttled. For many years Scapa Flow remained a place of bitter resonance for the German Navy.

But six weeks after the outbreak of the Second World War, *Kapitänleutnant* Günther Prien penetrated Scapa Flow in his boat, U-47, and managed to fire three torpedoes at the British battleship *Royal Oak*. Within minutes, the ship rolled over and sank with the loss of 833 lives. The Royal Navy had hardly recovered from Prien's attack when, four days later, the Luftwaffe showed its hand. In the face of intense anti-aircraft fire, four Ju 88s of I./KG 30 dived out of the morning sun and bombed *Iron Duke*, veteran flagship of Jutland but by then relegated to a training and depot ship. The ageing vessel was holed so badly that she had to be beached and abandoned.

Throughout March and April 1940, I./KG 30 launched further attacks on the anchorage, daring the response of the British guns. More ships were damaged and there were both military and civilian casualties and though the raids eased off as Luftwaffe commitment grew elsewhere, the British were left to face the unpalatable reality that the base at Scapa was not only vulnerable to underwater or surface attack, but to air strikes as well. The defences were hurriedly improved and by mid-April 1940, more than 100 heavy and light anti-aircraft guns were in position around Scapa, supported by 88 searchlights. By 1942, the entrances to Scapa Flow alone were covered by 37 guns and 52 searchlights.

The German plan of April 1944 did not represent the first time the British naval base had been considered a target for unconventional weaponry by the Luftwaffe; in 1943 a proposal was submitted whereby specially adapted Go 242 gliders would carry Italian assault boats directly into the anchorage. It was intended that one glider would carry one assault boat and its crew. However, despite several conversions being made, the operation came to nothing.

One area in which the Germans did not enjoy accurate intelligence was in the disposition of local British air defences and as *Oberst* von Greiff of the *Führungsstab* reported in the study of 1944:

> 'Very strong defences are to be expected in the target area. Exact information is not available, because our own radio listening network has only a range extending as far as the Wash. Ia [Staff Operations Officer] assumes that the airfields extending from the Firth of Forth to the north coast of Scotland will be occupied by 160-200 aircraft, comprising Spitfires, Hurricanes, Mosquitos and Beaufighters. It must also be assumed that the target will be surrounded by a ring of radar stations that will provide complete coverage of sea approaches.'

The Royal Navy anchorage at Scapa Flow in the Orkney Islands was the target eventually selected for attack by Mistel. 'Very strong defences are to be expected in the target area,' wrote Oberst von Greiff on 16 April 1944; 'The mission must be carried out in such a way that the Mistel will be detected by the enemy's radar so late that fighter defences cannot be brought to bear.'

A revealing revelation of the state of anti-aircraft defences in early 1943 can be found in the text of a letter from Air Marshal Sir Sholto-Douglas, AOC-in-C Fighter Command to General Sir Frederick Pile, HQ Anti-Aircraft Command:

> 'Collishaw[1] was in to see me yesterday. He is inclined to be critical of the state of readiness maintained by the AA gun defences at Scapa. He says that the gun crews are not normally by their instruments and guns and that they rely on getting a warning from the RDF system. As you know, provided an enemy aircraft remains under 50 feet, we get practically no warning at all of its approach and Collishaw thinks your people are living in a fool's paradise if they think they will get sufficient warning to man their guns before the enemy approaches. We do not want another Pearl Harbour at Scapa…'

On 27 April 1944, the Admiral Commanding Orkneys and Shetlands (ACOS) was 'more than a little disturbed' by the fact that a squadron of Spitfires which usually covered Scapa Flow and the Scottish coast was moved south from Castletown, near Thurso, as part of preparations for the invasion of France. He requested that a Fleet Air Arm Seafire squadron be moved in as a replacement. On 5 May 1944, in a terse message to the Admiralty, the Air Ministry stated that, in its opinion, one squadron at the Orkneys base at Skeabrae and a small detachment at Sumburgh were 'adequate.'

The British could have taken some comfort from the fact that after being shot down in a Ju 88 D-1 of 1.(F)/120 off the Shetland Islands in early March 1944, one of the German aircraft's crew told his British captors that 'flights to Scapa Flow were particularly unpopular on account of the AA defences there.'

[1] Air Commodore Raymond Collishaw, a Canadian who served with distinction in the RNAS during the First World War and then, during the Second World War served as commander of the Desert Air Force and later as commander of the Scapa Flow air defences for Fighter Command.

In his report, *Oberst* von Greiff added:

> 'The mission must be carried out in such a way that the *Mistel* will be detected by the enemy's radar so late that fighter defences cannot be brought to bear. Protection by our own escort fighters is not possible because of their lack of range (Stavanger to Scapa Flow is 510 km). Flights in bad weather or at night are not possible. An attack combined with bomber or torpedo-fighter groups, or conducted at high altitude, is also ruled out for the same reasons. The only remaining possibility is, therefore, to approach at very low level, pull up in front of the target at the last moment and then make the gliding attack.'

The 'gliding attack' was to be made from close range, closing in at 550-600 km/h at an angle of 20 degrees, with release of the lower component from a height of 700 metres and a range of 2 km from the target. It was considered that battleships should be attacked from the stern.

To guide the *Mistel* as they made their way across the North Sea, a series of floating FuG 302 C '*Schwan-See*' ('Swan-Sea') VHF radio navigation buoys was to be used, each with a range of 80-100 km at 200 metres. The buoys were to be laid out across the North Sea immediately prior to an attack being made. The *Schwan-See* was shaped like an ordinary bomb and dropped into the water by an aircraft. The *Mistel* Ju 88 lower component's three-axis autopilot and the Bf 109's FuG 16 Z VHF transceiver would ensure an accurate approach and safe return.[2]

On 16 April 1944, *Oberst i.G.* Eckhard Christian signalled the *Führungsstab's* intentions when he wrote: 'Make preparations for an attack on Scapa Flow.'

However, though certain logistical efforts were made to put the planned operation into action, a Scapa Flow attack force was not assembled until February 1945 (see Chapter Nine). The Allied invasion of France was to demand a more immediate role for the first operational *Mistel.*

[2] This is covered in more detail in a later chapter.

'A LUCKY STAR'

OPERATIONS IN THE WEST 1944 : PHASE ONE

Junkers technical personnel cycle out to an early Mistel S1 probably at Nordhausen in early 1944.

AS early as February 1944, the month that Holzbaur conducted his first test with a 'live' *Mistel* against the Møns-Klint in Denmark, the *Luftwaffe* took steps to establish its first operational *Mistel* unit.

As described in Chapter Six, during the early part of 1944, Hitler's mood of revenge permeated the *Luftwaffe's* high command. Operation *Steinbock*, the retaliatory bombing campaign against the British Isles, was under way. *Generalmajor* Peltz had been appointed by Göring as the '*Angriffsführer England*' (Attack Leader against England) in November 1943 and a hastily scraped-together force of bomber *Gruppen* was transferred to France from the East and the Mediterranean and placed under the command of IX. *Fliegerkorps*. Peltz knew that he had to make the best of what was available, since the widely differing capabilities of the aircraft assigned to him, together with the varying skills and experience of their crews, meant that he would need to keep operations as simple as possible. Throughout January and February 1944, Peltz sent his bombers to London and scattered targets throughout southern and eastern England. However, the tonnage of bombs dropped was paltry, with generally only fifty per cent landing in the target area. Furthermore, heavy losses and the shrinking size of the attack force meant that results were by no means the spectacular propaganda victories Hitler craved and, compared to the damage the Allied air forces were inflicting on German cities, they were pitiful. Typically however, Peltz was undaunted by the inevitable failure of *Steinbock*. In mid-February, he despatched *Oberleutnant* Horst Rudat, one of his young liaison officers on the staff of IX. *Fliegerkorps*, to Göring's country estate at Karinhall. It was time to unleash the *Mistel*.

Horst Rudat was born on 3 May 1920 in Wirtkallen, East Prussia and was a successful bomber pilot. Having passed through the *Luftkriegsschule* 5 at Regensburg-Obertraubling, he was posted to KG 55 on the Eastern Front and became *Kapitän* of 2. *Staffel* in November 1942. On 24 March 1943, Rudat was awarded the *Ritterkreuz* in recognition of the 315 missions he had flown, mainly against bridge targets and Soviet ammunition trains, as well as for supply flights to the trapped Sixth Army at Stalingrad. On 18 January 1943, his He 111 was one of the last to land at Gumrak airfield close to Stalingrad which had been surrounded by the Russians. Despite temperatures of twenty degrees below zero and appalling operating conditions, Rudat and his crew were able to fly out 27 personnel and boxes of important documents.

In the spring of 1944, Hauptmann Horst Rudat was appointed Staffelkapitän of the Ergänzungsstaffel, II./KG 101, later 2./KG 101, the first training and operational unit to be equipped with the Mistel. Rudat was awarded the Ritterkreuz while flying He 111s with KG 55 on the Eastern Front in 1943.

On 30 June 1943, Rudat was posted back to the Reich and by the end of the year was attached to Peltz's staff. Simultaneously, in January 1944, he was appointed a *Staffelkapitän* of the *Einsatzstaffel* II./KG 101 based at Varrelbusch. The precise function and activities of this unit at this time are not clear, but what is known is that this was a semi-autonomous *Staffel* with emphasis on the training of bomber pilots and navigators. An initial cadre of personnel was drawn from the *Verbandsführerschule für Kampfflieger* at Foggia and Tours.

During a brief audience with Göring, *Oberleutnant* Rudat was ordered to set up and command the *Luftwaffe's* first operational *Mistel* unit as a matter of the highest priority, a task for which he was promised full support. Together with four or five other pilots from the *Einsatzstaffel* II./KG 101, Rudat journeyed to Dessau to meet with Holzbaur. As Rudat recalled:

> 'Because of tight security measures, I had never previously heard anything about the *Mistel*. I therefore flew to Junkers at Dessau to receive detailed information about the type and from there to Nordhausen. On arrival, I found that initial flight-testing of the *Mistel* had already begun under the leadership of *Flugkapitän* Holzbaur and *Dipl.-Ing. Dr.* Haber, both of whom were regarded as the 'fathers' of the *Mistel*.'

The small Harz town of Nordhausen would gain considerable post-war infamy as the site of the notorious underground aircraft and rocket factory known as the *Mittelwerk* located beneath the anhydrite hills at Niedersachswerfen just to the north of the town. By mid-1944, more than 8,000 slave labourers, many of them drawn from the concentration camps, were toiling in the fetid, ammonia dust-filled air of the factory's tunnels. Nordhausen airfield, however, was located to the south of the town and served as a Luftwaffe training facility. Once Ju 88s began arriving at the airfield for refurbishment and *Mistel* assembly by the *Baustelle Schwab/Nordhausen* towards the end of 1943, Siegfried Holzbaur established a Junkers office close to the railway station.

Under the supervision of Holzbaur, Haber and Lux, Rudat and his small detachment began training. He recalled:

> 'I already had some experience flying the Ju 88, but had not previously flown the Bf 109. Instruction on Messerschmitt's fighter was brief. A few days later, I made my first flight with the *Mistel*. I have to admit that I did not feel very confident sitting high above the ground in a Bf 109 mounted to a Ju 88. Take-off proved to be a problem; control commands electrically transmitted from the upper to the lower aircraft seemed to take rather a long time reaching the Ju 88's control surfaces before they responded to the command. The pilot, therefore, had to anticipate every manoeuvre before it actually took place. During training with the *Mistel* S1, the Ju 88 was flown with a two-man crew, who were able to correct any bad mistakes made by the pilot of the Bf 109.
>
> 'Everything turned out well, however, and after take-off I was surprised to find how easy it was to control a large composite aircraft from a small fighter cockpit. I was particularly impressed by the accuracy of the three-axis, gyro-stabilised autopilot. During mock attacks, very little control movement was needed to keep the composite on course towards its target – a tree – once the aircraft had reached its final speed. Naturally, the biggest surprise was the feeling I got when I flipped the switch to separate the Bf 109 from the Ju 88. Thus was my first experience with the *Mistel*.'

However, Rudat soon realised that the facilities at Nordhausen did not offer the most practical or efficient environment in which to continue training his pilots for offensive operations. In the spring of 1944, Rudat transferred to an airfield at Kolberg, the 9th century town on the Baltic coast some 70 km east from the mouth of the Oder River. Equipped with about a third of the initial batch of 15 *Mistel*, he carried out some of the first aiming trials against the Møns-Klint.

By 12 March 1944, it seems that *Oblt.* Rudat's training detachment had been redesignated 2./KG 101, a further sign that *Mistel* operations were being viewed as autonomous and elements of the unit continued their training at Laon-Couvron in northern France.

Just over a month later, on 16 April, the *Luftwaffenführungsstab* issued orders that thirty-five men, probably ground crew and technicians, recently transferred to 2./KG 101, were to be relocated to Nordhausen, where they too would receive technical training on the composite. Both pilot and technical training continued throughout May, but the following month events suddenly, but not unexpectedly, overtook the Germans.

On 6 June 1944 the Allies landed on the coast of Normandy. An armada of some 6,500 naval and transport ships crossed the English Channel supported by 12,000 aircraft. By dawn of that day, 18,000 British and American paratroops were already on the ground, capturing key bridges and disrupting German lines of communications. The *Wehrmacht* at all levels was caught in disarray. At 1015 hrs *Generalfeldmarschall* Erwin Rommel, the commander of Army Group B, was informed of the landings. He was in Germany to celebrate his wife's birthday, but at once flew back to France, instructed by Hitler to drive the invaders 'back into the sea' by midnight. By that time, 155,000 Allied troops were ashore and consolidating their positions.

The Allied air effort during the first twenty-four hours of the invasion had been immense with sufficient capability to fly 14,500 sorties. By comparison, the performance of the Luftwaffe on the first day of the landings was woefully inadequate. In the early hours, the OKL teleprinters had chattered out a string of warnings and situation reports from the various French-based tactical commands, but the instruction to proceed with the relocation of home defence fighter units from the Reich to France, as planned, never materialised. OKL dithered with indecision, largely due to the threat of bad weather over central Germany which risked jeopardising the entire transfer.

Meanwhile, frantic efforts were made to launch some kind of determined response against the invasion fleet by the German bomber force. There were seven battleships, 23 cruisers, 105 destroyers, some 1,000 smaller vessels and more than 4,000 landing craft off the coast, but the sheer scale of Allied air strength made any question of the deployment of bombers and anti-shipping aircraft by day unthinkable. Elements of IX. *Fliegerkorps* flew some 175 sorties, of which anti-shipping operations – those which Göring had proclaimed to be 'the spearhead of the anti-invasion forces' – accounted for 25 per cent. Allied nightfighters and accidental German *Flak* took their toll. The launching of Hs 293 guided missiles against ships proved difficult because Allied escort vessels sent out jamming signals to block radio guidance systems. Something more was needed. Over the course of the next four days, German air reinforcements were rushed into France. Within a few days nearly 1,000 fighters had arrived from Germany, but their pilots had to contend with barely prepared emergency strips. On 8 June, more than 500 close-support sorties were flown and by the 10th, X. *Fliegerkorps* in southern France was bolstered by a further 45 torpedo-carrying Ju 88s and 90 long-range bombers transferred from Germany and Italy.

Among the various units ordered to move into France to engage the invasion forces was 2./KG 101 which was assigned to attack large Allied ships off the Normandy coast. By 10 June, the unit's ground and signals personnel had arrived by rail and established themselves on an airfield

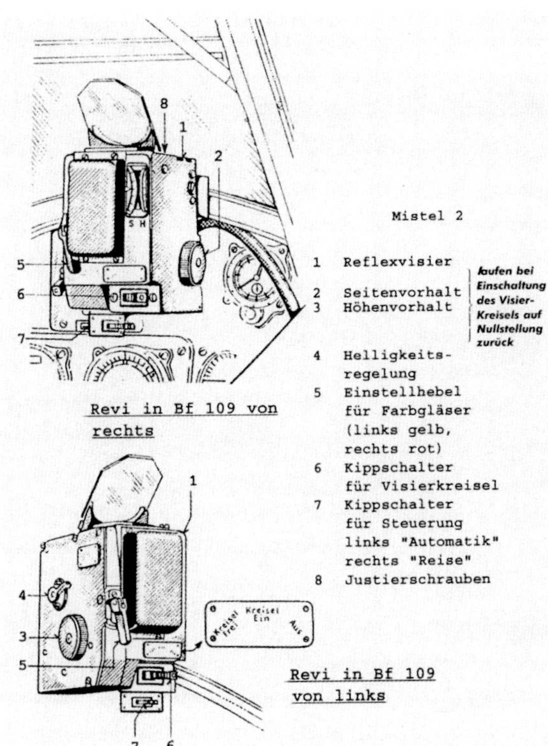

A page from the 'Mistel 2' instruction manual prepared by Junkers in May 1944 (issued August 1944), showing the installation of the reflex aiming sight in the Bf 109 of a Bf 109 F-4/Ju 88 A-4 combination.

Two Mistel S1s comprising Bf 109 F-4s mounted on what appear to be Ju 88 Cs. These aircraft are most likely undergoing tests at Nordhausen. Note the Mistel conversion numbers, blurred but just visible, on the Balkenkreuze of the Bf 109s.

near St. Dizier, 200 km east of Paris. However, preparations to fly in the *Mistel* had begun at Junkers' Nordhausen works several days earlier under the coordination of Siegfried Holzbaur.

One of the key personnel involved with transfer flights from Nordhausen to St. Dizier was *Feldwebel* Heinz Schreiber. Schreiber worked as an acceptance pilot on behalf of the RLM and between June 1944 and March 1945, he flew the *Mistel* in its various configurations on nearly 300 occasions, which made him one of the most experienced pilots on the type.

Just after the Allies landed in France, Schreiber was told to report to Holzbaur who briefed him on the *Mistel* development programme and the Luftwaffe's requirement to use the first 15 composite aircraft operationally against targets in Normandy. Schreiber's role would be to organise the transfer of the completed *Mistel* from the Nordhausen works to St. Dizier by the quickest and safest means possible.

Schreiber immediately flew to France in order to make sure that the airfield facilities there were adequate to accept

HEINZ SCHREIBER

HEINZ SCHREIBER was born on 27 April 1914 in Köthen, a small town to the south of Dessau. In many ways, his life was linked intrinsically with the Junkers aircraft firm. His father, Hans, worked as a *Flugzeugmeister*, or aircraft foreman, at the nearby plant where he had been employed since 1910. Heinz joined Junkers at Dessau in 1929. Because of his father's position and the fact that he was well known in the works, the young Heinz enjoyed a certain amount of privilege. He completed his apprenticeship on 30 December 1932 and on 18 June 1935 he became a *Bordmechaniker* (Flight Engineer). He made 36 training flights before embarking upon his first solo flight at Dessau on 2 September 1938 in an He 72 W.Nr.392, D-EIZI. It was normal practice to make some 100 training flights before going solo.

He continued to work as a *Bordmechaniker* until 14 March 1939, when he became an *Einflieger* (acceptance test pilot), for production aircraft. Though Schreiber was acquainted with Holzbaur, the Chief Test Pilot, the latter worked in the Experimental Department, whereas Schreiber was assigned to the Production Department and there was virtually no contact between the two men during the first half of the war.

Upon joining the Luftwaffe and completing basic military training, Schreiber was posted for advanced flying training to the *Flugzeugführerschule* C16 at Burg bei Magdeburg between May-July 1940, followed by a transfer to *Flugzeugführerschule* C9 at Altenburg on 4 September of that year. He then moved to *Blindflugschule* 6 at Wesendorf on 1 October 1941 before joining the *Uberführungs und Einfliegerkommando Jüterbog*, part of the *Flieger Sondergruppe Ob.d.L*, on 13 August 1942.

As a member of the *Uberführungs- und Einfliegerkommando Jüterbog*, Schreiber was based at various *Luftwaffe* repair facilities behind the front line and involved in the acceptance testing of aircraft that had either been repaired following battle damage or that had reconditioned 'war-weary' airframes, particularly aircraft manufactured by Junkers. In this capacity he saw service in Athens, then at the Junkers plant at Leipzig-Mockau and afterwards was assigned to facilities in Poland. On 7 April 1944, he was posted back to Dessau where he was involved in testing the Ju 88, Ju 188 and Ju 352 among others.

December 1932: a young Heinz Schreiber poses proudly with the item which completed his apprenticeship at Junkers Dessau. Six years later, he would become an acceptance test pilot with the company, probably making more Mistel flights, including ferry flights to 2./KG 101 in France, than any other pilot.

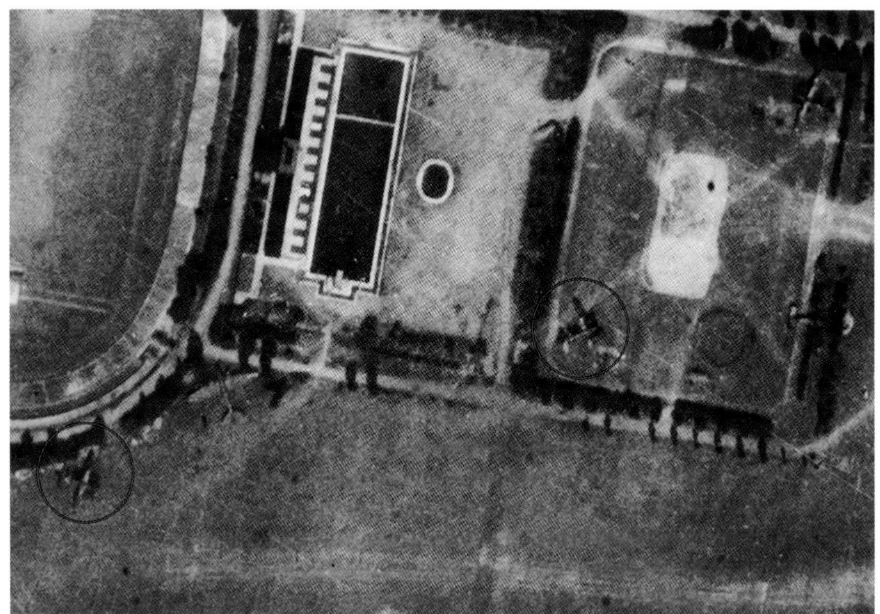

Two Mistel are visible – one either side of the building – in this Allied reconnaissance photograph of Nordhausen taken on 21 July 1944.

and operate the composites. On the afternoon of 10 June, he commenced his 1,140-kilometre journey from Nordhausen in the 'Ju 88 V-7'[1]. Staging via Rhein-Main and then St.Yan, south of Montceau-les-Mines in eastern France (the diversion was intended to avoid flying too close to the Invasion Front and any Allied fighters), he landed at St. Dizier just before 2200 hrs that evening to coincide with the arrival of 2./KG 101's ground contingent at the nearby marshalling yards.

Apparently satisfied with what he saw of the airfield's two 1,508-metre runways and support infrastructure, he returned directly to Nordhausen in a Ju 352 piloted by Junkers former Dessau-based Chief Test Pilot, *Flugkapitän* Wilhelm Zimmermann. That same evening, Schreiber flew on to Dessau to report to Holzbaur.

Schreiber believed that it was feasible for *Mistel* to fly direct from Nordhausen to St. Dizier. Holzbaur seems to have accepted Schreiber's word and wasted little time, immediately authorising the transfer of the first composite.

Early on the morning of 14 June 1944, a *Mistel* S1 comprising a Bf 109 (DM+UC) and the Ju 88 V9 (CN+FI) took off from the Nordhausen works en route

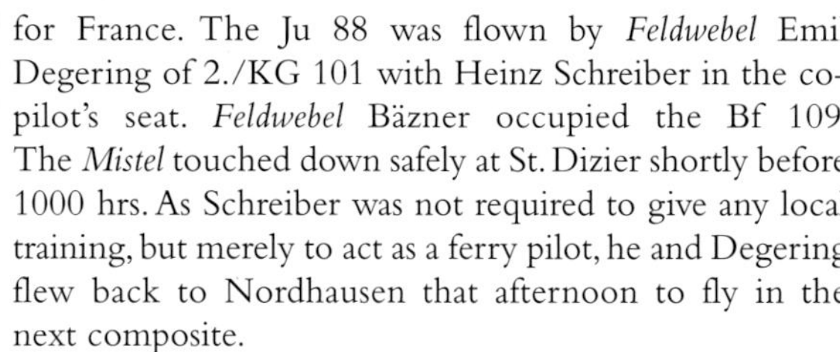

for France. The Ju 88 was flown by *Feldwebel* Emil Degering of 2./KG 101 with Heinz Schreiber in the co-pilot's seat. *Feldwebel* Bäzner occupied the Bf 109. The *Mistel* touched down safely at St. Dizier shortly before 1000 hrs. As Schreiber was not required to give any local training, but merely to act as a ferry pilot, he and Degering flew back to Nordhausen that afternoon to fly in the next composite.

Meanwhile, it seems other aircraft were arriving at Rudat's unit yet, remarkably, it was to be only hours before the Luftwaffe would lose its first *Mistel* to enemy action.

Throughout 14 June in Normandy, though the Americans had taken Quineville and Montebourg as part of their drive towards Cherbourg, the British were still struggling to advance towards Caen. The tanks of the *Panzer Lehr Division* put up a stiff line of resistance and even rocket-armed Hawker Typhoons of the 2nd Tactical Air Force could not break the German defence. By nightfall, the British were forced to withdraw. In the air, the American air forces bombed airfields, rail lines and communications targets south of the beachhead and south-west of Paris. Meanwhile, 221 Lancasters and 13 Mosquitos carried out RAF Bomber Command's first daylight raid since May 1943 when they attacked the German Navy's fast motor-torpedo boat base at Le Havre. These craft and other light naval forces were threatening Allied shipping only some 48 km away. Several hits were scored on the concrete-covered pens with 12,000-lb *Tallboy* bombs and few vessels survived the attack undamaged. By this stage, with their naval capability severely weakened, the Germans needed more than ever a weapon with which to strike at the massive armada off the coast and on the night of 14 June 1944 the *Mistel* underwent its baptism of fire.

Among the pilots of the *Einsatzstaffel* of KG 101 at St Dizier was *Oberleutnant* Albert Rheker whose service career is strong testimony to the calibre of pilots being assigned to fly the *Mistel* on its initial operations. After seeing service successively over England, North Africa, the Far North and the Mediterranean in Ju 88s, in December 1943 Rheker returned to the Reich having transferred from I. to II./KG 30. In April 1944 he was posted to KG 101's training base at Kolberg on the Baltic coast where he underwent brief and rudimentary training on the *Mistel*. It should be stressed that this would have involved conversion training from twin-engined aircraft to single-engine/single-seat fighter aircraft as well as

[1] 'Ju 88 V-7' as per entry in Schreiber's Flugbuch.

Oberfeldwebel Albert Rheker photographed at the completion of his training.

ALBERT RHEKER

ALBERT OTTO RHEKER was born on 29 March 1919 as the fifth child of Albert Rheker, a teacher, in Wiedenbrück (Westphalia). He joined the Luftwaffe in November 1938 and his service career illustrates the calibre of the relatively small number of pilots who flew the *Mistel* operationally.

After basic training in Detmold, in November 1939 he was assigned to *Flugzeugführerschule* C 12 at Prag-Rusin for training in multi-engine aircraft with flying weights of more than 5,000 kg, before moving to *Blindflugschule* 5 at Rahmel for instrument training which he completed in July 1940. Rheker's next posting was to *Ergänzungskampfgruppe* 3 at Krakau where he prepared to join his first operational unit; this was to be 9./LG 1 on 1 August 1940 with which he flew his first combat missions in Ju 88s over England. He would remain with *Lehrgeschwader* 1 until October 1942, transferring with III. *Gruppe* to the Mediterranean in early 1941. Between January and May 1941 and with the rank of *Leutnant*, he flew 27 missions there from Sicily. Between May and December he flew a further 67 missions over North Africa and Greece, including anti-shipping sorties and bombing attacks on Alexandria and Port Said. From November 1942 to the summer of 1943, he was engaged in thirteen anti-convoy flights in the Far North along the Murman Coast with I./KG 30, and had a brief secondment to the *Wettererkundungstaffel* 5 (meteorological unit) with whom he made one weather reconnaissance flight out to Jan Mayen island in the Arctic Ocean. He was promoted to *Oberleutnant* on 1 January 1943.

Albert Rheker was awarded the *Frontflugspange in Gold* on 17 March 1942 and the *Deutsches Kreuz in Gold* on 23 July 1943. He is believed to have flown in excess of 150 combat missions.

An operationally ready Mistel 1 probably from 2./KG 101 carrying the tactical number '2' applied to the rudder of the Ju 88. Compare this to the style of numbering applied to the Ju 88 in the photograph of another White '2' of 2./KG 101 seen at St. Dizier on page 73. Because the 'armed' Ju 88 was intended for 'Totaleinsatz', it is quite likely that tactical numbers were reused.

familiarisation with the dual-control composite. In May he was at Nordhausen and by June he was in France.

On the evening of 14 June 1944 *Oberleutnant* Rheker was briefed to fly one of the first *Mistel* missions against the Allied invasion fleet. Taking off from St. Dizier he made course west for the Seine, and from that river towards the landing area.

A few hours earlier, one hundred and seventy miles north of the Normandy coast at Hunsdon in Hertfordshire, England, Mosquito nightfighters of 410 (Cougar) Squadron, RCAF, were being readied for another nocturnal patrol over the invasion beaches. The Squadron had received its first Mosquito in October 1942 and the following year flew intruder sorties over occupied Europe and Germany. In early 1944, it had flown nightfighter interceptions against Luftwaffe bombers over southern England as part of the *Steinbock* offensive.

Flight Lieutenant Walter 'Dinny' Dinsdale from Eugene, Ontario and Flying Officer John Dunn from Winnipeg, Manitoba had been flying together as a crew since they had met at No. 54 Operational Training Unit in May 1943. Posted to 410 Squadron in August 1943, the pair commenced nightfighter patrols in October of that year flying Mosquito MK IIs and Mk VIIIs. Their first encounter with the Luftwaffe had come in early February 1944 when their aircraft 'grazed' a Ju 88 with its starboard propeller over North Weald. However, despite flying a number of operational sorties throughout the spring of 1944, Dinsdale and Dunn were denied any further opportunity to attack the Luftwaffe.

Then came the Invasion and 410 Squadron found itself operating as part of 2nd Tactical Air Force. Since the Allied air forces had attained air supremacy, several nightfighter units had been released from their defensive operations over Britain to fly protective patrols over the convoys heading for France as well as over the Normandy beaches. The main objective was to scout for any hostile aircraft which might interfere with Allied bomber operations and shipping. As John Dunn recalls:

> 'The 14 June was another operational day. Activity had increased over the beachhead area. In addition to enemy operations, there was also the danger from "friendly" *Flak* if you went below the designated *Flak* level. According to our logbook records, this would be our fifth trip to the beachhead area. Our first mission was on 6 June, 'D-Day', followed by trips on 7, 10 and 11 June. On 7 June, while lingering near a Lancaster, we were shot up slightly by a vigilant rear gunner!
>
> 'On the afternoon of 14 June, we carried out our usual 'NFT' (Night Flying Test) of aircraft, armament and radar. This was a Mosquito MK XIII –'O' (HK476), our favourite "Mossie" equipped with four 20 mm cannon and Mark VIII Air Interception radar.
>
> 'Prior to take-off from Hunsdon, we were briefed on the weather conditions, and intelligence indicated that Bandits were dropping "Window" over the beachhead area. We were airborne at 2235 hrs and set course for Fighter Pool No. 1 at the beachhead area. In the meantime, I switched the AI set to low tension to warm the AI cathode ray tube and set the oxygen control to 10,000 ft. Minutes later, I switched the AI set to high tension and then tuned the set to get the best possible picture. The capability of the scanner search was checked. This covered 180 degrees through the horizontal and 45 degrees above and below through the vertical. We arrived at Fighter Pool No. 1 at 2320 hrs. Under initial control of FDT 217 mobile Ground Control Interception (GCI)[2], we were vectored south, then 100 degrees following the Seine River, then

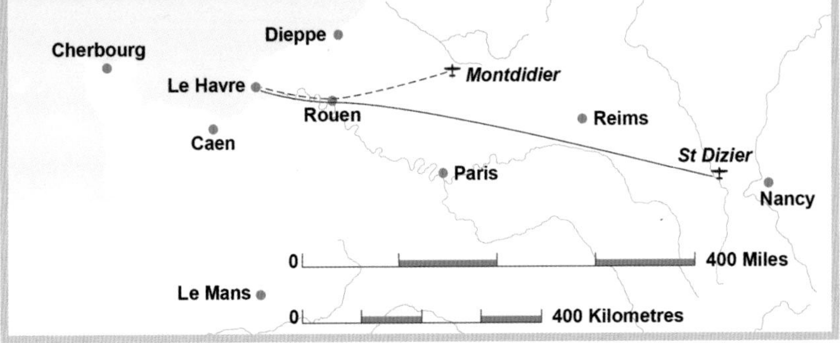

Normandy and north-eastern France showing 2./KG 101's base at St. Dizier. Pathfinders from I./KG 66 operated from Montdidier and made course for the Invasion coast via Rouen, the rendezvous point with the Mistel.

[2] This was a seaborne control unit.

Oberleutnant Albert Rheker photographed in tropical uniform while serving with LG 1 in the Mediterranean in 1942. He wears a newly awarded mission clasp in silver for the completion of sixty operational flights.

280 degrees. We experienced a heavy concentration of Window which flooded the cathode ray tube with spurious blips or contacts. I was finally able to select a solid blip at a range of 2,000 ft at 12 o'clock. I advised pilot immediately of "Contact!" and we climbed to 11,000 ft where a reasonable visual was obtained 23.35 hrs.'

The weather was good, with a few broken clouds, and Dinsdale was able to see his target quite clearly. It was moving slowly, so slowly that Dinsdale was forced to lower his wheels and flaps in order to avoid overshooting. He closed in from behind and below. John Dunn continues:

'Mobile GCI was advised of contact and visual and "chatter" with GCI was cut off while we assumed contact. We then closed to 1,000 ft astern of the Bandit, checked IFF, no resins, no battle stripes. We closed to 750 ft and made positive identification with the aid of Ross night glasses on a Ju 88 with what appeared to be a glider bomb attached to the upper fuselage. Identification was confirmed by my pilot, again with the aid of Ross night glasses. Strangely enough, there was no evasive action taken by the Bandit throughout this action.

'At 750 ft, my pilot opened fire with a short burst from our four 20 mm cannon; parts of the enemy aircraft burst into flames and it banked to port and went down in a steep dive. We followed on AI and visually. It hit the ground south-east of Caen at 2340 hrs. There was a massive explosion which lit up the whole countryside. Hedges, roads and buildings were visible.'

The Canadians' immediate belief was that their target was a type of airborne launching platform for a V-1 flying bomb. Only the previous day, the first V-1s had been fired at the British Isles from launch sites in the Pas-de-Calais, heralding the commencement of the flying bomb campaign. However, what Dinsdale and Dunn had most probably shot down was the *Mistel* of *Oberleutnant* Albert Rheker making its way to the coast. He was almost certainly flying Bf 109 'CD+LX' attached to Ju 88, W.Nr.10130, White '5'. It had taken a total of 15 rounds of 20 mm semi-armour piercing incendiary rounds and 17 high explosive incendiary rounds from Dinsdale's guns to despatch the composite. Dinsdale later told newspaper reporters:

'It was a very awkward thing and lumbered along like an old hippo at about 150 mph. I recognised it as a Ju 88 but couldn't figure out what the thing on top was. I thought it was one of their glider bombs mounted in a new way. It was on top, mounted between the rudder and the main

Flight Lieutenant Walter 'Dinny' Dinsdale (left) and Flying Officer Jack Dunn of 410 (Cougar) Squadron, RCAF, pose for a snapshot in front of their Mosquito HK476, the aircraft in which they shot down a Mistel of 2./KG 101 on the night of 14 June 1944. Dunn remembers, 'a massive explosion which lit up the whole countryside.'

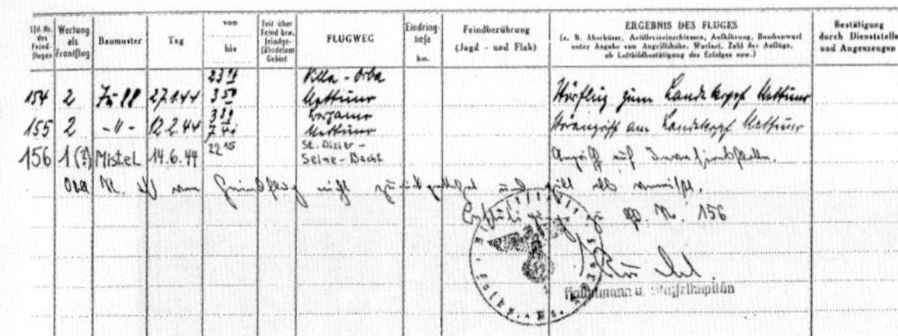

Lfd. Nr. des Feind-fluges	Wertung als Frontflug	Baumuster	Tag	von / bis	Zeit über Feind bzw. feindbesetztem Gebiet	FLUGWEG	Eindringtiefe km.	Feindberührung (Jagd - und Flak)	ERGEBNIS DES FLUGES	Bestätigung durch Dienststelle und Augenzeugen
154	2	[illegible]	2.7.44	[illegible]		[illegible]			[illegible]	
155	2	-"-	12.7.44	[illegible]		[illegible]			[illegible]	
156	1 (?)	Mistel	14.6.44	22.15		St. Dizier - Seine-Bucht			[illegible]	

Hauptmann u. Staffelkapitän

Albert Rheker's Staffelkapitän, Hauptmann Rudat, recorded in Rheker's Leistungsbuch, 'Oblt. R. has not returned from attack on enemy and is assumed as missing.'

wing. My first short burst hit the starboard wing and cockpit of the Junkers. I thought I had killed the pilot, but, of course, there was no pilot as the whole thing is controlled from the fighter on top. Carrying on for a few minutes, circling to port with the fire increasing, he then dropped away and crashed behind the German lines. The explosion lit up the countryside for miles around.'

In Oberleutnant Rheker's *Leistungsbuch* (service record book), his *Staffelkapitän, Hauptmann* Rudat, noted for 14 June:

'*Angriff auf Invasionsflotte. (Attack on Invasion fleet). Oblt. R. has not returned from attack on enemy and is assumed as missing.*'

The baptism of fire had resulted in the first combat loss – but no Allied ships had been touched.

Another machine fitting the description of a *Mistel* was claimed shot down that night by a Mosquito MK VIII flown by Flight Lieutenant John Corre and Flying Officer Bines of 264 (Madras Presidency) Squadron who were also on patrol over the landing area. As Corre reported:

'At 0008 hours, I was vectored on to a bogey flying at 8,000 feet on a vector of 140 degrees. At 0010 hours, my navigator F/O Bines gave me contact dead ahead 2 1/2 miles. We were then doing 280 IAS (indicated air speed). The target was not showing IFF and was doing corkscrew evasive action. We closed quite rapidly and at 0012, I obtained a visual on a twin engined mid-wing aircraft seeing the exhausts at 1,500 feet. I closed to 200 yards and identified it as a Ju 188. It appeared to have another single engine aircraft flying immediately above it but upon closer scrutinising, it appeared to be a glider bomb straddled on the Ju 188's back… I dropped back to 200 yards… I gave him a half second burst and he blew up and disintegrated. The main body of the Ju 188 went almost vertically into the sea and we saw a large greyish cloud of smoke where it had crashed. I gave murder over the R/T at 00.16 hours. The weather was a dark night, clear of clouds. The target was flying at 260 ASI and I fixed my position 25 miles west of Le Havre.'

The *Mistel* may have been piloted by *Oberfeldwebel* Heinz Lochmüller who was posted as missing. Rheker and Lochmüller were piloting two of five *Mistel* believed to have been airborne that night.[3]

These first encounters with the *Mistel* confirmed Allied suspicions that the Germans had an important new weapon and the next day Walter Dinsdale and John Dunn were summoned to London for an urgent debriefing by Air and Naval Intelligence. In the early hours of 16 June, as a result of this meeting, the British Admiralty dispatched

[3] According to Allied radio intercepts, five aircraft were operational.

This is almost certainly the Mistel 1 which Flight Lieutenant Dinsdale and Flying Officer Dunn shot down over France on the night of 14 June 1944: Bf 109 CD+LX/ Ju 88, W.Nr. 10130, White '5' was probably flown by Oberleutnant Albert Rheker of 2./KG 101 flying on assignment to the Einsatzstaffel.

With its hollow-charge warhead fitted, technicians check the cockpit of the Bf 109 of Mistel 1 'White 4' of 2./KG 101 at St. Dizier, June 1944. Note the fuse protector cap still fixed to the end of the *'Elefantenrussel'* warhead and the ladder access to the Bf 109.

a secret cipher message to all British and US naval forces taking part in Operation Overlord:

> 'The Germans are known to have developed a composite aircraft consisting of a bomber with a fighter mounted on top of its fuselage… From fighter combat reports on the night of 14/15 June, it is thought that the Germans are attempting to use this new weapon… Expected targets for these weapons are installations and heavy ships. If employed against the latter, evasive action is the best counter measure as the flight of the bomber cannot be adjusted after its release from the fighter.'

On 15 June, on paper at least, Horst Rudat was succeeded as *Staffelkapitän* of 2./KG 101 by *Oberleutnant* Alfred Pilz. In reality, Rudat stayed with the unit for some time and, as will be described, took part in at least one *Mistel* operation over Normandy.

That evening, at the headquarters of the *Luftwaffenführungsstab*, *Major* Bräu, an officer on *Generalmajor* Peltz's staff, advised *Major* Jakob, an adjutant on *General der Flieger* Karl Koller's staff that, of the remainder of the first fifteen *Mistel* expected from Nordhausen, the V9 and V10 were completed. The V11 was expected to be ready by 25-27 June with all aircraft from the V12 through to the V15 following over a five-day period ending at the latest 15 July. Koller promptly ordered another fifteen Ju 88s to be allocated urgently for *Mistel* conversion. However, his intentions were frustrated the next day when, during the mid-morning staff meeting, *Obst. i.G.* Eckhard Christian advised that it was very unlikely that any speeding up of the conversion process could be achieved. The additional fifteen aircraft had still not been made available from the Luftwaffe's repair shops and, furthermore, Bf 109 upper components were not available due to a lack of spare parts. Koller immediately appointed *Obst. i.G.* Eschenauer, the *Luftwaffenführungsstab's* chief supply officer, to locate spare parts from unserviceable aircraft.

There was a little light on the horizon when, just before midnight that night, Koller received word from *Major i.G.* Hauser that the 'first two' *Mistel* were reported as operationally ready at St. Dizier with a further two aircraft expected to be ready by 20 June and 'the remaining three' by 30 June. It is difficult to tell how realistic a forecast this was. Nevertheless, this news was considered important enough that *Luftflotte* 3, under whose command 2./KG 101 operated, requested approval from the *Luftwaffenführungsstab* to withhold the imminent transfer of the Bf 109-equipped nightfighter unit, I./JG 301, to the Reich until at least 20/21 June. By this time it was planned that 2./KG 101 would have commenced offensive operations against the Invasion fleet and with its initial supply of warheads expended, the need for fighter cover would thus diminish.

On 5 June, I./JG 301 had been transferred from München-Neubiberg to France in order to provide *Wilde Sau* nightfighter cover over the V-1 launch sites in the Pas-de-Calais. The *Gruppenstab*, under *Hauptmann* Wilhelm Burggraf, was based at St. Dizier and was thus in an ideal position to offer fighter escort for Rudat and Pilz's *Mistel*. Although it is not clear whether the two units were ever able to coordinate their operations on a regular or effective basis, in captivity *Feldwebel* Gromoll, a pilot from 3./JG 301, recalled his impressions of the *Mistel* to a fellow German POW:

'It is entirely filled with high explosives… Two tons… That's a lot… The pilot is above in the '109… He gets into the aircraft and can run all three engines from there… You can imagine how funny it looks…'

Supplies of new *Mistel* continued to trickle into St. Dizier. During the evening of 18 June 1944, *Feldwebel* Willi Döhring of 2./KG 101 ferried a *Mistel* S1, Bf 109, NA+YS fitted to Ju 88V8, CN+FK. He was accompanied by Heinz Schreiber with *Feldwebel* Bäzner in the Bf 109. This aircraft was assigned the tactical number White '1' by KG 101. The following afternoon Schreiber co-piloted another S1 to France, Bf 109, DE+VK, piloted by Bäzner, fitted to the Ju 88 V12, GI+QH, piloted by *Feldwebel* Schöppner. However, although new aircraft were arriving, ground-support equipment was lacking and without a heavy crane to mount and install warheads, the ground crews and technicians were forced to commandeer a large excavator for the purpose.

Attempts to begin operations in earnest began on the evening of 24 June when it seems five of the twelve available *Mistel* were prepared for an attack against an Allied convoy in the Bay of the Seine in which was reported to be the battleship, HMS *Nelson*. Accurate details of KG 101's missions at this time are sparse, but some fragmentary and conflicting reports have survived.

Oblt. Dipl.-Ing. Horst-Dieter Lux was at St. Dizier to witness this first operation. He wrote:

'Events are followed in central Germany tensely. Is everything in order? Is there anything amiss? Radio and telephones are in constant use, and the transport aircraft thunder ceaselessly to and from France and their home base. Even greater than this effort is the expectation placed in the *Mistel*. It is apparent to the High Command that, owing to the strength of the Allies' anti-aircraft defences, the time for the *Mistel* is past but still they believe in a lucky star. An operation in the evening twilight. An indescribable tension is felt by everyone. This is partly relieved as the five special aircraft, escorted by fighters, thunder into the evening sky. Mechanics stare after their charges and while waiting for their return begin puffing away on one cigarette after another and making monosyllabic comments. Cigarettes and an apparent industriousness hide the unbearable tension. The tension, however, is not relieved and they stare at the slowly moving hands of the clock with impatience. The radio operators scan the ether unceasingly.'

Fighter escort for the *Mistel* was to be provided by Bf 109s of I./JG 301, which had been operationally subordinated to X. *Fliegerkorps* for the mission. Additionally, a small formation of Ju 88 S illuminator aircraft from I./KG 66 were to drop LC50 illumination flares ahead of the composites. The 'pathfinders' were assembled on a satellite airfield close to I./KG 66's usual base at Montdidier and were led by *Leutnant* Hans Altrogge. They took off at 2218 hrs, following a course which took them west, directly over Rouen, towards the Bay of the Seine.

Altrogge noted: 'Flak: very heavy becoming light and medium in the Caen area. Also single engine fighter.'[4]

At St. Dizier, with warheads fitted comprising 70% Hexogen high-explosive and 30% Trinitrotoluol, *Oberleutnant* Rudat prepared his aircraft for take-off. As he recalled:

'After training, the experience with an armed *Mistel* was completely different. Apart from the certainty that in wartime somebody would always shoot at us, take-off was the most difficult part of the mission. If I remember rightly, the Ju 88's tyres were designed for a take-off weight of 12 tonnes; the *Mistel*, however, weighed at least 14 tonnes. In order to keep the weight of the composite to a minimum all non-essential equipment was removed from the Bf 109, and that included guns and radio equipment! Nevertheless, all four aircraft took off successfully. We took off in the early evening, when encounters with the enemy's day fighters were no longer expected and before nightfighters made their appearance. The entire *Mistel* operation was cloaked in secrecy. German anti-aircraft batteries along our route were only informed of our operation at the very last minute and were ordered not to fire. It was my bad luck that one of these batteries had not been informed in time. We were still climbing, when at a height of 1,500 metres we came under fire. My left engine was hit and stopped. Even today, many years later, I remember the feeling of sitting on top of an enormous warhead and being shot at by our own *Flak*. I still don't like the feeling!

'Because I was unable to feather the propeller of the dead engine, I lost speed rapidly and was unable to keep up with the other three *Mistel* of my *Schwarm*. The warhead was specially designed to destroy heavily-armoured targets. Ours, therefore, were to be battleships or cruisers in the Bay of the Seine covering the Invasion fleet, though any ship was an acceptable alternative.

'In the meantime it had grown dark. West of Le Havre, I noticed a British nightfighter and I became conscious of the fact that I had no means of defending myself – my guns had been removed. Because my Ju 88 tended to want to turn continually to the left, I decided to make a direct attack on the numerous landing craft saturating the coastline. Something would definitely be destroyed, even though I could not claim success for the destruction of a designated target. After aiming the Ju 88, I separated and immediately turned inland to escape the nightfighter.'

The 'British nightfighter' which Rudat had noticed was one of the several ADGB Mosquitos operating over the beachhead that night. At 2300 hrs the aircraft was on patrol 40 km west of Le Havre in clear skies and some 6 km west of the convoy which KG 101 had been assigned to attack, when its pilot and navigator noticed an 'unusual bi-plane' about 2 km away. Flying on a parallel course, the crew 'had a good view, lasting for 15 to 20 seconds.' They reported that the machine, 'had the appearance of a small aircraft attached to the top of a larger twin-engined type. It was possible to see between the two aircraft, and they appeared to be connected at the trailing edges of the main planes.'

As the crew of the Mosquito endeavoured to identify the mysterious aircraft, which had taken no avoiding action, the upper component separated and lifted away from the lower component, banked steeply, flew away at right angles and became,

[4] This was probably a Spitfire. At least one Spitfire from 130 Squadron was known to have conducted a night beachhead patrol and engaged a Ju 88 off Le Havre but was shot down by the bomber (see Foreman: *1944-Over the Beaches*, Air Research, 1994, pg. 280)

Mistel S2

Detail variations of Ju 88 G-1/G-6 and Fw 190 A-8/F-8 Mistel combinations

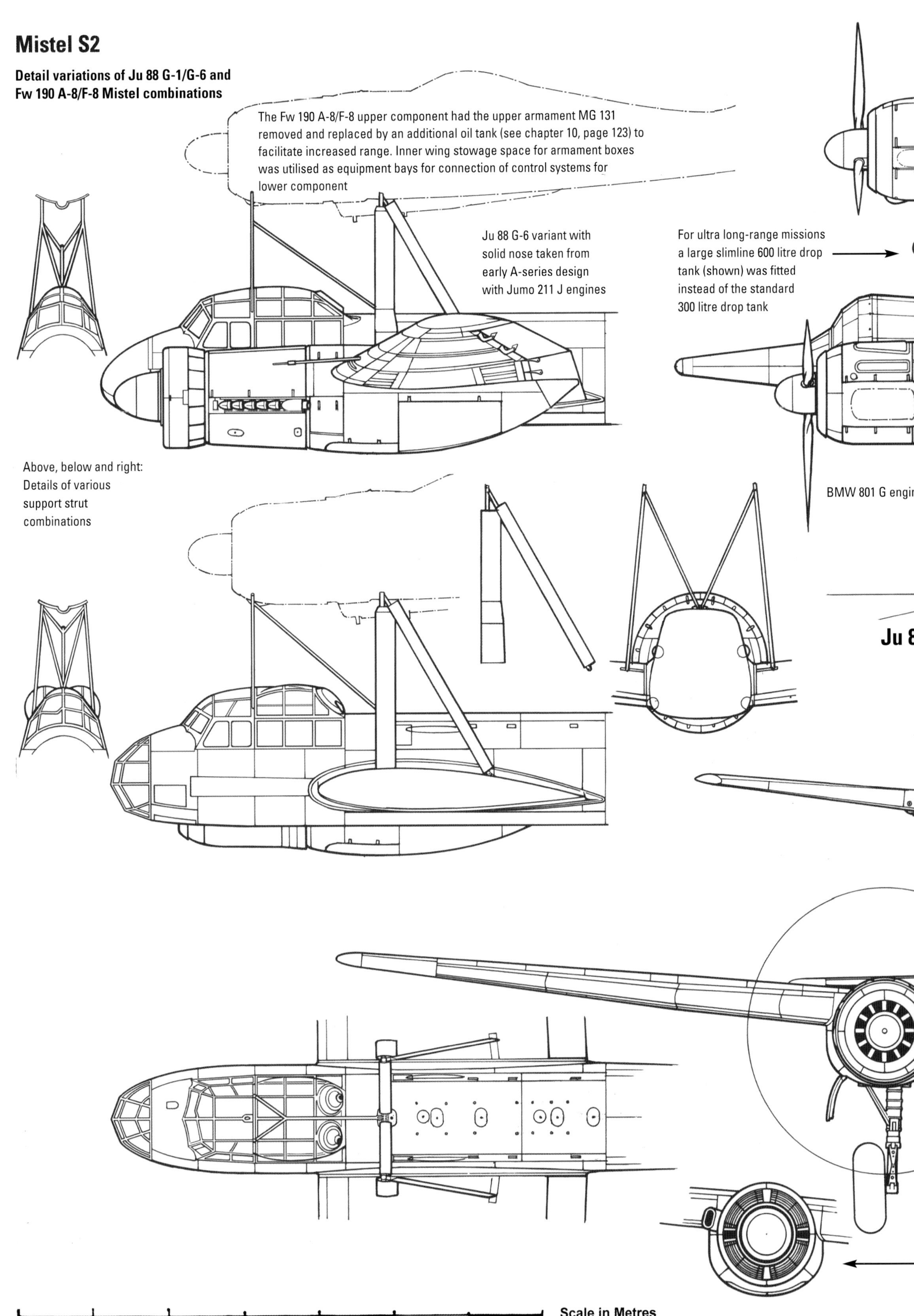

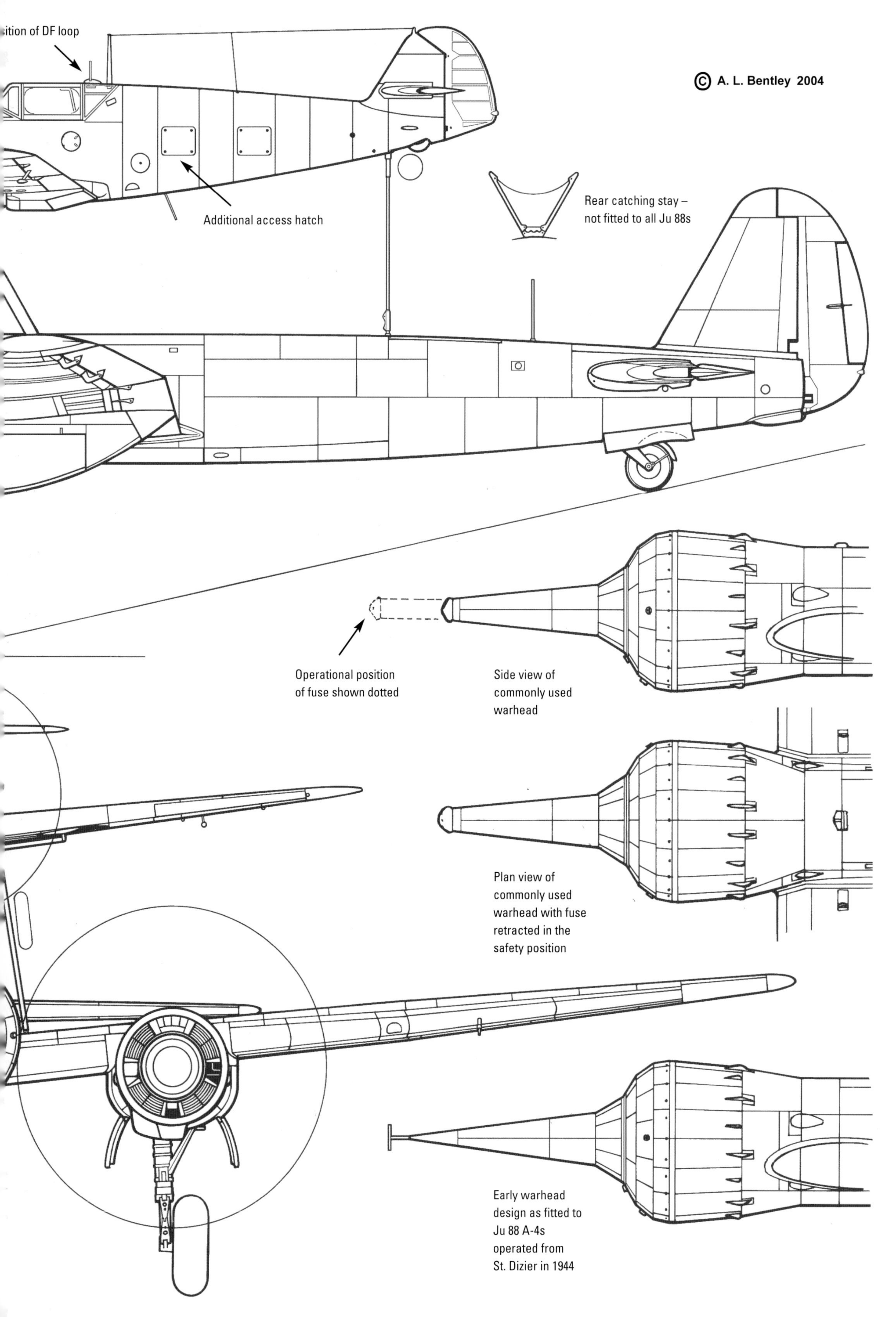
sition of DF loop
© A. L. Bentley 2004
Additional access hatch
Rear catching stay – not fitted to all Ju 88s
Operational position of fuse shown dotted
Side view of commonly used warhead
Plan view of commonly used warhead with fuse retracted in the safety position
Early warhead design as fitted to Ju 88 A-4s operated from St. Dizier in 1944

Mistel S1

Mistel combinations based upon the Ju 88 A-4 and modified Bf 109 F possibly with DB 605 engine

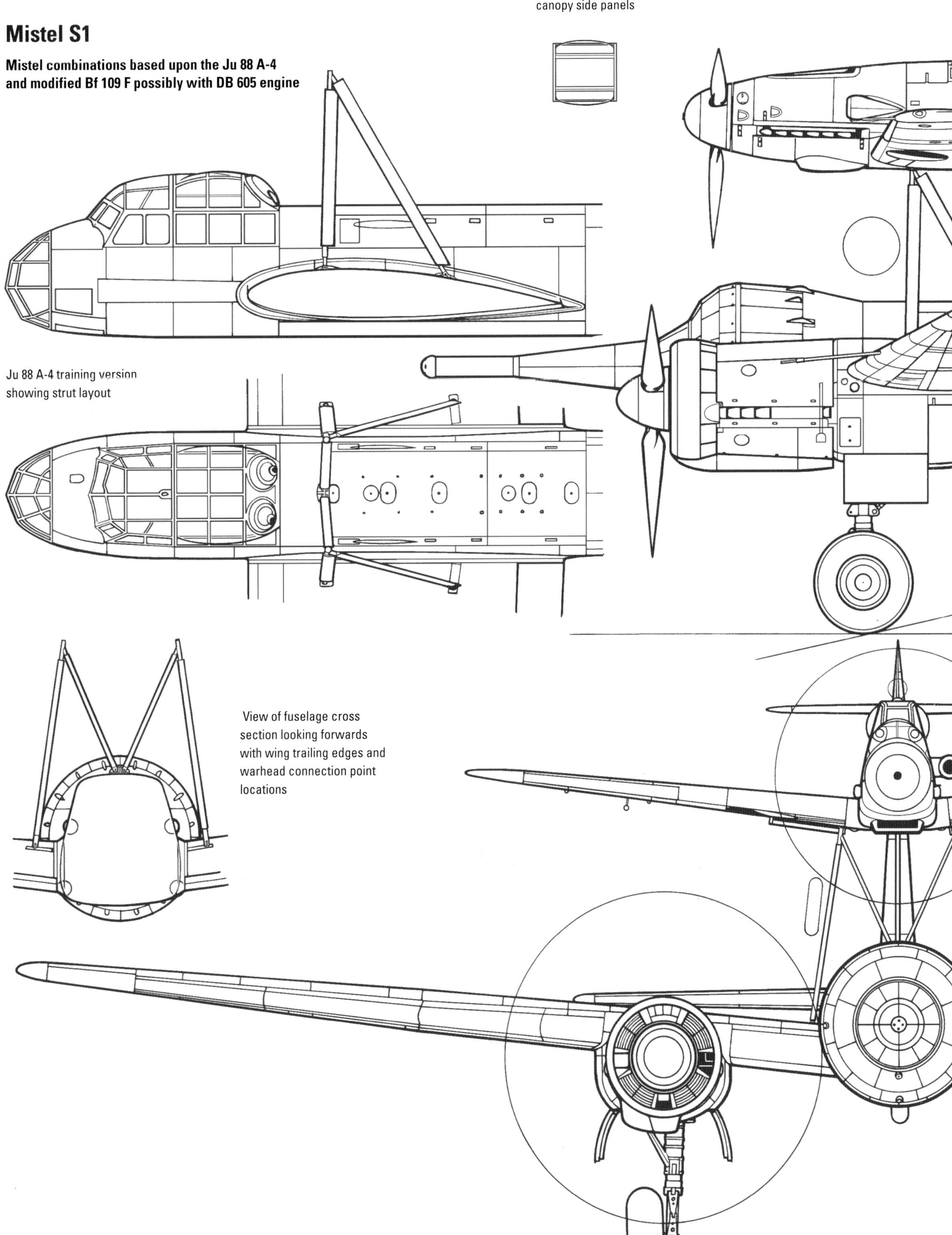

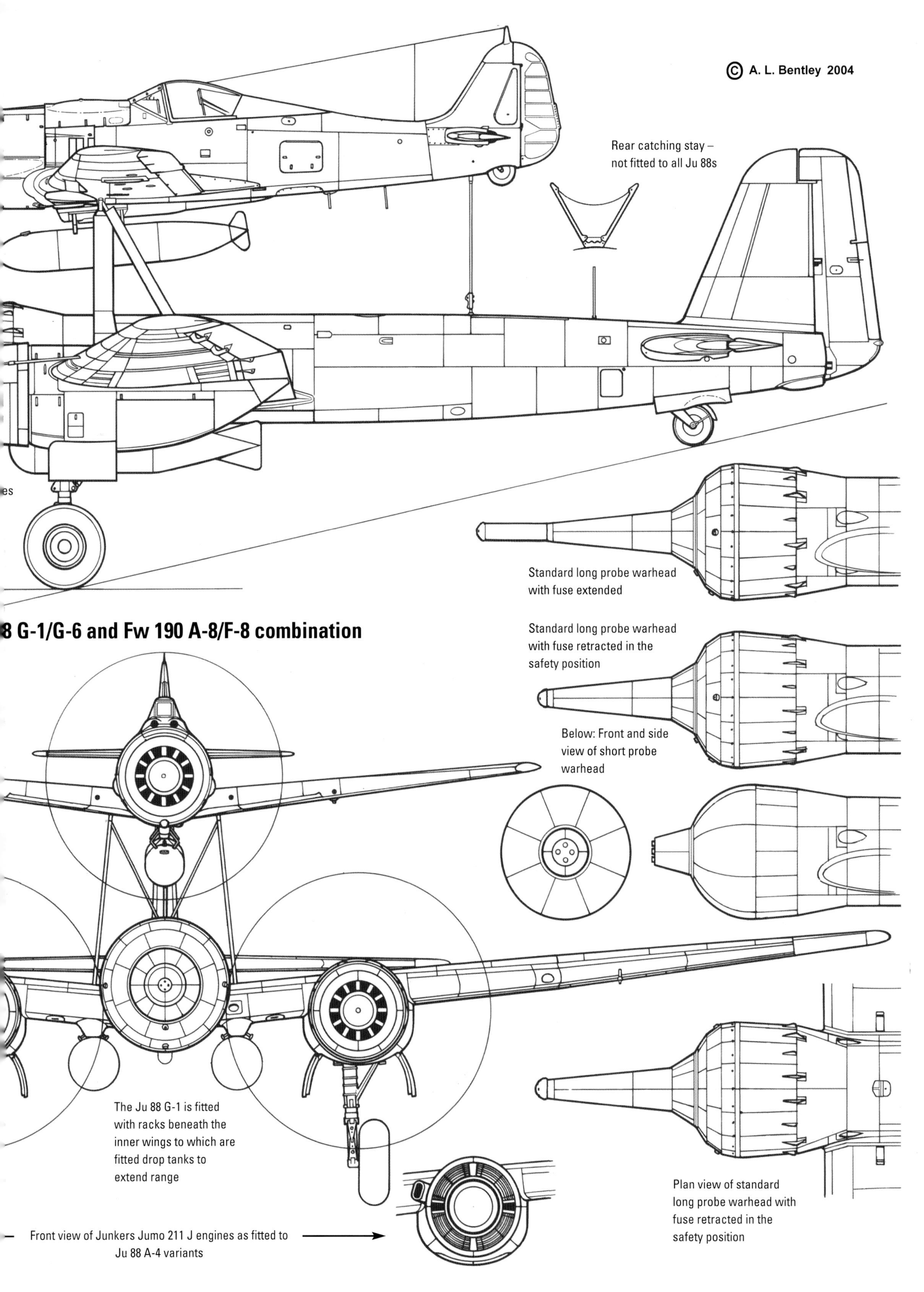
© A. L. Bentley 2004
Rear catching stay – not fitted to all Ju 88s
es
Standard long probe warhead with fuse extended
8 G-1/G-6 and Fw 190 A-8/F-8 combination
Standard long probe warhead with fuse retracted in the safety position
Below: Front and side view of short probe warhead
The Ju 88 G-1 is fitted with racks beneath the inner wings to which are fitted drop tanks to extend range
Front view of Junkers Jumo 211 J engines as fitted to Ju 88 A-4 variants
Plan view of standard long probe warhead with fuse retracted in the safety position

In what appear to be almost tranquil conditions, three operationally ready Mistel 1s, (White '1', '2' and '3'), of 2./KG 101 undergo checks at St. Dizier, France, in June 1944 prior to a mission over the Invasion Front. The machine to the far left, coded 'NA+YS'/'CN+FK', arrived at St. Dizier from Nordhausen on 18 June 1944, having been delivered by a crew comprising the acceptance pilot, Heinz Schreiber, Fw. Willi Döhring from 2./KG 101 and Fw. Bäzner, a flight engineer serving with Junkers.

Mistel 1 Messerschmitt Bf 109 F-4/Junkers Ju 88 A-4, 'White 1', 2./KG 101, St. Dizier, June 1944

Ordinary Seaman Les Gentry was a radio direction finder aboard HMS *Nith* when it was hit by a Mistel from KG 101. He tracked the German aircraft from dead astern until it was directly above the ship and remembered an 'enormous explosion'.

The 1,370 ton River Class frigate, HMS *Nith*, which was hit and severely damaged by a Mistel of KG 101 off the coast of Normandy on the night of 24 June 1944. The aircraft blew in the starboard side of the vessel, raking it with steel fragments. The ship's generator was put out of action, plunging *Nith* into darkness. Nine crew members were killed and 27 wounded.

'... lost against the land background. The larger aircraft then turned over on its back and dived straight into the sea, without showing any tendency to glide. It reached the sea in about three seconds. On striking the water it caused a terrific explosion, three miles east of the convoy. The separation of the two aircraft appeared hurried and ill-judged.'

Feldwebel Gromoll, a fighter pilot with 3./JG 301 was flying one of the Bf 109 escorts. As a POW, he later confided to a curious German paratrooper about what he saw:

'We flew escort to these aircraft; there were 20 Bf 109s to the right, left and above. At 2300 hours, we were over Rouen and from there went up to Le Havre. Bf 110s (*sic*) went on ahead to drop flares. We arrived there and the flares were hanging below us and we could see some large craft below. We were given the exact positions: *"That's a battleship, that's a cruiser; only go for the battleship and the cruiser."* Down it went. It dived and we kept our eyes open to see that there was no funny business; we fired like mad – a real diversion action. The AA started up and the lower aircraft dropped away; it disconnected a few hundred metres beforehand... the Ju 88 continued on its set course with its engines running at top speed. The pilot pulled away and the Ju 88 rushed at the battleship at a terrific speed.'

Elsewhere, another *Mistel* pilot, *Feldwebel* Saalfeld, experienced control difficulties and was forced to conduct an emergency separation. His Ju 88 also crashed into the sea. Another *Mistel,* which was apparently successfully launched at the enemy ships from a height of 245 metres, hit the sea and exploded close to HMS *Nith*, a 1,370-ton River Class frigate lying at anchor off Gold Beach.

Though originally built and launched as a frigate at Leith in February 1943 – after which she had performed as a convoy escort – *Nith* had been converted into a Brigade Headquarters Ship in February 1944. On 5 June, under the command of Lieutenant Commander D. Mansfield, she set sail for Normandy as part of the initial Overlord assault wave where she was to serve as Headquarters for 231st Infantry Brigade, which was assigned to land close to Arromanches. Upon arrival at her position, the ship, along with others in the task force, encountered fire from German shore-based batteries, but little damage was done. By 'D+1', the assault was completed and *Nith's* primary task had been accomplished. Her next assignment was to take up position in the approaches to the beach and to control incoming shipping during the 'build-up' phase on Courseulles.

Few first-hand accounts of what it was like to be on the 'receiving end' of a *Mistel* attack remain, but many years after the night of 24 June 1944, the events and their effects remain indelibly etched in the memories of survivors. Ordinary Seaman Les Gentry was a radio direction finder in HMS *Nith*; he remembers the KG 101 attack:

'Having left Southampton Water early on the evening of 5th June, we joined the main stream of ships heading for Normandy, where we dropped anchor off Gold Beach during the early hours of the 6th. Our responsibility was, as headquarters ship, to receive incoming craft and supply the necessary beaching instructions. After a few days, it seemed that, in the heavy traffic, it was difficult for incoming vessels to find the *Nith*. To overcome this, we painted the funnel and bridge structure in a bold red colour, in order to make ourselves more prominent. This may have solved one problem but brought about another, in as much that we began to receive attention from shore batteries along the coast. This caused us no harm, and in any case stopped, when a battle monitor[5] was brought near to us.'

'It became routine for us to remain at action stations from sunset to sunrise and on the 24th we closed up action stations as usual just before sunset, which would have been about 2200-2230. My action station was at the 291-Type radar set which was designed to locate aircraft as opposed to surface objects, and situated just beneath the overhang of the bridge, port side. On this particular evening the set gave trouble from the outset, and I was given permission by the bridge to close the set down and seek out the radar mechanic whose action station was in the starboard passage, possibly as fire party or stretcher bearer. As it turned out, he was extremely lucky to be taken away from that area. However, having applied his skills to the necessary repair, he asked me to try it out. On my first sweep, I had reached the bearing dead astern, when I picked up an aircraft at thirteen thousand, range closing. I reported to the bridge and was told to hold. The bearing remained steady all the way down to my last report which was: *'Target overhead, sir!'* This report was probably not heard on the bridge, as it coincided with an enormous explosion.'

Lieutenant Peter Meryon was second in command of *Nith* and from his position watched the *Mistel* as it approached the ship. He recalls:

'My action station was on the new superstructure – altered considerably to accommodate the Brigadier's 'war room' and staff accommodation – and in the open air, so I was able to observe and hear everything, though I was separated by some 100 feet from the bridge where the Captain was. I clearly remember that moonlit night, at action stations, hearing the droning of an enemy aircraft. Then I remember being aware of it aiming itself at us, then separating from the smaller aircraft above it. The aircraft continued on a descent towards us causing an enormous explosion alongside the ship.

[5] Battle monitor: a vessel smaller than a battleship and designed for coastal bombardment but much slower and therefore unlikely to be able to outrun attackers. As a result, there was a need for them to be more heavily armoured.

Afternoon summer sun casts shadows across the grass at St. Dizier as ground crew work on Mistel 1, 'White 2' of 2./KG 101, June 1944.

Mistel 1 Messerschmitt Bf 109 F-4/Junkers Ju 88 A-4, 'White 2', 2./KG 101, St. Dizier, June 1944

Lieutenant Peter Meryon was second in command of HMS *Nith*. He watched a Mistel approach the ship and remembers that the wing of the Ju 88 cut a lifeboat in half.

John Collins was attached to the personal staff of the Captain Group G.1 on board HMS *Nith* when it was struck by a Mistel off Normandy on the night of 24 June 1944. He remembered a 'dark shadow' passing overhead followed by a 'tremendous explosion'.

'Our seaboat – or, in civil terms, our lifeboat – was turned outboard at its davits "ready for an emergency" and the wing of the plunging aircraft cut the boat in half which gives some idea of how close the Ju 88 was when it hit the water.'

John Collins was a Joiner attached to the personal staff of the Captain Group G.1, the naval command set up to direct and coordinate all southbound sailings to Normandy. He had boarded *Nith* at Southampton and had been assigned sleeping quarters in the starboard passage. He recalls:

'I remember clearly the funnel and bridge being painted a "post box red" – an open invitation to any German to realise that *Nith* was more than just an escort vessel. On the night of 24 June, I was on the stern of *Nith* when there was a burst of AA fire which I believe was from the anti-aircraft cruiser *Scylla* which was some distance from our position. I started to walk towards the starboard passage and was about halfway between the stern of *Nith* and the starboard passage where I intended to take cover when I became aware of a sound which I thought to be like an underground train coming out of a tunnel into a station. I then saw this dark shadow pass over my head and almost immediately there was this tremendous explosion. The ship heeled over to port and from that moment on I have no memory of subsequent happening.'

Below the bridge, Les Gentry and his fellow shipmates prepared for the worst:

'We were ordered to "*Prepare to abandon ship*", but this was rescinded when it was realised that although the damage was down by the waterline, the ship had fortunately adopted a list to port, thereby lifting the damaged area clear of the water. The main damage occurred along the starboard passage, where nine men lost their lives and the number wounded amounted to twenty-seven.'

The *Mistel* had blown in the starboard side amidships and the entire length of the ship had been raked by steel fragments. Steam pipes in the boiler room had burst and the main generator had been put out of action. For a time *Nith* was without electricity but, working in almost complete darkness, the Chief Engine Room Artificer managed to activate the auxiliary power supply and the Chief Petty Telegraphist switched over the wireless sets to a battery supply and rigged temporary aerials to replace those that had blown down.

'I just remember the awful sight of maimed bodies, blood, flesh etc.,' recalls Peter Meryon, 'which, of course, we had to clear up after ascertaining that the ship herself was sound and not sinking.'

The impact of the *Mistel* had a profound effect on John Collins who had been about to enter the starboard passage of the vessel:

'Ever since that night, I have tried to remember what happened after the explosion, but have been unable to do so. I have had dreams and nightmares in which I see lights in the water, being on a vessel and seeing a green field on a hillside and someone saying, "That's the Isle of Wight". I do not remember returning to Southampton and going on leave to my parents' home in Oxfordshire until I was nearly there and I remember quite clearly an aircraft coming low towards me. I ran and took cover by a wall and a person said: "What did you do that for? It's only an experimental aircraft from the local Miles Aircraft company."

'I saw the doctor and told him of my loss of memory, but his response was: "You'll not get your ticket out of the Navy with that tale." I pointed out that I was in fact a volunteer and had no such wish to get out of the Navy but that I wanted to know what had happened. His reply was: "Official Secrets Act applies; you survived – isn't that enough?"'

Les Gentry:

'After the action, the ship was in a state of disarray with the loss of power; the Wardroom became a dressing station for the wounded, one of which was an ordinary seaman by the name of Salthouse, a Liverpool lad who was lying on some blankets on the deck. It was practice for officers to have a rating, usually a seaman, to act as a servant, and Salthouse was "flunky" to the navigating officer. I had gone to see how he was, when he asked if I would do him a favour. "Lofty," he said, "would you pull the blanket over my feet? I don't want the navigating officer to see that I'm wearing his socks." The thought of his concern over a pair of socks when he was lying there wounded is something that will always remain with me. The wounded were transferred to another vessel during the early hours and the dead were buried at sea at about 0700. We were then taken in tow to Cowes on the Isle of Wight by tug, where we undertook repairs in dry dock, which lasted for about four weeks, during which time we received a welcome period of leave."

Despite the severe damage inflicted upon HMS *Nith*, it was a relatively disappointing and unsatisfactory debut for the *Mistel*. Rudat and Saalfeld had been forced to jettison and the remaining pilots appear to have launched their aircraft without sufficient accuracy. Another *Mistel* is reported to have crashed on take-off at St. Dizier and one, possibly two, pilots were missing.

In a colourful account of the operation, *Oblt. Dipl.-Ing.* Lux recorded:

'At last, our ground crews begin to hear the first reports! Four pilots have landed at different airfields. The fifth is missing! There is no point in waiting; he will not return. Were they successful? Four large ships have been sunk! The *Wehrmacht's* report conceals this information; secrecy must be kept. English reports at that time spoke of aircrews who sacrificed themselves with their aircraft as they dived on their targets.'

Following the return of its Bf 109s to St. Dizier, KG 101 somewhat optimistically reported an 'attack on a battleship off Normandy.' There had apparently been 'hits on the stern.'

Upon the completion of his illumination flight, *Leutnant* Hans Altrogge returned to Montdidier and made a more measured observation:

'Three heavy cruisers and battleship, *Lorraine*, thought to have been *Nelson*, which KG 101 allegedly sank or damaged.'

In early July KG 101 is reported to have made another attack over the Bay of the Seine involving four *Mistel* again led by *Oberleutnant* Rudat and again escorted by Bf 109s from I./JG 301. A smokescreen prevented the results of their attack being observed at the time, though German reconnaissance later established that all four aircraft had apparently found targets. This is contradicted by the British Admiralty's reaction in its Weekly Intelligence Report for the week ending 7 July 1944 in which it was stated that:

> 'Attacks on shipping were made in the Seine Bay area on some nights, but with little success; whilst daylight activity against shipping off the beachhead was negligible. It had been known for some time that the Germans were experimenting with composite aircraft and these have now been reported in action against Allied ships... There is good reason to believe the penetrative force (of the warhead) is exceptionally high and that the enemy considers one hit capable of sinking a capital ship... The composite aircraft will unquestionably prove very vulnerable to fighter interception and both it and its separate Ju 88 component should be easy targets for AA defences.'

The Air Ministry took a similar view:

> 'The Ju 88 with special warhead is undoubtedly a formidable weapon if it can be brought to bear upon a suitable target. The abortive attack witnessed by the Mosquito crew, however, suggested difficulties in control which, allied to inherent vulnerability, must render success in operation extremely problematical.'

Indeed, throughout July 1944 the Allies were picking up more and more evidence of German composite activity. On 4 and 7 July, *Mistel* were seen by Allied reconnaissance aircraft at KG 101's training base at Kolberg and on 21 July, during a reconnaissance flight over Nordhausen, three composites – the greatest number so far – were seen. Three days earlier, on 18 July, one of 2./KG 101's *Mistel* was spotted in a shelter on the south side of St. Dizier airfield for the first time, just before eleven B-24s of the US Eighth Air Force dropped 31 tons of bombs onto the airfield as a target of opportunity. The *Mistel* had a lucky escape: post-strike photographs taken the following day revealed it to be undamaged and in the same position with no new craters around it.

The same day that the Americans bombed its airfield, 2./KG 101 received orders to carry out one of the last anti-shipping attacks to be ordered by IX. *Fliegerkorps* before the *Korps* moved into Holland following the withdrawal of German forces from France. The target was a French battleship anchored off the Orne Estuary. Escorted once again by fighters from I./JG 301 and with flare-dropping aircraft flying ahead, an unknown number of *Mistel* took off from St. Dizier and followed a course over Rouen and Honfleur towards the Orne. The raid was apparently unsuccessful and, to some extent, the *Luftwaffe* appears to have been duped.

For the Normandy landings to be successful, Allied planners had to establish a foothold on a coastline bristling with enemy defences *without* the help of a harbour. This problem was solved by prefabricating in Britain, an immense system of breakwaters, piers and landing stages which could be towed across the English Channel to Normandy and assembled offshore to form two complete artificial harbours. Operation 'Mulberry' became one of the most imaginative examples of war engineering ever attempted. One hundred and fifty floating steel caissons formed an outer breakwater, but in order to provide shelter for smaller craft such as landing craft and tenders, five short breakwaters, code-named 'Gooseberries', were formed from some sixty blockships including old tankers and

A Mistel lies in a blast pen on the south side of St. Dizier airfield on 17 July 1944. This photograph was taken by an Allied reconnaissance aircraft the day before St. Dizier was bombed by B-24 Liberators from the US Eighth Air Force. Note that there is already evidence of light and heavy bombing.

warships which were sunk close inshore. One of these vessels was the old French dreadnought, *Courbet*, whose engines had been removed and replaced by concrete. Moored off Sword beach in the 'Gooseberry 5' breakwater, she was deliberately festooned with an enormous Tricolour and Cross of Lorraine to give the impression of an active vessel and a small number Royal Artillery personnel remained aboard to man her anti-aircraft guns. She thus attracted several bomb and torpedo attacks by the Luftwaffe, including one by the *Mistel* of KG 101.

According to the war diary of the *Seekriegsleitung*, on the night of 25/26 July, five *Mistel* were sent out to strike against shipping in the estuary of the Orne; it was to be a disaster, with four of the composites being lost, though a direct hit was reported on a 'large vessel'. This was probably the *Courbet*.

Away from the battle front however, lack of operational success appears not to have dampened enthusiasm for the Luftwaffe's new weapon. To the contrary: by July 1944, at least one other aircraft firm was studying seriously the feasibility of constructing composite aircraft for offensive operations.

On 19 July, on the orders of the RLM, *Herr* Schöffel, a representative from the Focke-Wulf plant at Bremen journeyed to Junkers at Dessau to meet with *Flugkapitän* Karl-Heinz Kindermann, head of the company's Technical Service Liaison Office. Kindermann showed Schöffel around the Dessau plant and particularly the Ju 88 *Mistel* conversion line. Schöffel's subsequent report of 21 July 1944, '*Experience with the* Mistel *at Ifa,*[6] *Dessau*' offers an interesting insight into the *Mistel* conversion and production process at that time:

[6] Ifa = Junkers Flugzeugwerke

The old French dreadnought, *Courbet*, lies as a makeshift breakwater off Sword beach in July 1944. She is believed to have been a target for the Mistel of KG 101.

A picture taken from the 'Mistel 2' instruction manual showing the location of the auxiliary seat and handgrips beneath the Ju 88 as fitted with a warhead. The mechanic could operate the brakes of the Ju 88 in case of an emergency during taxying prior to take-off. Once the aircraft was ready for take-off, the seat would be dismantled and the mechanic would clear the area.

'No difficulties have been found during flight-testing. The paired aircraft are being delivered with the Ju 88's usual cockpit.

'The installation of the warhead at the operational base takes five hours. While moving the Ju 88 on the ground, the aircraft is fitted with a seat slung below the fuselage from where the brakes can be applied by two hand levers.

'Flight with the warhead presents no problems. In order to guarantee separation (of the upper aircraft), the rear support strut is designed to fold shortly before separation takes place. The resulting increase in the angle of incidence of the Me 109 substantially increases the lift (of that aircraft) and ensures clean separation from the Ju 88. According to the pilot, a particularly noticeable hard shock is felt at separation. Ifa is presently investigating whether the rear strut can be replaced by a simpler design.

'Care must be exercised with the mounting of the upper aircraft to ensure that no deviation to the approach to the target arises after separation because the lower aircraft will miss its target.

'All phases of the conversion of the Ju 88 were inspected. The fuselage is cut through at the position required for a new assembly joint. The forward and centre fuselage sections are fitted with new frames and four spherically-aligned joints in an extension of the fuselage mating strap. All of the fuselage equipment is removed.

'The delivery cockpit is fitted only with essential equipment in order to simplify the interface with the fuselage behind the cockpit. A second, rearward-facing seat for a flight engineer is added behind that for the pilot.

'A switch and equipment panel is fitted to the forward part of the fuselage joint. This is accessible not only from the rear seat but also from the ground after the warhead has been installed. The panel is fitted with engine starter, fuel injection pump, fuel tank transfer valve, fuel gauge, engine temperature and boost pressure gauges, propeller pitch control switch, split flap and undercarriage levers, fuse switch and stand-by compass, so that the Ju 88 can be prepared for flight from that position (i.e. from the flight engineer's position).

'The Me 109 is fitted with two throttles with explosively-separable fork end fittings on the throttle control linkage, engine revolution selection switch, turbo-supercharger pressure gauge and revolution counter, undercarriage and split flap levers, direction indicators for the three-axis gyro control unit and a switch for arming the warhead. Control inputs are provided by potentiometers.

'The structure for mounting the Me 109 consists of a forward truss comprising six struts and a simple foldable strut at the rear. The struts are made from steel tubes and have fork end fittings. The struts are faired. The electrical cables are routed inside the fairings. The connections to the fuselage and wing are made with bolts.'

Throughout August 1944, works testing continued apace at Nordhausen. Heinz Schreiber and fellow Junkers test pilots, Kuhlmann and Seibert, made more than twenty flights in *Mistel* S1s at the works. On the afternoon of the 8th, Schreiber and Kuhlmann effected their first airborne separation in Bf 109 NK+KD and Ju 88 5K+AK. More separations followed on the 9th (Bf 109 VQ+BK/Ju 88 BH+GB), the 10th (Bf 109 5T+YK/Ju 88 5K+AF) and then three in one day on 14 August (Bf 109 '24'/Ju 88 V4+SO, Bf 109 CI+MY/Ju 88 CR+CF and Bf 109 VQ+BK/Ju 88 RF+KR).

Both during flight and separation, the composite performed well and gave no problems. Schreiber told the author: 'Actually, flying the *Mistel* was nothing special. It was just a normal aircraft.'

In the light of the recent bombing raid at St. Dizier, elements of 2./KG 101 had moved to Metz-Frescaty to continue training. On 9 August, a *Mistel* S1 was 20 per cent damaged there following an emergency landing.

On the 2nd, the US Eighth Air Force made a return visit to St. Dizier. B-24 Liberators from the 448th Bomb Group dropped 36 tons of general purpose bombs across the western edge of the airfield, the south-west dispersal area and taxi-tracks. Although 13 aircraft were visible during the attack, no *Mistel* were observed and the bombing results were considered 'poor'.

Undeterred by the Allied raid, on the night of 10/11 August KG 101 launched another attack against shipping in the Bay of the Seine from St. Dizier. Once again, I./JG 301 was ordered to provide escort. The results are not known, but it was during this operation that an unexpected and extraordinary incident occurred. During the attack, one of KG 101's pilots became disorientated and began to fly north, across the English Channel. With fuel running low, the pilot decided to jettison his Ju 88 A-4 lower component, 5T+CK, and attempt to return to France.

Once separated, the Ju 88 flew on, crossed the English coast, and eventually crashed into open countryside at 2335 hrs with a 'tremendous explosion' at Slade Bottom Farm in the village of Binley near Andover, Hampshire. The force of the blast reportedly blew a man over some three miles away. Due to the open nature of the terrain, no damage occurred, though the impact created a large crater and the aircraft itself was 'smashed into small fragments.'

Luftwaffe ground crew, most likely belonging to KG 101, gather for a photograph with a civilian technician in a hangar at Burg in the early autumn of 1944. From the underwing letter visible, and from other photographs in this series, it is possible that the Ju 88 is CR+CF, an aircraft test-flown at Nordhausen on 13 and 14 August 1944 as the lower component coupled to Bf 109 CI+MY. The Ju 88 has had its cockpit section removed exposing the bulkhead in preparation for the fitting of a hollow-charge warhead.
A warhead could be fitted with relative ease by specialist Luftwaffe armourers.
To facilitate this process, four spherically-aligned quick-release bolts (the upper two of which are just visible) were fitted to the bulkhead for speedy removal of the crew compartment. The removal of the cockpit and fitting of the warhead took approximately one day and required a team of six mechanics, two armourers and a crane capable of lifting four tons.

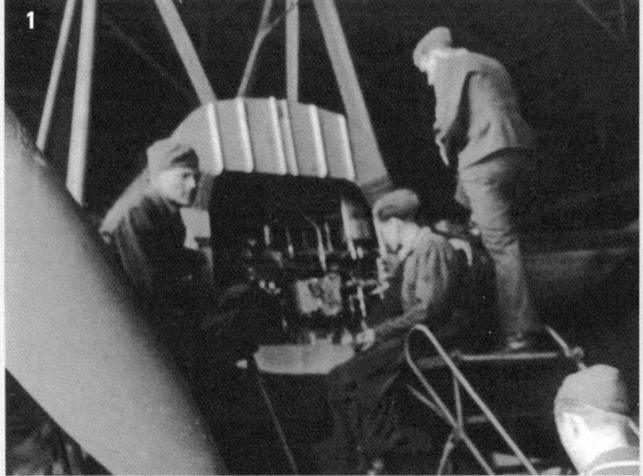

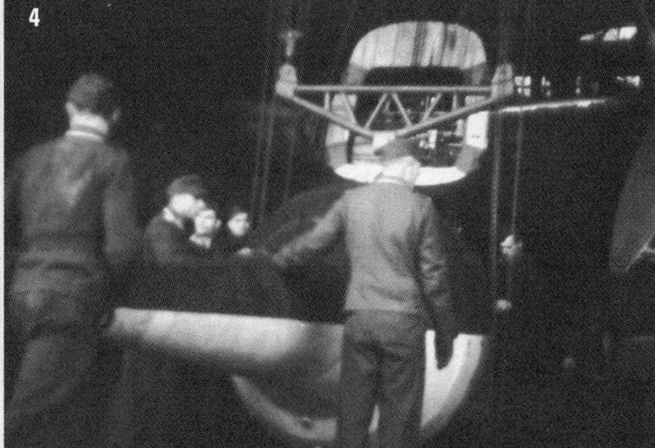

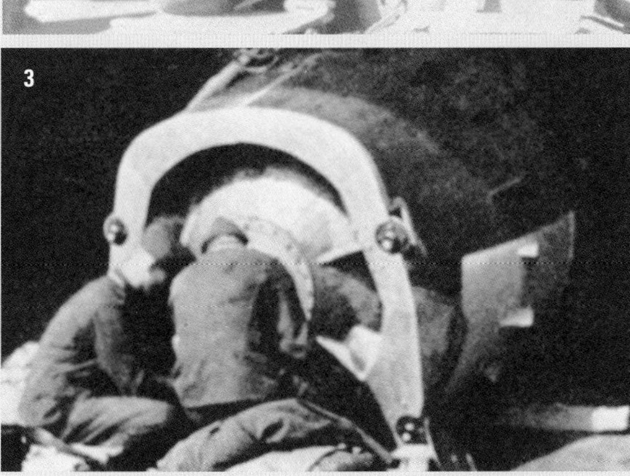

1. Ground crew prepare the bulkhead connections on the Ju 88.
2.& **3**. Armourers attend to the connections at the rear of the hollow-charge warhead.
The 1,700 kg of explosive and detonator for the main charge was placed at the rear of the warhead with a cone-shaped cavity or *Elefantenrüssel* ('Elephant's Trunk') tapering to 1.8 metres. The explosive charge comprised a mixture of 70 per cent Hexogen high explosive and 30 per cent Trinitrotoluol. Once the warhead was attached the Mistel had to be towed to its take-off position because the pilot of the fighter could not operate the brakes of the Ju 88.
4. With winch chains taut around its lifting lugs, the ground crew prepare to hoist the hollow-charge warhead towards the Ju 88 fuselage bulkhead.
5. Ground crew carefully pull the lifting chains, as the warhead leaves the ground.

Continues overleaf

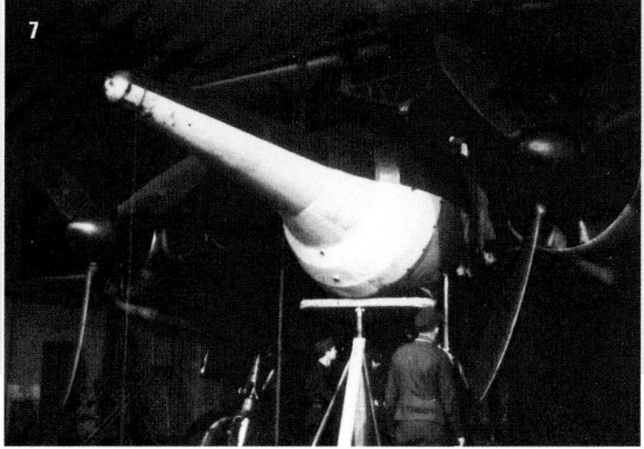

6. The massive hollow-charge warhead is hoisted towards the Ju 88 fuselage bulkhead as the lower component of the Mistel is made ready for operations. Note the underwing cross of the Bf 109 at top left of the photograph. **7**. The warhead is attached.

Despite its condition, the wrecked airframe offered British Technical Air Intelligence their first opportunity to analyse the effect and construction of a *Mistel* lower component. The shock waves of what they saw began to spread much further than the village of Binley. It was the task of F/O Constance Babington Smith, a hawk-eyed WAAF officer stationed with the Central Interpretation Unit at Medmenham, Buckinghamshire, to monitor long-term trends in German activity by studying the thousands of reconnaissance photographs taken by RAF aircraft over occupied Europe and the Reich. It was Babington Smith who had been key in spotting the launching ramps for Fi 103 flying bombs at Peenemünde in June 1943. Now, presumably from the photographs obtained from Kolberg and Nordhausen, she warned Air Intelligence about the *Mistel*. On 14 August 1944, a senior Air Intelligence officer wrote to a fellow officer:

> 'Capt. Rostow of AI2(a) informs me that in discussion with F/O Babington Smith at Medmenham, he learnt that she has serious suspicions of considerable activity by the Germans in connection with expendable aircraft. Please get in touch with her and find out the extent of her suspicions and the evidence which supports them.'

There was now a fear of yet another German terror weapon that could be fired indiscriminately at the British Isles. Sqn/Ldr. H.F. King of A.I.2(g), who had inspected the Binley *Mistel*, tried to soothe fears as best and as accurately as he could:

> 'There is no reason to believe that the fall of the aircraft near Andover was anything but fortuitous. It is known that a small number of composite aircraft carried out an anti-shipping operation off the beachhead on the night in question. The most logical explanation is that the control pilot of one of these aircraft got lost, found himself approaching the English coast, and released his lower component, leaving it to fly on inland.'

According to Allied radio intercepts, on 15 August a single, newly completed *Mistel* S1, or '*Beethoven Gerät*' as it was referred to, was delivered to St. Dizier from Hartmannshain, east of Giessen. Other *Beethoven Gerät* were ready for collection at a new assembly point at Christianstadt, approximately 15 km east of Sommerfeld in Lower Silesia. It was the first time the Allies had heard the code name '*Beethoven*'.

By mid-August 1944, German control of Normandy hung in the balance. Adolf Hitler knew he had to prevent the Allies from consolidating their hold in the area, but time was running out. *Generalfeldmarschall* von Kluge's Army Group B had failed in its critical drive on Mortain and Avranches. On the 12th, US forces captured Mortain, effectively signalling the end of any German hopes of holding back the Allied advance. Two days later, the Allies launched Operation Tractable, driving towards the nodal town of Falaise. Simultaneously, a westwards thrust was made towards Paris. On the 16th an angry *Führer* accepted that Normandy was lost. He sacked Kluge and replaced him with the more competent *Generalfeldmarschall* Model.

On 18 August, American forces reached the Seine, only 58 km from Paris. That same day, the Eighth Air Force's 3rd Bomb Division assembled a force of 116 B-17s to bomb St. Dizier, one of a range of bridge, airfield and marshalling yard targets to be struck that day.

A covert photograph of one of 2./KG 101's Mistel 1s as seen through the trees at the edge of St. Dizier airfield. The photograph was taken by a member of the French underground movement and was forwarded to London for evaluation.

SECRET A.I. No. 81522

D.D.I. (2)

Attached are photographs of a composite aircraft received from a French source. The photographs were taken at St. DIZIER. It is not known when the photographs were taken, but this was probably done in August.

For Group Captain.

A.I.1.(c)
13.9.44

A Mistel S1, Bf 109G, SK+ML/Ju 88 C-6 SC+CE, probably of KG 101, at an unidentified location, possibly Burg, in the early autumn of 1944. The Bf 109 was test-flown by the Junkers acceptance pilot Heinz Schreiber at Nordhausen on 17 August 1944, following which he flew it attached to the Ju 88 on 23, 26 (twice) and 29 August 1944 with Oblt. Dipl.-Ing. Horst-Dieter Lux at the controls of the bomber. Lux had been assigned to Junkers to oversee delivery of Mistel to KG 101 and later to KG 200 and KG(J) 30.

Just before 1500 hrs, the Flying Fortresses made their bomb run over the airfield at 14,000 ft scoring hits on hangars to the north west (which were destroyed) and dispersal areas and blast shelters to the south. The runway and taxiways were also hit and damaged. Amongst the 36 aircraft observed on the ground were five *Mistel*. At least ten of these 36 aircraft were thought to have been damaged.

Escort for the bombers was provided by 50 P-51 Mustangs from the 359th Fighter Group led by Major Niven K. Cranfill, which strafed the field between the individual Combat Wings' bomb runs. 'Clobbered St Dizier A/D,' Cranfill wrote, 'N, NW, NE, and SW corners, hangars, ammo or fuel dump, landing ground all plastered. Bomber formation excellent, re-assembly after target excellent... whole B-17 show admirable, easy to cover... no flak first pass, intense MG fire second pass. Left bombers 1634 at 12,000...'

The heavily damaged airfield was bombed again the next day by medium bombers from the US Ninth Air Force and a decision was made to pull back the elements of KG 101 at St. Dizier to Rhein-Main from where training at least could be continued.

With St. Dizier evacuated, Horst-Dieter Lux now returned to Nordhausen and, for the remainder of August, assisted Heinz Schreiber in making test flights on several newly completed *Mistel*, effecting a number of successful airborne separations.

By 24 August, most of the newly redesignated *Einsatzgruppe*/KG 101 was established at Rhein-Main, though the unit continued to carry out some training at Kolberg. Two days later, on the 26th, a *Mistel* S1, Bf 109 PH+IC/Ju 88 5K+AF, was ferried by a new crew from 3./KG 101 from Nordhausen to Biblis, an airfield east of the Rhine, between Darmstadt and Mannheim, ready for operations. *Unteroffizier* Kollecker was at the controls of the Bf 109, while *Unteroffizier* Conrad and *Oberfeldwebel* Klein manned the Ju 88. This *Mistel* had first flown eleven days earlier at Nordhausen, when Heinz Schreiber and Max Kuhlmann had made a test flight, followed by final check-out on the morning of the 26th prior to 3./KG 101 taking delivery.

Little was escaping Allied eyes, and it is probable that this was one of at least three *Mistel* spotted by F-5s of the US 7th Photographic Group when it reconnoitred Biblis.

Left: 'Clobbered St. Dizier A/D' was how the commander of an American fighter group described a mission on 18 August 1944. This strike photograph shows the effects of the US Eighth Air Force raid on 2./KG 101's base. The Ninth Air Force bombed the airfield the following day forcing the Mistel unit to withdraw.

Meanwhile, a number of former bomber pilots continued to join the *Einsatzgruppe*/KG 101 and amongst the recent intake was a young officer named *Leutnant* Balduin Pauli.

Balduin Pauli was born in München in 1923. Having completed his education at a boarding school in Landsberg/Lech he, like many other young men of the time, was keen to volunteer for war service. He recalls:

> 'When war broke out in September 1939, though we all wanted to volunteer we were refused on account of our young age. Furthermore, my father did not agree with my ambitions and I had to promise him that, if necessary, I would complete my school-leaving exam after the war! My father and a good friend of his, a *Major* with the *Luftgaukommando* in München, obviously had it in mind to prevent me from my intentions, but on 20 June 1940

Balduin Pauli photographed during his training with the Verbandsführerschule der Kamppflieger at Tours in early 1943.

Right: Taken whilst with the Verbandsführerschule der Kamppflieger at Tours in France in early 1943, Balduin Pauli (far left) lines up for a snapshot with his radio operator and observer. Pauli was later posted to 2./KG 101 and first flew the Mistel in August 1944.

I was called up to go through the tough basic training with the *Arbeitsdienst* (Labour Service) in Mittenwald for three months. Then, on 1 October 1940, I was drafted to *Fliegerausbildungsregiment* 43 at Kaufbeuren.

'At Kaufbeuren, I completed three months basic training and was then transferred to the *Fluganwärterschule* at Eger in the Sudetenland. In the spring of 1941 I was transferred again, this time to the *Flugzeugführerschule* A/B at Crailsheim, near Stuttgart, where I trained to be a pilot on various training aircraft. Within our cadre, I held a kind of position of trust, being an aide to our flight instructor.

'Due to my personal record and good performance in aviation, I was put forward for officer training in the Luftwaffe. I was honoured and agreed to comply, since refusal on my part would have been tantamount to being a "public enemy" and I would have had to face reprisals.'

'In the spring of 1942, I was transferred to the *Kriegsschule* at Fürstenfeldbruck for a further three months training before returning to Crailsheim. Then, in the summer, I was assigned to the *Kriegsschule* at Berlin-Gatow for completion of my officer training. Eventually, in January 1943, I was posted to the *Verbandsführerschule der Kamppflieger* at Tours in France to undergo operational training on bombers. [Author note: this unit was known as 3.(Erg.)/KG 60 to 31 January 1943 and as the VFS KG 101] In particular, we practised bombing methods and low-level flying predominantly on the Ju 88, but also with the Ju 87, Ju 52 and He 111. There were also several weeks of blind flying at Wesendorf. Shortly after that, in August 1943, with Mussolini's downfall and "revolution" taking place in Italy, we were formed up into a battle group known as *Gefechtsverband Sigl*. Our objective was to fly bombing missions over the Brenner, but we were actually sent to Udine to fly bombing raids in the Ju 88 against Tito's partisans before returning to Tours in October. In February

Right and opposite page: Luftwaffe personnel inspect Mistel S1, Bf 109 G, SK+ML/Ju 88 C-6, SC+CE. The man standing on the wing root of the Bf 109 has reached his position by using the access ladder just visible on the other side of the aircraft. Note the Reparaturwerkstatt (RW – works conversion number) '16', which has been crudely applied to the Balkenkreuz of the Bf 109.

Mistel S1 Messerschmitt Bf 109 G/ Junkers Ju 88 C-6, KG 101, autumn 1944

Friedrich-Karl Gottgetreu (far left) joined 2./KG 101 at Kolberg in late 1944 having undergone a fighter conversion course on the Bf 109 G-6. He considered the Mistel to have been a 'technically and tactically able aircraft'. He is seen here in Hungary whilst with 11./KG 2 during the summer of 1944.

1944, our special unit was placed on the strength of KG 54 and through to March 1944, I flew several missions over southern England and London, during which we attacked barracks and training camps. Then I returned to Tours.'

In mid-April 1944, Pauli was based at St. Dizier flying the Ju 88 S-3, until in early June, on orders from the IX.*Fliegerkorps*, he was posted to undergo fighter training at Burg. In June and July he flew both the Bf 109 and Fw 190 on training and familiarisation flights from Burg to St. Dizier. Then, on the night of 10 August 1944, he made his first flight in a *Mistel* with *Feldwebel* Degering of 2./KG 101 when he ferried a composite from Burg to St. Dizier. He did not fly the composite again until the evening of 13 September, when he undertook a training flight in a *Mistel* from Burg to Rhein-Main.

Also joining the *Einsatzgruppe*/KG 101 at Rhein-Main at this time was another former bomber pilot, *Oberleutnant* Friedrich-Karl Gottgetreu. Gottgetreu had originally served as a long-range reconnaissance pilot with *Fernaufklärungsgruppe* 101 at Perleberg before moving to the 3./*Fernaufklärungsgruppe* at Saloniki-Sedes followed by a tour of duty in Russia with 2.(F)/11. Gottgetreu recalls the way he found himself training for the *Mistel*:

> 'After a lengthy bout of jaundice acquired in Russia, I was transferred to 12./KG 51 with whom I received bomber training on the Ju 88 at Hildesheim and Wiener-Neustadt. However during the spring of 1944 KG 51 began to convert to the Me 410 at Hildesheim and since I wanted to stay on the Ju 88 I asked for a transfer to KG 2. This was granted and at the end of March 1944, I joined 11./KG 2 at Ferihegy in Hungary flying the Ju 188. IV./KG 2 flew a few missions over Rumania but was slated to be disbanded in September 1944. Most crews were transferred to other *Kampfgeschwader* and I found myself a member of 2./*Einsatzgruppe* 101, which a little later became 2./KG 101.'

Rather unexpectedly, Gottgetreu was first assigned to 3./*Jagdgruppe Ost* at Liegnitz for a 14-day conversion course onto the Bf 109 G-6 fighter. Upon completion of the course, he was sent to Kolberg where he reported to *Hauptmann* Rudat, still unaware of what was to come.

> 'Up to this time I had only the vaguest idea of what it was all about, since the existence of the unit was supposed to be secret. When I first saw the *Mistel* in Kolberg inside a hangar I was very impressed with the concept of a 'flying bomb'. I just stood there and stared at it in awe and tried to visualise how it would be to fly one of the things. *Hauptmann* Rudat was my *Staffelkapitän* while *Leutnant* Pauli was his adjutant. Conditions at Kolberg were very relaxed; an almost tranquil atmosphere reigned during my stay there. I even had my wife visit me there for a week, sharing my quarters on the base.
>
> 'I considered the *Mistel* to be a technically and tactically able aircraft, but in retrospect, I have to admit that its performance left a lot to be desired. Its qualities lay in the enormous destructive power of the warhead and in the

By means of a four-ton crane, a Bf 109 fighter is carefully hoisted towards a Ju 88. Note the tip of the warhead fitted to the Ju 88. Note also the mix of call sign code letters (CI) and tactical numbers (149), the latter probably used by the aircraft's previous operator, probably a training unit. Note also the Reparaturwerkstatt (RW – works conversion number) '8' applied to the fuselage and underwing crosses of the fighter.

The Bf 109 has been lowered onto the support struts fitted to the Ju 88 and the connections are secured by Luftwaffe personnel under the supervision of a civilian technician. Note the fuselage and underwing numbers and the blown canopy on the Bf 109.

Four Mistel are visible in this Allied aerial reconnaissance photograph taken over Nordhausen during the second week of September 1944.

upper component becoming an operational fighter after separation. The weakness lay in its weight, which really required smooth concrete runways for take-off, and its easy exposure to enemy action on account of it being not very manoeuvrable in the air.

'Conversion to the *Mistel* consisted first of all of a few familiarisation flights with the Bf 109 F, then up to about six flights at the controls of the lower component of the S1 – a Ju 88 A-4 – with the Bf 109 separating each time. Finally, you flew the S1 from the top component, a very tricky task at first. Again, it took a few flights to get used to the height above ground during take-off, the separation in flight being uneventful. Flight training was interspersed with ground school, dealing mostly with Bf 109 F cockpit operations while attached to the Ju 88 A-4.

'Following conversion training at Kolberg, I was transferred to 1./KG 101 at Rhein-Main, from where we were supposed to fly missions to the Invasion coast. We were quartered with local civilians around the airfield and driven daily to the old tower to await orders. I cannot remember too much of my time there, but one thing sticks in my mind; there was always talk about targets on the French coast, especially ships. We were told that one pilot, a *Feldwebel*, had sunk the French battleship *Courbet* on a previous mission over the Invasion area. But I never got around to flying the *Mistel* with the warhead attached.

'There were some *Mistel* under camouflage in the woods surrounding the airfield, but after waiting for two months with no action whatsoever, I asked for and got a transfer to the *Reichsverteidigung*. My posting was with II./JG 107 in Bad Vöslau in Austria and later with I./JG 108 in Müncheberg, flying the Bf 109 G-6 for which I had been trained.'

The inactivity described by Gottgetreu is given credence by Allied radio intercepts which, on 28 August, picked up an unspecified Luftwaffe command issuing orders to disband '*Einsatzgruppe* 101'. However, X.*Fliegerkorps* quickly countered this order by requesting it be delayed until 'the four remaining composite aircraft still on hand' had been launched on a mission planned for the night of 1 September in conjunction with *Sonderverband Einhorn*, a semi-autonomous unit formed from 2./KG 200 for the purpose of attacking ships with Fw 190s carrying 1,100 kg bombs.

There is little evidence to suggest such a mission took place, though in similar circumstances to those which occurred at Binley on the night of 10/11 August, two more *Mistel* lower components crossed the English coast on the night of 1 September, again wildly off course, coming down at locations some 150 miles apart. The first crashed at Warsop, north of Mansfield in Nottinghamshire at 2330 hrs, the explosion spreading debris over a quarter of a mile. The second blew open a crater 12 feet deep and 40 feet across at Hothfield, near Ashford in Kent, fifteen minutes later. The most likely probability is that these had been intended for shipping targets off the coast of France.

August gave way to September 1944 and the start of a wet, dismal autumn, the troops and armour of Montgomery's 21st Army Group advanced steadily across north-east France and Belgium and were closing on the port of Antwerp. Hitler had recognised its importance: 'It must be ensured,' he said, 'that the Allies cannot use the harbour for a long time.'

By defending the Scheldt, the *Führer* wanted to force the Allies to rely on long lines of communication, stretching as far back as Normandy and to signal that there would be no easy push into The Netherlands. On 5 September, with the US First Army driving towards the German border, the recently reappointed Commander-in-Chief West, *Generalfeldmarschall* von Rundstedt, signalled his troops: 'Soldiers of the Western Front! I expect you to defend Germany's sacred soil to the very last!'

In early September, the *Ritterkreuzträger* and bomber 'ace', *Oberst* Joachim Helbig was ordered to establish a new tactical air command, *Gefechtsverband Helbig*, with the objective of supporting German ground operations along the Reich's frontier with Belgium and The Netherlands. Of crucial importance was the destruction of potential key Allied crossing points over the Maas, the Waal and the Rhine as well as the continual harassment of enemy troops, armoured columns and communications centres. With a command post set up near Köln, Helbig was assigned the core units of LG 1, the Ju 88-equipped bomber unit he had commanded in Italy and Normandy and of which he

Ground crew appear as ghostly silhouettes in this photograph of a completed Mistel. Note the warhead has been attached, in all likelihood for training purposes.

was still *Kommodore*; NSG 2, a night ground attack *Gruppe* equipped with Ju 87s; and *Kommando Schenk*, a unit that had been carrying out limited bomber operations with the Me 262 in France and Belgium. In addition, according to the war diary of *Luftflotte* 3, on 7 September 1944 the 'remaining units of *Einsatzgruppe* 101' were also ordered to operate with *Gefechtsverband Helbig*.

On the morning of 13 September, *Luftflotte* 3 ordered 'all available' *Mistel* into action for an operation over the Albert Canal that evening. The target was to be a point near Beeringen, where armour from the British XXX Corps was crossing the Canal to threaten elements of *Kampfgruppe Chill*, a force assembled by *Generalleutnant* Kurt Chill who had pulled out of France in late August with the remains of three infantry divisions. However, it seems, for reasons so far unknown, that '*Einsatzgruppe* 101' did not deploy on this occasion and the British pushed on with their advance. Control of the *Mistel* unit was transferred from *Gefechtsverband Helbig* under whom, it seems, the composites had achieved little if anything and was passed to the direct guidance of *Luftflotte* 3.

Two days later, the US 7th Photographic Group once again flew over Biblis and photographed at least four *Mistel* on the airfield. Meanwhile, at Nordhausen, Heinz Schreiber and Horst-Dieter Lux continued to test newly assembled composites.

What was effectively to be the swansong of *Mistel* operations on the Western Front occurred just under two weeks later when '*Einsatzgruppe* 101' was ordered to make an attack on the Nijmegen Bridges.

In an unusually headstrong move, Montgomery had successfully persuaded Eisenhower that, under his control, the Allied Airborne Army could mount an air-ground thrust across the Rhine to form the spearhead of an advance into the German plain. Under the code name Operation Market Garden, the US 82nd and 101st Airborne Divisions would seize the Nijmegen and Eindhoven bridges respectively, whilst the British 1st Airborne Division would take the bridge at Arnhem. The disaster which befell British paratroopers at Arnhem has been well recorded, but for the American force, the capture of the Nijmegen bridge on 20 September, with the assistance of the British Guards Armoured Division, went relatively well.

The Luftwaffe then launched intermittent but determined attacks to destroy the lost bridge. On 27 September, under the coordination of *Gefechtsverband Hallensleben*, (Helbig had been wounded earlier in the month and replaced by *Oberstleutnant* Rudolf von Hallensleben, the *Kommodore* of KG 2), Fw 190s of III./KG 51 attacked bridges and roads leading into Nijmegen from the south while Ju 87s from NSG 2 bombed troops in the same area.

That night, four *Mistel* took off from Rhein-Main together with eight Ju 88 S bombers which had been seconded to *Einsatzgruppe* 101. One *Mistel* and two Ju 88s were forced to break off their attack and another *Mistel* went missing. The two remaining composites that were reportedly launched at the bridge missed the target.

So ended the *Einsatzgruppe's* brief and disappointing period of operations with the *Mistel*. Within days the unit was redesignated.

In an ardent conclusion to this somewhat unspectacular chapter of Luftwaffe accomplishment, Balduin Pauli, whose involvement with the *Mistel* would continue until the end of the war, recorded:

> 'The invasion could have been repulsed with the *Mistel*. Attacks with 400 to 500 *Mistel* should have been made on 6 June 1944. Germany could have fielded 500 to 1,000 old bombers – Ju 88s and He 111s – and the same number of pilots who were willing to fight. Hitler could then have withdrawn 3.5 million soldiers from the Western Front and thrown them at the Russians in the east to force them to call a ceasefire. Germany would then not have been forced to accept unconditional surrender. But Göring was a bungler; nobody could have been held back with just four *Mistel*.'

Mistel 1, Bf 109 CI+MY/Ju 88 CR+CF, is readied for operations, almost certainly at Burg, early autumn 1944. This is probably the same aircraft as seen in the photographs on page 77. Note the commom 'CI' code letters on the Bf 109, the underwing code letter 'R' on the Ju 88 and the location of the Reparaturwerkstatt (RW) on the Bf 109's fuselage Balkenkreuz. This Mistel 1 was flown by acceptance pilots Heinz Schreiber (inset) and Seibert at Nordhausen on 13 and 14 August 1944.

'HOW THE HELL AM I GOING TO HANDLE THIS MONSTER?'

OPERATIONS IN THE WEST 1944 : PHASE TWO

Final pre-flight checks are conducted to Mistel 1s at Burg, late 1944. These Huckepack (piggybacks) belong to either III./KG 66 or the unit into which it was soon redesignated, II./KG 200. According to former Mistel pilots, the generally poor quality of photographs showing operational machines is largely attributable to the fact that Luftwaffe personnel were threatened with court martial or even death if they were seen taking pictures of what was classified as a 'secret weapon'.

IN late September 1944, the 2. and 5.*Staffeln* of *Einsatzgruppe*/KG 101 were redesignated as 9. and 8./KG 66 respectively. Following its withdrawal from France, and like several other Luftwaffe bomber *Gruppen* based on the Western Front at this time, the unit entered a period of relative redundancy. Indeed, with the partial exception of anti-shipping units, a creeping disintegration of the German bomber force had been underway for most of that year. At this time, the priority facing the Luftwaffe was to get as many fighters into the air as possible to counter the Allied bomber offensive and consequently, resources, both in terms of training and aircraft were being channelled in that direction as a matter of necessity and urgency. During the first nine months of 1944, at least 25 bomber units had been disbanded, of which 80 per cent had been axed between July and September. Of the few remaining, activity centred on sporadic torpedo operations from Norway (KG 26), mining flights (LG 1), air-launched flying bomb operations against the British Isles (KG 53) and some sorties in the east (KG 4).

Paradoxically, KG 66 whose first *Gruppe* had operated over the Western Front with Ju 88s and Ju 188s as a *Zielfinder* (target illumination), electronic jamming and *Pfadfinder* ('pathfinder') unit during 1943-1944, was expanded with the creation of III./KG 66, which was to comprise 7. *Staffel* as a *Zielfinder* unit under *Oberleutnant* Pilz; 8. *Staffel* as an operational *Mistel* unit; and 9. *Staffel* based at Kolberg under Horst Rudat as an *Ergänzungsstaffel*. By 2 October 1944, *Luftflottenkommando West* was reporting that III./KG 66 was 'equipping and organising' with the *Mistel* at Burg near Magdeburg, aircrew and ground personnel being drawn from IV./KG 101 and a miscellany of other units. The *Gruppe* reported 15 *Mistel* on strength of which ten were serviceable. It is believed that contact between the two *Gruppen* of KG 66 was minimal if not non-existent, neither knowing of the other's location or operations.[1]

Hauptmann Kurt Capesius, Kommandeur of III./KG 66.

The new *Gruppe's* commanding officer was *Hauptmann* Kurt Capesius. Born in February 1919, Capesius was an Austrian bomber pilot who had flown missions over England with 9./KG 51 in the summer of 1940. On two occasions his Ju 88 was attacked by fighters but he managed to return his damaged bomber to the French coast. He then served successively in the Balkans and on the Eastern Front as *Staffelkapitän* of 10., 6. and 9./KG 51 between 1941 and 1942. He was awarded the *Deutsches Kreuz* in Gold on 7 December 1942 while an *Oberleutnant* with 9. *Staffel*, and was then appointed *Staffelkapitän* of 2./KG 101 in February of the following year. In May 1944, he served under *Generalmajor* Peltz on the staff of the IX. *Fliegerkorps* until August when he took over *Einsatzgruppe*/KG 101. His command of III./KG 66 became effective at the beginning of October 1944.

According to surviving records, the *Gruppe's* first attempt at operations took place on 3 October. In atrocious weather in the late afternoon five Bf 109 F-4/Ju 88 *Mistel* 1 took off from Burg to attack the Nijmegen bridge at

[1] According to correspondence and interviews conducted by Dutch researcher Marcel van Heijkop with former members of I./KG 66, there are no recollections of any contact with III./KG 66.

A convoy of British troops and armour rolls past a shot-up German transport close to the Nijmegen road bridge in Holland in late September 1944. The bridge was assigned as a target for five Mistel of III./KG 66 on 3 October 1944. The mission proved a disaster. Three composites crashed due to poor weather and one of the remaining two was shot down by Allied fighters.

Oberleutnant Balduin Pauli, formerly Staffelkapitän of 8./KG 66, was appointed to command 6./KG 200 which had been tasked with the operational deployment of the Mistel.

dusk led by *Leutnant* Balduin Pauli of 7./KG 66 who acted as a pathfinder, flying in a Bf 109 which left Burg at 1725 hrs. However, despite the presence of Pauli, events were to prove disastrous: in worsening conditions three of the composites went down in the forested hills of the Teutoburger Wald in the Bielefeld area. *Oberleutnant* Karl-Horst Polster and *Unteroffizier* Friedrich Scheffler crashed near Dissen, while *Unteroffizier* Paul Baranski separated his *Mistel*, his Bf 109 crashing into the Hollandskopf, a mountain near Borgholzhausen. The Ju 88 flew into a brickworks in Borgholzhausen but did not explode. The two remaining composites were unable to locate the target and their pilots are believed to have been forced to jettison their Ju 88s. One of the pilots, *Feldwebel* Franz Heckmann, was later recorded as lost when he was shot down by Allied fighters in his Bf 109 F-4 over the southern Netherlands, though it is not known for certain whether this was prior to jettison or not.

Three days later, possibly as a result of the loss of *Oberleutnant* Polster, *Hauptmann* Capesius appointed *Leutnant* Pauli as *Staffelführer* of 8./KG 66. However, Pauli's experience with the *Mistel* had, so far, been limited to a number of ferrying flights during the previous month and for the next few days he undertook a series of training and ferrying flights in *Mistel* between Burg and Altengrabow, which was used as a collection and storage field for composites being delivered from Nordhausen. By 10 October, the establishment of III./KG 66 was complete. Three days later, the *Gruppe* reported ten serviceable Ju 88s on strength.

An indication of how the Luftwaffe intended to use the *Mistel* during the impending Ardennes counter-offensive is given in a top secret document issued by *Reichsmarschall* Göring on 14 November 1944 and addressed to senior air commanders on the Western Front. Hitler planned to launch three armies along a 100 kilometre front from Monschau to Echternach which would thrust through the heavily-forested hill country of the Ardennes to cross the Meuse and take the vital port of Antwerp. In embarking upon such an audacious attack, the *Führer* was gambling that he could drive an armoured wedge between the American and British forces now advancing across north-west Europe and trap substantial American forces around Aachen to eliminate the threat posed to the Ruhr. A necessary prerequisite for success, however, would be offensive air support. In his '*Instructions for Preparation and Conduct of German Luftwaffe Operations for the Army Attack in the West*', Göring ordered that 3. *Fliegerdivision* should deploy,

> '... bomber and night ground-attack aircraft against reinforcements and reserves, especially at nodal points of communications. III./KG 66 (*Mistel*) and *Einhorn Staffel*[2] against important objectives such as bridges on flanks.'

In the meantime, training for such planned operations continued throughout November 1944, albeit sporadically. At Kolberg *Unteroffizier* Karl Müller joined Horst Rudat's 9./KG 66 from the *Jagdfliegerschule* at Stolp-Reiz on the Baltic Coast where he had trained on the Bf 109. Following a series of eight familiarisation flights in a *Mistel* S1, Müller flew a Bf 109 from Kolberg to Nordhausen, via Prenzlau and Neuruppin which took three days, where he formed part of a crew that would ferry a newly completed composite to III./KG 66's base at Burg.

Among the pilots assigned to convert to the *Mistel* were several experienced former bomber crewmen and blind-flying instructors: *Feldwebel* Toni Grögel for example, had qualified as a blind-flying instructor in Austria and then later flown combat operations with KG 6 and KG 100 during 1944 before being assigned to a fighter conversion course at Liegnitz in September of that year. In November, he was transferred to III./KG 66 at Burg and by mid-November was training with Balduin Pauli in a Ju 88 G-1 ready for *Mistel* operations.

Feldwebel Rudi Riedl was another former blind-flying instructor who was considered qualified and experienced enough to tackle the peculiarities of the composite bomber. A native of the Sudetenland, 24-year-old Riedl had wanted to fly since he was a small boy, as he recalls:

> 'As a little boy I "flew" from the boughs of a birch tree which swayed in the wind not far from my grandmother's home. It was a dream. My uncle had flown as a pilot in the Austro-Hungarian air force on the Eastern Front during the First World War and his life as a pilot had long interested me. In 1938, my stepfather, who owned a guesthouse, was sent to Dachau by the Nazis because of his opposing political views. I was given two choices: join the Army (or the Air Force) or go to Dachau as well. Every Monday and Thursday I had to report to the local Gestapo. Fortunately however, because of my uncle's influence, I was able to join the Luftwaffe as a trainee mechanic.'

Riedl qualified as a mechanic in 1938 and was then posted to *Stukageschwader* 77 based at Schweinfurt. He served with the *Stuka* unit during the subsequent Polish and French campaigns of 1939 and 1940 before commencing flying training as an *Unteroffizier* at the *Flugzeugführerschule* A/B 7 at Plauen where he trained on He 111s, Ju 86s, Do 17s and Ju 52s. In September 1941 he was transferred to *Flugzeugführerschule* (C) 9 at Pretzsch, north-west of Torgau on the Elbe, where he trained as a *Blindfluglehrer* (blind-flying instructor). In December 1942, whilst at *Blindflugschule* 1 at Waldpolenz/Brandis, he qualified to instruct on Ju 52s, Ju 86s and Ju 88s.

At the beginning of 1943, Riedl was promoted to *Feldwebel* and returned to Pretzsch to the renamed *Flugzeugführerschule* B9 where he served as an instructor

[2] 'Einhorn Staffel': A reference to *Sonderverband* (or *Sonderstaffel*) *Einhorn*, initially a semi-autonomous fighter-bomber unit equipped with Fw 190s fitted out to carry ultra-heavy (1,800 kg) bombs for use against bridge targets etc. Later redesignated 13./KG 200.

Above and right: Two views of a Mistel 1 dispersed in trees at Burg in late 1944-early 1945. These pictures show to advantage the 'Elefantenrüssel' ('Elephant's Trunk') warhead which measured 1.8 metres in length.

Feldwebel Rudi Riedl was a blind-flying instructor who was assigned to fly the Mistel in late 1944 with 6./KG 200. His first impression of the composite was as a 'monster'. He is seen here earlier in the war at the controls of a Dornier Do 17 whilst with the Flugzeugführerschule A/B 7 at Plauen.

Left: This operationally 'live' Mistel 1 crash-landed moments after take-off at Burg and its landing gear collapsed under the weight. Note how the support struts have disintegrated and the Bf 109's propeller blades have buckled from impacting with the Ju 88 lower component. Fortunately, the warhead has remained intact.

until June 1944 when the school was disbanded due to lack of fuel. Like Karl Müller, he was posted to the *Jagdfliegerschule* at Stolp-Reitz and received fighter conversion training on the Bf 109 G-12 and the Fw 190. The training was specialist from the point of view that it concentrated on attacking pinpoint targets. This was done by marking large crosses in sand and gravel pits at which pilots aimed, though no form of bomb could be spared to aid this training. Shortly afterwards, and along with nine other former instructors from *Flugzeugführerschule* B9, he was despatched by train to Kolberg for training on the *Mistel*. Arriving at Kolberg, Riedl's first encounter with the composite left him awestruck:

> 'When I saw my first *Mistel*, which was a training variant, I thought, "How the hell am I going to handle this monster?" I had to sit in the cockpit for a long time to get a feel for the machine, to understand how it worked and to come to terms with how high up I was. It's a very unusual feeling to be sitting six metres above the ground! Eventually however, after having checked out the instrumentation and controls, I began to realise that perhaps it was not going to be so difficult after all. But when I later saw the operational variant with that warhead mounted I was absolutely astounded! I thought, "How am I going to handle this? There is no other crew except me!"'

Riedl made a total of ten training flights in the *Mistel* at Kolberg, which was considered to be the standard number prior to embarking on operations. Six of these flights were aiming exercises, following which the complete composite returned to base. The remaining four flights involved separation exercises. On such flights there were occasional accidents. At the moment of separation, the natural inclination of the pilot in the upper component was to push the stick forward, causing the propeller blades of the fighter to strike the cockpit of the Ju 88 with fatal results for its crew. On one such training separation *Leutnant* Hans-Georg Brodesser's upper component collided with the Ju 88 lower component because Brodesser accidentally pushed the stick, causing the fighter to fall forward. The Ju 88 crashed and its pilot was killed.

The lower component of a Mistel 1 lies overturned in a field near Burg, late 1944.

'Starting and taxying in the *Mistel* was hard,' remembers Riedl. 'It was a real beast. Visibility was very restricted. Because of the height and angle at which the machine sat on the ground, you could only see the end of the runway when the tail came up and you were ready to lift off. Also, often when manoeuvring and turning into the take-off position, the tailwheel was known to come off and that was when there were accidents; machines slewed off the runway. But once the machine was airborne, there was no real problem. A little sluggish perhaps, but that was all. It has to be remembered that we were all experienced pilots – former instructors – not novices. In flight, the *Mistel* handled comparatively well, very like any other twin-engined bomber. The Junkers technicians who worked on matching the controls of the upper and lower components did a fantastic job.'

According to Allied radio intercepts, on the evening of 26 October 1944 *Luftwaffenkommando West* ordered I. and III./KG 66 to mount a 'concentrated operation with all serviceable aircraft' under the code name '*Kreuzzug*' (Crusade) against the sluice at Kruisschans on the River Scheldt, 8 km north-west of Antwerp. This operation was to include the *Mistel* of III. *Gruppe* and was to be mounted as soon as weather allowed and in a period of bright moonlight. It is not clear whether this operation was ever flown.

On the 27th, III./KG 66 reported 18 *Mistel* on strength with six serviceable plus 12 crews. The unit also had a further 11 Ju 88s of which nine were serviceable with 13 crews. Despite the unit's slowly growing contingent of personnel and equipment, it would not be long before it was redesignated. On 15 November 1944, *Oberstleutnant* Werner Baumbach, one of the officers who had visited Dessau in 1941 to inspect (and admire) Siegfried Holzbaur's theoretical *Grossbombe* concept, was appointed *Kommodore* of KG 200 and it would be this *Geschwader* along with just one other that would operate the *Mistel* for the rest of the war.

Much has been written about the activities of KG 200 and many post-war accounts have sensationalised the 'clandestine' nature of the work undertaken by the *Geschwader* prior to its restructuring in late November 1944. Formed officially on 21 February 1944 and placed under the command of *Oberst i.G.* Heinz Heigl, the real *raison d'être* of the unit stemmed from a need for coordinated control of aircraft assigned to agent-dropping duties. Such duties had, in the past, been the task of the *Gruppe Gartenfeld* which undertook missions on behalf of the SS-controlled *Reichssicherheitshauptamt* (RSHA – Reich Main Security Office) and which operated a mixed fleet of both German and foreign bombers and transport aircraft. This unit, together with its commander, *Major* Karl-Edmund Gartenfeld, was amongst the first to be integrated into I./KG 200 along with elements of the *Versuchsverband Ob.d.L.* All three *Staffeln* which constituted I. *Gruppe* were involved in agent-dropping, most of which were controlled by *Amt* VI, the Foreign Intelligence department of the RSHA. The *Gruppe's* operations ran from Finland to Persia, from Africa to Ireland, and utilised such diverse aircraft as Ju 188s, He 111s, Ju 290s, Do 24s, Ju 252s, and captured American B-17 and B-24 bombers. In July 1944 no fewer than 260 agents were dropped, 80 of these by 1. *Staffel* at distances up to 250 km behind enemy lines.

The II./KG 200 became operational at Hildesheim at the end of March 1944 under *Major* Jungwirt. Its 2. *Staffel* was commanded by a former glider pilot, *Oberleutnant* Karl-Heinz Lange, who believed that huge damage could be inflicted on the anticipated Allied invasion fleet by committed pilots who would launch manned glide-bombs at enemy ships and who were prepared to die in the attempt. Such radical operations were referred to as *Totaleinsatz* ('total commitment' or operations with expendable weapons and, in cases, crew) and *Selbstopfer* ('self-sacrifice'). Lange's idea eventually manifested itself in the form of a handful of Fw 190s laden with 1,100 kg bombs which were to be carried right onto a target. The unit trained up at Dedelstorf and Stolp-Parow and finally became ready for operations in late June 1944, by which time the whole scheme was cancelled by an order from a senior authority who apparently lacked the stomach for it.

All this changed in late October 1944, when Heigl, who had been suspected of complicity in the July 1944 bomb plot against Hitler, was replaced as *Kommodore* of KG 200 by Baumbach. Baumbach was an extremely experienced bomber pilot and a poster boy for the Nazi propaganda machine. Intelligent, urbane and a man of strong personality, he nevertheless courted controversy as a result of his outspokenness and, later in the war, his actions, opinions and moral viewpoints frequently clashed with those of the German leaders. Born on 27 December 1916 in Cloppenburg, he had yearned to become a 'flyer' since a student at the Clemens-August-Gymnasium. At the age of 14 he joined the *Hitlerjugend* and took up gliding. By 1935 he was involved in organising the *Rhön-Segelflugwettbewerbe* on the Wasserkuppe. The following year, he entered the Luftwaffe as a cadet at the *Luftkriegsschule* at Berlin-Gatow and on 1 January 1938, passed out as a *Leutnant*. Posted to KG 30, Baumbach first saw action in Poland when flying an He 111, he led a successful attack against Warsaw airfield despite encountering Polish fighters. On 28 September he was awarded the Iron Cross Second Class.

Following the conclusion of the Polish campaign, Baumbach's *Gruppe*, I./KG 30, converted to the Ju 88 and in the autumn of 1939 it flew some of the first missions against British shipping over the North Sea and off the coast of Scotland. On 16 February 1940, Baumbach bombed a British cruiser at Scapa Flow and other attacks followed around the Orkneys and Shetlands as well as off the Norwegian coast, where he accounted for a 10,000-ton cruiser destroyed. In late 1939, in an unusual aside, he was despatched on trips to Russia and Japan as a trusted

Major Werner Baumbach (left) in conversation with fellow Ritterkreuzträger, Oberleutnant Helmut Weinreich, during a visit to his former Gruppe, III./KG 30, at Leck in September 1943. Baumbach would become only the second bomber pilot to be awarded Oakleaves and the first to be awarded the Swords. He would end the war as Kommodore of KG 200. Weinreich later converted to flying single-engine nightfighters and was appointed Kommodore of JG 301 on 1 October 1943. He was killed a few weeks later on 18 November when his Fw 190 was hit by defensive fire as he shot down an enemy bomber.

diplomatic courier charged with carrying confidential RLM documents. He was awarded the *Ritterkreuz* on 8 May 1940, only the fourth bomber pilot recipient.

Following operations over France and The Netherlands in May 1940, Baumbach spent the winter of that year flying day and night missions over England, and on one occasion his Ju 88 was hit by *Flak* over London, suffering a failed engine. Baumbach was wounded but managed to return his aircraft and his crew to The Netherlands where he crash-landed. On 14 June 1941, in recognition of the 240,000 tons of enemy shipping he had accounted for by that time, the young *Oberleutnant* was awarded the Oakleaves to his *Ritterkreuz*, only the second bomber pilot to be so decorated. Just over a month later, promoted to *Hauptmann*, he took over as *Kommandeur* of I./KG 30. Throughout 1942, Baumbach was in action against shipping targets in the Crimea and the Black Sea. As his score reached 300,000 tons, he became the first bomber pilot to be awarded the Swords to the *Ritterkreuz*. In October 1942, he was promoted to *Major* and saw service in the Mediterranean.

Baumbach's friendship with *Generaloberst* Hans Jeschonnek, the Luftwaffe's fourth Chief of General Staff, allowed him to voice his criticism at certain members of the Luftwaffe High Command. One target was *General der Flieger* Bruno Lörzer, an old friend of Göring's who commanded II. *Fliegerkorps* in December 1942. Upon arriving with his unit at Comiso in Sicily, Baumbach wrote angrily to Jeschonnek on the 12th:

> 'I consider it my duty to give my views on the situation as I see it and I accept full responsibility if I express myself in harsh terms... It seems to me that General Lörzer, commanding II.*Fliegerkorps*, has shown no understanding of our situation... (no headquarters, clothing, feeding, telephonic network, bays, motor transport, repair and service staff)... So far we have seen nothing of the *Fliegerkorps*, much less the General. I have the impression, shared with other commanders, that there is a lack of overall direction and control... but I am telling you no more than the truth.'

Baumbach was duly relieved of his command and despatched to Berlin for a period to embark upon 'special duties' before returning to Italy in 1943 to take up successive staff positions with II. *Fliegerkorps* and *Luftflotte* 2. As *General der Kampfflieger*, a position he held for a brief period during late 1943, he was involved in the development and testing of the *Fritz-X* and the Hs 293 guided bombs.

Shortly after Baumbach's appointment as commander of KG 200, a reorganisation of the Berlin/Gatow-based *Geschwader* took place, effecting a change in the composition and operations of II./KG 200 thus:

Stab III./KG 66	became *Stab* II./KG 200 (*Hauptmann* Capesius)
7./KG 66	became 5./KG 200 (*Oberleutnant* Pilz)
8./KG 66	became 6./KG 200 (*Oberleutnant* Pauli)
9./KG 66	became 7./KG 200 (*Hauptmann* Rudat)

Oberleutnant Herbert Pilz, Staffelkapitän of 5.(Bel.)/ KG 200, the unit tasked with target illumination for the Mistel of 6. Staffel, KG 200.

Under this rearrangement and equipped with a small number of Ju 88s and Ju 188s, 5./KG 200 acted as a target illumination unit for the operational *Mistel* of 6.*Staffel* based at Burg, while 7./KG 200 at Kolberg (with elements at Nordhausen) became an *Ergänzungsstaffel* or replacement and training unit for 6./KG 200. On 28 November 1944, the *Gruppe* reported 24 *Mistel* on strength of which seven were serviceable. Two days later *Hauptmann* Capesius was awarded the *Ritterkreuz*.

As with KG 101 and III./KG 66, the Nordhausen conversion facility provided *Mistel* for II./KG 200.

Take-off and landing accidents were not uncommon as a result of the weight, size and lack of visibility from the upper component of the Mistel. With a 'live' Mistel, this was particularly dangerous. Here, a Mistel 1, Bf 109 DE+RB/Ju 88 FI+LL, purportedly flown by Oblt. Dipl.-Ing. Horst-Dieter Lux when it nosed over, lies in a field close to Burg in late 1944. Note the Reparaturwerkstatt (RW) conversion number '36', applied to the upper part of the Bf 109's fuselage Balkenkreuz. Lux had test-flown the Ju 88 of this Mistel at Nordhausen on 11 and 12 September 1944 accompanied by Heinz Schreiber in the Bf 109.

Rudi Riedl was transferred to Burg immediately after the completion of his training at Kolberg in December 1944. He remembers:

> 'At Burg our *Mistel* were hidden in cut-outs at the edge of the forest and were given additional concealment by covering them with fir branches. Prior to an operation, the aircraft were pulled out onto the runway by small tow-tractors. They were then always parked out in the open in a row ready for take-off. Because of the heavy weight of a *Mistel* combination and to avoid tyre bursts, careful efforts were taken to ensure that the runway was completely clear of any stones or debris prior to take-off. The warheads were delivered to the airfield by train from the same factory that made *Panzerfaust* anti-tank launchers. We pilots had our quarters in barracks on the airfield itself.'

Once at Burg, 6./KG 200 adopted an emblem for its aircraft in the form of an adaptation of the well-known German newspaper cartoon characters '*Vater und Sohn*' popularised by the artist Erich Ohser during the mid-1930s, and symbolising the upper and lower components of the *Mistel*, which by this time was also known amongst engineers, technicians and crews as '*Vater und Sohn*'.

By the end of November, trials had commenced with a new, enhanced version of the *Mistel*, featuring as an upper component the radial-engined Fw 190 coupled to a Ju 88 A-4 lower component. Essentially, the Fw 190 offered a marginally extended range over the Bf 109 F-4, coupled with the powerful BMW 801 engine. One of the first flights of this configuration, using Ju 88 A-4 CT+ZT, took place at Nordhausen on the 30th when Heinz Schreiber took to the air during the morning for an apparently trouble-free 15-minute test flight. However, further trials were abandoned due to the incompatibility between the 87 octane fuel grade of the Ju 88 A-4 and the 95 octane fuel grade of the Fw 190 A which prevented the fighter from drawing upon fuel from the bomber's tanks.

Additionally, by late 1944 significant numbers of the Fw 190 A-6 and A-8 fighter and F-8 ground-attack variants were available, which in itself forced further development and new design. *Dr.-Ing.* Fritz Haber, head of development, construction and flight trials for the *Mistel* project at Junkers offers a revealing perspective to the introduction of the Fw 190 as an upper component:

> 'Plans had been made to use the *Mistel* against targets behind the Russian Front. In order to be able to achieve the required range, it was proposed to use a combination comprising an He 177 and an Fw 190. This idea was quickly abandoned because of the difficulty in restoring the He 177s, parked and abandoned at various airfields throughout Germany, to a reliable flightworthy condition. Instead, orders were issued by the OKL after a few more months had elapsed to produce 150 *Mistel* aircraft based on the Ju 88 G-1 nightfighter and Fw 190 A-8 for this purpose. Incredibly, they were to be built and delivered within six weeks and the whole of the Junkers concern was mobilized in the attempt to fulfil this order within the stipulated timescale.'

The Ju 88 G-1 nightfighter, which had first appeared in the spring of 1944, proved itself a successful machine in operations but, most significantly, its BMW 801 air-cooled

'Vater und Sohn'
The *Staffelwappen* of 6./KG 200

IT is perhaps an ironic paradox that the *Staffelwappen* (emblem) adopted by 6./KG 200 for its *Mistel* was derived from the work of a man who openly criticised the Nazis and their policies. Erich Ohser was born the son of a customs officer in Untergettengrün in 1903. Subsequently a student of the *Kunstakademie* (School of Art) in Leipzig, he quickly made a name for himself as an artist and caricaturist during the 1920s. His lifelong friend and fellow artist, Erich Kästner, whom he met in Leipzig in 1924, described him as 'dark-haired, awkward and full of high spirits.'

Graduating from the *Kunstakademie*, Ohser and Kästner teamed up and for a while worked on the *Neue Leipziger Zeitung*, a local newspaper from which they departed under hostile circumstances in 1927. Moving to Berlin, Ohser took with him many of the nudes, portraits and landscapes he had sketched whilst in Leipzig and his reputation among the artistic fraternity of the German capital grew. Berlin inspired Ohser. He worked tirelessly, producing many brush and pencil sketches depicting scenes around the city's coffee houses and the *Reichstag* and reflecting the Nazis' rapid and audacious rise to power.

Erich Ohser photographed in his Berlin apartment at work on one of his cartoons in 1943. The emblem of 6. Staffel, Kampfgeschwader 200 was inspired by the 1930s 'Vater und Sohn' (father and son) cartoon characters of 'e.o.plauen', alias Erich Ohser. As a result of its design and principle, the Mistel was also known as 'Vater und Sohn'.

In 1929 he was commissioned to produce a series of satirical caricatures for the Social Democrat newspaper *Vorwärts*. In these sketches, his 'victims' – perhaps unwisely – included Adolf Hitler, the leader of the *Nationalsozialistische Deutsche Arbeiterpartei* (NSDAP) and Josef Goebbels, the recently appointed Reich Propaganda Leader of the NSDAP. Dedicated to his work, Ohser married Marigard Bantzer in 1930 and the birth of his son the following year brought some happiness into an otherwise frantic and reactionary lifestyle.

When the Nazis came to power in 1933, Ohser realised he was in danger of political retribution. In the naïve hope that he could somehow escape persecution, he burnt his original anti-Nazi caricatures and began to work with the *Berliner Illustrierte* for whom he created his *Vater und Sohn* series under the pseudonym 'e.o.plauen' (Erich Ohser from Plauen). This was a strictly non-political project since, in 1934, the Nazis had forbidden him to produce any work which contained unacceptable political reference. Between 1934 and 1937, Ohser plodded on with *Vater und Sohn*, the compromise with the Nazis at least affording him continued and considerable success as a popular commercial illustrator, though denying him his dream of ever becoming a truly great artist.

From 1940, Ohser was drafted onto Goebbels' populist newspaper *Das Reich* and thus reluctantly became a servant of the Nazi propaganda machine. Unable to accept the demands made of him, he was arrested in 1944 for making 'defeatist' comments. Whilst he was in *Gestapo* custody, Ohser's case was handled personally by Goebbels. The day before he was due to be brought to trial, Erich Ohser committed suicide.

KG 200 badge

Two large effigies of Erich Ohser's 'Vater und Sohn' cartoon characters are used to promote a winter-relief collection in wartime Berlin.

radials and those of the Fw 190 A-6 or and F-8 harmonised by utilising 95 octane fuel. Possibly the first pilot to fly the new combination was Horst-Dieter Lux who recounted:

> 'In the autumn of 1944 I made the first flight with the new Ju 88 G and Fw 190 combination. There were bugs, most of them related to the fly-by-wire system and the explosive bolts. Example: during one separation the two forward bolts exploded, while the one at the tail did not. I found myself in an abrupt stall and violent gyrations. My fighter separated from the bomber, which was flying slightly below me, showing a sizeable hole in the fuselage where normally the rear strut was attached. This told me that my fighter was carrying the 10-ft steel pole from its belly pointing straight down. I could not land with it. Fortunately, the aeroplane was still flying in a somewhat normal manner and I had enough fuel to do some thinking.
>
> 'My conclusion was to make a high-speed low pass over the airfield. Being fast would give me enough control and the chances were the pole would break off or at least bend backwards. It broke off.'

On 5 December 1944, Heinz Schreiber piloted an Fw 190, SR+GG, fitted to a Ju 88 G-1, PI+XU (the V2) for a 25-minute flight around Nordhausen. Things went relatively well and instructions were issued to the Junkers

Having been towed out of their wooded dispersals, no fewer than eleven Mistel of 6./KG 200, seven of them identifiable as Mistel 1s, are lined up on the runway at Burg prior to take-off in late 1944/early 1945. Careful efforts were made to keep runways clear of debris since the weight of a laden Mistel made tyre bursts a dangerous problem. Such a number of Mistel would have made a tempting target for Allied fighter-bombers.

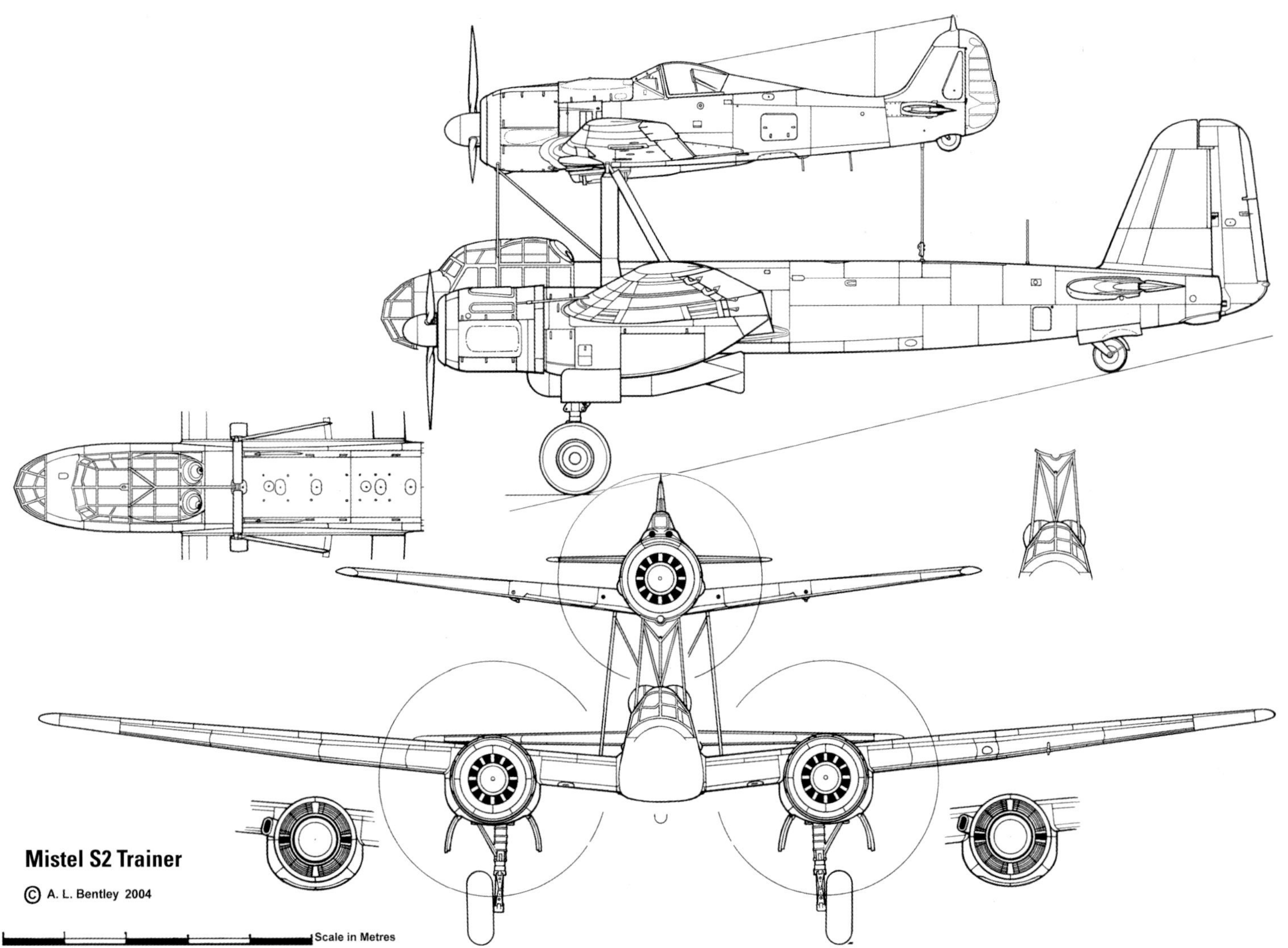

factory at Leipzig-Mockau to adapt 75 Ju 88 G-1 nightfighters for the *Beethoven* programme. These aircraft quickly began to arrive at Nordhausen and once support struts and an Fw 190 had been hoisted on top of each one, the completed *Mistel* were assigned individual *Reparaturwerkstatt* ('RW') or works repair numbers. For example, on 8 December, Schreiber tested 'RW 6' (Fw 190 TU+RW/Ju 88 G-1 PI+KB) and the next day, 'RW 9' (Fw 190 CV+JR/Ju 88 G-1 ST+BF). The *Feldwebel* conducted his first trial separation on the 7th in the same combination he had flown on the 6th, with further separations taking place throughout the month. Flight-testing with this configuration at Nordhausen continued throughout December and is known to have involved test pilots Schreiber, Kuhlmann and Brandenburg.

At a meeting of Department Fl.-E2 of the TLR in Berlin on 21 December, it was reported that 12 Ju 88/Fw 190 combinations had been completed, with another 20 due by 15 January 1945 and a further 30 by 15 February. However, such was the enthusiasm for the *Mistel* by this stage, that the order was extended to 100 units capable of attaining a range of 1,500 km to be available by 1 February and a further 100 capable of 2,500 km to be ready by 15 February at the latest.

Combined with an Fw 190 upper component, the Ju 88 G-1 was designated the *Mistel* 2 and trials with the variant initiated a simultaneous, but limited, familiarisation programme with the Ju 88 G-1 by II./KG 200. At Burg on 7 and 10 December, *Oberleutnant* Pauli accompanied *Feldwebel* Grögel and *Leutnant* Brodesser respectively on training flights in a G-1. The 21st found Pauli ferrying another G-1 together with *Oblt. Dipl.-Ing.* Lux from the collection depot at Altengrabow to Burg. Two days later, Pauli's logbook records that he made an operational flight in a live *Mistel*. Unfortunately, details of this mission are not known, though it is unusual in that Pauli took off from Burg in daylight at 1030 hrs and landed at Altengrabow 15 minutes later. It is possible that he was forced to effect separation and abort the operation.

In late December, Allied reconnaissance aircraft covered Burg, Kolberg and Nordhausen and identified *Mistel* at all three locations. Indeed, at the end of December, the first *Mistel* 2s were delivered to 6./KG 200 at Burg. By 10 January, the unit was reporting the following strength: 19 (13) *Mistel* 1s, 13 *Mistel* S2 trainers, one Bf 109 and one Fw 190 on strength. The 7.*Staffel* at Kolberg reported four *Mistel* S1s on strength of which three were serviceable. The *Stab* II./KG 200 and 5. *Staffel* accounted for twelve Ju 88s, nine Ju 188s and one Fw 190 between them.

Training progressed on the *Mistel* 2 and to assist pilots embarking on an operational take-off, the following checklist was prepared:

1) Trim the Ju 88 to 'zero'
2) Trim the Fw 190 to 'zero'
3) Set the Ju 88 landing flaps for take-off
4) Set the Fw 190 landing flaps for take-off
5) Set the Ju 88 propeller switch to '12 o'clock' position
6) Set the Fw 190 propeller to 'automatic'
7) Set rudder servo motor flick switch to 'take-off'
8) Hollow charge fuse switch to 'unprimed'
9) Set directional gyroscope to departure course
10) Undercarriage locking switch 'up' to lock
11) Check the transfer function of the rudder servo-motor on the Ju 88 rudder.

Below: Lt. Hans-Georg Brodesser of 7./KG 200 looks down from the cockpit of the Ju 88 G-1 lower component of a Mistel S2 at Kolberg in late 1944. Brodesser was a former flying instructor who is believed to have received training on the Me 262 and Ar 234 jets before ending the war flying the Mistel with II./KG 200.

By this stage, evidence points to increasing faith being placed in the new weapon: the OKL war diary reveals some concern about the fact that delivery of the 150 *Mistel* 2s ordered to be ready by 15 February was '*at risk through no delivery date instructions for the converted airframes*.' On 6 January, *Major* Wolfgang Schnaufer's NJG 4 based in western Germany had been ordered to hand over forty-three of its Ju 88 G-1s by 15 January latest 'for *Mistel* operations.' These aircraft were to be sent directly to the Junkers plant at Leipzig-Mockau for conversion into *Mistel* 2s. By the 10th, I./NJG 4 had confirmed that four G-1s were ready to transfer to Bernburg for conversion and that a further fifteen machines would be ready the next day. The *Gruppe* would then convert to the Ju 88 G-6.

The immediate difficulty facing II./KG 200 was to find suitable targets for its composite bombers. The challenge for Baumbach, Capesius and Pauli was how to fly a formation of large, lumbering *Mistel* unscathed and at low level through winter skies which were menaced by Allied fighters. Moreover, friendly fighter escort could not always be depended upon. One mission was planned in January to attack a French blockship in the Scheldt estuary close to the docks at Antwerp. The operation was designed to hamper Allied supplies through the port and support the Ar 234 jet bombers of the *Einsatzstaffel* III./KG 76 which was already conducting bombing operations in the area. Though III./KG 66 made preparatory reconnaissance flights over the estuary, the attack was eventually abandoned in favour of a much bolder operation.

An unidentified pilot looks down from the cockpit of a Ju 88 G-1 shortly before commencement of a training flight. Note racks for drop tanks.

Above: Two unidentified pilots of 7./KG 200 prepare for a training flight in a Mistel S2 on a winter's day at Kolberg in late 1944. One pilot wears flight helmet and lifejacket, while flying gloves and a parachute pack are visible on the ground. The lower component is a Ju 88 G-1. The man seen fourth from left would appear to be a civilian flight technician, possibly from Junkers.

Below: Pilots of KG 200 are fitted with parachute packs and harnesses during training at Burg in 1944. Note the rear support strut for the upper fighter visible above the Ju 88's fuselage.

The cockpit of an Fw 190 upper component of a Mistel S2 showing the added centre panel with automatic pilot control, propeller switch indicators, combination boost gauge and tachometers. On the left side are the throttles for the Ju 88 lower component and undercarriage switches and indicators.

A. Oil pressure for Fw 190
B. Combination of artificial horizon and turn and bank indicator
C. Air speed indicator
D. Altimeter
E. Rate of climb indicator
F. RPM
G. Fuel pressure for Ju 88
H. Fuel pressure for Ju 88
I. Unidentified
J. Unidentified
K. Switch from manual to autopilot control for Ju 88
L. Autopilot pitch control for Ju 88
M. Autopilot roll and turn control for Ju 88
N. RPM for Ju 88
O. RPM selector switch for Ju 88
P. Manifold pressure for Ju 88
Q. Manifold pressure for Ju 88
R. Throttle for right engine of Ju 88
S. Throttle for left engine of Ju 88
T. Throttle for Fw 190 (throttle has switch for manual propeller pitch control to be operated by the thumb)
U. Fuel switches for tank pumps
V. Pitch trim for Fw 190
W. Switches for instrument light intensity
X. Switches for instrument light intensity
Y. Remote control for radio
Z. Throttle friction knob

Antwerp was a vital supply port for Field Marshal Montgomery's 21st Army Group as it advanced across north-west Europe in late 1944/early 1945. It was assigned as a target for the Mistel of II./KG 200.

Below: Oberleutnant Herbert Pilz, Staffelkapitän of 5.(Bel.)/KG 200 (back to camera) discusses target details with a naval liaison officer prior to the planned mission to Antwerp docks. Also seen in this photograph are: (far left) Hauptmann Kurt Capesius, Kommandeur II./KG 200, Feldwebel Rudi Riedl (second from left) and Oberleutnant Balduin Pauli, Staffelkapitän of 6./KG 200 (fourth from left).

The three Staffelkapitäne of II./KG 200 in discussion on the runway at Burg in early 1945, allegedly prior to an aborted attempt to bomb Antwerp docks. From far left: Hauptmann Fiedler (in leather coat), Ia (operations officer) of II./KG 200; Hauptmann Horst Rudat (with Ritterkreuz), Staffelkapitän 7./KG 200; Oberleutnant Herbert Pilz, Staffelkapitän 5.(Bel.)/KG 200; and (with hands in pockets) Oberleutnant Balduin Pauli, Staffelkapitän 6./KG 200. Hauptmann Fiedler, who did not fly, was nicknamed 'Bohnenstange' ('Beanpole') on account of his height.

Three pilots of 6./KG 200 wait by one of their Mistel 2s as its engines are started and run up at Burg prior to the abortive mission to Antwerp in early 1945. From left: Feldwebel Rudi Riedl (without lifejacket), Feldwebel Willi Döhring and Feldwebel Emil Degering. Note the live warhead attached to the Ju 88, the ladder propped against the trailing edge of the wing of the Junkers with which the pilot would access the upper component fighter, and the drop tank fitted to the fighter, probably an Fw 190 and which, together with the wearing of lifejackets, suggests a long-range mission over water.

Feldwebel Willi Döhring of 6./KG 200 taps the side of his head in a clearly understandable gesture directed at the photographer at Burg, early 1945. Many pilots considered it to be a bad omen to take photographs immediately before a mission. Directly behind Döhring, and partially obscured, is Fw. Emil Degering. Both pilots had flown the Mistel with KG 101 in France. The Fw 190 component of the Mistel 2 seen behind the pilots has its engine running ready for take-off. Note the 'Elefantenrüssel' warhead fitted to the Ju 88 and the drop tank beneath the Fw 190.

'WE WERE ORDERED TO PRODUCE A GERMAN PEARL HARBOR'

Seen from the deck of HMS *Victorious*, the formidable anti-aircraft defences at Scapa Flow conduct a practice barrage. The Mistel of KG 200 would be expected to fly through such defences. Throughout the latter half of 1944, many of the big ships of the Royal Navy's Home Fleet regularly passed in and out of Scapa Flow; during June and July for example, the Fleet aircraft carriers *Indomitable, Victorious* and *Formidable* all visited and would have been considered high priority targets for *Drachenhöhle.*

IN January 1945, *Reichsmarschall* Göring retreated to his East Prussian country estate to avoid Hitler's increasing recriminations against the Luftwaffe. Göring craved a high-profile opportunity with which he could salvage his air force's reputation amongst the Nazi leadership and the people of Germany. The Luftwaffe had failed to push the Allied invasion back into the sea the previous June; it had failed to stop the Allies' round-the-clock bombing of the Reich's cities, transport system and production centres; it had failed to offer adequate cover to German ground forces on the Western and Eastern fronts throughout 1944; and its promises of new units equipped with jet fighters and bombers had yet to materialise in any substance.

Thus Göring ordered *Oberst* Baumbach to make preparations for one of the most radical and audacious operations ever to be considered by the Luftwaffe. The *Reichsmarschall* hankered back to a target which he had dreamed of attacking in mass at the outbreak of war. At the time his plan had been rejected by Hitler who feared retaliatory attacks on the Reich as a consequence; but with the *Mistel* he had the opportunity to fulfil his dream of launching an attack on the Royal Navy's anchorage at Scapa Flow. The code name *Drachenhöhle* (Dragon's Lair) was conjured up for the proposed operation.

Throughout the latter half of 1944, the big ships of the Royal Navy's Home Fleet regularly passed in and out of Scapa Flow. During June and July for example, the Fleet aircraft carriers *Victorious*, *Indomitable*, *Implacable*, *Indefatigable*, *Formidable* and *Furious* all passed through there, as did the battleships *Duke of York* and *Howe*.

On 11 December 1944, eleven Fleet Air Arm Seafires arrived at Skeabrae to bolster the air defence over Scapa already provided by a squadron of Spitfire IXs which had been transferred to the Air Defence of Great Britain from 2nd Tactical Air Force in September. Despite such defences, during late 1944 the Luftwaffe was able to conduct sporadic daylight reconnaissance missions over the

Despite local British air defences, during late 1944 the Luftwaffe was able to conduct sporadic daylight reconnaissance missions over the Shetlands and Scapa Flow using the Ju 88s and Ju 188s of 1.(F)/120 based at Stavanger-Sola in Norway. Carrying nearly 5,000 litres of fuel, some of which was stored in two jettisonable wing tanks, it was possible for a Ju 188 to make the five-and-a-half-hour return trip from Sola to the north of the Shetland Islands, south to the Orkney Islands, passing over Scapa Flow before heading east across the North Sea and back to Norway. The information gathered by these aircraft was crucial to the planning of *Drachenhöhle*.

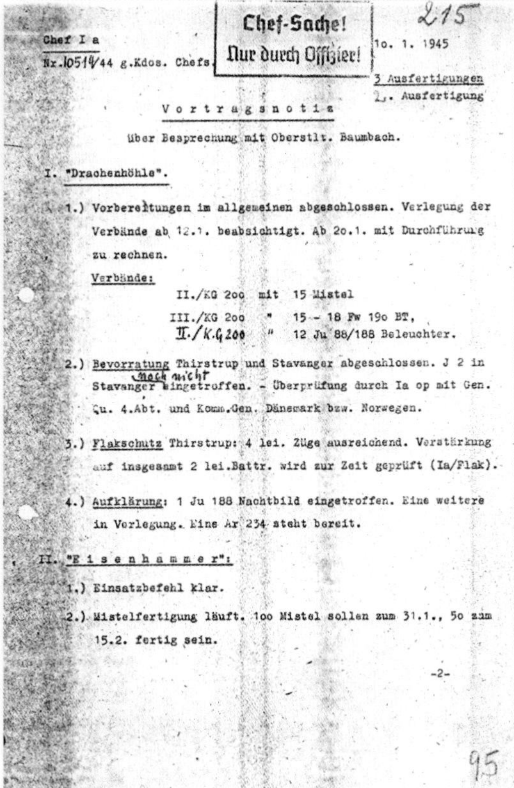

215

Chef I a
Nr. 10514/44 g.Kdos. Chefs.

Chef-Sache! Nur durch Offizier!

10. 1. 1945

3 Ausfertigungen
2. Ausfertigung

Vortragsnotiz

über Besprechung mit Oberstlt. Baumbach.

I. "Drachenhöhle".

1.) Vorbereitungen im allgemeinen abgeschlossen. Verlegung der Verbände ab 12.1. beabsichtigt. Ab 20.1. mit Durchführung zu rechnen.

Verbände:

II./KG 200 mit 15 Mistel
III./KG 200 " 15 – 18 Fw 190 BT,
II./K.G 200 " 12 Ju 88/188 Beleuchter.

2.) Bevorratung Thirstrup und Stavanger abgeschlossen. J 2 in Stavanger noch nicht eingetroffen. – Überprüfung durch Ia op mit Gen. Qu. 4.Abt. und Komm.Gen. Dänemark bzw. Norwegen.

3.) Flakschutz Thirstrup: 4 lei. Züge ausreichend. Verstärkung auf insgesamt 2 lei.Battr. wird zur Zeit geprüft (Ia/Flak).

4.) Aufklärung: 1 Ju 188 Nachtbild eingetroffen. Eine weitere in Verlegung. Eine Ar 234 steht bereit.

II. "Eisenhammer":

1.) Einsatzbefehl klar.

2.) Mistelfertigung läuft. 100 Mistel sollen zum 31.1., 50 zum 15.2. fertig sein.

-2-

95

First page of a *Luftwaffenführungsstab* paper dated 10 January 1945 on preparations for Operations *Drachenhöhle* and *Eisenhammer* (see Chapter Ten), both of which were intended to make use of Mistel composites. To provide reconnaissance for Drachenhöhle the Mistel, Fw 190 torpedo-bombers and Ju 88/188 'pathfinders' of KG 200 would be assisted by Ju 188 night reconnaissance aircraft as well as an Ar 234 which was on stand-by.

Shetlands and Scapa Flow using the Ju 88s and Ju 188s of 1.(F)/120 based at Stavanger-Sola in Norway. Carrying nearly 5,000 litres of fuel, including two jettisonable wing tanks, it was possible for a Ju 188 to make the 5.5 hour return trip from Sola to the north of the Shetland Islands, south to the Orkney Islands, passing over Scapa Flow before heading east across the North Sea and back to Norway. As late as 28 December 1944, a Ju 188, A6+FN, of 1.(F)/120 piloted by *Unteroffizier* Werner Grundmann took off from Sola with orders to obtain photographic cover of Scapa Flow and establish the number and type of vessels lying there. Unfortunately, the aircraft suffered an engine fire and was forced to make an emergency landing on the west coast of Scotland. Only one of the crew survived the landing.

Nevertheless, the lack of reconnaissance did not stop the Luftwaffe from proceeding with Operation *Drachenhöhle* as quickly as it could. The precise origins of the plan are not clear but, as related in Chapter Six, the *Luftwaffenführungsstab* had considered the possibility of an attack on the British naval base using *Mistel* in April 1944. At that time, however, the weapon was still untested, but the subsequent operations conducted by 2./KG 101 off Normandy in the summer did at least prove that, flown by trained and committed pilots, the weapon could be deployed to some effect.

In early January 1945, Baumbach visited II./KG 200 at Burg to meet with *Hauptmann* Capesius, *Oberleutnant* Pauli and *Oberleutnant* Pilz to discuss preparations for *Drachenhöhle*. Balduin Pauli, whom Baumbach despatched to Tirstrup to 'scout the area', recalled: 'We were ordered to produce a kind of German Pearl Harbor.'

By the 10th, Baumbach had marshalled the required forces from KG 200 for the attack. At a meeting with *Oberst* von Greiff of the *Luftwaffenführungsstab*, he advised that a total of fifteen *Mistel* from 6./KG 200 would form the core strike force, assisted by twelve Ju 88 and Ju 188 illuminator aircraft from 5./KG 200. These aircraft were ready for transfer to Tirstrup airfield in Denmark on 12 January, from where it was envisaged they could fly the operation at any time from the 20th. Furthermore, a force of fifteen to eighteen Fw 190 fighter-bombers of III./KG 200 were available for movement to Stavanger from where they would also take part in the attack equipped with new '*Bombentorpedo*' which were designed to detonate beneath ship targets. Baumbach intended to transfer these aircraft back to the Western Front for anti-shipping operations over the Scheldt estuary following the completion of *Drachenhöhle*.

Feldwebel Rudi Riedl of 6./KG 200 was one of the pilots assigned to take part in Drachenhöhle. During his low-level transfer flight to Denmark from Burg on 12 January 1945, his Mistel was threatened by the guns of wary German U-boats, their crews unfamiliar with the design of the composite.

The loss of the 1.(F)/120 Ju 188 on 28 December and the need for continued and reliable reconnaissance over the target area undoubtedly prompted the decision to allocate to Baumbach two Ar 234 B-2s originally intended for FAGr. 5. These jet aircraft possessed the necessary speed and range to conduct uninterrupted high-altitude daylight reconnaissance over the Orkneys. Added to these were two Ju 188 '*Nachtbild*' (night photographers) one of which had already transferred north, with the second machine en route.

On schedule, twelve *Mistel* S2s of 6./KG 200 transferred from Burg to Tirstrup on the morning of 12 January. However the day before, one pilot scheduled to take part in the operation, *Feldwebel* Rudi Riedl, had been ordered from Burg to 7./KG 200's base at Kolberg to assist with training; he recalls:

> 'I had just arrived at Kolberg by train when I received a teleprint message ordering me to return as quickly as possible to Burg where I was to collect my aircraft. When I got back to Burg I was told to fly immediately to Tirstrup in Denmark for a special operation. The other pilots had already departed. I just had time to pack my private papers and belongings into a suitcase and place them in the safety of the cellar under our barracks. The flight to Tirstrup from Burg took us directly north over Kiel towards the Danish island of Langeland. As we flew in low over Kiel harbour we passed some U-boats lying on the surface. Their crews did not recognise the lone *Mistel* as a friendly aircraft and considered us to be hostile, at which point they began tracking us with their deck-mounted guns. We tried to indicate that we were friendly by waggling our wings, but this seemed to have no effect and, rather worryingly, the guns still followed us. I eventually fired a recognition flare from the cockpit which thankfully seemed to convince them that we were not a "hostile", but nevertheless it was a hairy moment! Thankfully, I reached Tirstrup in one piece.'

In December 1944, Tirstrup airfield, located 30 km north-east of Aarhus on Jutland, was still being brought up to full operational status by the Luftwaffe, though facilities there were considered good enough to accept composite aircraft. There was one WNW/ESE runway 2,011 metres in length and one medium-sized hangar. Two dispersal areas lay to the north and south of the runway and more than 40 blast pens and shelters were located around the field in woods, protected by two heavy and 11 light *Flak* positions. The airfield headquarters and associated barrack huts were in the village of Stabrand, 1.2 km to the north, and a few more barrack huts were in the south dispersal area, but the KG 200 aircrew and staff were quartered in a grand manor house belonging to a shipowner at Møllerup about five kilometres south-west of the airfield.

When II./KG 200's aircraft arrived at Tirstrup they were rolled into the shelters and camouflaged. The same day, in a surprising demonstration of efficient logistics, the warheads arrived by train and were immediately fitted to the Ju 88 lower components of the *Mistel*.

The seemingly endless wait for good weather and suitable targets now began. On 14 January a telegram reached Baumbach advising him that two of the Ju 188s under *Hauptmann* Schenk, equipped with night cameras and allocated for the '*Sondereinsatz Scapa Flow*', had been delayed reaching Stavanger-Sola. They eventually landed in Norway on the 21st and were ordered to commence reconnaissance patrols immediately. These patrols proved extremely effective in locating the warships present in

Whilst in Denmark, the aircrew and staff of 6./KG 200 were quartered in a farmhouse at Møllerup, south-west of Tirstrup airfield.

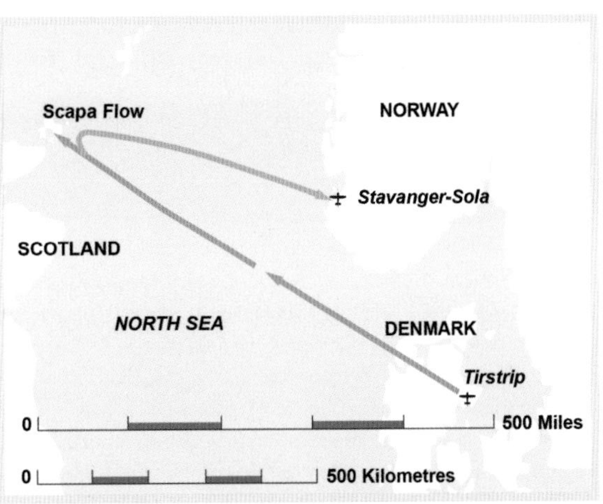

The planned outward route for *Unternehmen Drachenhöhle*. Having attacked Scapa Flow, the KG 200 pilots were to fly back across the North Sea to land at Stavanger-Sola in Norway.

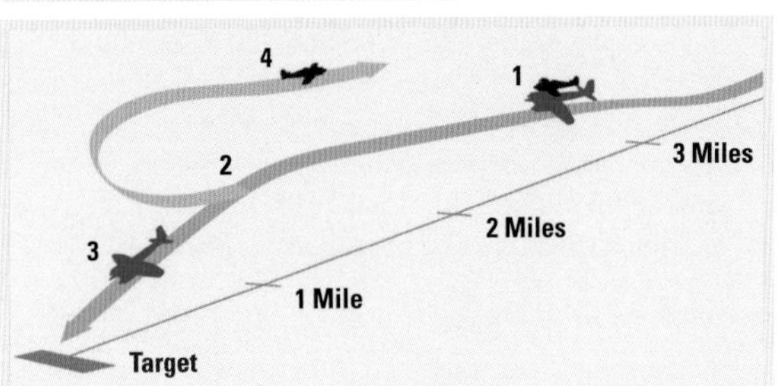

Method of Attack

1. Approach to within 3 miles of target at minimum height to avoid radar detection and climb to 2,500 ft for target identification.
2. Select target and commence attack, making final adjustments to auto-pilot on lower component.
3. Pilot effects separation and launch at 1 mile from target and at a height of 2,300 ft. Gliding attack at 20 degrees.
4. Pilot makes return course.

Scapa Flow and monitoring vessels arriving, departing or changing the position of their moorings.

'As far as the Scapa Flow attack plan was concerned,' remembers Rudi Riedl, 'we only received one proper briefing which took place in a large room of the country house near the airfield, in which was a large map of the Scapa Flow area. Each pilot was assigned an individual target since we received regular reconnaissance updates on British shipping movements – I knew exactly where my target ship was anchored. To help us further, at our base at Tirstrup, we had a large, specially built model of the harbour on which were laid scale models of all the ships known to be there. The real prize was to be assigned an aircraft carrier! It was felt amongst the pilots of 6./KG 200 that if the *Mistel* had been introduced earlier and in greater numbers, its effect against certain pinpoint targets, such as ships, could have been far more decisive. Any ship – no matter what size – if hit by a *Mistel*, would have gone under. There were to be twelve aircraft, no reserves, and the idea was to fly to the target in cloud so as to minimise the risk of being spotted by British patrols or Flak. Fuel for the outward flight would be drawn from the Ju 88 lower components and the amounts required had been calculated down to the last drop. Marker buoys had been laid out to guide us in. We were to adopt a line astern formation. We all wanted the mission to work, because we knew we would be decorated when we got back; there was even talk of the *Ritterkreuz*!

'Once the attack had been made, the plan was for our Fw 190s to climb as fast as possible to 7,000 metres and make for Stavanger which was the closest point for a safe landing. Both our forces in Norway and the Navy had been warned to expect us and the Navy had been briefed to watch out for any pilot unable to make it as far as Stavanger and who might have to bail out due to lack of fuel.'

The waiting played on the nerves of the handful of pilots. Riedl recalls:

'We spent most evenings playing cards, for example, *Skat* and *Doppelkopf*. We had to have some form of distraction. The long waits and the constant alerts generated a certain restlessness, which was not easily mastered. This in turn created a feeling of anxiety, which no one was prepared to admit for fear of being called an *Angsthase* ('scaredy-cat'). So in Tirstrup we all bought walking sticks to play ice hockey on the lake around the *Gutshof* (manor) at Møllerup where we were quartered. Our puck was a beer can until one of the pilots, Otto Linhard, was struck on the head and suffered concussion. Afterwards we were forbidden to play. Our *Staffelkapitän, Oberleutnant* Pauli, had much sympathy for our situation and allowed us a free hand. Nevertheless, he had us under control and knew that he could depend on us at any moment. So we had to devise something else. Growing a moustache was the answer! We lavished care and attention on them, but it did nothing for me; I just grew a weak beard. Pastry-eating was our favourite sport. After stand-down following an alert we would go to a café and eat cake by the centimetre. One day we entered the café sporting moustaches and with walking sticks swinging. I was in the first row. Oh dear! What a shock! We were confronted by none other than our *Kommodore, Oberst* Baumbach, and his assistant. I immediately tried to make a hasty exit, but it was not possible. The 'reinforcements' were too strong. You could have heard a pin drop. We quickly became well-mannered; whereas a few moments before we had been an unruly band, now we were like choirboys. He beckoned me with his forefinger. I presented myself, erect, but feeling weak at the knees. '*Riedl, you have until this evening to shave off your beard or have it entered in your pay book!*' After my reply, '*Yes, sir, Herr Oberst!*', he asked me, '*Why are you not wearing a moustache?*' I answered, '*I do not yet have one.*' There was only one choice, the order 'shave off beard' was obeyed. Later we were to learn from his assistant that the 'Old Man', who was seldom amused, laughed heartily over this incident. That is how we spent our leisure waiting for the '*Sondereinsatz Scapa Flow*'; we harboured no grudges – we just needed to ease our thoughts about "tomorrow".'

From certain evidence, it seems that one man becoming increasingly concerned about 'tomorrow' was Werner Baumbach. Indeed, one incident gave him good cause to be. At the beginning of February 1945, four *Mistel* 1s from 7./KG 200 at Kolberg were assigned to bolster the strength of the attack force in Denmark. These composites left Kolberg on the afternoon of 3 February and were flown by crews comprising members of 6./KG 200 and KG 30, whose personnel had recently undergone fighter training in preparation for either operations on the Me 262 or the *Mistel*.

Fritz Lorbach was one of the 6./KG 200 pilots assigned to fly a Ju 88 to Tirstrup that day; he recalls:

'On 3 February 1945, a part of 6./KG 200 was transferred from Kolberg to Tirstrup in Denmark. The whole detachment stationed in Kolberg comprised four *Mistel* with Me 109s and all their personnel. A stopover in Hagenow had been planned. Our *Staffelführer, Oberleutnant* Schiffer, and his crew took off first because of low cloud and made a good landing at Hagenow. The rest – three *Huckepacks*[1] with their pilots, Willi Kollhoff, Franz Pietschmann and I – flew in loose line astern formation from airfield to airfield listening out for warnings of approaching enemy aircraft, because our fighters were not armed. A group of fighters flew across our path before we reached Hagenow. I thought they were Me 109s. My mistake. They were Mustangs, as I discovered when they began to fire at us as we flew in closer formation over the airfield and I spotted the American markings...'

Feldwebel Fritz Lorbach of 6./KG 200. Lorbach was one of three pilots detailed to ferry Mistel from Kolberg to Tirstrup on 3 February 1945 and was bounced by P-51 Mustangs of the USAAF 55th Fighter Group: 'I thought they were Me 109s. My mistake.'

Lt. Col. Elwyn C. Righetti, Executive Officer of the 55th Fighter Group, claimed a Mistel destroyed near Hagenow on 3 February 1945. He wrote: '...before I could open fire, I discovered that the Buzz Bomb was actually a Focke-Wulf 190 fastened atop the heavy twin-engined aircraft. As I was closing to fire, the heavy aircraft seemed to be jettisoned, went into a shallow diving turn to the left.'

The *Mistel* had been bounced east of Hagenow by P-51 Mustangs from the US 55th Fighter Group which were returning home having escorted more than 900 B-17s on a raid to Berlin. The 55th FG had carved itself a formidable reputation; its aircraft had been the first from the Eighth Air Force ever to fly over the German capital and as 'ground strafers' its accomplishments were second to none. Lt. Col. Elwyn C. Righetti was the Group's Executive Officer. A skilled fighter ace of Franco-Latin descent and a tenacious pilot, Righetti would become the Eighth's top strafing ace with 27 aircraft destroyed and numerable locomotives to his credit. Righetti had just detached the 338th Squadron from the rest of the Group so as to make a low altitude ground sweep along the homeward-bound bomber track. Breaking into two flights, the Mustangs then hunted for targets of opportunity. Righetti, leading White Flight, reported:

Lt. Bernard H. Howes (front row left) of the 55th Fighter Group, seen here in a photograph taken at the Group's base at Wormingford, England, in 1944. Howes shot down at least one Mistel on 3 February 1945. One of his victims was probably Oberfähnrich Franz Pietschmann who was piloting a Ju 88 A-4 of II./KG 200.

"Near Boizenburg on the Elbe River I located a small hole in the unbroken overcast. Through the hole I could see two locomotives and called them in and started down. Visibility was about two miles and scattered fuzz on the overcast ran down in some places to 500 to 600 feet. I rolled out of my turn and started my final approach to the locos about four miles off. I had already assigned the locos and parts of the train to the flight. We were echeloned to the right with my position on the extreme left. At a distance of two miles from the train I spotted three piggyback aircraft at 1030 to me, at our same altitude of about 600 feet, headed almost directly at us, and half a mile off. I mistakenly identified them as Buzz Bomb-equipped He 111s and broke off rapidly, left and up, in a 200-degree chandelle, positioning myself on the tail of the middle one. I started firing two short bursts at 600 yards and missed. I swung into trail and closed to point blank range, firing a long burst. I saw many excellent strikes on the fuselage and empennage of the large aircraft and scattered strikes and a small fire on the fighter. Both aircraft, still fastened together, went into a steep dive straight ahead. I was about to overrun them and did not see them crash, but a few seconds later I saw a large explosion and spotted considerable burning wreckage.

'I still did not know what we were attacking; I turned slightly to port for another look. As I closed, and before I could open fire, I discovered that the Buzz Bomb was actually a Focke-Wulf 190 fastened atop the heavy twin-engined aircraft. As I was closing to fire, the heavy aircraft seemed to be jettisoned, went into a shallow diving turn to the left, and crashed and burned in a small hamlet. Apparently it carried no bombs, for the gasoline thrown from its tanks burned for some time, and I did not observe any unusually large explosion.

'The Fw 190, relieved of its load, snapped to the right and then began a wild evasive action. I drove up to 200 yards directly in trail, firing intermittently, and secured excellent strikes along the fuselage, wing roots, canopy, and induced good fire. Jerry went out of control and crashed straight ahead. At this time I noticed a few tracers too close and coming behind. I broke sharply left and up into a low cloud. I don't know who or what was firing at me, but it might have been the third Fw 190 having jettisoned its bomber.'

Also flying with White Flight was 23-year-old Lt. Bernard H. Howes from Brockton, Massachusetts who had shot down two German aircraft since his assignment to the Eighth Air Force the previous summer; he recalled:

'While pulling up from a first attack on a locomotive, I sighted a formation of three "pick-a-backs" flying in line at about 4,000 feet altitude. I turned into the second 'combo' with my wingman, Second Lieutenant Patrick L. Moore, following behind me. I fired a short burst from about 350 yards and at an angle of 90 degrees, observing strikes on the 190. As I fired, the Fw 190 atop the third unit was released. The propellers were all windmilling and the 190 seemed to nose up, then dropped nose down; it was apparently out of control and headed for the ground. The Ju 88 turned sharply left. I followed, firing short bursts. I fell outside the turn and momentarily lost sight of the Ju 88. Lt. Moore, following me, was in position and shot down the Ju 88. When I looked back, I saw it crash into the ground.

[1] *Huckepack* – German for 'piggyback' or 'pick-a-back'. As will be seen later in the book, this was one of at least three designations used by Luftwaffe personnel for the Mistel. The other two were 'Vater und Sohn' and, to a lesser extent, 'Nero'.

A Mistel S2 (Fw 190 A or F and a Ju 88 G-1, W.Nr.714633), Red '11', of 6./KG 200 seen close to its woodland dispersal at the edge of Tirstrup airfield in Denmark in the spring of 1945.

Mistel S2 Focke-Wulf Fw 190 A-8/Junkers Ju 88 G-1, W.Nr.714633, 'Red 11', 6./KG 200, Tirstrup, Denmark, February 1945

Two Mistel S2s of II./KG 200 caught on the gun camera film of Lt. Bernard H. Howes of the USAAF 55th Fighter Group, east of Hagenow, on 3 February 1945.

Lt. Bernard H. Howes closes in on a Mistel of II./KG 200 near Hagenow on 3 February 1945 as a member of its crew bails out.

The lower component of a Mistel banks low over the countryside near Hagenow, pursued by a P-51 from the 55th Fighter Group.

Oberfähnrich Franz Pietschmann of 6./KG 200 who was killed when his Mistel 'dived into the ground' following an attack by Mustangs of the USAAF 55th Fighter Group.

'After pulling up, I saw the first unit I had fired on at about 300 yards in front of me. There were flames coming out of the Fw 190, so I went after it again. I started firing and the "combo" turned into me and then dropped to treetop level. On a second pass, I set the right engine of the Ju 88 afire, and saw both aircraft crash into the ground.'

Howes also reported seeing at least one *Mistel* crash into a village where it 'blew up, destroying a mass of houses'.

Another Mustang pilot, Lt. Richard Gibbs, reported:

'I took the third and last one of the gaggle. I started firing on the Junkers at about forty-five degrees from about 800 yards, closing to about 300 yards with a two-second burst. I observed many strikes on the left wing root of the bomber, where it began to burn. After a short dive the fighter was released. It appeared rather unstable in the air, but managed to conduct violent evasive action. I fired a short burst from astern, beginning at about 200 yards and closing to zero yards. I saw strikes all over the aircraft and observed parts of the cowling and canopy fly off. There was also a fire in or around the cockpit. I overran the Fw 190 and skidded to the right, and looking back, I saw where it crashed into the ground.'

Fritz Lorbach recalled what happened when the Mustangs fell upon the German formation:

'Our altitude was 150 metres, that of the clouds 300 metres. The *Mistel* flown by Kollhoff and Lorbach separated, the Me 109s heading for the clouds, but they were shot down. Pietschmann's *Mistel* dived into the ground. Kollhoff made an emergency landing on the bank of a little river – the Sude, but was strafed on the ground; a member of his crew was killed and he was wounded in the elbow. The crew of my Ju 88 was not injured even though the left engine was on fire and I had to make an emergency landing in the woods.'

Oberfähnrich Franz Pietschmann was piloting Ju 88 A-4, W.Nr.8590, CK+WN, an aircraft which had first been tested for *Mistel* conversion at Nordhausen by Schreiber and Lux on 21 August 1944. Pietschmann was killed. His gunner, *Oberfeldwebel* Ernst Rübsam and his flight engineer, *Obergefreiter* Paul Giemsa, were also killed. As recounted by Fritz Lorbach, *Feldwebel* Willi Kollhoff suffered wounds when his Ju 88 A-4, W.Nr.3652, made an emergency landing, but his gunner, *Feldwebel* Franz Fischl, was killed. The aircraft was categorised by KG 200 as 80 per cent destroyed.

Pilots of the RAF Fighter Experimental Flight line up for a snapshot taken by F/O John Waters on a wintry day at Ford in early 1945. Seen together with the Flight's commander, S/L Bob Kipp, (fifth from left) are three of the four aircrew who took part in the Tirstrup raid on 14 February 1945: F/L Tony Craft (first left), F/O Roy Le Long (sixth from left) and F/O 'Mac' McLaren (third from right). Behind them is the Mosquito Mk VI belonging to the nightfighter ace, Wing Commander John Cunningham, who was visiting the unit at the time.

Although the American pilots reported the upper component fighters as 'Fw 190s', this conflicts with official German losses which, with one exception, lists the fighters as Bf 109s. However, one Fw 190 A-8, W.Nr.737989, piloted by *Oberleutnant* Otto Burkhard of KG 30, is listed as being lost by 6./KG 200 over Hagenow during the action and is probably the aircraft caught on Lt. Richard Gibbs' gun camera film. The other aircraft reported as lost that day were Bf 109 F-4 W.Nr.10053, the pilot, *Obergefreiter* Joachim Uhlig, attached to 6./KG 200 from KG 30, being killed, and Bf 109 F-4 W.Nr.13141, SK+MO, its pilot, *Oberfeldwebel* Arnold Klähn, attached to 6./KG 200 from KG 30, also killed.

The effect of this action upon German plans can only be speculated, but on 12 February 1945 an entry in the OKL War Diary records:

> 'Following discussions with the *Kommodore* of KG 200, the *Reichsmarschall* postponed the final decision to carry out Operation *Drachenhöhle* for three days.'

However, ten days earlier on 10 February, two Mosquito Mk.VIs of the RAF's specialist Fighter Interception Development Squadron (FIDS), had taken off at 0720 hrs from their base at Ford in Sussex briefed to 'patrol to Tirstrup', an airfield which had previously warranted little attention by the Allied air forces. The two aircraft ran into thick cloud down to sea level off the Danish coast and approximately 25 miles north-west of Sylt contact was lost with one machine which subsequently failed to return.

Another attempt to reach Tirstrup was made during the afternoon of 9 February by a pair of Mosquito Mk.VIs from the Fighter Experimental Flight [Ranger] (FEF) also based at Ford and piloted by New Zealander F/O Roy LeLong and F/L Tony Craft. However, the mission was abandoned when, once again, cloud brought visibility down to zero feet three minutes flying time from the island of Tuno in the Aarhus Bugt.

Like the FIDS, the Fighter Experimental Flight was one of a number of small semi-autonomous experimental and evaluation units forming part of the Night Fighter Development Wing which, in turn, was a branch of the Central Fighter Establishment (CFE) based at Tangmere. Formed on 27 October 1944 and equipped with the Mosquito Mk.VI long-range fighter, FEF was tasked with conducting and developing deep penetration daylight 'Intruder' missions under cloud cover, or 'Day Rangers', along the Baltic coast or over southern Germany. Sorties were usually despatched to a nominated target, usually involving the strafing of airfields with nose-mounted cannon, and on the return home trains or other transport targets were attacked. No bombs were carried. In February 1945 the unit was led by the highly experienced S/L Bob 'Kipper' Kipp, DSO, DFC, a former drugstore clerk from Kamloops, British Columbia who had previously flown with 418 Squadron, RCAF.

Another member of the unit was F/O John Waters who joined the Flight as a navigator in late 1944; he recalls:

> 'All members of the Fighter Experimental Flight were experienced and had completed at least one tour of operations – all except *me*: I was the only "sprog" member. So I was very lucky to have an experienced pilot from the start. They were all previous members of 418 Squadron or

Two Mosquito Mk VIs of the RAF's Fighter Experimental Flight in their revetments at the north-east corner of Ford airfield in Sussex, England in late 1944. Armed with four nose-mounted 20 mm cannon and .303 in. Browning guns, it was aircraft from this specialist unit which were detailed to attack 6./KG 200's base at Tirstrup in February 1945.

Flying Officer John Waters of the Fighter Experimental Flight flew as navigator on one of the Mosquitos which attacked Tirstrup on 14 February 1945: 'I can still see those 'pick-a-back' aircraft – and our frustration when the bloody guns got stuck. I can also still see the ground crews scattering, such was our surprise visit!

605 Squadron and two pilots from 23 Squadron. I have always assumed that 11 Group were determined to maintain an Intruder element of a few experienced crews when 418 and 605 Squadrons were posted to 2nd TAF after D-Day. The full strength was six crews (which we hardly ever were!), with replacements "as applicable".'

On 14 February, a third mission was planned for Tirstrup. Once again, Roy LeLong with F/O J.A. 'Mac' McLaren as navigator and Tony Craft with John Waters as navigator were picked for the job and at 0840 hrs, their two Mosquito Mk.VIs were airborne from Ford. Each aircraft was fitted with four 20 mm cannon and four .303-inch Browning guns in the nose. The Mosquitos flew towards Manston then set course over the North Sea at 'zero feet' and in clear weather with good visibility. Landfall was made at Stadil, north of Ringkobing, on the east coast of Jutland followed by another leg, across Jutland, then south to Tuno where the course was altered for the target. The time was 1056 hrs. John Waters remembers:

'Mac's job was chief navigator; mine was second navigator, just to keep a check, but mainly to make sure we were not "jumped". We had 50-gallon drop tanks, the fuel from which was siphoned into the wing tanks just before reaching the Danish coast. The pilot then pressed the "tit" and the tanks dropped off. But there was no such luck for us on this occasion; press as much as Tony Craft could, they refused to drop off and remained firmly secured to the wings throughout the trip! R/T silence was the order of the day, until one reached the target. But on reaching Mariager, Roy LeLong phoned up beseeching my pilot that it would be better for the Deity's sake to drop the bloody drop tanks. It was a fascinating but short conversation!

'This was a hard winter – ice and snow and floods all added to the excitement of map reading – and, in my humble opinion, Mac did a good job in finding the

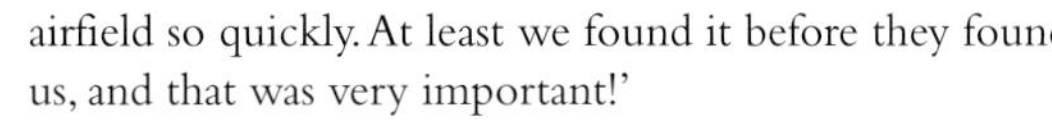

airfield so quickly. At least we found it before they found us, and that was very important!'

Shortly before 1110 hrs, the two Mosquitos closed in on Tirstrup and commenced their first attack run. John Waters continues:

'On what I assumed was a well-defended airfield such as this, we didn't want to hang around; this attack would have lasted no longer than 1 to 2 minutes. The whole essence was surprise – hence the low level – and as soon as the Hun gunners got going, we would have cleared off very smartly. I suppose it was like large-calibre clay pigeon shooting as far as they were concerned, and they were pretty good at it too! Once the Flak started, the *strict rule* was to *beat it*! There was, very much from the pilot's point of view, an art in strafing; if you came in too low, then you flew through the stuff which the cannon threw up. The four 20 mm cannon were not parallel to the fore and aft axis of the aircraft; the muzzles were inclined downwards, hence one needed a bit of height for strafing. But if you were too high, your navigator got the twitch because he could see where the Flak was coming from – neither very healthy! Since we were following Mac's map reading, I was "riding shotgun" and my first vision was a Fw 190 perched on top of a Ju 88.'

Down on the ground, the *Mistel* pilots of 6./KG 200 had left their quarters at Møllerup and were en route to Tirstrup. They had been advised that as a result of improved weather conditions, there was a fair chance that the Scapa Flow mission might be attempted that day. But as they neared the airfield, they heard the anti-aircraft guns firing. Rudi Riedl recalls:

'On the morning of the raid, we had all climbed aboard the Opel *Blitz* truck as usual for the short journey to Tirstrup. I was wearing all my flying gear ready for flight, including a life vest. We didn't make it as far as the airfield

Feldwebel Rudi Riedl's Mistel 2 'Red 12' of 6./KG 200 at Tirstrup, Denmark in early 1945. The Ju 88 G-1's (W.Nr. 714050) warhead has been fitted, suggesting an imminent operation and a primitive attempt has been made to conceal the composite from Allied aircraft. The 'RW' number visible on the Ju 88's rudder in the photograph (below) is the *'Reparaturwerkstatt'* or works conversion number applied by Junkers at Nordhausen.

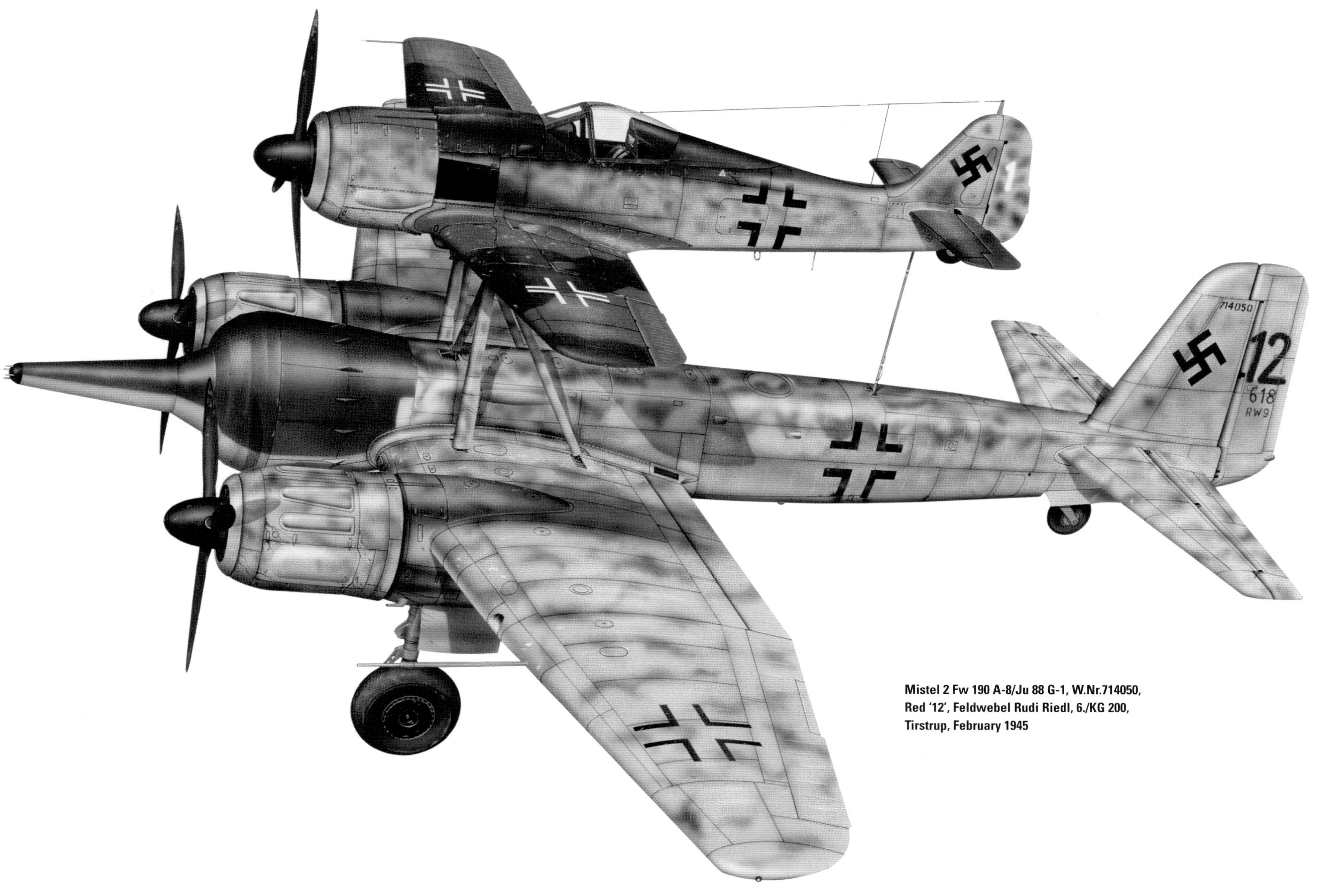

Mistel 2 Fw 190 A-8/Ju 88 G-1, W.Nr.714050, Red '12', Feldwebel Rudi Riedl, 6./KG 200, Tirstrup, February 1945

before the RAF arrived. I gazed upwards and saw two twin-engined fighters approach over the treetops in the distance, then there was one *Hell* of a commotion!'

Roy LeLong described his attack in his combat report:

'I approached the aerodrome from the East, the aerodrome being hard to find owing to snow and ice. On approach, I flew parallel to E-W runway on the South side. At first I could not see any aircraft, but finally saw about 5-6 Fw 190 and Ju 88 pick-a-backs with normal camouflage well dispersed in fir trees. My sight was u/s, so I used the plate glass for sighting, letting strikes hit the ground in front of one of these pick-a-backs. I pulled the nose up a little and saw many strikes on both the Fw and the Ju 88. Numerous personnel working around these E/A were scattered by the attack. I turned South into the next dispersal bay and made a similar type of attack on another pick-a-back also seeing strikes. I then turned West and attacked for a second time the first pick-a-back which I had previously damaged. This time both the Ju 88 and Fw 190 burst into flames. After breaking away from this last attack, light flak opened up at me, so we headed for our rendezvous at Mariager. Two columns of black smoke were seen long after the aerodrome was left.'

Seconds later, the second Mosquito made its first run. John Waters recalls:

'We were following, hugging the deck, young Waters busy looking all around to make sure we were not being jumped. But we were just too low on our first run and missed out...'

Tony Craft wrote after the mission:

'I approached Tirstrup from the East at zero feet. Flew down E-W runway and saw a Ju 88 painted black, to starboard in a wood to the North of the runway. Before turning starboard in an orbit to attack, I saw the Fw 190 and Ju 88 pick-a-back aircraft in flames subsequent to F/O LeLong's attack. I then attacked the Ju 88 from E-W and left it in flames (1110 hrs). Just after this attack, 3 light guns opened up at us from West of aerodrome.'

John Waters:

'Tony Craft obviously had a fixation on this black Ju 88 and we were too low to have a go at the 'pick-a-back' straight ahead. I think Roy LeLong did three runs and we did two. The Ju 88 would have been nailed on our second run. I can still see those 'pick-a-back' aircraft – and our frustration when the bloody guns got stuck (we hardly used any ammunition). I can also still see the ground crews scattering, such was our surprise visit! When the light *Flak* opened up, I suppose I got scared and too excited that I gave my pilot the ground speed to steer instead of the compass course – true inefficiency in the style of Pilot Officer Prune. The result was the two aircraft left the airfield in opposite directions which I insist foxed those Hun gunners! But once that *Flak* started Roy LeLong phoned us up and we quit *immediately*.'

Roy LeLong told a newspaper reporter afterwards: 'When we left, the composite and another plane were blazing furiously. We riddled another composite nearby.'

John Waters:

'We rejoined at the lake at Mariager and returned to base. I have a vivid memory of two men who stopped hoeing in a field and waved to us just before we crossed the coast. On arriving home, we taxied to dispersal, stopped the engines, undid our straps, took off our helmets and as I slid out backwards through the door, my pilot let go of the stick which just flopped to one side and *lo*! there were two *thuds* as our two wing tanks dropped to the ground! I quickly darted to our dispersal hut to hear two sergeant ground staff receiving what can only be described as a "right good bollocking" and a lot of nasty threats!'

British claims amounted to one composite destroyed and another damaged as well as a Ju 88 destroyed. In fact, II./KG 200 reported two *Mistel* 3 destroyed (Fw 190 A-8 W.Nr.380328/Ju 88 G-1 W.Nr.714623 and Fw 190 A-8 W.Nr.733683/Ju 88 G-1 W.Nr.714659) and one 15 per cent damaged (Fw 190 A-8 W.Nr.737388/ Ju 88 G-1 W.Nr.714150).

Ironically, the day before the British raid, Göring had decided to 'postpone' *Drachenhöhle* 'for the time being' and on the 14th, in a memo to senior officers, *Obst. i.G.* Christian of the *Luftwaffenführungsstab* noted that the operation was to be 'suspended temporarily... All preparations to be discontinued.' Units assigned to *Drachenhöhle* were to be released, though the *Mistel* assembled at Tirstrup were to remain there until further notice.

Though, ostensibly, German documents seem to attribute the sudden cancellation of the Scapa Flow attack to the juggling of fuel priorities (another operation using *Mistel* was being planned in the East – see Chapter Ten), the recollections of those who took part in the events of 14 February indicate an alternative and more intriguing scenario. In a revealing post-war testimony, Balduin Pauli, the former *Staffelkapitän* of 6./KG 200 wrote in a letter to former comrades:

'After the war, when I met Baumbach in Spain, he said the Reichsmarschall desperately needed a success as a matter of prestige, "his" Luftwaffe having been discredited so that he could show his face once again to the Führer. However, in Baumbach's opinion, the mission was not essential to the war effort and, in all probability, we stood to incur a casualty rate of about 80 per cent. So, using certain channels, he had deliberately betrayed the operation.'

Precisely what these 'certain channels' were remains unknown, but the pattern of events in England in February is also intriguing: on the 13th, S/L Kipp received a telephone call from Wing Commander S.N.L. Maude, DFC, a former commander of No.25(F) Squadron who worked at 'Operations 3' at HQ Fighter Command, Stanmore. John Waters remembers:

'At odd times there were "scrambled" telephone conversations between Wing Commander Maude and Bob Kipp. I have a suspicion that Maude had received information from some intelligence source and we received our instructions to go to Tirstrup. I'm pretty sure that we (LeLong, Mclaren, Craft and Waters) had no idea that we should find these composite aircraft there; I doubt if Bob Kipp did either, but he might have had some knowledge as a result of these telephone calls. The more I think about it, the only conclusion I can draw is that he fed us with ideas following those mysterious calls.'

Surviving 'Top Secret' documents show that British Intelligence were made aware of the *Mistel* at Tirstrup as early as the end of January. In a report to the Chief of Air Staff from the Assistant Chief of Air Staff (Intelligence) dated 28 February it is stated:

> 'An agent has reported at the end of January and on 19th February that a large quantity of *Mistel* aircraft have arrived on two airfields in Denmark.'

While the betrayal of the operation cannot be confirmed or denied with absolute certainty, there is no doubt that the operation was, once again, postponed. In its 'Points from Daily Conferences' for 16 February, the OKL war diary records that:

> 'The *Reichsmarschall* has decided that Operation *Drachenhöhle* cannot be carried out for the time being.'

And so the Royal Navy had escaped '*Drachenhöhle*'. But at least one of 6./KG 200's pilots was not so lucky:

> 'Once it was decided to cancel the operation,' remembers Rudi Riedl, 'we were eventually sent back to Burg. When we got back there, we found that the airfield had been bombed and my suitcase, into which I had earlier placed my belongings, had been stolen in the aftermath.'

A Ju 88 G-1 of 6./KG 200. This aircraft is typical of the nightfighter variants which were converted into Mistel, the support structure being visible behind the cockpit. Note the 'Reparaturwerkstatt' in the centre of the fuselage Balkenkreuz, the camouflage applied to the support struts and the large, crudely applied tactical recognition number '8' applied to the vertical stabiliser.

Ju 88 G-1, White '8', 6./KG 200, Tirstrup, Denmark, February 1945

Three Mistel lower components photographed at Tirstrup in mid-1945. Note the support struts for the upper component fighters which have been left in place. The Ju 88 in the foreground has had British Air Ministry markings applied to its fuselage and tail and RAF identification roundels applied to its underwing surfaces prior to its transfer to England.

Curious Danish civilians and military personnel inspect a Mistel S2 of 6./KG 200 at Tirstrup in June 1945. The tactical number 'Red 13' is visible on the rudder of the Ju 88.

A Danish officer poses for a photograph in front of a heavily camouflaged Mistel S2 at Tirstrup, June 1945. Note that the spinners and propeller blades have been removed from the Ju 88 probably for use on another aircraft.

Right: Former Luftwaffe ground crew at work on Ju 88 G-1, W.Nr.714633, Red '11' belonging to II./KG 200, at Tirstrup, Denmark in mid-1945. Comparison with the photograph above indicates that this could be the same machine being refitted with propellers and spinners prior to its being flown to England for further evaluation. Although this aircraft is fitted with BMW engines, suggesting a G variant, an earlier Ju 88 bomber nose has been fitted – see also photographs above.

Below: Ju 88 G-1, Red '11', formerly of 6./KG 200 and the same aircraft as the one seen in the photograph on page 101. This picture shows the aircraft at Tirstrup, still fitted with its upper component support struts but with its German national markings painted out prior to RAF roundels being applied.

Below: A close-up shot of the support struts of a Mistel S2 found at Tirstrup. Note the access ladder propped against the starboard wing of the Fw 190.

'PUT ALL OTHER MATTERS ASIDE AND CONCENTRATE ON THIS MISSION'

OPERATION *EISENHAMMER*

Twenty-seven-year-old Feldwebel Karl Russmeyer (right) of 3./KG(J) 30 was a former Ju 88 pilot who converted to Mistel at Prague-Ruzyne in February 1945. He recalled: 'When I first saw it, I was greatly astonished! I had no idea how I was going to fly it. Nevertheless, I regarded it as a challenge and got on with it.'

IN his study of Luftwaffe operations in Russia during 1942[1], *Generalleutnant* Hermann Plocher, who, during the year in question, served as Chief of Staff to V.*Fliegerkorps*, and Luftwaffe*nkommando Ost*, wrote:

'Keenly aware of the need to destroy the sources of Soviet military power, the responsible Luftwaffe command in the central area – at first the VIII Air Corps and later Luftwaffe Command East – nevertheless launched repeated air attacks against strategic objectives. The attacks, although strategic in character, caused only slight, temporary interruptions in the Soviet armament industry, and were really mere pinpricks which had no strategic impact on the war.'

He added:

'Special efforts were to be made against long-distance transmission lines carrying electric power from the deep interior of the Soviet Union to the industries in the general area of Moscow which were recovering from recent air attacks. Reconnaissance aircraft photographed Soviet power lines, and the intention was to send out planes using so-called electric cable bombs (*Seilbomben*) to interrupt the flow of current as completely and permanently as possible… Although the Commander in Chief of the Luftwaffe was keenly interested in the matter and was currently informed on the status of work done in preparation for such strategic operations, the studies were still incomplete at the end of 1942.'

Creative minds within the Luftwaffe staff had long dwelt upon the prospect of attacking an enemy's power sources. As early as 1936, *Oberst* Hans *Freiherr* von Bülow, an air theorist and head of the *Luftwaffenführungsstab's* Intelligence section, observed:

'The life of the large cities, the operations of innumerable factories and ever-growing portion of the transport system have to rely upon a constant and reliable supply of electric current. The importance of electricity for war industries hardly needs to be highlighted. The technical facilities for large generating and hydroelectric power plants are time consuming and expensive to construct, as well as extremely susceptible to air attack. The simultaneous destruction of most central electrical works will cause the instantaneous crippling of entire industries.'

Von Bülow's thinking had probably been influenced by developments in Russia where the electrification of industry represented technological progress and sophistication. Throughout the 1920s, and in line with Lenin's personal aspirations, the Soviet Union devised a modern and highly-centralised power generating system which spanned European Russia and comprised a number of large power stations linked by a high-tension grid. Indeed, Russia boasted that the concentration of its power

[1] *The German Air Force versus Russia*, Generalleutnant Hermann Plocher, USAF Historical Division, Aerospace Studies Institute, Air University, Arno Press, New York, June 1966.

systems was greater than Germany or the USA. However, such a vast and visible infrastructure was vulnerable to hostile intent.

By July 1943, one year after the Luftwaffe had launched its 'mere pinpricks' against Russian strategic targets and as German and Soviet armies clashed at Kursk, a report was being prepared quietly by a little known staff planner in an obscure department of the RLM in Berlin. The report echoed von Bülow's pre-war philosophy and proposed adopting the Soviet power supply system as the target for a systematic and coordinated strategic bombing attack by the Luftwaffe.

In early 1945, the technical and engineering specialist, Professor Dr.-Ing. Heinrich Steinmann was head of the innocuously titled 'Abteilung V 10' of the RLM's Luftwaffenverwaltungsamt (administration department). In this capacity he was the mastermind behind Unternehmen Eisenhammer, the plan to launch a mass air strike against the Soviet hydro-electric power infrastructure.

Professor Dr.-Ing. Heinrich Steinmann was born in Salzgitter on 1 August 1899. During his youth, he learned to fly gliders and also designed them, before serving as a frontier defence pilot in the First World War. Whilst a student at the *Technische Hochschule* at Braunschweig, he became instrumental in the construction of the *Deutsche Verkehrsfliegerschule* there. Later, his technical and scientific research work influenced numerous designs, building plans and patents and he was appointed Honorary Professor for Energy Studies, Power Plants and Long-Distance Cabling at the Military Technical Faculty of the *Berlin Hochschule*. As a respected member of the *Verband Deutscher Elektrotechniker* (VDE), his research in the field of energy economy found a great following among scientific experts.

At the outbreak of the Second World War, Steinmann was assigned as the *Oberregierungsrat* (Senior Administrator) of *Bauabteilung* 10 (Construction Section 10) in the Building and Construction Department within the RLM's *Technisches Verwaltungsamt* (Technical Administration Office) involved in the establishment of the Luftwaffe's ground organisation and responsible for all electronic and mechanical plant. In 1940 he was appointed as a technical adviser to *Studie Blau*, the Luftwaffe's appreciation of Great Britain's war potential, but he became frustrated by the numerous technical objections to his proposals to conduct air operations against British electric power stations and for the next two and a half years he returned to the more mundane task of designing power, heating and lighting systems for Luftwaffe ground installations.

In June 1943 however, he was once again summoned by the *Luftwaffenführungsstab* to produce a feasibility study of possible strategic air strikes against the Soviet electric power supply system. In his detailed plan, dated 31 July 1943 and entitled '*Recommendations for Air Attacks on the Power Supply of the Moscow-Upper Volga Region*', Steinmann concluded that 'a methodical and precisely conducted attack on the supply of electric current will result in the crippling of the armaments industry of the Moscow-Upper Volga region.' Well acquainted with Germany's over-burdened power situation, Steinmann stressed that only an attack mounted simultaneously across the entire network would be successful, since isolated raids would not produce such a cumulative impact.

However, the report was met with a degree of scepticism by Luftwaffe intelligence who felt that the target list proposed by Steinmann was too lengthy and that attacks on key industrial targets would produce more significant results. For weeks the report was shuffled from desk to desk until, on 9 November, in its '*Studie: Kampf gegen die Russische Rüstungsindustrie*' *(Plan for an Attack on the Russian Armament Industry)*, the Luftwaffe operations staff conceded:

> 'It is evident that we have missed the most favourable opportunities and that the difficulties in the meantime have become very great. Moreover, our airpower in the East is tied up today more than ever. In the meantime the Russian armament industry, measured by the quantity of supplies on the Russian Front, shows steady advances in production. If the Russian armament industry can continue to operate as undisturbed as it has been, it is to be expected that during the winter and next year (1944) it will turn out large quantities of aircraft, tanks, ordnance etc...
>
> 'Can the German Air Force no longer contribute to victory in the East if, instead of taking the place of artillery and dropping bombs in front of the infantry, it combats the root of the Russian offensive strength – the Russian armament industry?
>
> 'This study was made only as a result of the conviction that the elimination of perhaps large parts of the Russian armament industry will be of greater significance for the Eastern Front and, possibly, for the entire war, than the present direct support of the ground forces. It is necessary, however, to mass special forces for this and prepare for the task. When this will be possible (in view of the present position) cannot be said by this office; that depends on a higher decision.'

The point was that the Moscow area – the area assigned for attack by Steinmann – accounted for as much

On 9 November 1943, the Luftwaffe operations staff conceded that, 'If the Russian armament industry can continue to operate as undisturbed as it has been, it is to be expected that during the winter and next year (1944) it will turn out large quantities of aircraft, tanks, ordnance etc.' Shown in this photograph is the enormous Stalin Automobile Works constructed in a lonely valley in the southern Urals in 1941 and a major production centre for Soviet armaments. It was hoped that the damage caused by Unternehmen Eisenhammer, planned for early 1945, would seriously affect Russian armaments production.

as 75 per cent of the output of the armament industry. Undaunted by the delay in any positive response to his proposals, Steinmann set about producing a further report, this time centred around a strike against a range of Russian hydroelectric and steam power plants.

Steinmann's ideas received indirect support from *Reichsminister* Albert Speer, Hitler's armaments minister, and he made sure that the plan was brought to the attention of the *Führer*, as Speer has recorded in his memoirs:

> 'We had wooden models of the power plants made for use in training the pilots. Early in December I had informed Hitler. On February 4 [1944], I wrote to Korten, the new Chief of Staff of the air force, that "*even today the prospects are good... for an operative air campaign against the Soviet Union... I definitely hope that significant effects on the fighting power of the Soviet Union will result from it.*" I was referring specifically to the attacks on the power plants in the vicinity of Moscow and the Upper Volga. Success depended – as always in such operations – upon chance factors. I did not think that our action would decisively affect the war. But I hoped, as I wrote to Korten, that we would wreak enough damage on Soviet production so that it would take several months for American supplies to balance out their losses."

Nearly a year was to pass until, on 6 November 1944, *Reichsmarschall* Göring issued instructions that in the next full moon period a specially created force of ten He 177 bombers formerly of II./KG 100 based at Fassberg was to carry out an attack under the code name 'Operation *Burgund*' on the hydroelectric plants at Rybinsk, Uglich and Volkhovstroi. The bombers, which were to be placed under the operational control of KG 200 which, in turn, would act 'in closest cooperation' with *Professor* Steinmann, would carry the BM 1000 *Sommerballon* ('Summer Balloon') bomb which was already available in sufficient stocks at Prowehren. This type of bomb was divided length-wise into two halves, with one half filled with high explosive. When dropped over water, because of the location of the centre of gravity, which was low down on one side, the bomb stood on its nose, inclined from the perpendicular and with little pressure on the surface. Entering the water up-stream of a hydroelectric plant, the BM 1000 would be carried by a current flowing at over 0.5 metres per second to the grate of the operating turbine. It was designed to pass easily over any obstacles on the bed of the river. If the bomb exploded at the turbine grate, the resulting pressure wave would be transmitted through the induction channel and was sufficient to destroy the turbine cover. If in operation, the turbine then destroyed itself.

Preparations went ahead for the operation, with KG 200 aircrew and mine specialists from the Luftwaffe's *Erprobungsstelle* being despatched to secret locations under elaborate cover stories. However, such was the critical shortage of fuel at that time, that Steinmann was forced to beg 100 cubic metres of motor fuel from Goebbel's propaganda ministry which, with Göring's sanction, he then exchanged for an equivalent amount in aviation fuel from the Luftwaffe's fast diminishing reserves.

Unfortunately, Steinmann was dealt another blow when KG 200's planners calculated that a further 150 cubic metres of fuel would be needed for the operation. Furthermore, acute difficulties were experienced in servicing the He 177's 24-cylinder liquid-cooled Daimler-Benz 610 engines, for which parts were now in short supply. Because of these problems, the plan was eventually dropped.

Notwithstanding the difficulties in launching *Burgund*, the principle of striking at Soviet hydroelectric stations was not abandoned and the unavailability of the He 177 paved the way for the *Mistel*.

Despite efforts to keep the plans for *Burgund* secret, word of the Luftwaffe's intentions reached Speer who continued to take a personal interest in the discussion and planning of air attacks on the power stations and used his position to influence and hasten activity. He involved himself in arranging the order for the 100 *Mistel* mentioned in Chapter Eight. On 7 January 1945, in a document copied 'personally' to Speer, the Luftwaffe Chief of Staff, *General der Flieger* Karl Koller, introduced a new scheme under the code name, Operation *Eisenhammer* ('Iron Hammer') [see text box below]:

7 January 1945

An attack against electrical power production in the Soviet Union in the Moscow/Upper Volga region is to be carried out in one of the next moonlit periods (February-March). Time of the attack: dawn or early morning.

Code name 'Eisenhammer':

Preparation and execution of the attack is to be carried out by Luftflotte 6 to which KG 200 is to be assigned for the purpose. Orders are to be given verbally to the Kommodore of KG 200 by the Chief of the General Staff of the Luftwaffe.

Preparation for the attack is to be made in close collaboration with the General of Bombers and Minister Director Professor Dr. Steinmann (RLM, Department LD 10, Berlin-Templehof).

Targets for the attack:

1. Hydroelectric power plants at Rybinsk and Uglich.
2. Steam power plants at Stalingorsk, Kashira, Shatura, Komsomolsk, Yaroslav (2 plants) Aleksin, Tula, Balakhna, Gorki and Dzerzhinski.

Alternative targets are under consideration in order that the actual purpose of the attack will not be discovered: expedited for execution by Luftflotte 6 and report to Luftwaffe High Command, Intelligence.

Operational methods:

1. Ju 88/Fw 190 Mistel (combat radius: 1,500 km). Production of 100 by 1 February 1945 is to be expedited by all means (QMG 6.Abteilung).
2. BM 1000 F 'Summer Balloon' for additional use against hydroelectric power plants when the ice covering thaws.

Apart from a special flare-dropping Staffel, additional flare-dropping forces (He 111s, Ju 88 S-3s and He 177 Cs) are to be requisitioned urgently by KG 200. Possibly Luftwaffe High Command Intelligence will order detachments from I./KG 66 and KG 4 as necessary support.

When requested by KG 200, additional crews for the Mistel and marker aircraft are to be supplied by the Commanding General of Bombers. Arming and provision of the requisite He 177 C marker aircraft is to be supplied by the QMG 6.Abteilung. Crews and aircraft for the execution of the attack will be under the command of KG 200.

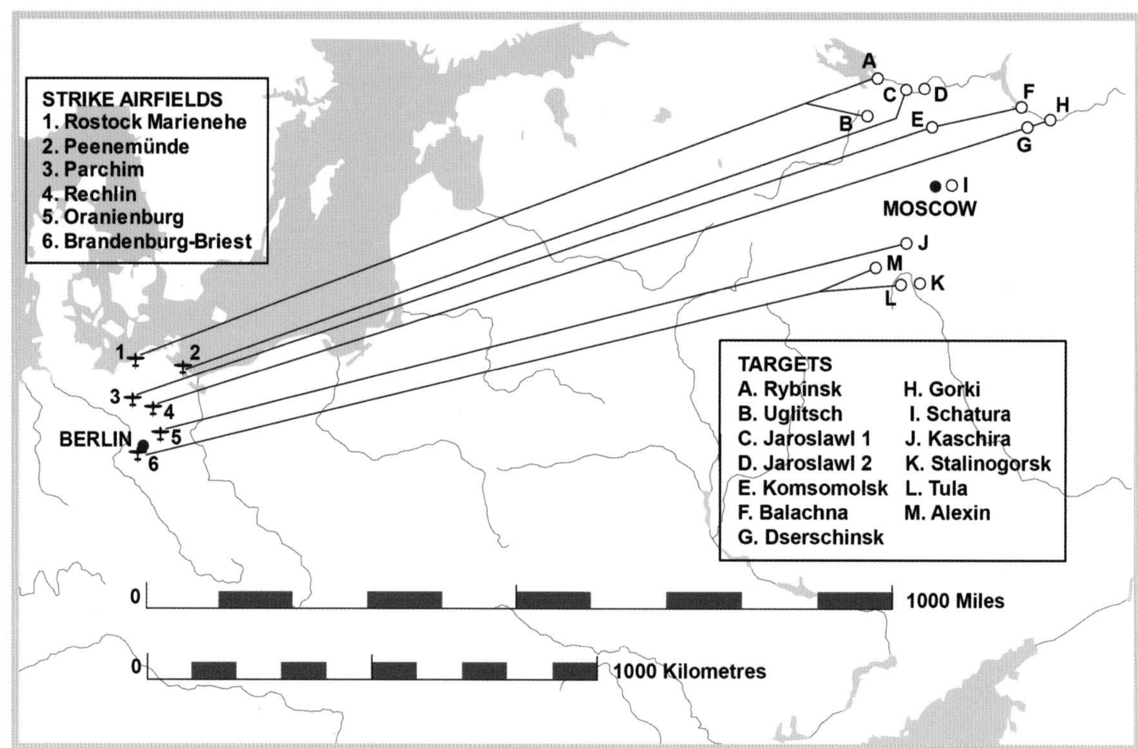

Operation *Eisenhammer:* planned strike airfields and targets

A summary of armament production in the Moscow/Upper Volga area at the time revealed how important the region was to the Russians:

Branch	Percentage of total production
Motor vehicles	90%
Ball bearings	50%
Light assault guns	60%
Overall ordnance production (anti-tank guns, AA guns etc., up to 50% of them field guns up to 15.2 cm)	16%
Medium tanks	25%
Airframes	27%

The region was also involved in electrical engineering and, to a limited extent, some extraction of raw materials.

Availability of the Fw 190/Ju 88 *Mistel* combination on the scale required by Koller's new plan was optimistic to say the least, but testing of this variant was still in progress at Nordhausen. Indeed, on the same day that Koller presented his proposals, the 'father' of the *Mistel*, Siegfried Holzbaur, was airborne from Nordhausen to Dessau in a new '*Mistel* 3' with Heinz Schreiber. For the next two months, Schreiber and another Junkers test pilot, Heinrich Osterwald, would conduct intensive pre-delivery testing on new *Mistel* at Nordhausen and Bernburg respectively. But with Operation *Eisenhammer* now being assigned top priority by the Luftwaffe, Junkers were under severe pressure to deliver.

On 10 January 1945, during discussions between officers of the Luftwaffe general staff and *Oberstleutnant* Baumbach, OKL demanded that in addition to the 100 composites required by the end of the month, a further 50 *Mistel* be ready by 15 February. Baumbach warned that II./KG 200 could provide only 15 trained crews and that these would be needed just to transfer completed *Mistel* from the Junkers assembly plants. In Baumbach's opinion, the supply of suitably trained pilots to mirror the increased production levels would be 'problematic'. As a possible solution, it was suggested taking on crews from the bomber units KG 30 and KG 40 which could be converted to the *Mistel* relatively quickly. The original intention had been to place pilots from both these units under the control of Peltz's redesignated IX(J).*Fliegerkorps,* which had been detailed to retrain redundant bomber pilots as jet fighter pilots for the defence of the Reich.

Although by this time personnel from KG 40 were no longer required for fighter conversion by IX.(J) *Fliegerkorps*, they had, at best, only limited experience on the Ju 88 and none on the Bf 109 or Fw 190. Conversely, the previously Ju 88-equipped KG 30 had been undergoing fighter conversion since the autumn of 1944 and was thus more suited to provide personnel experienced on both the Ju 88 and single-engine fighters. This made them ideal candidates for *Mistel* conversion.

Kampfgeschwader 30 – the so-called '*Adler-Geschwader*' ('Eagle Wing') – had been the first German bomber unit to take on the Ju 88 and flew it throughout the war. Formed in 1939, the *Geschwader* had served on virtually every major front to which the Luftwaffe had been sent, but with Germany's worsening military predicament the unit underwent an urgent metamorphosis: the Luftwaffe needed fighters and fighter pilots for the defence of the Reich and on 30 September 1944, KG 30 commenced its transition. The III. and IV. *Gruppen* were disbanded and I. and II. *Gruppen* were transferred by rail to airfields in the Prague and Königgratz areas, although many pilots were unhappy at having to abandon their trusty Ju 88s.

Following a short period of leave, efforts at conversion training began at Prague-Ruzyne, Prague-Gbell, Königgratz and Chrudim, south of Pardubitz, during October. Although a number of Ar 96s and Bü 181s were available for the job, conditions were generally very rudimentary. There had been heavy snowfalls at the end of 1944 and these had been followed by a quick thaw; airfields were caked with mud and throughout most of January the pilots at Chrudim were confined to their quarters where they occasionally studied fighter gun camera film and

20 February 1945: an Allied reconnaissance aircraft photographs seven of KG(J) 30's Mistel on the taxiways at Prague-Ruzyne.

Oberleutnant Heinz Frommhold and a canine friend pause for a rest on the roof of a military car during 3./KG 30's journey from Wesendorf to Chrudim in late 1944. Having reluctantly given up its Ju 88s, 3.Staffel converted to Bf 109 fighters. Frommhold was later assigned to fly the Mistel against Russian targets for Operation Eisenhammer and then over the River Oder in April 1945.

received visits from fighter pilots who lectured them on basic operational doctrine. A few pilots were sent to a *Jagdfliegerschule* at Rosenborn, south of Breslau, but since this school no longer had any Bf 109s, the instruction remained purely theoretical. As the writer of 3./KG(J) 30's *Staffelchronik* has recorded: 'For a frontline unit like KG(J) 30, these were hard times. We did not receive any more fighters, nor did we see any action in the *Reichsverteidigung*.'

Berlin-born *Oberleutnant* Heinz Frommhold was a young, but experienced bomber pilot who was assigned to Operation *Eisenhammer*; he remembers:

'After completing regular pilot training, on 6 December 1942, I was assigned with my crew to I./KG 60 which was in the process of being formed at Tours in France. I was to serve as both pilot and maintenance officer of 3. *Staffel*. The 1. and 2. *Staffel* were flying sorties against the Murmansk convoys from Banak where they were based with I. and II./KG 30. On 16 December, I was transferred to the *Stabsschwarm* of I./KG 60. In January 1943, 1. and 2. *Staffel* at Banak were disbanded and the rest of the *Geschwader* at Tours was transformed into a school for officers and named *Verbandsführerschule* KG 101. My crew and I were transferred to the *Erprobungsstaffel* of this unit. During 1943, we tested dive equipment, tactics and procedures, such as high-altitude bombing and the use of rocket-powered bombs, under operational conditions in northern Russia at Pleskau (Pskow) and at Foggia in Italy. On 26 May 1944, my crew was transferred to 3./KG 30 based at Le Culot near Louvain in Belgium and flew sorties with the Ju 88 S-3 over southern England, the Normandy beaches and against Allied troops and facilities in north-west France.

'At the beginning of December 1944, we were transferred to Chrudim, south of Pardubitz, and embarked upon conversion training onto the Bf 109. We were known as 3./KG(J) 30[2]. After a short course at the *Jagdfliegerschule* at Rosenborn, our future purpose became clear to us: we had to give up our careers as bomber pilots and join the fighters in the defence of the Reich. That was not easy for everyone; it meant parting with flight crews and mechanics with whom we had shared many joys and

[2] The designation 'KG(J)' indicated 'Kampfgeschwader (Jagd)' or 'Bomber Wing converted to Fighters'.

In January 1945, Oberstleutnant Bernhard Jope, seen here whilst Gruppenkommandeur of III./KG 100, was appointed Kommodore of KG(J) 30. It was proposed to put all Mistel units under his command for Unternehmen Eisenhammer.

A Mistel S2 of KG(J) 30 on the taxiway at Prague-Ruzyne in early 1945 with a tarpaulin draped over the cockpit of the Fw 190 upper component to keep out the rain. One of the unit's Fw 190s can also be seen, which was almost certainly used for familiarisation and conversion purposes, whilst in the distance two more Mistel are visible.

hardships and we would now be alone in the air. In other words we were to do the very opposite of everything we had done up until that time, but not without success. We were not really happy about flying fighter missions, but what had to be, had to be. So we stayed at Chrudim, but only moved our aircraft occasionally.'

Oberfähnrich Georg Gutsche was a pilot in III./KG(J) 30; he recalled:

> 'At the end of 1944, the experienced crews of KG 30 were torn apart. The observers, wireless operators and gunners were transferred to ground combat units while the pilots went to Pardubitz and Chrudim where they commenced retraining on the Bf 109 and had to make bad-weather landings and received radio communications training with ground stations. The few flights we made were without ground visibility and at night.'

Although most of the former bomber pilots found the transition to single-engined fighter aircraft relatively straightforward, the unit suffered the loss of its *Kommodore*, *Oberstleutnant* Siegmund-Ulrich *Freiherr* von Gravenreuth on the 16th, when his Bf 109 crashed into the ground following a high-altitude flight. The *Kommodore* of KG 100, *Oberstleutnant* Bernhard Jope, then took command of newly redesignated KG(J) 30. For Operation *Eisenhammer*, Koller proposed placing all *Mistel* – those of II./KG 200 as well as I. and II./KG(J) 30 – under Jope's central command.

Jope, a renowned bomber ace who had been awarded the *Ritterkreuz* in 1940 for sinking the 42,348 ton *Empress of Britain* whilst flying Fw 200s with KG 40, recalled his new command:

> 'At the time KG 100 was disbanded, I held the rank of *Oberstleutnant* and I was posted to take over command of *Kampfgeschwader* 30. This *Geschwader* had given up its bombers and its pilots were retraining on fighters. We expected that we would be assigned to fly Reich defence operations along with other units. Following a brief training course on the Fw 190 and Bf 109, I moved with my *Geschwader* staff to the airfield at Prague-Ruzyne.'

Of the entire installed power capability of the Moscow/Upper Volga area – 2.5 million kW – about 60 per cent, or 1.5 million kW output, were included in the projected *Eisenhammer* target list. It was anticipated that by using *Mistel* against these targets, approximately 60 per cent destruction could be achieved, representing a 40 per cent loss in output. In a generally optimistic report prepared for Göring on 18 January, Koller did at least acknowledge that there would be some difficulties in bringing off the attack, though these were not deemed to be insurmountable. Landing grounds close to the targets could still be found; four days earlier, *Oberst* von Greiff, the Operations Officer of the OKL *Führungsstab,* drew up a provisional list of airfields throughout West and East Prussia and within the command area of *Luftflotte* 6 which were to be assigned for the use of those units participating in *Eisenhammer*. These were Prowehren, Jesau, Wormditt, Hexengrund, Praust and Berent.

A pathfinder and illumination force would lead the *Mistel*, assisted by radio beacons and navigation specialists. This would comprise:

1. 23-25 'long-range' He 111 H-20s from II./KG 4.
2. 20 Ju 88s and Ju 188s from I./KG 66 modified to carry two additional 900-litre fuel tanks.
3. 10-12 Ju 88s and Ju 188s from 5./KG 200 suitably modified for long-range operations.
4. A reserve of 10-15 Ju 88s and/or Ju 188s. (This was redefined on 23 January as 15 Ju 188 D-2s under cooperation with the *General der Aufklärungsflieger*).

Göring – keen now for the success of a high profile Luftwaffe mission – did not keep Koller waiting long for authorisation to proceed. On 23 January, Koller wrote to

A Junkers Ju 88 S-3 of I./KG 66 at Tutow in March or April 1945. The Gruppe was tasked with providing illumination and 'pathfinder' support for the Mistel of KG(J) 30 and II./KG 200 during Unternehmen Eisenhammer. The aircraft has been draped with camouflage netting and, in accordance with instructions issued by OKL, has been fitted with auxiliary wing and bomb bay fuel tanks specifically for the operation.

Baumbach, *Oberst i.G.* Friedrich Kless on the staff of *Luftflotte* 6, *Oberst i.G* Erhard Krafft von Dellmensingen on the staff of IX.(J) *Fliegerkorps* and the *General der Kampfflieger, Oberstleutnant* Hans-Henning *Freiherr* von Beust; he confirmed that KG(J) 30 was to be removed from the jurisdiction of IX.(J) *Fliegerkorps* and was to be placed at the disposal of KG 200 for full-scale conversion to the *Mistel*. However, in a somewhat complex chain of command, and in line with original plans, *Oberstleutnant* Jope, the commander of KG(J) 30, was to assume day-to-day command of forthcoming *Mistel* operations, reporting to Baumbach.

Ten Ju 88s (four with dual controls) and 20 Fw 190s were to be assigned immediately to KG(J) 30 for conversion training. The strength of the unit was to be supplemented by drafting in 100 pilots from KG 40 and the now disbanded II./KG 100 and a total of 1,800 cubic metres of fuel was to be allocated for training and operations.

Bernhard Jope recalled the events of January 1945 at Prague-Ruzyne to the British aviation historian, Alfred Price:

'A few days after my arrival, I received orders to make myself and my senior officers available for a top secret briefing from officers of Göring's personal staff. The officers duly arrived and the main part of the briefing was given by a civilian professor from the intelligence department [author's note: this would have been Steinmann]. He began by telling us about *Beethoven-Gerät*, the code name of one of the "secret weapons" from which great things were expected. This one comprised an explosive-laden Ju 88 bomber, on top of which was rigidly mounted a Fw 190 or Me 109 fighter.

'The *Beethoven-Gerät* promised several advantages over a conventional bomber. It could deliver an extremely destructive warhead to a target with reasonable accuracy; moreover, if the attack was planned so that the approach was made during the hours of darkness and the target was reached at first light, the pilot made the dangerous return flight through the alerted enemy defences in a high performance fighter with an excellent chance of avoiding interception.

'The professor then went on to outline the operation which was in an advanced state of preparation, for which *Beethoven-Gerät* was to be used. Code-named *Eisenhammer*, it involved a large scale co-ordinated air strike on the important power stations feeding Russian industry in the Moscow and Gorky regions. These targets, comparatively small and well-protected by concrete, were almost invulnerable to attack by ordinary bombs. If we could deliver one or two *Beethoven-Gerät* warheads on each, however, it would be a different matter.

'We were then informed that our *Geschwader*, KG 30, was one of those chosen to fly the *Beethoven-Gerät* combinations during the *Eisenhammer* operations. So that was why all my pilots had been retrained to fly fighters… We learned that many of the combinations earmarked for the operation were ready and work on putting together the remainder was proceeding at the highest priority. The first of these aircraft would be delivered to Ruzyne shortly and training for the operation was to begin immediately. We left the two-hour briefing breathless with excitement. The enemy had been having his way for too long; now, at last, we could see a chance for us to strike back hard.'

A few days later the first *Mistel* trainers arrived with KG(J) 30; Jope was not impressed:

'It looked such an ungainly machine, sitting at its dispersal point. To get into the cockpit of the fighter one had to climb up a long ladder placed against one wing. Climbing it, I felt rather like a window cleaner! The cockpit of the fighter was about 18 ft high, which felt a bit odd; although when I was seated my head was in fact a little higher that it was when I was in a Focke-Wulf *Condor* on the ground. In the Fw 190 there was a small extra panel underneath the main instrument panel, which carried the instruments and switches necessary to control the Ju 88. There were separate controls to raise the undercarriage of the bomber after take-off.

'The big day came for my first flight in the *Beethoven-Gerät*. Possibly because I had expected all sorts of difficulties with this unusual aircraft, and therefore handled it even more carefully than was usual with a new type, my first flight was a bit of an anti-climax. I simply started up, taxied-out, took-off and tried a few turns to get the feel of the thing; it was all quite straightforward. So far as I can remember, none of my other pilots had any problems with the combination either. The initial flights were made with the lower component carrying little fuel and no warhead, so it was not very heavy and this made the combination easy to handle; during later flights the lower component was made progressively heavier.

'Cruising in the *Beethoven-Gerät* felt a little strange, as one was sitting in a fighter but the controls had the feel of those of a bomber. It handled like a normal Junkers 88, but there was a little more inertia during manoeuvres and so one had to be careful especially when close to the ground. During flight all three engines were kept running; on their power the combination was, perhaps surprisingly, about 50 kph faster than the equivalent version of the Ju 88 by itself. If there was an engine failure, the combination handled just like any other three-engined aircraft; if the centre engine failed there was no problem, because one was left with an ordinary twin-engined aircraft; if one of the bomber's engines failed, there was less of a tendency to swing than with a normal twin-engined type. Engine handling was in many ways similar to that of the old Junkers 52 three-engined transport. I personally never lost an engine while flying the *Beethoven-Gerät*, but I anticipated no serious problems if it had occurred.

'Throughout the flight, when controlled from the cockpit of the fighter, the Junkers 88's control surfaces were operated by a special type of automatic pilot. The pilot could select one of two positions: *Reiseflug* (cruising flight) or *Automatik*. The in-flight manoeuvres were made on *Reiseflug*; on this setting the movements of the stick and rudder pedals in the fighter were relayed electrically to the automatic pilot in the Ju 88, which then moved its control surfaces by the corresponding amount – it was probably the world's first fly-by-wire aircraft control system to enter service. On *Automatik* the autopilot held the aircraft on whatever heading or altitude had been established; this position could be selected to ease the pilot's workload on the way to the target, and was also used when the combination was lined up for the final dive to the target immediately before the pilot fired the explosive bolts to disengage the fighter."

Pilots and some ground crew from 3./KG(J) 30 arrived at Prague-Ruzyne from Chrudim on 4 February 1945. Training on the *Mistel* was limited mostly to take-offs and circuits around the field. To ensure a safe take-off, it was vital to line the *Mistel* up so that it sat absolutely straight on the runway. The *Staffel's* pilots found that the most difficult moment was the initial start until the tail lifted, when forward visibility finally became available and it was possible to make any necessary corrections. Up to this point, the throttle had to be handled with the utmost care. As soon as the wheels left the runway, the pilot needed to throttle back slightly and, at 300 metres, the flaps could be retracted. Though no major problems were experienced, one accident did occur when the support struts on one composite collapsed on landing and the propellers of the Fw 190 sliced through the canopy of the Ju 88, killing its pilot. It was only towards the end of the training period that one hour duration flights were undertaken in order to familiarise the former bomber pilots with the cramped confines of a fighter's cockpit for a longer period of time. The total training period lasted some 15 hours.

Oberfähnrich Georg Gutsche of III./KG(J) 30 was a very experienced bomber pilot, formerly a senior NCO; he remembers:

'We had barely become familiar with all-weather flying and blind landings, than we were ordered to convert to the Fw 190. Our fighter conversion ended quickly, and we were confronted at Prague-Ruzyne with a "flying contraption" for which we could see no use. It consisted of a Ju 88 with a Fw 190 mounted on three supports. The cockpit of the Ju 88 was manned by a training crew, while the pilot of the Fw 190 climbed into the cockpit by means of a five metre ladder. After I had made a few flights in the cockpit of the Ju 88, I found that the contraption was relatively easy to fly and to land. The same was also true for the pilot of the Fw 190, who after all had to steer the *Mistel*. This was made possible through the electrical steering connections that were located inside the three supports. During training flights, the pilots communicated with each other by means of the EiV system.[3] The Fw 190 pilot could control the flaps, the trim, and the propeller settings as well as the fuel tank pumps and the Ju 88's throttle. All the Ju 88's rudders could be manipulated so easily it was as if one were only flying the Fw 190. Stick synchronisation was outstanding. However as the pilot of the Ju 88, I was seriously concerned about the fact that the propeller of the Fw 190 was only 20 centimetres above my head! During a hard landing, the supports could collapse and the propellers could cut through the cockpit and smash the head of the pilot. Such a case did occur despite especially reinforced supports for the fighter.

'Practice flights were not only designed to master flying the *Mistel* but also emphasised attack exercises against ground targets. The pilots had to fly at the target and aim by means of a simple cross hairs gunsight. The Fw 190 pilot would take over control by means of a switch. The target was approached at 3,000 metres at a distance of 3-4 km, brought into the cross hairs of the gunsight and then the automatic targeting system took over. Normally, one course correction was necessary in order to hold the target in the cross hairs. The instructor pilot could see in his gunsight what mistake the student was making and could contact him via the EiV system. He could also take over the steering at any time. As soon as the target was in the cross hairs of the gunsight the Fw 190 pilot pushed the release button. In an emergency the Ju 88 could be blasted off with small explosive devices. During the instruction period, the instructor pilot took over the lower aircraft.'

Typical of the kind of pilot now training up on the *Mistel* at Ruzyne was 27-year-old *Feldwebel* Karl Russmeyer. Russmeyer had joined the Luftwaffe in July

[3] EiV (Eigenverständigungsanlage) = Intercommunication equipment used normally for use between a pilot and radar operator, but in this case adapted for the Mistel. It consisted of a throat microphone and headphones.

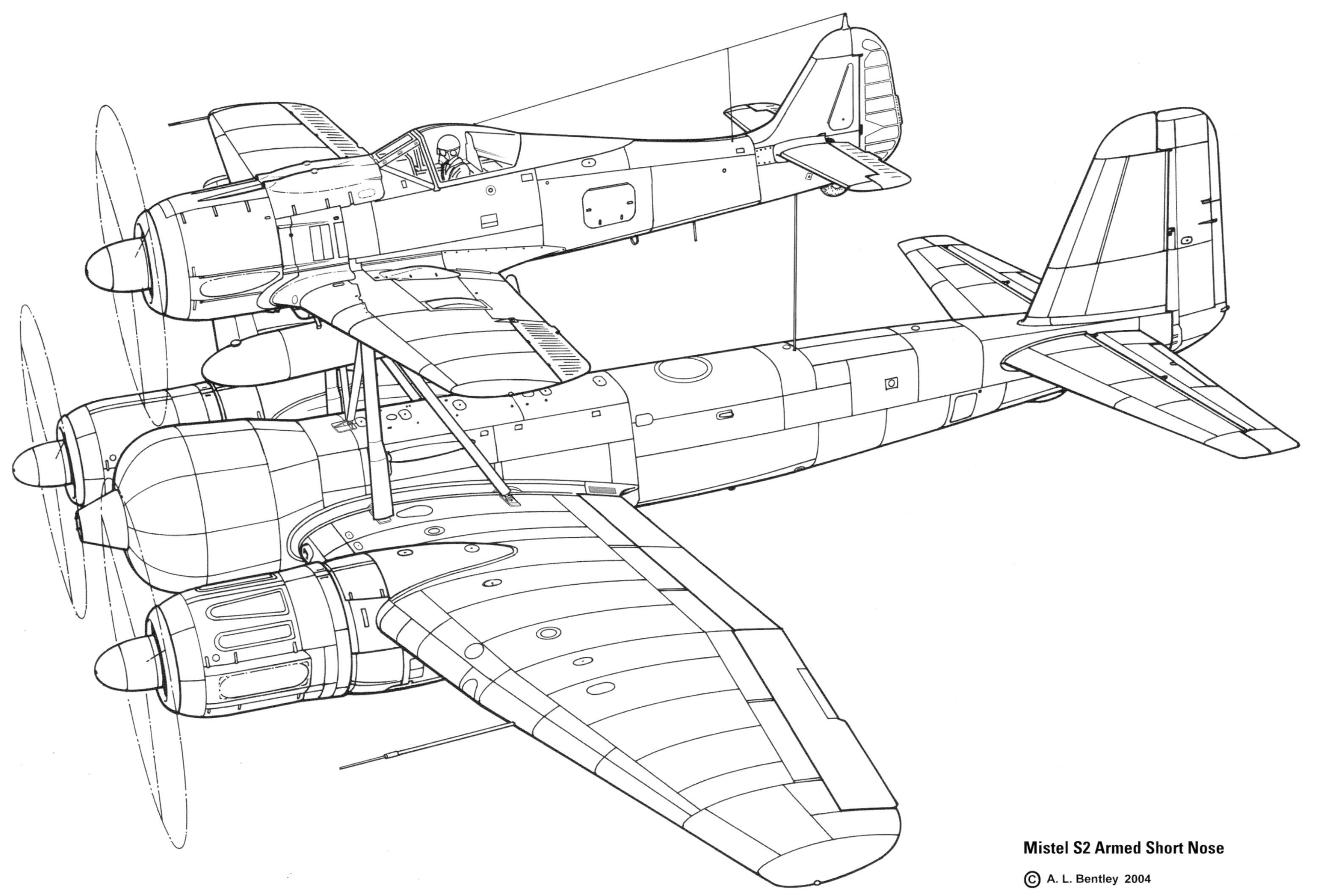

Mistel S2 Armed Short Nose

© A. L. Bentley 2004

1940 having served in an *Ausbildungs Regiment* at Schleswig where he initially wanted to train to become a flying boat pilot. From Christmas 1940 through to July 1943, he underwent training at the *Flugzeuführerschule* A/B 7 at Plauen, followed by the C-*Schule* at Bourges in France, then *Blindflugschule* (6) in Wesendorf where he flew the Ju 52, He 111 and Ju 86. In July 1943, he was posted to *Überführungsgeschwader West* at Villacoublay in France where he flew many different types including the Ju 52 and Ju 88. There was a Junkers production line at Villacoublay, from where Russmeyer delivered Ju 52s and Ju 88s to front-line units. In January 1944, he was transferred to IV./KG 30 at Aalborg in Denmark with which he underwent tactical and operational training on the Ju 88 before moving six months later to 3./KG 30 which was equipped with the Ju 88 S-3. The *Staffel* moved to Le Culot in France in July 1944 and for most of July, Russmeyer embarked upon anti-invasion sorties off the Normandy coast. He recalls:

'After the invasion, every front was in inescapable retreat as the war wound towards its bitter end. Our KG 30 was transferred to the Osnabrück area. On 19 September 1944, my crew along with the others of our *Staffel* flew its last mission on bombers. We attacked British troop concentrations near Eindhoven. Back at Achmer, we climbed down from our trusty Ju 88 S-3 and we were all really depressed.

'Following a spell of leave in Ribbesbüttel near Gifhorn, we began fighter conversion at Chrudim on 3 December 1944. I flew the Ar 96, the Bü 181 and finally the Bf 109, before taking leave of the defence of the Reich. *Oberfeldwebel* Ermert and I flew in a Fw 44 *Stieglitz* to Kasteletz near Olmütz for conversion to the Fw 190. Then, on 9 February 1945, we transferred to Prague-Ruzyne for conversion to the *Mistel* or, as we knew it, the '*Nero*'. When I first saw it, I was greatly astonished. I had no idea how I was going to fly it. Nevertheless, I regarded it as a challenge and got on with it. Of course, we weren't allowed to talk about the *Mistel* concept at the time, but my personal opinion was that it was a *Himmelsfahrt-Kommando* (a "Ticket to Heaven"). A good idea, but dangerous – very dangerous.'

On 9 February, Russmeyer made three circuits around Ruzyne in Ju 88 A-4, CI+WF and two flights in Fw 190 '3'. Two days later, he made a 30-minute flight in Fw 190 '8' before embarking on four short flights in Ju 88 A-5, DE+XM. Finally on 23 February, he climbed into Fw 190/Ju 88 G-1 *Mistel* '100' for the first time. He remembers:

'During training, the KG 30 pilots sat in the upper fighter and would make take-offs so that they could get a feel for where they were in relation to the ground. When the Ju 88 pilot thought that the upper pilot had a good enough "feel", he was then allowed to take over control of the *Mistel*. During flight, you could feel movement between the two aircraft. This was due to the lack of stiffness of the truss structure joining the aircraft. Once training was completed, the upper pilot was then expected to train new pilots in a similar way.

'From the top seat there was very poor visibility of the ground. At least one of our pilots was killed during training when, upon the pupil making a heavy landing, the supporting struts collapsed through the shock of touchdown and the fighter's propeller cut into the cockpit of the Ju 88 and killed its pilot. The unfortunate victim had the *Deutsches Kreuz in Gold*.

'Upon completion of our training at Prague-Ruzyne, we received a so-called *Russland-Notgepäck* ('Russia emergency pack).[4] At that moment, our area of intended operations became clear.'

Accidents did not cause the only problems. By early 1945, Prague-Ruzyne, like so many other airfields, was no longer immune from the attentions of Allied fighters; as Bernhard Jope recalled:

'During our training flights in the *Beethoven-Gerät* we had to keep our eyes open for Allied long-range fighters; by that stage of the war, nowhere was safe from them. On one occasion Spitfires carried out a low-level strafing attack on Ruzyne, shooting up some of our aircraft. Our Flak defences opened up, but the British pilots demonstrated their contempt for the gunners' efforts by performing victory rolls as they climbed away. We were most impressed by this display by the sporting Royal Air Force.'

According to Heinz Frommhold:

'All our crews thought the Ju 88 the best aircraft of all and I think we knew what we were talking about! The Ju 88 formed part of the *Mistel* and even though the two parts were assembled together as quickly as possible, we could see that every detail represented solid workmanship. If people like Lux and Holzbaur could fly the bastard thing then so could we! As far as flying the *Mistel* was concerned, it was a perfect aircraft despite its strange appearance. Take-off was tricky though, because you had to maintain direction without being able to see anything in front of the aircraft until it had enough speed so you could lift the tailwheel off the ground. Until that point, you had to take your chance! But as a matter of fact, I never saw a take-off where the pilot lost control of direction. In the air, you felt like you were flying an ordinary three-engined aircraft. True, you could not fly aerobatics with it, but I found I could handle it like any other 'bird' I flew, and I flew many of them. The BMW 801 D-2 engines were reliable: motors with good records in all the aircraft into which they had been installed. The steering system and transmission seemed perfect, though we did experience some breakdowns. However, I don't think this was down to the basic design, but rather to the fact that there was not enough time to eliminate all the 'bugs' and to train maintenance personnel sufficiently. Thus, it was not so much the aircraft that caused apprehension as the planned mission and the fact that we did not have our normal crews with us, neither on-board or on the ground. For '*Eisenhammer*', we lacked our normal organisation and we were supposed to take off from unfamiliar airfields, fly a crate we were not that familiar with and which had been serviced by ground crews whom we did not know.'

Though maintenance of the Fw 190/Ju 88 *Mistel* was eased somewhat by the common usage of the BMW 801 radial engine, continual movement on the ground, which needed tractors and equipment, proved a drain on stocks of diesel fuel. The daily consumption of diesel fuel at

[4] Russland Notgepäck – lit. 'Russia Emergency Pack': intended as a personal survival kit for German aircrew shot down or force-landing in enemy territory during Eisenhammer. It was to consist of mountain emergency gear, a pistol, emergency rations, medical supplies and other items. Further reference is given later in this chapter.

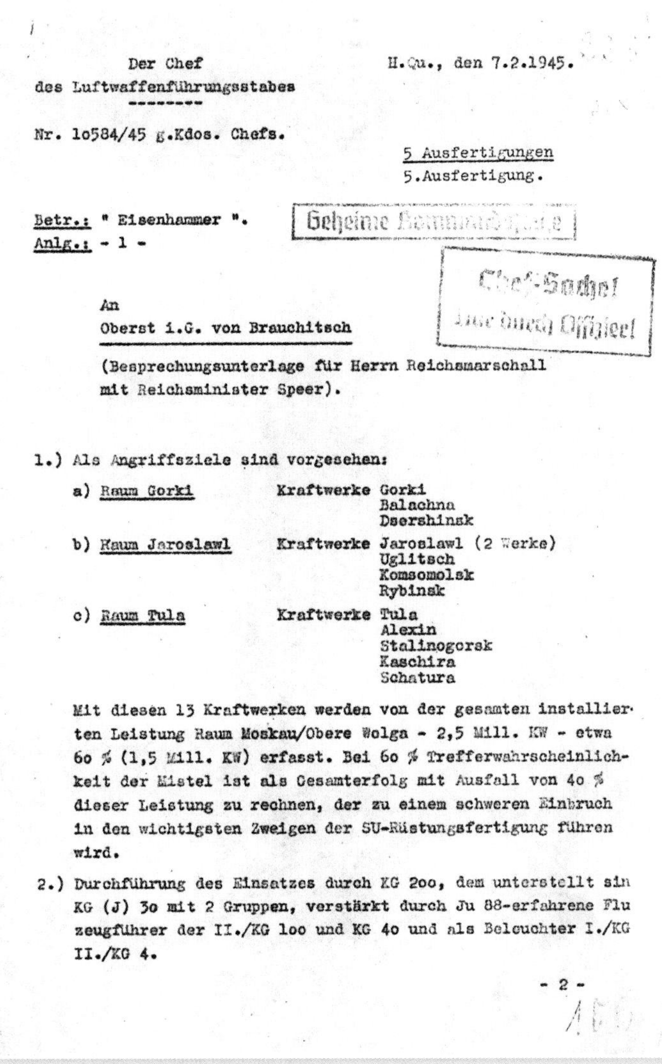

Der Chef
des Luftwaffenführungsstabes

H.Qu., den 7.2.1945.

Nr. 1o584/45 g.Kdos. Chefs.

5 Ausfertigungen
5.Ausfertigung.

Betr.: " Eisenhammer ".
Anlg.: - 1 -

Geheime Kommandosache

Chef-Sache!
Nur durch Offizier!

An
Oberst i.G. von Brauchitsch

(Besprechungsunterlage für Herrn Reichsmarschall mit Reichsminister Speer).

1.) Als Angriffsziele sind vorgesehen:

a) Raum Gorki	Kraftwerke	Gorki Balachna Dsershinsk
b) Raum Jaroslawl	Kraftwerke	Jaroslawl (2 Werke) Uglitsch Komsomolsk Rybinsk
c) Raum Tula	Kraftwerke	Tula Alexin Stalinogorsk Kaschira Schatura

Mit diesen 13 Kraftwerken werden von der gesamten installierten Leistung Raum Moskau/Obere Wolga - 2,5 Mill. KW - etwa 6o % (1,5 Mill. KW) erfasst. Bei 6o % Trefferwahrscheinlichkeit der Mistel ist als Gesamterfolg mit Ausfall von 4o % dieser Leistung zu rechnen, der zu einem schweren Einbruch in den wichtigsten Zweigen der SU-Rüstungsfertigung führen wird.

2.) Durchführung des Einsatzes durch KG 2oo, dem unterstellt sind KG (J) 3o mit 2 Gruppen, verstärkt durch Ju 88-erfahrene Flugzeugführer der II./KG 1oo und KG 4o und als Beleuchter I./KG II./KG 4.

- 2 -

First page of a document prepared by the Luftwaffe Chief of General Staff, General der Flieger Karl Koller, on 7 February 1945, for Oberst i.G. Bernd von Brauchitsch, adjutant to Reichsmarschall Göring, outlining the targets for Eisenhammer and the forces deployed. At this time, these were planned as two Gruppen from KG(J) 30 assigned to KG 200, supported by pilots with experience on the Ju 88 from II./KG 100 and KG 40, as well as pathfinders from II./KG 4.

Ruzyne was estimated at 200 litres because the *Mistel* had to be continually separated at the end of training so as to minimise the risk of damage from air attack.

In Berlin, evidence that competing interests were at work is contained in a minute from the OKL daily conference on 2 February:

> 'The *Reichsmarschall* agreed that the 100 *Mistel* aircraft planned by *Reichsminister* Speer, in addition to the 130 already in production or completed, will not now be built so as to allow industrial capacity to be freed for other purposes. The *Reichsmarschall* intends to confer with *Reichsminister* Speer.'

It is not known whether such conferral ever took place or with what result, but ten days later the OKL diarist recorded:

> 'Operation *Eisenhammer* will be carried out at all costs. Preparations will be expedited. The fuel required for the operation has been promised by OKW.'

The following day, 13 February:

> 'After the fuel required for Operation *Eisenhammer* had been provided by OKW, the *Reichsmarschall* decided that the operation will be prepared and carried out as soon as possible.'

Twenty-four hours later, KG 200, by this time assigned by Göring to supervise all aspects of *Eisenhammer*, confirmed that provided initial preparations were completed in time, it would be ready to undertake the operation 'as early as the end of February or beginning of March.' OKL seized the moment: *Oberst* Eckhard Christian of the *Luftwaffenführungsstab* wrote:

> 'KG 200's main objective is Operation *Eisenhammer*. All measures to be taken to accelerate preparations. Desired date of operation is the February/March moon period. As ordered, the *Kommodore* of KG 200, *Obstlt.* Baumbach, is responsible for preparation and execution; he must put all other matters aside and concentrate on this mission.'

Ten days later, on 24 February, General Koller sent out two emergency orders. The first of these was despatched to the *General der Kampfflieger, Oberstleutnant Freiherr* von Beust, instructing him to provide 'with immediate effect', on KG 200's request, 18 pilots experienced on the Ju 88 for 'special operations'. These were to be drawn from LG 1 at 'Top speed!' In another order addressed to *Generalmajor* Nielsen, Chief of Staff of *Luftflotte Reich*, 17 pilots from KG(J) 30 were ordered to be released for the same purpose.

> 'The Chief of Staff gives instructions for orders to this effect to be issued,' recalls the OKL war diary, 'as the best pilots are necessary for this operation if it is to be at all successful.'

Losses of valuable pilots were still being suffered by II./KG 200 during training; for example on 19 February, Ju 88 G-1, W.Nr.714230, crashed killing its pilot, *Feldwebel* Hermann Stolle and three ground personnel. The Fw 190 A-8 upper component, W.Nr.731420, was 45 per cent damaged. Alfred Lew, a pilot with 6./KG 200 recalled the incident:

'On that day, Stolle made a check flight with the *Mistel*. Hans Brodesser sat in the Fw 190. The Ju 88's undercarriage would not extend during the approach to land. Stolle increased his altitude to about 600 metres to allow Brodesser to separate over the airfield. Unfortunately, the Fw 190 did not immediately free itself from the rear strut fastening it to the Ju 88, and it pitched forwards between the cockpit and the left engine of the Ju 88. Brodesser made an emergency landing in the Fw 190 and was not injured. I witnessed the crash because I was due to make a training flight in the same *Mistel* afterwards. I wanted to make the check flight myself but Stolle talked me out of it. That's life.'

In addition to the resources demanded by Koller, the long-range Ju 290s of 2./FAGr. 5, a unit which had earlier in the month been due to disband, were placed under the command of *Major* Fischer's FAGr. 1 which, in turn, was placed under the command of KG 200 'for the duration of two special operations.'[5] These aircraft were required to function as pathfinders in the Moscow/Upper Volga area and to undertake reconnaissance after the attack.

On 5 March, Allied intelligence picked up a radio message from a *Professor* Immler in Ansbach ordering the collection of 60 maps from Jena which were to be made available by the 9th. At around the same time the airfields at Rostock-Marienehe, Oranienburg, Rechlin, Parchim, Briest and Peenemünde were designated for *Mistel* deployment. On 17 March *Luftgau* XI's depot at Lübeck was ordered to despatch a consignment of 17 BMW 801 engines, used by the Fw 190 A, F and G and the Ju 88, to Parchim and Marienehe. The airfields at Neubrandenburg, Tutow, Peenemünde, Garz, Barth and Pütnitz would be used by the Ju 88, Ju 188 and He 111 'illuminators' whilst the Ju 290s of 2./FAGr. 5 would operate from Lärz. Heinz Frommhold of 3./KG(J) 30 recalled:

'At the beginning of March 1945 we left our fighters in Chrudim and transferred to Peenemünde where there were live *Mistel* waiting for us and we thus had our first chance to look at these monstrosities. We had been told at Ruzyne what could be done with them, but what our forthcoming missions would be we only vaguely understood at that moment.'

Also on the 17th, *Mistel* pilots from both KG 200 and KG(J) 30 as well as crews from the pathfinder units assigned to *Eisenhammer* were ordered to Berlin for a week of intensive and top secret briefings. These were hosted by *Professor* Steinmann who would outline the political and strategic objectives of the operation; Siegfried Holzbaur who would cover technical aspects; the *Kommodore* and senior officers from KG 200 who would brief on tactical methods, and a host of other luminaries. With the aid of vast wall maps, Baumbach and his assistants outlined the attack plan. In the first leg, the whole attack force – *Mistel* led by Ju 88, Ju 188 and Ju 290 pathfinders – would fly north to Bornholm where the course would be changed eastwards across the Baltic to cross the coast north of Königsberg. Then, having flown over East Prussia and the old Soviet border, the second stage would take the formation along a highway from Minsk to Smolensk where it would split. One group of *Mistel* would turn south-east to attack Stalinogorsk and Tula while the remainder would continue east towards Gorki. North-west of Moscow, one section would make for Rybinsk.

Following the attack, the Fw 190 upper components would make for designated landing strips in the Kurland pocket, a salient of land just 150 km wide backing on to the Baltic and which the Red Army had rolled past during its advance into Poland. It was now defended by the remnants of Army Group North and protected by two *Gruppen* of fighters from JG 54. A consignment of 90 tons of fuel was flown into Kurland especially for the homeward bound upper component fighters.

The history of 3./KG(J) 30 records:

'During the middle of March as the training on the *Mistel* 2 ended, we began intensive target training at the *Luftkriegsschule* at Berlin-Gatow. The *Eisenhammer* targets were the steam and power plants around Moscow. The pilots were divided up into specific groups of three to six *Mistel*, each group assigned to a specific target. The briefings were detailed. Every group had its target presented to the minutest detail. There were aerial photographs taken from all directions and in all kinds of weather, as well as a three-dimensional model of the surrounding landscape. The groups spent many hours studying and discussing the best possible approach needed to destroy the turbine unit because this was the heart of the power plant. The targeting plans as well as the navigational plans were calculated and recalculated. The tight cockpit layout and emergency procedures were studied over and over again. Nobody doubted that they had the ability to manage this complicated machinery and also to pull off a perfect take-off. Some had serious worries about making such a long flight without a crew. The target briefing ended with a visit to the power plant at Spandau as well as a fly-over in a Ju 52, making approaches to the plant from various directions. The purpose was to acquaint us with the dimensions and the position of the specific targets (which would be illuminated). Whether theory and practice would coincide remained an open question.'

Karl Russmeyer was one of the 3. *Staffel* pilots who flew over Spandau; he recalls:

'*Professor* Steinmann was disappointed that his proposal, originally made in 1942, had been adopted almost too late. He was reserved when delivering his talk. But he was precise and did not waste words. What he said was convincing. Steinmann showed us that the most important part of the power stations were the turbine houses, for the simple reason that if the turbines were damaged, to repair them would take six months. The Russians were not in a position to build their own turbines. They were only capable of making temporary repairs and therefore were unable to replace them. Steinmann had the original photographs of the power house installations. Siemens had, in fact, delivered the turbines and had supplied the photos. These photos had been taken throughout the year and thus showed all the different climatic conditions, so that the targets would be recognisable under any circumstances. Because of these photos, our pilots would

[5] Operation Eisenhammer and Operation Drachenhöhle (see Chapter Nine).

not be surprised if there was bad weather and would always be able to recognise the targets. So that we would become even more familiar with our target, we were all packed into a Ju 52 and flown to and around 'the target' [Berlin-Spandau] and it was pointed out – "*That is the turbine house!*"'

If nothing else, the briefing had been well organised. Horst Dieter Lux was in attendance and remembered:

'This mission required a platform which would deliver a large explosive device with extreme accuracy. '*Huckepack*' was the only system which could do that. Fifty targets were selected and 120 pilots were picked. At a secure facility models of the targets were built. The pilots could study them under all kinds of conditions, day and night time, with and without snow, under good or bad visibility. It was a fantastic toy store. It kept the pilots busy, who for security reasons were not permitted to leave the premises.'

Many of the *Mistel* pilots were impressed by the levels of planning; as Heinz Frommhold remembered:

'Besides pilots of all ranks, there were a great number of generals, representatives from industry, economic advisors and "Golden Pheasants" present. We were warned about the strictest security and were not allowed to leave the premises. We were instructed about the operation and the targets and were given the details of how the operation was to proceed. We were divided into specific target units. Each power plant was to be targeted by between four and six *Mistel*. The targeting instructions were outstanding. Every detail was thought of and by using detailed maps, photo reconnaissance pictures and large dioramas, the targets were introduced to us. Each group spent hours working out the most efficient course of attack against the power stations. The turbine installations, as the heart of the power station, were the main target, and were to be totally destroyed. During a visit to the power station at Berlin-Spandau in a Ju 52 we were able to observe from the air the large expanse of a power station and were instructed as to where the heart of the station was. Course, headings, impact points (which were to be marked by the pathfinders) and target illumination was mentioned repeatedly and the proper documentation was handed out. In a general command session, the importance of the mission was made clear to us. Since the initially planned airfields in East Prussia were no longer available to us and the range was too great for a successful return of many machines, new landing fields were assigned to us inside the so-called Kurland Pocket. The question of whether planning and execution would mesh successfully was never answered. Despite the marking of the route and illumination of the target, pilots would reach their targets only after an eight hour night flight. Following the attack, the pilot had to return in a fully tanked up Fw 190 a distance of 1,200 km, about two-and-a-half hours flying time in broad daylight to the Baltic. Was that possible? Each pilot had to answer this question for himself. For most pilots, this was a mission that made them a little nervous, but they were young and had a devil-may-care attitude and believed nothing could be changed. Just like the briefings the personal equipment accorded us was excellent. In addition to a parachute, we carried mountain emergency gear, two flare pistols, a Walther 7.65 pistol, emergency rations in a backpack, medical kit in the knee pouch, a small pack with scissors, fishhooks, rope, 75,000 roubles and cartridges for the flare pistols. The Walther was strapped to the shin bone, watch and compass strapped to the wrist and there was a giant map with the course marked. How tight the cockpit of the Fw 190 was, one can only appreciate if one has sat in one.'

Amongst the contingent from 6./KG 200 was *Feldwebel* Rudi Riedl who had recently returned from Denmark where he had been due to take part in the ill-fated *Drachenhöhle* operation; he too remembers the unprecedented extent to which preparations were made:

'It was proposed that approximately 80 *Mistel* would put a number of hydroelectric dams out of action. We were brought together at the War Academy at Berlin-Gatow and there trained and prepared for possible operations. We had never before had so many prominent people in our company. Large models were available to us so that we could impress on our memories details of our targets. Timing was of the essence, because every drop of fuel was necessary for the return flight. A return flight to our point of departure could not be guaranteed with these suicide missions. The only course open to us was to fly to Kurland where a small airstrip was held by our fighting troops under the worst possible conditions. Each pilot had 75,000 roubles in a knapsack. We were expected to buy our freedom to the west in the event of an emergency landing. What an absurd thought – but then, nothing in wartime is impossible. Hitler could wait no longer. He pestered and pestered, but no one could change the weather – not even him! We had to have stable weather conditions to carry out the attack. All return flights were based on this condition. The attack was planned to take place towards the end of March. Our route was to be marked with coloured flares dropped by a "pathfinder" unit. We all followed a central marker. Eight to nine groups were foreseen; each had its own colour, which it was required to follow all the way to the target.'

Leutnant Hans Altrogge was a pathfinder pilot from I./KG 66; highly experienced on the Ju 88 S, his navigation and flying skills would be crucial to the success of *Eisenhammer*.

'By all standards, preparations for *Eisenhammer* were very thorough. I spent some five to seven weeks in total isolation with the other pilots at the *Kriegsschule* at Gatow. We were visited by experts in all different fields and we attended many briefings and lectures. These lectures included instruction on the Russian language, the Russian people and its culture, survival techniques and escape routes. Engineers who had built the power stations during the 1930s told us everything they knew about the plants and especially about the turbines which were the primary targets; where they were located within each station and which was the best approach. We were shown pictures taken from every angle in summer and winter. We had to learn everything by heart. By the end of it, I felt I had lived there all my life. You could have asked me things in my sleep.

'One thing however, was concerning every pilot: the mental stress of knowing that the return was very, very risky. Even with the most favourable wind and weather conditions, there was a fuel margin of about 3-5 per cent. That's equal to zero! It was very worrying for us that we had to plan our escape not as a remote possibility but as a very real option. Some decided that they would head south and take a dinghy and a pocket full of roubles with them, but as for me… well, I always liked the snow and planned to go north. All these years later, it is one of those things which makes me wonder how people can proceed with their duties even though they know that they are on a "*Kamikaze*" mission.'

Heinz Frommhold of 3./KG (J) 30 remembered:

'I was supposed to attack the power plant at Rybinsk with four other pilots. Just like the other target units and pilots, we spent most of our time going over and over our flight route so as to recalculate our navigational plan for the hundredth time and to acquaint ourselves with the peculiarities of the Fw 190 cockpit. We also made sure that all emergency equipment was checked out and tested for its practicality. We had no doubts about our ability to handle the complicated contraption and even to successfully take off with the overloaded machine, but the thought of flying eight hours without a crew brought a bit of uneasiness to the pilots. I was familiar with Rybinsk from a previous attack. I had lost an engine above the dam from anti-aircraft fire. Since you don't normally get hit in the same place twice and that the return flight with one engine was something perfectly clear cut, my worries began to dissipate.'

With the Gatow briefing over, the pilots were moved to their respective operational airfields. Many of the former bomber pilots found the next few days of gruelling preparations on unfamiliar airfields difficult without the back-up they received from their usual ground crews. Karl Russmeyer recalls:

'The planners knew that the chances of surviving the mission were very low and so while at Prague-Ruzyne we underwent a tough psychological examination to determine whether we had the right mental attitude for the operation.'

Meanwhile, at Junkers in Bernburg, Horst-Dieter Lux was focusing on technical experimentation to aid with the ranges and conditions which the *Eisenhammer* pilots were expected to encounter:

'While the pilots got familiar with their targets we, in industry, went into a three-shift production with 14,000 men. I had not too much to do with that, but my development and flight-testing kept me busy. With the forward thrust of the Russians, Germany lost vital air bases. This forced us to increase the range of the 'piggyback' from one day to the next. Eventually every cavity on the aeroplanes was filled with fuel. We also installed wing tanks.

'The Fw 190 was fitted with a long belly-tank which reached from two inches behind the propeller to the end of the fuselage. As time went on, range became critical and I had to tell the Luftwaffe. In order to be certain I was told to fly a simulated mission. The aeroplane assigned for the test had to have the exact weight of the operational version. The mass of the warhead was simulated with water and lead. We could not use the bomb because the lower aeroplane had to be brought back so that the residual fuel could be measured.

'I needed a pilot to fly the bomber and since the Luftwaffe decided to make it a combined test, they gave me one of theirs. All he needed to do was take control of the bomber after separation and land it. It sounds simple enough. It was not. Four pilots later, I found one who stuck it out. The others had left the project when they saw the test aircraft and experienced aborted attempts to fly the test.

'The Luftwaffe demanded a night take-off. The aeroplane was slowly, very slowly, pulled to the end of the runway. The gear which was originally designed for 10,880 kg, now had to carry more than 22,600 kg. While the aeroplane was towed it made unnerving noises and when the whole test had to be aborted because of sudden fog or some glitch in the complicated system, it became too much for the young pilots and they departed. There's no doubt it was very taxing. My flight in the fighter was over ten hours: six to the 'target' and four home. I was shoehorned into the cockpit with a lot of extra gear and instrumentation, special food, a Mae West and other survival gear. It was never a routine job to climb into that cockpit.

'Miraculously, after more than ten days of futile attempts to fly the test, everything fell into place. The night was dark but clear. The runway lights came on and I started the take-off run. At the last moment I broke ground. The flight card instructed me to reduce power immediately after being airborne. Had I done so, we would have crashed. I needed every ounce of power to stay airborne. With take-off power, I staggered on. The weight loss of used fuel was enough to finally get me closer to the prescribed power schedule. At daybreak we started to have trouble. The pumps on the external wing tanks on the bomber failed. This cancelled the test. I separated the fighter and let the bomber fly home while I continued with the test programme for the fighter's range.

'The flying was miserable. The long tank under the belly did not have enough baffles and the fuel was running either forward or aft, making the aeroplane pretty unstable. I was so busy trying to keep that rollercoaster under control that I was startled when the radio suddenly came alive. I was told to land immediately. Allied bombers with fighter escorts were approaching. For them, I would have been a sitting duck. I was tempted to jettison the belly tank, but we needed it to see how much fuel was left for our final range calculations. The half-full tank had all the makings of a bomb when touching the runway and grinding along on it. I decided to land on the grass and keep the tail up as long as possible. It worked. The tank did not explode or leak.'

Even as such testing and the *Eisenhammer* briefings were taking place however, events were rapidly overtaking German aspirations. By mid-March, the Soviet First Byelorussian Front was consolidating its position along the Oderbruch. The vital nodal point of the Küstrin 'fortress', spanning both the Oder and the Warthe rivers, was still in German hands, but General Berzarin's 5th Shock Army was about to advance on Golzow and Chuikov's 8th Guards Army was poised to take Kietz. On 18 March, just one day after the selected Luftwaffe crews arrived in Berlin, Koller advised Baumbach that even though the 'enemy offensive in the East may demand operations against the Oder bridges by units set aside for *Eisenhammer*' the operation was still regarded as of 'decisive importance even under present circumstances. Preparations for Operation *Eisenhammer* to be pressed on with determination to enable operation to be carried out during the March moon period.'

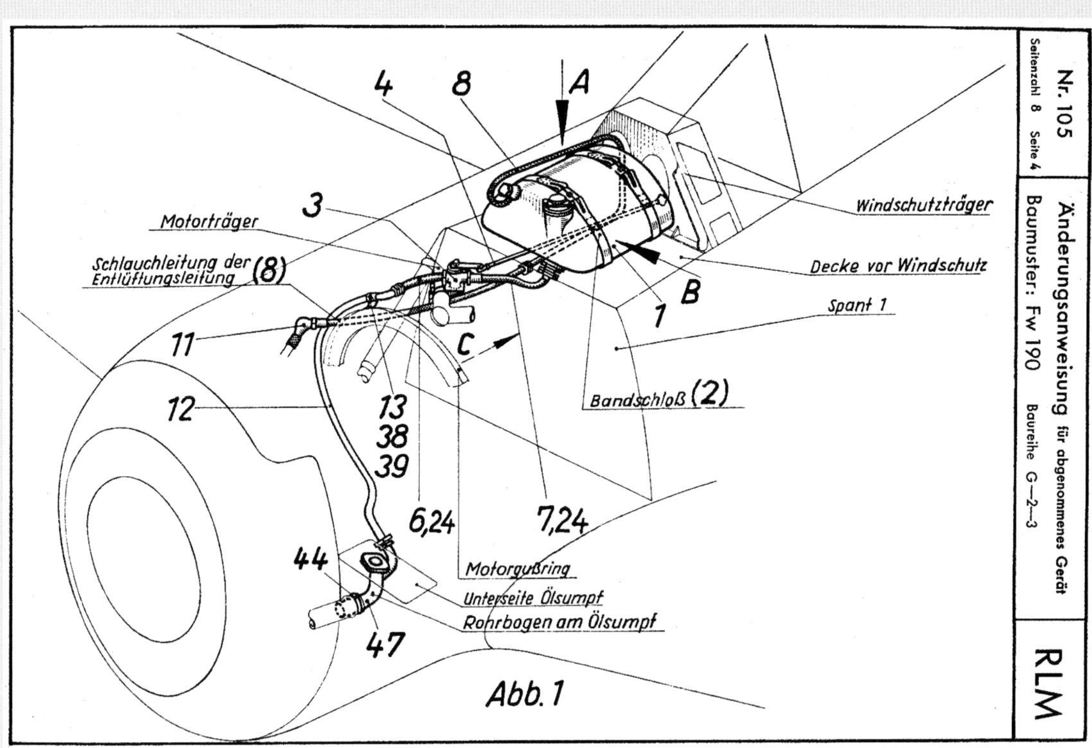

This drawing, issued by the RLM, shows the location of an auxiliary oil tank intended to increase operational range of the Fw 190. The tank is shown installed in the position normally occupied by two MG 131 machine guns in the Fw 190 G-2 and G-3 variants and would also have been applied to the Fw 190s used for the upper component of the Mistel.

Feldwebel Dietrich Deutsch, who had been assigned to take part in *Eisenhammer* from the disbanded 11./KG 30, recalled:

> 'Our take-off time was set between 1600 and 1900 hours. On all three of the possible days for the mission, we sat in our aircraft waiting for the signal. My airfield was Rechlin. The time went by without start orders coming through. We were somewhat disappointed because we did not know what was waiting for us; maybe infantry duty in a Luftwaffe field battalion. At the same time, we felt slightly easier that we did not have to fly the "suicide" mission.'

By 29 March, the garrison at Küstrin had surrendered under Soviet pressure. Zhukov's forces had now punched a bridgehead some 50 km wide and 10 km deep into the crumbling German defensive line. Berlin lay in reach. For the Luftwaffe, weather conditions were now also hampering plans. On the 30th, Christian was forced to advise Steinmann and Baumbach that *Eisenhammer* was 'postponed for the time being.' Aircraft and crews earmarked for the operation were to be released for operations against the enemy bridges over the Vistula, though they were to be 'pledged to secrecy, particularly in case of being taken prisoner. Operation *Eisenhammer* to be kept secret at all costs.'

Perhaps the final nail in *Eisenhammer's* coffin came on 10 April, when 103 B-24 Liberators from the US Eighth Air Force's 2nd Air Division bombed Rechlin-Lärz and destroyed 18 *Mistel*, a significant part of the attack force. Oddly, despite the flames resulting from the air attack, several of the *Mistel* warheads failed to detonate, but simply burned out slowly. At Oranienburg, the target for B-17s of the 1st Air Division, another five *Mistel* and six further Fw 190 upper components were destroyed when bombs fell upon the Lufthansa facilities in which they were hangared. The same day, in his operational orders, *Generaloberst* Robert von Greim, the commander of *Luftflotte* 6, issued orders to *Gefechtsverband* Helbig (see Chapter Thirteen):

> 'The execution of Operation *Eisenhammer* still takes priority, weather permitting, over all other missions.'

This determination is given credence by at least one pilot assigned to fly the *Eisenhammer* operation; Heinz Frommhold commented to the author:

> 'Back in 1945, I was sure we could make it; today, I still think that bearing in mind the situation behind the Soviet lines all the way to the Moscow area, we really could have made it. Not that it would have changed the course of the war, but we could have been successful in destroying a considerable number of power plants, especially since we knew that Soviet Flak forces in the target areas were considered insignificant.'

The possibility of attacking Soviet power installations also lingered on in the minds of those at the OKL. On 8 April 1945, *Major i. G.* Sandmann of the *Führungsstab* telephoned *Major* von Harnier, KG 200's operations officer, instructing him that *Major* Fischer and the Ju 290s of 2./FAGr. 5 were to be removed from Baumbach's personal jurisdiction and placed under the direct control of the OKL in readiness for a revised plan to be code-named Operation *Gertraud*. *Gertraud* foresaw an attack by up to 12 Ju 290s from 2./FAGr. 5 against three target groups of hydroelectric power plants (probably broken down into the Gorki, Jaroslawl and Tula areas). The operation was to be prepared in closest cooperation with *Professor* Steinmann and carried out no later than 18-20 April. The Ju 290s would be armed with BM 1000 F '*Sommerballon*' and BM 1000 G '*Winterballon*' mine bombs. The '*Winterballon*' – as opposed to the '*Sommerballon*' already described – was the code name for a variant of the SC 1000 bomb. It was fitted with a parachute brake and intended for deployment during the winter months. It was calculated that the BM 1000 G could penetrate ice up to 50 cm thick and could be safely dropped from high altitudes into as little as seven metres of water.

Following the cancellation of Eisenhammer at the end of March 1945, 2./FAG 5 was removed from Baumbach's personal jurisdiction and placed under the direct control of the OKL in readiness for a revised plan code-named Operation Gertraud which foresaw an attack by up to 12 Ju 290s against three target groups of hydroelectric power plants.

Shortly after the orders for Operation *Gertraud* had been issued, six of the twelve Ju 290s allocated for the mission were destroyed in Allied strafing attacks on north German airfields. Accordingly, on 14 April Koller ordered that all preparations for the planned operation be abandoned, and this finally marked the end of German hopes of destroying Russian hydroelectric power stations. However, even if *Gertraud* had taken place as scheduled, it is extremely doubtful if, at this late stage, it would have had any effect on the final outcome of the war. The Soviet offensive against Berlin, which effectively sealed the fate of the Third Reich, commenced on 16 April 1945 and by 24 April the city was virtually surrounded and the defending German armies in disarray. The truth was that the Red Army possessed sufficient reserves of equipment and munitions to offset the possible effects of a successful *Gertraud*, and could have completed the occupation of eastern Germany before any material shortages manifested themselves.

There is an intriguing postscript to the story of Operation *Eisenhammer*. According to Koller's version of events, on 18 April 1945 he held the following conversation with Albert Speer:

> '*Ministerialdirigent Dr.* Steinmann (*Professor*) has volunteered to let the front roll past him, go to the other side, that is, to the enemy [author's note: the Western Allies], and attempt, on the basis of his connections with the technical world, to make it clear to the enemy what it would mean to America and England if the Russians captured the German scientific installations and the German engineers. Steinmann believes that he can succeed in convincing them of the German viewpoint of the necessity of "Fighting the East". The man is decent and an idealist. How can we use him? Steinmann would only go, however, if he had specific orders from the *Führer* and he would never get them. The *Führer* will have us hanged if he ever heard that we have even been having such thoughts.'
>
> Speer: 'Do just as I have done. I let the front run all over my distinguished technicians and industrialists and works managers, kept them strictly together, and now they are working on reconstruction on the other side [author's note : the West] just as they did for me. This is all in the interests of the German people, I am only doing it for the German people… Steinmann should let the front roll past him and then work over there, but in his own interests, he should not start until the beheading wave has stopped here. The enemy must be told that a war can be lost and if the Germans do lose it, then it will be lost honourably; if the enemy treat us honourably, then we can enter into discussions with them. Steinmann will naturally not be given such orders by the *Führer*.'

'WHAT HAPPENS IF THE GERMANS TRY IT UPON LONDON?'

CHURCHILL, THE *MISTEL* AND THE THREAT TO 'THE FINEST TARGET IN THE WORLD'.

By August 1944, B-17 F, s/n 42-30353, which had originally served with the USAAF's 95th Bomb Group, had been seconded to the 'Aphrodite' project at Fersfield. It was later assigned to attack Herford in Germany on 5 December 1944. Note the television camera in the nose, the enlarged exit hatch with slipstream deflector and the smoke dispenser tank beneath the fuselage.

IN late June 1944, as KG 101 conducted its sporadic operations with the *Mistel* against the Allied invasion fleet off Normandy, the United States Strategic Air Forces (USSTAF) were developing their own method of remotely delivering an expendable, pilotless, heavy payload weapons system. Initially intended as a means of striking the V-1 flying bomb launch sites in northern France, 'Project Aphrodite' officially came into being on 23 June 1944. Under the Aphrodite plan, it was intended to guide stripped-down, war-weary B-17 Flying Fortresses fitted with radio receiving sets and carrying around ten tons of explosives towards appropriate targets. However, unlike the *Mistel*, the 'B-17 bomb' was to be flown by a pilot and radio-engineer, who would bail out once flight control had been established by an accompanying 'mother' aircraft which would then guide the unmanned 'robot' onto its target.

Experiments began using volunteer crews at Bovingdon in July 1944. Ten war-weary B-17 'babies' were made available, each aircraft having been stripped of its armour, turrets, bombing and oxygen equipment, co-pilot's seat and all other items deemed to be superfluous for a one-way mission. The first Aphrodite mission was attempted from Fersfield in Norfolk on 4 August and directed at concrete V-weapon launch sites near the French coast, but it proved a catastrophe when radio connection between one B-17 'baby', carrying 20,000 lb of TNT, and its B-24 'mother' failed and the aircraft crashed in England with its pilot still on board. The other 'baby' made it as far as France, but crashed some distance from its target.

The Americans tried again two days later, but with equally disappointing results; two more 'babies' went out of control and crashed into the sea.

In the meantime more sophisticated radio-guidance equipment was brought in and further experiments were undertaken by the US Navy in August 1944 under the code name 'Anvil'. In the first mission on the 12th, a PB4Y-1 Liberator 'baby' carrying 24,240 lb of high explosive was accompanied to the V-weapons site target at Mimoyecques by two PV-1 Ventura 'mothers'. Again, there was to be disaster; approaching the coast at Southwold, the 'baby' suddenly exploded at 2,000 ft, killing its pilot, Lt. J.P. Kennedy, the son of the US Ambassador to Britain, and his radio-control engineer.

Also in August, a special detachment from Wright Field arrived in the UK to test television-guided GB-4 bombs under the code name 'Batty'. The GB-4 had small glider wings, movable tail surfaces, a radio-control unit and a television camera mounted in the nose. A B-17 'mother' could carry two such bombs on underwing racks. Three Batty missions followed against the port of Le Havre, the U-boat pens at La Pallice and enemy installations at Ijmuiden. All failed. Either the bombs fell short or wide of their targets due to the malfunctioning of the television equipment or, in the case of the last mission, adverse weather forced the abandonment of the operation.

Throughout September and October, the Navy and the Air Force persevered with their respective experiments. Missions were flown to Helgoland and Hemmingstedt. In each case, the 'babies' were either hit by Flak, missed the

A B-17 'Aphrodite' 'mother ship' flies above a B-17 robot-bomb.

target, crashed into the sea or, in one case, landed in neutral Sweden. By 1 January 1945, a total of 19 war-weary bombers had been used with varying degrees of success in the Aphrodite, Anvil, Batty or Castor[1] programmes, seven against V-weapon sites, six against Helgoland, two at oil refineries and four at industrial targets in the Oldenburg area of northern Germany.

In November 1944, the USSTAF approached the British Joint Staff Mission in Washington with a proposal to move the Aphrodite launch fields to the Continent from where robots could be used more effectively against industrial targets. By the following month, there were known to be approximately 560 war-weary B-17s and B-24s in the European theatre of operations and it was estimated that 70 such aircraft would become available each month. The British hesitated in giving the USSTAF an answer and on 6 December, Air Chief Marshal Sir Charles Portal, the Chief of Air Staff, advised the War Cabinet Chiefs of Staff Committee:

> 'The destructive effect of one of these aircraft, should it fall in a built-up area, would be very considerable. It is estimated that complete destruction would be effected over a radius of 150 yards and serious damage over a radius of 300 yards. In addition, blast effects would probably be experienced at appreciably greater distances.'

Following due consideration, the British gave a measured response, suggesting to the Americans that they refine their 'development work' still further bearing in mind the considerable personnel and materiel resources that the project would need and the fact that experiments so far conducted had shown that it had,

> '... not always been possible to prevent the weapons falling on our own territory. This problem should be fully considered and the necessary steps taken to ensure safety before operations are undertaken.'

The Americans were stung by the attitude of the British; in January 1945, the Joint Staff Mission in Washington signalled:

> 'The US Chiefs of Staff do not consider it practicable at this time to install radio control in the war-weary aircraft. Possible improvements in accuracy by the use of radio control do not justify the additional time and personnel which would be required in further research... The limited travel of these aircraft aimed at large industrial areas should, we feel, result in considerable accuracy and produce a sufficient number of hits in the target area to warrant acceptability of this project... the US Chiefs of Staff request that an early approval be given to this project by the British Chiefs of Staff.'

On 15 January 1945, London signalled its approval, but without prior consultation with, or approval from, Winston Churchill. At this point, Churchill reacted and ordered approval to be withdrawn immediately. Alarm bells began to ring at the very highest levels of British command. Churchill's fear was that of possible German retaliation against London. Three pilotless and explosive-laden aircraft had come down in the British Isles during the previous summer (see Chapter Seven). The Prime Minister hurriedly scribbled a memo to Major General Sir Hastings Ismay, his Chief of Staff:

> 'What happens if the Germans try it upon London?'

On 22 January, Ismay, ever the diplomat, replied to Churchill:

> 'The Germans might try to use their war-weary bombers against London in the following ways:
>
> (i) Fly them to the target, pilot baling out prior to the attack.
> (ii) Air-launch them by means of a pick-a-back fighter, releasing the bomber over the target.
> (iii) Air-launch the bomber at some distance from the coast of this country, the bomber continuing to the target under mechanical-cum-radio control.
>
> 'The first method would entail an uneconomical wastage of pilots. The pick-a-back combination would provide a relatively easy target. The aircraft launched under method (iii) should make relatively easy targets for both fighters and AA guns owing to their size and speed, as compared to the flying bomb. The scale of attack would be limited by the availability of aircraft... The conclusion is that, if the enemy launched these attacks against London, incidents within the built-up area would be far more serious than those by the flying bomb; but the scale of attack is likely to be small and the incidents within the London area few... I much regret that you were not informed before the telegram was despatched, but the Chiefs of Staff felt sure that you would agree...'

Churchill remained unconvinced. On 26 January at a meeting of the Chiefs of Staff Committee, he opined:

> 'It should be a source of great satisfaction to the enemy that we should use such a weapon and might draw down heavy retaliation upon London, the finest target in the world. As a contribution to our offensive operations, the results likely to be achieved would be negative, whereas in the case of London this would certainly notbe so.'

It is known that the objective of the RAF raid on Tirstrup airfield in February 1945 was successfully accomplished and that, consequently, the German attempt to attack Scapa Flow with *Mistel* was foiled. But more than that, the raid offered proof to a somewhat indifferent

[1] Castor: Another name for the Aphrodite programme.

British Air Intelligence service that the Germans fully intended to employ explosive-laden composite aircraft in numbers against key targets.

'There is no doubt,' wrote a member of A.I.3B on 27 February, 'that the Germans now have available composite aircraft composed of Ju 88/Fw 190 as well as Ju 88/Me 109.'

Since the Tirstrup raid, the Allies had gathered increasing evidence of German composite activity. On 28 February, the Assistant Chief of Air Staff (Intelligence), wrote to Portal warning him of 'evidence' of,

> '... two impending operations, one involving the launching of V-1s possibly against London[2] and the other suggesting the reintroduction on a fair scale of *Mistel* aircraft... Instructions to an agent in London[3] suggest that London may be a common target for both operations, although... there is no other evidence to show that the *Mistel* operation will be directed against London. Since *Mistel* aircraft were operated against shipping in the Seine Bay at the time of Overlord, little has been heard of this aircraft until the beginning of this year. In the last two months and particularly in the last week, evidence has been accumulating...'

Throughout the second half of February 1945, reconnaissance aircraft photographed KG(J) 30's *Mistel* at Prague-Ruzyne on at least three occasions (13 on the 16th, 27 on the 20th and 17 on the 25th). Other composites were seen at II./KG 200's base at Burg, the Junkers plants at Halberstadt and Nordhausen, and some 12 machines remained at Tirstrup.

The intelligence chief continued:

> 'It is not known how, if at all, *Mistel* aircraft could be operated against London and it should be pointed out that we are now in the full moon period... It should also be pointed out that we have no idea what technique would be employed or would be necessary to operate *Mistel* aircraft against a distant target like London. It is tentatively suggested that the bomber component in the *Mistel* might be made to operate on the principle of a Diver[4], i.e. once released it might fly on automatic compass by locking the elevators. Nothing is known however, but it seems reasonable to suppose that since the early days of Overlord certain modifications have been introduced.'

The same day Ismay rushed a top secret memo to Churchill in which he warned:

During the first four months of 1945, Winston Churchill was wary of the Germans deploying Mistel against the British capital. On 12 April he signalled the US President: 'If the Germans have a number of war-weary bombers that could make the distance, London is the obvious and indeed only target.' Churchill is seen here with Air Chief Marshal Sir Charles Portal (right), the Chief of Air Staff.

> 'The Chiefs of Staff have received evidence of the possibility of renewed activity by German pick-a-back aircraft. The Germans are believed to have some 50 pick-a-back aircraft... There is evidence that the commander responsible for these aircraft has been in touch with the German pathfinder force and that an operation has been planned for tonight or, alternatively, the next night on which weather conditions are favourable. It is probable that this operation will be directed against London though it may be directed against Antwerp. Fighter Command are fully informed and have taken all possible steps.
>
> 'The Chiefs of Staff consider that the Minister of Home Security should be informed of the possibility of attacks by pick-a-back aircraft in addition to those by flying bombs and rockets. They do not recommend that the Civil Defence Services should be generally alerted as they doubt whether these attacks will achieve any great result, particularly as the prevailing moon conditions favour the defence.'

However, in the absence of any attack on London during the course of the following month – and also perhaps persuaded by senior air force commanders – President Roosevelt once again broached the subject of commencing Aphrodite operations. In a 'Personal and Top Secret' telegram to the British Prime Minister on 29 March 1945, he began to apply pressure:

> 'Your Chiefs of Staff originally concurred in the development and employment of this project but have recently withdrawn their concurrence because of the British Government's apprehension that retaliatory action against London by the Germans might result if pilotless bombers were employed.
>
> 'My Chiefs of Staff inform me that they consider this weapon to be most valuable in our all-out offensive against Germany... I am assured that pilotless bombers

[2] It would have been impossible for the Germans to ground-launch V-1 flying bombs against London by this time since the missile lacked sufficient range to reach the British Isles from Holland, the only option left available. However, limited air-launched V-1 operations had been carried out by the He 111s of III./KG 3 and KG 53 during the autumn of 1944, though many aircraft and crews were lost due to the inherent dangers involved in such operations as well as to RAF nightfighters and AA defences. V-1s were fired from the air at London, Portsmouth, Gloucester and Manchester. It is more likely that the 'operation' referred to here was to involve the V-2 rocket which was operated from mobile launch sites in Holland. More than 200 V-2s landed in the UK during January 1945, many of them in London.

[3] No German agents were known to have escaped capture by Allied intelligence in Britain during the war; this reference must therefore be considered in context and as an indicator to British fears of German clandestine penetration at the time.

[4] British code name for V-1 flying bomb.

PM has seen. Gen Ismay informed that Min of Home Security [illegible] informed.

JRC 28/2

243

OFFICE OF THE MINISTER OF DEFENCE

TOP SECRET

PRIME MINISTER

Since I reported to you on the 26th February on the possibility of a recrudescence of ground launched flying bomb attacks against London combined with an intensification of rocket attacks, the Chiefs of Staff have received evidence of the possibility of renewed activity by German pick-a-back aircraft.

2. The Germans are believed to have some 50 pick-a-back aircraft which consist of a fighter and a bomber, the latter loaded with some six tons of explosive. There is evidence that the Commander responsible for these aircraft is in close touch with the German Pathfinder force, and that an operation has been planned for tonight, or, alternatively, the next night on which weather conditions are favourable. It is probable that this operation will be directed against London though it may be directed against Antwerp. Fighter Command are fully informed and have taken all possible steps.

3. The Chiefs of Staff consider that the Minister of Home Security should be informed of the possibility of attacks by pick-a-back aircraft in addition to those by flying bombs and rockets. They do not recommend that the Civil Defence Services should be generally alerted as they doubt whether these attacks will achieve any great result, particularly as the prevailing moon conditions favour the defence.

H.L. Ismay.

28th February, 1945

In February 1945 Major General Sir Hastings Ismay (right), Churchill's Chief of Staff, warned the Prime Minister of an imminent attack by German composite aircraft: 'It is probable that this operation will be directed against London though it may be directed against Antwerp. Fighter Command are fully informed and have taken all possible steps.' In a report to the War Cabinet Chiefs of Staff Committee, Air Chief Marshal Sir Charles Portal (centre), Chief of Air Staff, wrote: 'The destructive effect of one (composite) aircraft, should it fall in a built-up area, would be very considerable... The contention of the Chiefs of Staff that the Germans might well use the composite aircraft against London even though we never used war-weary bombers against them, has never been in dispute.'

will be launched only from bases on the Continent which would appear to minimize the chances of retaliatory action against England. I believe that if the enemy were able to take effective measures he would have done so regardless of any use by us of pilotless aircraft... It is requested that you ask your Chiefs of Staff to reconsider their withdrawal of concurrence in this project.'

As a matter of 'duty', Churchill made sure that the telegram landed on Portal's desk. The Chief of Air Staff dismissed the American request. In his view there was no valid military justification whatsoever for the deployment of Aphrodite or any other pilotless weapon. Furthermore, now that Allied airpower reigned supreme across the skies of Europe, the number of worthwhile targets at which the weapon could be directed was limited and would narrow still further by the time it was ready for use. In a report to the War Cabinet Chiefs of Staff Committee on 10 April 1945 – the day that more than 1,600 heavy and medium bombers of the US Eighth and Ninth Air Forces bombed supply dumps, factories and airfields across Germany, destroying several *Mistel* in the process – Portal argued that:

'The previous main objection to the use of the weapon was political, namely that if the Germans used composite aircraft against London, the public would connect such an attack with the use of war-weary bombers by the Americans. The contention of the Chiefs of Staff that the Germans might well use the composite aircraft against London even though we never used war-weary bombers against them, has never been in dispute.

'The political objection, however, is by no means removed now that London appears to be on the point of deliverance from its long-sustained bombardment. It could be argued that the use of war-weary bombers against the enemy constituted a useless provocation and in fact a direct invitation to the enemy to retaliate by composite aircraft on London... It is therefore a question of deciding between the obvious advantages of accommodating the Americans, who are keen to try out this scheme, and the small political risk of allowing it to go forward. This is a matter for the Prime Minister to decide. I recommend therefore that we should tell him that this scheme would no longer have military results of any importance and might be held to have certain political disadvantages which he will wish to weigh against the natural desire to meet the President's wishes.'

On 12 April, Roosevelt died of a cerebral haemorrhage and two days later Churchill gave his successor, Harry S. Truman, his reply; marked 'Top Secret' and copied to the King and the Foreign Secretary, it shows the British leader in a wary but surprisingly compromising frame of mind:

'... if the Germans have a number of war-weary bombers that could make the distance, London is the obvious and indeed only target, and even a few very big explosions in London would be a very great disappointment to the people at this time when they had hoped that their prolonged ordeal was over... Having put these facts before you, I leave the decision entirely in the hands of your military advisers, and we shall make no complaint if misfortune comes to us in consequence.'

But by this time any fears that Churchill may have harboured over a possible *Mistel* attack on London were virtually groundless for, as we shall see in Chapter Thirteen, the Luftwaffe was using its remaining composites in a desperate attempt to stem the Soviet tide approaching from the East and threatening the German capital. In any case, on 17 April, the matter was effectively closed; Truman signalled Churchill:

'... it seems to me this project ... should not be pressed any further in Europe at this time. I am instructing my Chiefs of Staff accordingly.'

FROM THE DRAWING BOARD AND BEYOND

The DFS 228 V1 seen mounted to the Do 217 K V3 during testing at either Hörsching or Rechlin. Flights conducted under this arrangement revealed shortcomings in the DFS 228, forcing a redesign.

MISTEL PROJECTS AND VARIANTS

THROUGHOUT the Second World War German aircraft designers continued to search for ways to enhance technical performance and military value in their aircraft by using the *Mistel* method. From 1939 onwards a multitude of proposals was put forward by several firms, some more inventive or radical than others. As a result of the lack of original documentation however, it is difficult to include all such proposals in this study. Furthermore, in some cases, it is also difficult to differentiate between serious designs and those which, while perhaps well-intentioned, can be viewed as little more than whimsical.

Such inventiveness, for example, can be seen from the proposals which emanated from Junkers' *Abteilung Entwicklungsforschung* (Efo – Research and Development Department) which functioned as a separate entity from the company's main project office prior to 1942. Despite concentrating primarily on high-speed and jet-engined projects, several composite proposals were considered such as Dr. Molthan's plan for a '*Ju 90 mit angehaengten Flugzeugen Me 109*' ('Ju 90 with attached Me 109s'). Associated tests were conducted in Junkers' small, low-speed wind tunnel at Dessau on 21 and 22 June 1939. Another project, the EF 106, featured a 'Ju 88 with Me 109'; this underwent wind tunnel tests sometime in March 1942 and may have been a precursor to Siegfried Holzbaur's eventual *Mistel*.

Of more creative design was the enormous EF 101, a combination of a long-range, four-engined reconnaissance aircraft with a fully integrated, unspecified, single-engined, two seat parasite reconnaissance-fighter or survey aircraft. Considered between mid-September 1939 and mid-August 1941, the upper component had a wingspan of 70 m, a length of 26 m and was to be powered by four 24-cylinder Daimler Benz DB 613 double-inverted 'V' engines mounted on the wing leading edge and developing 3,500-4,000 horsepower. Range was planned to be 17,000 km with a maximum altitude of 12,000 m and a maximum speed of 760 km/h. The cockpit was to be pressurised and carry a crew of three to four, from where the aircraft's remote-controlled armament could be operated. This consisted of four FDL 131Z turrets each installed with two 13 mm MG 131 machine guns located on top of the canopy, on top of the fuselage aft of the cockpit and at two points beneath the fuselage.

The objective was to launch the parasite over its zone of operations, after which it would then climb, complete its mission and return to the carrier and hook up by means of arresting gear designed by the DFS. Although the arresting gear was actually built and installed for tests on an He 177, the project was never pursued.

From the end of 1943 until the summer of 1944, Daimler-Benz set up its own small, airframe design team which came up with a proposal to create a platform for its DB 007 turbofan engines which provided thrust of 1,150 kg. This centred on a turboprop-powered carrier aircraft capable of air-launching a twin-turbojet bomber offering a very favourable range/payload ratio and which could be directed at high speed against targets in North America. Eventually, design settled on a carrier aircraft fitted with

HeS 021 turboprops. It was to be a massive concept, boasting a 54-metre wingspan and including an undercarriage which would provide adequate ground clearance for the underslung bomber as well as being able to lift the combination's gross weight of 117,955 kg. The bomber component was to be powered by two 7,500 kg static thrust turbojets providing an envisaged high speed cruise of around Mach 0.8. It was to carry a bomb load of up to 30,000 kg plus a fuel load of 17,818 kg which would offer a range of 804 km.

By the spring of 1944, Daimler Benz realised that such plans were woefully unrealistic, though the company continued to work on projects favouring a DB 603 piston-engined carrier carrying a less powerful but aerodynamically refined bomber. The whole concept was eventually handed over to Focke-Wulf for further project work in February 1945.

The designs on the following pages were more pragmatic in their thinking in that they were either built and tested or that they were designed around airframes which were actually built or in advanced stages of design and acceptance by the RLM.

DFS 228 V1-Do 217K V3

High altitude rocket-powered reconnaissance trials

Evolved from the RLM's need for extremely high altitude reconnaissance and thus immunity from interception, the DFS 228 was originally foreseen as a test bed for research into supersonic flight, something which as early as 1940 the DFS considered feasible in the light of German rocket engine development of the time.

In 1941 however, the RLM's range and fuel requirements for such a project presented the DFS design engineers with a challenge. The plan was to carry or tow the small, wooden aircraft to an altitude of 10,000 m, then release it near to the area of reconnaissance, at which point the craft's rocket motor would be ignited in order to propel it, under its own power, to an altitude of 23,000 m. From this altitude the aircraft would then perform a series of intermittent shallow glides and steep climbs – using its rocket power – for some 45 minutes until the fuel load had been expended. The DFS 228 would then commence its reconnaissance run whilst in its long glide back to base, using Zeiss infrared cameras. By the time the craft had descended to 12,000 m, it was estimated that a distance of 748 km would have been covered since departure from its parent aircraft, with a further 300 km possible depending on thermal conditions.

Design centred around a clean mid-wing monoplane with the horizontal tail surfaces attached near the base of a single vertical fin. Wood was used wherever possible, the wing comprising a single laminated wooden spar with wooden ribs and plywood skinning. The fuselage incorporated three sections: a nose compartment; a centre section which housed the main section of the rocket unit and beneath which was fitted a retractable metal landing skid; and a tail cone which housed the rocket combustion chamber and tail skid. The principal exception to wood lay in the pressurised nose compartment which featured one hemispherical frontal and two smaller Plexiglas side panels in a metal two-skin structure with aluminium foil insulation between the inner and outer walls. The whole was sealed by a rear bulkhead. It was intended that internal pressure would commence at some 8,000 m and should be maintained up to 25,000 m. Power was to be supplied by a Walter 109-509A-1 bi-propellant liquid rocket motor.

Due to the complexities of its design and the demands of other projects, the first prototype, the DFS 228 V1, D-IBFQ, was not completed until 1943. In this particular aircraft, the pilot was to have been accommodated on a seat behind the Plexiglas panels which were fitted with electrically-powered hot air circulation to prevent frosting. Having reached a pre-determined height, the pilot would eject from the compartment by means of compressed air and make a normal parachute descent. For emergency escapes, the complete nose compartment could be jettisoned away from the aircraft by activating four explosive bolts connected to the bulkhead, after which a self-activating parachute would automatically deploy to stabilise and decelerate the rate of descent.

Initial trials with the DFS 228V1 mounted as an upper component in a *Mistel* configuration with the Dornier Do 217K V3 as the carrier were conducted at the DFS Hörsching and the *Erprobungsstelle* Rechlin. Some 40 flights were made, though no air-testing of the Walter rocket was undertaken. These flights revealed that the large pilot's cabin was very difficult to seal adequately. This was overcome by repositioning the pilot to a prone position on a horizontal couch, thus resulting in a smaller cabin area. This revised design was incorporated into the DFS 228 V2 which was rocket-tested but later virtually destroyed at Hörsching in May 1945. Two further aircraft had been planned for manufacture by the Wrede company at Freilassing which were to feature a Henschel-designed pressure cabin.

Another view of the DFS 228 V1 and the Do 217 K V3 at either Hörsching or Rechlin.

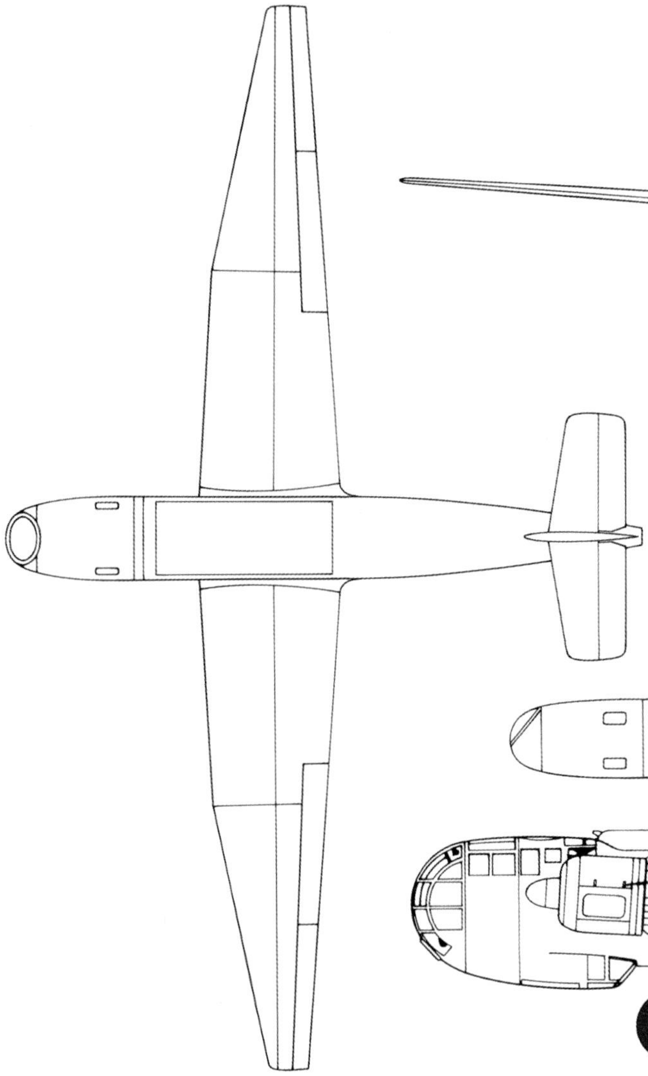

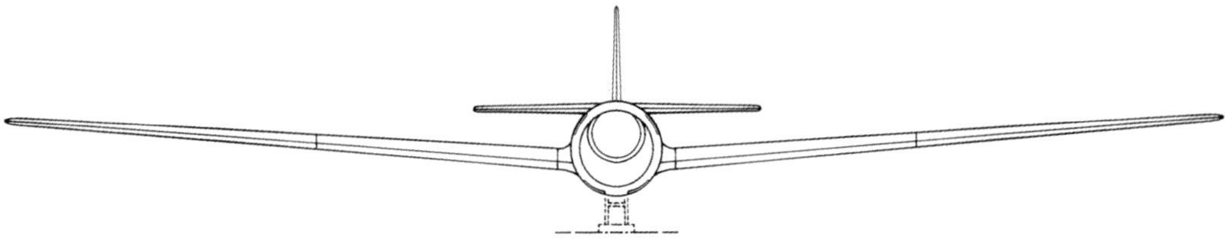

DFS 228 V1 and Dornier Do 217 K V3

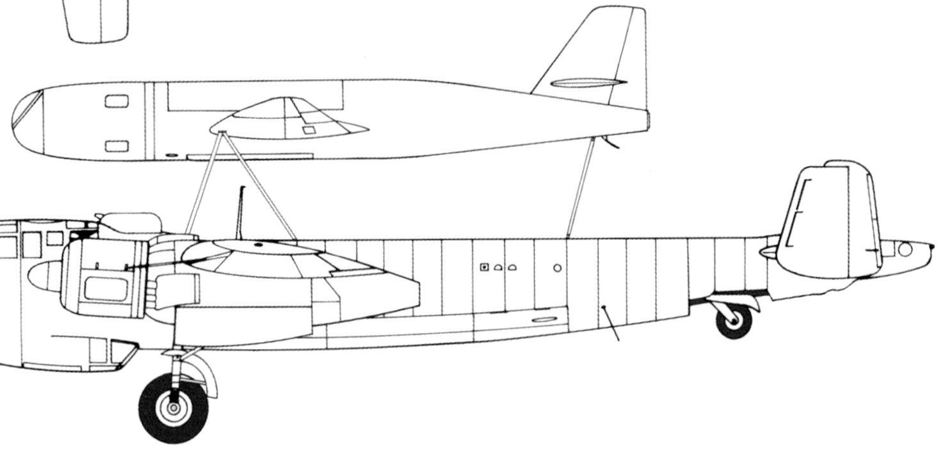

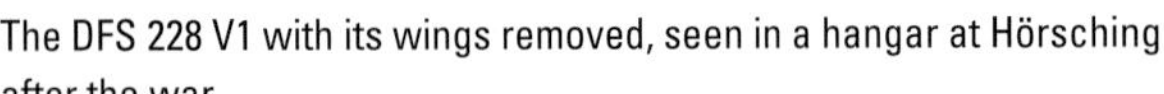

The DFS 228 V1 with its wings removed, seen in a hangar at Hörsching after the war.

Following a test flight, the DFS 228 V1 makes its approach at Hörsching. Having reached a pre-determined height, it was intended that the pilot would eject from the compartment by means of compressed air and make a normal parachute descent. For emergency escapes, the complete nose compartment could be jettisoned away from the aircraft by activating four explosive bolts connected to the bulkhead, after which a self-activating parachute would automatically deploy to stabilise and decelerate the rate of descent.

Me 328-Do 217 *Mistel*

High-speed, low-level fighter-bomber and carrier aircraft

IN July 1941, a series of design projects was undertaken by *Dipl.-Ing.* Rudolf Seitz, a project engineer in the Messerschmitt *Entwurfsbüro*, together with *Dipl.-Ing.* Prager and *Dipl.-Ing.* Mende, with the aim of producing a small, pulse jet-powered, air-launched parasite fighter plus a mounting, launching and retrieval system. The study was designated P.1079 and was produced in cooperation with the DFS at Ainring. By early 1942, the project had evolved into the P.1079/17 and on 31 March it was submitted to the RLM who assigned it the designation Me 328. Six versions of the Me 328 were proposed:

Me 328 A-1 – a fighter carrying two 20 mm MG 151 cannon
Me 328 A-2 – wider-spanned and incorporating two 20 mm MG 151s and also two 30 mm MK 103 cannon
Me 328 A-3 – as per the A-2 but with provision for in-flight refuelling
Me 328 B-1 – a fighter-bomber carrying a 1,000 kg external bomb load
Me 328 B-2 – the fighter-bomber equivalent of the A-2
Me 328 B-3 – designed to carry a 1,400 kg SD 1400 bomb

A wind tunnel model of the Me 328 showing engines fitted to the sides of the fuselage.

However it was to be several months later, in early 1943, that serious development work began. The Allied bomber offensive and the threat of an enemy invasion in the west, forced the Luftwaffe and its aircraft designers to search for ways to introduce cheap, quick-to-build and expendable fighter and fighter-bomber aircraft in large numbers. In March of that year the glider manufacturer, Jacob Schweyer Segelflugzeugbau, was commissioned to work with the DFS and Messerschmitt to build the Me 328. The company produced a wooden, mid-wing aircraft, with a circular-section fuselage featuring a raised cockpit canopy faired back and down to the base of the fin. The wingspan could be adjusted by means of detachable tips and electrical power was provided by wing-mounted air-driven generators. Self-sealing fuel tanks were housed in the rear fuselage and nose. Landing was to be accomplished using a retractable skid and the pilot was protected by a bulletproof windscreen.

The first three prototypes built in the DFS workshops had wooden wings and sheet steel fuselages to which were fitted standard Bf 109 tailplanes. Power was to be provided by two Argus pulsejets. Various configurations were tested in the Messerschmitt wind tunnel at Augsburg. Firstly the jets were mounted on pylons each side of the fuselage with the tailpipes extending below and beyond the tail fin but this proved unacceptable due to severe vibration which resulted from the close proximity of the engines. A second arrangement with the engines mounted in the wings so that the tailpipes terminated below and in front of the tail unit also resulted in the fuselage being subjected to the effects of the pulsating jet efflux, but this second arrangement was considered preferable to the former. However, the attraction of the scheme lay in the fact that it was estimated that for every Bf 109 or Fw 190 completed, four Me 328s could be built, largely due to the simplicity of the Argus units.

On 7 December 1942, *Dipl.-Ing.* Felix Kracht of the DFS Ainring, a well-known pre-war sports flier, had drafted a report for GL/C-E 2 and the RLM in which he proposed using either a fully armed Do 217 E or Do 217 M bomber as a carrier aircraft for the Me 328 for the purpose of aerodynamic trials. The respective specifications were as follows:

	Do 217 E	**Do 217 M**
Fully armed	10,250 kg	10,640 kg
Crew	400 kg	400 kg
Fuel load	1,250 kg	1,440 kg
Lubricants	225 kg	250 kg
Me 328	3,600 kg	3,600 kg
Total weight	**15,725 kg**	**16,330 kg**

Based on these specifications, Kracht calculated the following take-off and flight performance:

	Do 217 E	**Do 217 M**
Take-off distance (concrete runway)	800 m	810 m
Take-off distance (grass field)	990 m	950 m
Airborne distance up to 20 m (concrete)	1,120 m	1,100 m
Airborne distance up to 20 m (grass)	1,300 m	1,250 m
Climb rate at ground level	4.4 m/sec	4.8 m/sec
Maximum altitude	6 km	7.5 km

Since these calculations indicated that the performance differences were marginal, the Do 217 E was used on the grounds that it was available in numbers. Standard airfields were adequate for take-off and Kracht promoted the structural and aerodynamic virtues of the Me 328 which were suitable for the task envisaged. Furthermore, the lack of propeller turbulence from the Me 328 would mean a shorter and safer take-off.

The Me 328 V1, without pulsejet ducts, was subsequently mounted on top of a Do 217 E, JT+FL, in a *Mistel* arrangement and preliminary trials were undertaken at Hörsching during the autumn and winter of 1943. The attachment and support frame incorporated strain and pressure gauges to measure the forces on the fighter and, later, the upper component was released from the Dornier at altitudes between 2,750-5,500 m and at speeds of between 145-245 km/h.

The results of these tests showed that, though the Messerschmitt was aerodynamically sub-standard, in general terms it was good enough to proceed further. At this point, it was envisaged that the aircraft would be used as an expendable, piloted missile for deployment against bomber formations where it could be pole-towed towards a target. As an A-series fighter, also rigid-towed, a ground landing would be made rather than a reconnection to the parent aircraft.

Hitler was to indirectly influence future plans for the Me 328 when in late 1943 as the war situation became increasingly difficult for Germany, he demanded that he have more fast bombers with which to make low-level attacks on enemy troop and vehicle concentrations if needed. Thus the A-series was abandoned and work progressed on the B-series. It was proposed to carry the

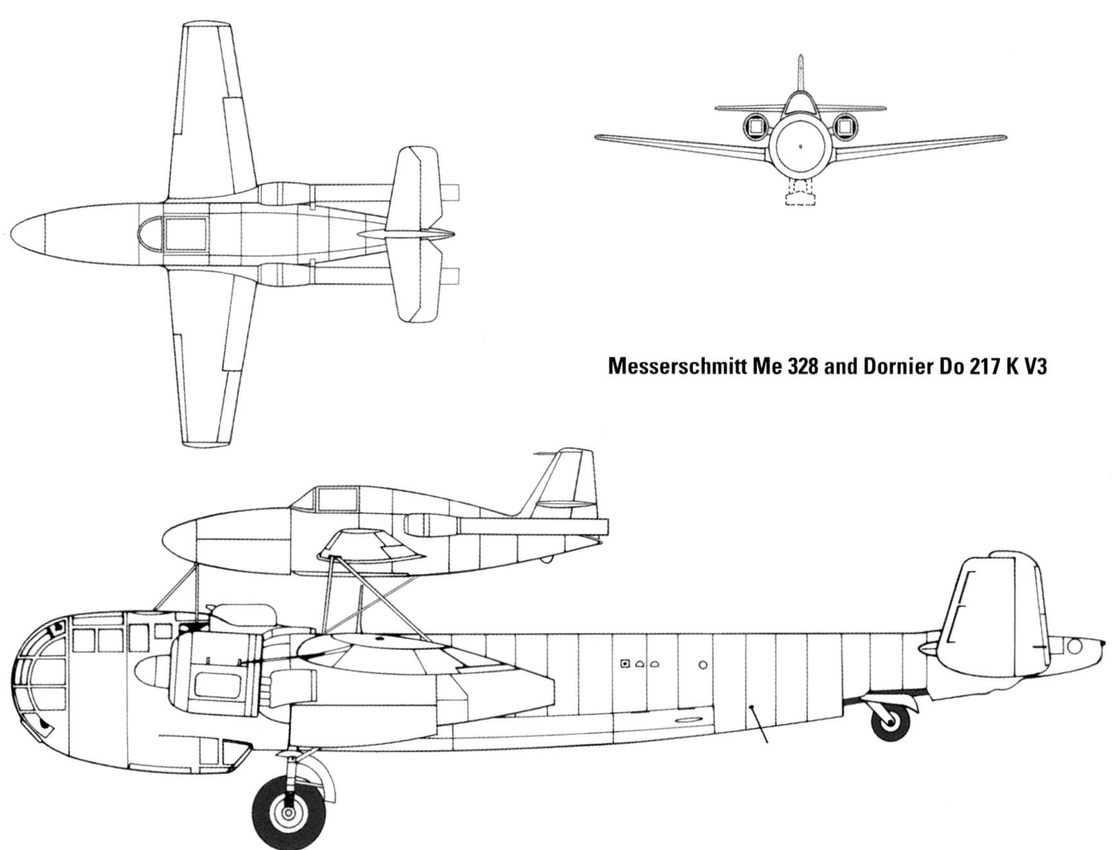

Messerschmitt Me 328 and Dornier Do 217 K V3

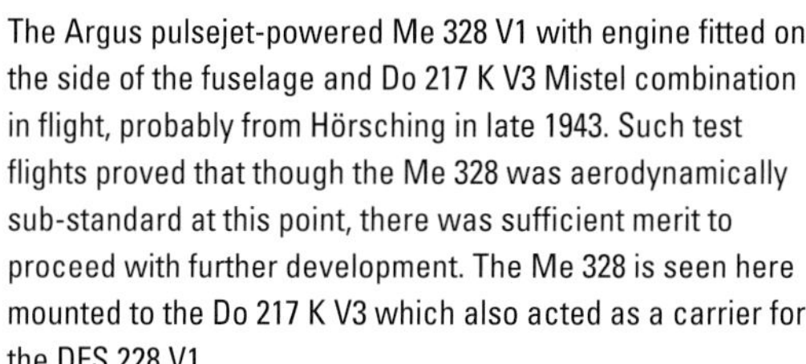

The Argus pulsejet-powered Me 328 V1 with engine fitted on the side of the fuselage and Do 217 K V3 Mistel combination in flight, probably from Hörsching in late 1943. Such test flights proved that though the Me 328 was aerodynamically sub-standard at this point, there was sufficient merit to proceed with further development. The Me 328 is seen here mounted to the Do 217 K V3 which also acted as a carrier for the DFS 228 V1.

Two views of the support frame as fitted to the Do 217 K V3 which incorporated strain and pressure gauges to measure the in-flight forces on the modified Me 328 V1.

Me 328 as close to the area of operations as possible on a carrier aircraft, whereupon it would attack and then return to its carrier to refuel and operate as an escort fighter for the carrier. Several carrier aircraft were proposed, with interest focusing mainly on the Heinkel He 177 or Junkers Ju 388. However, problems surrounding the pulsejets were never satisfactorily resolved and a further version was planned utilising Junkers Jumo 004 B turbojets installed in the fuselage. But this, in itself, eliminated the benefits of cheapness and simplicity.

Finally, in April 1944, some attempts were made to equip 5./KG 200 with an unpowered version of the Me 328 as a piloted glider bomb. These proposals were ultimately abandoned in favour of a piloted version of the Fieseler Fi 103, the '*Reichenberg*'.

Focke-Wulf Fw 190/Ta 154 *Mistel*

IN early July 1944 following the appearance of the first Junkers-built *Mistel* 1s, the RLM issued Focke-Wulf's *Entwurfsbüro* (Development Office) at Bad Eilsen with a specification for a '*Mistel* Ta 154 A/Fw 190 A-8 *Beethoven*' combination. The RLM hoped to develop a *Mistel* which would comprise a war-weary Fw 190 A, of which there were plentiful numbers equipping the fighter units in the *Reichsverteidigung*, and the cheap-to-build, wooden Ta 154 fighter as its lower component.

Though Focke-Wulf complied with the RLM's request to investigate such a project, it had already studied the possibility of using a Ta 154 for both upper and lower components of the planned composite. However, according to a Focke-Wulf report: 'This is not possible since there would be too much weight on the landing gear and the structure of the aircraft.'

The sleek design of the Ta 154, with its distinctive nose wheel, had first been authorised by Kurt Tank in 1942 following a specification requirement from the RLM for a two-seat, twin-engined, wooden fast-attack bomber but by October 1943, influenced by the air war waging over the Reich, this was amended to become a fast nightfighter.

Though governed to a great extent by shortages of light metals, many prominent figures at the top of the German aeronautical hierarchy, including *Reichsmarschall* Göring, felt attracted by the prospect of an all-wood fighter; it was an opportunity to reply to the British de Havilland Mosquito, the so-called 'Wooden Wonder', which was ranging deep and untouched into Europe on photo-reconnaissance and bomber missions.

Throughout the second half of 1943 and the first half of 1944, trials were conducted with a variety of Langenhagen-assembled prototypes ranging from the Ta 154 V1 which first flew in July 1943 and incorporated Jumo 211F engines, through to the V8 which first flew in April 1944 and used Jumo 213A engines. The V2 was fitted with flame dampers and FuG 212 *Lichtenstein* radar; the V3 was the first aircraft of the type to carry armament in the shape of four 20 mm MG 151s, whilst the V4 was adapted to include 2 x 20 mm MG 151s and 2 x 30 mm MK 108s.

However, there were problems: the V4's starboard engine fell away in flight and the aircraft later crashed; the V5 developed leaks and collected water in the gun bays; the V6 suffered from rusting and various technical failures; and the V7 was also found to be unfit. The V9 (the first machine to be built at Poznan) crashed on landing in April 1944 as a result of hydraulics failure. Pilots complained of the lack of lateral and rearward visibility and on 6 May, whilst conducting the fifth flight of the Ta 154 V8, two test pilots were killed when fire suddenly broke out in the right engine, which resulted in a fatal crash.

In March 1944, the first of twenty-two pre-production Ta 154 A-0 night fighters was delivered, featuring more powerful Jumo 211N engines and, just over two months later Tank, fearful that the RLM was about to cancel the whole Ta 154 programme, persuaded the *General der Jagdflieger*, Adolf Galland, to fly the aircraft to assess it for himself. On 2 June 1944 both Galland and *Oberst* Werner Streib, the *Inspekteur der Nachtjagd* (Inspector of Night Fighters), flew the V14 but subsequently expressed disappointment in its performance, particularly its potential for catching and matching the British Mosquito.

A fortnight later the fourth Ta 154 A-1 was destroyed in a crash and on 28 June another such machine was lost when its wing was reported as having broken up in flight due to faulty glue. In the interests of safety, Kurt Tank ordered production to be stopped. Göring was furious and accused the aircraft designer of attempting to sabotage his own product.

On the verge of cancellation, there was a small flicker of hope. On 17 July 1944, having received the RLM's instruction to look at a *Mistel* option, *Herr* Schöffel from the Focke-Wulf *Entwurfsbüro*, visited Junkers at Dessau to observe the *Mistel* conversion process. He subsequently produced his feasibility study on a Ta 154 A/Fw 190 A-8 combination. Unlike the original intention to build a twin Ta 154 combination, the Fw 190 proposal appeared more promising:

> 'With this (Ta 154 A/Fw 190 A-8) combination there are no fundamental difficulties from a structural point of view. The heavy take-off weight (up to 15 tons) is still possible for the landing gear if a concrete runway is used. A landing of the combination is not possible.'

As with the Junkers designs, Schöffel proposed maintaining a normal Ta 154 cockpit for transfer flights, but replacing it with a 'large explosive charge', probably 2,500-3,500 kg for use against 'a suitable target'. 'For a mission as an "aerial torpedo" where total loss of the aircraft is inevitable,' Schöffel wrote, 'the inexpensive Ta 154 is especially suitable.' His report continued:

> The Fw 190 will be attached atop the Ta 154 by means of special connecting struts. Take-off must take place from a concrete runway because of concerns regarding the overloaded landing gear. The good stable rolling characteristics of the nose wheel promise good take-offs.
>
> In flight, the control of the main landing gear, flaps, steering, trim and the operation of the engines are initiated from the Fw 190. During approach to the target, the Fw 190 takes fuel from the tanks of the Ta 154, in order to conserve enough fuel for the return flight. The approach to the target is aided by TSA 1.[1] Separation is accomplished by means of explosive bolts. The Ta 154 will be kept at altitude and on course by means of a modified Patin three-axis steering mechanism.
>
> **Modifications to the Ta 154 A:**
>
> **1) Fuselage**
> The fuselage can be separated at rib no. 5 using four bolts. The forward fuselage can be attached for transfer purposes with a simplified cockpit. It will be possible to exchange the cockpit configuration with the explosive configuration in a few hours.
>
> **2) Landing gear**
> The main landing gear will be used as is. Hydraulic pressure in the oleo legs must be increased from 60 to 97 atü [atmospheres]. The nose wheel has to be attached to the explosive charge by means of a strut attachment connected to an explosive bolt and will be jettisoned after take-off. The main gear can be retracted hydraulically since in regard to the take-off aids, the hydraulic system will not be removed. If it should prove impossible to attach the nose wheel to the explosive charge, then either a makeshift skid mechanism that can be jettisoned after take-off will be needed or take-off will have to be accomplished by means of a take-off trolley.

[1] The Zeiss TSA (Tiefwurf- und Schleuderanlage) 1 bomb dropping sight.

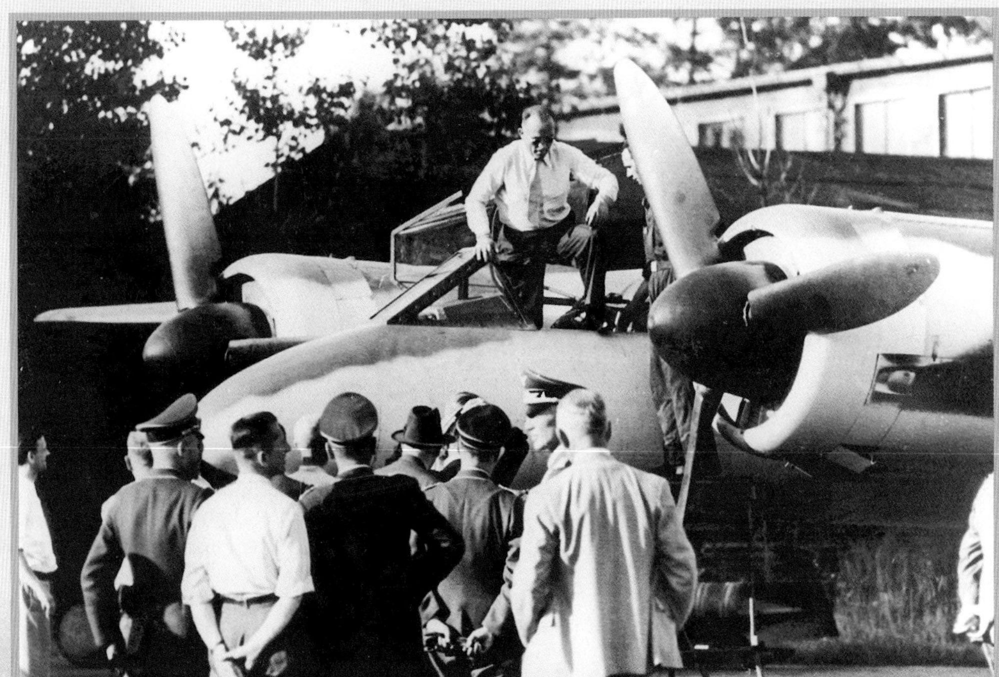

Following a test flight, Professor Dr.-Ing. Kurt Tank climbs from the cockpit of the Ta 154 V1 at Hannover-Langenhagen in July 1943 to be greeted by an assembly of Luftwaffe officers and Focke-Wulf personnel.

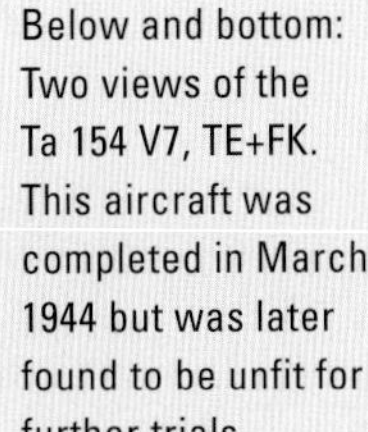

Below and bottom: Two views of the Ta 154 V7, TE+FK. This aircraft was completed in March 1944 but was later found to be unfit for further trials.

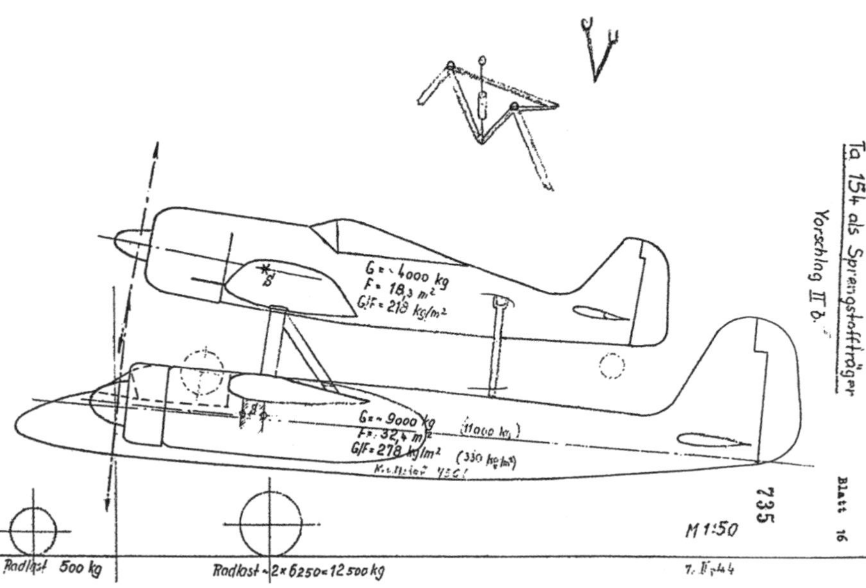

A Focke-Wulf drawing dated February 1944, showing the intended structure of a planned Fw 190/Ta 154 composite variant. The version seen here was designated a Sprengstoffträger' – or 'explosives carrier' – which was intended to be flown into enemy bomber formations and detonated to cause dispersal or simply used against large fortified targets.

3) Tail unit
No changes.

4) Steering
Steering will be effected by means of a three axis steering mechanism. Therefore two operational possibilities exist.

a) Approach: servo steering by means of a potentiometer.
b) Separated flight: self-steering by means of remote control for altitude steering.

5) Wing unit connections
Connection fittings for strut framework to be designed.

6) Engines
Engine control is effected from the Fw 190. The fuel lines are equipped with explosive bolts. The fuel tanks will be changed to make it possible for the Fw 190 to take fuel from the tanks of the Ta 154. For this reason C 3 fuel is also to be used in the Ta 154.

7) Equipment
Weapons and radio equipment will not be carried. Remaining equipment will be determined by the type of mission and must be cleared on a case-by-case basis. For transfer flights, the cockpit will be equipped with only the most necessary instruments.

8) Strut Framework
The framework for the attachment of the Fw 190 consists of one stand made up of six struts connected to the wing of the Ta 154 with two upper connection points and a rearward-positioned simple snap strut which connects the two rear fuselage sections. The attachment to the Fw 190 and the explosive bolts work in such a way that, at separation, the snap struts break first, followed by the front bolts. This will result in a quick and safe separation of the two aircraft.

9) Explosive Device
The explosive device will be attached to the fuselage with four bolts and the joint will be glued over. Provisions for the reinforcement of the nose wheel will have to be made.

The weight of the explosive charge depends on the location of its centre of gravity. It is possible, by use of ballast in the rear fuselage, to increase the allowed weight to five times the weight of the ballast.

Modifications to the Fw 190

On the Fw 190, fittings for the strut attachments connecting to the Ta 154 will have to be installed. The extra equipment will be determined by the requirements of a mission. Amongst other things two throttles, the directional instruments as well as the regulator for the three axis steering, the switches for the special flaps, landing gear, trim and explosive charges will be installed.

When deployed operationally, it was proposed that the *Mistel* would fly to within one kilometre of the target, at which point the Fw 190 pilot, having aimed the machine, would effect separation with the fighter's throttle set at full power, while full throttle on the Ta 154 would be delayed for a few seconds by means of a timing switch.

In his report, Schöffel also outlined the main advantages and disadvantages of the planned composite; they were:

Advantages
Firstly, due to its lack of sophisticated instrumentation, the Ta 154 could be cheaply and relatively easily produced. Secondly, and as with the Junkers' composites, the whole configuration requires only one pilot.

Disadvantages
The loss of a Ta 154 following every mission even if a target could not be located; bad visibility for the pilot (the Ta 154 would be practically invisible to the pilot of the Fw 190); even after separation it would be impossible to follow the Ta 154 for any distance; the angle of the *Huckepack* arrangement meant that forward visibility was poor. Furthermore, sluggish flight characteristics were predicted, which would be especially dangerous when confronted by fighter attack. Complicated modifications were needed to install a quick separation mechanism and, finally, the *Mistel* would be easily recognised by enemy fighters even at a great distance.

Notwithstanding any of these factors, during Schöffel's visit to the Junkers works at Dessau in July 1944, *Herr* Emmert of the RLM stressed to the Focke-Wulf technician the 'urgent need' for the Ta 154/Fw 190 combination. According to Schöffel, Emmert said that: 'the RLM expects the first conversion to be ready by the end of August 1944.'

Information on the required design and conversion resources was requested and completion deadlines were also required for the first, tenth and fiftieth aircraft as well as details of where production was to take place. However, the loss of seven Ta 154s incurred during a USAAF bombing raid on Hannover-Langenhagen airfield in early August 1944, combined with the troublesome performance of the remaining aircraft, most probably diminished further interest in the project. Plans were also drawn up to use Fw 190/Ta 154 *Mistel* combinations for use against Allied bomber formations as '*Pulkzerstörer*' (formation destroyers). The intention was for an explosive-laden Ta 154 to fly into a group of bombers where it would be detonated by the pilot of the separated Fw 190 controlling aircraft. Tests were apparently prepared at Eschwege but no further details are known.

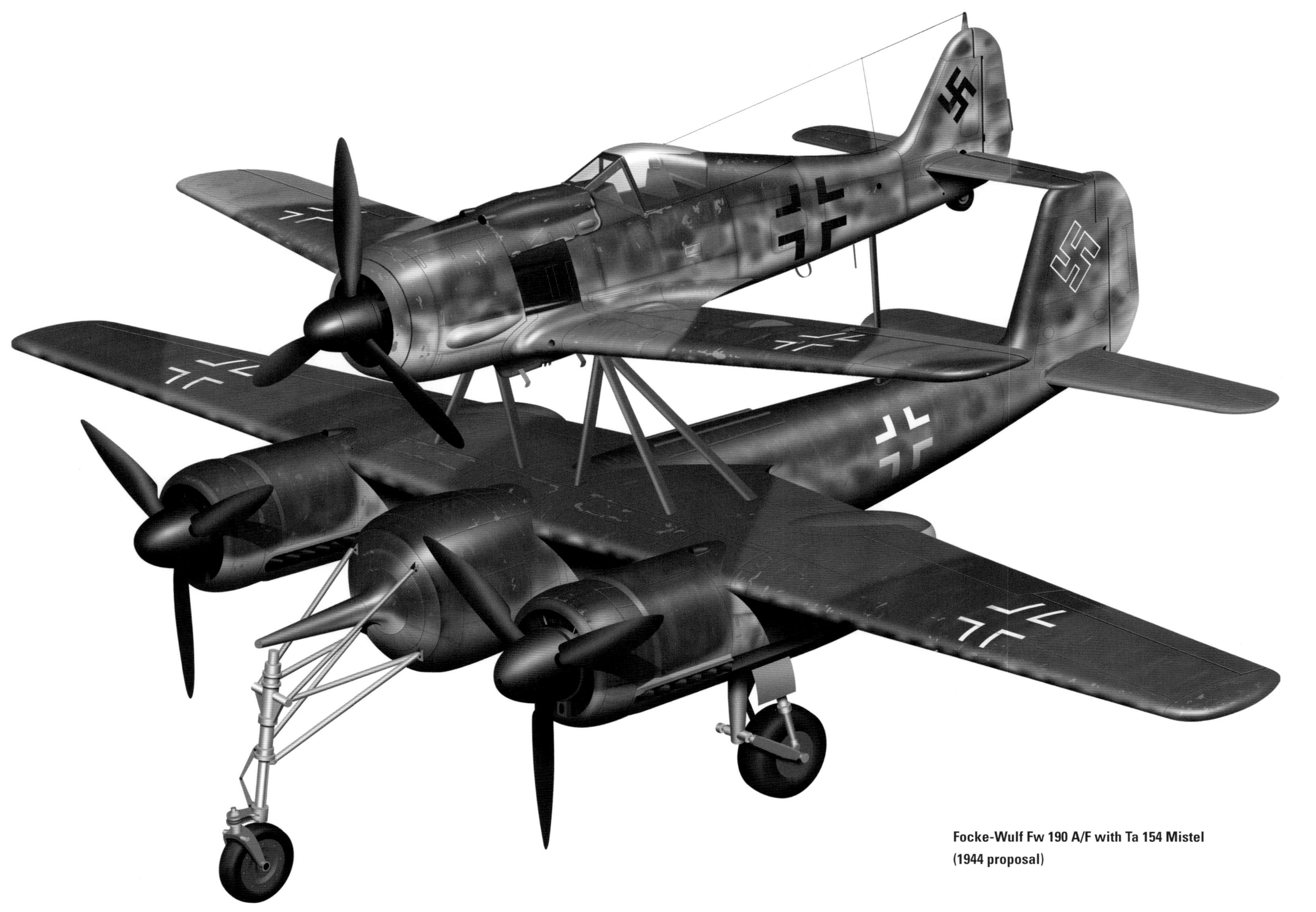

Focke-Wulf Fw 190 A/F with Ta 154 Mistel
(1944 proposal)

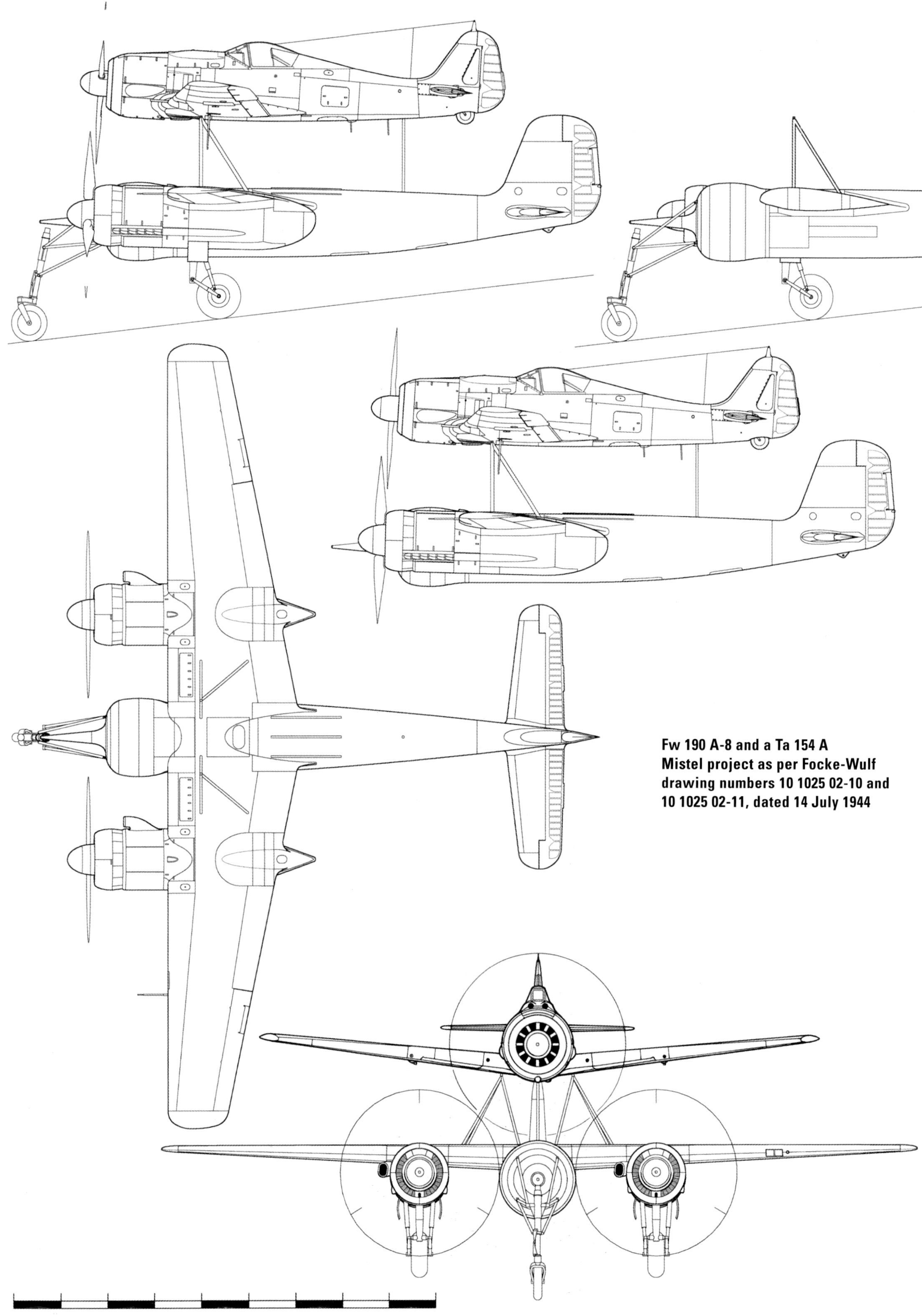

Fw 190 A-8 and a Ta 154 A Mistel project as per Focke-Wulf drawing numbers 10 1025 02-10 and 10 1025 02-11, dated 14 July 1944

Mistel 3

THE *Mistel* 3 series was built or planned in three basic configurations, though within these configurations there were variations.

The *Mistel* S3A, a training variant developed from the warhead-carrying *Mistel* 3 which proved unacceptable because of octane incompatibility difficulties, comprised either an Fw 190 A-8 fighter or Fw 190 F-8 ground-attack fighter-bomber mounted onto either a standard Ju 88 A-4 or, in some cases, a Ju 88 'A-6/U' (A-7), a largely redundant anti-shipping conversion variant of the balloon, cable and wire-cutting Ju 88 A-6. The difference in fuel octanes used by the Ju 88 A-4 (87) and the Fw 190 A (95) prevented the upper component from drawing fuel from the lower component, thus making the composite unsuitable for combat operations but feasible for training. In the case of the Ju 88 'A-6/U' (A-7), any remaining wire-cutting devices and rear fuselage ballast as well as the FuG 200 *Hohentwiel* anti-shipping radar sets and/or cameras were removed prior to *Mistel* conversion. Other plans centred around a Ju 88 G-1 or G-10 lower component.

In early January 1945, a radical proposal was drawn up by the RLM for a so-called '*Führungsmaschine*' or ultra-long-range pathfinder. By adopting the *Mistel* principle, it was planned to use a long-range Ju 88 H-4 *Zerstörer* as the lower component beneath an Fw 190 A-8 which would serve as its dedicated escort fighter.

The Ju 88 H-4 had been derived from the Ju 88 H-1 long-range reconnaissance aircraft and H-2 *Atlantikzerstörer* which were planned to play a key role in German air operations over the Bay of Biscay during 1943-1944. Resembling a 'stretched' Ju 88 G-1 complete with BMW 801D engines, well armed with up to six MG 151/20 cannon and fitted with external fuel tanks, the Ju 88 H-2 was capable of attaining a range of 5,000 km and a speed of 550 km/h at 6,000 m. Equipped thus and aided by a nose-mounted FuG 200 *Hohentwiel* search radar, it was ideally suited to offer badly needed protection for German U-boats returning to French ports from Atlantic patrols. By June 1943, an order for twenty such aircraft had been added to the prototypes already under construction. On 2 November the first prototype H-1 flew and, by the end of March 1944, five H-1s were serving with 3.(F)/123 with another three available, though by July only two survived and were withdrawn. Only one Ju 88 H-2 is known to have been completed by Junkers at Merseburg. The Ju 88 H-3 was intended as a FuG 200-equipped reconnaissance variant, but never progressed beyond the drawing board.

The *Mistel* 3B proposed mounting an Fw 190 A-6 or A-8 above a Ju 88 H-4 airframe which was to be fitted with a SHl 3500D warhead with *Splittereinlage* (fragmentation liner). The 95 octane fuel for the fighter on its outbound flight was to be supplied from the H-4's fuselage tanks while the wing and external tanks held 87 octane fuel for the *Zerstörer* itself. By 11 February 1945 the department of the *Chef* TLR put forward a requirement for no fewer than 130 *Mistel* 3B combinations, though it also recognised that the planned commencement date of 15 February was not possible due to 'general difficulties, as well as an increased range requirement'. It was reported that 60 of a total of 130 SHl 3500D warheads had been 'filled' by 17 February and were on their way to a *Luftmunitions-anstalt* (Air Munitions Establishment). The filling rate was estimated at ten warheads per day. KG 200 was reported as demanding a new deadline of 1 March 1945, presumably for Operation *Eisenhammer*.

The *Führungsmaschine* pathfinder, which was also required for *Eisenhammer* and other long-range tasks, evolved from the *Mistel* 3B with the Ju 88 H-4 retaining its three-man crew as well as a pair of ETC 504 bomb racks intended to carry two 900-litre drop tanks. An MG 131 was to be mounted in the rear cockpit and a Telefunken FuG 240 *Berlin* centimetric airborne interception radar was to be housed in a large, bulbous nose fairing. In mid-February 1945, KG 200 requested the supply of 50 such combinations.

The upper Fw 190 escort fighter, which was supported on connecting struts featuring thicker, more streamlined fairings than used in previous *Mistel* types, was adapted to carry two 270-litre *Doppelreiter* auxiliary fuel tanks mounted on its upper wing surfaces. Designed and developed as a result of collaboration between *Herr* Klemm of Focke-Wulf's *Entwurfsbüro* at Bad Eilsen and Georg Madelung, Ulrich Hütter and Fritz-Dietrich J. Reder of the *Forschungsanstalt Graf Zeppelin* at Stuttgart-Ruit, these 'flattened' *Doppelreiter* fuel, personnel or provisions containers were intended to offer low drag and minimal reduction in air speed. To investigate the principle of the *Doppelreiter*, the first mock-ups were built of wood with the interior painted with a fuel-proof lacquer. Test flights were undertaken between 17 July and 23 August 1944 using an Fw 190 A-8 and an Fw 190 G-2. Results were very positive and further tests were performed using an Fw 190 carrying a standard 300-litre drop tank which revealed a 33.8 km/h loss of speed, whereas an Fw 190 fitted with fully tanked *Doppelreiter* lost only 13.7 km/h. Some problems were experienced, however, when the aircraft fitted with the wing-mounted tanks proved unstable in flight due to the positioning of the rear fuselage fuel tank. Though the other aircraft had its fuel tank removed, to a great extent this negated the *raison d'être* for installing the *Doppelreiter*.

On 25 September, *Fl. Stabsingenieur* Heinrich Beauvais, a fighter aircraft test pilot from the *Erprobungsstelle* Rechlin delivered Fw 190 A 'White 7' fitted with *Doppelreiter* to *Jagdgruppe* 10, the Luftwaffe's testing and evaluation unit under *Major* Georg Christl. JGr 10 made flights with the *Doppelreiter* full and landing empty, and noted a loss of 15 km/h against normal flying speed. Furthermore, with the fuel in the tanks having been expended and the resultant change to the aircraft's horizontal axis, it was noticed that the aircraft became susceptible to a 'snaking' effect in flight though the unit did comment favourably on the tanks' superior standard of construction. Further flights were made with the tanks removed but with the fittings left in place. A provisional order was made for 300 *Doppelreiter* tanks.

The fuel capacity for the *Führungsmaschine* was planned as follows:

For the Ju 88 H-4 (87 octane):

In the wings:	2 x 415 ltr inner tanks	830 ltr/600 kg
	2 x 425 ltr outer tanks	850 ltr/620 kg
In the fuselage:	1. tank	1,220 ltr/900 kg
	2. tank	1,220 ltr/900 kg
	3. tank	1,220 ltr/900 kg
	5. tank	1,220 ltr/900 kg
	6. tank	1,050 ltr/780 kg
External load:	2 x 900 ltr drop tanks	1,800 ltr/1,320 kg
In the Fw 190:	2 x 270 ltr Doppelreiter	540 ltr/400 kg

Continued on page 142

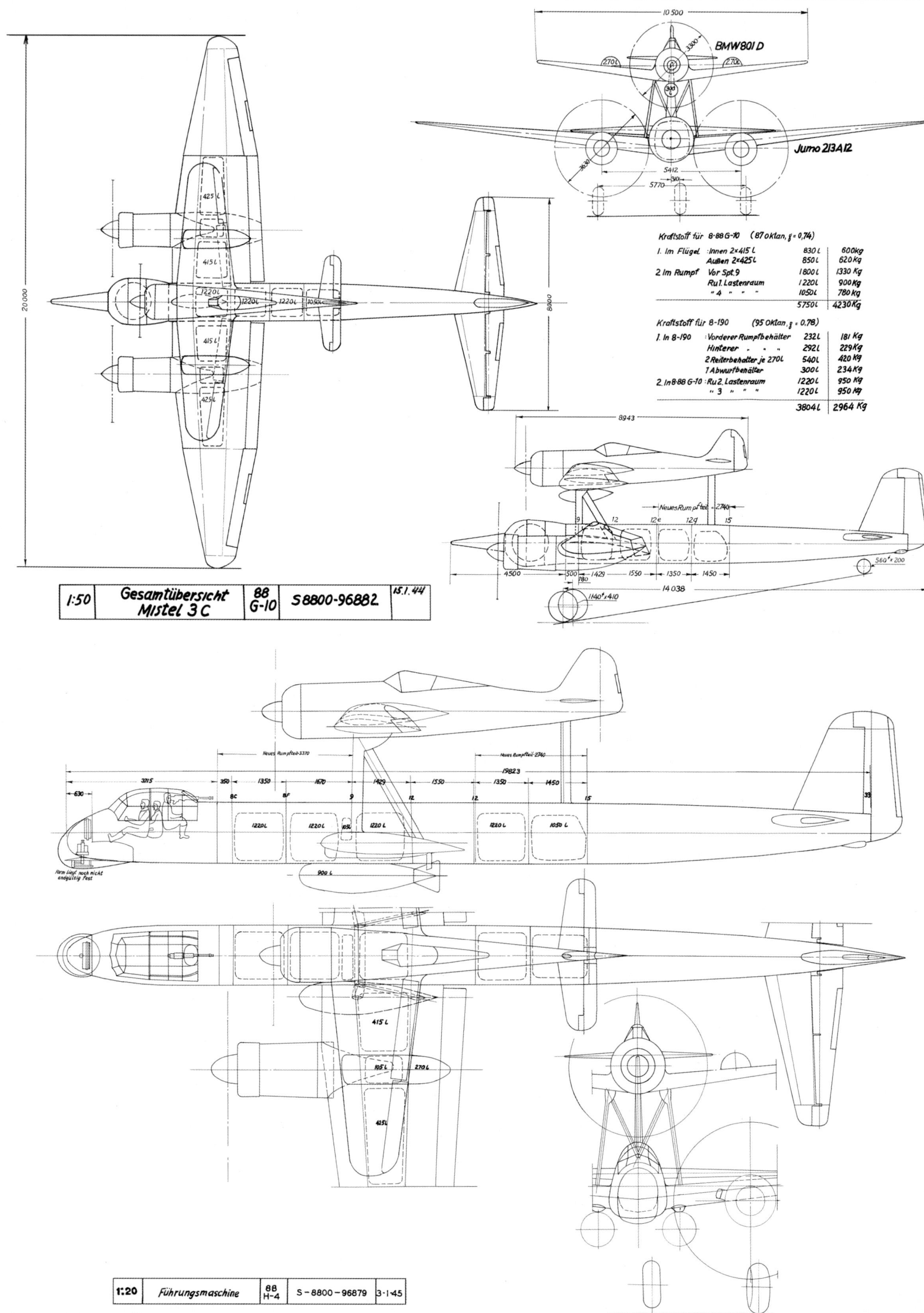
10 500
BMW 801 D
Jumo 213 A 12
5412
5770
Kraftstoff für 8-88 G-10 (87 Oktan, γ = 0,74)
1. Im Flügel :Innen 2×415 L 830 L 600 kg
Außen 2×425 L 850 L 620 Kg
2 Im Rumpf Vor Spt. 9 1800 L 1330 Kg
Ru 1. Lastenraum 1220 L 900 Kg
" 4 " " " 1050 L 780 kg
5750 L 4230 Kg
Kraftstoff für 8-190 (95 Oktan, γ = 0,78)
1. In 8-190 :Vorderer Rumpfbehälter 232 L 181 Kg
Hinterer " " " 292 L 229 Kg
2 Reiterbehälter je 270 L 540 L 420 Kg
1 Abwurfbehälter 300 L 234 Kg
2. In 8-88 G-10 :Ru 2. Lastenraum 1220 L 950 Kg
" 3 " " " 1220 L 950 Kg
3804 L 2964 Kg
20 000
8000
8943
Neues Rumpfteil 2740
4500
1429
1550
1350
1450
14 038
1140 × 410
560 × 200
1:50 Gesamtübersicht Mistel 3 C 88 G-10 S 8800-96882 15.1.44
Neues Rumpfteil 3370
Neues Rumpfteil 2740
19823
3715
1350
1670
1429
1550
1350
1450
1220 L
1220 L
1220 L
1220 L
1050 L
900 L
Form liegt noch nicht endgültig fest
415 L
270 L
425 L
1:20 Führungsmaschine 88 H-4 S-8800-96879 3-1-45

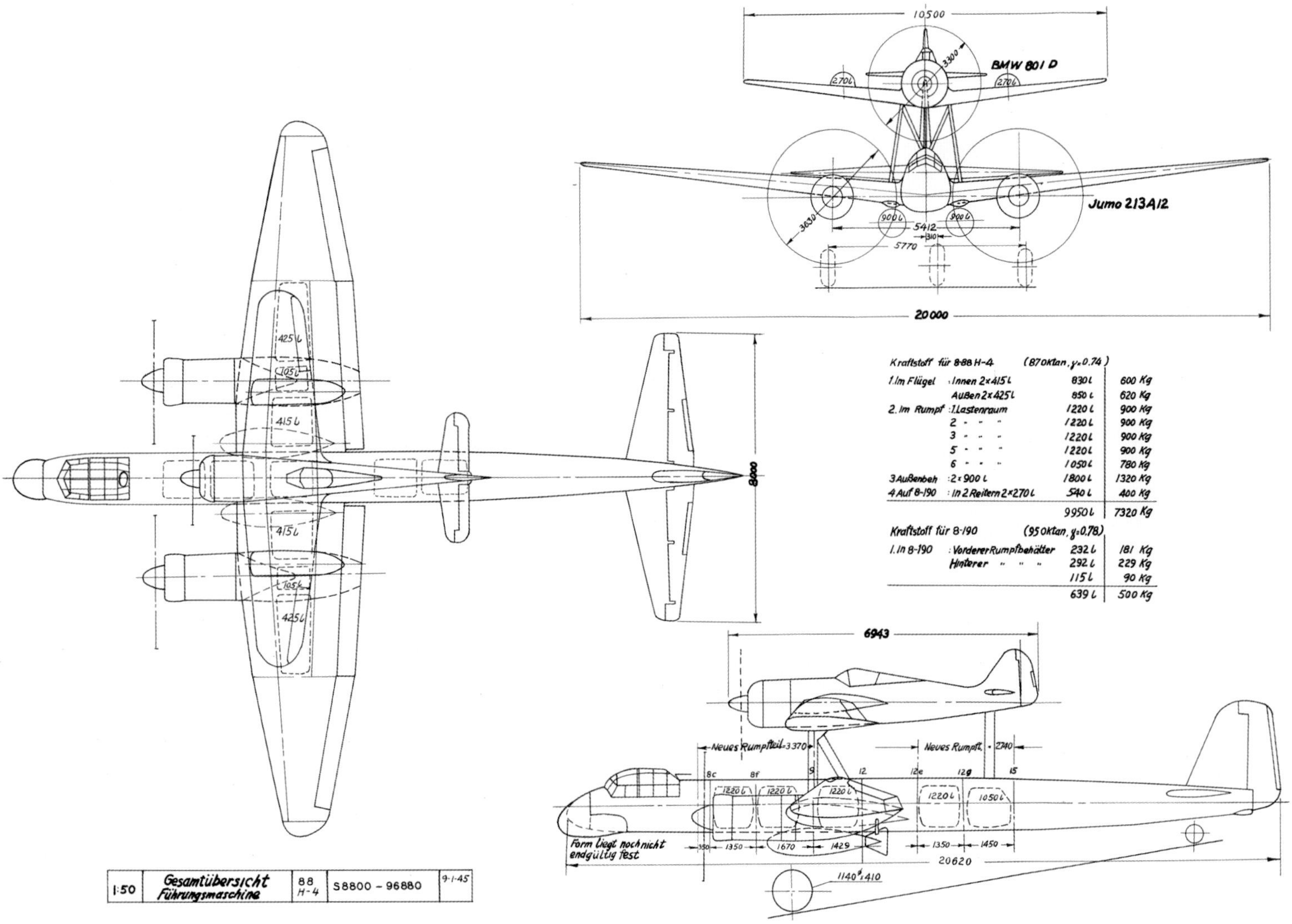

10500
BMW 801 D
Jumo 213A12
20000

Kraftstoff für 8-88 H-4	(87 Oktan, γ=0.74)		
1. Im Flügel	: Innen 2×415 L	830 L	600 Kg
	Außen 2×425 L	850 L	620 Kg
2. Im Rumpf	: 1. Lastenraum	1220 L	900 Kg
	2 " "	1220 L	900 Kg
	3 " "	1220 L	900 Kg
	5 " "	1220 L	900 Kg
	6 " "	1050 L	780 Kg
3 Außenbeh	: 2×900 L	1800 L	1320 Kg
4 Auf 8-190	: In 2 Reitern 2×270 L	540 L	400 Kg
		9950 L	7320 Kg
Kraftstoff für 8-190	(95 Oktan, γ=0.78)		
1. In 8-190	: Vorderer Rumpfbehälter	232 L	181 Kg
	Hinterer " " "	292 L	229 Kg
		115 L	90 Kg
		639 L	500 Kg

6943
Neues Rumpfteil 3370
Neues Rumpft. 2740
Form liegt noch nicht endgültig fest
20620

1:50	Gesamtübersicht Führungsmaschine	88 H-4	S8800 – 96880	9-1-45

A wind tunnel model of an Fw 190 fitted with mock-up moulds of wing-mounted Doppelreiter auxiliary fuel tanks. This configuration was intended for use in the Mistel 3C and the proposed Führungsmaschine.

Two views of Fw 190 A 'White 7' showing the installation of Doppelreiter wing-mounted fuel tanks. Fw 190s serving as upper component fighters in the Mistel 3 and Führungsmaschine configurations would have been similarly converted.

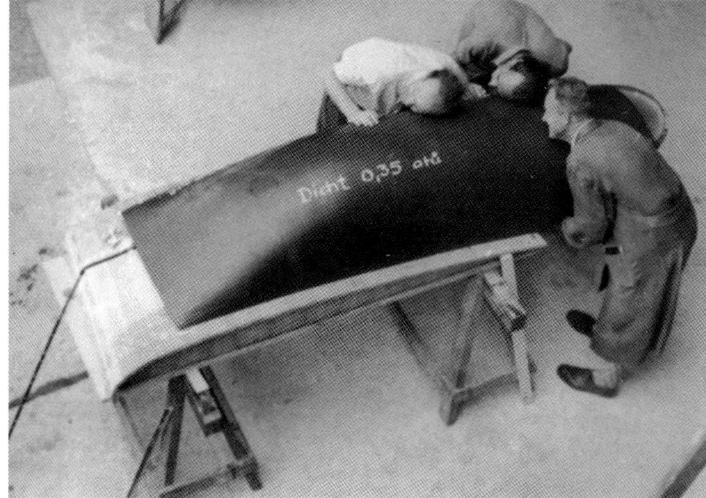

Left and above: Civilian personnel seen during construction and testing of Doppelreiter wing-mounted fuel tanks.

The internal construction of a Doppelreiter wing-mounted fuel tank.

Technicians lift a Doppelreiter wing-mounted fuel tank onto the wing of Fw 190 A White '7' at the Erprobungsstelle Rechlin. This aircraft was later flown by Rechlin's fighter specialist, Fl. Stabsingenieur Heinrich Beauvais to Jagdgruppe 10, the Luftwaffe's testing and evaluation unit.

Far right: White '7' shown in flight with the Doppelreiter wing-mounted fuel tanks.

For the Fw 190 (95 octane)

Front fuselage tank:	232 ltr	181 kg
Rear fuselage tank:	292 ltr	229 kg
	115 ltr	90 kg

The *Mistel* 3C was foreseen as a long-endurance composite, the upper Fw 190 component to be fitted with *Doppelreiter* wing tanks. In order to bear the excessive weight of the combination, the Ju 88 was to have had a third wheel and leg added to the main undercarriage which was to be jettisoned after take-off. In early January 1945, the *Chef* TLR stipulated that as far as the *Mistel* 3C was concerned, 'after stoppage of the 100 units ordered, only three prototype combinations and ten pathfinder aircraft to be built by Junkers.' By 11 February however, further development of the *Mistel* 3C was 'deferred' on the orders of *Reichsminister* Speer.

Performance data was as follows:

Fuel load Ju 88 G-10	6,130 kg
Fuel load Fw 190 with 2 x *Doppelreiter* and drop tank	1,064 kg
Total	7,194 kg

Take-off weight	23,600 kg
Max. speed at sea level	320 km/h
Max. speed at 4,000 m (13,123 ft)	340 km/h
Range	4,100 km

The *Mistel* S3C was intended as a training variant incorporating either an Fw 190 A-8 or F-8 mounted onto a Ju 88 G-10 long-range *Zerstörer* as the lower component. Powered by either Jumo 213 A or BMW 801 engines and armed with six MG 151s, manufacture of the Ju 88 G-10 commenced in 1944 with the first aircraft completed by Junkers at Dessau in March 1945. However, shortly afterwards, series production was abandoned and it was decided to use all finished airframes – thought to have totalled ten – as *Mistel*, though only one machine, W.Nr.460066, was converted.

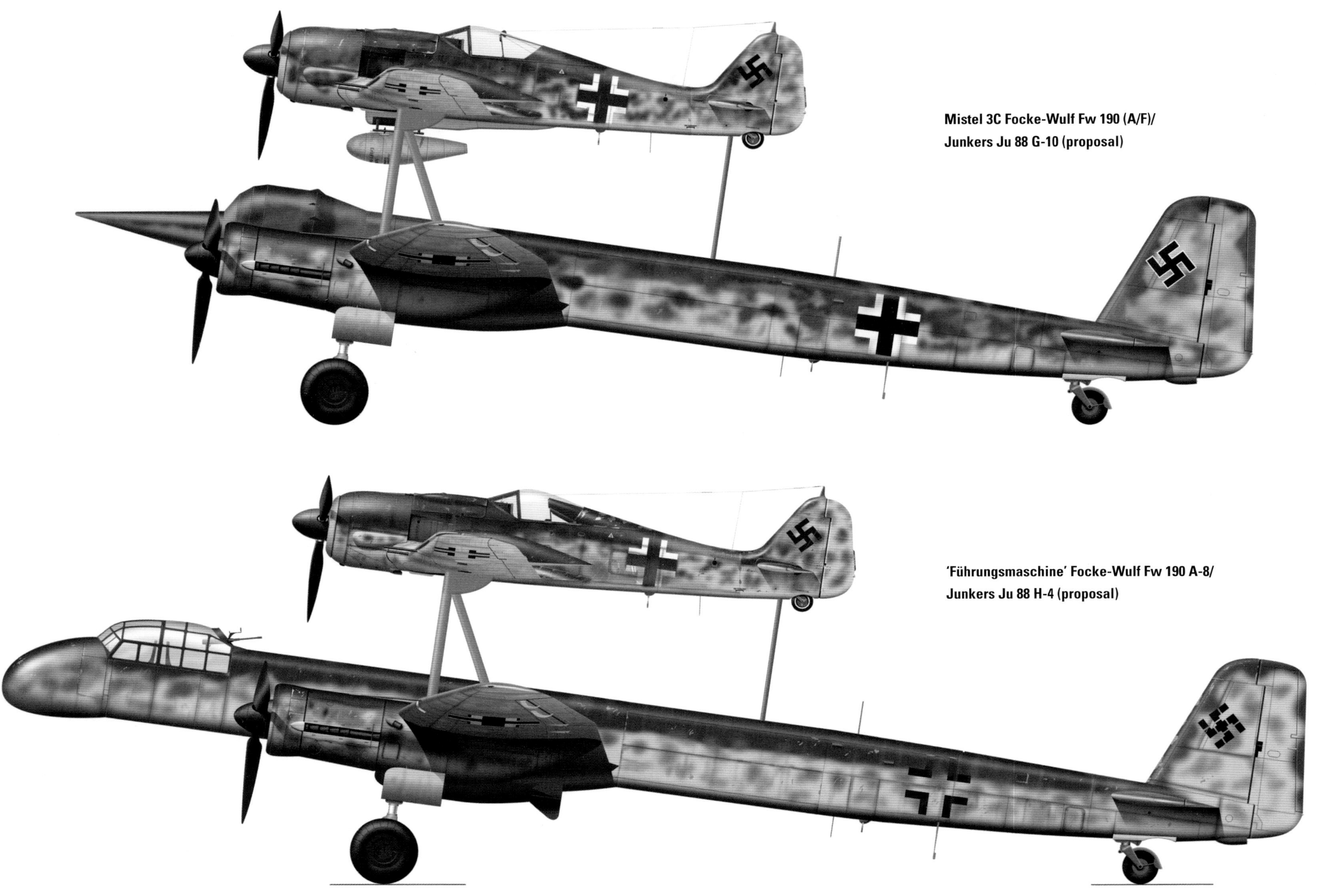

Mistel 3C Focke-Wulf Fw 190 (A/F)/
Junkers Ju 88 G-10 (proposal)

'Führungsmaschine' Focke-Wulf Fw 190 A-8/
Junkers Ju 88 H-4 (proposal)

Fw 190/Heinkel He 177 *Mistel*

BY the autumn of 1944, the Luftwaffe's ability to mount effective strategic bomber operations was at an end. Nevertheless, Germany's airfields were littered with hundreds of redundant bomber aircraft which had been stripped for parts and their crews split up for emergency fighter training or for service in ground units.

One aircraft to end its largely problematic service record in such a way was the Heinkel He 177 *Greif*[2] and of more than 1,000 machines built, some 900 ended up abandoned or on scrapheaps by the end of the war. Conceived originally as a dive-bomber, the He 177 had been intended as Germany's main 'strategic' bomber, but during some of its earliest operations in Russia it was plagued by engine fires in the coupled DB 610 inverted engines, these and other mechanical problems earning it a poor reputation. Ultimately, the He 177 was used only in numbers on sporadic bombing missions over the British Isles in the first half of 1944 and as an anti-shipping aircraft by KG 40 over the Atlantic and the Mediterranean. Some 90 aircraft were placed on the strength of KG 1 in mid-1944 for operations in the East, but a lack of fuel and interference on the part of Göring, who relegated the He 177s to attacking Soviet tanks, ensured that any strike power they possessed was nullified.

As early as the summer of 1944, *Oberst i.G.* Heinz Heigl, the *Kommodore* of KG 200, wrote a memo to the commander of IV.*Fliegerkorps*, stating that the planned Ju 88/Fw 190 A-8 *Mistel* combination would have a range of some 1,500 km whilst an He 177/Fw 190 A-8 combination would attain a range of 3,300 km. Furthermore, ten major Soviet power stations lay within range of such a *Mistel* if Prowehren was used as a take-off base, which was also home to KG 1's He 177s. With Heigl replaced by Baumbach and the subsequent planning for Operation *Eisenhammer*, it was decreed that as many as possible of the He 177 A-3s and A-5s parked on airfields across Germany, Denmark and Norway should be brought to flight readiness by the end of 1944 and converted to *Mistel*.

On 20 November 1944, Heinkel offered to commence work on a *Mistel* prototype at the Eger plant and advised that a second could be built within 15 days. The company also estimated that it would take 5,000 man-hours per airframe to convert 50 He 177s. At the beginning of December, despite the fact that work had not commenced on the two prototypes, the RLM placed an order for 50 *Mistel* conversions, though this quantity was later reduced to 20 in order not to endanger production of the He 162 *Volksjäger*.

Though the prototypes had still not appeared by 7 December, ten days later *Luftflotte* 6 asked that 50 He 177s be converted to *Mistel* as soon as possible for operations on the Eastern Front. Simultaneously however, doubts grew about the bomber's technical suitability for such a lower component.

Rescheduled delivery dates for the first and second prototypes were set at 1 February and 15 February respectively, and it was agreed that production should switch from Eger to Nordhausen, though ultimately the worsening war situation prevented any further development.

[2] 'Griffon'.

It was proposed that the Lippisch DM-1 test glider was to be carried to altitude by a Siebel Si 204 in a Mistel configuration and then released to assess low-speed characteristics.

Siebel Si 204/Lippisch DM-1

Low speed research

IN the autumn of 1944, a group of students at the universities of Darmstadt and München commenced design work on a test glider known as the DM-1 ('DM' = 'Darmstadt' and 'München'). This group was known as the *Flugtechnische Fachgruppe* and it had been commissioned to design and build the DM-1 by *Dr* Alexander Lippisch who had formerly worked at Messerschmitt in Augsburg on the Me 163 development programme.

Installed in his new post at the *Luftfahrtforschungsanstalt* (LFA) in Vienna, Lippisch worked on various high-speed aerodynamic matters as well as a delta-wing aircraft project. In conjunction with the DFS, he began to look at ways in which to integrate ramjet propulsion with delta wing design to produce a fast interceptor. Consequently, in late 1944, Lippisch produced a design for the LP-13a, a ramjet-powered, pure delta-wing aircraft intended to develop speeds up to Mach 2.6 using powdered coal as fuel.

As a preliminary part of the design project, Lippisch assigned the *Flugtechnische Fachgruppe* which, by November 1944, had been bombed out of its premises and relocated to Prien, to construct the DM-1 for the purposes of obtaining data on low-speed handling.

The DM-1 emerged as a delta-wing aircraft with a large delta fin, extending almost to the front tip of the wing with symmetrical elliptical sections used for both fin and wing which were of two spar wooden construction with plywood skinning. The craft rested on a tubular metal nose wheel undercarriage, which retracted not by folding but by being drawn up into special recesses.

The DFS proposed that the DM-1 should be carried to altitude in a *Mistel* configuration, mounted on top of a Siebel Si 204 and then released to assess the low-speed characteristics. The DM-1 was almost completed by the time it was captured by the Americans who later moved it to the USA for flight and wind tunnel testing.

Mistel 4

Messerschmitt Me 262 *Mistel*

BY 1944, the problem with the conventionally powered *Mistel* was its vulnerability to enemy fighters before the lower component could be released at its target. Therefore, on 28 November 1944, the Messerschmitt *Projektbüro* at Oberammergau put forward a proposal to use two Me 262 jet aircraft as the upper and lower components of a new *Mistel*. The upper component was to be an

262. Misteleinsatz. Geheime Kommandosache

I. Leitflugzeug.
Mit Bomberkanzel und 2 Mann Besatzung, 2 MK 108
Startgewicht: 6985 kg
Kraftstoffvorrat: 2133 kg (900 + 170 + 900 + 600 ltr.)

II. Stoffträger.
Ausführung A: Alle Räume mit Flüssigstoff gefüllt, Rumpfspitze gepanzert,
Startgewicht: 9917 kg
Kraftstoffvorrat: 1494 kg (900 + 900 ltr.)
Flüssigstoffmenge: 4460 kg

Ausführung B: Rumpfspitze aus Baustoff geformt, in den übrigen Räumen Baustoffblöcke
Startgewicht: 11650 kg
Kraftstoffvorrat: 1494 kg (900 + 900 ltr.)
Baustoffmenge: Geheime kg

Ausführung C: Rumpfspitze aus Baustoff, in den übrigen Räumen Flüssigstoff
Startgewicht: 10125 kg
Kraftstoffvorrat: 1494 kg (900 + 900 ltr.)
Gesamte Stoffmenge: 5210 kg (2450 kg Baustoff + 2760 kg Flüssigstoff).

III. Startgewichte der Gespanne:
Ausführung A: 16902 kg G/F = 390 kg/m²
Ausführung B: 18635 kg G/F = [illegible] kg/m²
Ausführung C: 17110 kg G/F = 395 kg/m²
Ges.Kraftstoffmenge 3627 kg = 4370 ltr.

Der Startwagen kommt mit rund 2000 kg noch hinzu.

Oberammergau, 28.11.44.
Pr/Mtz/Sto

Me 262 A-2a/U2, a fast bomber variant fitted with a specially enlarged wooden front fuselage featuring a glazed nose and upper panel, known as the *Bomberkanzel* (bomber nose), in which a bomb-aimer would lie prone to operate a *Lotfe* 7H bombsight with which he would aim the lower component at its target. It was estimated that this upper component would have a take-off weight of 6,985 kg with a fuel load of 2,570 litres.

Three different versions of the lower component were proposed, *Ausführung* A, B and C. Version A was to have an armoured fuselage nose with liquid explosive; Version B was to have the forward fuselage formed of solid explosive with similar material in other fuselage areas; and Version C was to have the forward fuselage of Version B but with liquid explosive in the other areas. The following weights were estimated:

The Lotfe 7H gyro-stabilised bombsight as fitted into the glazed 'Bomberkanzel' of the Me 262 A-2a/U2. To the left is the switching key and supplementary bombsight.

Me 262 A-2a/U2, W.Nr.110484, is towed across Rechlin airfield in early 1945. Visible beneath the camouflage drape is the distinctive wooden nose section with its glazed cone, the 'Bomberkanzel', designed to accommodate a prone bomb-aimer and Lotfe 7H gyro-stabilised bombsight. It was proposed to use such a variant of the Me 262 as the upper component of the Mistel 4. The other Me 262 seen in the photograph is believed to be W.Nr.130015, the second V1 prototype.

	Take-off weight	Fuel Reserve	Explosive weight
Carrier Aircraft	6,985 kg	2,133 kg	none
Ausführung A	9,917 kg	1,494 kg	4,460 kg
Ausführung B	11,650 kg	1,494 kg	6,030 kg
Ausführung C	10,125 kg	1,494 kg	5,210 kg

The first combination would have a total take-off weight of 16,902 kg, the second of 18,635 kg and the third 17,110 kg.

The combination was to take off on a purpose-built, five-wheeled trolley developed by Rheinmetall-Borsig which was boosted by four Walter 501 rocket units. After the combination had taken off and the rockets had burnt out, the trolley was jettisoned.

Two Me 262s were delivered for conversion as *Mistel* during December 1944 but, as far as is known, the composite never flew before the end of the war. The combination was given the designation *Mistel* 4.

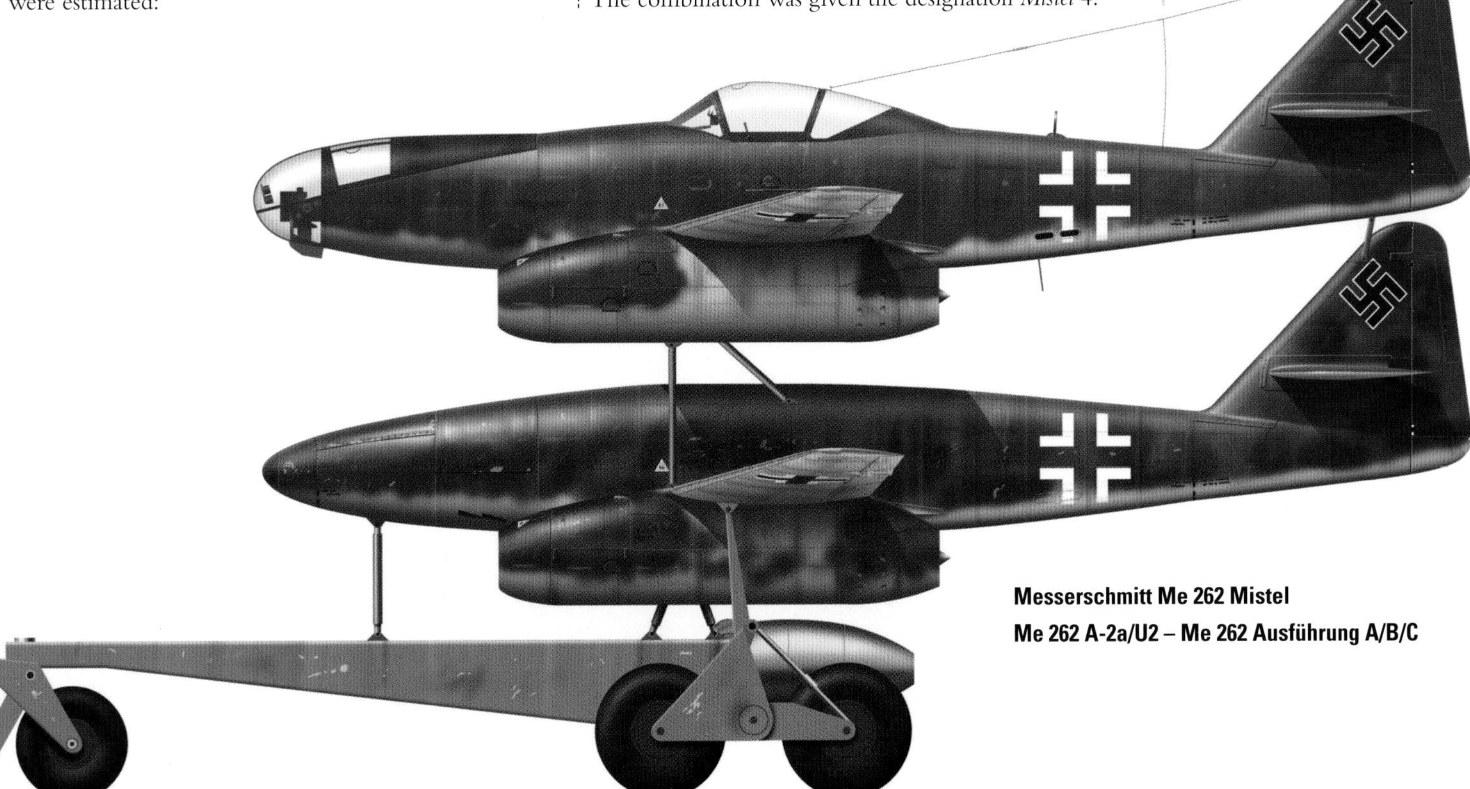

Messerschmitt Me 262 Mistel
Me 262 A-2a/U2 – Me 262 Ausführung A/B/C

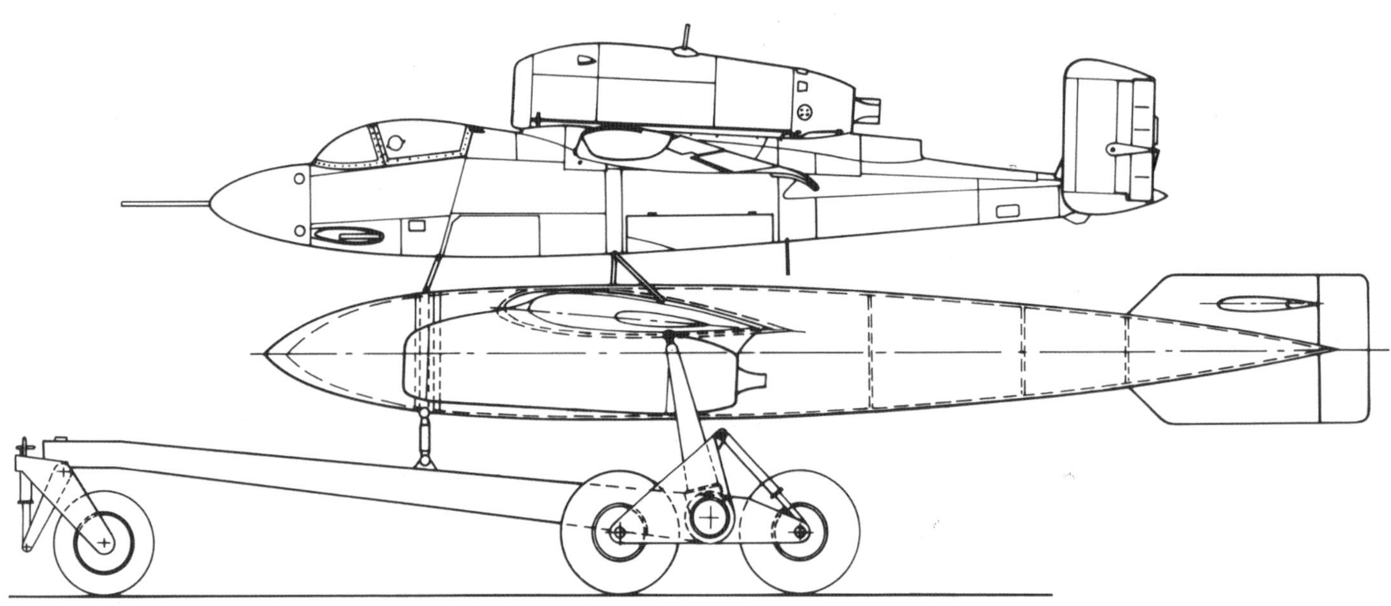

Mistel 5 He 162/ E377 a (powered), November 1944

An SC 1800 bomb on its transport cradle. It was intended to mount such a bomb without its tail unit in the nose of the E377.

Mistel 5

PLANNED in November 1944, the concept behind the *Mistel* 5 was to use the Heinkel He 162. Known as the *Volksjäger* (Peoples' Fighter), the He 162 was a cheap-to-build, jet-powered 'emergency' fighter. Constructed from non-strategic materials in relatively few man-hours, the He 162 was considered by some to be the ideal delivery vehicle for a powered version of the E 377, known as the E 377a, as described in the *Mistel* 6. The E 377a was to be fitted with a pair of BMW 003 A-1 engines. The weight breakdown of the *Mistel* 5 was as follows:

Undercarriage	2,000 kg
Warhead (2 t or SC 1800 without tail unit)	2,000 kg
Engines (2 x BMW 003 A1)	1,330 kg
Accumulated weight	5,530 kg
Equipment (horizontal steering)	30 kg
Accumulated equipped weight	5,360 kg
Fuel in wings	1,000 kg
Fuel in fuselage	3,500 kg
Starting fuel and lubricant	40 kg
Ballast or disposable (burning) liquid	500 kg
Accumulated weight	5,040 kg
Flight weight of E 377	10,400 kg
Flight weight of Ar 234	2,900 kg
Flight weight for Mistel without start trolley	13,300 kg
Start trolley with 4 x Walter RATOs each producing 1,500 kg thrust for 30 seconds	4,000 kg
Take-off weight for Mistel with take-off trolley	17,300 kg

	He 162	E 377	
Wing area	11 m²	25 m²	
Span	7.2 m	12.2 m	
Length	9.05 m	6 m	
Take-off weight with take-off trolley	17,300 kg		
Wing load	478 kg/m²		
Flight weight without take-off trolley	2,900 kg	10,400 kg	(13,300 kg)
Wing loading	259 kg/m²	416 kg/m²	(675 kg/m²)
Flight weight over target at max. depth of penetration	2,900 kg	5,900 kg	(8,800 kg)
Wing load	259 kg/m²	236 kg/m²	
Fuel	870 kg	4,500 kg	(5,370 kg)
Warhead		1,800-2,000 kg	

Other carrier aircraft considered for use in this configuration were the Me 262 and the Ju 268, the latter based on the E 377, for which Arado lacked the necessary development and production capacity. In mid-January 1945, Junkers had calculated that a range of 1,600 km with a maximum speed of 820 km/h at 6,000 m altitude was attainable. Though the project was reported to have been 'in preparation in its final form' in March 1945 and a low-speed wind tunnel test on a '*Mistel* 5 twin jet aircraft' was carried out at Junkers Dessau on 19 April, no such *Mistel* were ever produced.

Mistel 6 and Arado *Mistel* projects

IN early September 1944, the Arado Flugzeugwerke discussed a proposal for an aircraft to be carried beneath the Ar 234 C jet bomber. This was to be the Arado E 377 and it was to form the mid-wing purpose-built lower component of a *Mistel*. The project was to be unpowered and have either a 2,000-kg hollow-charge warhead or an SC 1800 bomb mounted in the nose. Additional fuel could be carried in the rear fuselage giving the combination a theoretical range of 2,000 km.

Following a meeting between representatives of the RLM and Arado in Berlin on 4 and 5 September 1944, it was reported:

> '... special care needs to be taken with the aerodynamic design of the connections between the two aircraft. If possible, the distance between the two fuselages has to be increased. Due to the incremental development of 300-500 kg of thrust, two of the connections could be installed on the payload aircraft.
>
> Wood is the only material for construction at this time. We have to distance ourselves from synthetic materials until development has been completed.
>
> The start dolly should be designed in such a way that as well as a take-off with 20 tonnes, a landing with 12-14 tonnes can also be accomplished. The purpose of this is to be able to transfer the empty payload carrier (without fuel and explosives) to the airfield where the mission is to originate. For this purpose a good aerodynamic design for the take-off dolly is necessary. The axle and the wheels need to be aerodynamically faired. The possibility of a jettisonable rather than a standard dolly was also discussed. There are no advantages gained other than more efficient transport from the mission airfield back to the transfer airfield. In order to connect the Ar 234 C3, the payload aircraft and the start dolly, special tools have to be on hand such as lift cranes, jacks, etc.'

This composite was evidently intended for use against such targets as merchant ships of 12-15,000 tonnes and various ground targets. It was envisaged that an explosive charge of 2 tonnes would be mounted in the nose of the lower aircraft but that a large steel housing with explosive capability would be required to ensure a successful attack against such merchant shipping. For ground targets, a thinly housed explosive charge with more explosive content and possibly 500 kg of liquid explosive in the tail would be appropriate. It had apparently been suggested that this tail charge might be replaced by a 500 kg bomb, but according to *Herr* Demann of the RLM, this would not have the same effect as the liquid explosive.

The lower component was to have been launched in a flat dive with the use of a Revi gunsight or a front and rear periscope gunsight. The explosive nose was to be developed in such a way that it could be installed at the mission airfield.

In the final plan, no control surfaces or undercarriage were to be fitted to the E 377 because of the expense involved and the missile was intended simply to be aimed at its target and launched. Rheinmetall-Borsig had developed a 20 tonne take-off trolley onto which the expendable aircraft could be hoisted. The Ar 234 mother aircraft would then be lifted on top and connected to it by struts fitted with explosive bolts. Take-off was accomplished with the aid of four Walter rocket units, the five-wheeled trolley being jettisoned shortly afterward in the manner of the early Ar 234 prototypes.

Mistel 6 weight specifications

Undercarriage	1,970 kg
Warhead (2 t or SC 1800 without tail unit)	2,000 kg
Accumulated weight	3,970 kg
Equipment (horizontal steering)	30 kg
Accumulated equipped weight	4,000 kg
Fuel in wings	1,000 kg
Fuel in fuselage	3,500 kg
Ballast or disposable (burning) liquid	500 kg
Accumulated weight	5,000 kg
Flight weight of E 377	9,000 kg
Flight weight of Ar 234	10,000 kg
Flight weight of Mistel without start trolley	19,000 kg
Start trolley with 4 x Walter RATO units each producing 1,500 kg thrust for 30 seconds	4,000 kg
Take-off weight for Mistel with take-off trolley	23,000 kg

	Ar 234 C	E 377	
Wing area	27 m²	25 m²	
Span	14.4 m	12.2 m	
Length	12.8 m	6 m	
Take-off weight with take-off trolley	23,000 kg		
Wing load	442 kg/m²		
Flight weight without take-off trolley	10,000 kg	9,000kg	(19,000 kg)
Wing load	370 kg/m²	360 kg/m²	
Flight weight over target at max. depth of penetration	8,250 kg	4,500 kg	12,750 kg
Wing load	306 kg/m²	180 kg/m²	245 kg/m²
Fuel	3,100 kg	4,500 kg	7,600 kg
Warhead		1,800-2,000 kg	

Another Arado project was the E 381 parasite fighter. Echoing the concept of the Me 328, Arado proposed carrying a small, rocket-powered fighter beneath an Arado 234 C which would be able to get close enough to an enemy bomber formation to ensure success. Naturally, the midget fighter was to feature extensive armour plating so that the pilot, who would lie in a prone position, the small rocket engine and the fuel tanks were all to be housed within an armoured tube. A single 30 mm MK 108 cannon was to be mounted above the fuselage with 45 rounds of ammunition contained in the port wing. The whole

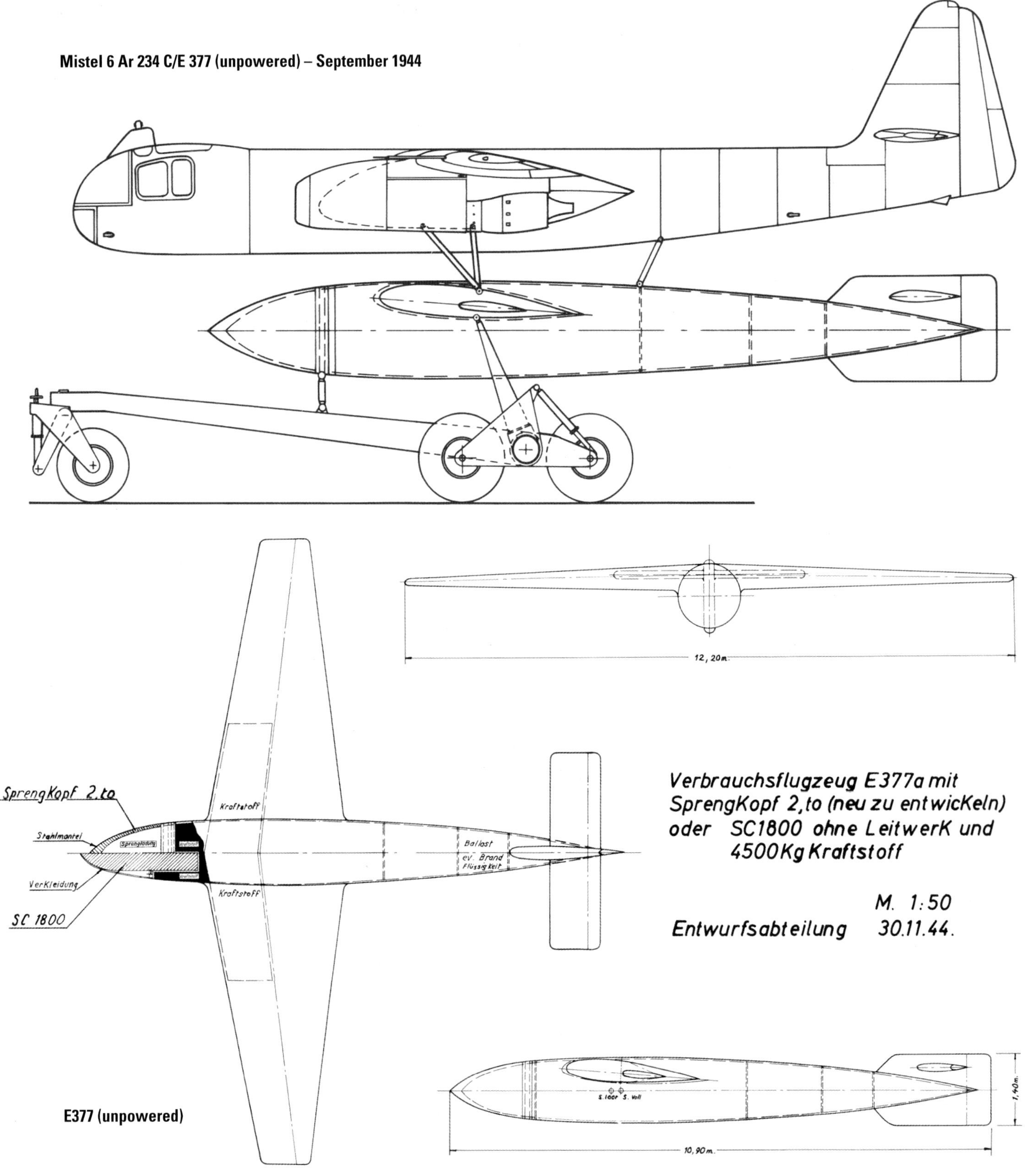

Mistel 6 Ar 234 C/E 377 (unpowered) – September 1944

E377 (unpowered)

configuration was considered sufficient to make two attacks before the pilot had to cut the engine so as to reserve fuel for landing on a suitable airfield or main road using a spring-loaded skid and a small braking parachute. It was intended to recover the E 381 from its landing site by a special truck which could carry two such aircraft.

In mid-January 1945, the TLR issued a specification stating that the *Mistel* 6 should be capable of attaining a range of 1,300 km with a maximum speed of 720 km/h at 6,000 m altitude. The idea progressed no further than the planning stage; no prototypes were completed and by mid-February 1945 the *Chef* TLR had officially abandoned any further development work.

Assigned the name '*Huckepack*' and thus within the scope of this study, was the radical October 1944 proposal featuring a Fieseler Fi 103 flying bomb mounted above the fuselage of a Ar 234 C. This was seen as a progressive and improved step in attempts to conduct air-launched flying bomb operations such as those which had been carried out against the British Isles by the He 111s of KG 3 and KG 53 during the second half of 1944. The slow speed of the He 111, particularly when burdened by an Fi 103 load,

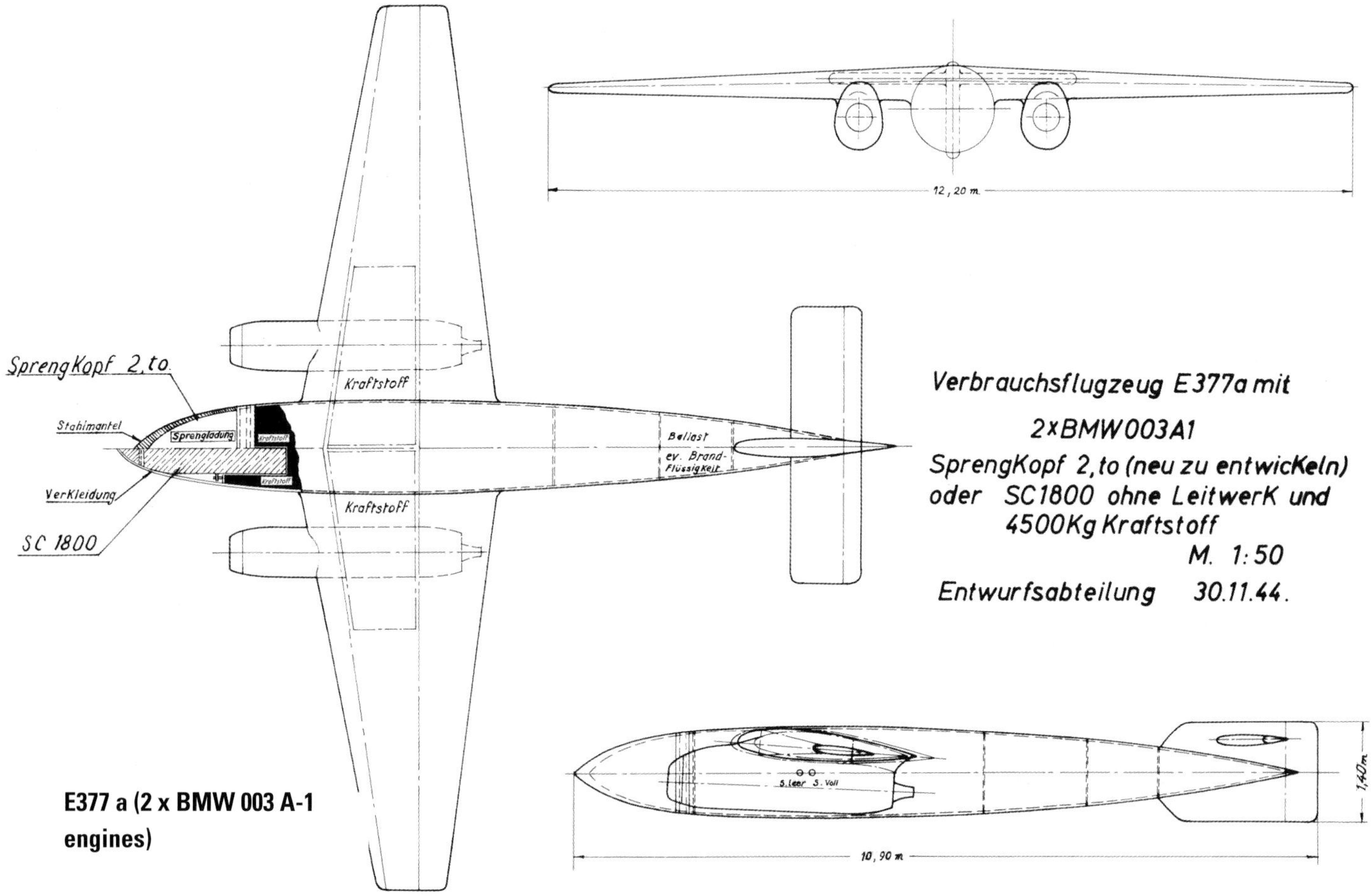

SprengKopf 2,to

Stahlmantel

Sprengladung

Kraftstoff

Verkleidung

SC 1800

Ballast
ev. Brand-
Flüssigkeit

12,20 m

Verbrauchsflugzeug E377a mit
2xBMW003A1
SprengKopf 2,to (neu zu entwickeln)
oder SC1800 ohne LeitwerK und
4500Kg Kraftstoff
M. 1:50
Entwurfsabteilung 30.11.44.

1,40m

10,90 m

E377 a (2 x BMW 003 A-1 engines)

An undated proposal (probably latter half of 1944) by Fieseler for an Fw 190 A-8/Fi 103 flying bomb Mistel combination

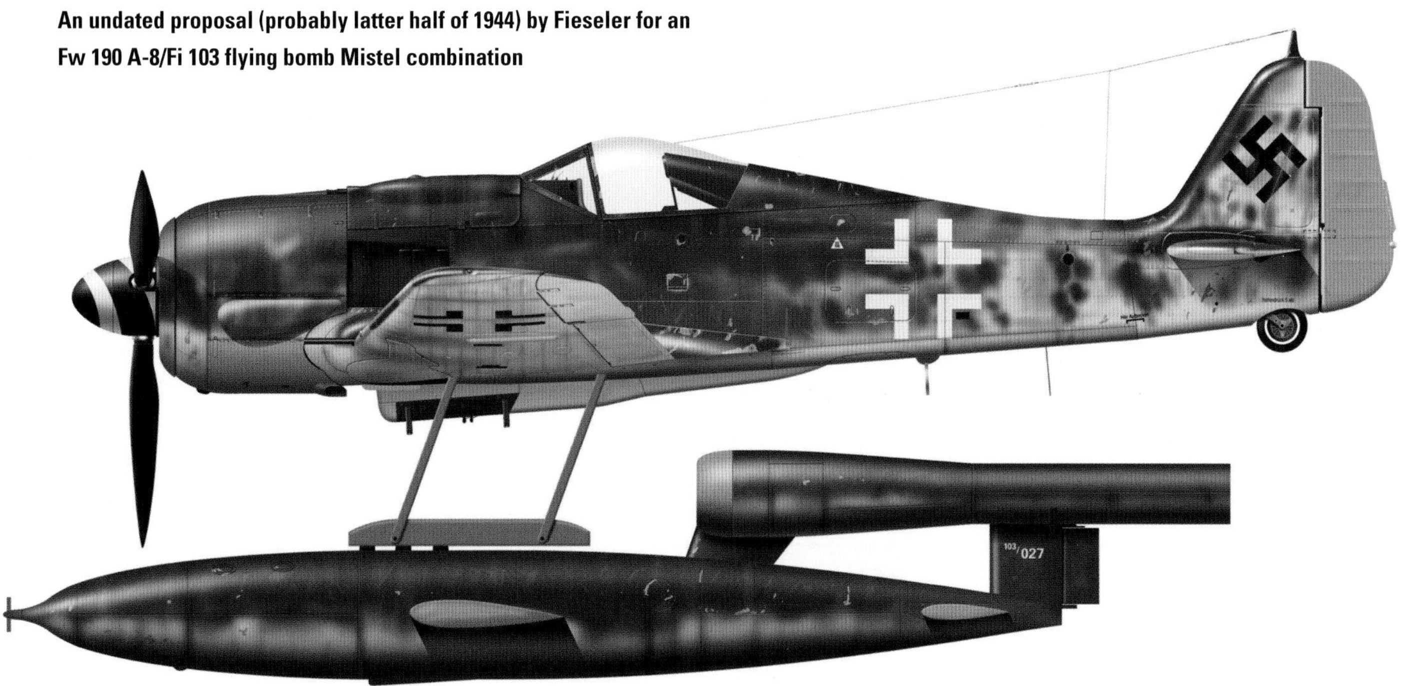

rendered it vulnerable to fighter attack, especially by RAF night fighters which patrolled the eastern coast of Britain. The Ar 234 was an altogether different story and it was intended that the Fi 103 be raised above its Ar 234 carrier by large hydraulic arms immediately prior to firing. However, as far as is known, work did not extend beyond conceptual design.

Fw 190/Fieseler Fi 103

EVIDENCE exists of a *Mistel* proposal to combine an Fw 190 fighter or fighter-bomber upper component with a Fieseler Fi 103 flying bomb lower component. Unfortunately, on the single document discovered to date, no reference to the originator or date of the proposal is given.

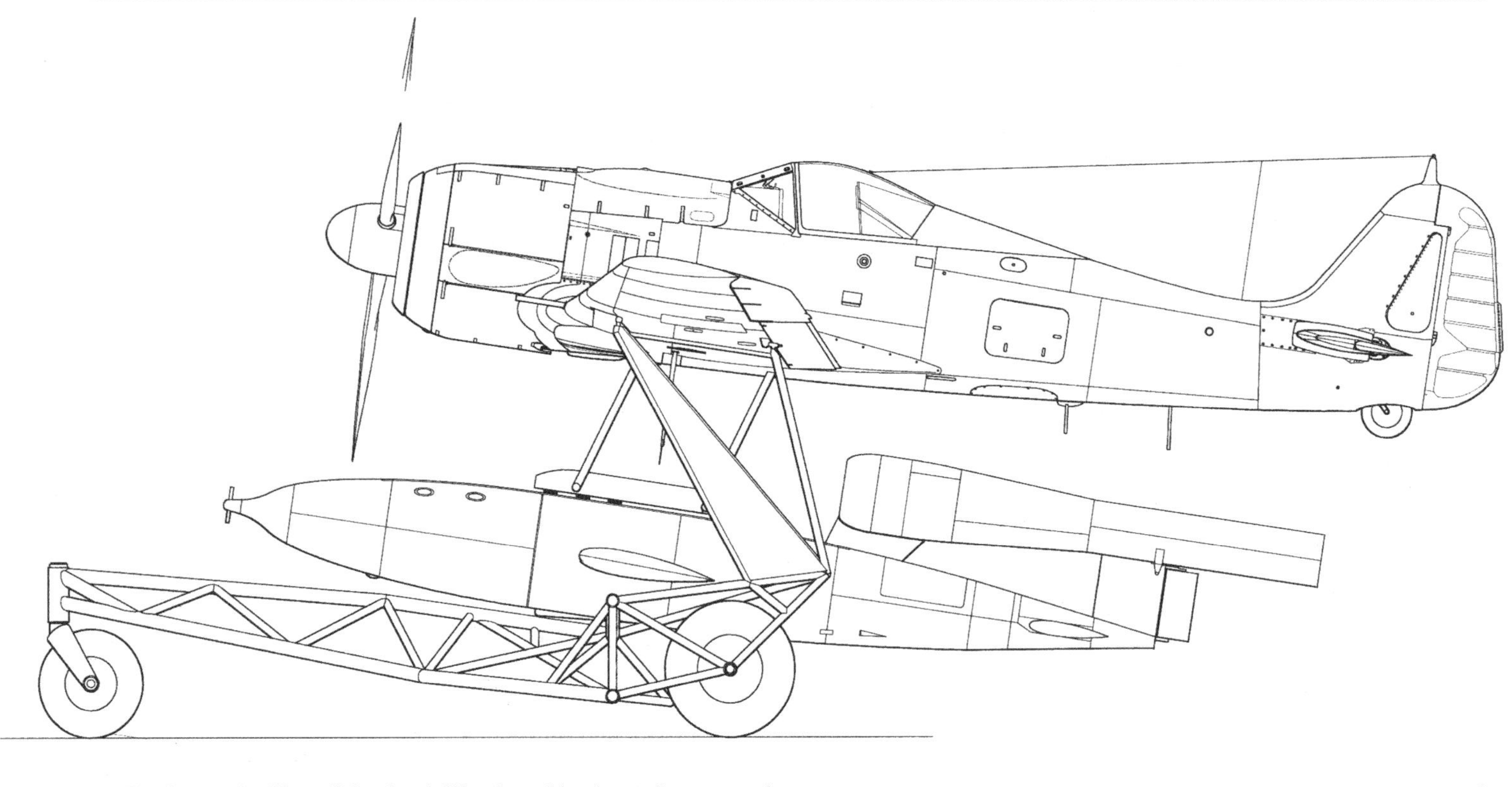

The Fw 190 A-8/Fi 103 flying bomb Mistel combination on its proposed take-off trolley

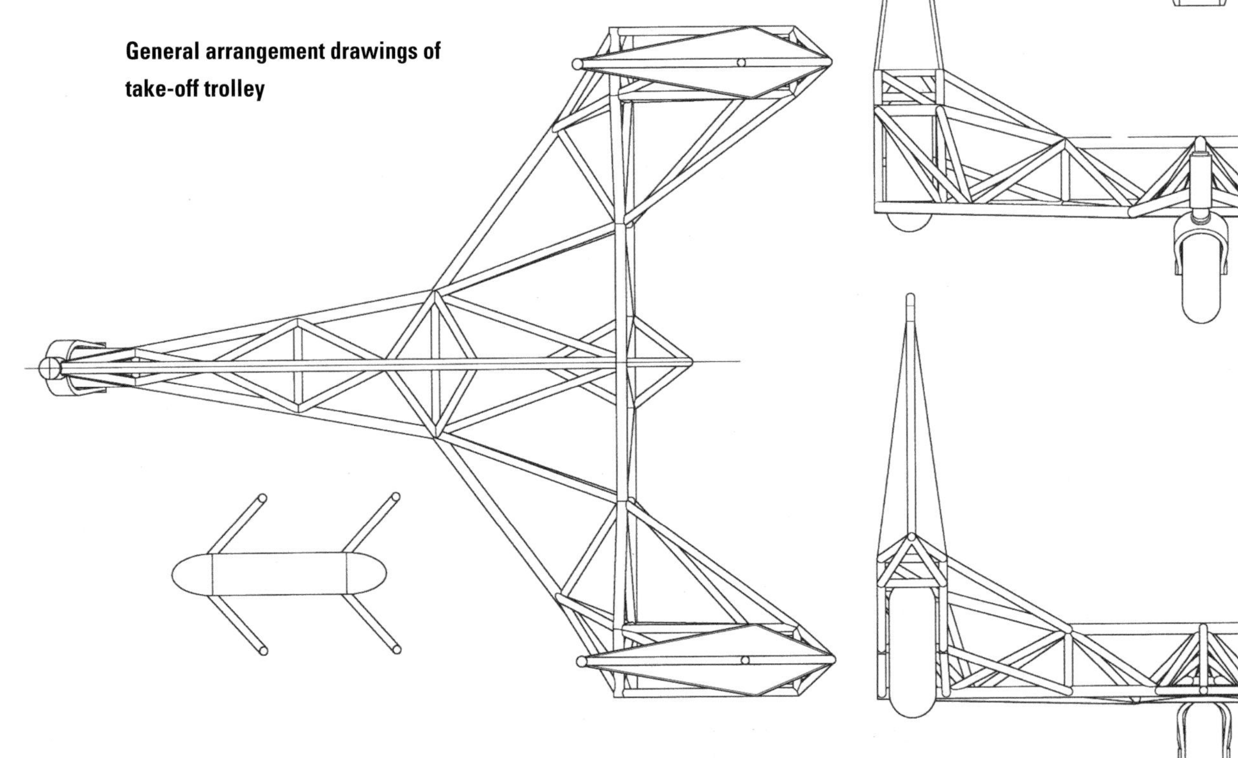

General arrangement drawings of take-off trolley

Ju 88 *Selbstopfer*

IN the surviving files of the *Luftwaffe Führungsstab*, there is record of a discussion held with *Oberstleutnant* Baumbach on 10 January 1945 who was 'investigating the replacement of *Reichenberg* [the Fieseler Fi 103 R *Reichenberg*] by a piloted *Mistel* as an SO-*Geräte*.' The piloted *Mistel* was proposed as a Ju 88.

'*Reichenberg*' was the code name applied to the Fi 103 A-1/Re 3 and Fi 103 A-1/Re 4 trainer and operational variants of a piloted Fi 103 flying bomb intended as part of the Luftwaffe's *Selbstopfer* (Self-Sacrifice) operations, also referred to as *Totaleinsatz* (Total Commitment). However, nothing more is known of the *Mistel* proposal investigated by Baumbach.

'WITCHES' DANCE'

On 12 January 1945 the Soviet Army opened its last great offensive against Hitler's forces and towards the end of that month its armour was racing through East Prussia towards the River Oder, the last great barrier before Berlin.

The Russians will suffer the bloodiest defeat imaginable in front of Berlin.

Adolf Hitler to *General der Flieger* Karl Koller, 17 April 1945

For the Luftwaffe *there is only one categorical imperative, and that is to destroy these bridges with all available means…*

Oberst Joachim Helbig, Commander of *Gefechtsverband Helbig*, 23 March 1945

As early as 15 January 1945, in a brave aside, an SS officer on Hitler's staff was heard to quip in his leader's presence: 'Berlin will be most practical as our headquarters; we'll soon be able to take the streetcar from the Eastern to the Western Front!'

Even if a somewhat candid remark, it was not without reality. As February began, temperatures in the East rose and the snow melted, thawing the ground. As the Third Reich inexorably fell apart, it was a grave time for the German people and their armies. Upper Silesia had been lost to the Soviets and in East Prussia, German forces were being worn down. On the 2nd, as the Russian spearhead reached the Oder at Zellin, Hitler ordered *Reichsführer*-SS Heinrich Himmler and his Army Group Vistula to maintain a line on the Oder upstream from Schwedt and around Stargard in preparation for an attack by the 2nd Guards Tank Army and to hold back any Soviet thrust into Pomerania or West Prussia. The Germans clung on to the bridgeheads at Küstrin and Frankfurt-on-the-Oder, but the Russians seized key points north of Küstrin and south of Frankfurt. On 5 February, as Stalin, Roosevelt and Churchill met at Yalta to discuss the political problems of post-war Europe, the Red Army crossed the Oder again at Brieg, 40 km south of Breslau. Two days later, the river was crossed at Fürstenberg, some 96 km from Berlin. During mid-February, the Second Belorussian Front pressed its attack through the woods and swamps of West Prussia. Himmler's Army Group somehow checked the enemy advance and it ground to a halt on the 19th. By the 14th, as the fires raged in Dresden following the Allied bombing of the city, the Third Belorussian Front and First Baltic Front had isolated Königsberg. It seemed nothing could stop the Soviet advance.

German Volkssturm troops arm themselves with Panzerfaust anti-tank missiles on the Oder Front in early 1945.

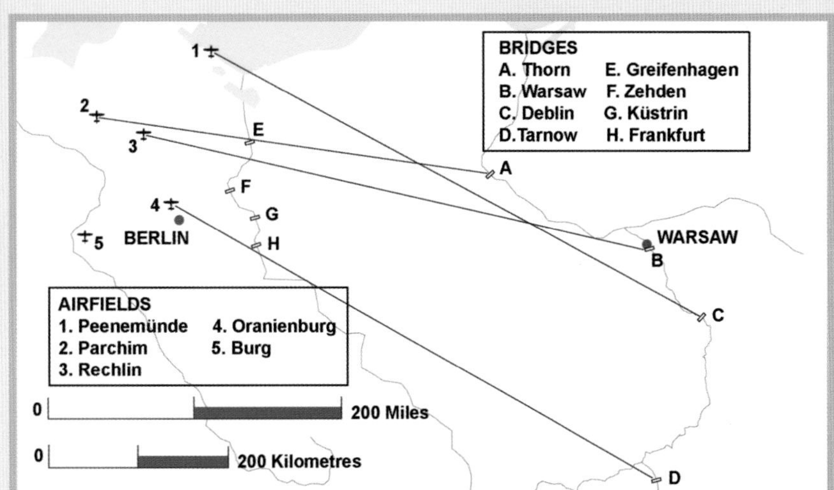

Mistel airfields and assigned bridge targets – Eastern Front, February-April 1945.

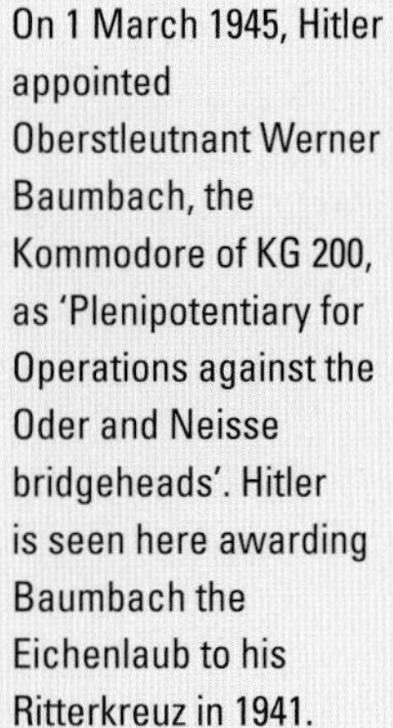

On 1 March 1945, Hitler appointed Oberstleutnant Werner Baumbach, the Kommodore of KG 200, as 'Plenipotentiary for Operations against the Oder and Neisse bridgeheads'. Hitler is seen here awarding Baumbach the Eichenlaub to his Ritterkreuz in 1941.

Thursday, 1 March 1945

Following a devastating 50-minute artillery barrage combined with strikes directed at German positions by ground-attack aircraft, Marshal Georgi Zhukov, commander of the Soviet First Belorussian Front, launched a major advance north towards Kolberg and the Baltic coast. The Germans were caught in disarray; panic broke out in the rear and roads in the area became congested with refugees streaming west. Amidst the collapse of his defence in the northern sector of the Eastern Front, Adolf Hitler was convinced that his senior and regional military commanders had failed him. He immediately initiated his own measures to deal with the Soviet threat and created the post of 'Plenipotentiary for Operations against the Oder and Neisse bridgeheads'.

However, instead of selecting a *Wehrmacht* or *Waffen-SS* ground commander for the role, the *Führer* appointed the *Kommodore* of KG 200, *Oberstleutnant* Werner Baumbach, to assume responsibility. Following a brief telephone discussion with the young bomber ace at the KG 200 *Gefechtsstand* at Stendal in the early hours of the morning, Hitler issued a *Führerbefehl* from his headquarters in Berlin:

> 'I assign *Oberstleutnant* Baumbach with the destruction of all enemy crossing points over the Oder and the Neisse. *Oberstleutnant* Baumbach is empowered to use all means available to him from the *Wehrmacht*, armaments industry and the war economy and is to co-ordinate them to bring about the required results. He is subordinated to the Commander-in-Chief of the Luftwaffe[1] and his assignment will be undertaken within the area of *Luftflotte* 6. Mission orders will originate from the Commander-in-Chief of the Luftwaffe under agreement of the Chief of the *Oberkommando der Wehrmacht*.[2]'

As mentioned in Chapter Ten, Baumbach was already working under the auspices of *Luftflotte* 6, preparing for the planned *Eisenhammer* operation against the Soviet power stations. Of the air fleets covering the Eastern Front, *Luftflotte* 6, under the command of *Generaloberst* Robert *Ritter* von Greim, was the strongest. In January 1945 it held on strength 194 day fighters, 14 bombers, 373 day and night ground-attack aircraft, plus 283 reconnaissance aircraft. Throughout the spring of 1945, the fleet would be supplemented by fighter *Gruppen* transferred from the West.

Despite the pressures of organising *Eisenhammer*, within hours of Hitler's order being issued Baumbach quickly marshalled the air units directly under his command for a first strike against the railway bridges at Warsaw, Deblin and Sandomierz. These three bridges were deemed 'absolutely vital for the logistics support of the entire Soviet front.'

The iron bridge at Deblin was 450 metres in length and had been partially destroyed by German guns during the Russian advance but had since been repaired. The 480-metre wooden bridge at Sandomierz allowed thousands of trains across the Vistula to keep the First Belorussian Front supplied (it needed 25,000 tons of supplies per day) and was thus a priority target for the Luftwaffe. The Chief of Staff of *Luftflottenkommando* 6 issued a comprehensive assessment of the constraints of Soviet logistics and its dependence on railways and bridges:

> 'The continuous logistical support of enemy forces currently on the offensive in Eastern Germany as well as their resupply for future offensives will be impossible to carry out without a railroad network. As a result, during their rapid advance, the Soviets have, with strong forces, repaired the main railway lines. Most important in this regard was the rebuilding of the decisively important Vistula bridges. The railroad bridges at Deblin and Warsaw were declared usable by our reconnaissance units. The Sandomierz railway bridge was already finished before the beginning of the offensive on 12 January, but is now unusable because of ice. The other important railway bridges at Modlin and Thorn have to be assumed to be almost ready for use.

Baumbach assigned an attack force under the command of *Oberleutnant* Pilz, *Staffelkapitän* of 5./KG 200, to strike at the first three bridges. It comprised three *Angriffsgruppen* (attack groups) of *Mistel* from 6./KG 200 based at Burg. The Deblin group would comprise five *Mistel* 3s guided by three Ju 88 or Ju 188 *Zielfinder* aircraft from 5./KG 200; the Sandomierz group would comprise three *Mistel* 3s with three *Zielfinder*, whilst another six *Mistel* 3s with a further three *Zielfinder* would strike the Warsaw bridge.

[1] Reichsmarschall Hermann Göring
[2] Generaloberst Heinz Guderian

Following a pre-dawn weather reconnaissance by 5./KG 200, during which conditions would be reported back to Burg every thirty minutes, the attack force was to be brought to readiness at 0900 hours. Following take-off, the three *Angriffsgruppen* would fly in close formation until rendezvous was made with the fighter escort provided by II. *Fliegerkorps*. The whole formation, including fighters, would then make for Jüterbog-Damm where the three groups would split and head for their respective targets.

On the approach to the targets, which would be marked with flares, the *Mistel* were to remain close to the cloud ceiling to avoid enemy fighters and effect separation at 1,000 metres. Once the lower components had been launched, the Bf 109 fighters were to return to assigned landing fields at Stolp-Reitz, Vietzker-Strand and Kolberg, while the Fw 190s were to make for Kamenz, Finsterwalde, Dresden, Grossenhain, Weidengut, Benneschau, Prossnitz, Costelit or Olmütz-Süd. The pathfinders were to return to Burg having filmed the results of the attack with both hand-held and robot cameras. However, as the morning progressed, the weather deteriorated and at 1050 hrs, the mission was cancelled.

Elsewhere, a *Mistel* 3 belonging to *Major* Karl-Heinz Greve's I./KG(J) 30 crashed due to technical reasons at Prague-Ruzyne. The Fw 190 pilot, *Feldwebel* Heinz Buberl, was injured and the Ju 88 pilot, *Oberfähnrich* Paul Iffländer, was killed and one member of the ground personnel also injured. An Fw 190 A-5, W.Nr. 4415, of II./KG 200 was damaged on take-off from Enschede and an Fw 190 F-8, W.Nr. 581613, from the unit was damaged following undercarriage collapse at the same airfield.

Friday, 2 March 1945

During reconnaissance sorties over Denmark and Germany, Allied aircraft photographed 12 *Mistel* at Tirstrup, left there from the aborted *Drachenhöhle* operation, and 16 composites belonging to KG 200 at Burg.

During the morning, two P-51D Mustangs flown by Lt. Myron Becraft and Lt. G.A. Robinson of the US 363rd FS, 357th FG made seven strafing passes each over Kamenz airfield. With their fuel and ammunition running low, the P-51s left, leaving 'several' Fw 190/Ju 88 *Mistel* burning on the ground.

Ten newly-assembled *Mistel* destined for II./KG 200 were destroyed or damaged on the ground during an Allied fighter-bomber attack on the assembly airfield at Altengrabow, 30 km east of Burg. They were:

***Mistel* 1**

Bf 109 undamaged/Ju 88 A-4 W.Nr. 3808, lower component 10% damaged

Bf 109 undamaged/Ju 88 A-4 W.Nr. 2565, lower component 10% damaged

***Mistel* 3**

Fw 190 A-8 W.Nr. 680524/Ju 88 G-1 W.Nr. 714534 destroyed

Fw 190 A-8 W.Nr. 960539/Ju 88 G-1 W.Nr. 714908 destroyed

Fw 190 A-8 W.Nr. 730955 coded TO+KO/Ju 88 G-1 W.Nr. 712322 destroyed

Fw 190 A-8 W.Nr. 380971/Ju 88 G-1 W.Nr. 714141 destroyed

Fw 190 A-8 W.Nr. 731012/Ju 88 G-1 W.Nr. 714414 coded NN+XT destroyed

Fw 190 A-8 W.Nr. 739222 50% damaged/Ju 88 G-1 W.Nr. unknown 30% damaged

Fw 190 A-8 W.Nr. 960541 10% damaged/Ju 88 G-1 W.Nr. 714804 10% damaged

Fw 190 A-8 W.Nr. 173938 10% damaged/Ju 88 G-1 W.Nr. 714287 10% damaged

Hitler's appointment of *Oberstleutnant* Baumbach as his 'Plenipotentiary' for the bridgeheads was endorsed when Göring ordered that Baumbach was authorised to draw upon the bomber and fighter-bomber units of *Luftflotte* 6 in order to fulfil his task provided 'he has the necessary means (fuel etc.). The orders also stated that:

> 'In the case of special units such as artillery, combat engineers and the *Kriegsmarine's* special units [mini-submarines, frogmen etc.], he is authorised to make requests to the High Commands of the respective arms of service. He is also empowered to approach and deal directly with these branches of the Armed Services at local command level.'

Baumbach was also to work directly with *Reichsminister* Speer and local NSDAP officials to secure equipment when and where necessary and also to make full use of any specialist equipment available from the *Erprobungsstellen*.

Saturday, 3 March 1945

Such was Adolf Hitler's concern regarding events on the Oder Front that he made a surprise visit to Busse's Ninth Army at Schloss Harnekop, only his second such visit to a front-line command HQ during the war. Though word of his visit served to boost morale somewhat, his driver reported him 'unusually withdrawn' on his return journey.

On 3 March 1945, Adolf Hitler made a surprise visit to the Oder Front, following which he was reported as being unusually withdrawn.

'No special developments on the Oder or Neisse fronts,' wrote Josef Goebbels, the Nazi Propaganda Minister. 'South of Küstrin, however, the enemy succeeded in widening his bridgehead west of Görlitz by a few hundred yards reaching the high ground. Violent Soviet attacks in East Prussia once more failed against the unflinching resistance of our defences.'

Sunday, 4 March 1945

An entry in the diary for the *Chef der TLR* for the week ending 4 March 1945 records:

> 'The DFS have completed the installation of wire guidance in a *Beethoven* combination. Testing in flight without separation it gave faultless direction transmission. Testing with separation and target aiming run follows immediately.'

Monday, 5 March 1945

In the north, the First Guards Tank Army had reached the Baltic, isolated Kolberg and made contact with the left flank of Second Belorussian Front. On the Oder, a Russian rifle division, reinforced by armour and artillery, was in position in the Zellin bridgehead; the Soviets prepared to consolidate their position in this sector of the river.

Oberst Joachim Helbig, as commander of Gefechtsverband Helbig, was tasked with coordinating air operations against the Oder bridges under the control of KG 200.

Having recovered from wounds suffered during an Allied strafing attack at Vogelsang in September 1944, *Oberst* Joachim Helbig was appointed by Baumbach to establish a new *Gefechtsverband Helbig*, subordinate to KG 200, and charged with coordinating air attacks against the Oder bridges. It will be remembered that in the autumn of 1944 Helbig commanded a *Gefechtsverband* of the same name, charged with supporting German ground operations along the Reich's frontier with Belgium and The Netherlands. This re-established command, comprising 15-20 personnel, had no connection with the previous one, other than in name and in the identity of its commander. The *Geschwaderstab*/LG 1 was to form the headquarters element of *Gefechtsverband Helbig* and was to transfer its operational elements by road in wood-burning trucks and buses from its base at Schwerin/Zippendorf to the headquarters of *Luftflotte* 6 at Treuenbrietzen. The II./LG 1 was to follow by rail. Individual elements of KG 200 were also ordered to prepare for assignment to the *Gefechtsverband*. Helbig was appointed Baumbach's 'exclusive representative' with *Luftflotte* 6 and all 'bridge attack specialists' with the *Wehrmacht*, *Luftwaffe*, *Kriegsmarine* and the *Waffen*-SS were ordered to report to him and render full support.

Thirty Ju 88 A-4s of II./LG 1, together with bombs and bomb racks, were also placed at readiness to transfer to a new base for 'special operations' as a component of *Gefechtsverband Helbig*. Helbig issued orders for the *Gruppe* to be supplemented by eight crews from I./EKG 1. I./LG 1, which was not assigned to the *Gefechtsverband*, was placed under the control of 14. *Fliegerdivision*.

Meanwhile, in a report to Baumbach, Helbig outlined his strategy for the campaign against the Oder and Vistula bridges. Helbig believed that it was necessary to conduct 'immediate attacks against the crucial Oder and Vistula rail bridges' combined with 'sudden attacks on the most important Oder bridges during the first days of the enemy offensive against Berlin.' With the limited resources available to him, and in the knowledge that operations had to be conducted in the shortest possible time and with the utmost urgency, Helbig proposed the following four-stage plan:

> '*Operation One*' would utilise the most skilled pilots to deploy *Mistel*, guided bombs and day and night bombing with the heaviest calibre bombs against bridge targets. Bomb specialists from the *Erprobungsstelle* at Rechlin were to be called in together with naval frogmen and assault boats. The heavy calibre bombing attacks were to be carried out by the best crews from II./LG 1, supplemented by additional crews from I./EKG 1.
>
> '*Operation Two*' called for frogmen and demolition squads to be used on a limited basis and as diversions for continuous night bombing missions carried out by II./LG 1 using phosphorus and small calibre fragmentation bombs. These operations were to be supplemented by *Selbstopfer* (SO 'self-sacrifice') missions flown by volunteers in war-weary Bf 109s and Fw 190s carrying 1,000 kg bombs, as well as minelaying operations assigned to the He 111s of III./KG 53. In his report of 5 March, Helbig stated that these operations would have as their objective, 'the destruction of the bridges by all possible means.'
>
> '*Operation Three*' was to use 'all possible methods' from *Operations One* and *Two*, together with more intensive *Mistel* and SO attacks and a large-scale attack by naval frogmen. Major demolition attacks were to be conducted against each bridge, utilising at least one company of paratroops. Helbig wrote: 'All these options must be evenly distributed amongst all the bridge targets using careful planning.'

The fourth operation proposed a 'war of sabotage' against 'bridges still in our hands west of the Oder and Elbe and the rivers in between.' Helbig foresaw using the local population to effect his plan, who were to be supplied with weapons, communications equipment and 'underground depots'.

Helbig also recognised that '*Operation One*', 'with its limited resources can accomplish limited objectives. Because of material considerations and the military situation, a crucial decision will have to be made between Operations One and Two.'

Tuesday, 6 March 1945

The Fw 190 A-8, W.Nr. 171597, piloted by *Oberfeldwebel* Gerhard Rosenberg of I./KG(J) 30 was destroyed at Prague-Ruzyne during a training flight due to engine failure. Rosenberg escaped with injuries.

Four He 111s of the *Versuchskommando*/KG 200 took off from Parchim at 1617 hrs, each aircraft carrying one Hs 293 guided bomb, and attacked the north bridge at Göritz just over an hour later. This *Kommando* had been formed from *Lehr- und Erprobungskommando* 36 at Garz, a test unit for the Hs 293 and other guided bombs. The attack was made at an altitude of 1,200 metres and under light enemy anti-aircraft fire. As the attack force pulled away, the *Flak* became more intense. The Heinkels were escorted by eight Bf 109s from I./JG 4, which shot down two Yak_9s, at 1725 hrs and 1737 hrs respectively. One He 111 missed the target because of Flak, but the bridge was damaged as a result of the attack. One aircraft crash-landed with three shell holes in one wing and an engine.

Generaloberst von Greim advised his staff at *Luftflotte* 6:

> 'Bridges of all kinds are key elements in the major enemy attacks against Berlin and the heart of the Reich. Their timely and continuous destruction by all necessary actions on the part of all branches of the *Wehrmacht* is of decisive importance, not only for the outcome of this battle, but possibly the war.
>
> '*Oberstleutnant* Baumbach coordinates, by means of all possible resources at his disposal, the unity of all elements of the Luftwaffe, the Army and Navy in their attacks against enemy bridging attempts over the Oder and Neisse between Göritz and Stettin. This destruction is to take place as soon as these bridges are established. Special importance is placed on the destruction of those bridges where major breakthrough attempts are identified or where a shift in troop concentration is anticipated.
>
> 'In cooperation with the Army and Navy, he must make sure that in the light of the fuel shortage, Luftwaffe attacks are only to be flown against bridges, after Army and Navy actions are repulsed or are impossible to carry out.
>
> 'In particular, Luftwaffe units are to be handled in the following manner:
>
> a.) Missions by KG 200 with special units (remote-controlled bombs, *Mistel* etc.) – directly under *Oberstleutnant* Baumbach.

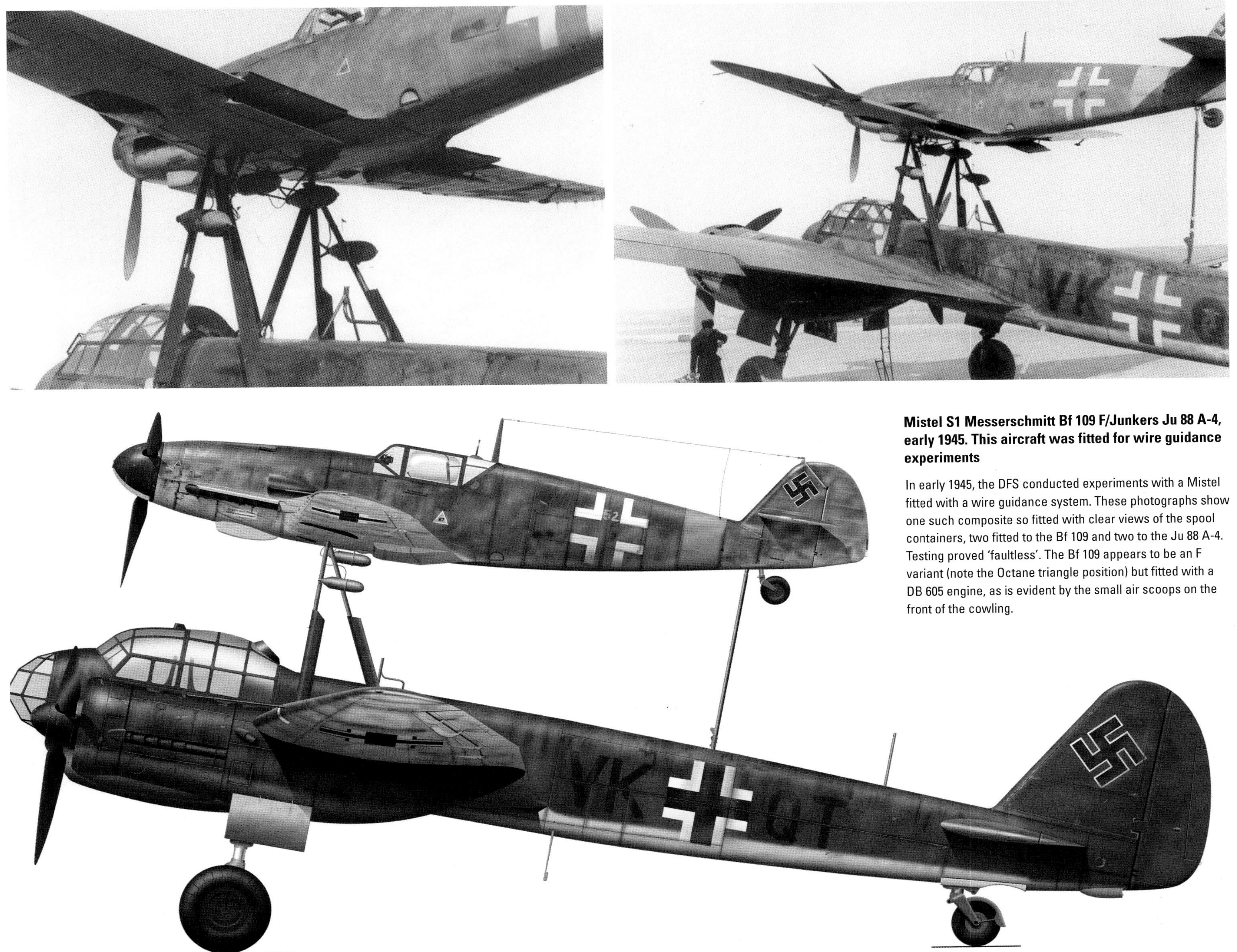

Mistel S1 Messerschmitt Bf 109 F/Junkers Ju 88 A-4, early 1945. This aircraft was fitted for wire guidance experiments

In early 1945, the DFS conducted experiments with a Mistel fitted with a wire guidance system. These photographs show one such composite so fitted with clear views of the spool containers, two fitted to the Bf 109 and two to the Ju 88 A-4. Testing proved 'faultless'. The Bf 109 appears to be an F variant (note the Octane triangle position) but fitted with a DB 605 engine, as is evident by the small air scoops on the front of the cowling.

b.) Ground-attack missions by the ground-attack units of the II. and VIII. *Fliegerkorps* in conjunction to the above orders by the Chief of Staff.
c.) Night ground-attack units of the II. and VIII. *Fliegerkorps* if needed with illumination, same as (b.)
d.) Trials and missions by all other Luftwaffe technical means now under development, such as '*Wasserballon*', the spraying of phosphorus or burning oil etc.
e.) The use of all methods in which the element of surprise plays a role, especially against bridgeheads where concentration of forces are noticeable. The use of SD 2 bombs with delayed action fuses against especially important bridgeheads.'

With Helbig taking charge of the tactical initiative for the campaign against the bridges and bridgeheads, Baumbach decided to drop his 'Plenipotentiary' title in favour of the more immediately recognisable '*Fliegerführer 200*'. He saw his position as mainly a planning and liaison role and he placed members of *Professor* Steinmann's office (see Chapter Ten) on his staff.

Wednesday, 7 March 1945

Colonel General Chuikov's 8th Guards Army commenced a sustained attack on Kietz with a view to cutting off Küstrin.

A *Mistel* 3 of II./KG(J) 30 was lost at Geussnitz due to engine failure, Fw 190 A-8, W.Nr. 739134 rated 100% destroyed and its pilot, *Oberfeldwebel* Heinz Busse, killed. The Ju 88 G-1 lower component, W.Nr. 710612, was 60% damaged.

Sixteen Fw 190s of I./SG 1 attacked the Oder bridge at Zellin, scoring hits on the bridge and other hits to the west of it. Nine Ju 87s of 15./SG 151 attacked the Oder bridge at Aurith, though hits against the bridge were not observed. Escort for this operation was provided by three Fw 190s of *Stab*/JG 11 and 16 Fw 190s of III./JG 11 led by the *Geschwaderkommodore*, *Major* Anton Hackl. Twelve Yak-9s were sighted, with one shot down at 09.25 hrs.

Thursday, 8 March 1945

Gefechtsverband Helbig reported the following Order of Battle:

Stab/LG 1	Ju 88 S-1 and S-3
II./LG 1	Ju 88 S-1 and S-3
'Part of KG 200'	*Mistel* 1 and 3, Ju 188 A-2, E-1 and E-3, Ju 88 A-4 Bf 109 F-4 and Fw 190 A-8

Luftflottenkommando 6 issued orders for a strike against the pontoon bridges and rope ferries at Göritz, using Hs 293 guided bombs and *Mistel*. Fighter cover was to be provided by and under cooperation with II. *Fliegerkorps*, comprising two Fw 190 D-9s of *Stab* and 16 Bf 109s of III./JG 4 led by the unit's *Kommodore*, *Major* Gerhard Michalski. A small ground-attack force of Ju 88s and Ju 188s was to fly ahead of the main formation to counteract the anticipated enemy smokescreen.

Gefechtsverband Helbig deployed four *Mistel* for the attack supported by two Ju 88s and five Ju 188s, all from II./KG 200, the Junkers carrying AB500 weapons containers loaded with SD 1 bombs. The formation took off between 0900 and 0920 hrs, maintaining radio silence, and the first *Mistel* was over the bridges between 1000 and 1012 hrs. Low cloud base at 3,000 metres prevented a surprise attack and the Ju 88s and Ju 188s had to attack simultaneously with the *Mistel*, making a gliding approach run from 3,000 metres down to 800 metres, bombing anti-aircraft positions around the target to enable a safe approach for the composites. One Ju 188 crewed by *Obergefreiter* Flakner and *Unteroffizier* Post was shot down by Flak. One *Mistel* narrowly missed the south bridge at 1006 hrs and hit the west bank of the river between the two bridges leaving a large crater, but the centre of the north bridge was destroyed.

In his memoirs[3], Colonel General Chuikov, commander of the Soviet 8th Guards Army, wrote of the time he first witnessed the *Mistel* in action:

> 'Lacking the strength to repel our attacks on the bridgehead the enemy struck back with every means he had, including unmanned auto-piloted aircraft packed with explosives. I first saw this "secret weapon", which Goebbels had so widely advertised, in action on the Oder in early February[4], when our engineers were building the first bridge across the river at Górzyca (Göritz). It was a fine sunny day. General Pozharsky and I were at an observation post nearby when we noticed a twin-engined aircraft flying low from the west. Passing over Height 81.5, it began to lose altitude and about 300 metres from the river it dived, hit the ground and exploded. The Germans used four such planes in an attempt to blow up the bridge but none hit the target. They made huge craters without, however, causing much damage. We wondered whether the game was really worth the stakes. The employment of such an expensive weapon against a bridge under construction was unjustified extravagance.'

Although *Major* Michalski was able to claim one Yak 9 shot down from a formation of ten sighted, the fighters found it difficult to be effective during the operation and in its monthly report, *Stab*/JG 4 stated that:

> 'Cooperation with KG 200 with regard to escort has shown that as a result of the (low) speed of the *Huckepack* aircraft, it was difficult to provide effective defence in the target area. Moreover, the loose formation of the *Huckepacks* makes escort very problematic.'

Another *Mistel* was lost as a result of a technical failure when *Feldwebel* Friedhelm Elger, believed to have been with II./KG 200 and flying Bf 109 F-4, W.Nr. 6380, was forced to bail out near Belzig at 0932 hrs. He was posted as missing. Several days later, one of Elger's fellow pilots, *Leutnant* Rudi Dewenter, wrote to his comrade's parents to explain the events of their son's last flight.

On 8 March 1945, Bf 109s of III./JG 4 escorted four Mistel from II./KG 200 which were assigned to attack rope ferries and pontoons at Göritz. The fighters found their mission difficult. Here, pilots of 9./JG 4 gather near a Bf 109 K-4 at Jüterbog-Damm in March 1945.

[3] *The End of the Third Reich*: Marshal V.I. Chuikov, Progress Publishers, Moscow, 1978.
[4] This is unlikely; Chuikov probably means early March.

Dewenter, Rudolf, Leutnant
21.March 1945
L60 174, Lg. ka. Berlin

Dear Frau and Herr Elger,

I am sure you will be surprised to hear from me. Your memory of me must be fleeting at best – sadly I must admit that my letter is of a serious nature.

On 8th March, we flew a mission, which included 'Tietge'[5]*. His aircraft was hit and burned. 'Tietge' left his aircraft without incident with his parachute. The opening of the chute was observed by many of his comrades, so it is almost certain that he reached the ground safely. Up to this point everything went fine. Unfortunately, the wind blew him over enemy occupied territory.*

With this report, I have certainly brought you sad news. I can feel your pain and sorrow bearing in mind the close relationship you had with your son. I have known your son for two years and learned to value him as a person. You will probably remember our trip to Italy. We experienced both serious and happy hours in Italy and we always got along well. You can understand that 'Tietge's' fate has affected not only me but also the whole Staffel. These are no empty laments or expressions of sorrow on our part, but we feel connected to you and you should know that you are not alone in your sorrow.

Please do not regard these as empty words and promises which I now convey to you as cheap consolation. You may certainly rest assured that you will see your son again after the war. I know that I am unable to take away your uncertainty with my optimistic efforts but please take my well intentioned words to heart and trust me and the organisation for which I work to give you all the support and help you might need.

Heil Hitler!

I remain yours,
Rudi Dewenter

Feldwebel Friedhelm Elger bailed out over Soviet-held territory when his Mistel suffered a technical failure near Belzig on 8 March 1945.

A Ju 188 A-2, W.Nr. 180447, of II./KG 200 was damaged by Flak near Fürstenwalde, no further details.

Friday, 9 March 1945

Another attack on the Göritz bridges was planned by *Luftflottenkommando* 6, using three *Mistel* against each bridge in conjunction with ground-attack aircraft, but the operation was cancelled due to adverse weather conditions.

An Allied reconnaissance aircraft identified four *Mistel* on Dessau airfield.

Saturday, 10 March 1945

In its orders for 11 March 1945, *Luftflottenkommando* 6 stated:

> 'Orders for II. *Fliegerkorps* and *Gefechtsverband Helbig* remain unchanged. Any advantageous weather conditions, even of the shortest duration, are to be used to carry out attacks on the Göritz bridges.'

An Fw 190 A-7, W.Nr. 638933, of II./KG (J) 30 was destroyed at Melnik during *Mistel* training. The pilot, *Leutnant* Eberhard Ramminger, was killed.

Monday, 12 March 1945

Following a meeting between *Oberstleutnant* Baumbach, *Generalleutnant* Kienzel and SS-*Gruppenführer* Lammerding, Chief of Staff to the *Reichsführer-SS* Heinrich Himmler in his capacity as commander of Army Group Vistula, Baumbach drafted the following stark memorandum:

> **Re: Attacks against the Oder bridges in the area of Fürstenberg-Schwedt**
> With reference to: Presentation by *Oberstleutnant* Baumbach to Army Group Vistula – *Gen.Leutnant* Kienzel and SS-*Gruppenführer* Lammerding.
>
> With the use of all three branches of the *Wehrmacht* presently available and the currently available material

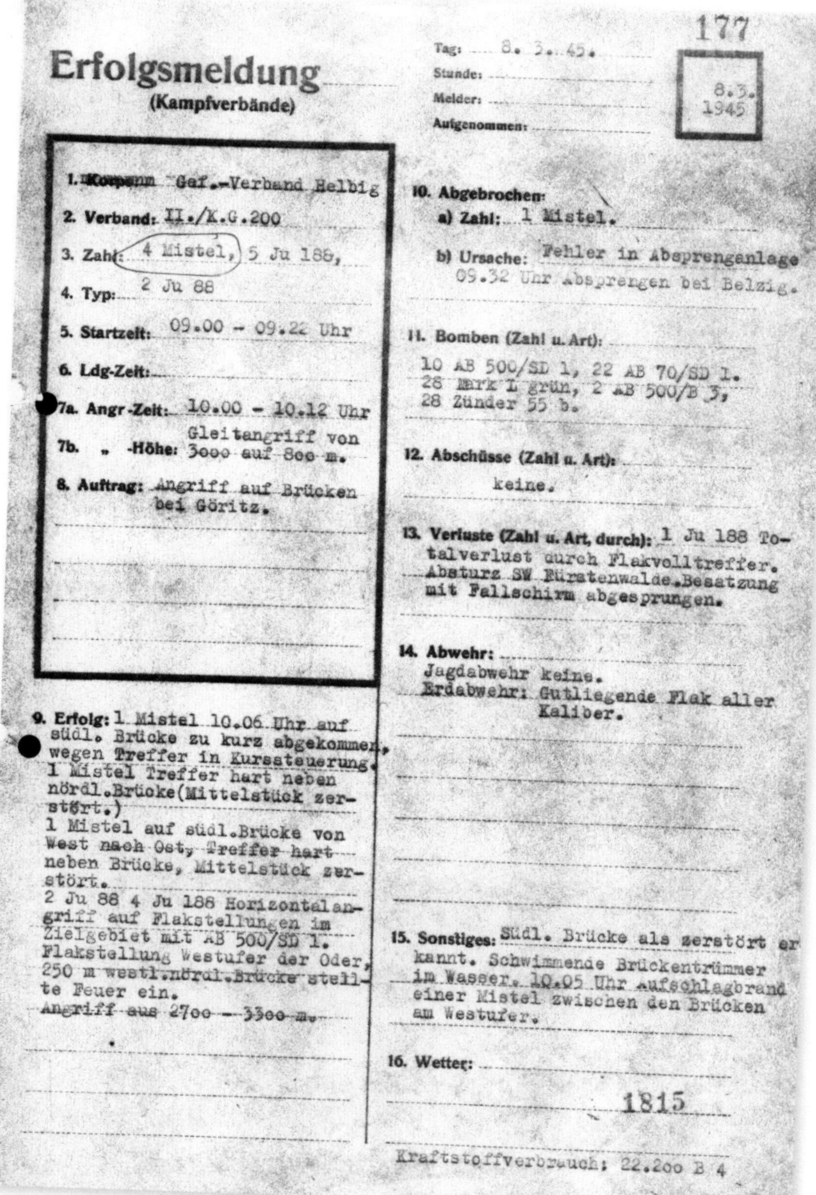

177

Erfolgsmeldung
(Kampfverbände)

Tag: 8. 3. 45.
Stunde:
Melder:
Aufgenommen:

8.3.
1945

1. Kommando: Gef.-Verband Helbig
2. Verband: II./K.G.200
3. Zahl: 4 Mistel, 5 Ju 188,
4. Typ: 2 Ju 88
5. Startzeit: 09.00 – 09.22 Uhr
6. Ldg-Zeit:
7a. Angr.-Zeit: 10.00 – 10.12 Uhr
7b. " -Höhe: Gleitangriff von 3000 auf 800 m.
8. Auftrag: Angriff auf Brücken bei Göritz.

9. Erfolg: 1 Mistel 10.06 Uhr auf südl. Brücke zu kurz abgekommen, wegen Treffer in Kurssteuerung. 1 Mistel Treffer hart neben nördl. Brücke (Mittelstück zerstört.)
1 Mistel auf südl. Brücke von West nach Ost, Treffer hart neben Brücke, Mittelstück zerstört.
2 Ju 88 4 Ju 188 Horizontalangriff auf Flakstellungen im Zielgebiet mit AB 500/SD 1. Flakstellung Westufer der Oder, 250 m westl. nördl. Brücke stellte Feuer ein.
Angriff aus 2700 – 3300 m.

10. Abgebrochen:
a) Zahl: 1 Mistel.
b) Ursache: Fehler in Absprenganlage 09.32 Uhr Absprengen bei Belzig.

11. Bomben (Zahl u. Art): 10 AB 500/SD 1, 22 AB 70/SD 1. 28 Mark I grün, 2 AB 500/B 3, 28 Zünder 55 b.

12. Abschüsse (Zahl u. Art): keine.

13. Verluste (Zahl u. Art, durch): 1 Ju 188 Totalverlust durch Flakvolltreffer. Absturz SW Fürstenwalde. Besatzung mit Fallschirm abgesprungen.

14. Abwehr: Jagdabwehr keine. Erdabwehr: Gutliegende Flak aller Kaliber.

15. Sonstiges: Südl. Brücke als zerstört erkannt. Schwimmende Brückentrümmer im Wasser. 10.05 Uhr Aufschlagbrand einer Mistel zwischen den Brücken am Westufer.

16. Wetter:

1815

Kraftstoffverbrauch: 22.200 B 4

Mission report prepared by KG 200 for the Mistel and bombing attack against bridges at Göritz on 8 March 1945.

[5] Probably a familiar term used by Friedhelm Elger's friends and family.

resources, (especially the fuel situation within the Luftwaffe – daily available fuel amount for *Luftflotte* 6: 80-90 cubic metres), it is impossible to destroy and keep destroyed all the Oder bridges. The current weather conditions also provide a degree of uncertainty in respect of full-scale commitment by all Luftwaffe attack units.

For these reasons, the only possibility that exists is that the enemy activity in the Oder bridgehead and any major offensive can only be hindered seriously by Army Group Vistula. Luftwaffe attacks can only accomplish a disruption of enemy offensive preparations. Accordingly, a fundamental and timely decision is necessary to attack the important troop concentrations at the appropriate Oder crossings.

Suggestions:

1. Constant disruptions by Luftwaffe attack units, dependent on available fuel supplies. Also offensive actions by special units of the Navy and Army.
2. The provision of enough fuel for a major attack by the Luftwaffe, supported by all available forces of the *Wehrmacht*, on the first day of the enemy offensive.
3. To support these decisive attacks against the Oder bridges, it seems appropriate to keep Luftwaffe special units (*Mistel* and SO attacks) at the ready. An attack before the beginning of the offensive cannot be attempted for the above mentioned reasons. Because of the limited forces available, a premature frittering away of forces should be avoided at all cost.
4. An attack with Luftwaffe special units mentioned in Item Three should be carried out immediately against the important bridges over the Vistula, independent of the start of the enemy offensive.
5. In conclusion, it is apparent that bearing in mind the fuel set aside for the bridge attacks, a decisive halting of the imminent enemy offensive and the destruction of the bridges during the offensive is impossible.

We ask Army Group Vistula to present these conclusions to higher authority.

Baumbach

Simultaneously, *Oberst i.G.* Friedrich Kless, Chief of Staff of *Luftflottenkommando* 6 admitted to OKL that mounting successful attacks against the Oder bridges was proving to be virtually impossible:

'Experience to this point has shown, and will also demonstrate in the future, that wooden bridges will only be out of service for a short term if air mines or fragmentation bombs are used. The burning of bridges provides greater success. Bomb types currently available are unsuitable for this purpose.

It is therefore suggested that production of current developments of incendiary bombs with hard to extinguish materials (tar-phosphorus mixture) should be accelerated and delivered for operational use as quickly as possible and if possible. It has to be pointed out however, that long-range planning in this case is futile, since deployment of such bombs is too late.'

Tuesday, 13 March 1945

A *Mistel* 3 of II./KG(J) 30 crashed on landing at Prague-Ruzyne. Ju 88 G-1, W.Nr. 714212, was stated as 80% damaged, with *Oberfeldwebel* Franz Meier, the pilot, wounded and *Oberfähnrich* Eberhard Dubhorn, the radio operator, also injured. The upper component, Fw 190 A-8, W.Nr. 734393, was destroyed and its pilot, *Oberfeldwebel* Alfons Welzel, was killed. One member of the ground personnel was also injured in the accident.

Twelve *Mistel* were photographed by an Allied reconnaissance aircraft on Nordhausen airfield.

SS-*Brigadeführer* Lammerding ensured that Baumbach's memorandum of the previous day was brought to the attention of the *Reichsführer*. Himmler duly signalled SS-*Gruppenführer* Hermann Fegelein, his liaison officer at the *Führer's* headquarters in Berlin:

Lieber Fegelein!

1. As you know the *Führer* has ordered *Oberstleutnant* Baumbach to use the Luftwaffe to destroy the Oder bridges in the area of Fürstenberg-Schwedt.

2. *Oberstleutnant* Baumbach reports the following: Because of the fuel situation it is impossible for the Luftwaffe to destroy and to keep destroyed all Oder bridges. Besides that, the weather provides another adverse factor. Furthermore, *Luftflotte* 6 has a daily fuel allocation of only 80 to 90 cubic metres.

3. Within the realm of the possible, *Oberstleutnant* Baumbach suggests the following:
a. Constant nuisance raids by special units of the Navy and constant, well-planned artillery attacks by the Army.
b. Supply and accumulation of enough fuel to make a major Luftwaffe attack possible.
c. The availability for action of special Luftwaffe units (*Mistel* aircraft, SO-attack forces) at the start of the enemy offensive.

4. I am asking you to report to the *Führer* with *Oberstleutnant* Baumbach's report and suggestions. Obviously, from my current location, I am unable to determine if it is possible to supply *Oberstleutnant* Baumbach's *Geschwader* with the fuel he needs to keep up continuous attacks on the bridges.

Heil Hitler!

Yours, H. Himmler

Friday, 16 March 1945

The Ju 88 G-1 lower component, W.Nr. 714129, of a *Mistel* 3 of II./KG(J) 30 was destroyed at Dresden-Lösnitz due to engine failure. The pilot, *Leutnant* Krahme, and a mechanic, *Oberfeldwebel* Schönieger, were both listed as missing. The Fw 190 upper component was undamaged.

Allied reconnaissance aircraft photographed two *Mistel* on Neuruppin airfield and a further nine at Oranienburg.

Sunday, 18 March 1945

At 0515 hrs, the Russian 69th Army at Lebus penetrated as far as Schönfliess railway station, but was subsequently driven back to its original position on the Küstrin-Frankfurt railway line.

In the air, eight P-51 Mustangs from the 383rd FS of the Eighth Air Force's 364th FG were amongst the 733 fighters despatched to offer escort to heavy bombers returning from a raid on Berlin and other targets. Red Flight caught a composite taking off 'from an airdrome on the western tip of Parchim.'

Mistel S2 Focke-Wulf Fw 190 F-8 '50'/ Junkers Ju 88 G-1, W.Nr.746, RW 93, 6D+ES, location unknown, 1945

A Luftwaffe NCO clambers along the fuselage of the Ju 88 lower component of a Mistel S2 Fw 190 F-8 '50'/ Ju 88 G-1, W.Nr. 746, RW 50, +ES. This composite is believed to have been photographed at Löbnitz at the end of 1944 or early 1945 and again at Gardelegen in 1945. The Fw 190 F-8 carries the Reparaturwerkstatt number '50' in the centre of its fuselage Balkenkreuz and is fitted with an ETC 501 bomb rack. Note also the crude wooden access ladder.

Lt. John C. Hunter (above) and Lt. Edward Chlevin of the US 364th Fighter Group jointly accounted for the destruction of a Mistel west of Parchim on 18 March 1945.

Lt. John C. Hunter claimed the Fw 190 upper component destroyed while Lt. Edward Chlevin accounted for what was thought to be the 'He 111 K' lower component. This was probably an aircraft from KG(J) 30.

General der Flieger Koller signalled Baumbach, acknowledging firstly that demands on the Oder Front may supersede immediate military intentions and, secondly, that the time to utilise a second *Mistel* unit in the battle for the bridges had arrived:

> 'Enemy offensive in the East may demand operations against Oder bridges for units set aside for '*Eisenhammer*'. *Fliegerführer* 200, in cooperation with *Luftflottenkommando* 6, will prepare for the destruction of Oder bridges and prevention of new bridges being laid. Preparations to cover target selection, planning of attacks and related technical problems as well as of ground organisation, preparation of orders and briefing of crews, to be carried out without influencing preparations for Operation '*Eisenhammer*'.
>
> '*Fliegerführer* 200's task to operate against Oder and Vistula bridges (via *Gefechtsverband Helbig*) is unaffected by planning and preparation of *Mistel* operations by KG(J) 30 against Oder bridges.'

Tuesday, 20 March 1945

Three *Mistel* were photographed by an Allied reconnaissance aircraft on Bernburg airfield.

Thursday, 22 March 1945

Soviet forces broke out of the Görlitz bridgehead, heading north, cutting Küstrin off from its rear communications. Advancing respectively from the Kienitz and Lebus bridgeheads, the 8th Guards Army and 5th Shock Army struck across the Küstrin corridor and united around Golzow.

Surrounded by low-lying marshland, the fortress town of Küstrin was sited on an important Oder crossing point, just 80 km east of Berlin. Its history was grim and one German poet stated that he could never think of the place without imagining it under a grey November sky; its core took the form of a citadel on an island in which the future Frederick the Great had been imprisoned by his brutal father. In 1758, the town had been virtually flattened by Russian howitzers. In 1945, it was a complex of industrial sites and factories which sprawled across the banks of the Oder and the Warthe, approachable only by roads which were narrow.

Following extensive reconnaissance sweeps across central Germany, the Allied air forces observed the largest quantity of *Mistel* so far seen on enemy airfields: 22 at Burg (6./KG 200), five at Nordhausen (Junkers), nine at Oranienburg (KG(J) 30) and six at Bernburg (Junkers).

Assembly and delivery of new *Mistel* continued throughout February and March 1945; Heinz Schreiber had been making test and ferry flights of newly assembled *Mistel* 3s from Nordhausen, sometimes making two to three flights per day in different composites, and Heinrich Osterwald undertook similar flights at Bernburg. The Ju 88 G-1 lower components were now assigned a '*Reparaturwerkstatt*' number (works repair number) for identification.

Friday, 23 March 1945

Following Koller's instruction to Baumbach on the 18th, *Oberst* Helbig issued orders to KG(J) 30 to immediately commence operations on the Oder Front:

Combat Instructions for KG 30

1.) Evaluation of the enemy situation on the Eastern Front shows, without doubt, that the enemy considers the rail bridges over the Vistula and near Krakau as well as the Oder bridges, as paramount for the continuation of his final push, which has the destruction of Germany as its goal.

2.) For the Luftwaffe there is only one categorical imperative, and that is to destroy these bridges with all available means and if necessary with the full commitment of the personnel involved. Here, and as contained in other battle orders, KG 30 is ordered to participate in a major role:

KG 30 will carry out, as rapidly as possible, the destruction of the Vistula bridges. Anticipated targets:
Railway bridge near Thorn
Both railway bridges near Warsaw
Deblin railway bridge
The railway bridge at Dunajec, east of Krakau

Every bridge, six *Mistel*. Details of the execution of missions to be through *Kommodore* of KG 30 with coordination of *Gefechtsverband Helbig* and *Luftflottenkommando* 6.

b.) KG 30 to prepare immediately for a mission against the Oder bridges in the area of Oderberg-Zehden in such a way that the mission can be carried out within 12 hours. Current priority targets: the bridges between Fürstenberg-Zehden. The mission in this area of enemy concentration is to be carried out at the time of the great offensive against Berlin. Time: any time.

3.) KG 30 is responsible for the acquisition of all target maps, exact approach routes, navigation and target marking. All forces that had been involved in Operation '*Eisenhammer*' are to be made available for this mission.

Signed
Oberst Helbig

Eight *Mistel* were photographed by Allied reconnaissance on Rechlin-Lärz airfield and another two at Nordhausen.

Saturday, 24 March 1945

The Order of Battle and a surprisingly high strength return for *Gefechtsverband Helbig* was reported as follows:

II./LG 1	Ju 88 A-4	24 (15)
II./KG 200	Ju 88 A & S	18 (8)
	Ju 188 A & E	9 (8)
	Mistel 1	14 (7)
	Mistel 2	2 (0)
	Mistel 3	13 (5)
Versuchskommando/KG 200	He 111	19 (11)
	Do 217	8 (4)
		107 (58)

Josef Goebbels noted:

'In the Küstrin sector the enemy brought up fresh reinforcements, having suffered extraordinarily heavy losses on the first day of fighting. In spite of these reinforcements the weight of his attack was somewhat reduced. In this sector, 66 Soviet tanks were destroyed and

A Mistel 2 probably of II./KG(J) 30 at its camouflaged dispersal at Oranienburg in March 1945. The Ju 88 G-1 has been fitted with an SHL 3500 'short' fuse ('Sprengkopf ohne Elefantenrüssel') and carries a 900-litre fuselage-mounted drop tank, whilst the Fw 190 F-8 is fitted with a 600-litre drop tank.

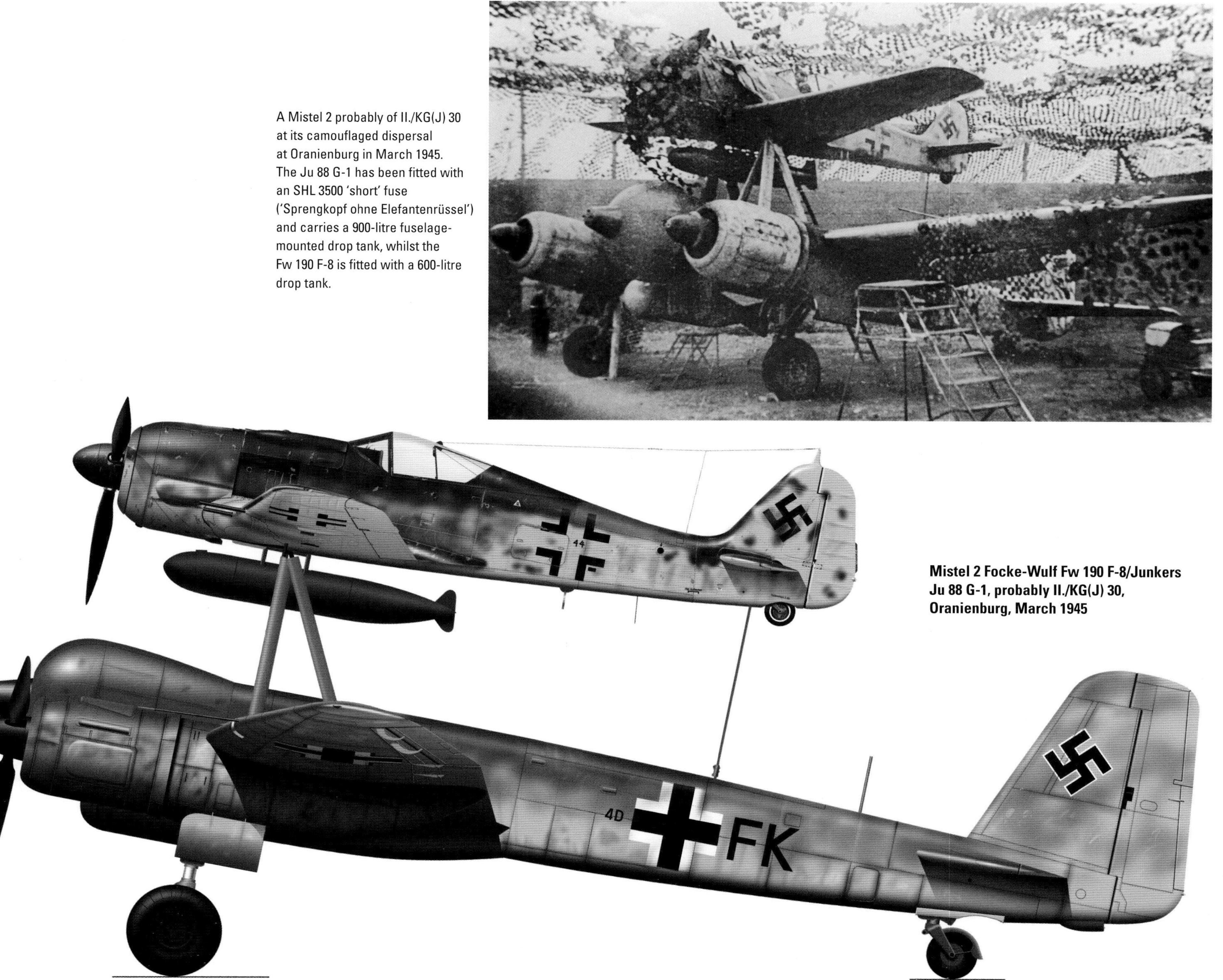

Mistel 2 Focke-Wulf Fw 190 F-8/Junkers Ju 88 G-1, probably II./KG(J) 30, Oranienburg, March 1945

116 the previous day. In the light of the numbers of men and materiel in action the enemy success was extraordinarily small. He was able to extend his two bridgeheads north-west and south-west of Küstrin only by some 92 metres. The two bridgeheads succeeded in joining up on a front of about 457 metres. OKH reports that access to Küstrin has been re-established.'

Sunday, 25 March 1945

On the Western Front, General George S. Patton's US Third Army was now across the River Rhine between Mainz and Worms. A bridgehead had been established at Oppenheim and American troops and armour were now crossing the river to the east bank in increasing numbers. Further north, Montgomery's 21st Army Group had 'bounced' the Rhine around Wesel and cleared that town of German resistance by the 25th.

From 22 March, *Luftwaffenkommando West* launched a series of attacks against the American pontoon bridges and troop and vehicle concentrations near Oppenheim using the Ju 87s of NSG 1 and the bomb-carrying Bf 109s and Fw 190s of JG 53 and JG 2. But their ordnance was not powerful enough to sink the pontoons.

During the evening, four *Mistel* 3s of 6./KG 200 took off from Burg and, led by five pathfinders from 5./KG 200, attacked the pontoon bridges near Oppenheim scoring probable hits on the northern bridge and its eastern abutment.

Leutnant Alfred Lew of 6./KG 200. A former He 111 pilot, on 22 March 1945 he was assigned to attack the pontoon bridges over the Rhine near Oppenheim with a Mistel. His composite was set on fire by a direct hit from anti-aircraft fire before release.

Taking part in this attack was the former instructor, *Leutnant* Alfred Lew. 'Fred' Lew had joined the Luftwaffe in July 1940 and from January 1941 until June 1942 attended the A/B *Schule* at Plauen, before moving to the *Flugzeugführerschule* (C9) at Pretzsch/Elbe. On 1 April 1943, he commenced a flying instructor's course at Pretzsch before spending a three-month stint as a trainee staff officer at the *Luftkriegsschule* 9 in Tschenstochau. From June to September 1944 he saw operational service, flying He 111s with the *Einsatzgruppe* of the 2. *Fliegerschuldivision* at Borissow before taking up a post as a blind-flying instructor at Burg in September 1944. He transferred to 6./KG 200 in January 1945 and commenced conversion to the *Mistel*. The fateful Oppenheim mission was his first in the *Huckepack*; he recalls:

> 'We had five Ju 88/Fw 190 *Mistel* combinations ready for the Oppenheim Rhine bridge attack. Around 1700 hrs, four *Mistel* took off, the fifth combination having broken down on the airfield. We were accompanied by five Ju 88 and Ju 188 *Beleuchter* from our 5. *Staffel*. Since take-off in a *Mistel* was always a dangerous affair, the air raid siren was sounded at Burg to clear the field of personnel for their own safety. This time, however, things went according to plan and the four remaining *Mistel* got off the ground without problem. Following a wide left turn, our formation headed towards the Rhine. Initially, we were at 1,500 metres, but soon climbed to a cruising altitude of 2,000 metres. The approach flight took two and a half hours. As it began to turn dark, so I saw the River Rhine glittering below us in the moonlight. Meanwhile, our *Beleuchter* aircraft had dropped their signal flares, but still, I could not recognise the bridge. I flew a full circle to orientate myself, but as I did so, I ran into heavy American anti-aircraft fire. In order to locate the target, I descended to 1,500 metres and then – *Bang*! – I was hit. My *Mistel* lurched to port and went into a spin on its back. As I was no longer able to control the machine, I decided to separate my Fw 190 while simultaneously diving away from the *Mistel*. At 300-400 metres, I finally managed to regain control over my aircraft and got away from that terrible Flak and headed east towards Burg.
>
> 'In the darkness and flying on instruments, my return flight became quite hairy and I flew off course. I found myself approaching the River Elbe. Since the Russians were by now quite close, it was dangerous to cross the river. Fortunately, I reached the Elbe at Torgau. Now my experience as a flying instructor at Pretzsch became very useful and I managed to find my way home. At 2200 hrs, I landed safely at Burg. One *Mistel* pilot, *Feldwebel* Brendhof, another former flying instructor at 'C9' did not make it back from the mission. The success of the operation was virtually nil.'

Feldwebel Erich Brendhof of 6./KG 200 and his Fw 190 A-8, W.Nr. 680150, were posted missing. Another Ju 88 bomb component crashed following release and a Ju 88 pathfinder was also missing.

In the East, five He 111s of *Versuchskommando*/KG 200 equipped with Hs 293s attempted to attack the Göritz bridges over the Oder, but they were forced to abort their attack due to intense anti-aircraft defences.

A Ju 188 A-2, W.Nr. 180402, of 5./KG 200 suffered 20% damage at Burg in an emergency landing following engine failure.

Four *Mistel* were photographed by an Allied reconnaissance flight over Dessau airfield and a further four were seen at Nordhausen.

Monday, 26 March 1945

Thirteen *Mistel* of KG(J) 30 were photographed by an Allied reconnaissance aircraft at Oranienburg.

Tuesday, 27 March 1945

In what was to be one of Germany's last offensive actions of the war, *General* Busse's Ninth Army comprising 20. and 25. *Panzer-Grenadier Divisions*, *Führer-Begleit* and the scratch *Panzer Division 'Müncheberg'*, struck northwards from the Frankfurt bridgehead, with the aim of relieving Küstrin. At first, the Russians were taken by surprise and a number of German tanks managed to reach the outskirts of Küstrin, but their supporting infantry was later caught in open ground by Russian artillery and the main advance petered out after gaining less than three kilometres.

Wednesday, 28 March 1945

Küstrin remained cut off and surrounded by Russian forces.

Fuel shortages were beginning to take effect. *Fliegerführer* 200 was heard by Allied radio decryptors asking whether a stock of eight tons at Perleberg could be used by *Mistel* for ferrying purposes.

Thursday, 29 March 1945

Following a series of attacks by the Soviet Air Force, Küstrin was subjected to heavy artillery bombardment during the morning, before units of the 82nd and 35th Guards Rifle Divisions stormed the town. By midnight, the remaining German troops still holding the town under *Generalleutnant* Rheinefarth, managed to fight their way out.

With the capture of the town, the Soviets now held a bridgehead about 50 km wide and 7-10 km deep and were in a position to begin preparations for the final drive on Berlin, the first priority of which was to rebuild Küstrin's heavy capacity bridges.

Above: With the capture of Küstrin on 29 March 1945, the Russians' first priority was to rebuild the bridges blown by the retreating Germans.

Right: An aerial reconnaissance photograph of the Steinau railway bridge taken by 2.(F)/100 on 23 March 1945.

Below right: A sketch prepared by the staff of Luftflottenkommando 6 following the KG 200 Mistel attack on the Steinau railway bridge over the River Oder on 31 March 1945. Immediate post-strike reconnaissance showed serious damage to the western end of the bridge as a result of a Mistel hit, probably that which was seen to hit the centre section.

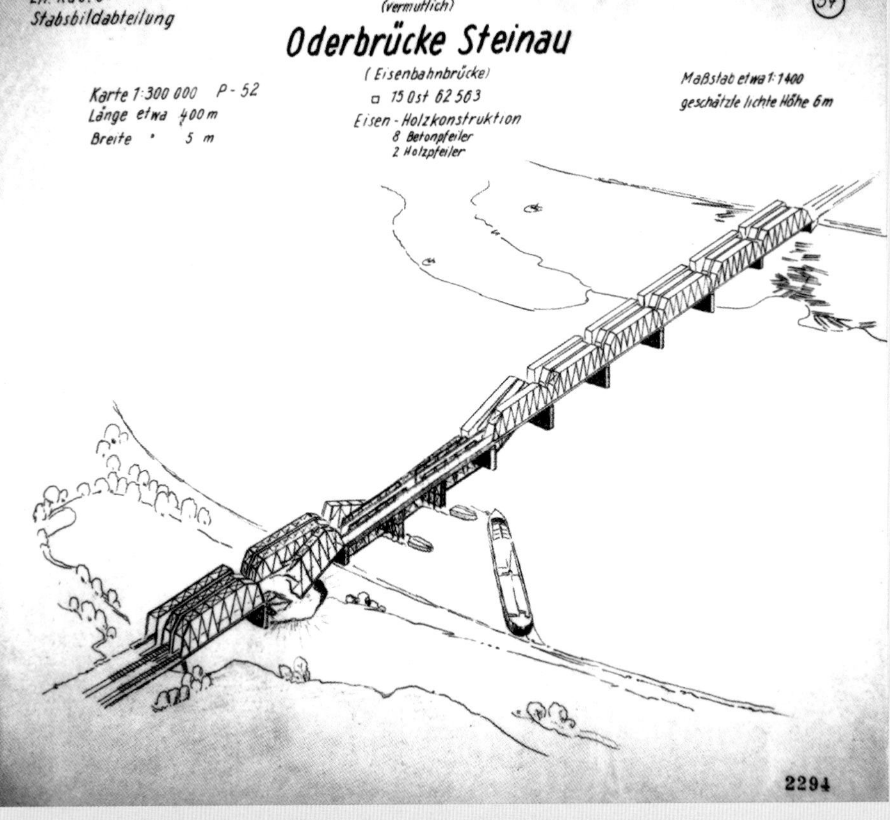

Saturday, 31 March 1945

Six *Mistel* 1s from 6./KG 200 took off from Burg around 0730 hrs to attack the railway bridge at Steinau some 300 km to the east of their base. Total radio silence was observed. Two Ju 88s and two Ju 188s from 5./KG 200 flew as *Zielfinder* and long-range escort, and had been briefed to conduct diversionary attacks against both the bridge and Steinau railway station using eight SD 1000 and 30 SD 70 bombs. Additionally the *Mistel* were assigned a fighter escort consisting of 24 Bf 109s from JG 52 based at Schweidnitz which would rendezvous with the KG 200 formation over Waldenburg.

Shortly after take-off at 0736 hrs, one *Mistel* suffered a hydraulics failure at 70 metres and was unable to retract its gear. The pilot effected separation with the warhead unarmed, which hit the ground near Genthin. Another *Mistel* made it as far as the rendezvous with the fighters near Waldenburg, when the engine of the Bf 109 F-4 cut out. Its pilot was unable to restart and commenced a return course to Burg. Eighty minutes later, the port-side engine on the Ju 88 started vibrating and separation was effected with the live warhead in the Prettin-Torgau area. The lower component was seen to explode in a field. The Bf 109 crashed near Prettin and was listed a total loss, the pilot escaping with a broken leg.

One Ju 188 flew ten minutes ahead of the main formation and upon reaching Schweidnitz fired a recognition flare as the signal for the waiting fighters to take off. The main formation followed, making a left-hand circuit at 2,000 metres over Waldenburg. Once the Bf 109 escorts had assembled in the air, the fighter leader waggled his wings as the signal for the formation to proceed. Three *Schwärme* covered the *Mistel* and three *Schwärme* escorted the 5./KG 200 machines.

A third *Mistel* got as far as Görlitz at which point the Bf 109's engined failed. Emergency separation took place near Lauban and the fighter crash-landed near Görlitz with 60% damage. Then, at 0845 hrs, the composites endured friendly fire from local light Flak, despite the apparent recognition of German markings. The German gunners believed the *Mistel* to be aircraft from a specially camouflaged enemy unit.

The remaining composites reached their target at 0905 hrs and launched glide attacks through 6/10 cloud and light Flak from 2,500 metres descending to 200 metres. The first *Mistel* was launched with a rudder failure at the centre section of the bridge, but the effect of the impact was not observed amidst the Russian smokescreen. Following launch, the pilot of the Bf 109 strafed Soviet infantry positions before climbing and turning for home. The second composite scored a direct hit on the eastern section of the bridge and the third also hit the centre section following a trouble-free launch, although the effect of impact was not observed.

Immediate post-strike reconnaissance showed serious damage to the western end of the bridge as a result of a *Mistel* hit. The Ju 88s and Ju 188s inflicted 'serious damage' to Steinau railway station and scored hits on the western bridgehead and at the eastern exit to the station.

In his post-mission report on 4 April, *Oberstleutnant i.G.* Mahlke on the staff of *Luftflottenkommando* 6 wrote of the lessons learned as a result of the Steinau attack:

> 'A 50% technical malfunction rate is very high. Since older aircraft were used, future missions must expect to incur technical problems at a similar level. The long inactivity of the aircraft led to unforeseen technical problems which even good maintenance cannot cure. The intended longer-range missions will be compensated by using better aircraft. The mission deployment of six *Mistel* for one bridge target should be viewed as the minimum for a successful attack.
>
> 'In the case of daylight missions, fighter escort must adjust to the loose formation of the *Mistel*. The *Mistel* unit reported that fighter escort during the operation was good. The fighters, naturally, find it difficult to fly such missions due to the great distances between the *Mistel*. In order to save fuel and for security reasons, (especially during moonlit nights and ideal cloud cover), it is suggested that missions be undertaken without fighter cover.
>
> 'Target reconnaissance pictures indicate good effect against the railway bridge despite a minimal spread effect in the target area. This requires great skill on the part of the *Mistel* crews.'

Meanwhile 11 *Mistel* were photographed by Allied reconnaissance on Bernburg airfield and a further four at Burg. At least two *Mistel* were reported slightly damaged during Allied strafing attacks on Bernburg.

That night the Allies bombed Nordhausen, destroying or damaging 3,000 houses and inflicting heavy damage to transport facilities. There were 8,000 casualties. The airfield escaped major damage.

Wednesday, 4 April 1945

During the day, Allied reconnaissance photographed a *Mistel*, most likely from KG(J) 30, at Prague-Ruzyne whilst, at Parchim, another four were observed, probably from the same unit.

Friday, 6 April 1945

During the late afternoon, an unknown number of *Mistel* from I./KG(J) 30 were prepared for a mission over the Oder. *Oberfähnrich* Georg Gutsche recalled:

> 'From Rechlin, our mission field for Operation '*Eisenhammer*', we were ordered to attack the Oder bridges south of Stettin, over which came the supplies for the Russian armies attacking the northern sector of the front. Take-off was set for 1700 hours. The aircraft were lined up one behind the other with engines running. My *Mistel* was the second one in line. From my cockpit, I could not see the horizon because the nose of my Fw 190 was pointing up too high. The procedure was to move all three throttles in a synchronised manner so that the *Mistel* stayed on the runway. With sufficient airspeed, the stick could be pulled back and the undercarriage and flaps retracted. You then throttled back, adjusted the airscrews and made a steady climb. After reaching our combat altitude of 2,000 metres, I could see the front, the fires and the impact of mortar explosions. The heavy haze made visual orientation very difficult, but the Oder River was easy to make out as a silvery band. The bridge that I was looking for was a dark line across this band. I was "welcomed" by heavy anti-aircraft fire so I put the *Mistel* into a dive, switched on the fully automatic control system, pulled down the cross hair sight and aimed at the bridge. When the target drifted out of the cross hair sight, I corrected and the automatic control system put the target squarely into the cross hair again. At about 1,000 metres distance, I squeezed the trigger that automatically armed the warhead, and I separated the *Mistel*. My Fw 190 climbed as it released itself from the heavy weight of the Ju 88. As I pulled away, I noticed a lightning flash in the river bed below me that quickly went out. Without much difficulty I returned to my home field.'

Saturday, 7 April 1945

By this time *Gefechtsverband Helbig* comprised:

II./KG 200 (5. and 6 (*Mistel*)./KG 200)
II./LG 1
I. and II./KG(J) 30 *Mistel*
Elements of I./KG 66
II./KG 4
Versuchskommando/KG 200

In accordance with *Oberst* Helbig's orders of 23 March, KG(J) 30, which until this date had been held ready for *Eisenhammer*, commenced operations against the Vistula bridges. During the morning, operational orders arrived at the headquarters of *Oberstleutnant* Hans Heise who had taken over from Jope as *Geschwaderkommodore*. Heise was a very experienced bomber commander who had been awarded the *Ritterkreuz* in September 1942 whilst serving in Russia. He had subsequently led KG 51, KG 2 and KG 40.

Under the somewhat uninspired code name Operation '*Weichselbrücken*' (Operation Vistula Bridges), Heise was ordered to prepare 24 *Mistel* from I. and II./KG(J) 30 to destroy the enemy-held bridges near Thorn, Warsaw and Deblin as well as a Soviet headquarters near Tarnow. Airfields allocated to the mission were Peenemünde, Oranienburg, Parchim and Rechlin-Lärz with take-off for the six *Mistel* 3s at each airfield set for midnight.

Things got off to a bad start when 134 B-17s of the Eighth Air Force's 3rd Air Division bombed Parchim during the afternoon, dropping more than 370 tons of high explosives and incendiaries. Three hangars and six accommodation blocks were destroyed and various installations and workshops were heavily damaged. Some 30 aircraft were destroyed including four *Mistel*. The runways were badly cratered and it was estimated that it would take two days to restore them to serviceable standard. This meant that the (undamaged) *Mistel* assigned to attack the Thorn bridges could not move and it was therefore decided to divert the composites based at Oranienburg, which had previously been allocated to strike at Tarnow, to attack the targets at Thorn. However, just as the operational plans were being changed, the weather turned bad and the mission was postponed.

At 2130 hrs orders came through from Helbig to prepare for operations urgently, although at Oranienburg receipt of this order was delayed. Eventually the first composites rolled out onto the runway and their engines were run up, but an engine on one *Huckepack* failed to turn over and this *Mistel* blocked take-off for the others. By the time the runway had been cleared, the official take-off time had passed and the mission was aborted.

It was to be no better at Peenemünde, as *Oberleutnant* Heinz Frommhold of 3./KG(J) 30 later described:

> 'During that morning the boredom of inactivity was suddenly interrupted with the order: '*Combat readiness late afternoon!*' The mission was not *Eisenhammer* but an attack on the bridges across the Vistula near Deblin about 100 km south of Warsaw. The attack would be initiated with six *Mistel* from Peenemünde. Further attacks against Thorn, Warsaw and Tarnow were planned from other airfields. There were supposed to be 24 *Mistel* on this mission; for us, that was a big surprise, although there was still doubt in our minds that we would ever fly to Rybinsk some day. But... this was a mission and we were eager to go because we wanted to show what the *Mistel* could do.
>
> 'Flight preparation was no problem. The flight plan would take us over Schneidemühl and Kutno to the Vistula estuary north of Deblin. The return would be due west to the Warthe River, then north to Posen, to Stargard and then directly to the airfield. All turning points and the target – a railway bridge – were supposed to be illuminated. Flying time was estimated at five hours. The weather was supposed to be good: visibility 30 km; cloud 3/10 Cumulus with Cirrus above.
>
> 'At 2300 hrs, we were ordered to our aircraft. We climbed up to the cockpits of the Fw 190s with the aid of a four-and-a-half metre ladder and made ourselves "comfortable" in the confines of the very tight space. My problem, at 1.66 metres, was much less than that of the pilot ahead of me at 1.86 metres. Then the siren went off: it was just like an air raid siren. Everyone not directly involved in the *Mistel* take-off took cover. A minimum of manpower was to be put at risk, in case one of the hollow-charge warheads went off by accident. At the same time, the electrical and hydraulics specialists conducted their last checks on the steering mechanism. The "thumbs up" was given. Meanwhile, the mechanics had connected the engines to the starters and when the signal was given, I started the engine of the Fw 190 and then the left and right engines of the Ju 88. All three BMW 801 D2s started without any problems. Then I ran through my checklist: trim at zero; flaps in the '*Start*' position; propeller setting first at twelve o'clock then to '*Automatic*'; rudder to '*Start*' position. A quick glance at the release button for my highly explosive 'companion'. Safety on! Turn on compass and set landing gear lock. Now I could give my hand signal for take-off. I must admit that my heart beat faster than normal. Meanwhile, the first aircraft had rolled to the starting position and accelerated into the darkness, where it disappeared.'

Returned from leave and recently married, Oberleutnant Heinz Frommhold poses for a snapshot at either Prague-Ruzyne or Chrudim in early 1945. Under the direction of his Staffelkapitän, Oberleutnant Rudolf Kainz, Frommhold would coordinate the Mistel operations of 3./KG(J) 30.

This lead composite was piloted by *Hauptmann* Peter-Heinz 'Pitt' Nolte, the *Staffelkapitän* of 4./KG(J) 30. Nolte was a *Legion Condor* veteran who had gone on to serve with KG 1 and KG 3 and at one point in 1943, he had been an adjutant to *General der Flieger* Koller. Nolte's *Mistel* had not yet reached take-off speed when the port tyre of the Ju 88 G-1 burst. As the entire weight of the composite fell onto the port wheel rim, the port undercarriage leg collapsed under the strain and this also caused the starboard leg to fail. As the Ju 88's belly hit the ground, the struts supporting the Fw 190 A-8 buckled so that the upper component slid onto the Ju 88 and the two aircraft swung off the runway and collapsed onto the grass.

Heinz Frommhold was in the *Mistel* behind Nolte; he recalled:

> 'Suddenly – barely visible over my engine – sparks flashed all across the furthest third of the runway and then small flames appeared. Down below, next to me, a red light blinked. My first thought was: "*The warhead is going to go sky high! Get out!*" I don't know how, but within seconds, I cut the engines and was sprawled flat on the ground. Behind me, the pilot in the next take-off position showed reactions as fast as mine.'

The warhead on the *Mistel* began to burn. The mission leader immediately called off the operation and clambered down from his cockpit, ordering all personnel to evacuate the runway area. As the runway was closed and sealed off, so the warhead continued to burn yet did not explode, much to the amazement of all those now watching from a safe distance. Eventually, the airfield fire crews set about extinguishing the fire and, as they did so, a foam-covered figure emerged from the darkness 'cursing violently.' It was *Hauptmann* Nolte, unhurt and carrying his parachute under his arm. Only the facts that the runway was completely unusable and the allocated take-off time had been missed, convinced him to abandon his thoughts of a second attempt in another aircraft.

Another *Mistel*, piloted by *Feldwebel* Lukaschek, swung off the runway, crashed into a revetment and exploded. Lukaschek was killed.

Elsewhere, five *Mistel* managed to get airborne from Rechlin-Lärz, but the first one into the air at 0023 hrs was attacked by a Russian nightfighter and the pilot was forced to make an emergency separation and shortly afterwards belly-landed his Fw 190 A-8. Two more composites had fuel transfer difficulties and the pilots bailed out over Müncheberg and Güstrow, whilst a fourth machine experienced stability problems and its pilot also abandoned his aircraft. Only the one remaining *Mistel,* flown by Austrian pilot, *Oberfähnrich* Burkhardt Winkler-Hermaden of 1./KG(J) 30, reached the railway bridge at Warsaw. He recalled:

'I took off at 0025 hrs in *Mistel* No. 36/RW 111 from Rechlin-Lärz with orders to destroy the railway bridge over the Vistula at Warsaw. The approach was uneventful and after two hours in the air, I reached Warsaw. The heavy Flak defences immediately went into action. I was able to make out the target since a few flares were still illuminating the Vistula bridges. I immediately went into attack. Despite the strength of the defences, I was able to get close to the target. Having obtained the right angle of attack, I was ready to separate in my Fw 190. Nothing happened and I was forced to fly right over the target and try to gain altitude again. The density of the Flak increased and I was caught in a searchlight beam. I was only able to escape by adopting violent defensive manoeuvres and then tried to climb for another attack. I tried the emergency separation procedure to get rid of the Ju 88 as I made my attack. Still the attempt at separation failed. I had no alternative but to pull up again with the *Mistel* intact and expose myself to further anti-aircraft fire. I could not escape the searchlights. After once again having gained enough altitude, I went into a steep glide approach, my airspeed rose drastically and I pulled the *Mistel* up steeply. It worked! The Ju 88 broke away at the normal separation points and I was free. Now, nothing else for it but head west!

'Once away from the Flak and the searchlights, I noticed that I had lost my auxiliary fuel tanks during the violent manoeuvre which I had had to perform to get rid of my explosive "guest". I decided to go to a favourable altitude and throttled back on my engine to save fuel and increase my range. I tried to call up Prague-Ruzyne on the radio. I did manage to make contact; the response was, "*Please wait.*" Then a crackling noise and I lost contact. Stubbornly, I continued heading west and eventually crossed the front lines whereupon I began firing recognition flares. However, despite firing several flares, not a single airfield turned on its lights.

'My calculations told me that I must be somewhere around Berlin or even further west. I changed my heading to the south. My fuel supply dwindled and I was out of emergency flares. Soon I knew that I would have to prepare for a parachute jump. It was a very dark night – no lights in sight. *Get ready to jump*... how many times had I practised that procedure? Theoretically, it was: *Unbuckle, jettison the canopy, give the stick a kick with your boot, get thrown out, count '21, 22, 23' and pull the ripcord.* One hard jolt and I swayed under the open shroud of my parachute at 2,500 metres, surrounded by darkness. The only sound was the air rushing around the chute. Suddenly, a loud *thud*... my aircraft had exploded upon impact with the ground. All my flares were gone and I could not see the ground. Moments later however, I could make out the shape of a forest below and I pulled on the lines of the parachute to try to avoid it. Then I was down and I was lying on my back in a field. Happily, I clawed at Mother Earth. It was five in the morning; four and a half hours since take-off. Physically, I was in good shape, so I gathered up my parachute and thought about which direction I should take. It began to get lighter and I noticed a few houses – a village! I knocked at the first illuminated window. The window opened and I identified myself as a German airman. "*Yes, yes, we can see that,*" said a voice. "*We make the flying suit you are wearing; our contribution to the war effort!*" The village was called Lautern and was near Bamberg. I later tried to search for the wreck of my Fw 190. There was just a large crater in the ground, small pieces of wreckage, nothing else. From the town hall, I contacted my unit. I told them I would make my way to Rechlin-Lärz. After four days of hitchhiking via Berlin, I reached my unit.'

Oberfähnrich Burkhardt Winkler-Hermaden (left) of 1./KG(J) 30 made a dramatic attack on the railway bridge at Warsaw on 7 April 1945. His Mistel was subjected to intense anti-aircraft fire and initially failed to launch. Winkler-Hermaden is seen here with his navigator in Paris whilst on leave in early June 1944. His Staffel was operating out of Orly on mining missions off the south coast of England.

Meanwhile, at Parchim, other pilots of I./KG(J) 30 were waiting for their order to take off. As *Ofhr.* Georg Gutsche recalled:

'The day's target was the Oder bridges again and we were to start from Parchim. Around noon however, a formation of B-17s destroyed the runway and we could not take off. We were driven to Rostock-Marienehe in order to fly a mission against the bridges near Greifenhagen. Really there were two bridges: one normal bridge and one pontoon bridge right below the water's surface which were both used by the Soviets. This time the haze was so bad that during the first approach I could barely make out the bridge and so I flew a second approach and released the payload more or less haphazardly. The return flight presented no problem at all. The "Christmas tree" (landing lights) was on when I landed. Then something happened that can only be called pure "pilot's luck". My aircraft landed on the right wheel first and broke to the right.

With some hard right rudder action, I was able to bring the aircraft on a parallel course to the runway. But about 50 metres away, almost as if in a dream, I saw a triangle in front of me as I brought the Fw 190 to a standstill. Some infantrymen suddenly appeared in front of me screaming "*You just took our tent with you!*" I climbed out of my aircraft and found myself standing on a concrete block. The wheels of my aircraft had rolled between several of these concrete blocks – a very good reason to have a birthday celebration!'

Helbig viewed the events of 7 April as a fiasco and made his views very clear in his report of the following day:

1. Cause: Most likely far too much weight on the tyres (aircraft parked too long in one place).
2. Night take-off: Although night take-offs are not considered to be the reason for the breakdowns, *Oberst* Helbig has the impression that the possibility of night take-offs was overestimated. Therefore, in the future, only daylight take-offs or sufficiently illuminated take-offs are intended.

Sunday, 8 April 1945

A *Mistel* 3 with *Leutnant* Reinhard Glaubig of I./KG(J) 30 as pilot was damaged at Rostock-Marienehe.

Monday, 9 April 1945

The city of Königsberg surrendered to the Russians.

Tuesday, 10 April 1945

Luftflottenkommando 6 ordered *Gefechtsverband Helbig* to launch another *Mistel* strike against the Steinau railway bridge and also against the Autobahn bridges across the Bober and the Queiss under the code name '*Hexentanz*' (Witches Dance). On 10 April, *Oberst i.G.* Kless issued the following directive to VIII. *Fliegerkorps* at Senftenburg and II./KG 200 at Burg.

Re: Fighter cover for the *Mistel* attacks against the Autobahn bridges over the Bober and Queiss and the repeat attack on rail bridge at Steinau.

1.) VIII. *Fliegerkorps* is to provide fighter cover for the attacks against:

a.) Reichs-Autobahn: bridges to be attacked by 4 flights (16 aircraft) per target.

b.) Steinau bridge to be attacked by 6 flights. Fighter escort to be flown in close as well as loose support formation. Each type of support should be flown in equal numbers.

2.) The attack on the Reichs-Autobahn bridges should originate from Welzow airfield, and the attack against Steinau from Schweidnitz airfield.

3.) Details for take-off time for the fighters, as well as assembly altitude and time, and execution of the escort mission will be planned between all individual units involved. It is imperative that all details are worked out meticulously between units and all problems solved to assure a successful mission before take-off.

After the attack (the launching of the *Mistel* against the targets), the fighters are free to attack targets of opportunity (especially locomotives). The difficulty of this escort mission will come from the loose *Mistel* formations. The *Mistel* have orders to fly formation as closely as possible.

4.) Notification of mission date and assembly times will come under the code name '*Hexentanz*' (Witches Dance). The attack details for the bridge at Steinau will be issued under the code name '*Steppenritt*' (Ride over the Steppes). These orders will be issued by *Gefechtsverband Helbig* directly to the appropriate units.

5.) Notification for the I. *Flakkorps* will be issued on the day of the mission from *Luftflottenkommando* 6 Ia Flak. Approach routes for the units will remain unchanged.

Signed,
Kless, *Oberst i.Gen.Stab*

One of the pilots due to fly on this operation to Steinau was a veteran bomber pilot, thirty-year-old *Oberst* Herbert Kuntz. A native of Diefflen in the Saar, Kuntz had flown missions in the He 111 over the British Isles from Norway with 3./KG 100 during 1940. He then saw action over Malta, Crete, North Africa, the Suez Canal, the Red Sea and Russia, including Stalingrad, with II./KG 26. On 14 March 1943, he was awarded the *Ritterkreuz*, having sunk 16 ships and damaged another eleven. He then joined

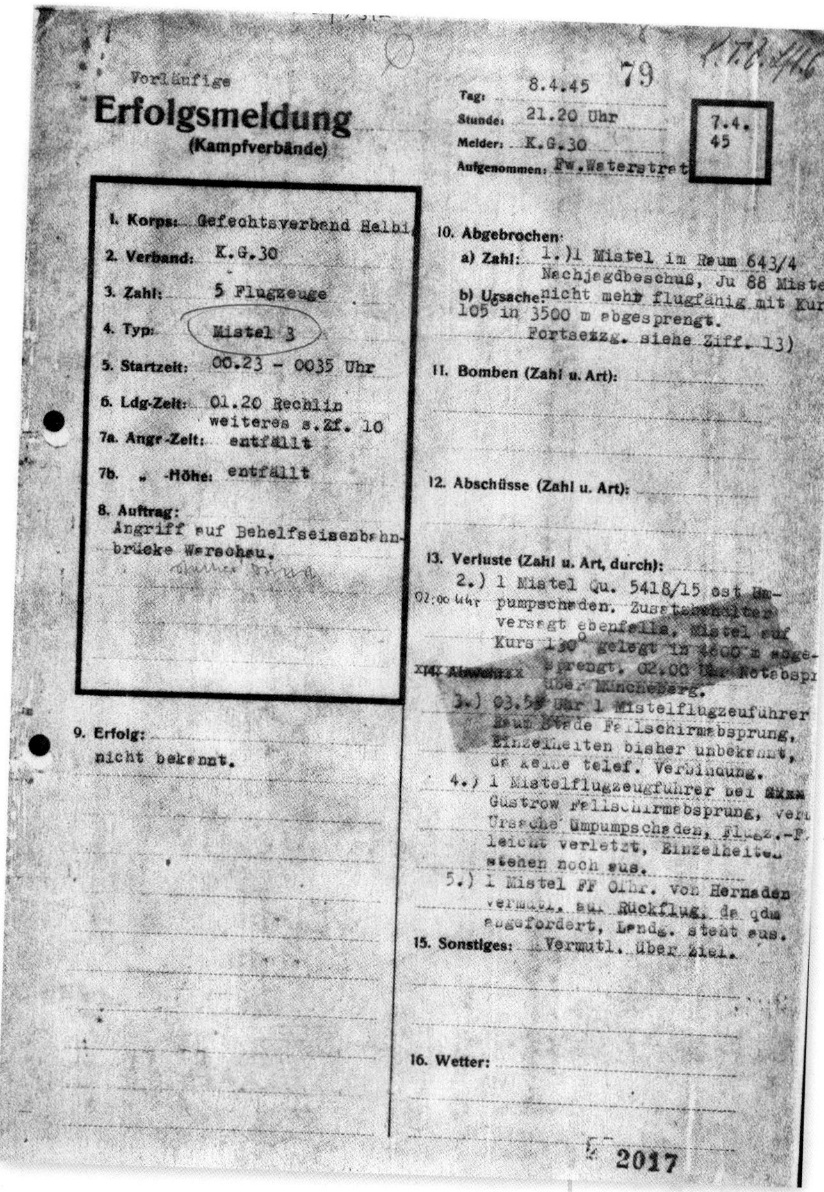

Vorläufige
Erfolgsmeldung
(Kampfverbände)

Tag: 8.4.45 79
Stunde: 21.20 Uhr
Melder: K.G.30
Aufgenommen: Fw.Waterstrat
7.4.45

1. Korps: Gefechtsverband Helbig
2. Verband: K.G.30
3. Zahl: 5 Flugzeuge
4. Typ: Mistel 3
5. Startzeit: 00.23 – 0035 Uhr
6. Ldg-Zeit: 01.20 Rechlin weiteres s.Zf. 10
7a. Angr.-Zeit: entfällt
7b. " -Höhe: entfällt
8. Auftrag: Angriff auf Behelfseisenbahnbrücke Warschau.
9. Erfolg: nicht bekannt.

10. Abgebrochen:
a) Zahl: 1.) 1 Mistel im Raum 643/4 Nachjagdbeschuß, Ju 88 Mistel
b) Ursache: nicht mehr flugfähig mit Kurs 105 in 3500 m abgesprengt. Fortsetzg. siehe Ziff. 13)
11. Bomben (Zahl u. Art):
12. Abschüsse (Zahl u. Art):
13. Verluste (Zahl u. Art, durch):
2.) 1 Mistel Qu. 5418/15 ost Umpumpschaden. Zusatzbehälter versagt ebenfalls, Mistel auf Kurs 130° gelegt in 4600 m abgesprengt. 02.00 Uhr Notabsprung über Müncheberg.
3.) 03.5? Uhr 1 Mistelflugzeugführer Raum ?rde Fallschirmabsprung, Einzelheiten bisher unbekannt, da keine telef. Verbindung.
4.) 1 Mistelflugzeugführer bei Güstrow Fallschirmabsprung, ver... Ursache Umpumpschaden, Flugz.-F. leicht verletzt, Einzelheiten stehen noch aus.
5.) 1 Mistel FF Ofhr. von Hernaden vermutl. auf Rückflug, da qdm angefordert, Landg. steht aus.
15. Sonstiges: Vermutl. über Ziel.
16. Wetter:

2017

The report prepared by KG 30 on 8 April for the previous night's attempt by five Mistel to strike a railway bridge at Warsaw.

A heavily concealed Mistel 2 belonging to 6./KG 200 parked at its dispersal area at Burg, April 1945 prior to a mission. Note what appears to be evidence of an unusual camouflage scheme on the fuselage of the Ju 88 and the tactical number '9' applied to the underside of the warhead cone.

Oberst Herbert Kuntz, a Ritterkreuzträger and experienced bomber pilot, was assigned to II./KG 200 in March 1945 and underwent training on the Mistel. However, his one and only opportunity to fly the aircraft operationally was frustrated by Allied air operations.

11./KG 100 as *Staffelkapitän* in a training supervisory capacity before being appointed to command 2./KG 100. I./KG 100 was then redesignated III./KG 1 in May 1944 with which unit Kuntz flew the He 177.

In the spring of 1945, Werner Baumbach approached Kuntz and suggested he transfer to II./KG 200 so as to lend that unit his experience. It seems Kuntz may have been outspoken about Göring's policies and that a transfer to a *Mistel* unit was considered 'appropriate'. Arriving at Burg in March 1945, he was given a very rudimentary introduction to the *Mistel* – no tactical instruction or any form of organised training. Nevertheless, the first four or five training flights he did receive were undertaken in the Ju 88 lower component accompanied by an instructor with the rank of *Oberfeldwebel*. Once these were completed, he then made a further two or three short familiarisation flights in the upper component Fw 190. Kuntz recalled that he encountered very few problems during this short 'training' period, with the instruments generally performing well.

During his final *Mistel* training flight however, Kuntz flew the Ju 88, accompanied as usual by the *Oberfeldwebel*. Above, in the Fw 190, was a young *Oberleutnant*. Having made a circuit around Burg, the composite made its touch down. Unfortunately, the *Oberleutnant* disregarded the *Oberfeldwebel's* urgent order to throttle back the Ju 88's engines and so the *Mistel* rolled at too high a speed towards the airfield boundary where its landing gear ran into soft, wet, sandy soil. The composite slowly nosed over. Fortunately, the two occupants of the Ju 88 were able to escape, but in the Fw 190 the *Oberleutnant* remained trapped upside down in the cockpit, soaked with fuel and rendered unconscious by the fumes. He was eventually extricated by rescue personnel.

On 10 April 1945, Kuntz was ordered to take part in the mission to Steinau. Take-off was set for 1800 hrs and Kuntz privately planned to fly past the target, thus avoiding the westward facing anti-aircraft defences and to make an attack approach from the east. At 1500 hrs that afternoon however, II./KG 200's base at Burg was heavily bombed by 147 B-17s from the US Eighth Air Force's 95th, 96th, 100th and 360th Bomb Groups as part of a more wide-ranging attack mounted against the network of airfields defending Berlin. The raid was to prove catastrophic for the German units based there. Hangars and workshops were badly damaged and at least 200 bombs fell on the runways and taxi tracks. Caught up on the receiving end of this attack was *Oberleutnant* Helmut Reinert, a member of 1./F 22, a reconnaissance *Staffel* equipped with the Ar 234 jet. Reinert had been flying the Arado since the beginning of the month and remembered:

> 'The parking area for our Ar 234s was located in the pine forest south of some Junkers 'piggybacks' and the Autobahn running west-east from Köln to Berlin. The airfield was subjected to bombardment from wave after wave of American Flying Fortresses during the early afternoon. It was a beautiful spring day, clear sky, but somewhat hazy. I was standing in front of the control tower on the runway side together with some other crews. We heard the roar of multiple engines in the air somewhere north of us. We thought: '*There go the Yankees against Berlin again.*' And then we saw the faint outline of a Flying Fortress moving south. For a moment we just couldn't believe that this time it was our turn! Everybody scrambled like Hell! I briefly hesitated about whether I should jump into one of the many "one-man holes" or whether I should try to make it to a bomb shelter under the control tower. I chose the latter, thank God. The first wave of bombs was already hitting the far end of the runway. The deafening roar of explosions, coming nearer with each new wave and the convulsive shaking of the buildings were truly out of Dante's *Inferno*. And then there

The wreckage of at least three Mistel of II./KG 200 litter the crater-pocked surface of Burg airfield following the USAAF raid of 10 April 1945. Hangars and workshops were badly damaged and at least 200 bombs fell on the runways and taxi tracks.

Oberleutnant Helmut Reinert of 1./F 22, who witnessed the effects of the American raid on II./KG 200's base at Burg on 10 April 1945.

was sudden silence! It was over. The roar of aircraft engines gradually faded away. Screams for help could be heard. We were covered with dust.

'South of the control tower in a forested area were all the accommodation and administrative buildings and vehicle garages as well as holding areas for several 'piggybacks' – Ju 88s with Fw 190s mounted on top. These received relatively minor damage. However, there were numerous fires. Evidently, some incendiary bombs had been dropped there. Despite the lack of water, hordes of people were swarming about like ants trying, slowly, to get things under control, particularly with one Ju 88 'piggyback' whose warhead had caught fire! It was a very tense moment! The entire area was cleared of people and, somehow, a very brave crew was able to get near enough to extinguish the blazing nose without an explosion. Four of our aircraft were lost.'

The damage inflicted to the targeted airfields was severe; at Burg, all hangars were destroyed and the runways declared unusable. At Oranienburg, five *Mistel* and six Fw 190s were destroyed during a raid there. The Lufthansa facilities were burned down, with two killed and eight wounded. At Rechlin-Lärz, the runway was left unusable and 29 aircraft were destroyed with a further 45 damaged. One of these was a 'Me 109/Ju 88 pick-a-back' destroyed on the ground by a P-47 Thunderbolt piloted by Lt. Dennis A. Carroll of the USAAF's 62nd FS, 56th FG, during a strafing run.

Elsewhere, a lone *Mistel* 3 from 6./KG 200 operated from Peenemünde against the rail and road bridge at Neuhammer spanning the Neisse River, south east of Görlitz. Its pilot, *Feldwebel* Carl-Ernst Mengel, was a former Luftwaffe flying instructor who had been posted to II./KG 200 from the *Flugzeugführerschule* B9 at Pretzsch/Elbe where he had taught on Ju 88s. Having received basic training on the Bf 109 at Stolp during the winter of 1944, Mengel was then given conversion training to the *Mistel* at Burg. He recalls:

A fire crew hoses down the smouldering remains of a Mistel 2 destroyed during the USAAF raid on Burg on 10 April 1945.

'I flew my last operational sortie from Peenemünde on 10 April 1945. My target was the viaduct (railway and road bridge) over the Neisse, south-east of Görlitz. I was fired on by a Russian MiG while I was descending steeply towards the viaduct. After separating from the Ju 88, there was smoke in the cockpit and the propeller pitch indicator needle was swinging towards the "feather" position. I quickly switched off the propeller pitch control but I could only coax 220 km/h out of the '*Mühle*' (crate), even at full throttle. Because the left undercarriage leg was hanging down and the ground was coming ever closer, I

Feldwebel Carl-Ernst Mengel was a flying instructor with the Flugzeugführerschule B9 before he transferred to 6./KG 200. He launched a Mistel at a viaduct south-east of Görlitz on 10 April 1945, but his Fw 190 was attacked by a Russian fighter shortly afterwards.

extended the right undercarriage and made a landing in open country. Thank heavens the Fw 190 did not tip over on its nose. I put in a call to the *Fliegerhorst* Görlitz and the machine and I were picked up. The next day, I was sent by rail through the burning ruins of Berlin back to Usedom. Although six Fw 190s were available at Görlitz, nobody would give me one. A few days later they were blown up!'

Oberleutnant Rudolf Kainz, Staffelkapitän of 3./KG(J) 30.

Following KG(J) 30's recent operations, *Oberst* Helbig produced a bleak assessment:

1.) Fundamental problems:

1.) Due to the *Mistel's* complexity and the difficult combination of so many technical prerequisites, a successful mission can only be flown if:

a.) The unit has enough operational experience with this aircraft. In the case of KG 30 this experience was lacking.

b.) That the unit has a single, precisely defined mission and that all details for this mission are worked out. There should be no parallel mission planned. Until 6 April, the units designated for Operation '*Eisenhammer*' had to be diverted to attack the Vistula bridges. Due to the complicated technical nature of the *Mistel* this is impossible because of organisational and leadership reasons.

Feldwebel Karl Russmeyer of 3./KG(J) 30 launched a Mistel at one of the Küstrin bridges on 27 April 1945 and noticed how a 'giant cloud of smoke' rose from the target.

2.)For similar reasons as under no. 1.) a *Mistel* unit at this time, even with more operational experience, can only achieve limited success under variable operational requirements (target changes, night missions, weather and fighter escort by day).

3.) The *Geschwader* overestimated its capabilities in terms of night take-off and night attack. The first mission with a new aircraft at night can only be successful if circumstances prove fortunate and not from any of one's own doing. These circumstances were taken into account when, with suitable weather conditions, the Vistula bridges were attacked. The *Geschwader* took all these circumstances into account and acted upon them and did all that was needed to master the situation.

2.) Particular problems:

1.) Take-off preparations have to be handled by the *Kommandeure* and *Staffelkapitäne* in a more intensive manner because of technical and organisational problems. Above all they have to act more responsibly. Furthermore, the unit has to act as a cohesive military unit, and under no circumstances should a broken up unit be used on possible other missions such as Operation '*Eisenhammer*'.

2.) The take-off weight problem will be a problem in the future because of the long periods that the aircraft are parked. The number of take-off accidents will increase. The rough surfaces of the airfields at Rostock and Peenemünde require tyre changes even before aircraft can take off. At this time the required replacements are not available and will be unavailable in the future when one considers the current production and raw material situation.

3.)For similar reasons (namely the duration of aircraft parking time) there are problems in flight with the fuel transfer pumps. These had all been checked out thoroughly on the day of the mission.

4.) The return during the darkest of nights in the Fw 190 by pilots who have no single-seat nightfighter experience, (and despite all navigational and landing aids) has:

a.) a negative and morale lowering effect on the pilot.

b.) an unjustifiable risk of loss of pilot and aircraft.

5.) The mission is to be set based on the official special weather report which gives a specific timetable, independent of weather reconnaissance aircraft reports. The command then has the only right to influence the cancellation of the mission.

6.) Weather reconnaissance can be divided into two types:

a.)If a weather reconnaissance aircraft is to be used (if early enough and for possible defensive reasons) for a *Mistel* operation, then the return landing of this aircraft should be within 45 minutes of the *Mistel* mission start (not 1½ hours as the *Kommodore* of KG 30 reported).

b.) A weather reconnaissance aircraft of a long-range reconnaissance *Gruppe* is to be in the air around the clock and should provide constant weather reports. This would provide better and more secure weather information about the target area. The report should then be transmitted in the air at least 1½ hours ahead of the mission and should be listened to by the unit about to take off.

7.)From the point of view of point no. 5 and no. 6, the briefing has to be held in such a way as if the mission is actually going to take place. The pilots can only be reached 1½ hours before commencement of a mission with difficulty. A communication system has to be established (such as five red flares from ground command or at take-off) to cancel a mission.

Signed, Helbig

The same day that Helbig drafted his report, 3./KG(J) 30 under *Oberleutnant* Rudolf Kainz arrived at Rostock-Marienehe having staged via Pardubitz, Prague-Ruzyne and Peenemünde. The unit's flying personnel comprised *Oberleutnant* Heinz Frommhold, *Oberfeldwebel* Schlicke, *Feldwebel* Casanova, *Feldwebel* Ermert, *Feldwebel* Kinder, *Feldwebel* Karl Russmeyer, *Unteroffizier* Kurt Kesten, *Unteroffizier* Karl Merkle, *Unteroffizier* Stulier and *Unteroffizier* Karlheinz Wiesner. For some weeks the unit had been dispersed in preparation for *Eisenhammer*; the *Staffel's* diary of events records:

'The 3. *Staffel* assembled at Rostock-Marienehe and was together again after two months. The pilots and ground personnel arrived in buses from the scattered '*Eisenhammer*' airfields, with those from Peenemünde and Fürth arriving by train. The train journey ended at Tangermünde on the Elbe River. All equipment had to be transferred to *Staffel*-operated transport. This proved to be insufficient and much equipment had to be destroyed. At Marienehe, the

A Mistel S2 with Oberst Herbert Kuntz at the controls of the Fw 190 lifts off the runway at Burg on a training flight, April 1945. Note a second composite just visible in the background.

Below: Burg, April 1945. Oberst Herbert Kuntz adjusts his throat microphone as he sits in the cockpit of an Fw 190 forming the upper half of a Mistel S2, the shadow of which can be seen on the ground below.

Above left and above: Oberst Herbert Kuntz had a lucky escape when, as pilot of a Ju 88 lower component, the landing gear of his Mistel became mired in soft, wet soil following a high speed landing at Burg and the entire composite nosed over. Kuntz and his co-pilot were able to escape, but the Oberleutnant in the Fw 190, soaked with fuel, became trapped upside down in his cockpit and passed out as a result of the fumes. Eventually, rescue personnel extricated him alive. Note the red tactical number '5' applied to the rudder of the Ju 88's vertical stabiliser.

Left: The undersurface of the starboard side wing of the Fw 190 is visible to the right of this picture. The fighter appears to have been pushed backwards off the support structure, the apex of which has impaled the ground. The Focke-Wulf's propeller blades have narrowly missed the Ju 88's cockpit.

Mistel 2s on the airfield had to be brought to operational status immediately which presented the ground crews with round-the-clock work. The pilots, meanwhile, had to prepare themselves for a new type of mission – the destruction of the Oder bridges. That meant formation flying with fighter protection. These new orders had been issued by the KG 200 Plenipotentiary for Bridge Destruction. The ground personnel arriving from Fürth were informed about *Eisenhammer* and were able to stare at the fighter with the giant remote-controlled bomb for the first time.'

Wednesday, 11 April 1945

During the evening, *Mistel* from II./KG 200 attacked the Autobahn bridges over the Queiss and Bober rivers. One *Mistel* was shot down, but its Fw 190 upper component escaped. The results of the mission are not known.

On this occasion, the composites were provided with a fighter escort and were guided to their targets by Ju 188 bomb-carrying pathfinders of I./KG 66. This *Zielfinder* unit played an invaluable role in not only guiding the composites but also acting as both escort and ground-attack support by strafing and suppressing enemy anti-aircraft sites around the target. It was usual for the *Zielfinder* to fly at the same height and some 3-4 km ahead of the *Mistel*, with one aircraft acting as a guide for between two and four *Huckepack*.

By April 1945, 24-year-old *Leutnant* Hans Altrogge was *Staffelkapitän* of 1./KG 66, now acting under the direction of *Gefechtsverband Helbig*; he had flown the Do 217, Ju 88 S and Ju 188 on bombing and pathfinding operations over England and the Western Front throughout the second half of 1943 and 1944 and was very experienced in nocturnal illumination and radio-jamming operations. He also remembers flying as a pathfinder for *Mistel* operating against the bridges or '*Lotse für Mistel*' (Guide for *Mistel*):

'I did 25 illuminator missions over the London area and most of our operations were conducted, out of preference, at night. Our targets were quite clear, but tactics were left down to us. The *Mistel* operations however, were usually attempted in daylight or at dusk from Peenemünde. The risk here was definitely greater as we navigated the *Mistel* in sight of the ground. The *Mistel* remained at sight distance. Flying height, according to the objective of the mission, ranged between 300 and 3,000 metres. We signalled when and where to separate the Ju 88 'missile'. The *Mistel* pilots ran a high risk from the start on account of their restricted visual range. During the flight they were effectively fixed in motion. Once released, however, they could move considerably more easily and faster than we could. Therefore, they were meant to protect us as an escort on our return flight. In practice however, those boys were so relieved when they were 'loose' that they just got the Hell out of it!'

Leutnant Hans Altrogge (centre), the Staffelkapitän of 1./KG 66 flew a number of 'pathfinder' missions in Ju 188s for Mistel attacking bridge targets over the Oder and Neisse rivers in April 1945. He considered the risks faced during such operations as 'definitely greater' than the illumination missions he flew over London the previous year. Altrogge is seen here with his crew at Montdidier, France in 1944.

During the mission on 11 April, Altrogge and his crew took off from Peenemünde at 1744 hrs and having guided the *Mistel*, dropped eight SD 70 bombs on a *Flak* position south of Sagan, on the Queiss, from 3,000 metres, returning to Neubrandenburg at 2012 hrs. Another Ju 188 from I./KG 66, Z6+RM, piloted by *Leutnant* Ernst-Karl Fara, took off from Peenemünde exactly thirty minutes earlier and also dropped the same payload as Altrogge's aircraft.

Thursday, 12 April 1945

The Soviet First Belorussian Front conducted preliminary attacks with a view to expanding the depth of the Küstrin bridgehead in order to assemble large troop concentrations there.

Around 10 April, four of the eight or nine *Mistel* which were on the strength of 6./KG 200 were transferred from Burg to Peenemünde and were assigned to attack the bridges at Küstrin, accompanied by a fighter escort and the *Zielfinder* of I./KG 66. Pilots known to have been due to fly this mission were *Feldwebel* Rudi Riedl and *Unteroffizier* Karl Müller. A course was set from Peenemünde to Strausberg where a rendezvous would be made with the fighter escort.

Another KG 200 pilot, Fritz Lorbach, remembers the start of the operation which took place on 12 April:

'The evening prior to the mission, our *Huckepacks* were lined up on the runway at Peenemünde facing into the wind. During the day we had received our orders concerning our targets, the bridges at Küstrin. We had spent the night in our barracks speculating: *What if this or that happened... What would happen if we veered off the runway*? The whole airfield was covered in bomb craters but the damage to the concrete runway had been repaired immediately. Rudi Riedl was to be the third of the four lined up for take-off. The *Mistel* were staggered so that one could still take off should the other fail to start.

Feldwebel Fritz Lorbach of 6./KG 200. Together with Willi Büllesfeld he marked the take-off points for his unit's Mistel by hammering marker pennants into the earth at the side of the runway at Peenemünde on 12 April 1945.

'In the morning, we discovered the wind had turned and was blowing at 15 km/h in the opposite direction. It was felt that a start from the other end of the runway was not possible because of the extra stress it would have imposed on the *Mistel's* undercarriage. Therefore, it was decided to take off with a tailwind. Willi Büllesfeld and I volunteered to mark the point of lift-off for the aircraft. We clamped red, yellow, green and white marker pennants and a hammer under our arms and set off. At the third *Mistel*, Willi Büllesfeld clambered up the pilot's ladder to wish Rudi '*Hals und Beinbruch*' (Good Luck) and '*bleib g'sund*' ('come back in one piece'). He clambered back down the ladder with tears in his eyes, which I had not thought possible. We then carried on to set out the markers, spacing them between 1,200 and 1,800 metres from the start position. The normal take-off, depending on the strength of the wind, was 800 to 1,000 metres. Then we crawled into the nearest bomb crater and hardened ourselves against the worst. The first *Mistel* rolled in a straight line, it rolled and rolled until, at 1,800 metres, it lifted off and at first climbed normally until suddenly it began to climb very steeply. Luckily, he was already beyond the edge of the airfield. The pilot separated his Fw 190 and made a smooth landing. The *Mistel's* lower component rolled to the right and plunged into the Baltic. The second rolled about 1,000 metres, then the left tyre burst and he headed straight for us. We didn't stay to watch. We disappeared into the crater. Nothing happened. We peered over the edge. The fire brigade, experienced men and young girls called-up for service, had already pulled the pilot out of the burning heap. Strangely, the warhead did not explode, it burnt with the wreck. The third pilot, Rudi, prepared for take-off. His was an example straight out of the textbook, but what else could be otherwise expected after Willi's '*Hals und Beinbruch*'? Despite the crash and the burning aircraft, the *Mistel* lifted off at 1,600 metres and turned left on course for Strausberg. The longest take-off run was 2,200 metres.'

The fourth aircraft failed to take off, though it is unclear why.

Once airborne, Rudi Riedl steered a course towards Strausberg He recalls:

'Our orders for the *Mistel* attack on the railway bridges at Küstrin on 12 April 1945 called for us to fly from Peenemünde to Strausberg at low level where we could hide ourselves from Allied fighters that roamed around Germany like fish in a large ocean. Our fighter pilots at the time were making a superhuman effort; they hardly had time to rest before being pitted against overwhelming odds.

'I found it fun flying at about 100 metres above the ground. Near Strausberg we had to climb to combat altitude and fly a complete circuit while awaiting our fighter escort. I looked around nervously. I couldn't see anything. Suddenly, there was an enormous shadow over me. I was shocked to the core. I couldn't believe my eyes; an Me 109 was sitting on my right wing. The chap must have dived on me like a hawk. He looked at me with astonishment. I thought to myself: "*You scoundrel, do you want to bring us both down?*" ... or so I thought for a brief moment. Laughingly, the rascal waved to me and we greeted each other like two old friends. Together, we flew to Küstrin.

'Everything in the air and down on the ground was very quiet – no Flak, nothing. We flew on for quite some time

Feldwebel Rudi Riedl of 6./KG 200 flew a successful attack against one of the Küstrin bridges: 'The lower component hit the first section of the three-section bridge which flew into the air and landed on top of the next section.'

Feldwebel Willi Büllesfeld of 6./KG 200; 'tears in his eyes...'.

together in this funny formation; we were allies on an extremely dangerous mission. We played out our parts with feeling. I recognised by the way he flew that he must have been an Ace. He flew around me like a golden eagle protecting its eyrie and I knew that he would not let anyone near me. I felt secure. Nearer the target he flew even closer to me and with his thumb pointed downwards at my target. We must have crossed the front line because all hell broke loose. I was so surprised; after all, this was my first operational sortie. The target lay before me ringed by a hail of fire.

'As I made my attack dive, my fighter escort climbed away to stay beyond range of the enemy Flak. All I could see around me were black clouds from the Flak. Occasionally, as well as these black clouds, I could see little flashes of light from the tracer – just like when you throw more wood onto an already burning fire. I don't actually remember pressing the button to activate the separation, but my diving speed was 600-650 km/h. The lower component hit the first section of the three-section bridge which exploded and landed on top of the next section.'

During Riedl's attack the forces on his aircraft at such a diving speed had not only distorted and buckled the connection between the two components, but had also twisted one wing of his Fw 190. Following separation, Riedl found himself dazed and flying upside down just above a forest on the east bank of the Oder. He had completely lost his sense of direction and had to reorientate himself for his return flight. Such was the damage to his aircraft that it could only be flown back to base in a sideways, crab-like manner. As he gathered his senses, he found himself flying low over a column of refugees fleeing from the advancing Russians.

It was dark by the time he returned to Strausberg. He made a side-slip landing because of the damage incurred to the wing of his fighter. He recalls:

'On landing at Strausberg – it was by then quite dark – I went to report the results of my attack at the operations room. A young chap in his flying overalls was sitting there on a table. I knew him immediately: it was my escort. Relief showed in his face as we stood and clapped each other on the shoulder. He had been greatly worried: he had lost sight of me among the barrage of fire as I released myself from

In mid-April 1945, the great metal girder bridges spanning the River Oder at Küstrin were assigned as targets for the Mistel of 6./KG 200.

the Ju 88 below me. We thought we deserved a drink. We walked over to the canteen and shed our flying kit. I was astonished. Before me stood an *Oberleutnant* and holder of the *Ritterkreuz*. He noted my surprise and reacted immediately, gesturing to his decoration: 'This doesn't change anything.' A long conversation followed. He told me that, on receiving orders to provide fighter escort for a "secret bird", he had picked the first on the list. That was me. His curiosity had been more than satisfied, even by the fireworks created by the Flak. He said: "*The whole of the Russian Army must have fired at us, but you hit the first third of the bridge*." He said this with some respect in his voice and I felt a little proud. We had more than one drink that night and toasted our guardian angel (or angels – there must have been more than one).'

'Next morning, as we stood together while my machine was being refuelled, we found it difficult to express our feelings. Something was weighing us down, which we could not put into words or accept. We shook hands for a long, long time. There was regret in his eyes and a strange feeling came over me. The situation forced us to go our separate ways. He took off first, his feelings in turmoil, waggling his wings in farewell. I stared after him for a long time, knowing how he felt. I took off a little later, but first I had trouble with my very battered Fw 190. A notice on the steps to the cockpit stated, *"Not Cleared for Flight."* At first I thought it was a joke and threw the notice away. A red-faced senior engineer and author of the notice, hurried over and severely reprimanded me. I demanded to speak with the representative from Baumbach's staff. That stopped him. He gave me some well meaning words of advice, but I knew myself in what state my ruffled bird was. After all, I had managed to keep it in the air from Küstrin to Strausberg. I just did not want to leave my companion where it was, it had supported me all the way home. It was the most difficult take-off I had had to make. The Fw 190 and I slowly wandered towards Peenemünde. It was my last flight for the Luftwaffe. It was 13 April 1945. That was what neither of us could accept. It's good to remember that meeting at 2,000 metres over Strausberg.

'Many weeks after this mission, whilst I was a POW at Grossenbrode, I met a German paratrooper who had been defending a position close to the bridge, only some 100 metres away from the nearest Russian positions. He told me that as my lone *Mistel* had flown over the bridge, all the German paratroops began waving and cheering as if to say "*At last! Our long awaited secret weapons have arrived!*" Not exactly a "secret weapon", but there you are!'

Also operational against the Küstrin bridges from Peenemünde during the day were four *Mistel* from KG(J) 30. A Ju 88 S *Zielfinder* of I./KG 66 flown by *Leutnant* Hans Altrogge led the attack. The Junkers flew three kilometres ahead and 460 metres above so that the four *Mistel* could see it. As the formation embarked on the glide towards the target, Altrogge waggled his wings as the signal for the *Mistel* to launch. After separation, the Fw 190s strafed the Flak batteries. No successes were confirmed though all pilots believed that they had delivered their missiles successfully.

Saturday, 14 April 1945

Five Soviet divisions accompanied by 200 tanks attempted, unsuccessfully, to storm the Seelow Heights, west of Küstrin. Sergeant Fritz-Rudolf Averdieck was a soldier with 90.*Panzergrenadier Regiment*, 20.*Panzergrenadier Division*. In mid-April 1945, he was one of those defending the Küstrin area and witnessed a *Mistel* attack. He recorded:

> 'Several quiet days followed as a result of the weather being misty. There were some sporadic air attacks by day and night, including incendiaries, and the Russian artillery participated with smoke shells putting an end to any ideas of launching an attack. Then on Easter Sunday we were assigned to some new positions. The expected attack had yet to occur. We set up our command post in a large farmstead. From 1 to 13 April we went through a completely quiet period, although the Russians fired their smoke shells repeatedly. During a visit to the 1st Battalion, I had the opportunity to examine Russian-occupied countryside and the place where we had stopped their attack. About 50 to 60 tanks stood shot up in a small area. I listened to the radio a lot… catastrophic news from the Western Front. *Reichsmarschall* Göring drove past once on a visit to the neighbouring parachute division. Appeals and orders arrived to hold the Eastern Front at all costs, and to hold on to our positions and command posts to the last man… Then on the last evening, we were offered something new. A Ju 88 with a fighter sat on top appeared under heavy Soviet anti-aircraft fire. Suddenly, the lower aircraft was released and dived on its target, and a massive explosion followed. As there was a shortage of fuel, the bomber had been filled with explosives and deliberately used in this manner. The soldiers dubbed this phenomenon '*Vater und Sohn*' – 'Father and Son'…'

At least three *Mistel* from I./KG(J) 30, piloted by *Unteroffizier* Kurt Kesten, *Unteroffizier* Karl Merkle and *Unteroffizier* Karlheinz Wiesner, took off from Rostock-Marienehe to attack one of the bridges at Küstrin. During take-off Wiesner, an experienced Ju 88 pilot who had flown with I./KG 30 since the summer of 1943, became aware that his *Mistel* felt 'sluggish'. He was unaware that the metal tow-bar from the tractor which had towed him out to his start position on the runway at Marienehe, was still fixed to his aircraft! Having lifted off the ground, he completed a circuit around the airfield, before the bar detached itself from his aircraft and dropped onto a field.

The *Mistel* proceeded to their target and Karl Merkle later wrote the following report:

Unteroffizier Karlheinz Wiesner (left) and Unteroffizier Karl Merkle pose for a snapshot in Italy in 1943. Both pilots went on to fly the Mistel with 3./KG(J) 30 in April 1945.

Unteroffizier Kurt Kesten of 3./KG(J) 30 flew a Mistel to attack one of the bridges at Küstrin on 14 April 1945. The results of the mission are not known. Kesten is seen here in France in late August 1944 having been awarded the Iron Cross First Class.

Take-off at 1740 hours from Marienehe.
Target: Oder bridge north of Küstrin.

Mission report: We had excellent fighter cover from four *Schwärme* of JG 11 before the actual attack. Within the area of well-aimed Soviet anti-aircraft fire they turned towards the front. My explosive payload received heavy Flak damage. I made a wide easterly turn towards my target. Time: 1942 hours, altitude 1,800 metres. Flat approach from the south-east to west-northwest and towards the Oder, the fourth and last *Mistel*. Suddenly close at starboard a Soviet Yak-3. I look back and suddenly receive serious hits and am wounded by cannon shells. As it turned out later, my instrument panel was completely shot up. Furthermore, there were 24 holes in the wings and fuselage of the fighter. There are four holes in the propeller. I immediately pushed the release lever and the explosive-laden lower component felt as if it was shot off. At 2020 hours, I made a belly landing.

Allied radio interceptors picked up evidence to indicate that five *Mistel* and fighter escort from unidentified units carried out attacks on the bridges at Görlitz South and Schaumburg. No other details are available.

The grim reality about conditions on the *Mistel* airfields was getting through to the highest quarters. In his diary entry for 14 April, the Chief of the Luftwaffe General Staff, *General der Flieger* Karl Koller, recorded his daily meeting with Hitler:

'…there are supposed to be at least 250 bomb craters filled with water on the landing strip at Oranienburg. (I attempted to describe how such an airfield looks.) Most airfields are repaired within two days, but Oranienburg will take three weeks. I tried to contrast this with railway repairs, but it made no difference. The *Führer* ordered Bormann to have representatives of the Party check the airfields to see what the Luftwaffe was doing. He wound up by ordering that all bombed airfields were to be repaired overnight.

'(These imputations were so unjustified and hurtful that I was very offended. On my way home I was almost driven to despair and wanted to report sick. Even the strongest nerves couldn't take this. But what can we do about it in an emergency? Just continue to do one's duty as a soldier.)'

Monday, 16 April 1945

The Soviet First Belorussian and First Ukrainian Fronts commenced their main attacks around Küstrin while, simultaneously, holding attacks were carried out by the left wing of the Second Belorussian Front. The Red Army was assisted by large numbers of close-support aircraft which hindered German response and artillery operations. They also used the SU-152 assault gun bearing a formidable 152 mm gun.

In the face of far greater numbers on the Russian side, the German Ninth Army had to cover a 130-km front with just 235,000 men, 833 tanks and assault guns and some 4,000 artillery pieces and mortars.

Four *Mistel* from 6./KG 200 were assigned to attack the Küstrin bridges. They were to be guided, once again, by Ju 188s from I./KG 66. For this operation, the *Huckepack* were flown from Burg to Parchim and made ready, whilst the Ju 188 *Zielfinder* flew in from Neubrandenburg and Rostock. To the detriment of the mission planners however, the Allied air forces chose this day to launch large-scale fighter sweeps and strafing missions against airfields throughout Germany and Czechoslovakia. The skies were teeming with Allied fighters. Indeed, the US VIII Fighter Command despatched 15 groups which accounted for a record 747 German aircraft claimed destroyed on the ground. Ninth and First Tactical Air Force fighters claimed another 30 shot down.

Leutnant Ernst-Karl Fara of I./KG 66 (second from left) flew a Ju 188 'pathfinder' for the Mistel of 6./KG 200 during their mission to Küstrin on 16 April 1945. They narrowly missed an encounter with Allied fighters during take-off. Fara's observer was Obergefreiter Leonhard Häussler (seen far left). In his logbook, Häussler recorded: 'Six Thunderbolts over the field at take-off.' Fara and Häussler are seen here with other members of their crew at a chateau near Avelin in France in 1944.

Leutnant Ernst-Karl Fara of I./KG 66 was ordered to fly one of the Ju 188 pathfinders, Z6+HM. This unit had been busy: the previous night 20 of its Ju 88s and seven of its Ju 188s had launched an attack on the bridge over the Aller at Rethem. According to visual observation three hits were scored, though four aircraft were damaged and another reported missing. Fara remembers the events which occurred at Parchim:

Flying Officer D.J. Bazett of 411 Squadron, RCAF. Bazett shot down the Fw 190 upper component of a KG 200 Mistel 2 south-west of Parchim on 16 April 1945.

'We received an order on 16 April 1945 to fly as an escort for a *Mistel* mission. Four Ju 188 crews (one as reserve) were chosen. We were one of them. Our mission was to serve as pathfinders, to get the fighter escort into position, to find and mark the target and to attack any anti-aircraft fire at the target. The *Mistel* were stationed at Parchim.

'We took off at 0925 hrs from Neubrandenburg and landed at Parchim at 0947 hrs. We were the first aircraft to land at Parchim and waited for our companions at the airfield. The first aircraft approached and set its right wheel down first and promptly broke it off on the runway. The pilot was able to hold the aircraft on the left wheel long enough not to cause too much damage. The runway was cleared in order to lengthen it for the mission.

'Our reserve aircraft was now out of action and furthermore its crew was to have served as the lead crew. I now had to take the lead. There was a mission briefing and each crew was assigned a specific duty.

'Take-off was at 1700 hrs for the *Mistel*. We, on the other hand, took off when the situation demanded. We also had to keep the *Mistel* together once they were in the air. We observed the tedious procedure necessary to get these contraptions into the air. The *Mistel* were pulled with tractors to the runway, then the tailwheel of the Ju 88 was lined up with the runway. Then a ladder was provided for the pilot in order for him to climb into his Me 109, the engines of the Ju 88 were started and only at that point was it the turn of the Me 109 to crank up. Finally came take-off. Naturally all this took time.

'As soon as the *Mistel* were airborne and forming up, there was an air raid alarm. An American bomber unit with fighter escort was flying over the airfield. We left the immediate environs of the airfield and looked for cover. The *Mistel* continued to take off and were ordered by radio to fly to Neubrandenburg airfield where they were to circuit and try to maintain formation until we could get there. The anti-aircraft batteries were able to keep the American fighters at a distance. I was at dispersal with my crew when a courier on a bicycle called for a crew from KG 66. I asked him what he wanted. One of our aircraft had fly to Neubrandenburg, to meet the *Mistel*.

'It was a touchy situation since American fighters were still very close to the airfield. I notified my two other crews and we returned to the field with misgivings. I told my crew that we would sell our lives as dearly as possible. The radio operator was to go in first and turn on all the main switches in the aircraft, especially the ones that operated the defensive armament. Next, the turret gunner should get in and man his cannon and search the sky. Next, I would enter the aircraft and lastly the engineer and observer.'

Fara's observer was *Obergefreiter* Leonhard Häussler. The entry for this day in his logbook records: '*Six Thunderbolts over the field at take-off.*'

Fara continues:

'Suddenly, my turret gunner shouted: "*A fighter is coming straight for us! Should I open fire?*' I said: "*Keep him in your sights and fire only when he does. Maybe he won't see us.*" I placed my trust in our new "day camouflage" – we had only received it shortly before for the '*Eisenhammer*' mission. Because of our very low altitude and the fact that he came out of very bright sunlight, it was almost impossible for him to see us. That is what happened as he turned away from us.'

'For take-off, I sneaked between two *Mistel*, pulled up, retracted the landing gear and remained at treetop level. Carefully, I turned to the east. Close by, a *Mistel* was shot down by a fighter and crashed into a farmhouse. The only thing that remained was a cloud of dust.'

It is likely that the *Mistel* Fara and his crew had seen shot down was a victim, not of the USAAF, but of a Canadian-flown Spitfire. In the air around Parchim at that time was a number of Spitfire IXs of No. 411 Squadron, RCAF, which had been ordered to conduct armed reconnaissance/fighter sweeps over central and eastern Germany that evening. F/Lt D.C. Gordon was leading the squadron and later reported:

'I was leading 411 Squadron on an Armed Recce. After an hour of hunting for enemy MT, we crossed over Parchim aerodrome where there was a Ju 88 starting to take off but when he saw Spitfires above, he closed his throttles quickly and slewed off the runway. We then orbited looking for any airborne enemy aircraft and spotted a Ju 88 with an Fw 190 pick-a-back on it. I closed to 500 yards astern and opened fire. At the same time the Fw 190 separated from the Ju 88. On this burst, large pieces flew off the Ju 88 and it caught fire and crashed. In hitting the ground it made a tremendous explosion.'

Flying with Gordon was F/O D.J. Bazett who later reported:

'I was flying Red 2 in 411 Squadron. My leader sighted a Ju 88 and Fw 190 pick-a-back and attacked with strikes on the Ju 88. The Fw 190 was launched and broke port. My leader told me to follow the Fw 190. On my first one-second burst from approximately 300 yards I observed strikes on the fuselage. A couple of succeeding bursts were ineffective. I settled down and my last one-second burst obtained strikes on the engine port side. The aircraft started to burn, turned on its back and hit the deck from about 200 feet, bursting into flame. I claim one Fw 190 destroyed.'

F/Lt Gordon confirmed the destruction of the Fw 190 upper component – probably the last *Mistel* to be shot down in combat by the Allied air forces, though the identity of its pilot is not known.

Meanwhile *Leutnant* Fara's Ju 188 was heading east:

'Since we were flying in the opposite direction of the American bomber stream, we quickly lost sight of it. Eventually, we climbed to our operational altitude and soon we saw a *Mistel* in front of us. I flew above the *Mistel* and took the lead. Soon my squadron mates with the rest of the *Mistel* joined us and we headed for the target. The target, the bridges at Küstrin, were shrouded in mist and difficult to see and as a result, we could not make out the effectiveness of the attack. Nevertheless we dropped our fragmentation bombs into the anti-aircraft positions and then turned for home. On the way back, I pulled the Ju 188 up because I saw fires in front of me. Later I realised that they were campfires, most likely from refugee columns heading west.'

Twenty-five-year-old *Feldwebel* Toni Grögel of 6./KG 200 was one of the *Mistel* pilots sent to attack Küstrin that day; he recalls:

'My last operation was on 16 April 1945 from Peenemünde. The target was one of the Oder bridges at Küstrin and I managed to destroy it. I saw *Unteroffizier* Hans Kempzo shot down over the target. The bridge was confirmed destroyed on 17 April by aerial reconnaissance.'

Tuesday, 17 April 1945

Luftflottenkommando 6 requested *Gefechtsverband Helbig* via *Luftwaffenkommando Nordost* at Biesenthal to prepare a mission using '*Huckepack* operations' to destroy the railway bridge at Steinau. Fighter escort was to be provided but no further evidence exists to indicate that this operation was flown this day.

During the afternoon however, seven *Mistel* from 3./KG(J) 30 were readied for take-off from Peenemünde for a mission against the bridges at Küstrin. In total, it was planned to despatch three *Angriffsgruppen* drawn from the *Staffeln* of I. *Gruppe*. However, at Oranienburg and Marienehe, the first *Mistel* crashed on take-off and the remainder had to remain on the ground. Details of any subsequent successes achieved by I./KG(J) 30 are not known. However, only two pilots returned. One of the two, *Oberfähnrich* Georg Gutsche, who had belly-landed in his Fw 190 at Werneuchen reported:

'The Americans came again at noon to bomb our airfield. However, this time the ceiling was so low that they had to look for other targets. We were able to take off and our targets were the Oder bridges near Küstrin. I was barely over the front when I received hits in the wings of the Ju 88. The shells exploded between the wings and also damaged the wing of the Fw 190. The *Mistel* turned towards the left. Right rudder did not change the situation, and I had no choice but to blast the Ju 88 away. After that it was very difficult despite full application of right rudder to steer my "lame duck" Fw 190 towards the west. I was getting ready to use the parachute, but I suddenly saw a red wingtip light. That could only be a friendly aircraft heading for a friendly airfield. I followed and suddenly saw the landing lights of an airfield. The machine in front of me turned into a final approach and landed. The lights went out immediately. I fired my emergency flares and the lights came on again and I attempted to land. Landing gear and flaps were not operable. I killed the throttle and hit the ground. At an altitude of one metre and at a speed of 270 km/h, I reached the end of the runway in a flash. I pulled up again slowly and carefully made a 180-degree turn. This time I had to come down. Again I fired my flares. Again the lights came on. Throttle in. At 270 km/h, I skidded along the ground, hands in front of my face. The fighter slid onto the grass and somersaulted. My emergency field was Werneuchen. Besides myself, another pilot from the mission landed there.'

Gutsche flew the *Mistel* against targets at Stettin, Greifenhagen and Steinau and survived the war.

Wednesday, 18 April 1945

On the morning of 18 April, Zhukov renewed his assault on the Seelow Heights, more than ever determined to break through the German defences. The 47th Army aimed at Wriezen. The 3rd Shock supported by 9th Guards Tank Corps attacked towards Kunersdorf, while the 5th Shock Army drove towards Reichberg and Münchehof. The fighting raged all day and the Russians pushed their way forward in all sectors.

During the night of 18/19 April, a formation of 26 Ju 88s and Ju 188s from unknown elements of *Gefechtsverband Helbig*, though most likely LG 1 and I./KG 66, attacked the bridgehead at Barby on the Elbe. The results of the attack were not observed. There were no losses.

Thursday, 26 April 1945

The Russians broke through at Prenzlau.

Feldwebel Kurt Kesten was one of 3./KG(J) 30's pilots briefed to conduct an operation against various bridge targets along the Oder, Neisse and Bober rivers. He remembers:

'While waiting to take off, I had could see *Unteroffizier* Merkle's *Mistel* behind me while ahead the three engines of *Hauptmann* Röschlau's *Mistel*, which had started first, howled as he slowly rolled for a take-off. We then saw the "double-decker" swing slightly to the left and thought it would ground loop, but although Röschlau was able to correct it, the landing gear of the Ju 88 struck a railway embankment at the edge of the airfield. Suddenly the Fw 190 was alone in the air and the Ju 88 slid with broken and retracted landing gear into an adjacent field. Meanwhile, the Fw 190 climbed to altitude and turned as if the pilot was going to make an exemplary landing approach, but the collision with the embankment had caused his aircraft to lose speed and take off too late. In shock, we now watched as the aircraft stalled, went into a half-roll, crashed and sank into the '*Bodden*', a nearby bay on the Baltic coast. Although the altitude before approach seemed high enough for Röschlau to save himself by parachute, he was apparently unable to do so. For us, there were a few worrying minutes as we were rescued from our lofty four-and-a-half metre high narrow perches by means of simple wooden ladders. But the feared explosion of the "super bomb" never came. After this take-off attempt we walked back to our quarters in a very depressed state.'

Friday, 27 April 1945

At 3./KG(J) 30's base at Rostock-Marienehe, *Feldwebel* Karl Russmeyer's *Mistel* was towed out to its starting position; as he recalls:

'On the 27th, the *Mistel* were lined up early for take-off. My mission for the day was the bridge over the Oder near Küstrin. After the briefing, we walked over to the aircraft where the hard working ground crews were waiting for us. Each steering setting was checked out one at a time. The check for the Fw 190 I carried out alone, based on a checklist which every pilot had to carry around his neck.[6] Finally, all three engines were running and I was the last pilot to signal the removal of the chocks. I soon rumbled at full throttle down the runway, but this time without any sign of ground looping. I quickly reached take-off speed and lifted off the runway. What a good feeling to be up and to be able

[6] See Chapter Nine.

Feldwebel Toni Grögel of 6./KG 200 succesfully attacked one of the Küstrin bridges with a Mistel on 17 April 1945: 'The bridge was confirmed destroyed.' Grögel had previously been a bomber pilot with KG 6 and KG 100 before converting to the Bf 109 in September 1944.

Unteroffizier Alfred Hansen flew Ju 88s with KG 51 in 1944 before joining 6./KG 200 with which he flew the Mistel against bridge targets on the Oder Front in 1945.

Above and right: A Mistel 1 is prepared for operations on the taxiway at Burg, April 1945. The Bf 109 carries a yellow fuselage band, indicative of an aircraft formerly deployed on the Eastern Front and the Reparaturwerkstatt number '39' can be seen in the centre of the Balkenkreuz. Note the tactical number 'Red 6' visible on the rudder of the Ju 88. A Mistel S2 can be seen to the left.

to use autopilot without any problems. Since the take-off distances between such sluggish aircraft had to be far apart, I soon found myself alone. Slowly, I reached proper altitude and found the visibility as bad as at take-off. Now and then I had problems in finding the most obvious landmarks which had been clearly marked on my map. The silvery course of the Oder I discovered only after I had flown too far to the north. Maybe that was the reason it was so quiet around me – and on the ground there was no indication that this river was being fought over.

'As I reached Strausberg on an easterly heading and flew over the railway tracks to get to the bend in the Oder, I reached the front. Here our troops were locked in mortal combat with the Russians. Flak also made itself noticed; only fighters were still absent. The target, Küstrin, drew closer and the bridges were visible in the haze. My target was the road bridge. With a few corrections, I was able to bring my aircraft into the correct approach pattern and soon after I was in the glide to release my explosive companion. A few more corrections and I had the bridge in my sights and the remote control for the Ju 88 could be activated. After the separation and as I was pulling up, I noticed that I hit only the western bridge moorings since a giant cloud of smoke rose from this location. With the depressing thought that the Red Army could no longer be stopped and that Berlin and the war would soon be lost, I flew my Fw 190 at treetop level back to Rostock-Marienehe. The two *Mistel* which started ahead of me on that day did not return.'

Monday, 30 April 1945

Four *Mistel* 2s of 3./KG(J) 30 at Marienehe were assigned to make a strike against the Oder bridges between Tantow and Greifenhagen. The four *Huckepack* were rolled out onto the runway line astern, starting carts next to them and the ground crews waited for the arrival of the pilots. *Oberleutnant* Heinz Frommhold later recalled:

'At around 1000 hrs, I climbed into the third *Mistel*. Immediately, rudders were checked prior to take-off. Then the siren sounded and I received the signal to start the engines. All three started immediately and sounded good. Looking over my pre-flight checklist, I made the necessary adjustments and gave the signal that I was ready. The two *Mistel* in front of me took off without mishap. The first one left the airfield in a flat right turn and the second one had just lifted off the runway, when I was given permission to take off with a green lamp. The precarious feeling in my stomach – just like the one I felt during my first take-off – gave way to the conviction that what they could do, I could do.

'Carefully, I pushed the throttle forward, the left one before the other two. The contraption moved, picked up speed and I thought to myself: "*Keep straight on the runway!*" Every uneven stretch of runway seemed like a leap over a ditch and with every bump I swayed four and a half metres over the ground. Every rudder correction seemed to be a gamble. I had the feeling that my air speed was not picking up fast enough and the crate rumbled on, until finally the tailwheel came off the runway. Ahead of the Fw 190's engine I could see the striped edge of the runway and I knew that I was going straight. The bumps stopped – it seemed like an eternity to me – and my *Mistel* was airborne! A quick check on the air speed indicator: I was OK. Retract landing gear! As I reached the edge of the runway and I throttled back, I felt much better. The three BMW 801D2 engines ran a little rough, but then my ears were used to the sound of the Jumo 213.

'Obviously well trimmed, the *Mistel* seemed to climb all by itself. The air speed increased and the altimeter passed the 300-metre mark. Flaps gradually reduced and I turned on a heading of 120 degrees towards Pasewalk, following the others. Automatically, I synchronised the engines, a quick check of the engine dials and I switched the rudder to automatic. Everything was fine! In front of me and slightly above, I saw the *Mistel* which had taken off before me. They had reached cruising altitude. A look around: other than the two of them, the sky was empty. Below us, at 800 metres, we saw the first Cumulus clouds that seemed to become denser towards the east. When I reached 3,000 metres and wanted to go to autopilot and pushed the control column slightly forward in order to bring the variometer to 'zero', the aircraft continued to climb. I pushed the control column forward a little harder, and then as hard as I could, but the nose of the Fw 190 just did not want to go down. The crate continued to climb. I became a little worried when I thought about the very first flight of a *Mistel*. From what I had been told, the *Mistel* had gone into a steep descent from which it did not recover. I checked everything – all the rudder controls were OK. The control light showed that the rudders were functioning normally. I had taken the aircraft off autopilot. The climb increased and air speed began to slowly decrease. I pushed the throttle forward and the air speed stabilised. I tried to remember whether I noticed any change in the elevator setting during my climb – no, everything had been normal. I switched all the rudder settings to "take-off" in order to see if this would bring a change – nothing! I could not stop the climb. Then I remembered the "up" and "down" switch for the autopilot. Neither the descent nor the climb setting brought any change. I tried the same again with the autopilot on – no reaction. Meanwhile, the Fw 190's nose had gone up again and air speed was falling again. I did not know what to do and slowly I began to panic! Despite full throttle, the forward air speed had gone down to 200 km/h. Under the circumstances, I had no other alternative than to launch the Ju 88. I throttled the Fw 190 to full power and activated the switch that would separate the Ju 88. A jolt, and the Fw 190 climbed steeply – minus the load. To the right, I observed my Ju 88 climbing to the south-east.

'Depressed, I returned to Marienehe and landed. For a time, I was plagued by the question of what I had done wrong. An hour later, the other pilots landed. One had been attacked by a fighter and had to separate his dangerous load before the approach to the target. After a successful approach, the other had observed an explosion. He could not tell if he had hit the target. The fourth one, an *Unteroffizier*, did not return from this mission. A few days later, the *Staffel* left Rostock-Marienehe for an uncertain future.'

Saturday, 5 May 1945

Following the cessation of operations, some of 3./KG(J) 30's pilots, such as *Unteroffizier* Kurt Kesten and *Unteroffizier* Karlheinz Wiesner transferred to *Schlachtgeschwader* 3 with whom they spent the last few days of the war flying fighter-bomber missions in Fw 190 Fs.

The majority, however, left Rostock-Marienehe and were transported by truck to Eberswalde where they were to be incorporated into the III. *Germanische SS Panzer Korps*. However, when the *Geschwaderkommodore*, *Oberstleutnant* Heise, reported to the corps headquarters, SS-*Obergruppenführer* Felix Steiner, commander of Eleventh SS *Panzerarmee*, refused to waste 'inexperienced Luftwaffe personnel in ground combat.'

Steiner advised Heise to march with his *Geschwader* towards the River Elbe. By the morning of 5 May, all *Staffeln* had reached a newly designated assembly point at Ülitz, between Schwerin and Ludwigslust. The front here was extremely fluid and enemy troops, either Soviet or American, were anticipated in the area at any time. KG(J) 30 dug in ready for their last battle – as ground troops. However, concern at being captured by the Russians prompted *Oberstleutnant* Heise to make contact with the Americans who, by then, had crossed the Elbe near Bleckede.

On 7 May at 1700 hrs, the *Geschwader* reported officially for the last time. Upon dismissal, KG(J) 30 was disbanded. Individually, or in small groups, the former *Mistel* pilots and their ground crews, made their way to the western shore of the Elbe. By the evening of 8 May, most of 3. *Staffel* was in American captivity on Hagenow airfield.

Tuesday, 8 May 1945

The Allies captured the components of at least four former II./KG 200 *Mistel* still at Tirstrup in Denmark which, on paper, had been assigned to IV./KG 200; these aircraft had been left in Denmark following the cancellation of Operation *Drachenhöhle* and were reported as:

Fw 190 A-8	W.Nr.732100
Fw 190 A-8/R6	W.Nr.733682
Fw 190 A-8	W.Nr.733759
Fw 190 A-8	W.Nr.960964
Ju 88 A-4	W.Nr.142492
Ju 88 A-4	W.Nr.144032
Ju 88 G-1	W.Nr.714633 (PI+XI)
Ju 88 G-1	W.Nr.714656

Thought to have been taken at Gardelegen in mid-1945, Soviet troops are seen here posing for a photograph on a rare Bf 109 G/Ju 88 A-4 combination.

This Mistel combination is believed to have been used for training flights for operations against the bridges in the east.

CONFIDENTIAL
HEADQUARTERS
UNITED STATES STRATEGIC AIR FORCES IN EUROPE
Office of Asst. Chief of Staff A-2

COPY NO. [illegible]

TECHNICAL INTELLIGENCE)
REPORT NO.........A-389)

AAF Station 379
APO 633, U S Army
14 May 1945

SUBJECT: Inspection of FW 190/Ju 88 Composite Aircraft.

1. A composite aircraft was inspected on the Merseburg airfield. This type consisted of a FW 190 A-8 mounted on a Ju 88 G. Although this craft is being reported on, other variations of the composite aircraft were found. On the Bernberg airfield both Ju 88 and Ju 188 aircraft were being used. However, the FW 190 has been the controlling aircraft in all cases.

2. In the general [illegible] five large airfields have been [illegible] more composite aircraft on it than any other [illegible] of these have been found in all. The aircraft inspected [illegible] good condition. Some of the FW 190's on the [illegible] operational aside from a few minor adjustments

MISTEL | FINALE

As the Allied armies ranged deep into Germany during the final weeks of the Second World War, so they came upon former Luftwaffe airfields littered with hundreds of abandoned German aircraft of all types – some damaged, some intact. For many Allied troops it was the first time they were able to inspect the enemy's aircraft at close quarters. Often these encounters were the source of considerable astonishment and bewilderment, particularly in the case of jet and rocket-powered aircraft. But at certain airfields, British, American and Russian soldiers and airmen were greeted by possibly the most striking sight of all – the Mistel composite.

The pages that follow contain just a sample of some of the photographs taken officially and unofficially by Allied soldiers as they discovered the Luftwaffe's 'Huckepack' aircraft.

Above and below: Two views showing Mistel combinations using what appears to be a Ju 88 C variant with Jumo 211 engines (above) and with a G model with BMW 801 radials (below).

Mistel S2 Focke-Wulf Fw 190 A-8 '97'/Junkers Ju 88 G-1, W.Nr. 590153 Merseburg (see also pgs 200-209). In the background is Mistel S2 Focke-Wulf Fw 190 A-8 '87'/ Junkers Ju 88 G-1, W.Nr. 714237.

Mistel S2 Fw 190/Ju 88 G-1 Gardelegen, May 1945
(Page 184 lower photo to 186)

Mistel S2 Fw 190 F-8 '90'/Ju 88 G-1 W.Nr. 714790, Ludwigslust, May 1945

(Page 187 to 192)

Mistel S2 Focke-Wulf Fw 190 F-8 '90'/Junkers Ju 88 G-1, W.Nr. 714790, Ludwigslust, May 1945

Mistel S2 Focke-Wulf Fw 190 A-8 '87'/ Junkers Ju 88 G-1, W.Nr. 714237 and Focke-Wulf Fw 190 A-8 '97'/ Junkers Ju 88 G-1, W.Nr. 590153, Merseburg, May 1945

(Page 194 to 209)

Mistel S2 Focke-Wulf Fw 190 A-8 '87'/ Junkers Ju 88 G-1, W.Nr. 714237, Merseberg, May 1945

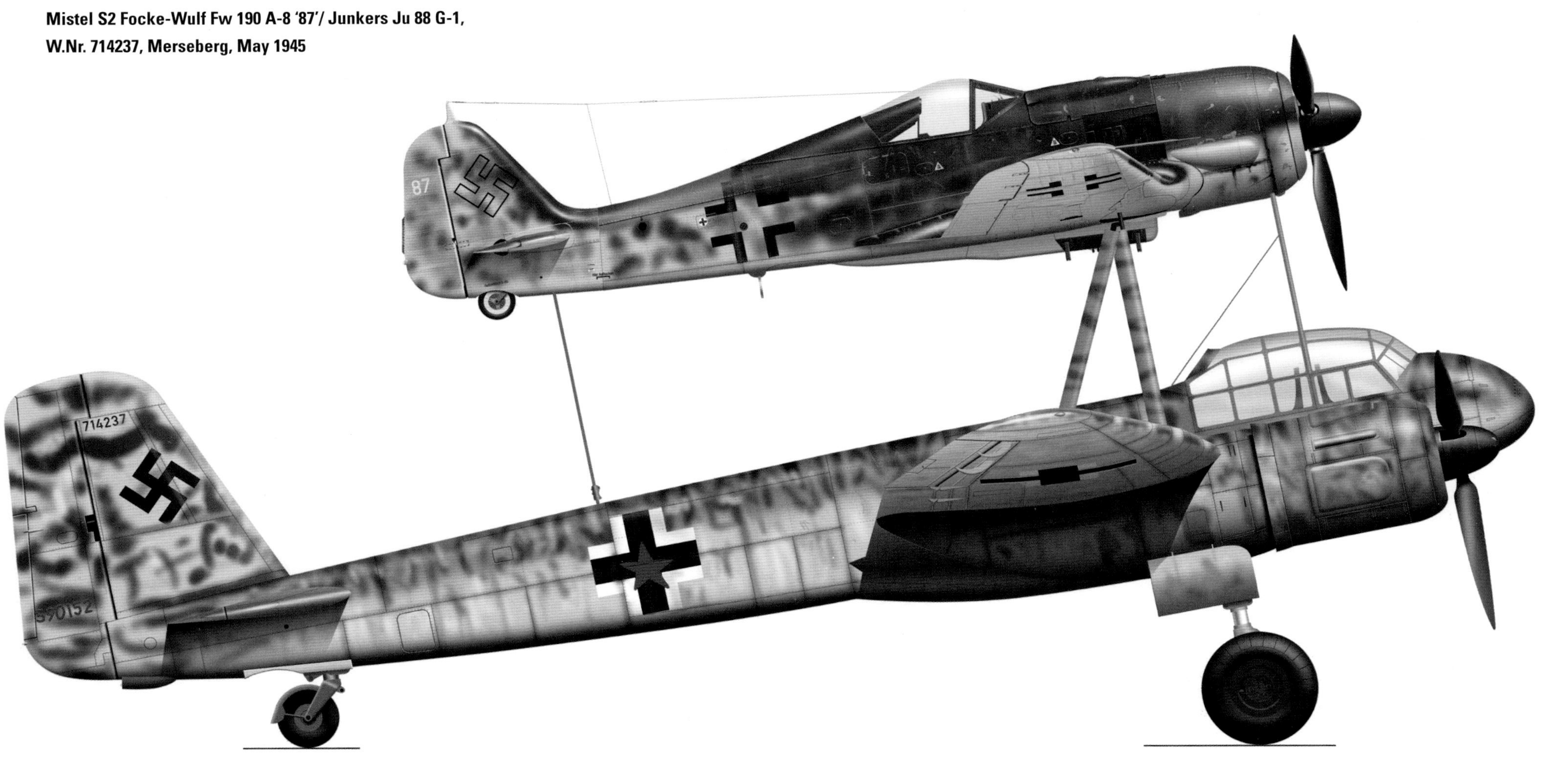

Mistel S2 Focke-Wulf Fw 190 A-8 '97'/ Junkers Ju 88 G-1, W.Nr. 590153 Merseburg, May 1945

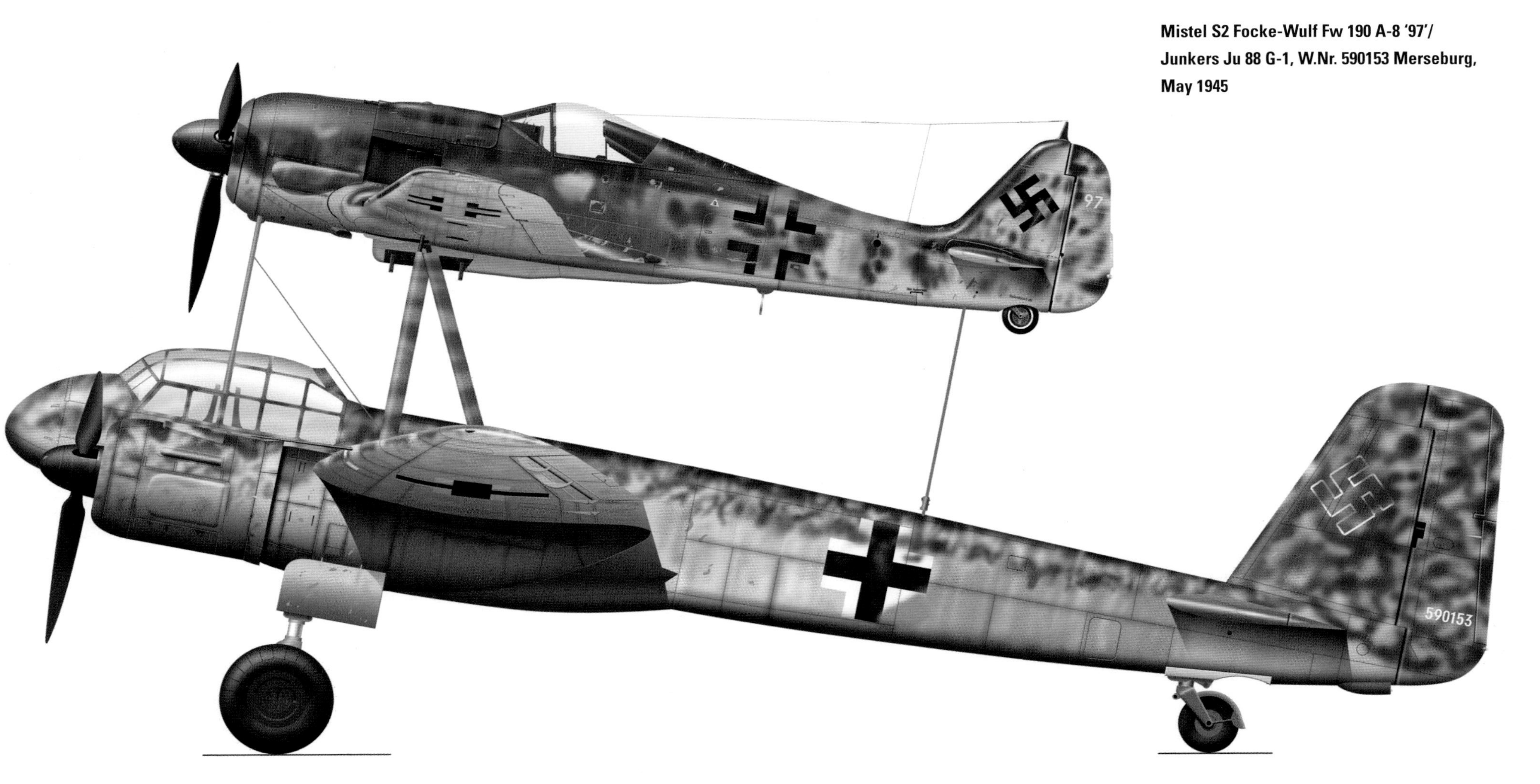

590153

Note the fuselage code 'C9' visible aft of the Balkenkreuz on the Ju 88 denoting a nightfighter formerly of NJG 5 taken over for Mistel conversion.

CONFIDENTIAL
HEADQUARTERS
UNITED STATES STRATEGIC AIR FORCES IN EUROPE
Office of Asst. Chief of Staff A-2

COPY NO. 1

TECHNICAL INTELLIGENCE)
REPORT NO........A-389)

AAF Station 379
APO 633, U S Army
14 May 1945

SUBJECT: Inspection of FW 190/Ju 88 Composite Aircraft.

1. A composite aircraft was inspected on the Merseburg airfield. This type consisted of a FW 190 A-8 mounted on a Ju 88 G. Although this craft is being reported on, other variations of the composite aircraft were found. On the Bernberg airfield both Ju 88 and Ju 188 aircraft were being used. However, the FW 190 has been the controlling aircraft in all cases.

2. In the general area of Merseburg five large airfields have been inspected, and each had more composite aircraft on it than any other type. Over 50 of these have been found in all. The aircraft inspected were in relatively good condition. Some of the FW 190's on the Merseburg airfield were operational aside from a few minor adjustments and the only apparent reason for abandoning them was because of the lack of fuel. The additional instruments, controls, and wiring were already installed, but they had not been mounted on one of the bombers. A large factory on the perimeter of the Bernberg airfield was engaged in making new Ju 188 aircraft and modifying Ju 88 and 188 night-fighters and bombers. All these were to be used for composite aircraft. The modifications consisted of removing all the equipment, putting on a new nose and completely rewiring the aircraft. New engines were installed in all of the aircraft.

3. In view of the number of craft found and the fact that Ju 188's were being built for this purpose, it is believed that the GAF had planned an all-out last offensive with this weapon to do as much damage as possible at some later date.

4. None of the aircraft inspected could have been used operationally without further modification. With the existing equipment now installed, a crew of two would have to be in the bomber. For this reason it is believed that the aircraft in this area were engaged on a large training program for the final operation.

5. Captured drawings which accompany this report show that considerable modification will be necessary before the existing aircraft could be used as planned. These show that two types of special noses can be installed to carry the charge. With either of these the existing nose, controls, seats, and other equipment would have to be removed from the bomber. In that event no personnel could ride in the bomber to start it and get it off the ground for the fighter pilot. This being the case, the controls now installed in the bomber would have to be led up to the fighter. The drawings also show two additional fuel tanks have been installed in the rear fuselage of the bomber.

6. Method of Attaching the Aircraft.

a. The weight of the fighter is carried by a set of two struts on each side. The top of each set is attached to the lower surface of the fighter wing below the spar at the jack point. The bottom of the struts are bolted to the forward and rear spar, respectively, of the bomber wing, just outboard of the spar joint at the root. A diagonal bracing leads down from each jack point, and the bottom of the two members are bolted together on a pad on top of the bomber fuselage above the forward bomb bay bulkhead. A single small balancing strut is attached to the under surface of the fighter just forward of the tail

-1-
CONFIDENTIAL

wheel, and the bottom is attached to the frame forward of the dinghy compartment. The rear strut is unfaired. However, all of the others are well streamlined by a thin metal fairing.

b. The lines from the fighter to the bomber are led thru the starboard diagonal bracing. They are connected at the under surface of the fighter fuselage by a metal tube which is inserted into the ends of the flexible lines. Although the ends of the lines are safety-wired about the metal tube they should disconnect easily when the aircraft separate.

c. The electrical leads from the fighter pass under the cockpit to the port wing gun well, where they are connected to multiple sockets which are flush with the under surface of the wing. Plugs fitting into these sockets are held in place like all German electrical connections. However, they will disconnect when the two aircraft separate. All of these leads pass thru the port diagonal bracing to various stations in the bomber.

d. Connections to the two bomber throttles are led thru the port wing of the fighter to the jack point, where they pass thru the forward main brace fairing to the bomber wing and are connected here to an override on the throttles installed in the bomber. An explosive bolt is inserted in a turnbuckle of the throttle controls below the wing surface. The electrical wiring to these two bolts is interconnected with the remainder of the system which leads to the other explosive bolts in all of the struts.

7. Safety Bracing.

a. Mounted above the cockpit of the bomber, where the after part separates when it is jettisoned, is a heavy steel strap. Leading upwards from this strap on each side is a rod brace with cross bracing between the two. Attached to the top of this bracing is another strap which has the same contour as the under side of the fighter cowl ring under which it is placed. Supporting this structure from the rear is a forked brace which leads back to the bracket on top of the bomber fuselage which holds the bottom of the diagonal braces.

b. This forward bracing does not support any of the fighter weight while it is attached to the bomber, as the bracing is 2" below the cowl ring. As the center line of the fighter is approximately 15 degrees downward to that of the bomber, there is some possibility of it hitting the nose of the bomber when the two aircraft separate. This being the case, it is believed that this front bracing acts as a bumper to bounce the nose of the fighter into the air, when necessary, so that it will climb free of the bomber.

8. Additional stressing of aircraft.

a. It was not necessary to stress-up the fighter other than in a small section near the tail where the pad which holds the tail brace is attached. All of the bombers had double skin, and the nose former just forward of the cockpit has been reinforced. Another thickness of skin and additional formers have been added to all of the bomb bay bulkheads. Three inch steel channels with cross bracing have been added in the small space between the forward bomb bay bulkhead and the after cockpit bulkhead. The removable panel below the forward bomb bay has been heavily built-up with another thickness of skin and more heavy stringers.

9. Fighter equipment.

a. The equipment left in the fighter is standard. An MW 50 tank has been added. An oil tank is fitted into the space normally occupied by the two over-engine MG 131s.

-2-
CONFIDENTIAL

CONFIDENTIAL   TI Rpt. A-389 14 May 45

b. The armament has been removed from the fighter. However, an ETC 501/XII A-1 carrier with a Schloss 500/XII/C shackle, remains installed.

c. The cockpit arrangement remains basically the same, but some additional controls for the bomber have been added. The majority of these are on a special panel extending down to the floor of the cockpit between the pilot's legs. The new instruments and controls will be shown in photographs appended to this report.

10. Bomber equipment.

a. The original instruments and controls remaining in the aircraft consist of the tachometer, boost gauge, and throttles. The mag. prop pitch control switches, and the starters are mounted on a new panel on the left side of the pilot's seat.

b. The landing gear switches are mounted on a new panel in the position where the mag switches are normally found. A notice on the panel reads, 'Do not switch on while on the ground".

c. The radio equipment on the after cockpit bulkhead has been removed. A special small wooden panel has been mounted in this space just aft of the entrance hatch door. Mounted on this panel are the electrical master switches, oil temperature gauges, oil and fuel pressure gauges, fuel contents gauges, pump switches, tank selector, compass, hydraulic pump controls, and the automatic pilot switch. Leading from this panel to a small box are wires which connect with the switches controlling the three axes of the automatic pilot, which must be turned on before it will function.

d. The armament and the rear gun ring and other protection have been removed. 2 x Schlosslafette 1000/500/XI carriers are still installed below the wings.

11. Course Control.

a. The Master Compass, the "S" Compass and an Askania three-axis automatic pilot are installed in the rear of the bomber fuselage. The fighter pilot controls the flight of the bomber by two of the normal type thumb controls which are connected with the apparatus in the bomber. One of these is mounted on the fighter control stick, and it affects actions on the rudder and ailerons, which are hooked in together. The other control is on the new panel between the pilot's legs. It affects the elevators only. By this manner the fighter pilot controls the bomber and presumably sets the bomber in a shallow dive on the target before the two aircraft separate.

12. Fuel Capacity.

a. In all cases the fighter carries C-3 fuel while the bomber carries B-4 (although one aircraft used fuel from the tanks of the other). Inspection revealed that the fighter could draw fuel from the bomber to give it a greater range than normal. However, there is no indication that the bomber can draw fuel from the fighter as the accompanying drawings state. Also, no provision has been discovered for installing a bulging tank above each wing of the fighter as the drawings indicate.

b. The drawing lists two categories which are given below; one giving the fighter the maximum of fuel, while the other gives the maximum to the bomber.

-3-
CONFIDENTIAL

CONFIDENTIAL   TI Rept.A-389, 14 May 45.

Case I

Fuel for Ju 88 G-10

Inner wing tanks 2 x 415	830 L
Outer wing tanks 2 x 425	850 L
Jettisonable wing tanks 2 x 900	1800 L
Fuselage tank #1	1220 L
Fuselage tank #4	1050 L
	5750 L - Total

Fuel for FW 190

Forward fuselage tank	232 L
Rear fuselage tank	292 L
Wing tanks 2 x 270	540 L
Jettisonable belly tank	300 L
Ju 88 fuselage tank #2	1220 L
Ju 88 fuselage tank #3	1220 L
	3804 L Total

CASE II

Fuel for Ju 88 H-4

Inner wing tanks 2 x 415	830 L
Outer wing tanks 2 x 425	830 L
Fuselage tank #1	1220 L
Fuselage tank #2	1220 L
Fuselage tank #3	1220 L
Fuselage tank #4	1220 L
Fuselage tank #5	1050 L
Jettisonable wing tanks 2 x 900	1800 L
FW 190 wings tanks 2 x 270	540 L
	9950 L Total

Fuel for FW 190

Forward fuselage tank	232 L
Rear fuselage tank	292 L
MW 50	115 L
	639 L Total

13. Explosive charge.

a. No trace of any of the charges to be used could be found on any of the airfields where these aircraft were stationed. The attached drawings reveal that there are two entirely different types of explosive noses which can be used. One type is rounded when seen from the front. However, a side view shows that from the tip aft it slopes up toward the bottom of the bomber fuselage to give the aircraft the appearance of having a drooping nose. The other type is round and the diameter increases in cross-section until it nearly reaches the forward end where it is sharply rounded off. On the end of this is a long slim funnel-like extension which resembles a stinger.

14. Miscellaneous.

a. An additional main wheel is fitted below the belly of the bomber, and it is attached to the heavily reinforced cover plate below the forward bomb bay. A special type connection is made with two eye bolts at the forward end for the main support. A forked brace from the wheel is attached to a fitting at the rear of the panel.

b. The bomber priming tank is located in the rear fuselage and is filled thru a cap set in the solid panel which now covers the removed PoGe 6 loop.

Basic report prepared by /s/ Charles E. Thompson, Capt., AC
Approved by /s/ John O. Gette, Jr., Lt. Col. AC

H.D. Sheldon, Col. A.C.

GEORGE C. McDONALD
Brig. Gen., U.S.A.
Asst. Chief. of Staff A-2

-4-
CONFIDENTIAL

USAAFE Technical Intelligence Report date 14 May 1945 containing a detailed description of a Mistel 2 found at Merseburg.

Bernburg, April 1945

The recently destroyed wreck of a Mistel S smoulders on the taxiway at the Junkers airfield at Bernburg. This was the scene which welcomed troops of the US Ninth Army's 113th Cavalry Group when they arrived there on 16 April 1945. In the background is a Mistel S3C (the subject of several photographs on the following pages) and a Ju 88 G-10 with fuselage-mounted support frame fitted ready for conversion into a Mistel.

Two photographs taken from the opposite viewpoint which shows to advantage the 'stretched' fuselage of the Ju 88 G-10 W.Nr. 460065, and its recently installed Mistel support frame, Bernburg, April 1945.

Mistel S3C Fw 190 A-8, W.Nr. 961243/Ju 88 G-10 W.Nr. 460066, Bernburg, April 1945

(Pages 213 to 215)

Mistel S3C Fw 190 A-8, W.Nr. 961243/Ju 88 G-10 W.Nr. 460066, Bernburg, April 1945

Mistel S3C Fw 190 A-8/Ju 88 G-10, Bernburg, April 1945

(Pages 216 to 217)

Like so many Luftwaffe aircraft found by Allied forces all over Germany in 1945, this Mistel combination has been deliberately sabotaged.
The photo at right shows it before this was done. Note (below and opposite page) how the front support frame is pushed forwards and the struts are jammed up in the open undercarriage wells of the Fw 190. Also as a result of the sabotage, the rear of the Fw 190 has dropped down towards the fuselage of the Ju 88 so that the Focke-Wulf's tail wheel is almost touching the Junkers.

In the foreground a Ju 88 fitted with Jumo engines and support struts for a Mistel combination lies abandoned on a concrete runway having been sabotaged at an unidentified location in Germany. The Ju 88 in the distance also appears to have been deliberately sabotaged. An explosive device has been put just behind the trailing edge of the wing and the remaining fuselage has tipped onto its nose due to the force of the explosive.

Mistel S2 Fw 190 A-8/Ju 88 G/H-1, W.Nr. 714633 'Red 11', Schleswig, Winter 1945-1946

(Pages 218 lower photo to page 220)

A member of the RAF's No. 409 Repair and Salvage Unit smiles for the camera from the wing of Mistel S2 Fw 190 A-8/Ju 88 G/H-1, W.Nr. 714633 'Red 11', seen on the snow-covered airfield at Schleswig in the winter of 1945-1946.

Five views of Mistel S2 Fw 190 A-8/Ju 88 G/H-1, W.Nr. 714633 'Red 11', seen at Schleswig during the winter of 1945-46. Both components of the Mistel have been given a crude whitewash as winter camouflage and RAF roundels and tail markings have been applied.

The snow has melted and Mistel S2 Fw 190 A-8/ Ju 88 G/H-1, W.Nr. 714633 'Red 11', sits at Schleswig awaiting an uncertain fate in early 1946. The Ju 88 had been one of those allocated to take part in the 'Drachenhöhle' operation of February 1945.

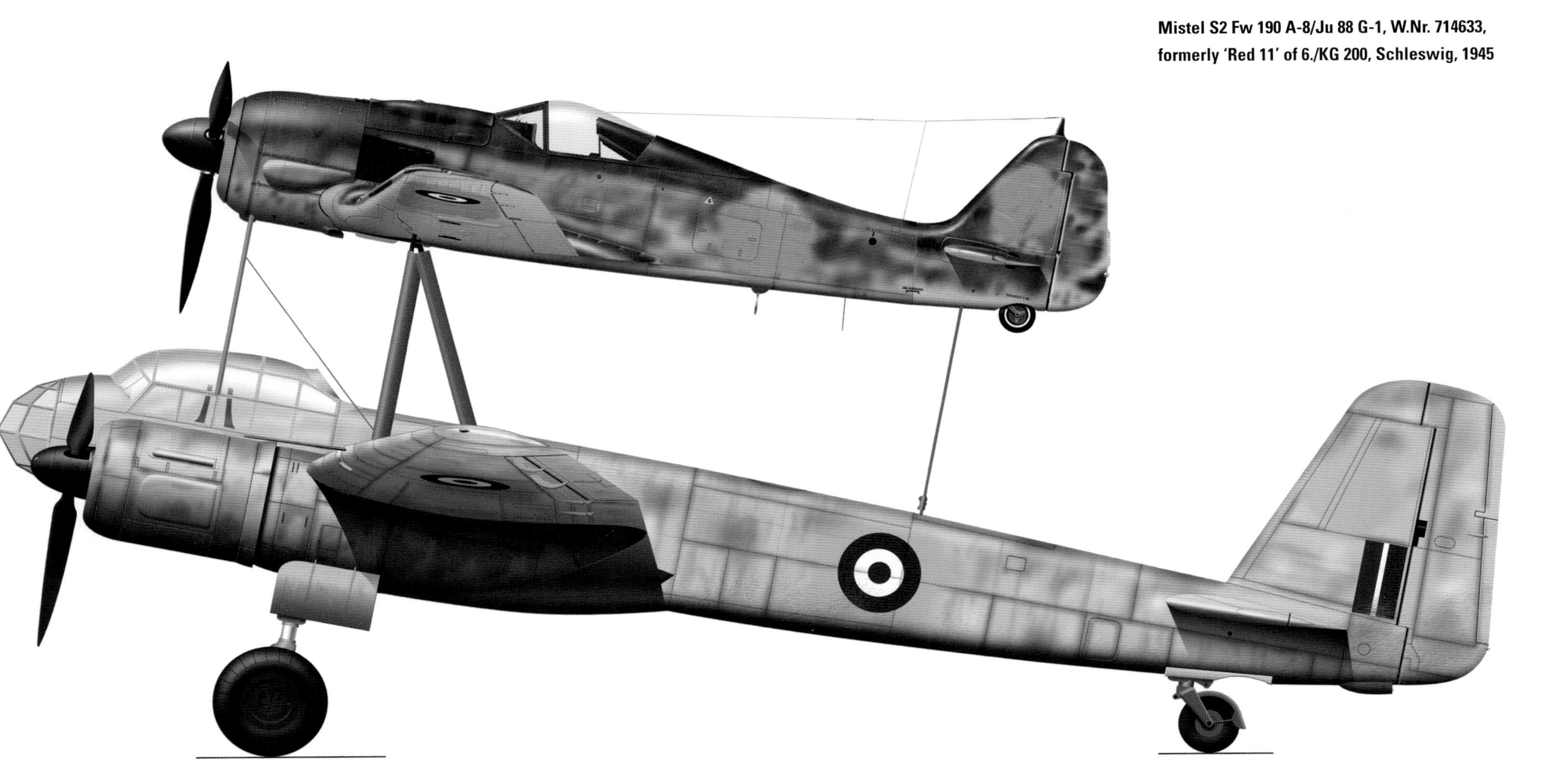

Mistel S2 Fw 190 A-8/Ju 88 G-1, W.Nr. 714633, formerly 'Red 11' of 6./KG 200, Schleswig, 1945

Mistel S3A Fw 190 W.Nr. 733759/Ju 88A W.Nr. 2942 (recoded Air Min 77), Royal Aircraft Establishment Farnborough, England, October 1945

Ju 88A, W.Nr. 2942, formerly from a Mistel of II./KG 200 found at Tirstrup in Denmark, was recoded 'Air Min 77' by the British and ferried to Schleswig, northern Germany on 30 July 1945. It was separated from its Fw 190 upper component at Schleswig and was subsequently flown to the Royal Aircraft Establishment at Farnborough on 21 September 1945 by F/L Taylor, where it was eventually 'reunited' with the Focke-Wulf. The last known whereabouts of the Ju 88 was the Farnborough 'scrap area' on 15 December 1946.

Mistel S3A Fw 190, W.Nr. 733759/Ju 88A, W.Nr. 2942 (recoded Air Min 77) seen at the 'German Aircraft Exhibition' at the Royal Aircraft Establishment at Farnborough in October 1945. It is unlikely that the curious British visitors would have been aware that this was probably one of the KG 200 aircraft intended for operations over Scapa Flow in February 1945!

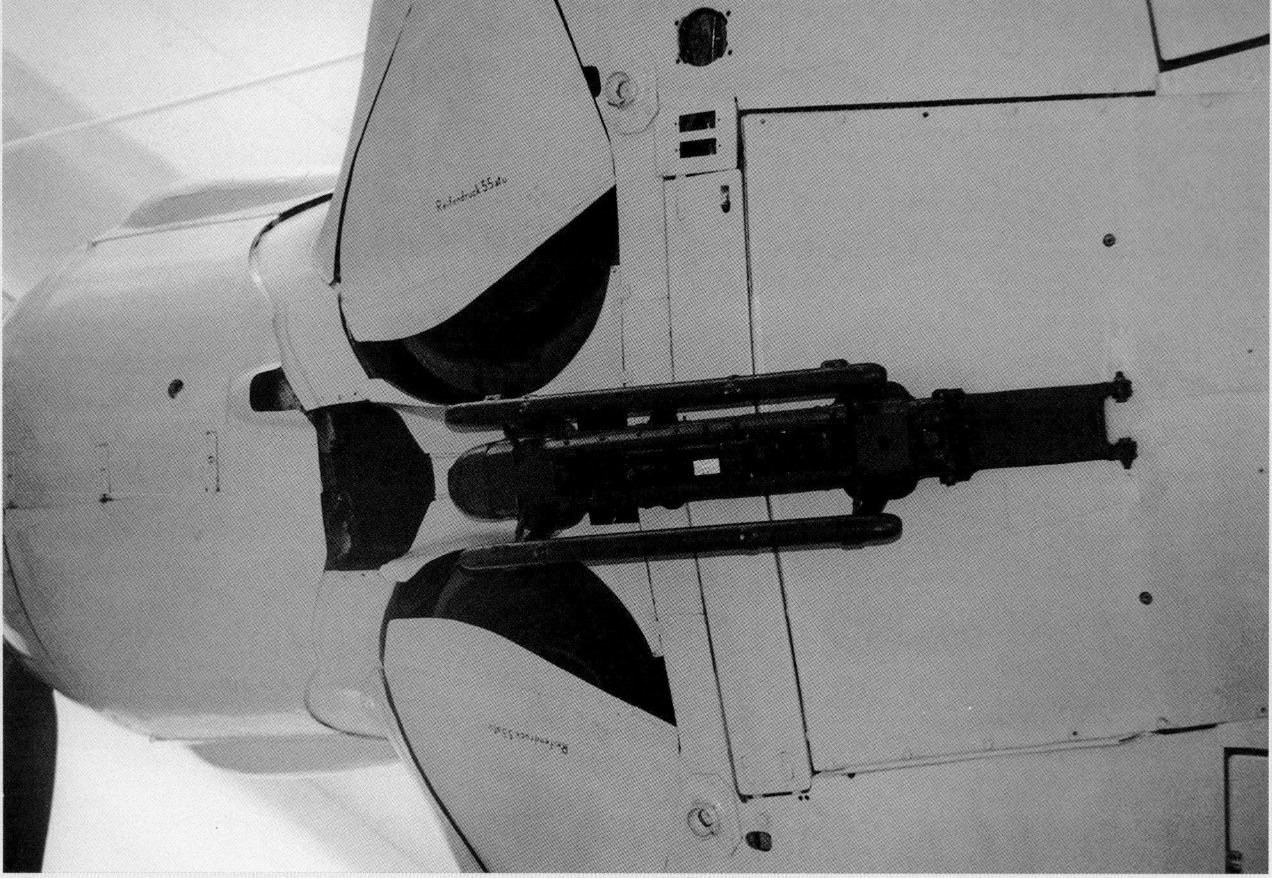

An underside view of the Fw 190 A-8 in the Imperial War Museum, London. This aircraft, W.Nr. 733682, originally formed the upper component of a Mistel S3 of II./KG 200 at Tirstrup, Denmark in 1945. The aircraft was ferried to the UK via Schleswig. The details of the underside modifications show the locating sockets for the mounting struts and cut-outs in the skin to allow the connecting services and fuel pipes to pass through. The left side gun ammunition bay door has been shortened to provide the space for most of the services to pass through, suggesting that the inner wing guns could not be fitted. The top cowl gun location was occupied by an extra oil tank giving long-range capability, leaving only the outer wing gun bays for armament.

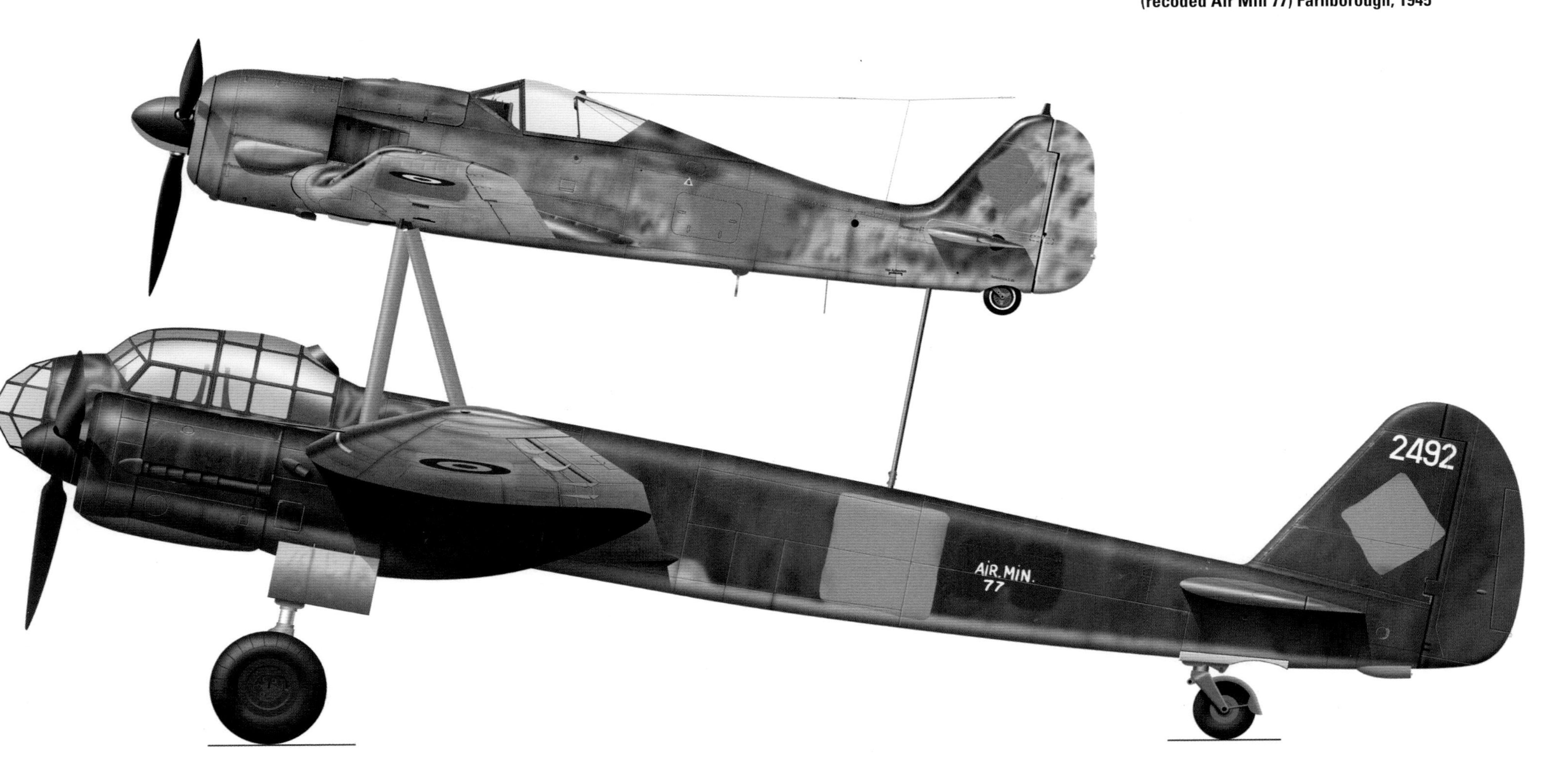

Mistel S3A Fw 190, W.Nr. 733759/Ju 88A, W.Nr. 2942
(recoded Air Min 77) Farnborough, 1945

Visitors to the 'German Aircraft Exhibition' at the Royal Aircraft Establishment in Farnborough inspect the Do 335 A-12, W.Nr. 240112, which had been brought to England from Oberpfaffenhofen in September 1945, whilst in the background, next to a Ju 52, Mistel S3A Fw 190, W.Nr. 733759/ Ju 88A, W.Nr. 2942 (recoded Air Min 77), towers above the other aircraft.

Charles Cain, reporter from '*The Aeroplane*' magazine, poses for a photograph in front of Mistel S3A Fw 190, W.Nr. 733759/Ju 88A, W.Nr. 2942 (recoded Air Min 77), at Farnborough in October 1945. The rear of this photograph is inscribed: 'Wet and windy – taken in front of the 'father and son' 'V' – or revenge weapon Junkers Ju 88 A6 missile and the Focke-Wulf Fw 190A parent plane, at the Royal Aircraft Establishment, Farnborough on Monday, October 29, 1945. Look of abject misery and appearance of total exhaustion is the result of six hours concentrated inspection of new British and German aircraft plus the thought of trying to describe the scene in one page of *The Aeroplane Spotter* which goes to press less than 24 hours hence!'

„Firmenschrift"

Geheim!

Mistel 2

Bedienungsvorschrift-Fl.

Teil I

Klarmachen zum Abflug
(Stand ~~Mai~~ Juli **1944**)

Ausgabe ~~Juni~~ August **1944**

Mistel 2 Instruction Manual
May-August 1944

The following pages are extracted from a facsimile of an original Junkers Bedienungsvorschrift (Operating Instruction Manual) for the Mistel 2, dated May-August 1944.

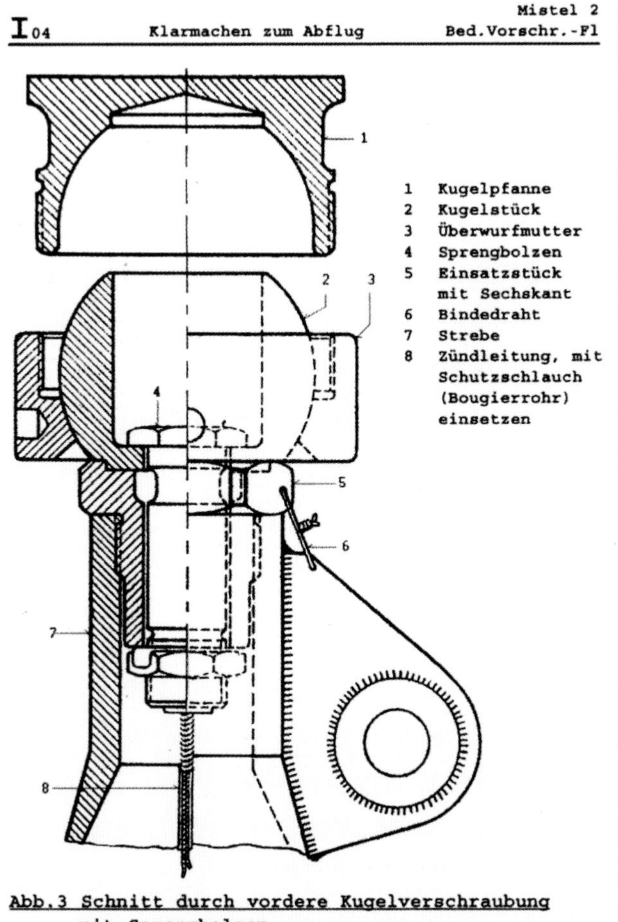

I 04 Klarmachen zum Abflug Mistel 2 Bed.Vorschr.-Fl

1 Kugelpfanne
2 Kugelstück
3 Überwurfmutter
4 Sprengbolzen
5 Einsatzstück mit Sechskant
6 Bindedraht
7 Strebe
8 Zündleitung, mit Schutzschlauch (Bougierrohr) einsetzen

Abb.3 Schnitt durch vordere Kugelverschraubung mit Sprengbolzen

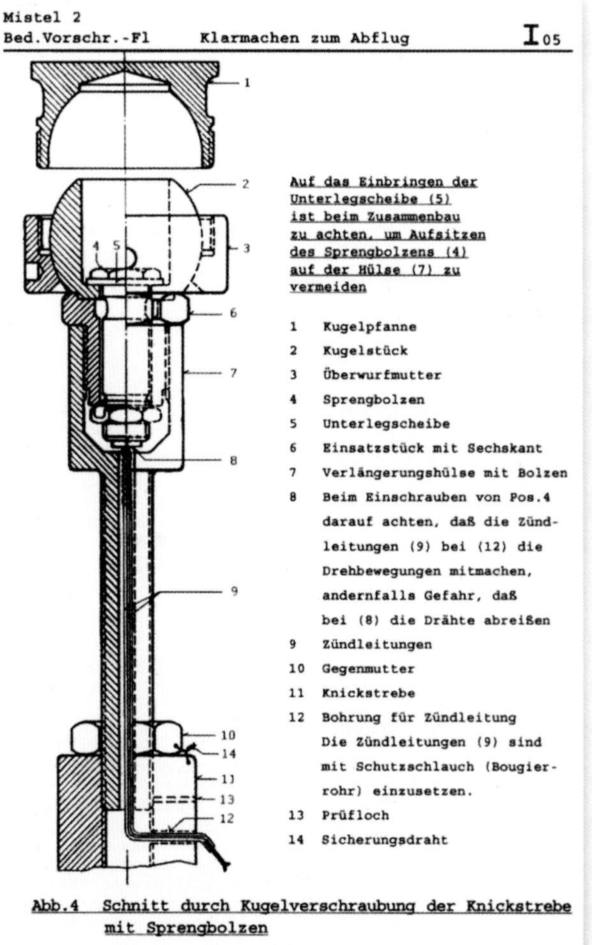

Mistel 2 Bed.Vorschr.-Fl Klarmachen zum Abflug I 05

Auf das Einbringen der Unterlegscheibe (5) ist beim Zusammenbau zu achten, um Aufsitzen des Sprengbolzens (4) auf der Hülse (7) zu vermeiden

1 Kugelpfanne
2 Kugelstück
3 Überwurfmutter
4 Sprengbolzen
5 Unterlegscheibe
6 Einsatzstück mit Sechskant
7 Verlängerungshülse mit Bolzen
8 Beim Einschrauben von Pos.4 darauf achten, daß die Zündleitungen (9) bei (12) die Drehbewegungen mitmachen, andernfalls Gefahr, daß bei (8) die Drähte abreißen
9 Zündleitungen
10 Gegenmutter
11 Knickstrebe
12 Bohrung für Zündleitung Die Zündleitungen (9) sind mit Schutzschlauch (Bougierrohr) einzusetzen.
13 Prüfloch
14 Sicherungsdraht

Abb.4 Schnitt durch Kugelverschraubung der Knickstrebe mit Sprengbolzen

I34 Klarmachen zum Abflug Mistel 2 Bed.Vorschr.-Fl

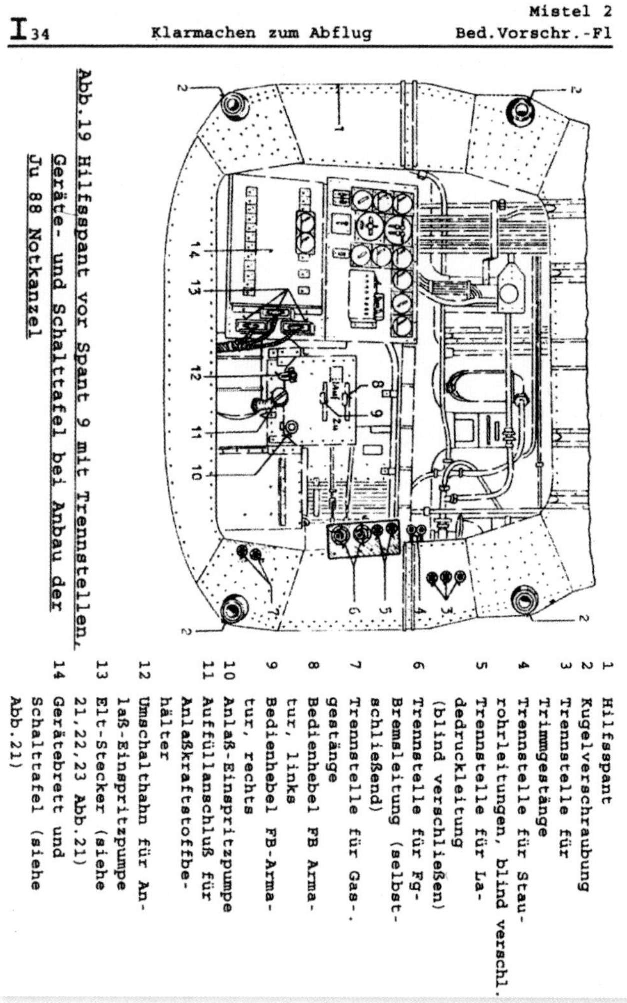

Mistel 2 Bed.Vorschr.-Fl Klarmachen zum Abflug I35

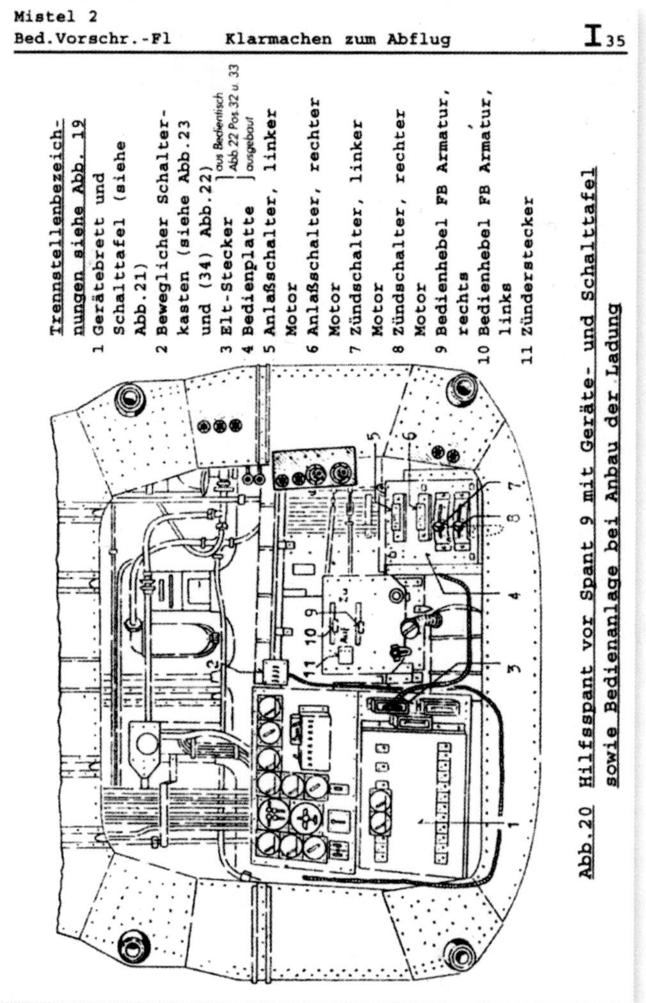

I36 Klarmachen zum Abflug Mistel 2 Bed.Vorschr.-Fl

Zahlenerklärung zu Abb.21: Gerätebrett und Elt-Schalttafel in Ju 88 A-4 vor Spant 9

1 Schmierstofftemperatur-Anzeigegerät, rechter Motor

2 Vierfachdruckmesser Kraftstoff - Schmierstoff

3 Schmierstofftemperatur-Anzeigegerät, linker Motor

4 Kraftstoff-Vorratsmesser

5 Meßstellenumschalter

6 Kraftstoff- und Schmierstoff-Vorratsmesser

7 Kühlstofftemperatur-Anzeigegerät, rechter Motor

8 Kühlstofftemperatur-Anzeigegerät, linker Motor

9 Betätigungsschalter für Kühlerklappen rechter Motor

10 Betätigungsschalter für Kühlerklappen linker Motor

11 Führertochter-Kompaß

12 Zündschalter für Ladung

13 Prüflampen für Zündstromkreisprüfung der Ladung

14 Kreiselüberwachungsschalter (zu Pos.11)

15 Kippschalter für Kennleuchten

16 Umpumpschalterkasten

17 Kippschalter für Kraftstofförderpumpen der Entnahmebehälter

18 Kippschalter für Kraftstoffumpumpen :
Schalter 1,2 und 8 nicht angeschlossen
Schalter 3: Vorderer Rumpfbehälter
Schalter 5: linker Tragflügel-Außenbehälter
Schalter 6: rechter Tragflügel-Außenbehälter

19 Amperemeter

20 Voltmeter

21 Stecker (rot) für Anlassen, Zündung, Brücke für LRg 12 bzw. Achsenschalter

22 Stecker (gelb) für Neunlampengerät, Drehzahlwahlschalter, Segelstellungsschalter links

23 Stecker (blau) für Wendezeiger, Netzausschalter, Drehzahlmesser, Segelstellung rechts, Fahrwerk, Horizonttochter

Mistel 2 Bed.Vorschr.-Fl Klarmachen zum Abflug I37

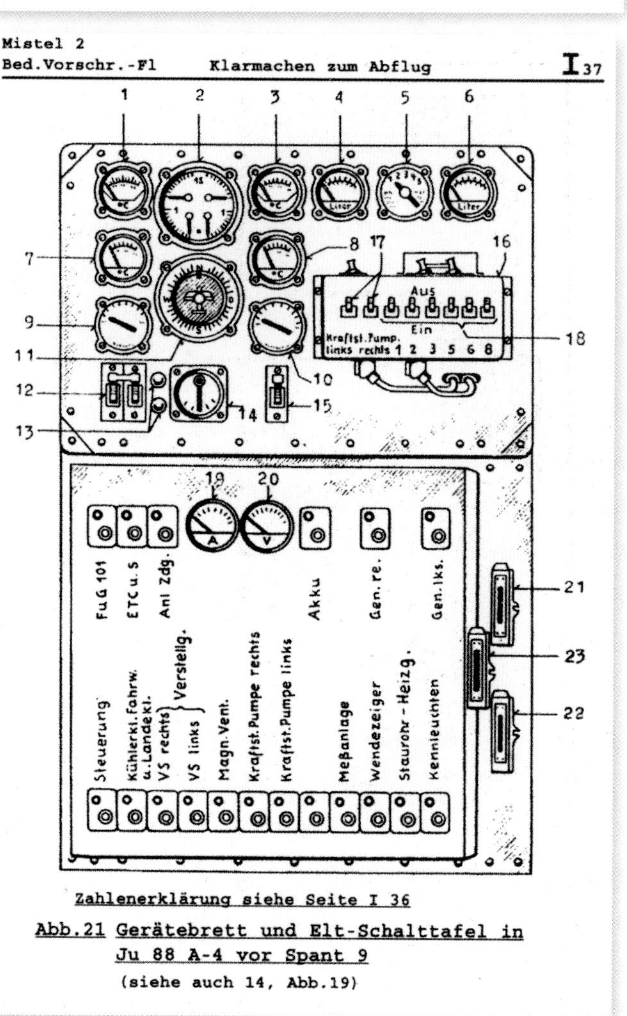

Zahlenerklärung siehe Seite I 36

Abb.21 Gerätebrett und Elt-Schalttafel in Ju 88 A-4 vor Spant 9
(siehe auch 14, Abb.19)

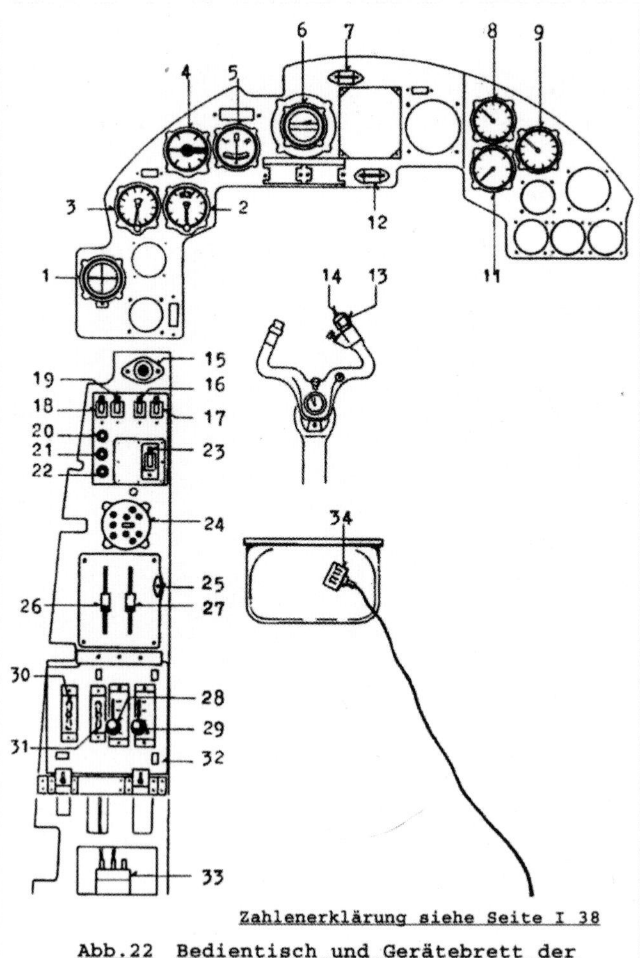

Zahlenerklärung siehe Seite I 38

Abb.22 Bedientisch und Gerätebrett der Ju 88 A-4 Notkanzel

I38 Klarmachen zum Abflug Mistel 2 Bed.Vorschr.-Fl

Zahlenerklärung zu Abb.22
Bedientisch und Gerätebrett der Ju 88 A-4 Notkanzel

1 Notkompaß
2 Fein - Grob-Höhenmesser
3 Fahrtmesser
4 Stauscheiben-Variometer
5 Wendezeiger
6 Horizonttochter
7 Schieber für Betriebsdatentafel
8 Ladedruckmesser, linker Motor
9 Ladedruckmesser, rechter Motor
10 Nummer ist frei
11 Drehzahlmesser
12 Schieber für Deviationstafel
13 Richtungsgeber LRg 12 (totgelegt)
14 Kuppelschalter
15 Netzausschalter
16 Drehzahlwahlschalter, links
17 Drehzahlwahlschalter, rechts
18 Segelstellungsschalter, links
19 Segelstellungsschalter, rechts
20 Druckknopfschalter Landeklappe und Höhenflosse "Ein"
21 Druckknopfschalter Landeklappe und Höhenflosse "Start"
22 Druckknopfschalter Landeklappe und Höhenflosse "Aus"
23 Kippschalter für Fahrwerk
24 Neunlampengerät
25 Hebelbremse
26 Drosselhebel, linker Motor
27 Drosselhebel, rechter Motor
28 Zündschalter, linker Motor
29 Zündschalter, rechter Motor
30 Anlaßschalter, linker Motor
31 Anlaßschalter, rechter Motor
32 Bedienplatte
33 Stecker (rot)
34 Beweglicher Schalterkasten

II08 Flugbetrieb Mistel 2 Bed.Vorschr.-Fl

6. Zielanflug — Wegen Sichtbeschränkung der Bf 109 ist das Ziel seitlich mit Steuerungsstellung "Reise" anzufliegen. Je nach taktischem Erfordernis in entsprechender Entfernung und Bahnneigung abkippen und Ziel mit Visier in Fadenkreuzmittel aufnehmen. Visierkreisen entfesseln (6, Abb.16 und 17). Erst nach deutlicher Auswanderung des Zieles solange nachsteuern nach Seite und Höhe (2 und 3, Abb.16 und 17), bis das Ziel in Fadenkreuzmitte ruhig liegt.

7. Absprengung — Prüfe, ob die Selbstschalter (2 und 3, Abb.14) für Sprengung gedrückt sind. Rote Lampe (7, Abb.15) am Gerätebrett der Bf 109 muß leuchten.

Nach Beendigung des Zielanfluges Höhenruder leicht ziehen, Kippschalter (9, Abb.15) für Absprengung neben roter Lampe entsichern und umlegen.

Absprengvorgang siehe Baubeschreibung.

Im Falle des Versagens der Absprengung, Höhenruder stark ziehen, um die erforderliche Anstellung der Bf 109 zu bekommen, da Knickstrebe nicht einknickt, Notabsprengschalter (8, Abb.15) entsichern und umlegen.

8. Landung — Landung mit Gespann erfolgt grundsätzlich von Ju 88 aus. Zu beachten ist, daß beim Ausfahren der Landeklappe auf Landestellung die Höhenflosse erst fährt, wenn Landeklappe voll angestellt ist.

Lastigkeitsänderungen wie bei Ju 88 A-4.

Zulässiges Höchstlandegewicht 13,5 t.

Landung mit Ladung ist grundsätzlich verboten.

Mistel 2 Bed.Vorschr.-Fl Wartung III05

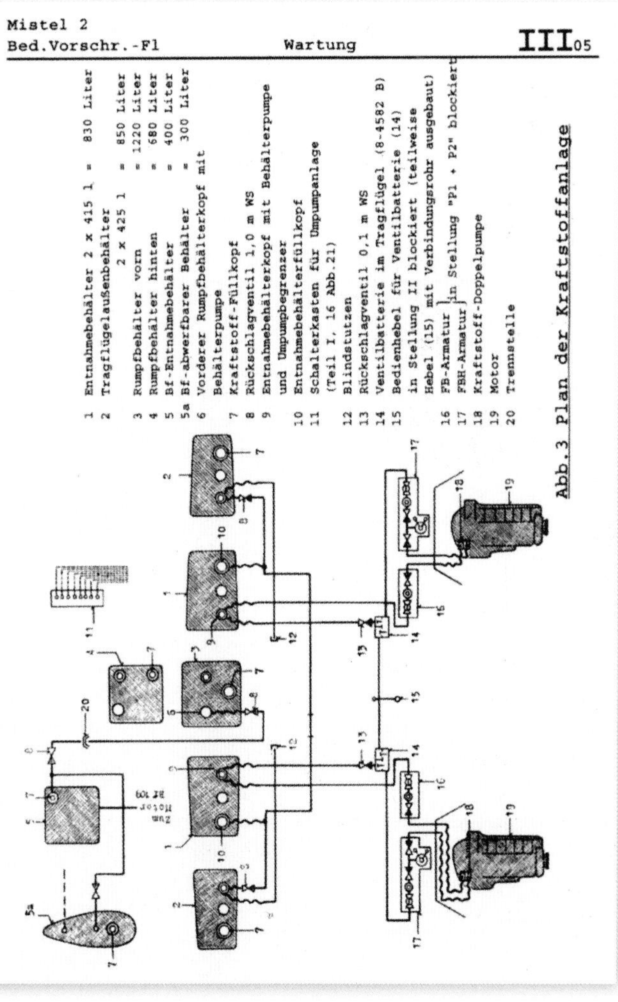

Abb.3 Plan der Kraftstoffanlage

Table of Ranks

The table below lists the wartime Luftwaffe ranks together with their equivalent in the Royal Air Force and the US Army Air Force:

Luftwaffe	Royal Air Force	U.S.A.A.F.
Generalfeldmarschall	Marshal of the RAF	Five Star General
Generaloberst	Air Chief Marshal	Four Star General
General der Flieger	Air Marshal	Lieutenant General
Generalleutnant	Air Vice Marshal	Major General
Generalmajor	Air Commodore	Brigadier General
Oberst	Group Captain	Colonel
Oberstleutnant	Wing Commander	Lieutenant Colonel
Major	Squadron Leader	Major
Hauptmann	Flight Lieutenant	Captain
Oberleutnant	Flying Officer	First Lieutenant
Leutnant	Pilot Officer	Lieutenant
Oberfähnrich	(leading cadet)	(leading cadet)
Fähnrich	(cadet)	(cadet)
Stabsfeldwebel	Warrant Officer	Warrant Officer
Oberfeldwebel	Flight Sergeant	Master Sergeant
Feldwebel	Sergeant	Technical Sergeant
Unterfeldwebel	–	–
Unteroffizier	Corporal	Staff Sergeant
Hauptgefreiter	–	Sergeant
Obergefreiter	Leading Aircraftman	Corporal
Gefreiter	Aircraftman First Class	Private First Class
Flieger	Aircraftman	Private

In addition, the Luftwaffe used the term '*Hauptfeldwebel*'. This was not a rank. A *Hauptfeldwebel* (colloquially called *'Spiess'*) was the NCO administrative head of a company or corresponding unit (*Staffel*, battery etc.). His rank could be anything from *Unteroffizier* to the various *Feldwebel*.

Glossary

Angriffsgruppe(n)	Attack group(s)
'Beethoven'	Project name for German composite development
Blindflugschule	Blind-flying school
Diplom-Ingenieur (Dipl.-Ing.)	Diploma Engineer – academic engineering title
Einsatzgruppe	Operational Group
Ergänzungstaffel	Operational Conversion/ Training Squadron
Erprobungsstelle	Test Centre
Fliegerausbildungsregiment	Flight Training Regiment
Fliegerführer	lit. Flight Leader (area command)
Fliegerkorps	Flying Corps
Flugkapitän	Flight Captain
Flugzeugführerschule	Pilot training school
Führungsstab	General Staff
Gefechtsverband	Air battle group
General der Kampfflieger	Commanding General of the Bomber Arm
Generalluftzeugmeister	Chief of aircraft procurement and supply
Gerät	Device
Grossbombe	Super bomb
Gruppe	Group
Gruppenkommandeur	Commander of a Gruppe
Huckepack	lit. 'Piggyback' – nickname for composite aircraft
Jagdgeschwader	Fighter Wing
Kampfgeschwader (KG)	Bomber Wing
Kampfgeschwader (J)	Former Bomber Wing converted to Fighters
Kommodore	Commander of a Wing
Luftflotte	Air Fleet
Mistel	lit. 'Mistletoe' – code name for composite aircraft
Mistelschlepp	Mistel method of 'towing' or carrying
Oberkommando der Luftwaffe (OKL)	Luftwaffe High Command
Reichsluftfahrtministerium	Reich Air Ministry
Reichsverteidigung	lit. Air Defence of the Reich
Ritterkreuz(träger)	Knights Cross (holder)
Schleppgestell	Towing frame
Schwere Hohlladung (SHL)	Heavy hollow charge
Sondereinsatz	Special operation
Staffel	Squadron
Staffelkapitän	Squadron Commander
Technischer Amt	Technical Office
Vater und Sohn	'Father and Son' – nickname for composite aircraft
Verbandsführerschule	Unit leaders' school
Wehrmacht	Germany Army
Zielfinder	Target illumination aircraft/'pathfinder'

Source Notes

Chapter One
UKNA/AIR 1/214 and AIR 1/215 - RNAS Felixstowe Daily Reports – May 1916

Chapter Two
Biographical Notes on Noel Pemberton Billing by P.Jarrett: Private – in author's collection

Chapter Three
UKNA/AIR8/321 "Composite Aircraft – Prime Minister's Questions"

Chapter Four
Start of Flying Machines (Hugo Junkers of Dessau, Germany): United States Patent Office, No. 1,703,488, Patented Feb.26, 1929
Volume III (S.Germany), Sheet No. 3, Airfield, Ainring, A.I.2(b) Report, Revised 24.2.1943
Private biographical notes on Fritz Stamer compiled by Stephen Ransom (unpublished, 20.4.1998)
DFS Anstaltsleitung – Zeugnis (Karl Schieferstein): Walter Georgii, DFS Ainring, 16.8.1945
Hermann Zitter – Lebenslauf & Anlage: Hermann Zitter, 29.8.1950 & 28.4.1986
Untersuchung des "Mistel-Schleppverfahrens" mit den Aggregaten DFS 230 & Kl 35 und DFS 230 & Fw 56 (Stösser): Fritz Stamer, Deutsche Forschungsanstalt für Segelflug Ernst Udet, Ainring, 22.10.1942
Untersuchung des "Mistel-Schleppverfahrens" mit den Aggregat DFS 230 & Bf 109 E: Fritz Stamer, Deutsche Forschungsanstalt für Segelflug Ernst Udet, Ainring, 8.1.1944

Chapter Five
Siegfried Holzbaur – Letter, 9.5.1986 (Private)
Biographical notes on Siegfried Holzbaur compiled by Dipl.-Ing. Karl Kössler
Was war Mistel?: Paper by Dr. Fritz Haber, undated (via Rose)
Untersuchungen über die Mistel-Anordnung Ju 88 A-4 – Bf 109 F: Deutsches Forschungsanstalt für Segelflug "Ernst Udet", 17.6.1943
Bericht über die Flugerprobung des Mistelgespann MI S 2 "Beethoven": Deutsches Forschungsanstalt für Segelflug "Ernst Udet", (Ziegler), 9.2.1944

GL/C-E 9/IV B, GL/C-Nr. 25580/43(E 9/IVB) g.Kdos., App.Nr.1545, gef.Kn.4.11.43, *Betr. Entwicklungsverhaben "Beethoven"*
OKL-FüSt.Ia/Flieg (Rob.) I.A. Nr. 11228/44, 2.6.1944 (via Rose)
Interrogation of Dipl.-Ing. E.A.Marquard (sic) by A.D.D., D.4.P., 27 March 1945, BIOS Interrogation Report No. 128, 5 September 1946
UKNA/AIR40/186 *German Composite Aircraft – Extract from N.A. Stockholm, 7.6.44*
The Capital Ship (C.S.) Bombs: Paper compiled by RAF Bomber Command (Intelligence Unit) D/Arm.D (via Carter)
A&AEE Report AEE/766 – Lancaster I R.5609 April/May 1943 (via Carter)
UKNA/AVIA18/909 A&AEE Report ATO/G.53 *5,000 lb C.S. Bomb*

Chapter Six
Beethoven-Gerät: Ausgesteuertes, unbemanntes Flugzeug für Totaleinsatz: Junkers document, undated
Luftwaffenführungstab Ia op, 16 April 1944, Studie über die Einsatzmöglichkeiten der Mistel
Luftwaffenführungstab Ia/T, 16 April 1944: Technische Unterlagen für Einsatz Mistel
Luftwaffenführungstab Ia. Nr. 9532/44, 16.4.1944: Studie mit technischer Anlage
UKNA/AIR16/689 – *Defence of Scapa Flow*
Die 1.(F)/120 von April 1940 bis heute: private paper by *Major a.D.* Hugo Löhr, 26.9.1991 (via Wadman)
The Mistel Scapa Flow Attack Plan: Unpublished paper by Dr. Alfred Price

Chapter Seven
Author's interview with Heinz Schreiber, Braunschweig, 22 February 1999
Heinz Schreiber Flugbuch No. 2 (via Schreiber)
Hans Altrogge Leistungsbuch (via Altrogge)
Correspondence author-Fred Gottgetreu, June-October 1998
Quarterly Review, Horst Rudat, 1976 as contained in *Mistel und Huckepack* – private paper by Alfred W. Krüger, 6 June 1997 (via Krüger)
Chef des Luftwaffenführungsstab Nr.4532/44, Tagesverlauf am 15/16.6.1944, 10. Ang. and 11. Ang, 15.6.1944 (via Irving)
Erfahrungsaustausch über Mistelanordnung bei Ifa in Dessau, 19.7.44 (Reisebericht Schöffel): Focke-Wulf Flugzeugbau GmbH, Bremen (via Ransom)*Die vorletzte Waffe*: *Dipl.-Ing.* Horst-Dieter Lux, *'Aus den Geheim archiven des zweiten Weltkrieges, aktuelle bilder zeitung*, Düsseldorf (undated)Account by Jack Dunn (Addendum No.1 to Combat Report 410/21, 14 June 1944) private unpublished (Dunn via Fochuk)
Form 'F' Pilot's Personal Combat Report, 410 (RCAF) Squadron, Serial 410/21, 14 June 1944 (Dunn via Fochuk)
Correspondence Les Gentry and Peter Meryon, formerly HMS *Nith*, to author, October/November 1999 and correspondence John Collins to author, April 2000
HMS Nith: Lt. P.J.Davey, unpublished manuscript, via Gentry
Ultra Decrypt XL 8673 (via Beale)
Ultra Decrypt T309/68 HP 366 (via Wadman)
Ultra Decrypt XL5718 (via Wadman)
UKNA/AIR16/2029: 83 Group Intelligence Summary re Composite Aircraft (via Pegg)
UKNA/AIR20/7704 Luftflotte 3 KTB
UKNA/AIR37/635 No 85 Group Intelligence Summaries 13-195 (1944)
UKNA/AIR40/186 Interpretation Report No. L.252: Composite Aircraft at Biblis and Nordhausen
UKNA/AIR40/2687: T229/97, T227/2 and T292/65
UKNA/AIR50/104 Personal Combat Reports – 264 Sqdn.
UKNA/ADM223/163 Admiralty Weekly Intelligence Summary No. 227 w/e 14.7.1944
UKNA/AIR40/701 Interpretation Report S.A.2421: Attack on St. Dizier airfield, 2.8.1944
UKNA/AIR40/717 Interpretation Report S.A.2598: Attack on St. Dizier airfield, 18.8.1944
UKNA/WO208/4134 CSDIC(UK) SRA 5510
Reported Attack on Convoy by German Composite Aircraft: AI2(g), 30.6.1944 (via Wadman)
Bomber Command Intelligence Digest No 4 – German Composite Aircraft, 3.7.1944 (via Wadman)
Liegeplätze und Stellenbesetzung KG 101 – private document via Carlsen

Chapter Eight
Interview Rudi Riedl – author, Bremen, 22.4.1998
Balduin Pauli Flugbuch (via Pauli/Riedl)
Karl Müller Flugbuch (via Riedl)
Heinz Schreiber Flugbuch (via Schreiber)
Was war Mistel?: Paper by Dr. Fritz Haber, undated (via Rose)
Ultra Intercepts HP 4667, 27.10.1944 and HP 4871, 28.10.1944 (Kitchens via van Heijkop)
ADI(K) No. 398/1945: *A Short History of KG 200*, 9 October 1945 (via Kitchens)
UKNA/AIR40/2426 *Interrogation of German and Italian Prisoners of War*, October 1945-February 1946
UKNA/AIR40/1460 (A.I.12/USSTAF/N.22) *OKL Intelligence Report No.22: The Ardennes offensive, December 1944: Plans, scope and inquest Lagebericht der Fachabteilung Fl.-E 2 (Nr. 16834/44), 21 Dezember 1944* (via Smith)
Bomber und Jäger zugleich: unpublished article by Dr. Balduin Pauli
Geoff Thomas unpublished draft/notes on Mistel and KG 200 (via Thomas)
Sonderverband Einhorn: Nick Beale (unpub.)

Chapter Nine
Interview Rudi Riedl – author, Bremen, 22.4.1998
Balduin Pauli correspondence with author (via Riedl and Teuber), 7.2.1999
Fritz Lorbach personal recollections, 9.5.1998 (via Riedl)
Karl Müller *Flugbuch* (via Riedl)
Lillian Howes correspondence with author and personal papers, 1998
John Waters correspondence with author, 3.11.1998, 17.11.1998, 29.11.1998, 29.12.1998
UKNA/AIR40/2687 T422/7 and T426/108
UKNA/AIR16/689 – *Defence of Scapa Flow*
UKNA/AIR34/280 – *Interpretation Report No.L.717 – German Composite Aircraft*, 7 March 1945
UKNA/AIR24/641, AIR24/642 and AIR24/643 – *Fighter Command ORB Appendices*
ADI(K) Reports No. 127/1944 and No. 29/1945 (via Wadman)
Beethoven-Gerät: Ausgesteuertes, unbemanntes Flugzeug für Totaleinsatz: Junkers document, undated
Luftwaffenführungstab Ia op, 16 April 1944, *Studie über die Einsatzmöglichkeiten der Mistel*
Luftwaffenführungstab Ia/T, 16 April 1944: *Technische Unterlagen für Einsatz Mistel*
Luftwaffenführungstab Ia. Nr. 9532/44, 16.4.1944: *Studie mit technischer Anlage*
Chef Lw. Fü.St. Nr.10514, 10.1.1945
Das Oberkommando der Luftwaffe Kriegstagbuch (1 Februar-7 April 1945) NARS/T-321 Roll 10 via Irving
Genst.Gen.Qu.6.Abt.Nr.1420/45 Aircraft losses 3.2.1945
Die 1.(F)/120 von April 1940 bis heute: private paper by Major a.D. Hugo Löhr, 26.9.1991 (via Wadman)
The Mistel Scapa Flow Attack Plan: Unpublished paper by Dr. Alfred Price
Sonderverband Einhorn: Nick Beale (unpub.)
The Story of "418" – The City of Edmonton Intruder Squadron, RCAF: 1945, via Wadman

Chapter Ten
Reminiscences of Fred Lew (via Riedl)
Rudi Riedl correspondence with author, May 1999
Interview– Karl Russmeyer, Alfeld, 24 February 1999
Correspondence and interview Hans Altrogge – Marcel van Heijkop, January 1999
Elektronische Zeitschrift: Volume 58, No. 39 30th September 1937 (via TU Berlin)

Studie: Kampf gegen die Russische Rüstungsindustrie (Plan for an Attack on the Russian Armament Industry): Special Document Section Report No. 125, 2.12.1947 (via Smith & Thomas)
Kr-g.Kdos.Chefs.-m.Anschr.Uberm., 6.11.1944 (via Kitchens), Chef der Generalstabes d.Lw. Nr. 10496/45, 7.1.1945 (via Kitchens), Chef der Generalstabes d.Lw. Nr. 10514/45, 10.1.1945 (via Smith), OKL FüSt Nr.19011/45, 14.1.1945 (via Kitchens), Chef der Generalstabes d.Lw. Nr. 10564/45, 18.1.1945 (via Kitchens), Chef der Generalstabes d.Lw. Nr. 10552/45, 23.1.1945 (via Kitchens), OKL FüSt Nr.10597/45, 14.2.1945 (via Smith), Chef der Generalstabes d.Lw. Nr. 10620/45, 24.2.1945 (via Kitchens), Chef der Generalstabes d.Lw. Nr. 10621/45, 24.2.1945 (via Kitchens), OKL FüSt Nr.19040/45, 21.2.1945 (via Smith), OKL FüSt Nr.19044/45, 21.2.1945 (via Kitchens), OKL FüSt Nr.190654/45, 18.3.1945 (via Smith), OKL FüSt Nr.10685/45, 30.3.1945 (via Smith)
Geschichte der 3.Staffel, Kampfgeschwader 30 1939-1945 (Wien, 1991)
Die Unternehmen "Eisenhammer", Weichselbrücken und Brückenbekämpfung "Oder". Das Kampfgeschwader 30 von Oktober 1944 bis zum 7. Mai 1945 (Ein Beitrag zur Geschichte des KG 30). Zusammengestellt von H. Frommhold (unpub. paper via Frommhold)
Kurzer Abriß der Technischen und Taktischen Einsatzgrundlagen der I./KG 66 (Zielfindergruppe West) in verschiedenen Kriegsphasen – Hans Hebestreit, 1979 (via van Heijkop)
UKNA/AIR40/2423 *Interrogation of German and Italian Prisoners of War*, July-August 1945 (ADI(K) No. 358/1945)
UKNA/AIR40/1486 *KG 200 Monkey Business Part 1 – II./KG 200 and Mistel* (3A Summary No. 41)
The Collapse viewed from Within – The Memoirs of General Koller, the German Chief of Air Staff: ADI(K) Report No.348/1945 (via IWM)

Chapter Eleven

Expendable Aircraft – German Intentions (A.I.3B, 27 February 1945 via Smith)
UKNA/AIR8/838 *Use of War Weary US Bombers* (War Cabinet Chiefs of Staff Committee and Appendices COS(44) 1016(0), 5.12.1944, COS(W) 579, 15.1945, COS(45) 81 (0) 25.1.1945 and COS(45) 246 (O) 10.4.1945, Prime Minister from President Roosevelt No.T.362/5, No.728 29.3.1945, Prime Minister to President Truman No.T.472/5, No.2 14.4.1945, President Truman to Prime Minister No.T.500/5 No.5, 17.4.1945.)
UKNA/PREM3/111A *Crossbow – Post Attack June 1944-May 1945* (Records of Prime Minister's Office)

Chapter Twelve

'Ju 90 mit angehaengten Flugzeugen Me 109': Junkers Schnellbericht (Molthan), Dessau, 26 June 1939 (via Ransom)
Index of Junkers Wind Tunnel Test Reports: US Naval Technical Mission in Europe, October 1945, Technical Report No. 437-45 (via Ransom)
Untersuchungen über Startmöglichkeiten 8-328 "Mistel-Schlepp" 8-328 auf Do 217: Kracht, DFS 'Ernst Udet', Ainring, 7.12.1942 (via Rose)
Kurzbeschreibung: Mistel Ta 154 A-Fw 190 A-8 "Beethoven": Focke-Wulf Flugzeugbau GmbH, Bremen, 14.7.44 (via Creek)
262. Misteleinsatz: Pr/Mtz/Sto, Oberammergau, 28.11.44 (via Creek)
Aktennotiz über Besprechungen im RLM am 4 und 5.9.1944 (7. September 1944) (via Creek)
References to Mistel Composite Aircraft contained in Chef TLR documents: private notes compiled by Mike Norton, undated (via Norton)

Chapter Thirteen

Reminiscences of Alfred Hansen (via Riedl)
Reminiscences of Toni Grögel (via Riedl)
Reminiscences of Fred Lew (via Riedl)
Reminiscences of Fritz Lorbach (via Riedl)
Reminiscences of Herbert Kuntz (via Krüger)
Reminiscences of Carl-Ernst Mengel (via Riedl)
Rudi Riedl interviews and correspondence with author
Interview– Karl Russmeyer, Alfeld, 24 February 1999
Interview– Heinz Frommhold, Bernried, 12 September 2000
Interview– Karl-Heinz Wiesner, Bernried, 12 September 2000
Correspondence and interview Hans Altrogge – Marcel van Heijkop, January 1999
Karl Russmeyer Flugbuch (via Russmeyer)
Leistungsbuch Hans Altrogge (14.4.1943-1945) via Altrogge
Leistungsbuch Leonhard Haussler (via van Heijkop)
Reminiscences of Helmut Reinert (via Wadman)
Die Unternehmen "Eisenhammer", Weichselbrücken und Brückenbekämpfung "Oder". Das Kampfgeschwader 30 von Oktober 1944 bis zum 7. Mai 1945 (Ein Beitrag zur Geschichte des KG 30). *Zusammengestellt von H. Frommhold (unpub. paper via Frommhold)*
Geschichte der 3.Staffel, Kampfgeschwader 30 1939-1945 *(Wien, 1991)*
Treffpunkt Straussberg 2000 m: *private article by Rudi Riedl, undated (via Riedl)*
Ein Einsatz mit Hindernissen: *private article by Karl-Ernst Fara, undated (via van Heijkop)*
Kurzer Abriss der Technischen und Taktischen Einsatzgrundlagen der I./KG 66 (Zielfindergruppe West) in verschiedenen Kriegsphasen – *Hans Hebestreit, 1979 (via van Heijkop)*

Selected documents:

OKL/Gen.Qu.6.Abt. Flugzeugunfälle und Verluuste bei den fliegenden Verbänden, Lfl.kdo 6. Führ.Abt. Nr. 1865/45 (Der Führer Br.301/45), 1.3.45, Kampfgeschwader 200 Br.B.Nr.1713/45, 1.3.45, Lfl.kdo 6. Nr.122, 1.3.45, Lw.Füst.Ia. Nr.1350/45, 2.3.45, Lfl.kdo 6. Führ.Abt.I Nr.3224/45 3.3.45, Lfl.kdo 6. Führ.Abt.I/Ic. Nr.2710/45, 4.3.45, OKL Füst, Nr. 19050/45, 5.3.45, Brückenbevollmächtiger Baumbach Brückenkämpfungsvorhaben, 5.3.45, Organisationsvorschlag gleichzeitig Befehlsentwurf (Helbig), 5.3.45, OKL Lw.Org.St Nr.1030/45, 10.3.45, Lfl. 6 Nr.85/45, 6.3.45, OKL Füst. Nr.20342/45, 6.3.45, Gef.Verband Helbig Erfolgsmeldung, 6.3.45, Lfl.kdo 6 Führ.Abt. Nr. 3390/45, 7.3.45, Einsatzbefehl Lfl.kdo 6 Nr. 134, 8.3.45, Lfl.kdo 6 Führ Abt.I/Ia, Nr.3055/45, , Gef.Verband Helbig Erfolgsmeldung, 8.3.45, Lfl.kdo 6 Führ Abt.I Nr.3541/45, Eisatzbefehl Lfl.kdo 6 Nr. 140 für den 11.3.45, Lfl.kdo.6, Chef 4, Nr,119/45, 12.3.45, Bevollmächtiger für Brückenkämpfung, 12.3.45, Reichsführer-SS, Ia 73 3057/45, 13.3.45, Bevollmächtiger für Brückenkämpfung Ia Nr. 0210/45, 23.3.45, OKL Füst. Nr.10676/45, 26.3.45, Lfl.kdo 6 I Nr. 2482/45, 30.3.45, Lfl.kdo 6 Führ Abt. I Br.B.Nr. 2548/45, 4.4.45, Lfl.kdo 6 Führ Abt. I, Nr. 2675/45, 8.4.45, Lfl.kdo 6 Führ Abt. I Nr.5453/45, 9.4.45, Lfl.kdo 6 Führ Abt. I, Nr. 2725/45, 10.4.45, Gefechtsverband Helbig Nr. 0285/45, 10.4.45, Lfl.kdo 6 Führ Abt. I Nr.2860/45, 17.4.45.
BA-MA, RL 21/5 Fl.H.K. Bernburg (via Carlsen)
UKNA/DEFE3/570/KO714
UKNA/AIR40/186, AIR 40/841
Gordon and Bazett, 411 Sqn. RCAF Combat Reports (via Fochuk)

Bibliography

(Airlines of the World – Lufthansa) Across the Atlantic – Mail Operations 1930-39: File 713, Sheet 09, World Aircraft Fact Files, Aerospace, London, 1997
Aus den Geheim Archiven des Zweiten Weltkrieges – Die vorletzte Waffe: Dipl.-Ing. Horst-Dieter Lux (aktuelle bilder zeitung, Düsseldorf)
Flugsport, XXVII, Heft 18, 4.9.1935
Flugsport, XXVIII, Heft 5, 4.3.1936
Mistelschlepp: Article by Fritz Stamer in *Der Flieger* (date unknown)
Vom Mistelstart zum Sänger-Projeckt: Aerokurier, 9/1986
Der Propeller – Werkzeitung der Junkers Flugzeug- und Motorenwerke AG, Heft 9/12 Sept.-Dez. 1943 (Private)
50 Jahre Turbostrahlflug: Deutsche Gesellschaft für Luft- und Raumfahrt e.V. – DGLR-Symposium am 26. Und 27. Oktober 1989 (via Ransom)
Das war keine 'Wunderwaffe' – Ein Jäger flog den Sprengstoff-Bomber: Dr Balduin Pauli, *Jägerblatt*, 1984
Fliegerführer 200: J.Richard Smith, *Archiv* (Gruppe 66: International Society of German Aviation Historians), No. 3, Autumn 1966
Mistel im Einsatz – Ein Bericht von Hans Lächler: *Flugzeug*, Nr. 6 Dezember 1988/Januar 1989, Flugzeug Publikations, Illertissen
Hitlerjunge Baumbach – Ritterkreuzträger Baumbach:, Signal Magazine
Beethoven Gerat Bf 109 F-4 & Ju 88 A-4: *'Il Notizario'* (Journal of IPMS Italy, 1982, Vol. 13, No. 2) and Aldo Zanfi (1980)

Daimler-Benz Air-launched Bombers: Hugh W. Cowin, Air Pictorial, June 1981
Startverfahren für Schnellstflugzeuge (Patentschau): Flugwelt 1955, Heft 12
Unbekannte Focke-Wulf-Projekte (II) – Projeckt eines Schnellbombenträgers für 30t Nutzlast: aerokurier, 9/1964
Grey, C.G: *On the Mayo Composite Aircraft, The Aeroplane*, 16 February 1938
Short-Mayo - The Composite Aircraft Described in Detail: *Flight*, 17 February 1938
Jarret, Philip: *PB's Dream Machines,* Air Enthusiast 51 (1993? date not known – via S. Ransom)
Jarret, Philip: *The Incredible Pemberton Billing*, Aircraft 'SixtyNine
A Day to Remember: FlyPast Magazine, March 1991 (via Fochuk)
Das Huckepack Flugzeug wird 50 Jahre alt!: Luftfahrt International, No.23, October 1977
The Hugo Junkers Biography: Horst Zoeller/The Hugo Junkers Home Page, http://ourworld.compuserve.com/homepage/hzoe/ju_bibl.htm
The Times Atlas of the Second World War: Ed. John Keegan, Times Books, London 1989
The Rise and Fall of the German Air Force 1933-1945: (HMSO) Arms and Armour Press Ltd, Poole, 1983
Warfare in the Third Reich – The Rise and Fall of Hitler's Armed Forces: ed. Christopher Chant, Smithmark Publishers, New York, 1996
Aders, Gebhard: *History of the German Night Fighter Force 1917-1945*, Janes Publishing Company, London, 1979
Barnes, C.H.: *Shorts Aircraft Since 1900*, Putnam, London, 1967
Barrymore Halpenny, Bruce: *Fight for the Sky – True Stories of Wartime Fighter Pilots*:, Patrick Stephens, Wellingborough, 1986
Bartz, Karl: *Swastika in the Air – The Struggle and Defeat of the German Air Force 1939-1945*, William Kimber, London, 1956
Baumbach, Werner: *Broken Swastika – The Defeat of the Luftwaffe*, Robert Hale, London, 1986
Beauvais, Heinrich; Kössler, Karl; Mayer, Max; Regel, Christoph: *Die Deutsche Luftfahrt: Flugerprobungsstellen bis 1945,* Bernard & Graefe Verlag, Bonn, 1998
Bennett, Air Vice-Marshal D.C.T.: *Pathfinder,* Frederick Muller Ltd, London, 1958
Bruce, J.M.: *British Aeroplanes 1914-18*, Putnam, London, 1957
Brütting, Georg: *Das Buch der Deutschen Fluggeschichte – Band 3*, Drei Brunnen Verlag, Stuttgart, 1979
Brütting, Georg: Das waren die deutschen Kampfflieger-Asse 1939-1945, Motorbuch Verlag, Stuttgart, 1975
Chuikov, Vasili I.: *The End of the Third Reich*, MacGibbon and Kee, London, 1967
Churchill Winston S.: The Second World War, Volume III, The Grand Alliance, (Cassell & Co, London, 1950)
Conyers Nesbit, Roy: *An Illustrated History of the RAF*, Colour Library Books, Godalming, 1990
Cooper, Matthew: *The German Air Force 1933-1945 – An Anatomy of Failure*, Janes Publishing Co. Ltd, London, 1981
Corum, James S. and Muller, Richard: *The Luftwaffe's Way of War – German Air Force Doctrine 1911-1945*, The Nautical and Aviation Publishing Company of America, Baltimore, 1998
Craig, William: *Enemy at the Gates – The Battle for Stalingrad*, BCA, London, 1973
Dabrowski, Hans-Peter: *Mistel: The Piggy-Back Aircraft of the Luftwaffe*, Schiffer Publishing, Atglen, PA, 1994
Dierich, Wolfgang: *Die Verbände der Luftwaffe 1935-1945 – Gliederungen und Kurzchroniken Ein Dokument,* Verlag Heinz Nickel, Zweibrücken, 1993
Dierich, Wolfgang: *Kampfgeschwader 55 'Greif' – Eine Chronik aus Dokumenten und Berichten 1937-1945*, Motorbuch Verlag, Stuttgart, 1994
Dressel, Joachim & Griehl, Manfred: *Die Deutschen Raketenflugzeuge 1935-1945*, Motorbuch Verlag, Stuttgart, 1989
Duffy, Christopher: *Red Storm on the Reich – The Soviet March on Germany, 1945*, Atheneum, New York, 1991
Erickson, John: *The Road to Berlin*, Weidenfeld and Nicolson, London, 1983
Essame, Major General H.: *Normandy Bridgehead*:, Macdonald & Co, London, 1971
D'Este, Carlo: *Decision in Normandy – The Unwritten Story of Montgomery and the Allied Campaign*:, Collins, London 1983
Ethell, Jeffrey L.: *Komet – The Messerschmitt 163*, Sky Books Press, New York, 1978
Filley, Brian: *Junkers Ju 88 in action – Part 1*, Squadron/Signal Publications Inc, Carrollton, 1988
Foreman, John: *1944 – The Air War over Europe June 1st-30th: Over the Beaches*:, Air Research Publications, Walton-on-Thames, 1994
Freeman, Roger A.: *The Mighty Eighth War Diary*, Janes Publishing, London, 1981
Gellermann, Günther W.: *Moskau ruft Heeresgruppe Mitte: Was nicht im Wehrmachtbericht stand – Die Einsätze des geheimen Kampfgeschwaders 200 im Zweiten Weltkrieg*, Bernard & Graefe Verlag, Koblenz, 1988
Gilbert, Martin: *Second World War*, Weidenfeld and Nicolson, London, 1989
Goodall, Michael H.: *The Norman Thompson File*, Air Britain (Historians) Ltd, Tunbridge Wells, 1995
Gray, John M.: *The 55th Fighter Group vs The Luftwaffe*, Specialty Press, North Branch, 1998
William, Green: *Warplanes of the Third Reich*:, Macdonald & Janes, London 1979
Griehl, Manfred: *Junkers Ju 88 – Star of the Luftwaffe*, Arms and Armour Press, London, 1990
Griehl, Manfred and Dressel, Joachim: *Zeppelin! The German Airship Story*, Arms & Armour Press, London, 1990
Griehl, Manfred and Dressel, Joachim: *Heinkel He 177-277-274 – Ein luftfahrtgeschichtliche Dokumentation*, Motorbuch Verlag, Stuttgart, 1989
Hardesty, Von: *Red Phoenix – The Rise of Soviet Air Power 1941-1945*, Smithsonian Institution Press, Washington DC, 1982
Hastings, Max: *Bomber Command*, Michael Joseph, London 1979
Hayward, Joel S.A.: *Stopped at Stalingrad – The Luftwaffe and Hitler's Defeat in the East, 1942-1943*, University Press of Kansas, Lawrence, Kansas, 1998
Held, Werner; Trautloft, Hannes; Bob, Ekkehard: *JG 54 – A Photographic History of the Grunherzjäger,* Schiffer Military History, Atglen, 1994
Heinkel, Ernst: *He 1000*, Hutchinson, London 1956
Hess, William N.: *Zemke's Wolfpack – The 56th Fighter Group in World War II*
Hewison, W.S.: *Scapa Flow in War and Peace*, Bellavista Publications, Kirkwall, 1995
Hinchcliffe, Peter: *The Other Battle – Luftwaffe Night Aces versus Bomber Command*, Airlife, Shrewsbury, 1996
Hinsley, F.H.: *British Intelligence in the Second World War, Volume 3 Part 2*:, HMSO, London 1988
Hooton, E.R.: *Phoenix Triumphant – The Rise and Rise of the Luftwaffe*, Arms and Armour Press, London, 1997
Hooton, E.R.: *Eagle in Flames – The Fall of the Luftwaffe*, Arms and Armour Press, London, 1997
Hozzel, Paul-Werner: *Recollections and Experiences of a Stuka Pilot 1931-1945*, (Private Publication), 1978
Irving, David: *Göring – A Biography,* MacMillan, London, 1989
Irving, David: *The Rise and Fall of the Luftwaffe - The Life of Erhard Milch,* Weidenfeld & Nicolson, London, 1973
Kahn, David: *Hitler's Spies – German Military Intelligence in World War Two*, Hodder and Stoughton, London, 1978
Kens, Karl Heinz & Nowarra Heinz J.: *Die Deutschen Flugzeuge 1933-1945*, J.F. Lehmann Verlag, München, 1961
Ketley, Barry & Rolfe, Mark: *Luftwaffe Fledglings 1935-1945 – Luftwaffe Training Units & their Aircraft*, Hikoki Publications, Aldershot, 1996
Kracheel, Kurt: *Flugführungssysteme – Blindfluginstrumente, Autopiloten, Flugsteuerungen*, Bernard & Graefe Verlag, Bonn, 1993
Kuhn, Volkmar: *German Paratroops in World War II*, Ian Allan, Shepperton, 1974
Lewin, Ronald: *Ultra Goes to War,* Grafton, London 1988
Lucas, James: Storming Eagles – German Airborne Forces in World War Two, Arms and Armour, London, 1988.

MacDonald, Charles B.: *The Battle of the Bulge*, Guild Publications, London, 1984
Molloy-Mason, Herbert: *The Rise of the Luftwaffe 1918-1949*, Cassell, London 1973
Maynard, John: *Bennet and the Pathfinders*, Arms and Armour, London, 1996
Middlebrook, Martin & Everitt, Chris: *The Bomber Command War Diaries – An Operational Reference Book: 1939-1945,* Penguin Books, Middlesex 1985
Mowthorpe, Ces: *Battlebags – British Airships of the First World War*, Wrens Park Publishing, Stroud, 1995
Mrazek, James E.: *Prelude to Dunkirk – The Fall of Eben Emael*, Robert Hale & Co., London, 1972
Muller, Richard: *The German Air War in Russia*, The Nautical and Aviation Publishing Company of America, Baltimore, 1992
Myhra, David: *Secret Aircraft Designs of the Third Reich*, Schiffer Publishing, Atglen, PA, 1998
Neitzel, Sonke: *Der Einsatz der deutschen Luftwaffe über dem Atlantik und der Nordsee 1939-1945*, Bernard & Graefe Verlag, Bonn, 1995
Overy R.J.: *The Air War 1939-1945*, Stein & Day, New York, 1981
Pegg, Martin: *Luftwaffe Ground Attack Units 1939-45*, Osprey Publishing, London, 1977
Penrose, Harald: *British Aviation – The Pioneer Years 1903-1914*, Putnam, London, 1967
plauen e.o.: *Leben und Schaffen 1903-1944 (Sonderausgabe):* Sudverlag, Konstanz, 1993
Plocher, *Generalleutnant* Hermann: *The German Air Force versus Russia*, USAF Historical Division, Aerospace Studies Institute, Air University, Arno Press, New York, June 1966
Poolman, Kenneth: *Focke-Wulf Condor – Scourge of the Atlantic,* Macdonald & Janes, London 1978
Price, Alfred: German Air Force Bombers of World War Two, Volume One, Hylton Lacy, Chalfont St Giles, 1968
Price, Alfred: Focke-Wulf 190 at War, Ian Allan Ltd, Shepperton, 1977
Prien, Jochen and Rodeike, Peter: *Jagdgeschwader 1 und 11 – Teil 3: 1944-1945*, Struve-Druck, Eutin, undated
Read, Anthony & Fisher, David: The Fall of Berlin, Hutchinson, 1992
Rose, Arno: Mistel: Die Geschichte der Huckepack-Flugzeuge, Motorbuch Verlag, Stuttgart, 1981
Sharp, C. Martin & Bowyer, Michael J.F.: *Mosquito*, Faber and Faber, London, 1971
Shores, Christopher F.: *Pictorial History of the Mediterranean Air War – Volume 1*, Ian Allan Ltd, Shepperton, 1972
Smith, J.R. & Kay Antony L.: *German Aircraft of the Second World War*, Putnam, London, 1989
Smith, J.Richard: *Focke-Wulf – An Aircraft Album:*, Ian Allan, Shepperton, 1973
Smith, J.Richard: *The Focke-Wulf Fw 200* (Profile 99), Profile Publications, Windsor, July 1971
Smith, J.Richard & Creek, Eddie J.: *Arado 234 Blitz*, Monogram Aviation Publications, Sturbridge, 1992
Smith, J.Richard & Creek, Eddie J.: *Me 262 Volume One*, Classic Publications, Burgess Hill, 1998
Smith, J.Richard & Creek, Eddie J.: *Me 262 Volume Two*, Classic Publications, Burgess Hill, 1998
Smith, Peter L.: *The Naval Wrecks of Scapa Flow*, The Orkney Press, Kirkwall, 1989
Späte, Wolfgang: *Test Pilots*, Independent Books, Bromley (undated)
Speer, Albert: *Inside the Third Reich*, Weidenfeld and Nicolson, London 1970
Spenser, Jay P.: *Monogram Close-Up 22: Moskito*, Monogram Publications, Boylston, 1983
Stahl, P.W.: *KG 200 – The True Story*, Janes Publishing, London, 1981
Steel, Nigel & Hart, Peter: *Tumult in the Clouds – The British Experience of the War in the Air, 1914-1918*, Hodder & Stoughton, London, 1997
Stüwe, Botho: *Peenemünde West – Der Erprobungsstelle der Luftwaffe für geheime Fernlenkwaffen und deren Entwicklungsgeschichte*, Bechtermünz Verlag, Augsburg, 1998
Stewart, P.A.E.: *Airborne Aircraft Carriers*, published in *The Aeronautical Journal*, Royal Aeronautical Society, June 1973
Suchenwirth, Richard: *The Development of the German Air Force 1919-1939*, Arno Press, New York, 1970
Tapper, Oliver: *Armstrong Whitworth Aircraft Since 1913,* Putnam, London, 1973
Taylor H.A.: *Fairey Aircraft Since 1915,* Putnam, London, 1974
Terraine, John: *The Right of the Line: The Royal Air Force in the European War 1939-1945*, Hodder & Stoughton, London, 1985
le Tissier, Tony: *Zhukov at the Oder – The Decisive Battle for Berlin*, Praeger Publishers, Westport, 1996
Turner, John & Nowarra Heinz J.: *Junkers - An Aircraft Album*, P.St. Ian Allan, London, 1971
Whitehouse, Arch: *The Zeppelin Fighters*, Robert Hale, London, 1968
Whiting, Charles: *Battle of the Ruhr Pocket,* Pan Books, London, 1970
Wiesinger, Günter / Schroeder, Walter: *Die Österreichischen Ritterkreuzträger in der Luftwaffe 1939-1945*, Herbert Weishaupt Verlag, Graz, 1986
Winterbotham, F.W.: *The Ultra Secret*, PBS, London 1974
Vajda, Ferenc A. & Dancey, Peter: *German Aircraft Industry and Production 1933-1945*, Airlife, Shrewsbury, 1998.
van der Vat, Dan: *The Good Nazi – The Life and Lies of Albert Speer,* Weidenfeld and Nicolson, London 1997
Ziemke, Earl F.: *Battle for Berlin – End of the Third Reich:*, Macdonald and Company, London, 1968
Ziemke, Earl F.: *Stalingrad to Berlin – The German Defeat in the East*, US Army Center of Military History, Washington DC, 1968
Zindel, Ernst: *Die Geschichte und Entwicklung des Junkers-Flugzeugbaus von 1910 bis 1945 und bis zum endgültigen Ende 1970*, Deutsche Gesellschaft für Luft- und Raumfahrt, Köln, 1979

Index